DILLON O'LEARY

OCT- 71

North American Indians in
Historical Perspective

Consulting Editor: ANTHONY F. C. WALLACE University of Pennsylvania

NORTH AMERICAN INDIANS

in Historical Perspective

Edited by ELEANOR BURKE LEACOCK,

Polytechnic Institute of Brooklyn,

& NANCY OESTREICH LURIE,

University of Wisconsin–Milwaukee

RANDOM HOUSE  NEW YORK

Preface

Despite the recent appearance of new books on the Indian peoples of America, none has had quite the same perspective as that which gives direction to the present one. Through her work on the Montagnais-Naskapi people of the Labrador peninsula, Eleanor Leacock has tried to define more clearly the long period of Indian cultural reintegration that followed European encroachments in the New World. Nancy Lurie has long been concerned with documenting that this cultural reintegration is still very much operative and that it has led to a present "Indian Renaissance," despite the popular cliché of the "vanishing American." The writings of Julia Averkieva, who took a lead in initiating the present work, have focussed on the development and change of institutional forms in Indian society. All of the anthropologists who contributed to this book share a general interest in the history of Indian-White relations and in attempting to interpret them from an Indian standpoint. The focus of this book, therefore, is on recent Indian history and its exemplification of constantly emerging ways of dealing with and adapting to new circumstances.

This book began at the Seventh International Congress for Anthropological and Ethnological Sciences, held in Moscow in the summer of 1964. There a number of Russian and American specialists in North American Indian studies met each other for the first time, and the easy camaraderie that seems to typify anthropological gatherings promoted enduring international friendships and a desire to further the interaction evoked by the Congress. The formal papers on American Indians and the shoptalk during periods of relaxation led to the suggestion made by Julia Averkieva and Irina Zolatarevskaya of the Soviet Union to Eleanor Leacock that perhaps a good vehicle for continuing international endeavors would be a book to which both Americans and Russians would contribute. As the idea took shape, Leacock and Lurie agreed to coedit the original English version, and Averkieva and Zolatarevskaya planned to handle translation and editing for publication in the Soviet Union. Since many more Americans than Russians are North American specialists, it was obvious that the contributors would be mostly Americans and that the Russian contribution would devolve upon Averkieva and Zolatarevskaya, who have done field work in North America. However, it was the two Russian scholars who broached the idea of the book and who drew up the initial list of contributors.

From the beginning it was clear that the body of the book would consist of case studies that broadly represented America north of Mexico, and as the project developed, the group of contributors was enlarged so that major geographic and cultural areas would be included. In addition, D'Arcy McNickle was asked to set the prehistoric and early historical background, and Lurie was asked to write a final chapter on contemporary Indian attitudes. Zolatarevskaya planned to write on the relationship between colonialism and revitalization movements.

All who agreed to participate had other commitments to fulfill, so it was understood that deadlines would not be too immediate. Liaison with our Russian colleagues was expedited by the fact that Lurie spent 1965–1966 as a Fulbright-Hay Lecturer at the Danish University at Aarhus and, thanks to a grant from the Wenner-Gren Foundation for Anthropological Research, was able to spend the Easter holidays of 1966 in the Soviet Union and discuss progress on the book with Averkieva and Zolatarevskaya. She was also able to present them with a draft of her chapter, which was then circulated among the other contributors for comments and suggestions.

During the annual meetings of the American Anthropological Association at Pittsburgh in November 1966, a special dinner meeting was arranged and was attended by most of the American contributors. It was then that William Sturtevant brought to our attention that two European ethnohistorians, Theodore Brasser of Leiden and Christian Feest of Vienna, were eminently qualified to provide information on the Atlantic coast, Brasser having also done field work with the remnant tribes of the Northeast.

At the gathering of 1966 the authors of the book discussed the changing patterns of Indian-white contact relations, which seemed to be replicated from place to place, and the possibility of using these sequential changes as a coordinating theme of the book. It was agreed that the subject should be explored further at another meeting of at least several days, where the contributors would have a chance to discuss each other's work in detail. The Wenner-Gren Foundation was approached and agreed to arrange a conference at the foundation's center at Burg Wartenstein, Gloggnitz, Austria, August 7 to 14, 1967. All the contributors were invited, as well as Christian Feest, whose participation in the discussions was most valuable. Other, unexpected, commitments prevented Downs and Averkieva (who was to be in Canada at that time) from joining the group; and to our regret and sorrow, Zolatarevskaya's failing health precluded travel and soon prevented her from taking any active part in the project. However, immediately after the conference, Leacock was able to visit Moscow to consult with our Russian colleagues and to bring them a tape recording of the conference discussions.

The Burg Wartenstein gathering accomplished its purposes of establishing a useful organizational framework for the book and of allowing for full discussion of many questions, both general and specific, about various phases of Indian-white contact from group to group. It also enabled the editors to discuss each individual chapter with its author. In bringing together into one book the work of many people, there are always somewhat arbitrary decisions to be made about the balance between the advantages of authorship based on firsthand acquaintanceship with material and the disadvantages (or so they are generally considered) of resulting inconsistencies in style and emphasis. We are grateful for the good-natured patience of our colleagues in conceding to requests to rewrite or cut portions of their chapters and for bearing with the delays in bringing the book to completion that were occasioned by our other responsibilities.

We also wish to express our gratitude to the Wenner-Gren Foundation and, particularly, to its Research Director, Lita Osmundsen, whose experienced handling of the Burg Wartenstein conference made our meeting so rewarding. We are grateful to the many persons who have read individual chapters and offered suggestions to their authors, and we wish especially to thank Anthony F. C. Wallace for his careful evaluation of, and suggestions for, the book as a whole. For invaluable assistance in preparing the manuscripts, we are indebted to Martha Livingston. Finally, we would like to dedicate our efforts to Irina Zolatarevskaya, whose warm hospitality made the editors' stays in Moscow so pleasant, and who played so important a part in the initiation of this book.

ELEANOR BURKE LEACOCK   NANCY OESTREICH LURIE

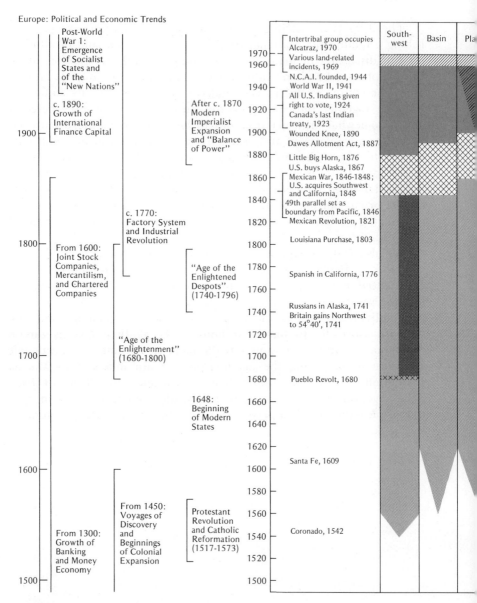

Europe: Political and Economic Trends

Early contacts and development of Contact-Traditional Culture. May include hostilities, but native societies are still politically autonomous.

Competition and conflict; threat to land base and political autonomy. May be marked by overt hostilities, but not necessarily.

Changes in Indian-White Relationships in North America in Historical Perspective.

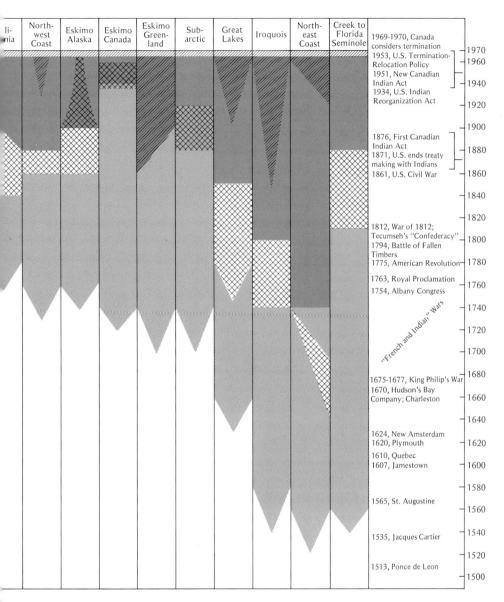

li- nia	North- west Coast	Eskimo Alaska	Eskimo Canada	Eskimo Green- land	Sub- arctic	Great Lakes	Iroquois	North- east Coast	Creek to Florida Seminole	

1969-1970, Canada considers termination — 1970

1953, U.S. Termination-Relocation Policy — 1960

1951, New Canadian Indian Act — 1940

1934, U.S. Indian Reorganization Act — 1920

— 1900

1876, First Canadian Indian Act — 1880

1871, U.S. ends treaty making with Indians

1861, U.S. Civil War — 1860

— 1840

— 1820

1812, War of 1812; Tecumseh's "Confederacy" — 1800

1794, Battle of Fallen Timbers

1775, American Revolution — 1780

1763, Royal Proclamation — 1760

1754, Albany Congress

"French and Indian" Wars — 1740

— 1720

— 1700

— 1680

1675-1677, King Philip's War

1670, Hudson's Bay Company; Charleston — 1660

— 1640

1624, New Amsterdam — 1620

1620, Plymouth

1610, Quebec

1607, Jamestown — 1600

— 1580

1565, St. Augustine — 1560

— 1540

1535, Jacques Cartier

— 1520

1513, Ponce de Leon — 1500

Administrative stabilization; reservation or comparable situation. May be marked by continuing threats to Indian land and community identity.

Emergent reintegration; involves "Pan-Indian" or "nationalistic" aspects in terms of Indian interest and self-determination in relation to the encompassing nation.

Contents

*North American Indians in
Historical Perspective*

1   *Introduction*[1]

ELEANOR BURKE LEACOCK

The first Americans north of Mexico have figured as little more than a few stereotyped and contradictory images in most accounts of the New World. They are generally regarded as savages with no past and no future, sparsely inhabiting a continent, and childlike both in their generosity—"selling" Manhattan Island for $24 worth of "trinkets"—and in their ferocity—scalping the victims of battle. In the West they have been seen as a jumble of opposites, as the earlier "only good Indian is a dead Indian" attitude has given way to a latter-day Hollywood "good Indian" peacemaker juxtaposed against the "bad Indian" fighter. Only most recently can a "good" Indian fight for his people's independence. Contemporary Indians are seen as a beaten people on reservations, sharing in a general "culture of poverty," a curiosity for passing tourists, while the notion persists, despite census figures to the contrary, that Indians are "vanishing" as a racial and sociocultural entity.

The "American Indian unit," usually given in the fourth grade in elementary school, may have colorful projects on wigwam-building and firemaking. However, with at best a "noble savage" tinge, it does not do much to improve the picture. Indeed, in elementary and high school, and even in college, it is still the North European, come to these shores to seek freedom and equality for all, who strides almost alone through the pages of American development. The variety and complexity of his relationships with the peoples of other continents are passed over. The other people are presented mainly as difficult and disturbing: people with red-brown skins, impolitely residing here first and unwilling simply to disappear; black-skinned peoples brought to work as slaves under a sun said to be too hot for whites; almond-eyed peoples also supposedly well-suited for long hours of drudgery. Later, too, according to the myth, came other whites from South and East Europe to make their way in the land of peace and plenty. Only recently has Spanish St. Augustine in Florida been granted its priority over Jamestown as the "oldest settlement"; and the further priority of several Southwestern Pueblos is still unrecognized. As the history of the land unfolds, the Anglo-Saxon magnanimously, and with but occasional falterings, draws on his rational view of the world to move this assembly of other peoples along with him on his onward, upward course.

This historical myth, ever more frayed, has been coming under increasing criticism. However, despite the growing number of scholarly works that aim to reconstruct the actual nature of relationships among many peoples of Europe, America, and Africa in the New World, more effort is needed in order to achieve a rounded perspective of New World history and its intertwined attempts of most men to live and a few to dominate. Some whites came to reap profits from new wealth in land, trade, and slaves; others were escaping from the land hunger of Europe; and many were at least temporarily pressed into servitude. Some blacks were slaves and some were "free," but both have been ever struggling toward what became a formal commitment of a new nation, that all men have "inalienable rights" to "life, liberty and the pursuit of happiness." Meanwhile, the first Americans, red-brown men with a more egalitarian way of life, tried to cope with the instability of strangers who exploded from a few scattered colonies into an engulfing wave of settlements.

The present book is a contribution toward a more balanced understanding of the New World. It is a partial reconstruction of the political and cultural history of the first Americans during the near five centuries in which the face of their lands was being transformed. The coverage is far from complete; necessarily the book is but a sampling of what there is to be written. However, the chapters that follow illustrate the variety of Indian experience in the New World north of Mexico. With the past millennia of Indian history as a background, they document Indian ways of coping with the events of the past 500 years, the basis for a contemporary assessment by Indians of their common position and purpose in the midst of a still alien people.

The Expansion of Europe

Schoolchildren are told of the romance between Pocahontas and John Rolfe, but they are not told of the challenge thrown out to John Smith by Pocahontas' father, Powhatan, or Wahunsonacock. "Why will you take by force what you may have quietly by love?" Wahunsonacock asked. "Why will you destroy us who supply you with food? What can you get by war?" He called on John Smith to have the English put away their guns and swords, saying:

> I am not so simple as not to know that it is much better to eat good meat,
> sleep comfortably, live quietly with my wives and children, laugh and be

merry with the English, and trade for their copper and hatchets, than to run away from them, and to lie cold in the woods, feed on acorns, roots and such trash, and be so hunted that I can neither eat nor sleep [Forbes, 1964, 55].

The people of North America had known fighting before. The next chapter, by D'Arcy McNickle, tells how myriad peoples spread over the lands of the New World, jockeying for place, often peacefully, sometimes at war, with parties of young men raiding against neighboring peoples for honor and booty and to establish or protect rights to surrounding lands. To the south, in the lands of the Aztec and Maya, and down to the Andes of the Inca, nascent city-states grew through conquest into empires. However, the invasion from Europe brought conflict of an altogether different dimension; it meant fighting for sheer survival. For millennia, history had meant for the inhabitants of America the surmounting of varied problems, but always within a land that was their own. Now history had taken a new and drastic turn, as Europeans burst into a continent they took as theirs to exploit.

At Buffalo, New York, two centuries after Wahunsonacock called on John Smith to live in peace, the Seneca Indian Red Jacket spoke to a missionary by the name of Cram, saying, "An evil day came upon us [when] your forefathers crossed the great waters, and landed on this island." Red Jacket continued:

Their numbers were small; they found friends, and not enemies; they told us they had fled from their own country for fear of wicked men, and came here to enjoy their religion. They asked for a small seat; we took pity on them, granted their request, and they sat down amongst us; we gave them corn and meat; they gave us poison in return. The white people had now found our country, tidings were carried back . . . At length their numbers had greatly increased; they wanted more land; they wanted our country. Our eyes opened; and our minds became uneasy. Wars took place; Indians were hired to fight against Indians, and many of our people were destroyed. They also brought strong liquors among us; it was strong and powerful, and has slain thousands . . . [Forbes, 1964, 57].

Contemporaneous with the new problems with which American Indians were coping were the problems on the other side of the Atlantic of transition to "modern Europe." During the fifteenth and sixteenth centuries the growth in power of the business classes sufficiently undercut the last remnants of the feudal economic and social order to promote the development of centralized nation-states and usher in the so-called Age of Absolutism. Strong monarchies grew up in the seventeenth century and flourished for the succeeding 200 years. As an ideological corollary the Protestant revolution of North Europe legitimized the business ethic, while it also freed capital and property previously in the control of the Church of Rome.

Underlying the distortion of the roles played by many peoples in American history is a distorted version of these developments in Europe. They are commonly described as almost wholly internal matters, with colonies of secondary importance until the growth of large-scale imperialism in the nineteenth century. There is a glossing over of the extent to which the Age of Exploration and the time of the commercial revolution where periods in which the accumulation of capital from the lands of Africa, Asia, and the Americas were paving the way for the industrial revolution.[2] Eric Williams writes of the significance for England of the triangular trade in manufactured goods, slaves, and raw materials that she conducted with Africa and the West Indies:

> The triangular trade . . . gave a triple stimulus to British industry. The Negroes were purchased with British manufactures; transported to the plantations, they produced sugar, cotton, indigo, molasses and other tropical products, the processing of which created new industries in England; while the maintenance of the Negroes and their owners on the plantations provided another market for British industry, New England agriculture and the Newfoundland fisheries. By 1750 there was hardly a trading or a manufacturing town in England which was not in some way connected with the triangular or direct colonial trade. The profits provided one of the mainstreams of that accumulation of capital in England which financed the Industrial Revolution [1966, 52].

Dissimilarities in the development of European countries at different periods were expressed in differing interests in the Americas and in varying types of relations each country attempted to set up with the Indians. These variations concerned, first, the relative importance of missionizing activities, trade, and settlement and the extent to which Indians might be pressed into a serf or slave status; second, the governmental policies of the different European countries; and finally, the nature of competition among them. Relations with Indians also varied over time as Europe, profiting from the wealth gained from the new colonies, developed the determined and commonly brutal pattern of world domination which, in the period of its decline, was passed on to that precocious offspring, the United States.

In the sixteenth century, Spain, fresh from the reconquest of her territory from the Moorish kingdoms, and expanding through Europe both in the north and south, was the first to take advantage of the newly discovered Americas. Looking for gold, she settled primarily on silver to fill the coffers of the court, and she forced Indians to work in the mines under intolerable conditions. The conquistadors and their successors, largely landless gentry, set up haciendas dependent on Indian labor. Only superficially did they follow the lines of the feudal manor, for they were not aimed at self-sufficiency, but oriented toward the market for agricultural produce, both in the mining centers and in Europe. Priests, whose ideological goal was to save human souls, extended the power of the Church by setting up missions that were also economic enterprises. Mining entrepreneurs, landholders, churchmen, and the new class of bureaucrats representing the interests of the crown all jockeyed for position within the uneasy confines of a supposedly common concern for the glory of Spain.

The Spanish Empire was built largely in those parts of Central and South America where class lines were already being drawn in Indian society and where a farming population was accustomed to supporting the luxury of a theocratic state apparatus with elaborate pomp and ritual. Some years ago Ruth Benedict (1932) pointed out that conditions were otherwise to the north, where more egalitarian villagers were not habituated to working for others, and where ranking ritual and lay leaders had to show some direct justification for their existence. The attempt to transform the Pueblo Indians of the Southwest into docile laborers for the Spanish missions was brutal, but ineffective. In the Southeast, Spanish holdings were more strategic than economic in purpose. The continual efforts by both the Spanish and English to press the Indians of this region into slavery were in the main unsuccessful, and slaves to work the land were brought from Africa, where people from "high" cultures were already familiar with the practice of working for others.

During the seventeenth century, English trade became firmly established in the New World. Within a few decades after 1670, when the English established a settlement in Charlestown, the Indians had become dependent on a variety of English trade goods—metal tools and cooking utensils, cloth, rum, and especially guns—with which the Spanish were unable to compete. In time the trading phase of Indian-European relations in the Southeast gave way to one dominated by the pressure of settlement. Increasing numbers of Europeans moved into the Southeast following the French and Indian Wars and continued to do so after the Revolutionary War, despite repeated formal agreements not to encroach further upon Indian lands. The growth of plantations, which were producing great wealth in cotton and tobacco with African slaves, was not to be hindered by anyone, and responding to the strong urging of President Jackson, Congress passed the Removal Bill. During the 1830s almost the entire Indian population of the Southeast, including Cherokee and Creek plantation holders, was forcibly exiled to Oklahoma. Charles Hudson writes, ". . . the Southeastern Indians exhausted their resources of fur-bearing animals very quickly. After they were gone, the only resource they had that interested European colonists was land, and this they got by removal, a political expedient that was gentle in name only" (1967, 81–82).

In the northerly United States and in Canada, trade, along with the competition among the mercantile countries of France, Holland, and England, dominated relations with the Indians from the beginning. Whereas the French were more involved in this trade during the sixteenth century, England, the "nation of shopkeepers," less saddled than France by anachronistic feudal institutions, became dominant during the seventeenth.

Throughout the temperate areas trade was soon accompanied by settlement, and colonial relations were established with settlers who furnished raw materials and agricultural produce to the "mother country" in return for manufactured materials. The Indian trade in hides and furs became secondary and then obsolete in the coastal areas; its centers moved ever farther west and north. In 1830 the American Fur Company was still the largest single concern in the United States (Nute, 1927), but it went into receivership in 1837. In the far north, where agriculture was not possible with the technology available, Indian and Eskimo lands were left virtually intact until the recent encroachment upon them by an industrialized white world, interested in exploiting their wealth in minerals and timber and in establishing air bases, weather stations, and the like.

In addition to north-south variations in Indian experiences with invaders from Europe, there were differences from east to west. Along the eastern shore and up the rivers there was an early and long period of missionizing, trade, and warfare, during which various groups of Indians were caught in the competition among the European powers. Then the number of colonizers grew enormously, and they entered into fierce competition for land with the settled village-living Indians. Soon, except in the North, only fragments of former populations were left on little pockets of land.

In the central areas around the Great Lakes and the Plains, trade goods and new epidemic diseases often preceded even the first explorers. Horses that had perhaps escaped from an expedition led by Francisco Coronado into the Southwest in the sixteenth century had proliferated rapidly in the great grasslands of the West. As the chapter by Gene Weltfish shows, by the time settlers moved into the Plains, a highly mobile culture based on the hunting of buffalo on horseback had replaced the early agricultural way of life centering in the river valleys. Trading centers, farms, railroads—all represented an obstreperous new nation, bursting to extend its domains from sea to sea. The long period of relatively autonomous incorporation of new traits into Indian economic and social forms in the central areas of the continent was ended in the nineteenth century in a few decades of fierce conflict and final defeat. However, Indian groups in this area were able to maintain their integrity and preserve their languages, religion, and other cultural traditions.

When the westward push of the United States reached California, the attitude of the settlers toward the Indians was simple and brutal: They should be exterminated. The California Indians were not the intrepid warriors of the Plains; yet as James Downs points out in his chapter on California, to hunt them was considered a sport. Even Indians who had previously lived in Spanish mission settlements often faced massacre. Further to the north along the heavily wooded North Pacific coast, the fishermen subsisting on the rich marine resources of the area had been profiting from trade with the Russians since the eighteenth century, which had encouraged further elaborations of their already rank-oriented culture. They became engaged in occasional battles to preserve their independence, but as Julia Averkieva shows in her chapter on the Tlingit, they were not seriously challenged until, in the twentieth century, they were pressed to the wall by the Euro-Canadian usurpation of their fisheries and woodlands.

The western Eskimos, too, were early involved with Russian trade and, at times, in bitter and losing conflicts. In Greenland, as Charles Hughes discusses in his article, Eskimo experiences with Danish settlers were altogether on a different order. In the central arctic zone prolonged contacts did not take place until the twentieth century.

Five Phases of Indian History

Despite the variety of historical relations between Indians and new-comers, which unrolled over many centuries, it is possible to discern five general phases. These phases are far from clear cut, and they vary greatly in their length and specific features as one moves from area to area. As has already been indicated, and as will be documented in detail in the pages that follow, the history of each area, indeed of each people, is too complex to fit any neat scheme. However, the delineation of five general types of Indian-white relations focuses on some major differences in the kinds of problems with which the Indians and their leaders had to cope at various times during the past four and three-quarters centuries.

Phase I, late precontact, with its manifold adaptations to varying types of environment, is described in D'Arcy McNickle's chapter. These adaptations have generally been described in terms of nine "culture areas." The concept of a culture area implies definable boundaries and internal cultural homogeneity, neither of which existed, and it does not allow for evolutionary development through time. However, if these limitations are kept in mind, the concept can be useful for indicating the nature of broad variations in Indian society, population density, and patterns of land use and ecological adaptation that existed during the period when Europeans were first coming to the Western Hemisphere.

Each chapter in this text deals with a culture area or a major people thereof. The nine areas are:

1. The Southeast, where the culture of agricultural peoples had reached a peak in the development of town life and in elaborate ceremonial centers that had apparently declined by the sixteenth century.
2. The Northeast, where village life based on horticulture faded off into the nomadism of northern hunters.
3. The Plains, in precontact times an extension of the eastern agricultural areas, although also the home of some buffalo hunters. In later historic times the Plains became the center of a culture type based on horse nomadism, generally thought to represent the way of the "typical Indian."
4. The Southwest, where food-producing villagers had experienced a cultural decline from an earlier period, and where people practicing simpler forms of gardening or subsisting by hunting and gathering also dwelt.
5. The Great Basin, between the Rocky Mountains and the Sierras, where peoples depended on hunting and the gathering of nuts and other wild vegetable foods.
6. California, where agriculture was not practiced, but where in some parts of the area dependable supplies of acorns and other foods enabled a relatively settled village life. The chapter on California by James Downs, which indicates the variety of both its languages and cultures, suggests the enormous complexity of Indian cultural history in this one region alone.
7. The Northwest coast, where plentiful resources enabled a richer life for fishermen than did early agriculture.
8. The subarctic, inhabited by hunters of caribou, moose, and other game.
9. The Eskimo area, with the ingenious adaptation of its people to the exploitation of sea mammals along the Arctic coasts.

Societies dependent on some combination of hunting, fishing, and gathering are often called "simple societies" because they do not have the complex social and political forms afforded by more productive economies. However, as the chapters on California and on the Ute and Paiute, the Eskimo, and the Canadian hunters illustrate, the intimate knowledge of an area, its resources, and the techniques required for exploiting them successfully are anything but "simple" in hunting and gathering economies. Indeed, they often call for a variety of skills and a degree of technical ingenuity on the part of the average adult that is considerably greater than that required in our button-pushing civilization. The ability to weigh situations and make quick decisions on possibly life-and-death matters is not something unusual to a hunter and gatherer, but is expected in the normal course of events. Nor is social life among such peoples merely a matter of following "blind custom." That rituals and traditions are well established and deeply revered does not mean that a fine sense of interpersonal relations is not required for maintaining the group cohesion necessary for survival.

Phase II commences with early contacts, either directly with explorers, missionaries, and traders or indirectly with goods traded through neighboring tribes. The extent to which a reintegration of Indian institutions followed these first contacts has often been underestimated. It has been all too common for anthropologists to assume that the cultural information they were gathering from elders about life styles that stretched back to the beginning of the nineteenth century and even earlier represented pre-Columbian society. Cases in point are the assumptions that individualized patterns of fur trapping in the north woods and the virtually total dependence on the buffalo in the Plains were aboriginal. Indian-white contacts during this phase, which extended over several generations for most Indian societies, were relatively equal and commonly of a mutually beneficial nature. The common Indian preference for contractual relationships with whites—as reflective of interacting but not merging societies—may well stem from this early period. So also may concepts of the "golden age" that Indians still dream of recapturing, with modifications appropriate to modern conditions.

Phase III was the period of large-scale settlement and of serious conflict and other pressures. Disruption, and at times virtual annihilation, were caused by new diseases as well as by warfare. However, in great sections of the North, in place of settlement, permanent trading posts were established, upon which Indians and traders were mutually dependent. Thus, there was less disruption in this area and a continuation of the essential features of the second phase.

Phase IV was a period of relative stabilization and the institution of governmental controls, in most cases involving the establishment of reservations. During this phase a recurrent assertion of the Indian desire for independence took the form of religious revitalization and the belief in many of the cults—such as the Ghost Dance which culminated in the Sioux outbreak of 1890–1891—that on a stated day the white man would be swallowed up by the sea, or otherwise destroyed, and Indian lands regained. Military reprisals by the United States against the more militant Indian cults brought home the futility of hoping to prevail over whites. With the creation of reservations or the Indian withdrawal into areas the whites did not covet, adaptations became increasingly directed toward maintaining social boundaries through passive resistance, manipulating white sources of power, and continuing to make selective adaptations from white culture in order to survive as Indian enclaves.

Phase V, the recent period, has been marked by the emergence of a new sense of national consciousness and common purpose and by attempts to achieve effective political organization and the viable social and cultural reintegration of Indian institutions within the context of contemporary industrial society.

Trends in Indian Social History

Arguments about the future of the first Americans have commonly focused on two alternatives: should Indian culture and identity be "preserved" and ways found for Indians to support themselves "as Indians," or should Indians be helped to "assimilate" and become absorbed into the "mainstream of American life"? One thesis of this book is that these are not the only two alternatives; that Indians have played a role in American history, and that they still have a role to play, neither as "museum pieces" nor as individuals lost in the "melting pot," but as Indians of the twentieth century. Indian traditions and experiences have neither fossilized nor disappeared; Indian ways of today are not those of centuries ago, but they are nonetheless Indian. Indian cultural traditions have continued to grow and change, and there has been constant integration of innovations into characteristically Indian ways and Indian views. Today there is a strong interest in redefining these ways. A 1966 editorial in the National Congress of American Indians bulletin, *The Sentinel,* states:

> There seems to be an intellectual acceptance of technological society and a real desire by American Indians to learn what American society is and how one finds economic security in it. At the same time there is an ever increasing rejection of the social values of the "mainstream" and a return to Indian values [Steiner, 1968, 299].

An example of how persistent Indian cultural autonomy can be is afforded by a Wisconsin community of various Algonkian groups originally from Massachusetts. As reasonably well-off farmers, they view themselves as "assimilated," but nonetheless they adhere to certain values that they perceive as distinctively Indian. Describing community attitudes, Marion Mochon writes:

> Most important is the relation of man to the natural world and to the deity. They perceive a necessity for harmony in the universe; man's obligation in maintaining this harmony obliges him to refrain from destroying his natural environment, the forest, rivers, lakes, etc. A second value is sharing—goods and money—within the family and with other Indians. Sharing within the family is typified by the giving of large gifts—a television or refrigerator, for example—when funds are available, and expecting aid in the form of shelter, food, and money when in need. Related to this value is the feeling that whites are rapacious in their struggle for material success and that such behavior is contrary to the Indian scheme [1968, 184].

Such attitudes are not disembodied perpetuations of ancient Indian values, but a fuller delineation of those traditional attitudes that have been of particular importance in Indian relations with white society. In Indian societies of the past the precursors of such attitudes were probably implicit—simply taken for granted as the way people normally behave. It was later that they became stressed in terms suited to the Indian battle for freedom and for cultural integrity. Today, when the Indian fight for independence has become transformed into an attempt to re-shape viable and meaningful community lives, such attitudes are being sharply defined and their political significance is being drawn. For instance, Vine Deloria, Jr., former Administrative Director of the National Congress of American Indians, is quoted as saying:

> We Indians have a more human philosophy of life. We Indians will show this country how to act human. Someday this country will revise its constitutions, its laws, in terms of human beings, instead of property . . . [Steiner, 1968, x].

Deloria is only one among many younger, college-educated Indians who are today challenging the "American way," in which they see goods and services produced for individual profit rather than for the fulfillment of community needs. Interestingly enough, comparable attitudes are increasingly finding expression in contemporary white society; and alienated white students, who are searching for some living embodiment of the humanism and cooperativeness espoused by Judeo-Christian tradition but contradicted by Euro-American institutions, journey to Indian reservations, and thence, perhaps, to the setting up of communes. The adolescent faddist aspect of this "back to the Indian" movement ob-

scures the relevant historical fact that out of their particular experience,
Indians (as well as other so-called backward peoples of the heretofore
colonial world) have an important statement to make. They have a
valuable perspective to bring to bear on the problems of a technologically overdeveloped and socially underdeveloped Western world, a world
that endangers itself and all humanity by the increasingly fruitless and
dangerous proliferation of ever more inefficiently efficient techniques of
consumption and destruction.

In the past the perspectives of tribal societies have been stated in
generalized terms, usually by anthropologists. Anthropologists have traditionally felt called upon to make it clear that man is not innately the
aggressive competitive creature he may appear to be from a Euro-
American vantage point, but that he has lived and can live cooperatively
without dominating or exploiting his fellow-man. Although greed, hate,
envy, and cruelty certainly cannot be eradicated from human life, they
need not be such predominant themes. Today it is no longer anthropologists, but young Indians themselves, acutely conscious of their differences
with white society, who are actively exploring the more cooperative
Indian way. The scrutiny takes on special relevance now that there is
widespread concern as to whether technologically advanced society must
inevitably lead to a bureaucratized and robotlike life, or whether it can
be restructured so that people can understand and make decisions about
the social processes that affect them.

Societies organized along the lines of those found among American
Indians at the time of contact have been called "stateless societies." In
such societies, villages or groups of villages are politically autonomous,
although they recognize common "tribal" ties of language and culture
and are linked with other villages through ties of kinship and often of
social and ceremonial interchange. In 1691 the missionary Casanas wrote
of the Caddoan-speaking peoples ranging from Louisiana and Texas
north to the Dakotas:

> These allied tribes do not have one person to govern them (as with us, a
> kingdom is accustomed to have a ruler whom we call king). They have only
> a *xinesi*. He usually has a subordinate who gathers together four or five
> tribes who consent to live together and to form a province or kingdom, as
> it might be called—and a very large one too, if all these tribes had one
> person to rule over them. But such a head they have not, and I, therefore,
> infer that this province in New Spain is called "Teijias" (Friend)—which
> really expresses just what they are because each tribe is a friend to all the
> others [Swanton, 1942, 170–171].

Within each group, decisions expressed by chiefs or clan elders must
reflect, or be affirmed by, consensus among adult members of the group.
Robert Lowie, describing the Crow Indians of the Plains, wrote:

How shall we conceive the ancient chief?—a good "valiant" man. He was neither a ruler nor a judge and in general had no power over life and death—he decided when and where his followers should move and pitch camp [1935, 5].

The emphasis on consensus required techniques of decision making that involved hearing everyone out so that bases for compromise could be found. In her closing chapter Nancy Lurie touches on some of the implications of these techniques for interpersonal relations. Here, again, their cultural heritage is being explored by contemporary Indians. An editorial in *American Aborigine,* organ of the National Indian Youth Council, refers to the Indian concept of leadership as based on the "unity and solidarity for the benefit of all" and contrasts it with European concepts that are seen as based on "the belief of dividing people against themselves so that they can be easily controlled." Some of the skills called for in Indian leaders, the editorial states, are "the willingness to listen to what [the] . . . group desires" and the ability "to wait and be patient for the real issues to come to the surface before drawing . . . conclusions" (Steiner, 1968, 310–311). Such definitions of leadership ability are not foreign to European thought as *ideals;* Indian society, however, afforded the objective basis for their enactment.

The autonomous band or village unit, in which chiefs or clan elders came to decisions on the basis of feeling out group interest and sentiment, is sometimes referred to as "atomistic" in that no individual commands power or place in the social system beyond that directly flowing from his or her personal attributes. The term can be misleading, however, in that it de-emphasizes the many linkages that existed among groups of like interests. Atomism as applied to northern Algonkian hunters, whose groups break up to scatter over wider territories when game is scarce, often implies that close group ties do not exist. In fact, close ties are maintained despite physical distances. The term has also confused aboriginal mores with the individualized trapping practices that followed intensive involvement with the fur trade.

While atomism and individuality have been emphasized for hunting and gathering groups, the cohesion of agricultural groups has often been seen as repressive of individuality. This has been particularly true of Pueblo Indians of the Southwest, where the charge of witchcraft may be used to discourage ambitious individuals. However, as D'Arcy McNickle points out, one is in this case looking at a community that has actively fought to maintain its cohesiveness for the last 400 years. This battle for cohesion and autonomy continues today, although many younger members who become wage laborers splinter off and set up households away from the pueblos. As for practices of witchcraft, trials were first introduced among the Pueblo Indians by Spanish missionaries in the early seventeenth century, and dissident Indians were killed as witches.

It is a truism to say that the very existence of society inevitably involves some compromise between group interest and individual leeway for full expression of sentiment. However, to interpret the nature of this compromise in Indian society in terms of our own tendency to equate the expression of individuality with laissez-faire competitiveness (which, although anachronistic, we still do) can only lead to distortion.

The possibility of reaching consensus in Indian society, while still allowing considerable leeway for individual expression, followed from the common interest that obtained, both among individuals and among constituent groups of a tribe. This correspondence of interest was based on the unquestioned access of all tribesmen to the source of subsistence, the land. Thus, while there were constant early references to the respect accorded a chief, whose word was unquestionably "obeyed" (or so it appeared to the outside observer), there were also many references to the egalitarianism of Indian life. In his *History of the American Indians*, James Adair wrote in 1775:

> Their whole constitution breeds nothing but liberty; and when there is that equality of condition, manners, and privileges, and the constant familiarity in society, as prevails in every Indian nation, and through all our British colonies, there glows such a cheerfulness and warmth of courage in each of their breasts, as cannot be described [Pearce, 1965, 47].

Almost literal equality of possessions existed among some peoples. For example, among the Canadian hunters and the Great Basin gatherers, food supplies were neither plentiful nor dependable enough, given existing techniques for exploiting them, to afford the luxuries of relative wealth and high status. However, in most Indian societies some inequalities existed; but they pertained to luxuries, not to necessities. The question on which there remains considerable disagreement pertains to societies in which rank was highly developed: those of the North Pacific coast and along the northern shores of the Gulf of Mexico, fanning out to the Atlantic coast and into the central states. It is uncertain to what extent status in these areas had reached the point where chiefly decisions no longer expressed consensus, but instead reflected the vested interests of ranking ritual and lay chiefs. In her chapter Julia Averkieva deals with this question in some detail as it pertains to Northwest coast society.

In any case, Indian societies north of Mexico were quite different from those of Mexico and the Andean area, where farming populations supported elaborate royal and religious hierarchies. Not only were internal classes well developed in these southern areas, but conquering tribes collected tribute from defeated peoples and employed standing armies to control them. North of Mexico, when serious disagreements arose within a village or town and consensus became impossible, the precedent was for groups to bud off and form their own autonomous unit. This was probably an age-old expedient related to the need to keep a group from becoming too large to subsist successfully on the resources of an area. Where land pressures developed, raiding parties of young men warred against bordering tribes, thereby defining the tribal domains.

On the whole, however, relationships among different tribal groups were peaceful, with an ease of movement, trade, and intermarriage among them. Indeed, there was more of a cosmopolitan character to Indian life than one might think, a quality that has often been retained. The ease with which Indians travel, expecting and receiving hospitality from real and fictive kinsmen in widespread areas, contrasts sharply with the provincialism that is found among farmers of European descent, where the movement is to the city, leaving the elders behind, but not back and forth. Hospitality was traditionally accorded to strangers and could even be extended to individuals from groups with which one might be at war.

The trade and the warfare that followed the European involvement with North America were both of a different order from what had obtained in earlier Indian society. Salt had been the one necessity traded; most trade had been for variety and novelty, and if for better materials, not markedly better ones. Metal tools brought by Europeans, however, enormously enhanced an individual's ability to procure food and to manufacture clothes and equipment; and increasingly over the years clothes themselves were acquired through trade, as well as guns and ammunition and foods that were compact, storable, and transportable. Formerly, there had been a limit to the number of furs and hides that could be used, but with trade they began to acquire a value through exchange that was far beyond their previous value for use. When hoarded by an individual in a manner that would have made no sense in early Indian economy, furs and hides could be exchanged for virtually an entire livelihood. Therefore, lands with fur-bearing animals began to take on a significance much greater than they had when they were the source of immediate necessities. The invasion of fur-yielding lands traditionally hunted by others and the maintenance of a middleman role in the fur trade became additional functions of Indian war. At the same time the Indians faced a new kind of warfare with Europeans for the right to their lands. Thus, over a period of time the practice of sporadic raiding by parties of young men, bent on acquiring honor and prestige and in the process maintaining the tribal boundaries, gave way to more total war, first for trapping lands and trade routes, and increasingly, for tribal lands and independence. Such changes have been most fully stud-

*Naskapi woman setting a rabbit snare; Northwest River, Labrador
(photo by Richard Leacock).*

ied among the Iroquois, who, as discussed in the chapter by William
Fenton, were actively involved in the fur trade and in the competition
among the British, French, and Dutch for priority along the Atlantic
coast.

The new trade introduced new bases for both cohesion and fragmentation in Indian society. Trade for basic necessities loosened the economic
basis for cohesion upon which the "stateless society" was based. The
introduction of commodity exchange cut at the reciprocity of kin relations in Indian society and weakened the foundation for traditional
forms of leadership. During the early days of trade ambitious chiefs
could enhance their position by playing the role of intermediary between tribe and trader, as often happened among Algonkian peoples;
and with the new wealth afforded by trade, ranking members of a group
could consolidate their upper-status position, as they did on the Northwest coast.

New forms of warfare could also be destructive of groups not prepared to meet them or, on the other hand, could help strengthen the
position of chiefs and encourage more centralized political apparatuses

than had previously existed. The strengthening of chieftainship was further aided by the European assumption that a chief could make and enforce decisions about tribal matters that had traditionally required a continuing consensus among the constituent units of a tribe. Thus, a composite of influences determined the political history of each group. These influences included the needs or demands presented by the newcomers, the nature of a group's exploitation of environmental resources and its settlement pattern and population density, the precedents set by its relations with other Indian groups, and always the indefinable factor of individual genius whereby great leaders might or might not come to the fore to meet a particular historical moment. For example, among central Algonkians such as the Miami and Shawnee, the introduction of fur trading meant that initially large agricultural villages broke up into small trapping and trading bands. At a later period strong chiefs emerged to deal with the political and military aspects of the fight for freedom, such as Tomah among the Menominee in the 1820s.

Concomitant with economic and political adjustments to new conditions were changes in Indian social organization. In stateless societies a person's relationships to others through blood and marriage define his rights and duties. The production and distribution of food and other materials and the allocation of usufructuary rights to land and its resources are arranged primarily through kin connections. Relatives are grouped into categories and each category carries with it expectations for behavior with respect to other kin groups. For example, one's mother's sisters are often referred to by the same term as one's mother, and one can turn to them, when necessary, for "motherly" advice and help. Similarly, one's father and the father's brothers may be grouped under one term, and paternal uncles may play an attenuated father role. Certain cousins are often addressed and treated as siblings. These are the children of one's mother's sisters and father's brothers. However, the children of one's mother's brothers and father's sisters are commonly differentiated from other cousins, and those of opposite sex may be preferred marriage partners. Often one's mother's brothers are very important, and the term referring to them may also include their male children and grandchildren in the male line. And so on, across the generations and extending, upon marriage, into various in-law categories. Variations in the delimitations of categories and in distinctions between terms used when talking about persons and when talking to them are virtually endless, so that the study of kinship has become very complex. However, knowledge of some basic kinship principles is far from esoteric, for it reveals the socioeconomic structure of the societies that employ them.

Kin ties were relatively loose and informal among hunters and gatherers of the north woods and the Great Basin area. However, they were highly institutionalized in relatively settled village societies. This was so whether such societies were agricultural or whether they subsisted on regular and plentiful supplies of fish or wild vegetable foods. Apparently where some hundred or more people stayed together more or less permanently, taking in a major part of their food supply at a particular season, it was important to regularize the use of land and distribution of food; the formal organization of kin ties was the means through which this was accomplished. In American Indian society the basic unit that functioned on a day-to-day basis was made up of close kin, both immediate lineage members and marriage partners, and the ties became attenuated as they fanned out. The categorical relationship with a person, whether friend or stranger, defined expectations for behavior toward him or her. The treatment of war captives illustrates the extent to which kin ties underlay relations. A captive might be tortured and killed; but he might also be adopted by a particular family, usually to make up for a kinsman lost in battle. In time he could become a loved and revered member of the group. Kin ties were to some extent also maintained across tribes. Marrying into another tribe sometimes called for the creation of a fictional clan in order to validate the establishment of new ties, as was also sometimes done where white paternity was involved.

Two basic principles of American Indian social organization that are widely distributed around the world are *exogamy* and *unilineality*. The principle of unilineality means that kin are counted on one side only. Thus one "belongs" to the kin group of either one's mother or one's father. Although the other parent's family is recognized and important, it is as another family, not one's own. By comparison with bilateral descent and formal recognition of both mother's and father's families, a unilineal system means that discrete, nonoverlapping groups persist over generations. However, as a corollary to these discrete groups, the principle of exogamy, whereby one marries outside of one's kin group or clan, results in myriad links that bind bands, villages, or tribes together.

The significance for human history of reckoning descent through the female line (matrilineality), by contrast with the male line (patrilineality), has been a focus for argument ever since Lewis Henry Morgan first documented the prevalence of kinship organization in stateless societies and posited matrilineality to be prior. Matrilineality is common in societies practicing simple forms of agriculture, where daily work in the fields is done largely by women, while men tend to hunting. Matrilineality predominated among American Indian agriculturalists, and usufructuary rights to fields were passed down in the female line. However, a shift toward patrilineality often occurred rapidly with the new economic and political relationships with Europeans that encouraged reckoning of descent through the male. Trade, stepped-up warfare, and wage work all augmented the position of the men, while traders, missionaries, and government officials acted upon the assumption of paternal descent. For instance, summarizing the information on one southeastern group, Eggan writes:

> There are numerous statements in [Grant] Foreman [*The Five Civilized Tribes*] indicating the efforts—and successes—of missionaries, teachers, and government agents in changing the attitudes and mode of life of the Choctaw. The facts that women worked in the fields and that a father—in accordance with the matrilineal system of inheritance—failed to provide for his own children particularly worried the missionaries. New regulations regarding land were introduced that emphasized the position of the man as head of the family. Marriage was regulated by law, widows were entitled to dower rights, and children could inherit their father's estate. The leaders no longer came from the clans but were elected by the adult male members of the district, and the old town rituals were largely replaced by the church and its activities.
>
> The effect of these changes on the social organization of the Choctaw was to break down the clan and kinship structures and to emphasize the nuclear family and the territorial tie. . . . In general terms, these changes indicate a shift from a matrilineal to a patrilineal, or bilateral emphasis . . . [1966, 29].

In the Southeast in general, Eggan writes, "the relationships of a father to his child were strengthened at the expense of the mother's brother," and "the father came to own land and property and to be the head of an elementary family." As a result "the clan was weakened, losing its corporate functions and political power, and matrilineal descent was no longer of much significance" (1966, 39).

The reckoning of kin ties bilaterally, on both mother's and father's sides, was widespread throughout western and northern North America when Indian societies were first described by interested observers. In some cases there was a greater emphasis on the maternal line, in others on the paternal line. Some societies were altogether patrilineal. There are considerable differences of opinion about the historical depth of these practices. Since descriptions of Indian relationship terms everywhere followed earlier contacts, it is difficult to resolve questions about precontact systems with certainty. However, the prevailing opinion is that hunting societies would logically be *patrilocal*, and groupings would tend to form around the men due to their preeminent role in the procuring of food. Matrilineality, it is assumed, followed the emergence of agriculture as economically predominant, when women, the gatherers of wild vegetable foods, developed the techniques of domestication. As a student, I myself accepted this view, but field work among the Montagnais-Naskapi of the Labrador Peninsula persuaded me otherwise. The society of these hunters was *matrilocal* until a trapping-trading economy, together with missionary and government influences, caused a shift to patrilocality. Other aspects of social organization among Canadian hunters are discussed in the chapter by June Helm and Eleanor Leacock, and a shift from matrilineality to patrilineality is dealt with in Averkieva's chapter on the Tlingit of the Northwest coast.

Whatever the history of formally delineated kin groupings may have been among American Indians, an adverse change in the status of women subsequent to European contact is clear. Early observers noted the high status of women as evidenced by such things as the inheritance of houses and land in the female line and the considerable influence women held in the making of group decisions. However, some writers saw the hard and heavy work done by Indian women as evidence of a low status. For instance, in *An Essay on the History of Civil Society,* published in 1767, Adam Ferguson wrote that the labor of Indian women was "a servitude, and a continual toil, where no honors are won; and they whose province it is, are in fact the slaves and helots of their country" (1966, 83). Indeed, the economic contribution of Indian women to the group was considerable; they tended the crops and gathered wild foods, snared small animals, manufactured clothes and utensils, often built the houses, and so on. Where men brought in virtually the entire food supply, as among the Eskimos, the work of women preparing skins for clothing and other purposes was still essential.

That such work led to a more egalitarian than subservient status follows from the structure of Indian society. A woman's duties were not carried out in the confines of the nuclear family, in which women were socially and legally secondary to men. Rather, women worked as part of a group of related families that usually shared the same house, lodge, or tipi and constituted the socioeconomic unit on a day-to-day basis. Since such groups were in turn bound by a network of reciprocal relations to other such groups, no person, man, woman, or even child was dependent on another individual, but depended on the group as a whole. According to the principle of consensus, in Indian society decisions were not made for others; every adult participated in making decisions concerning his or her area of responsibility in consort with others of like interests and needs. Hence, the participation of women in the making of decisions pertaining to their economic activities, and hence, their generally "equal" status.

As previously noted, Eggan has reviewed material on the decline of matrilineal institutions among agriculturalists of the southeastern United States, as men became heads of individual families owning their own tracts of land. Hamamsy has documented parallel types of changes in more recent times among the Navaho of the Southwest as men increasingly turned to wage earning. This undercutting of the woman's economic contribution has been accompanied by a change in residence patterns after marriage from matrilocal (where the new husband joins the wife's family group) to patrilocal or neolocal (where the young couple moves to a new location). Along with their loss of economic independence, Hamamsy notes, women were also losing "their security and power within the family" (1957, 111).

As for hunters, the importance of women in decision making among the Montagnais-Naskapi was recorded with disapproval by the seventeenth-century Jesuit Father Le Jeune, who also spoke of the men preferring "to take the children of their sisters as heirs, rather than their own" (Thwaites, 1906, V, 181; and VI, 255). In recent times there has been a shift from an informal tendency toward matrilocality among the several families hunting together and sharing one large tent to a patrilocal-patrilineal orientation centered on the working of individual trap lines by a man and his sons (Leacock, 1955). The hunting group stayed together, consuming the meat and depending on the leather clothing and tent covering made by the women. With the exchange of furs for staple foods, such as flour and lard, as well as for cloth and canvas, the work of women became obviated; and keeping the group together impaired the efficiency of trapping. Accordingly, men began to leave their dependent families near the post to go alone into the interior to trap.

A rather extreme case of how the social significance of women's economic contribution could be undercut when their duties were performed for individual men in the context of the nuclear family is afforded by Oscar Lewis' discussion of "Effects of White Contact upon Blackfoot Culture." A lively trade in tanned buffalo hides required the cooperation of wives to tan the skins, and chiefs and wealthy men literally bought wives with horses. By the nineteenth century, wives were less often sisters, as had been the traditional Indian practice; the marriage age of women had dropped to preadolescence; and the number of wives had increased to as many as ten or eleven, by which number their status was that of virtual slaves. However, this should not be taken to mean that the status of women in Indian society is necessarily low today. Indian women continue to play an important role in the family configuration and may participate actively in tribal organizations and affairs.

Despite the trend toward an independent nuclear family structure of the Western type, broader kin ties have remained important among many Indian groups. Unfortunately, the ties usually noted are those that seem to be clear remnants of older usages. Recurring patterns, such as, for example, grandparent-centered households (Leacock, 1949), have seldom been analyzed as adaptations of older forms to new conditions. Contemporary social practices and attitudes among American Indians are often debated either as vestiges of aboriginal personality and life style or as purely contemporary responses to poverty, discrimination, and isolation. As previously noted, Indian ways and views partake of both, but strictly speaking are neither. They are the product of Indian history, which for the past 500 years has included the constant meeting of challenges thrown out by an alien people come from Europe in overwhelming numbers.

In Conclusion

In a richly documented study of "savagism" as an American idea, Roy Harvey Pearce discusses the ideological role Indians played for those "Renaissance Englishmen who became Americans." Pearce writes:

> . . . the American before 1850—a new man, as he felt, making a new world —was obsessed to know who and what he was and where he was going, to evaluate the special society in which he lived and to know its past and its future. One means to this end was to compare himself with the Indian who, as a savage, had all past and no future. The final result was an image of the Indian as man out of society and out of history [1965, 135].

This image was internally contradictory: on the one hand, the Indian was roving, untamed, cruel; but on the other, he was free, proud, at one with nature, the "noble savage" who began to appear in eighteenth-century literary periodicals as a critic of American society. The noble savage image was in keeping with a major intellectual tradition of seventeenth- and eighteenth-century Europe, the tradition of "primitivism," "the belief that other, simpler societies were somehow happier than one's own," Pearce writes. According to him, there was the need on the part of new Americans who were exploring the nature of their society "to recover that portion of the primitive self which civilization had corrupted and, in the process, to lay bare the faults of civilization" (1965, 136). Yet the Indian's role as critic was ephemeral, and the noble savage was ultimately seen as part of the past, part of the "childhood of man in America" (1965, 195), whose eradication or transformation was the justifiable task of civilization.

However, the Indian as critic of American society was more than a fiction, and the ambivalent image of the Indian held by whites was more than an internal battling with the "savage" element in society. Indians have always posed a living criticism and a challenge to be met in practical political terms. The communal nature of Indian society, with the security it afforded an individual, was apparently of such appeal in early seventeenth-century Virginia that severe penalties were imposed on whites who ran away to join Indian groups. Washburn raises the need for research as to why so many whites wanted to do so (1957, 51). In the colonial Southeast the runaway slaves who joined Indian bands increased the dread of alliance between Blacks and Indians. "Nothing can be more alarming to Carolinians than the idea of an attack from Indians and Negroes," stated the British Superintendent of Southern Indian Affairs in 1775 (Willis, 1963, 161). A few years earlier the governor of South Carolina had explained to his successor in office that "it has been allways the policy of this govert to creat an aversion in them [Indians] to Negroes" (Willis, 1963, 165). Willis documents the various ways in which a divide-and-rule policy was carried out, with slaves used as soldiers against the Indians and Indians used to catch runaway slaves. Despite the considerable aversion that existed between the two groups, fraternization continued, and in 1825 the formally educated Cherokee David Brown wrote of the "presumption" that the Cherokee would free their slaves and send them home (McNickle, 1949, 232–233). McNickle comments on the significance such a sentiment had at this time, just prior to the forced removal of southeastern Indians to Oklahoma:

> More than the growing prosperity of the Cherokees, more than their adaptation to civilized modes of life and their increasing population, this suggestion that the Cherokees might be contemplating the freeing of their slaves must have set many Georgians to thinking that the time had come to take action [1949, 233].

In the post-Civil War years the student of Iroquois society Lewis Henry Morgan saw the comparison between "civilization" and "savagery" as both a censure and a directive for future social development. "Since the advent of civilization, the outgrowth of property has been so immense," Morgan wrote, "its forms so diversified, its uses so expanding and its management so intelligent in the interests of its owners, that it has become, on the part of the people, an unmanageable power." It could have no real future. Morgan continued, "The dissolution of society bids fair to become the termination of a career of which property is the end and aim; because such a career contains the elements of self-destruction." To Morgan American society was moving toward "the next higher plane . . . to which experience, intelligence and knowledge are steadily tending." He saw this as "a revival, in a higher form, of the liberty, equality and fraternity" of society organized along kinship lines (1963, 561–562).

Indian observers, noting the same contrast in two ways of life, were somewhat less optimistic about the outcome. A contemporary of Morgan's, Black Elk, of the Oglala Sioux, came east to Chicago and New

York in 1886 to see if he could learn from the ways of the whites something of help to his people. "I did not see anything to help my people," he stated, and continued:

> I could see that the Wasichus [white men] did not care for each other the way our people did before the nation's hoop was broken. They would take everything from each other if they could, and so there were some who had more of everything than they could use, while crowds of people had nothing at all and maybe were starving. They had forgotten that the earth was their mother. This could not be better than the old ways of my people . . . [Forbes, 1964, 66].

The same point is being made by Indian leaders of today. Young college-educated Indians, seeking what they feel to be most meaningful in the traditions of their elders, speak of the Indian way, as quoted above in Vine Deloria, Jr.'s statement, as organizing society "in terms of human beings, instead of property." The context is advanced industrial society, which threatens not only humanistic values but the earth itself. It is not that Indian society was a utopia or represented the answers for today. It is rather that from the history of Indian experience, first in cooperative societies, then, in Tocqueville's words, as "a little colony of troublesome strangers in the midst of a numerous and dominant people," certain themes have emerged as most meaningful. These are the philosophical commitments that man is part of nature and that each man is in a very real sense part of other men and the living memory of ways in which these commitments were embodied in social realities. The relevance for America is that today, when men are faced with the necessity of controlling their own society or perishing, Indians are saying with conviction that they have done it in the past and can do it again. Using the rhetoric of Red Power, they are now insisting on the "right to determine our own destinies, . . . the right to decide for ourselves how we want our lands used, how we wish our children to be educated, and how our reserves will be run" (*NARP Newsletter,* 1968, 3).

NOTES

[1] I am indebted to the other participants in this volume for critical suggestions on this chapter, as well as to Marvin Gettleman and Louis Menashe, historians, and to Murray Wax.

[2] As an example, the volume of the Harper-American Heritage Textbook Series, edited by William Langer (New York and London: Harper & Row, 1961), entitled *Western Civilization—Paleolithic Man to the Emergence of the European Powers,* takes the reader, in great detail, into the eighteenth century

with less than a half-dozen passing references to European colonization. Other general histories are usually a little better balanced. Two notable books contributing to a counter-perspective are W. E. B. DuBois, *The World and Africa* (New York: Viking, 1946), and Eric Williams, *Capitalism and Slavery* (New York: Capricorn, 1944).

REFERENCES

BENEDICT, RUTH
1932 Configurations of culture in North America. American Anthropologist 34:1–27.

EGGAN, FRED, AND HAROLD H. SWIFT
1966 The American Indian, perspectives for the study of social change. Chicago: Aldine Publishing Company.

FERGUSON, ADAM
1966 An essay on the history of civil society. D. Forbes, ed. Edinburgh: University of Edinburgh Press.

FORBES, JACK D.
1964 The Indian in America's past. Englewood Cliffs: Prentice-Hall.

HAMAMSY, LAILA SHUKRY
1957 The role of women in a changing Navaho society. American Anthropologist 59:101–111.

HUDSON, CHARLES
1967 Acculturative stages in the southeast. Working Papers in Sociology and Anthropology, 1 (2). University of Georgia Department of Sociology and Anthropology.

LEACOCK, ELEANOR
1949 The Seabird community. *In* Marian W. Smith, ed. Indians of the urban northwest. New York: Columbia University Press.
1955 Matrilocality in a simple hunting economy (Montagnais-Naskapi). Southwestern Journal of Anthropology 11:31–47.
1967 North American Indian society and psychology in historical perspective. Proceedings of the 7th International Congress of the Anthropological and Ethnological Sciences, Moscow, IV.

LEWIS, OSCAR
1942 Effects of white contact upon Blackfoot culture. Monographs of the American Ethnological Society VI.

LOWIE, ROBERT H.
1935 The Crow Indians. New York: Holt, Rinehart & Winston.

MCNICKLE, D'ARCY
1949 They came here first, the epic of the American Indian. New York and Philadelphia: Lippincott.

MOCHON, MARION JOHNSON

1968 Stockbridge-Munsee cultural adaptations: "assimilated Indians." Proceedings of the American Philosophical Society 112:182–219.

MORGAN, LEWIS HENRY

1963 Ancient society, Edited, with Introduction by Eleanor Leacock. Cleveland and New York: World Publishing.

NATIVE ALLIANCE FOR RED POWER

1968 NARP Newsletter. Vancouver, B.C. June-July.

NUTE, GRACE LEE

1927 The papers of the American Fur Company: a brief estimate of their significance. American Historical Review 32:519–538.

PEARCE, ROY HARVEY

1965 The savages of America, a study of the Indian and the idea of civilization. Baltimore: Johns Hopkins Press.

STEINER, STAN

1968 The new Indians. New York: Harper & Row.

SWANTON, JOHN R.

1942 Source material on the history and ethnology of the Caddo Indians. Bureau of American Ethnology Bulletin 132.

THWAITES, R. G., ED.

1906 The Jesuit relations and allied documents. 71 vols. Cleveland: Burrows Brothers Company.

WASHBURN, WILCOMB E.

1957 A moral history of Indian-white relations: needs and opportunities for study. Ethnohistory 4:47–61.

WILLIAMS, ERIC

1966 Capitalism and slavery. New York: Capricorn Books.

WILLIS, WILLIAM S.

1963 Divide and rule: red, white, and black in the Southeast. The Journal of Negro History 48:157–176.

2 *Americans Called Indians*[1]

D'ARCY McNICKLE

The Americans called Indians wrote no histories, and their past was only dimly told in oral tradition and legend. When strangers came to write about the land that had been theirs, the Indians somehow turned into flora and fauna and were hardly visible as men. Their global experience had been reduced to scattered footnotes in world history. Yet the crossing into a new world and the long trek spanning two continents and 9,000 miles of mountain and prairie, desert and jungle, were in their magnitude the equivalent of anything man had experienced elsewhere.

The Americans called Indians shared what is probably man's oldest characteristic—his inclination to wander. Unlike most animals, whose lives are spent within a limited radius of the place of their birth or who return in seasonal cycles, the human species began at once to break away from homelands. As a hunter and gatherer of foodstuffs, man explored the fearful unknown of all climates and regions, including the troublesome world within himself. He became adventurer and poet.

These qualities the Indian people shared. It is not necessary to speculate on how early man, the predecessor of the American Indian, stumbled into the Western Hemisphere northeastward out of Asia in pursuit of game animals. He simply radiated into all beckoning biospheres of the Old World and continued into the New, without any awareness that he had bridged two worlds. Wherever he paused along the way, he named the land and learned to live within it. Like all men from the beginning, he built upon his past and enlarged his future. He tamed a wild grass and built an entire way of life upon it. He constructed fabulous cities in the most incredible jungle and mountainous terrain. He composed songs and legends that told of his adventures. In all of this the Indian was not unique, and neither was he disjoined.

The failure to see the red race within the great tradition of mankind is what has been most difficult for Indians to accept in the accounts they read of themselves and their ancestors. The Europeans who stumbled upon what they were pleased to call the New World wrote of their discoveries, their conquests, and their accomplishments as if no human experience had been before them. Even when Europeans incorporated into their languages the myriad place names that Indian tongues had attached to the land, it was as if these had been invented by Europeans. The sound of the original Indian word was so often corrupted that, indeed, it might have come from an alien source. The attitudes and assumptions of these early contacts have continued to give color and substance to descriptive writings of these first Americans.

The Indian, as he came to be dealt with in the histories written by other men, was diminished in various ways. His part in the development of New World society was reduced to inconsequentiality, if not to mere obstructionism. When his manners and morals were described, the Indian seemed to exist in a world devoid of logic or sentiment or dynamics. It was a world that had stood still, seemingly, since its own dark creation.

Still later, when studies of human development became more sophisticated, the employment of the "ethnographic present" served as a kind of cookie-cutter device that clipped away and discarded that which was antecedent or subsequent. Indian life came from nowhere and went nowhere.

It is not possible even now to construct a sequential account of the peopling of the Western Hemisphere, with times and places spelled out. It is a history made up of fragments and inferences woven around gaping discontinuities. The material offered in these pages cannot correct these deficiencies, but it is offered at a time when there seems to be an awakening concern for the small peoples of the world. Though we may not have learned how to comprehend other lives except in terms of our own lives, there may now be a readiness for understanding. Notwithstanding the gaps in the narrative, the Indians may at last emerge from a legendary past and from the superficialities of the roles assigned to them in other men's histories.

The Search for Beginnings

Only gradually has speculation about the first peopling of the New World yielded to scientific field methods and published data. Of course, until tree-ring counts, radiocarbon analysis, and other precise dating methods were developed, beginning about forty years ago, all attempts to fix a time depth for pre-European settlement had to rely on speculation. Moreover, as Wilmsen observes, "modes of thought at any given time were firmly rooted in the ethos of that time and were severely circumscribed by the extent of knowledge then current" (1965, 172). This meant that Europeans began by looking to the Bible and to their own historical antecedents for answers to the enigma thrust at them by a hitherto unknown race. Later, when discoveries about early man that were made in the Old World began to afford a deeper perspective on human history, some students of New World antiquities, still looking to Europe, rashly ascribed comparable dates for some discoveries in the Americas. The refutation of such assertions, most effectively by scientists associated with the Smithsonian Institution, discouraged further claims for American antiquity. Not until the discovery at Folsom, New Mexico, in 1926, of man-made artifacts in clear association with extinct Pleistocene mammals were reference points available on which to base age estimates.

Some reasonably accurate bench-mark dates have now been established, or have been generally accepted, but unfortunately the spatial distribution of such dates adds to complexity instead of clarity. It is not yet possible to follow a chronological trail from a point of origin to the flowering of civilization in the two continents. Such a sequence may never be established, for reasons that will become clear later in this chapter.

The earliest established dates are derived from sites approximately mid-continent in North America, while others, perhaps equally old, are found in Mexico and South America. It would appear from such evidence that settlement occurred almost simultaneously over a wide area of the two continents, which is not likely. Reasonable time must be allowed for people to move, to explore, to adapt to local conditions. The sites to which these first dates are attached were occupied by accomplished hunters, with sophisticated stone weapons, which probably were not carried out of Asia but must have evolved in the New World—again suggesting an interval of time.

It is generally inferred that the first settlers came down from the North and, still earlier, from the Asiatic mainland. The North, at different times and in varying locations, was burdened with sheets of ice of thousands of feet in depth. Also, there were times when sea levels were low and a land bridge as much as 1,000 miles wide connected North America and Asia at the Bering Strait (Hopkins, 1959).

The last major ice thrust reached its climax and began to recede about 12,000 years ago. This coincides approximately with some of the earliest "accepted" dates for the mid-continent occupation sites. These sites, significantly, are south of the farthest thrust of glacial ice, which extended to the Missouri River in the West and to the Ohio River in the East. This probably means that men had reached the North American continent sometime prior to the last maximum glaciation.

How far back in prior time men reached this continent cannot be established from present knowledge. It is questionable whether the full story will ever be known, because then-existing land masses are now under water or have been scoured by glacial drifts.

Evidence for earlier occupation may result from more extensive knowledge of the Asiatic origin of the migrating population. Two rather distinctive cultural traditions are involved; one is older than the other, but the antecedents of both are remote in time. One of these traditions, the Eastern Asiatic, is characterized by a stone-work technology referred to as "chopper-scraper," a descriptive term applied to an assemblage of artifacts that are, typically, of igneous rock, fist-sized or smaller, fabricated into tools or weapons by fracturing or flaking to form a cutting or scraping edge. Material of this sort has been found, for example, at Choukoutien Cave in northern China, the occupancy of which covers a period of several hundred thousand years. Even more remotely, the chopper-scraper type of implement can be traced to the dawn of human history in eastern and southern Africa.

The other tradition derives from central Siberia and, ultimately, from North Africa, Europe, and the Near East. It reflects a considerable advance in the technique of shaping stone implements. Flakes are struck from a rock core and then carefully worked into a cutting or thrusting point. Both faces of the flake or chip are thinned to a fine edge by applying pressure with a pointed bone or other tool. Weapons and tools so fashioned have been recovered in the Lake Baikal region of Siberia, at a time depth estimated at 20,000 B.C. Archeologists who have studied the material see similarities between these Siberian specimens and early New World stone work. The resemblance is to the technique employed, not to any close similarity of appearance between the artifacts of the two areas.

The question of when the first migrations occurred may ultimately be determined by comparative studies of technological development. A scattering of evidence throughout the two continents suggests occupation as early as 30,000 years ago or even earlier. As yet, the suggestion is not widely accepted, but evidence does not disappear by being ignored or denied respectability.

One proponent of the earlier horizon theory, Alex D. Krieger (1964), advances the descriptive term *Pre-Projectile* for the period characterized by a limited range of tools and implements that could conceivably have accompanied a people migrating out of the older Eastern Asiatic tradition. Occupation at that time level would have limited access to the environment, and this too seems to be indicated by the sites thus far reported. The absence of spear points and finely flaked cutting edges, for example, suggests that hunting equipment was not highly specialized and that animal kills may have been accomplished by the use of wooden clubs, sharpened stakes, or other relatively inefficient implements. The association of crudely made human artifacts with extinct animal species (at least thirty such species and genera were identified at one site) suggests great antiquity, even where datable material has not been obtained or a reported date is subject to substantial reservations (Willey, 1966).

The absence of clearly established dates has thus far impeded acceptance of the evidence for a Pre-Projectile stage of development in the Americas. It is recognized, nevertheless, that a number of recorded sites can best be explained in terms of a crude technology of great antiquity.

When New World settlement is viewed from the point in time for which firm dates have been established, two features are apparent: The technology was capable of producing a variety of finely wrought tools, and man had spread all over North America south of lingering ice masses and perhaps over much of South America as well.

The time range involved here, supported by numerous radiocarbon dates, is between 15,000 B.C. and 5000 B.C. (Krieger, 1964; Jennings, 1968). The culture stage is variously referred to as Paleo-Indian, Upper Lithic, and Big Game Hunting, among others. Spear or lance points (arrowheads occur much later) are delicately chipped along both faces to achieve a sharp cutting edge. These points, from even the earliest sites in the series, are often channeled or "fluted" from the base part way up the face (Clovis type) or along the entire length of the blade (Folsom type), indicating great virtuosity in the art of stone chipping or flaking.

The distinctive type and workmanship reflected in this stone work is native; that is, the development took place in the New World. The technical knowledge may have been carried by early migrants out of Eurasia, but thus far no counterparts of the carefully fluted points have been discovered anywhere in the Old World.

While the economy was presumably based on big game hunting and the remains of mammoth and other extinct mammals are invariably associated with the human artifacts of the period, the ecological adaption was not limited to a single-minded pursuit of big game. It happens that the sites most commonly discovered and studied appear to be of the nature of "kill sites," where game animals were brought down and butchered. In some of the most spectacular finds, projectile points were discovered in actual association with the animals' bones. The material objects are usually those that a hunter might carry in the chase. Only rarely, as at the Lindenmeier Site in northern Colorado, have campsites been located that appear to have been occupied for protracted periods. In such instances a more varied inventory of stone and bone implements is found. Certainly small game was taken, and quite possibly other natural food substances were used, although no milling stones for grinding wild seeds are associated with the period.

The growing ability to make use of the varied resources of the land is demonstrated by the spread of this early population. By at least 8000 B.C., the big game hunter, with his specialized skills and equipment, had spread over the continent from the Rocky Mountains eastward to the Atlantic and from the retreating ice fields in the North down through Mexico and well into South America. The Strait of Magellan was reached soon after 7000 B.C., which gives an idea of how thoroughly and rapidly, in relative terms, the continents were covered. West of the Rocky Mountains, where the mammoth and other big game were not found, other kinds of hunters with a different tradition of stone work—a blade that tapered toward each end like a willow leaf—worked their way out of the Northwest (perhaps out of Eurasia as a separate tradition) and reached Mexico and the southern continent, presumably by a different route (Butler, 1961).

Not only had man occupied the northern continent, wherever habitable, but he had begun to make the regional adaptations that would characterize Indian society into historic times.

A major readaptation was forced upon these early hunters by the disappearance of certain of the game animals upon which they had subsisted. The mammoth, for example, whose dismembered skeletons are found so frequently in association with the fluted spear points of this period, had disappeared by about 8000 B.C. The mastodon, another variety of elephant, perished at about the same time or may have survived for a slightly longer period. This loss, without replacement of major animal types, was a peculiar characteristic of the final stages of the Ice Age in North America, as, indeed, it was in other parts of the northern hemisphere. It is reported that among the larger animals, no fewer than thirty-three genera became extinct during the Wisconsin, or terminal, stage in North America (Martin and Wright, Jr., 1967). Among those that Indians pursued as game animals were the native American horse, camel, a four-horned antelope, and an archaic bison. Hunting continued as a way of life into historic times, at least in the Great Plains, but the animals pursued were the modern bison and various deer and antelope species. Hunting persisted also in the nonagricultural North, of course, again with the substitution of modern animal species for those that became extinct.

There is as yet no satisfactory explanation for this relatively sudden disappearance of animal species, which had the effect of profoundly reshaping human life in the postglacial age. As the diminished biological environment became felt, new adaptations to subsistence needs followed.

The Archaic Mode

The succeeding period or cultural stage, designated the Archaic, is characterized by fuller exploitation of resources, with regional variations, and by an expanding population. The period began about 6000 B.C., earlier in some areas, and for some historic tribes it remained the basic scheme of life into modern times, with refinements in technology and social practice.

The inventory of tools and equipment was generally much greater and more versatile than in previous times, and variations in the assemblages reflect the habitat where settlement occurred. It was a gathering or foraging economy, in which game animals might still have provided a major food supply, but all manner of wild seeds, fruits, berries, nuts, roots, and fleshy plants were utilized. Along fresh-water streams and lakes and salt-water shores, fish and shellfish were taken in abundance with traps and weirs and specialized gear. Substances other than stone and bone were fabricated into utility objects. Especially common and diagnostic of the period are devices for grinding wild seeds or other vegetable matter. These take two particular forms: (1) a nether milling stone, called a *metate* (which is a Nahuatl word), and a hand-operated roller or abrader, called a *mano;* and (2) a hollowed-out stone or wooden mortar and a cylindrical stone or wooden pestle.

While a generic term, such as *Archaic,* might imply a certain universality of meaning, what is distinctive here is the range of adaptation. There was both a lateral spread of new lifeways across the continent and an evolutionary development upward through time. The disappearance of fluted points (the big game arsenal) was not immediately followed by the appearance of milling stones. At most of the sites studied, the early fluted points are followed by other (Plano) shapes and sizes of projectiles, suggesting modified hunting practices for the pursuit of different game species. Milling stones appear in the upper (later) strata.

The eastern half of the continent, where the Archaic way of life was first studied, a woodland environment, with abundant streams and a long shoreline, offered the greatest possible variety of natural resources. The tools and implements associated with the area indicate the many ways in which the people learned to exploit that environment with adzes, chisels, and mauls for woodwork; bone fish hooks, harpoons, and stone net sinkers; bone needles and awls used in basketry; fiber cordage for traps, fishlines, and snares; especially prepared milling stones for crushing hard shell nuts; and a wide variety of stone points, drills, knives, axes, scrapers, and so forth.

Prepared grave sites showing that burials were accompanied by gifts suggest new ceremonial practices. The corpse was probably painted in preparation for burial, as traces of red ocher are frequently found in the grave site. Turtle-shell rattles almost certainly point to the presence of shamanism (Caldwell, 1958).

In the Far West, where large game animals of the Ice Age were first to disappear or never flourished, the Desert Culture, which is equated with the Archaic, had its beginnings as early as 8000 B.C. Because of the extreme aridity of much of the area, as in the Great Basin, southeastern California, southern Arizona, and northern Mexico, agriculture never became established (except in some local situations), and the historic tribes occupying these desert environments have retained much of the basic cultural adaptations of their ancient forebears.

Seminole Indian women, Seminole Reservation, Florida, in traditional dress, standing before platform house (chickee).
(Courtesy, United States Farm Security Administration. Photo by Mydans.)

As is generally true of the Archaic stage of development, the Desert Culture is distinguished by an almost total exploitation of available resources. In an environment so stark and waterless, nothing could be wasted and nothing overlooked as a possible source of sustenance. The totality of resource use is illustrated at Danger Cave, located at the western edge of the Great Salt Desert in Utah. Some sixty-five different plant species, the seeds and other parts of which were used for food, were identified, all of them species still found in the immediate vicinity. More than 1,000 flat milling stones were also found in the deposits, the earliest of which was radiocarbon dated at 8500 B.C. (Jennings, 1968).

The Archaic period saw the beginnings of more settled communities. Even where people of necessity followed seasonal cycles of food gathering, supplemented by small game hunting, their movements were scheduled and purposeful. The rootless nomadic tribesman of later literature was already a fiction. Massive shell middens along the ocean shore and along an inland stream where fresh-water mussels abounded give evidence of prolonged periods of occupation. The first villages appeared late in the period, as at Wapanucket in southeastern Massachusetts (Griffin, 1964). At the opposite side of the continent, California, with its abundant marine resources and vast oak groves yielding acorns for food, provided an environment that favored large permanent settlements and concentrations of population. Only the fishing Indians of the Northwest Coast could equal the Californians in density of population.

Every ecological niche, to use the biologist's term, appears to have been occupied during the course of the Archaic stage, that is, by 2000 B.C. In the far North, the last major migrations out of northeast Asia brought the Eskimo and Athapaskan-speaking people into the Arctic zone and the interior of the continent, where they made their own highly specialized adaptations to sea and tundra and boreal forest. As the ice retreated from its southern perimeter, people carrying the Eastern Archaic tradition pushed upward into Canada until they encountered and occupied a common front with the ancestors of Algonkian-speaking tribesmen moving in behind the diminishing ice.

Occupation of the northern continent was complete.

The characteristic features of the Archaic period, as reported from numerous sites, need to be emphasized, because they prepared the way for the changes that would create the conditions in which the Indians were living when Europeans first encountered them.

Among these characteristics was a kind of moving, venturing spirit that induced people to try new environments and to invent the tools to go with the new conditions. Within a time span of several thousand years exploitative competence grew, populations expanded, and numerous environmental hazards must have been neutralized. At a site in Tennessee, where a number of burials were found, almost one-fifth of the skeletons were of adults beyond sixty years of age, some past seventy, which would indicate that the population had arrived at a reasonable life expectancy (Lewis and Lewis, 1961).

trade

There is good evidence that trade routes were established during this period, which would mean that individuals or small groups traveled to other regions and learned about other people—a familiar pattern in later Indian society. Olivella shells were carried from the coast of California far into the interior. Copper was traded out of the Lake Superior region eastward and southward many hundreds of miles. Rocky Mountain obsidian was made into projectile points in Illinois, Iowa, Wisconsin, and elsewhere in the Middle West. Shark and alligator teeth were found in the Ohio Valley.

Exchanges of technical information and ideas doubtless account for the spread of basketry and textile weaving, once these arts appeared on the horizon. The Desert Culture or aspect of the Archaic Tradition may have fostered these developments, as did also the metate-mano milling stones; at least the dates for these developments appear to be older in the Desert Culture province than elsewhere.

Another characteristic that would seem to have significance for the future was a factor of technology itself. In their foraging activities the people learned to identify varieties of plants and their economic uses. They became familiar with growth cycles and the influences of seasonal variations of rainfall and frost lines on plant life. They developed methods and structures for preserving and storing food products. They experimented with ways of preparing food. Some of these food processes, as in the preparation of acorns and manioc, with their bitter and poisonous juices, were complicated and must have involved considerable trial and error learning.

These cultural acquisitions, taken together, contributed to the transition that would lead to the practice of agriculture and to larger, stable communities of people—to the Indian world as it came to be.

The First Farmers

Beginning at about 1000 B.C., the cultural stream that had carried man and material artifacts southward out of northern North America reversed itself, like channeled tidewater at the end of its run. Thereafter, the flow was northward. The details of such a shift can only be suggested here, but the possible reasons for it become clear after a quick look at developments in southern Mexico.

Desert culture subsistence, with characteristic milling stones, storage

baskets, digging sticks, and related food-gathering equipment, appeared
in the Mexican highlands before 7000 B.C.; between that date and
2000 B.C. the economy had shifted from hunting-gathering to an agricultural base in which domesticated plants provided an ever-expanding
proportion of food production (Mangelsdorf, MacNeish, and Willey,
1964).

Plant domestication may have more than one point of origin, at least
different plants or different species of a given plant seem to appear for
the first time at separate locations. One major center was the Tehuacan *corn*
Valley in southeastern Mexico, near the modern city of Puebla. Here in
a number of dry caves and open sites, from which some 1 million individual bits of cultural data were collected and sorted out, the full course
of change from hunting-gathering to village agriculture has been reconstructed (MacNeish, 1964b).

The region produces wild varieties of a number of plants that came
under cultivation. The first to be domesticated appears to be a variety
of squash, at some time during the interval 7000–5000 B.C. In a later
sequence specimens of corn are found, evidently at an early stage of
domestication. The refuse in which the first specimens occur has a radiocarbon date of 5000 B.C. At the same time level were found remains of
avocado, chili peppers, and gourds (used as containers). Later, amaranth
(pig weed), tepary beans, zapotec, and squash were added, some of these
probably still in the wild state.

Maize was not fully domesticated; that is, it was not crossbred with
other genetically related species to form new strains for another 2,000
years. But after about 2500 B.C. plant cultivation throughout Meso-
america expanded rapidly.

An unexplained phenomenon in the history of maize development is
the occurrence of a primitive form of corn at Bat Cave in southwestern
New Mexico at an occupational level dated 3500 B.C. (Dick, 1965). The
region (Plains of San Augustine) yields no specimens of wild corn; thus
it is unlikely that domestication occurred locally. Later deposits in the
cave produced specimens leading up to fully evolved modern corn, suggesting a continuing importation from an originating center, presumably
Mexico. No diffusion from Bat Cave to other locations in the Southwest
occurred at the early date, and when corn appears elsewhere in the
region, some 2,000 or more years later, it is a fully evolved type.

By 1000 B.C. squash and the red kidney bean had followed corn into
the Southwest, and agriculture had made its beginnings along with settled
villages and pottery. House architecture (the so-called pit house) probably derived from the North, but the pottery appears to have its proto-
types in what is now northwestern Mexico (Willey, 1966).

Maize cultivation appears in the eastern part of the continent

(Eastern Woodland) at a slightly later time. But it is possible, of course, that perishable vegetable material failed to survive in the humid climate of the East, and this may account for the apparent absence of corn remains until sometime after 1000 B.C. Domestication of native plants—among them Chenopodium (goosefoot), sunflower, and amaranth—has been suggested for the Adena culture stage before corn shows up in occupation sites (Griffin, 1964). This spread of agriculture, in any case, was not eastward from the Southwest, but from two apparent Mesoamerican sources—the Valley of Mexico and along the Gulf Coast of Mexico out of Guatemala.

Except in the East, where rich soils and abundant rainfall favored plant growth, agriculture never entirely displaced the Archaic foraging adaptation in other areas of North America. A major exception was in the desert valleys of southern Arizona, where the Hohokam people practiced an intensive irrigation agriculture. It may be significant of the relationship between intensive agriculture and institutional growth that the Hohokam people, with their irrigated lands, adopted more traits out of the Valley of Mexico (the ceremonial ball court, truncated pyramid platforms, the jacal house type) than did other people of the Southwest (Reed, 1964).

Elsewhere in the West and Southwest, farming was marginal and, after an initial spread over the region, tended to withdraw to watered valleys. This was true, for example, of the Anasazi (Basket Maker–Pueblo) experience. People of this tradition carried agriculture northward into Utah, an adjacent strip of Nevada, and the western half of Colorado. Most of these outlying Anasazi settlements had pulled back to the Rio Grande and other irrigable valleys before A.D. 1200, leaving the country north and west of the Colorado River to Desert Culture foragers who, in historic times, would be the Shoshone and Paiutes (Reed, 1964).

The experience with agricultural limitations was not confined to the West and Southwest. In the upper Mississippi Valley–Great Lakes region incipient farmers encountered the same problem. The short growing season of the north proved inhospitable to maize, which had been introduced from the evolving Mississippi culture of the south sometime after A.D. 700. By A.D. 1200 agriculture had been abandoned, and the people returned to an older pattern of hunting and fishing, with wild rice as the principal plant food. Farther west, in northern Iowa, a similar effort to establish an agricultural base proved unsuccessful (Griffin, 1964). In the Great Basin and the Plateau country, where the Desert Culture was the initial adaptation, as well as in the High Plains, river and creek bottom farming was simply an addition to the old foraging-hunting style of life.

It was a life-style that fitted perfectly the kind of social organization that must have been developing throughout the West and northward to the Arctic. This was an unstratified, egalitarian, kinsmen-oriented group, cooperating in small units, and maintaining an intimate association with the natural environment. The people of these regions remained apart from the agriculturally induced urbanization that, in the Southeast and in Mesoamerica, divided populations into ruling hegemonies and voiceless masses.

The People

The Americans called Indians had physical form; they were not abstract phantoms. They had words for themselves and for other people they knew or encountered. They moved within, and were adapted to, a physical environment.

To express the reality behind such seemingly self-evident statements, it is necessary still to weave with speculation and inference. The physical form is varied, but not so varied as to exceed a basic homogeneity. Languages have survived as the speech of living people, without indicating clear origins or precise chronologies. Territories were occupied, but the occupation leaves unsettled the probabilities of lineal descent from the men who left the buried hearths and the spear points and tools of those first camps. These are uncertainties still, but within them are the lineaments of a race of man.

In even the earliest descriptions by incoming Europeans it was recognized that the Indians were physically a distinct people with "copper-colored skins" and coarse black hair—"almost like the hairs of a horse's tail," Columbus remarked (quoted in Washburn, 1964). Only much later, when more Indians had been observed, was it recognized that the Indian population was not, in fact, all of a single type. Skin color varied from ivory to the darkest brown. Hair form ranged from the coarse black of Columbus' observation to shades of brown and degrees of waviness. Stature and body build showed great variability. With respect to the Mongoloid features that are generally considered to be typically Indian—the slanting eye fold, the low-bridged nose, the smooth, straight brow, prominent cheek bones, scantiness of beard and body hair—these are not all equally manifested by all Indian population groups.

When skeletal material became available and comparative studies could be made between prehistoric and recent or contemporary crania, it was apparent that at least two rather different physical types were involved in the peopling of the Americas. The earliest skulls, going back 10,000 years or more, represented by some ten or more specimens (such finds have been uncommon), and widely distributed in both continents, are long-headed; that is, the distance from front to back of the head tends to be considerably greater than the distance between the sides of the head. The presumption is that the first settlers in the New World shared this characteristic.

Long-headed populations persisted in most areas of North America, at least where data are available, for several thousand years. Then, at varying time intervals, the trait gave way to broad- or round-headedness or to a kind of half-way stage, termed *mesocephalic*. In some regions, moreover, the two physical types were contemporaneous, at least briefly. This seems to have occurred in eastern North America, where Adena and Hopewell people in the Ohio Valley and adjoining areas shared a cultural continuum that began in Adena times at about 1000 B.C. and attained its full elaboration in the Hopewell period, which lasted until about A.D. 250. What studies of the skeletal material seem to show is that the Adena population, predominately round-headed, moved in among an earlier (Woodland) long-headed people; but the Hopewell population, in part contemporaries of the Adena and ultimately its cultural successors, was again long-headed (Willey, 1966).

In the Southwest a similar shift, but perhaps not so marked, occurred between Basket Maker III and Pueblo I times, that is, between A.D. 450 and A.D. 750.

Various interpretations of the physical data have been offered to account for these population shifts. Most common, at least in early studies, was the notion of an actual invasion or displacement of people by latecomers equipped with superior exploitative tools and techniques. This may still account for the sequence of events in some instances, but recent studies have suggested other possibilities that take into account more of the factors involved.

When the full range of measurable physical traits came to be correlated, the differences exhibited at different time levels and in different geographical zones seemed too diverse to be contained within a single inbreeding population. Two possible explanations suggested themselves: either the migrating population was already a hybrid of two or more constituent strains, in which case buried traits would surface in succeeding generations; or migration occurred in a series of waves, each composed of a stable, homogeneous population.

Such physical anthropologists as E. A. Hooton and J. B. Birdsell looked for American origins in various Old World ethnic stocks, some of which were non-Mongoloid or antedated the emergence of the specific Mongoloid type. The American Indians, according to this view, represented an amalgam of very old genetic strains that was formed before migration to the New World occurred.

The second view, favoring the idea of multiple, sequential migrations, has been offered by several students, most persuasively perhaps by G. K. Neumann (1952). He proposed eight physical types, representing different migrating groups separated in time and in geographical distribution. The earliest, in terms of settlement and distribution, was designated Otamid, a long-headed type. It is represented by the human skull discovered at Midland, Texas, which may be 20,000 years old. The most recent of Neumann's types were the Inuid (Eskimo) and Deneid (Athapaskan tribes), which entered the New World as recently as 4,000 years ago.

The recent trend is toward a restatement of the basic homogeneity of the New World physical type, in which greater allowance is made for the dynamics of genetic process in accounting for variability. In this view, offered by T. D. Stewart (1960) and M. T. Newman (1953, 1962), among others, a relatively homogeneous incoming population spread thinly over the wide expanses of the two continents, beginning as far back as perhaps 30,000 years ago. The variety of physical environments encountered favored permanent settlement, once an ecological balance had been achieved. This in turn favored isolated breeding groups, in which, given the time lapse now deemed possible, natural selection, mutation, and genetic drift would bring about modifications in the gene pool itself. The basic homogeneity was not lost, but it came to be expressed as highly variable population.

The shift from long-headedness to round-headedness, in this view, was not an all-at-once happening such as might have occurred by the displacement of an early population by later invaders. It was rather a gradual process, brought about by interbreeding, or it may even indicate an ongoing evolutionary process within the human race, the evidence for which extends beyond the Americas.

Whatever the differences of interpretation, it is generally agreed that the Americans called Indians have no counterparts in Asia nor anywhere else in the world. For all that they differ among themselves, they are one people. The impression expressed by a Spanish traveler, Francisco de Ulloa, as early as 1772, "If we have seen one Indian, we may be said to have seen them all, their color and make are so much alike" (Stewart and Newman, 1951, 19), remains essentially accurate. In Stewart's words, "It is safe to say that no population of comparable size has remained so uniform after expanding, in whatever time has been involved, over such a large land area" (Stewart 1960, 259).

Language

The variability expressed in physical form has its counterpart in groupings of some half-dozen basic language stocks, each containing a broad band of cognate tongues ranging from locally differing dialects, with some interchange of communication possible, to mutually unintelligible languages so distantly related that only sophisticated analysis can demonstrate even inferential kinship. The gross number of more than 2,000 separate, identifiable languages spread throughout the two continents gives an idea of the possibilities for interpreting movement in time and space.

Indian languages, like other aspects of Indian existence, have been studied from earliest times for clues to origins and relationships with other peoples of the world. Word lists were gathered and compared with other world languages. Since any comparison of unrelated languages will reveal by pure chance a small percentage of identical or nearly identical sounds, it is possible to "discover" affiliations between native American tongues and such unlikely languages as modern Welsh. As language study progressed beyond simple sight comparisons and knowledge was gained about internal structure, it became increasingly evident that the languages of the New World had no immediate progenitors in any part of the Old World.

The situation was roughly comparable to that which emerged from studies of the genetic composition of the American race. Whether initial settlement was accomplished by speakers of a single language or of several languages, the time lapse of from 15,000 to 30,000 years was sufficient to account for the great diversity that ultimately developed. A process of environmental adaptation might produce such variance, for example, as Eskimo preoccupation with snow and the large herbal vocabularies of the desert tribes. Such adaptive modifications, of course, are quite apart from the internal stresses and divergencies that normally bring about change in language behavior.

It is possible, as Swadesh (1964) suggests, that the earliest migrating languages were lost, either by absorption in later speech styles or simply by the extinction of the speakers. If any of these very early languages survived into historical times, as he indicates, they are probably to be found in isolated areas of South America and apparently bear no relationships to any of the extant linguistic divisions. The most recent language group to reach North America is the Eskimo-Aleut or the "Bask-Dennean" of Swadesh's terminology, which includes Eskimo-Aleut as well as Nadene. This is also the only group whose antecedents can

be traced with some certainty to Old World roots. Even here, the division
is of such antiquity—at least 4,000 years—as to elude identification with
any specific language group.

Like the spread of man himself over the world, languages divide from
parent stocks and are carried into new territory, where, isolated from
the original speakers, and possibly in contact with tongues of a different
origin, they develop along their own internal dynamics and, in turn, sub-
divide into dialects and separate new languages. In this view, the languages spoken in the Americas, while they may have no immediate progenitors outside of the hemisphere, are seen as part of a world community of linguistic kin.

From Prehistory to History

The native world that existed before permanent settlers moved in
from Europe is less remote and inscrutable than it seemed last century
when the great mounds of the Ohio and Mississippi Valleys and the
monumental works of Middle America were first contemplated (and
pillaged). Clearly such accomplishments, it seemed, were beyond the
capacities of the unlettered savages who roamed the forests and deserts.
The better understanding we now have of aboriginal America can be
traced to a lessened parochialism growing out of wider knowledge of
man's evolutionary development, but it also traces to the extensive ethnographic studies and historical reconstructions published within the
century. It is now possible for anyone seriously interested in American
beginnings to read about the Sioux or the Iroquois, the Aztec or the
Maya, and to realize that New World society was experienced at many
levels.

What is not yet possible, with only a few exceptions, is to establish
clear lines of descent between contemporary tribes and prehistoric
groups. The archeologist is often able to describe the precontact style of
life of a people, on the material level at least, with some of the fullness
of detail that an ethnographer obtains from a study of a contemporary
community. But the archeologist's people disappear like evening
shadows, while the ethnographer, working with historical material, is not
certain of the antecedents of his contemporary community. Cultural
sequences that flourished through 1,000 years pass into oblivion, seemingly without remainder.

Throughout the Southeast, for example, a highly successful agriculture permitted the growth of large population centers, which in some
instances approached true urban developments. The cultural florescence
that accompanied this population growth resulted in an elaborate art

and ceremonial life and marked social stratification that endured from about A.D. 500 until as late as A.D. 1650, yet the tribes that were residing in the Southeast when Europeans entered the area seem suddenly diminished. A partial explanation no doubt arises from the fact that the chroniclers who accompanied the earliest expeditions of discovery and conquest were looking for the familiar and, not finding it, described what was not present and overlooked what was evident. They wrote of nonexistent European-model kings and kingdoms and dismissed as heathen extravagance the ceremonial practices they happened to observe. The chroniclers, unfortunately, were not social scientists.

A further, and perhaps more telling, explanation can be attributed to the actual reduction and scattering of populations resulting from epidemics spawned by initial contacts with Europeans in the sixteenth and seventeenth centuries (Sears, 1964) and from border wars, as in Virginia in 1622 and 1644. In Swanton's monumental compilation (1953), in which the author tried to locate geographically the tribes of North America in and around the year 1650, one finds constant reference to amalgamations of shattered tribal remnants, of tribal refugees seeking the protection of still powerful groups, and of total extinction of such once potent hierarchical states as that created by the Natchez. The monumental structures of the flourishing Southeastern culture are nowhere mentioned in association with the tribes that Swanton catalogued.

The ceremonial splendor that must have marked the life revolving around the massive temple mounds at Etowah in northern Georgia, for example, is not reflected in the early accounts of the Cherokee people, whose ancestors created the mounds and the culture that gave rise to them. It is believed that the Busk, or Green Corn, ceremony of the historic Cherokees and of other Southeastern tribes is a survival of an earlier religious theme (Sears, 1964).

The only other major Southeastern tribes whose identity with prehistoric settlement areas has been creditably established are the Creek, Choctaw, and Chickasaw, who moved in late prehistoric times into the coastal regions between northwestern Florida and the mouth of the Mississippi River. The great ceremonial center at Moundville in west central Alabama, one of the largest urban developments in the Southeast, may have been ancestral to these tribes.

In the Northeast region the lines of descent from prehistoric settlements to identifiable tribal communities are only slightly less obscure. As the Hopewell culture complex of the Ohio River Valley declined as the major influence after about A.D. 250, various regional variants prospered. Some of these experienced their own developmental sequence and were still evolving as political units when first contacts were made with Europeans. The high artistic achievements of Hopewell times were not recaptured by these later emerging groups, but they benefited from a more developed agriculture in some areas and from influences spreading northward out of the Southeast and perhaps ultimately out of Mexico and Middle America.

One such development was the northward spread from a germinal center at Cahokia (near modern St. Louis) along the Mississippi River to the upper reaches of that river and eastward along the Great Lakes. Here it is identified archeologically as the Oneota culture, which gave rise to the Iowa, Missouri, Oto, and Winnebago—all Siouan-speaking tribes of historic times. The movement occurred during the period A.D. 700–1200; and when the northern end of the population spread found agriculture a precarious economic base, it reverted to an earlier hunting-gathering style of life.

Still farther north, across northern Wisconsin and around the north shore of Lake Superior, various Algonkian groups can be identified. Some of these, with neighboring Siouan groups, shared in the Effigy Mound complex of the upper Mississippi Valley, one of the final phases of the Hopewell culture, expressed as an elaborate concern with burials and in ceramic design.

Perhaps the most studied and best delineated transition from prehistoric to historic times centers on the Iroquoian people of the lower Great Lakes and central New York. Within this general area from about A.D. 1000 the Owasco culture flourished, a regional adaptation of the Woodland tradition with borrowings from the vanishing Hopewell radiance. Some domesticated food plants were grown, at least corn and beans, supplementing the basic hunting and gathering way of life. By A.D. 1200 the longhouse was in use, and palisaded village clusters began to appear, indicating an expanding semi-sedentary population. Squash was added to the garden crops, forming the Indian trinity of plants, and a localized pottery style had emerged. All of these were distinguishing features of the Iroquois people when they were first encountered by Europeans, as by Cartier in the St. Lawrence Valley in 1534 (Griffin, 1964; Jennings, 1968).

The varied regions within the Plains area present the same discontinuity between archeological remains and identifiable tribesmen of the early chronicles, even though some cultures survived as viable, though modified, communities until well into the nineteenth century. The archeological sequences have, in fact, been so extensively worked out, as a consequence of the salvage operations precipitated by the construction of dams within the Missouri River basin, that Plains prehistory is perhaps now better understood than that of any region outside of the Southwest. Even so, it is still not possible to document clear lines of descent from prehistory to contact history for more than a handful of Plains tribes.

The earliest recorded encounter between Europeans and Indians living between the Rocky Mountains and the Mississippi was chronicled by the Coronado Expedition of 1541, in what is now western Kansas. The Indians, referred to as *Querechos* by the Spanish, are now thought of as having been representatives of the Athapaskan (Apachean) people who had only recently entered the Southwest from the far North.

Occupation of the Plains can be traced back at least 12,000, possibly 15,000 years, and through a series of developmental stages. But only in the latest of these, the Plains Village stage, beginning before A.D. 1000, is it possible to make at least tentative identification with tribes of the historic period. The descriptive term refers to a time when corn-growing Indians occupied the fertile valleys of all the major streams flowing eastward out of the Rockies, in permanent villages of earth-covered houses. They made a sturdy, durable pottery and utilized a variety of materials in fashioning household tools and utensils. After the horse reached the Plains from Spanish settlements in the Southwest at the beginning of the eighteenth century, some tribal groups abandoned farming (which provided a precarious economic base in some areas) and became highly mobile hunters; but others among the Plains Village tribes maintained their fixed settlements and used the horse only on semiannual hunts into the neighboring countryside.

Perhaps the best known among these latter were the Mandan villages on the upper Missouri River, where the Lewis and Clark expedition spent the winter of 1804–1805. The Mandans were first visited, however, by Sieur de La Vérendrye in 1738, when they occupied nine separate, but closely affiliated, villages. When Lewis and Clark wintered with them, the villages had been reduced to two, and the population was perhaps one-third of what it had been in the previous century (Swanton, 1953).

The archeological record includes several sites along the Missouri River between what is now Yankton, South Dakota, and Bismarck, North Dakota, the earliest of which has been dated at A.D. 710 (Wedel, 1964). Mandan tradition makes reference to earlier locations downriver from the Missouri–Heart River junction where they were living when they saw white men for the first time (presumably the Vérendrye party). At least some of these traditional village locations correspond to the excavations carried out along the Missouri River.

The Pawnee bands and the related Wichita constitute another group whose antecedents can be traced into the archeological past. They were among the indigenous tribesmen whom Coronado encountered on the western Plains in 1541, and in any case they had dwelt upon the Plains in their earth-covered houses since at least A.D. 1100, according to dated sites attributed to them. The earliest of these sites are in Nebraska along the lower Platte River and the Republican branch of the Kansas River.

Wichita settlements were farther south, in Kansas, along tributaries of the Arkansas River.

The Pawnee bands moved northeastward, to the Loup River above its confluence with the Platte, in the years just preceding the coming of Europeans to the New World. This migration seems to have been part of a general population shift beginning after A.D. 1450, when numerous small, scattered settlements were abandoned and larger centers were constructed nearer the Missouri River or along its main tributaries. That a succession of drought years was responsible for this movement is inferred from tree-ring data compiled in recent years. During the period 1471–1518 in North Dakota, for example, the data show a total of forty years of prolonged drought, alternating with brief intervals of normal, or above normal, moisture. The dry years, moreover, were characterized by heavy dust storms that buried some abandoned sites under deep layers of silt (Jennings, 1968). The new sites were built within defensive stockades, and houses were bunched closer together than had been the practice of earlier times; thus, it can be inferred that a certain amount of forceful collision accompanied the search for better watered homelands.

One further effect of this late population shift was a certain blending of regional cultures, with borrowing intensified by increased tribal contacts. The house type, for example, which throughout the Plains prior to the fifteenth century had been rectangular or square in shape, with excavated floors and a central fire pit, was changed to a circular structure, earth covered as before, and sometimes as large as 80 feet in diameter. Agriculture in this later period was practiced more intensively, and large numbers of food storage pits suggest surpluses for trade or as a supply to carry the communities through lean years. Quite possibly the increased production resulted from the growing of improved strains of corn from the East, where much of the Plains culture originated.

While the association of historic tribes with archeological sites is just beginning to be delineated in the Plains area, the antecedents of many of the Southwestern tribes have been known, or reasonably inferred, for some time. The record of cultural development in the Southwest is, indeed, better known than in any other region of native America, and in at least one instance the record of continuous occupation to historic times is only exceeded perhaps by recent discoveries in the Tehuacan Valley of southern Mexico.

Ventana Cave in southern Arizona near the Mexican border (and inside the Papago Indian Reservation) has an occupation history covering more than 10,000 years. The lowest level of the cave contained cultural materials of the Big Game Hunting stage, along with the fossilized remains of such extinct mammals as the horse, four-pronged

antelope, tapir, sloth, and the dire wolf. At 6000 B.C. or earlier the occupants of the cave were primarily foragers rather than hunters, as is suggested by the occurrence of milling stones for seed grinding. In the
archeological time scale this corresponds approximately with the emergence of the Cochise, a regional variant of the Desert Culture. Three
stages (in time) of the Cochise tradition are generally recognized:
Sulphur Springs, Chiricahua, and San Pedro. The last of these is marked
by the introduction of pottery and the beginnings of agriculture. This
detail is mentioned here because all three stages are found at the various
levels of occupation in Ventana Cave. In fact, the cave was used as campsite or living quarters all through the Hohokam Period, beginning about
100 B.C., and continuing into historic times. The topmost deposits contained pottery and other material objects of modern Papago Indians
(Haury, 1950).

It is not possible to say, of course, that the original occupants of the
cave were the lineal ancestors of contemporary Indians. The Papagos
speak a dialect of the Piman language, a component of the Uto-Aztecan
group that extends from southern Idaho to Central America. Unlike
material artifacts, language cannot be recovered from archeological deposits. However, from internal evidence of language divergence and
spread, Swadesh (1964) estimates that Uto-Aztecan was centered in the
Southwest at least by 1000 B.C. and possibly much earlier.

A similarly continuous chronology, though of shorter time span, can
be demonstrated for the modern Pueblo peoples of the Rio Grande Valley,
western New Mexico, and the Hopi villages of Arizona. These and their
predecessors, the Basket Maker people, together referred to as the
Anasazi (a Navaho word meaning "ancient ones"), have occupied
approximately the same territory since the early years of the Christian
Era. Through all this time, they have been village-dwelling farmers,
gradually elaborating their technologies and style of life until the coming
of European settlement at the end of the sixteenth century. At a slightly
earlier time, beginning about 300 B.C., the Mogollon culture of southwestern New Mexico and southeastern Arizona had acquired agriculture
and pottery, presumably from Mexico, and these and other traits were
carried north to the Anasazi country. In fact, the Mogollon people themselves are believed to have assimilated with the Anasazi, and their descendants may be the Indians of Zuni and other Pueblos (Martin and
Rinaldo, 1960).

Still another center of cultural development of some antiquity
occurred in the Southwest—Patayan along the lower Colorado River.
Like the Mogollon, the Patayan represents a gradual regional adaptation
out of the basic desert or Archaic culture of the Southwest. Differences
of opinion exist in assigning a beginning date for this development,

marked by flood-water irrigation, cremation of the dead, and specialized pottery forms, but it was in existence at least by A.D. 600 (Willey, 1966). The modern Yuman tribes—that is, Mohave, Walapai, Havasupai, Maricopa, and Yuma—are thought to be the descendants of this early riverine adaptation.

The Athapaskan-speaking people, the Navaho and Apache, entered the Southwest in very late prehistoric times, perhaps not earlier than the fifteenth century, and, of course, have persisted in approximately the same areas they occupied when first encountered by incoming Europeans.

The Arctic

Sequences of settlement and adaptation in the Arctic and the Subarctic interior have not been clearly defined as yet, although occupation dates have been pushed back to greater time depths. Part of the problem of determining time relationships in the North is that cultural styles tend to persist without striking changes over long periods, even when the probabilities are that shifts of population occurred. It would seem that once man had developed the essential tools and technologies for life along the Arctic sea, in tundra country, and in the boreal forest, he had little reason and scant inducement to experiment with new devices. Gaining a livelihood became highly specialized, and maintaining an ecological balance was the essential concern.

Certain broad time horizons have been designated, or at least suggested, but these do not always fit into an early-to-late progression. Earliest is a Pre-Eskimo period, with a possible beginning date of 16,-000 B.C. at British Mountain on the Arctic coast, just east of the Alaska-Canada boundary. Other sites that belong to this time period are found at Kogruk in the Brooks Range, tentatively dated at 8000–6000 B.C., and perhaps the Palisades complex at Cape Krusenstern north of Kotzebue Sound, which appears to be "very old" (Giddings, 1960).

Some Pre-Eskimo sites of only a slightly later time period yield stone projectile points similar in style and workmanship to the fluted and, later, Plano, points characteristic of the Big Game Hunting period of the Great Plains. Still other sites contain leaf-shaped points that closely resemble the Old Cordilleran tradition of the Pacific Northwest and Interior Plateau. Since the dates for this northern material generally tend to be later in time than the Plains and Northwestern forms, it is assumed that the diffusion was from the south northward, in what Collins refers to as the phenomenon of "Arctic retardation" (Collins, 1964). Influences from the South were late in reaching the Arctic, due to distances and difficulties of travel. What is probably remarkable is that contact of any extent was maintained when travel was probably accomplished on foot.

At later intervals, not in sequence and not spatially related, are the Northwest Microblade Tradition and the Arctic Small-Tool Tradition. The former extends from the interior of Alaska, where it may have originated, into neighboring Yukon Territory and southeastward into the Canadian Northwest Territories. The possible chronological range may be from as early as 6500 B.C. until as late as 1000 B.C. This was a hunting culture subsisting on land mammals, all of modern species, with no significant changes in the economy during that period, except for an apparent population increase toward the end.

The Arctic Small-Tool Tradition evidently developed along the Bering Sea coast, from which it spread eastward following the Arctic coast all the way to Greenland. The time interval is from about 4000 B.C. to 1000 B.C., and eventually it blends with incoming Eskimo cultures. At Cape Denbigh on Seward Peninsula, where the tradition is most clearly defined, the subsistence seemed to be based on the hunting of sea mammals as well as inland caribou (summarized in Willey, 1966).

Eskimo culture appears late on the scene, sometime after 2000 B.C. and possibly as late as 1000 B.C. It is not likely that the culture was formed in Asia and moved intact as a language, a population shift, and a way of life, although it is sometimes described in a manner to leave that implication. It is a hunting culture, reflecting various adaptations to geographical regions, to available resources, and to types of sea and land game animals. While the spread of the culture is principally along seacoasts—the Pacific coast of Alaska and the Arctic shores from Siberia to Greenland—inland waterways and caribou hunting grounds were equally a part of the yearly round.

Much of the territory identified as Eskimo country was occupied by less specialized, earlier hunting peoples, some of whom may have been Eskimo-speaking; and much of what is characterized as Eskimo culture represents the spread of ideas, technologies, and material artifacts to these earlier inhabitants. In this respect, cultural development in the North was largely a matter of internal development, as was the case elsewhere on the continent. The transition from big game hunting to foraging and, finally, to agriculture in more southerly regions was a process through time, not a displacement of people, although some population shifts doubtless took place. Even when physical invasion occurred, the likelihood is that the older population was absorbed by the invaders; or, in fact, the invaders might have been absorbed, disappearing as a recognizable foreign entity.

It is clear that influences from the circumpolar regions of Eurasia did enter into the combination of traits and life-styles, even into the physical composition that is recognized as specifically Eskimo. But what is equally clear from recent archeological findings is that the region facing the Bering Strait, including both shores, was the center from which specialized tools and skills for subsisting in the harsh northern climate spread throughout the Arctic environment. It was not, in other words, simply a bleak and hostile region through which people passed on their way to other and more friendly places, but was rather an area of cultural stability where generations of hunters and fishermen slowly acquired and passed on the skills and knowledge needed in the North (Giddings, 1960).

In its development, Eskimo culture moved in two directions, spatially and ecologically. One spread, and it may be the older trend (sites have been dated at 1000 B.C.), was southward along the Pacific shore into the Aleutians and the Gulf of Alaska. The other movement was to the north, around the northwestern shoulder of Alaska, and eastward all the way to Labrador and Greenland.

In its southern outreach the cultural adaptation was influenced by a milder climate, more abundant and more accessible resources, and the presence of non-Eskimo people of the Northwest Coast of the United States. The development in this southern sector was away from classical Eskimo, in material artifacts as well as in language.

This is not to say that Eskimo culture was without its regional variants, but in its diffusion northward and eastward it was primarily an adaptation to a climate of extreme cold, of timberless land masses, of long winter nights, of ice and blowing snow, where survival depended on making effective use of the very elements that could destroy—hence, the snow house and sophisticated winterized clothing made from animal skins and furs. The uniformity of this eastward thrust of more than 6,000 miles, in subsistence practices and in language, is remarkable among the cultures of the world, as Collins has indicated (Collins, cited in Giddings, 1960).

The Northwest Microblade Tradition gave rise to an inland type of adaptation, in somewhat the same fashion as the Arctic Small-Tool Tradition fostered the Eskimo development. Some time after 1000 B.C. the fine flint work that characterized the Microblade Tradition disappeared and was replaced for the most part by polished stone woodworking tools and by weapons and tools fashioned out of bone and antler. Copper also came into use. And increased use was made of wood and bark for household purposes. The environment was primarily a coniferous forested area, with many streams, lakes, and marshes, spreading from Yukon Territory, possibly from the interior of Alaska, into the Northwest Territories, and eastward across the northern parts of Alberta, Saskatchewan, and Manitoba. It was a culture of hunters and trappers, to which the designation *Denetasiro* has been given. The early phase of this forest culture dates from about A.D. 300, and it continued into historic times. Of interest here is the suggestion that the *Denetasiro* hunters were the immediate ancestors of the historic Athapaskan tribes (MacNeish, 1962) who ranged generally north of the Algonkian-speaking Cree and Blackfoot Indians.

Retrospect

What has been reviewed here, all too briefly, is a long history of ecological adaptation, of people learning the infinite variety of the land and accommodating themselves to it. Though details have been generalized or omitted (sometimes for the simple reason that they are not known), certain characteristics or themes are strikingly apparent.

Foremost, perhaps, is an underlying homogeneity that persists as a kind of nucleating core within great diversity—of physical type, language, subsistence base, social form, ceremonial style, and technological level. The Spanish traveler Ulloa remarked on it in 1772, as noted earlier, referring specifically to physical types. A modern student scans the whole sweep of contemporary Indian life and remarks:

> Amid all the variety of customs among present-day Indian communities in the United States and Canada, an impression of similarity grows as one becomes acquainted with successive reservations. . . . Similar trends in the replacement of material culture, similarities in dialects of English, likenesses in kinship behaviors and types of extended families, comparable growths of nativism and adaptations of ceremonial life, and even what one feels to be nearly identical constellations of personality traits thrust themselves on one's attention [Spicer, 1961, 1].

It would almost seem that something in the land itself and in its challenges compelled a certain kind of human adaptation. Perhaps it is not fortuitous that the Indians in their creation stories conceive of man as emerging from the underworld, the earth. First Man and First Woman do not spring fully formed from the sea or from the head of a God, and not from any Word. They are weak and imperfect beings faced with imminent doom, which they escape by calling upon their brothers of the earth, sky, and water—badger, beaver, turtle, ant, raven, chipmunk, blue jay, dragonfly—the cast of characters varies from region to region, but the theme is well-nigh universal. Man and the animals are equally involved in making the world. Nowhere in these stories is man portrayed as a superior being, as the master of those who come to his aid. It is a world, moreover, in which moral judgments are never pronounced. When triumph occurs, it is likely to result from some

A Western Apache warrior and the weaponry with which his people fought the United States army in the late nineteenth century.
(Courtesy, United States Bureau of Indian Affairs.)

act of chicanery, with a jocular twist, not from inherent nobility or as virtue's reward. And defeat is due to some human foible or piece of stupidity, again laughable, not because evil deserves to be defeated. Man is always earthbound, with no grandiose presumptions about himself or his destiny.

The land in its infinite variety, its immensity of space, stretching to empty horizons, and its first loneliness, compelled respect, and moving through it man saw himself in perspective against thundering waterways and crashing mountains. Not only was his stature held to lifesize, but he recognized himself as but one of the features of that infinite landscape, and he made no prior claim because he was alive and sentient. What he was, he owed to that which was around him, and he gave back what he could of himself. The idea of reciprocity became the core of his social existence.

That was the nature of the adaptation that the Americans called Indians achieved in the New World.

The individual could stray from this model, legitimately. He could stand up before his peers and brag shamelessly about his bravery, his skill as a horse thief, his trophies of war. He could spend hours on his personal adornment, polishing his hair and weaving into it bits of fine fur and gaudy ribbon, until he was a regular turkey cock. (Many a trail-worn, foul-smelling explorer and trader offered curled-lip comment on this trait.) He could pile up mountains of personal possessions and give them all away, as witness to his open-handed generosity. Such behavior was ostentatious, but a formalized and accepted pattern. It was not, as the early observers concluded, a matter of the individual building a reputation at the expense of less competent tribesmen. The element of competition was totally lacking. When speaker followed speaker in council, each in his splendor, and told of his exploits and flourished his trophies, they were not vying with each other. It was the group that responded in pride of achievement. Even the least could say, "We are a great people."

Dorothy Lee remarks on this quality in Indian life when she writes of the Sioux: "A boy had a duty to develop himself, to increase in hardihood, in physical prowess, in skill, in bravery, because through enhancing himself he enhanced his society" (1959, 62).

The individual found himself within the group and had no role outside of it, and yet he was under no compulsion. He acted out his community role, because that was who he was. He could also be a deviant and not seek to distinguish himself in acts of public service, and the group responded by accepting him in that role, thus keeping him viable. The autonomy of the individual was never diminished, whatever social pressure was brought to bear. In describing the Navaho view of life, Kluckhohn and Leighton observe:

> While the individual is always seen as a member of a larger group, still he is never completely submerged in that group. There is an area of rigidity where what any given person may and may not do is inexorably fixed, but there is likewise a periphery of freedom . . . Rights of individuals, including children, over their immediate personal property, are respected to the fullest degree, even when their wishes run counter to the obvious interests of the family [1947, 228].

A closely parallel pattern is described by Weltfish for the Pawnee: "Neither personal relations nor the personnel of the household were cramped within a fixed kin structure. The individual personality was not trimmed down to fit the kin structure, but the structure was used to realize the individual personality" (1965, 50). At another place, she says: "One thing is clear, no one is caught within the social code. Against the backdrop of his natural environment, each individual stands as his own person" (1965, 57).

Writing specifically in the same study about political control within Pawnee society, Dr. Weltfish remarks:

> They were a well-disciplined people, maintaining public order under many trying circumstances. And yet . . . there was no code of rules of conduct nor punishment for infraction. There were no commandments nor moralizing proverbs. The only instigator of action was the consenting person [1965, 5].

The Pueblos of the Southwest might seem to stand in sharp contrast with what has been just described, for social control among the Pueblos was a tightly woven mesh of restraints and compulsions that apparently left the individual few opportunities for autonomous action (see Dozier in Spicer, 1961). In fact, the individual was the apparatus of control. The community was not hierarchically organized, and no one was left out. The individual functioned qua individual, but he also functioned as the community. Ridicule and gossip could be directed at him to keep him in line, but he also could be the gossiper when someone else got out of line, including institutional leaders.

It is also pertinent perhaps to remark that the Pueblos have lived under the threat of extermination or dissolution for a longer time than any other Indian group in North America and have adopted defenses against such threats. Enforced conformity has been the price they have had to pay for maintaining their societies, as at Taos where in recent years there has been bitter opposition to voting in state or national elections and to the introduction of electric power into the pueblo. In aboriginal times, it would seem, nonconsenting, or dissident, groups could, and did, break away, as happened at Hopi within the present century. There is now no place for the dissenter to go, except into exile.

These similarities of attitude and practice, spread over the continent, are indicative of what must be another characteristic of life in the New World before the coming of Europeans. People moved about, bearing ideas, curious about what other people were doing, borrowing from each other. A common theme of the narratives grandfathers spun for their young audiences in evening firelight had to do with journeys, fabled or otherwise, in which strange and friendly people were encountered and magical gifts were obtained.

"When they were departing, the Wildcats said to the Bear party:

'You must surely come again next year and visit us, and teach our people to weave baskets like that one.'" Thus concludes one of the California tribal stories recorded by Jaime de Angulo (1953, 160). Like all such folk tales, the attitudes and behaviors described are woven out of the fabric of the culture. Animal-people are expected to have such attitudes and to behave that way, because that is the way of the people.

The principal routes over which people traveled were in many cases well established long before Europeans came to "discover" and "explore" the continent. Perhaps the oldest in all of North America was the long trade route extending from southern Arizona through western Mexico and eventually reaching Middle America. It was down this road that Cabeza de Vaca fled after his shipwreck on the Texas coast and his harrowing six years of captivity and wandering westward; and it was up the same road that Coronado marched in 1540 with 200 horsemen, 70 foot soldiers, 1,000 head of livestock—and 1,000 Indians to carry burdens and show the way. Much of the cultural borrowing between the indigenous cultures of the southwestern United States and the Valley of Mexico followed this, or other similar, routes.

Carl Sauer, the geographer, retraced the route some years ago, many sections of which still showed the wear of generations of foot travel, and afterward he wrote:

> In the New World the routes of the great explorations usually have become historic highways. . . . For the explorers followed main trails beaten by many generations of Indian travel. There was, in varying degrees, intercommunication and exchange of goods between Indian villages or tribes. . . . Explorers, being sensible men if their explorations succeeded, used Indian guides, who took them over Indian roads [1932, 6].

When Henry Kelsey traveled upcountry from Hudson Bay in 1690, the first white man to reach the interior of the continent from the North, he traveled with Indians who knew the waterways and portages all the way to the Saskatchewan prairies.

At every port of entry touched by the first Europeans, travel routes reached far back into the hinterland. The French coming up the St. Lawrence Valley, as well as Dutch and English in the Hudson and Mohawk Valleys, stimulated trade nerves, the impulses of which reached 1,000 miles beyond the headwaters. Long before a white man ever saw a Sioux or Cheyenne or Blackfoot Indian, the lives of these tribes were affected, just as in aboriginal America farming Indians found their lives enriched by new breeds of corn coming north out of Mexico.

In the Canadian Rockies in the 1920s, Marius Barbeau collected stories told by various Salishan tribes about the new world that was to come when life "would be easy" (1923). From internal evidence within the stories, Barbeau estimated that the mythical events recounted had their origins in encounters between Indians and white men that actually occurred generations earlier in time, at far distant places. The instrument that was to make "life easy" was the steel ax.

The Flathead, or Nez Percé, Indians (the record is not clear as to the tribe) who traveled from the Northwest all the way to St. Louis in the 1830s to persuade a priest-missionary to come to their country were responding to counsel they had received from Iroquois Indians working as canoemen for the Hudson's Bay Company. The Iroquois tribesmen, some of whom married into these Plateau tribes, assured their hosts that the Black Robes possessed special powers that would help them defend themselves against the aggressive Blackfoot and Crow Indians, already possessed of guns, who were encroaching on their hunting grounds.

What is suggested by the network of trade and travel routes, many of which have been traced through historical records, and by the legends preserved in tribal memory, is a native world in which people moved freely, and ideas presumably moved with them. The traffic that takes place within contemporary Indian society and results in the similarities noted by Spicer cannot be a recent development. Rules of hospitality and institutionalized gift giving are so deeply imbedded in traditional behavior as to supply a common theme in tribal legends and creation stories. Visitors occupied a privileged place in any camp, and, of course, visitors were expected to exchange stories. Host and guest learned from each other.

Looking back over the record reviewed here so briefly, it seems clear that the great changes that occurred as the Americans called Indians moved from a basically hunting subsistence to one of food gathering and finally to crop growing (where soil and climate permitted) came about quite naturally through channels that were always open. It was not a static world, and it was not a world in which violence flared whenever a tribesman crossed his frontiers into the territory of a neighboring people. That has been the stereotype, and it is totally unfounded.

The prehistory of the New World, or what we have been able to learn of it, is not disjoined from contemporary Indian society. The history of any people at any point in time is a continuity, a process out of its own past. Indians travel today back and forth across the continent, often without funds, without transportation of their own— going to meetings, to powwows, or simply to visit. In a certain radical respect, it is still their continent, however much it has been made over. Apparently they never read the official reports and scholarly works that predict or lament their imminent transformation into average urbanites fixed within a social orbit. In his study of the Cree Indians of Canada some years ago, David Mandelbaum remarked on this characteristic:

The Plains Cree took to riding on the trains to visit distant bands of their own people, or of other tribes, whose reserves were close to the railroad lines. The visitors came back home with a knowledge of new dances, new games, new moccasin types which were soon taken over by the rest of the band [1935].

A Cree Indian could go the length of Canada, and always find a welcome among his tribesmen. The pattern has not changed.

"A Pawnee child was born into the community from the beginning, and he never acquired the notion that he was closed in. . . . He was literally trained to feel that the world around him was his home" (Weltfish, 1965, 57).

Only such people trained to look outward upon the world, and trained also in the niceties of receiving a guest—only such a people could have extended so willing a hand as the Indians offered to the incoming Europeans.

"They are a loving people, without covetousness," Columbus wrote of his first encounter with the Americans he called Indians (McNickle, 1949).

NOTE

[1] The preparation of this paper was made possible by a faculty grant from the University of Saskatchewan, Regina Campus.

BIBLIOGRAPHY

ANGULO, JAIME DE
1953 Indian tales. New York: Hill and Wang.

BARBEAU, MARIUS
1923 Indian days in the Canadian Rockies. New York: The Macmillan Company.

BUTLER, B. R.
1961 The old Cordilleran culture in the Pacific northwest. Idaho State University Museum, Occasional Papers, no. 5.

CALDWELL, JOSEPH R.
1958 Trend and tradition in the prehistory of the eastern United States. Memoir 88, American Anthropological Association 60(6), part 2: 22 and 29.

COLLINS, HENRY B.
1964 The arctic and subarctic. In Prehistoric man in the new world. J. D. Jennings and Edward Norbeck, eds. Chicago: University of Chicago Press.

CROOK, WILSON W., JR., AND R. K. HARRIS
1958 A Pleistocene campsite near Lewisville, Texas. American Antiquity 23:233–246.

DICK, HERBERT W.
1965 Bat cave. School of American Research Monograph, no. 27.

GIDDINGS, J. L.
1960 The archeology of Bering Strait. Current Anthropology 1 (2):121–138.

GRIFFIN, JAMES B.
1964 The northeast woodlands area. *In* Prehistoric man in the new world. J. D. Jennings and Edward Norbeck, eds. Chicago: The University of Chicago Press.

HAURY, EMIL W.
1950 The stratigraphy and archaeology of Ventana Cave, Arizona. Albuquerque and Tucson: University of New Mexico and University of Arizona presses.

HOPKINS, DAVID M.
1959 Cenozoic history of the Bering Land Bridge. Science 129 (3362):1519–1528.

JENNINGS, JESSE D.
1968 Prehistory of North America. New York: McGraw-Hill.

KLUCKHOHN, CLYDE, AND DOROTHEA LEIGHTON
1947 The Navaho. Cambridge: Harvard University Press.

KRIEGER, ALEX D.
1964 Early man in the new world. *In* Prehistoric man in the new world. J. D. Jennings and Edward Norbeck, eds. Chicago: University of Chicago Press.

LEE, DOROTHY
1959 Freedom and Culture. Englewood Cliffs: Prentice-Hall.

LEWIS, THOMAS M. N., AND MADELINE K. LEWIS
1961 Eva, an archaic site. Knoxville: University of Tennessee Press.

MACNEISH, RICHARD S.
1964a Investigations in the southwest Yukon. R. S. Peabody Foundation for Archaeology, Papers 6 (1).
1964b The origins of new world agriculture. Scientific American 211 (5)29–37.

MCNICKLE, D'ARCY
1949 They came here first. New York and Philadelphia: Lippincott.

MANDELBAUM, DAVID G.
1935 European factors in Plains Cree culture. Paper presented before the thirty-fourth annual meeting of the American Anthropological Association, December 27, 1935.

MANGELSDORF, PAUL C., RICHARD S. MACNEISH, AND GORDON R. WILLEY
1964 Origins of agriculture in Mesoamerica. *In* Handbook of Middle American Indians, vol. 1. R. Wauchope, ed. Austin: University of Texas Press. pp. 427–445.

MARTIN, PAUL S., AND JOHN B. RINALDO
1960 Table Rock Pueblo, Arizona. Fieldiana: Anthropology 51 (2):129–298.

MARTIN, PAUL S., AND H. E. WRIGHT, JR., EDS.
1967 Pleistocene extinctions. New Haven: Yale University Press.

NEUMANN, G. K.
1952 Archeology and race in the American Indian. *In* Archeology of eastern United States. James B. Griffin, ed. Chicago: University of Chicago Press.

NEWMAN, MARSHALL T.
1953 The application of ecological rules to the racial anthropology of the aboriginal new world. American Anthropologist 55 (3):311–327.
1962 Evolutionary changes in body size and head form in American Indians. American Anthropologist 64 (2):237–257.

REED, ERIK K.
1964 The greater southwest. *In* Prehistoric man in the new world. J. D. Jennings and Edward Norbeck, eds. Chicago: University of Chicago Press.

SAUER, CARL O.
1932 The road to Cibola. Berkeley: University of California Press.

SEARS, WILLIAM H.
1964 The southeastern United States. *In* Prehistoric man in the new world. J. D. Jennings and Edward Norbeck, eds. Chicago: University of Chicago Press.

SPICER, EDWARD H., ED.
1961 Perspectives in American Indian culture change. Chicago: University of Chicago Press.

STEWART, T. D.
1960 A physical anthropologist's view of the peopling of the new world. Southwestern Journal of Anthropology 16 (3):259–273.

STEWART, T. D., AND M. T. NEWMAN
1951 An historical résumé of the concept of differences in Indian types. American Anthropologist 53 (1):19–26.

SWADESH, MORRIS
1964 Linguistic overview. *In* Prehistoric man in the new world. J. D. Jennings and Edward Norbeck, eds. Chicago: University of Chicago Press.

SWADESH, MORRIS, *et al.*
1954 Time depths of American linguistic groupings. American Anthropologist 56 (3):361–377.

SWANTON, JOHN R.
1953 The Indian tribes of North America. Bureau of American Ethnology Bulletin 145.

WASHBURN, WILCOMB E., ED.
1964 The Indian and the white man. Garden City: Doubleday.

WEDEL, WALDO R.
1964 The Great Plains. *In* Prehistoric man in the new world. J. D. Jennings and Edward Norbeck, eds. Chicago: University of Chicago Press.

WELTFISH, GENE
1965 The lost universe. New York: Basic Books.

WILLEY, GORDON R.
1966 An introduction to American archaeology, vol. I. Englewood Cliffs: Prentice-Hall.

WILMSEN, EDWIN N.
1965 An outline of early man studies in the United States. American Antiquity 31 (2):172–192.

WORMINGTON, H. M.
1957 Ancient man in North America, 4th ed. Denver Museum of Natural History.

3

The Coastal Algonkians: People of the First Frontiers T. J. C. BRASSER

The following account will be focused on the native population of coastal New York State. Material on the other Indians of the Middle Atlantic seaboard has been brought in to illustrate the general historic background of dramatic events starting with the arrival of the Schwunuk, "the people from the sea." Few of the natives remain; epidemics and conflicts with the invading whites resulted in the extinction of whole tribes, many bands retreated into the interior, and only a thin scattering of Indians survive in their ancient homeland. Both physically and culturally these eastern remnant groups represent the result of human adjustments over a period of about four centuries. A fair amount of documentary source material covers this period of culture change, and increasing archeological research supplements the picture drawn from these documents. Yet modern studies are rare and usually of a preliminary nature, as is this paper.

Prelude to Contact

The whole region from the Carolinas to central New England was fairly uniform as an ecological area and covered by immense forests. The marshy coastal plain is broad in the south and diminishes in a narrow strip to the north. Having cleared the land by slash-and-burn activities, the people settled in semipermanent villages, surrounded by extensive gardens bordering the shallow and tidal streams. In spring, after the corn was planted, the greater part of the people moved into temporary camps situated along the coast or the fall line of the rivers. They passed the summer there, fishing and gathering huge quantities of shellfish and drying a good portion for winter consumption. In September the people returned to the villages for the harvest of corn, beans, squash, and pumpkins and for the accompanying harvest festivals. Autumn was a period of collective hunting drives and the gathering of wild fruits and nuts in the surrounding forests, which were cleared of their cumbersome undergrowth by annual brush burning. Taking this economic pattern into consideration, we have little reason to believe that the country was a virgin wilderness when the Europeans arrived.

These lowlands as well as the broad river valleys were, in Indian times as in the present, the most densely populated portions of the entire area. Surprisingly enough, however, the greatest concentration was to be found northeast of present New York, where the coastal plain becomes rather narrow. If James Mooney's computations are right, there was a density of around ninety individuals per 100 km² in coastal New York and Connecticut as opposed to approximately thirty-five in coastal Virginia and North Carolina. Kroeber suggests that this heavy population in the Northeast might be related to the fact that the coastal plain is narrow with uplands nearby, thus providing a great variety of subsistence opportunities (Kroeber, 1939, 141–142, 145). In late autumn the people moved to their hunting grounds along the upper river courses toward the rugged uplands, frequently camping in rock shelters and passing the winter there.

The western border of this area is formed by the Appalachian Mountain ranges, building up and spreading to the coast in New England. This rough country was little frequented by the Indians, and archeological evidence strongly reveals its isolating effects. Throughout the coastal belt, however, lakes and streams provided waterways, and along a network of forest trails news, goods, and people reached the villages from far away. As might be expected, a geographical setting like this produced no sharply differentiated cultures. Regional variation as detected by the archeologists is largely of a ceramic nature; early historical records indicate some variety of a nonmaterial nature.

One of the most obvious distortions in popular descriptions of the area concerns the nature and size of the aboriginal sociopolitical unit. The tribal maps are a case in point. They give the impression that large autonomous regional groups or tribes were originally in existence, whereas the evidence available indicates that the aboriginal units were very small. The territory of these units consisted of the lands around a river system surrounded by the little-frequented watersheds and the fall line or seashore. Coastal territories tended to be smaller than those more inland because of the heavy dependence upon the sea as a source of food. From New England southward the longhouse type of dwelling indicates that these local groups consisted of a number of extended families that shared in the usufruct of the land.

Cultural relations with neighboring groups were intrinsically linked to the water routes. Important among these relations were the kinship ties, especially those of the several leading lineages. Both in Virginia and southern New England these "noble families" may have formed the upper class of a nascently stratified society. The chief was married polygynously and received tribute from his people so as to be able to house and feed visitors. During religious festivals he assumed the role of master of ceremonies. Latent political ties existed between several adjoining local groups in that their leaders were related by intermarriage. Confederacies on this basis may have existed in pre-contact times, although they did not provide economic benefit. Due to a low level of sociopolitical integration, such confederacies soon may have broken up again. Thus, the tribal map shows a situation relevant to a later period. The term "Delawaran" as used in this paper covers a large number of local groups, remnants of which combined and formed the Delaware tribe in the eighteenth century.

First Contact: The Traders Phase (c. 1550–1700)

The events surrounding the first contact between alien groups of people are important to the understanding of subsequent acculturation. But what are we to consider as the first relevant contact along the Middle Atlantic seaboard?

This episode must have taken place somewhere within that hazy period of protohistory, starting either with the Viking explorations of coastal New England, say about A.D. 1000, or with the voyage of Verrazano in 1524. The Viking stories spread along the European seaports and lived long enough for Columbus to hear of them. When Columbus sailed to the West, the Viking colony in Greenland was coming to its end. It is not unlikely, however, that the relatives of the Vikings in Iceland used to visit the fishing grounds off the American coast by that time. At any rate, the Norman, Breton, and English fishermen were going there annually at least since A.D. 1500.

The sixteenth century was one of rapidly increasing knowledge of the whole coast as well as of the St. Lawrence valley. Fishermen operated mainly in the North, slave raiders mainly in the South; and an occasional explorer left posterity his logbook. They traded with the Indians—furs against red stroud, iron nails, knives, hatchets, beads, brass kettles, and liquor. Along with the items traded to the Indians went a range of infectious diseases, and the changes resulting from them were probably of far greater importance than all the trade goods together. Periodically epidemics ravaged the native populations, who lacked immunity to these diseases. Now here, then there, thousands of Indians were killed by them, and refugee remnants brought the microbes even more inland. Wahunsonacock, the Powhatan chief, said to John Smith, "I have seen two generations of my people die. Not a man of the two generations is alive now but myself." Massasoit, the Wampanoag chief, remarked, "Englishmen, take that land, for none is left to occupy it." Similar statements are known from the Delawarans.

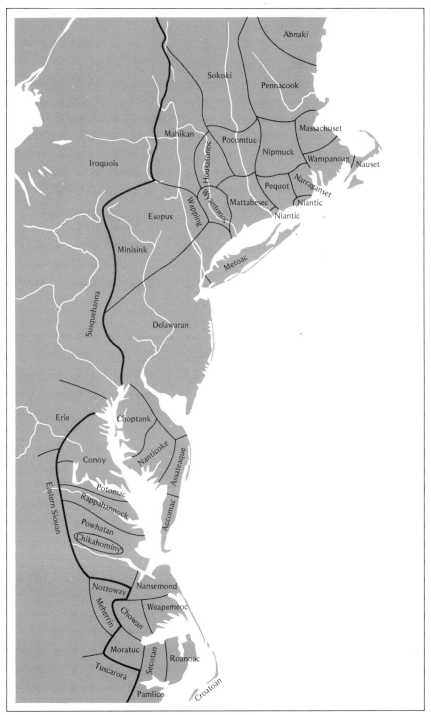

Figure 3.1. The Coastal Algonkians and their western neighbors, after the formation of larger political units in the early seventeenth century. This map is a revised version of Kroeber's Middle Atlantic Slope, comprising the area from present-day southern Maine southward into North Carolina.

In the meantime the fur trade was penetrating the area. With this as their major purpose, French vessels had been visiting the St. Lawrence valley regularly since 1535. As far south as the Potomac River, trade goods were disseminated through the Northeast, transported along old Indian routes by native middlemen. Mortality was increased by the growing number of intertribal wars, for which there was now an additional incentive: direct access to the trade goods and the enlargement of trapping grounds. Latent political ties were strengthened, and by integration as well as conquest, local groups combined into confederacies or "tribes." Throughout North America the rise of such confederacies would indicate the arrival of the shifting traders' frontier. Armed with more effective weapons of European origin, northern Algonkians drove the Iroquoians out of the St. Lawrence valley before 1581; it was a war that would have repercussions throughout the Northeast. Many of these Iroquoian refugees joined their relatives in what is now New York State and continued their desperate wars against invading enemies. Their hope to regain control of the St. Lawrence valley received a severe blow in 1609, when the French definitely sided with their Huron and Algonkian enemies and established a trading post at Quebec.

The arrival of the so-called Laurentian Iroquois and the formation of the Iroquois Confederacy is regarded by archeologists as the expansion of cultural influences from the interior toward the Atlantic coast, particularly in the lower Hudson valley. Pressure from the interior caused intensive warfare and social upheaval as well as some vaguely comprehended population movements. In Pennsylvania the Susquehanna had to move downriver to Chesapeake Bay by 1580. They seemed somehow to have maintained their role as middlemen in the French trade, however. They got furs from their own territory as well as from subjected Delawarans.

In the interior the Mahican and related Housatonics, Wappingers, Esopus, and Minisinks held their ground against expanding Iroquois. Their traditions tell of a confederacy they formed, perhaps as a defensive measure against these troublesome neighbors. Coming from their direction, the Pequot arrived on the eastern Connecticut coast. Driving off the local Niantic, they carved out a territory in the drainage system of the Thames River.

The early seventeenth century saw the rapid establishment of English, Dutch, and Swedish trading posts along the Middle Atlantic seaboard, repeating the processes that had developed in the St. Lawrence valley, thus starting off a series of conquest wars among the coastal Algonkians. Several groups, such as the Powhatan, Pequot, and Wampanoag, extended their power. The Mahican confederates attacked the Delawarans along the lower Hudson River shortly after, if not before,

1620. Part of these people withdrew to western Long Island at the expense of Metoac territory; others fled behind Staten Island and settled in New Jersey. Such was the position of the Mahican proper that even the eastern Iroquois were forced to pay them tribute. The important role of the Mahican leaders in intertribal politics started in those days and continues up to the present time with their descendants among the Stockbridge in Wisconsin.

Never abundant in the coastal plain, fur-bearing game began to disappear rapidly. But the coastal Indians struck upon another source of income: the production of shell beads called "wampum." Formerly used as a traditional token of homage, wampum was in enormously increased demand after the Dutch developed its use as small change among themselves, as well as for the fur trade, and induced the nearby English to acquire the beads for their Indian trade, too. Eastern Long Island was particularly rich in material for wampum production, motivating the Pequot to subjugate the area. To the fur traders, however, the coast was losing its interest, and they began to move their posts upriver.

The contest for trade control between the Mohawk Iroquois and the Mahicans had already started in 1614, when the first traders arrived on the upper courses of the Hudson River. The tide turned definitely in favor of the Iroquois when the Dutch founded a permanent trading post there in 1623. It did not take long before the Dutch noticed that a pact with the Iroquois would be more profitable than with the neighboring Mahicans. By trading directly with the Iroquois, the Dutch followed the policy of the early Virginian colonists, acquiring a strong position by befriending inland enemies of the local natives. With the founding of Fort Orange, now Albany, New York, the "golden age" of the Iroquois dawned and the downfall of the Algonkians began. From the foregoing it appears that this florescence was not due to a cultural superiority of the Iroquois as has been postulated formerly. Although most of the Mahicans were forced to withdraw east of the Hudson River by the liaison between the Iroquois and Fort Orange, intermittent warfare kept the Iroquois on the defensive in their settlements west of Schoharie creek.

All along the coast the Indian trade opened up the river courses, and with minor differences in each river valley, the story repeated itself. By 1632 the Pequot were no longer able to keep the traders down the rivers. A trading post was set up at what is now Hartford, Connecticut, starting off the disintegration of Pequot power over its subject tribes and culminating in the defeat of the Pequot in 1637. When the Swedes founded their posts in the Delaware valley, the Susquehanna cleverly maintained their power over the local natives by entering into a pact with these whites.

Increasingly armed with Dutch guns, the Iroquois were extending their power far and wide. The quest for new trapping grounds was the major reason for these campaigns, as their own territory had become pretty well exhausted by 1640. They also turned upon the coastal Algonkians, attacking those who were still involved in the fur trade and demanding an annual tribute of wampum from them. The Mahican made the best of a bargain by an alliance with the Iroquois, thus maintaining, as representatives of the latter, some of their former control of the lower Hudson Indians. At the same time, however, they sided with the Sokoki, Pocumtuc, and Pennacook in their wars against the Iroquois and, if possible, actually joined them. These wars brought about the gravitation to the French of several New England tribes. The geographical as well as political situation of the Mahicans explains their careful maneuvering between French and English interests. It was not until the English authorities intervened and the Iroquois allowed the Mahicans to participate in their midwestern fur trade that there was finally peace in 1671.

At last the Iroquois were able to direct all their attention to their Susquehanna rivals. When the latter were defeated in 1675, their control of the Delawarans passed to the Iroquois. About that time, however, the bottom fell out of the fur market because of changes in European taste as well as the virtual extermination of beaver in the area. Insofar as the trade at Albany continued, it was based upon furs imported from the Great Lakes region by Iroquois and members of the old Mahican Confederacy.

In view of the early impact of the Europeans, who brought disease, trade goods, and war, we presume that even the earliest reports do not give us a picture of the aboriginal community as it was before contact. Not only do these reports indicate extensive taking over of material items, but they also betray the vast changes in the demographic make-up of the area. Moreover, cultural responses to the new situation were developing from within the native society. Many of these changes will remain forever obscure to us, but some of them we sense in the early accounts, however vague these are.

With the annual return of white traders and their subsequent founding of a permanent station at the traditional summer fishing place of some local group, related neighboring groups changed their summer resort and assembled together near the trading post. Several of these groups were mere remnants of former units; and no longer able to maintain their social life independently, they united into a larger tribal organization. The sociopolitical organization of these tribes included no new ideas, but went along traditional kinship lines that had been given broader scope. Apparently, a clan structure as was present among the Iroquois was only adopted by their direct Algonkian neighbors, who tried to fit the old local groups into this pattern.

Leadership of such an Algonkian tribe was in the hands of a prominent lineage, usually of the local group in whose territory the trading center was established. This choice was not wholly of native origin; the traders tended to deal with the natives through the local chief and to support his aspirations.

The fur trade added a new value to the possession of land, and the Indians became more conscious of the exact boundaries of their territories. Moreover, private gain and ownership were stimulated by the practices of the European traders, resulting in the rapid development of a mosaic of family-owned hunting grounds within each tribal territory.

The fur trade brought new goods but necessitated significant readjustment in socioeconomic customs. In the balanced system before contact, labor was well divided between the sexes, but after contact the men were seriously diverted from their normal activities to meet the demands of the traders. The Indians employed more of their time in trapping fur-bearing animals or in the manufacture of wampum, and the responsibilities of the women increased. Thus, the balance in food production was disturbed. The food production of the males further declined if they went into business as middlemen, and this situation often resulted in continual warfare. Increasing mortality resulted from these wars as well as from frequent epidemics. Increased mortality plus the male's shift from his traditional economic activities probably influenced the change in the native kinship system to one characterized by matricentrism. Of course, the most obvious changes were visible in the material culture. All the traits listed for the late prehistoric period continued in diminishing ratios, making way for the addition of artifacts of European manufacture. Aboriginal forms tended to persist but were made of imported material. For a long time imports like steel hatchets were primarily status symbols and only secondarily utilitarian. The price of all these riches was the economic dependence of the natives, resulting in poverty and chronic malnutrition after the loss of the fur trade.

The Shrinking of a World: The Settlers Phase (*c.* 1620–1700)

One of the reasons the traders moved upriver was the arrival of the colonists and the subsequent expansion of their settlements. Due to their opposite interests they often were on bad terms with each other.

The number of English immigrants before the middle of the seventeenth century was above 30,000. Those who survived the first trials of pioneer life, along with their progeny, numbered about 50,000 in 1650, and this population was about equally divided between the colonies on the Chesapeake Bay and those on the New England coast. Between these two areas, in the drainage system of the Delaware and Hudson rivers, settled a few thousand Dutch, Finns, Swedes, and, later, the English and Palatine Germans, now known as the Pennsylvania Dutch. In the course of time the world shaped by these settlers was to serve as a background to Indian culture as importantly as the ecological environment did in precontact days.

The Indians who met the first settlers were long accustomed to face-to-face contact with whites; they were already armed with guns and had some idea of what to expect from the strangers. The settlers, however, introduced a selection of European culture different from that of the traders. This became evident from the very start of settlement, when the colonists wanted to buy land.

Though cautious, the Indians were generally friendly. They were quite willing to help the settlers in their need for land, but of course, in the only way they knew. Land, from the Indian viewpoint, was an inheritance from their ancestors, to be held in trust by the tribal chief for future generations, and, thus, it could not be sold. In return for their annual tribute, the chief allowed his people to share in the usufruct of the land. Along the same lines any stranger could be admitted to the territory of a chief, and the Indians made their first adjustment to the settlers in terms of existing native conditions. That the whites would demand exclusive possession did not occur to the natives, and the idea was unacceptable to them. Ultimately, however, the Indians came to realize that negotiations with the whites meant irrevocable loss of their land. In the face of the European advance the Indians became restive and complained of the settlers' activities. The contrasting views of Indians and whites created tensions that inevitably resulted in open warfare.

The reaction of the colonists was another new experience to the natives, unprepared as they were for a war of utter devastation and wholesale massacre. They were shocked at this style of warfare, which was waged against the Pequot in 1637, the lower Hudson Delawarans in 1643–1644, the Esopus in 1660–1663, and all New England tribes in 1675. After each of these wars there followed a period of uneasy peace in which the survivors regrouped; small groups were incorporated into larger tribes or withdrew into the interior. The decrease in native population was hastened by the rise of degenerative diseases such as tuberculosis and syphilis, exacerbated by sociocultural conditions prevailing among the Indians. Uprooted, their food resources destroyed, the Indians took refuge in the use of liquor. The combination of venereal

disease and death

and epidemic diseases struck at both the Indian health and birth rates; by 1680 there were probably no more than 14,000 Indians in central and southern New England and only 8,000 Algonkians in New York and New Jersey.

By a combination of Indian resistance, opposition of the fur traders, and the later French and Indian Wars, expansion of colonial settlement was made nearly impossible for a long time. This delay was of vital importance to the adaptive development of native cultures in the interior and, in turn, to the increased power of resistance displayed when the westward-moving frontier reached them. People like the Iroquois owed a great deal to the resistance of the coastal Algonkians, and both peoples were well aware of this. It was to the advantage of the Iroquois to maintain close contacts with the traders and to keep the settlers out of their territory. Iroquois control of the coastal Algonkians was stimulated by the desire to use these coastal groups as a buffer along the settlers' frontier. In their turn the Iroquois were of growing importance to the Colonies as a buffer against French incursions. Thus, colonial authorities preferred to support them in their political aspirations. After 1655 the Dutch Reformed Church at Fort Orange even acted as agent for the coastal Delawarans in their payment of tribute to the Iroquois. When the coastal Algonkians were no longer able to check the expansion of the settlers, the Iroquois invited, or simply ordered, the Algonkian remnants to withdraw inland, thus keeping an Indian population around their own lands as long as possible.

Inevitably, each of the coastal wars ended in the defeat of the Indians, and each of these defeats was a milestone in the increasing control of the native society by the colonial governments. Generally speaking, government control increased with the improvement of communication and of means to enforce the regulations. From evidence of several regulations until around 1643 it is obvious that there was strong sentiment against doing anything that might cause ill feeling or start an uprising among the natives. The numerical preponderance of the Indians plus the fact that white settlements usually were widely scattered forced the colonial authorities to take precautionary measures.

Within this development two periods can be recognized: one is a period in which the colonial authorities cautiously played a game with powerful Indian politicians; the other, which followed, is a period in which the tables were being turned. East of the Hudson River the break between these two periods was formed by the murder of Miantonomo in 1643. As Chief Sachem of the Narragansetts he was a man of great influence far beyond his own large tribe. Miantonomo, not King Philip, was the only leader among the coastal Algonkians who realized that the tribes should unite into one great war against the whites. His message had already reached the lower Hudson Delawarans when he was killed by Uncas, chief of a band of Pequot renegades called Mohegans. Individuals of Miantonomo's type were in the minority. More were like Uncas. For their own safety and gain they sided with the colonists, and having won the colonists' confidence by the betrayal of rival chiefs, they set out to conquer neighboring tribes. Once they had succeeded, they "sold" the land from under the feet of subjected peoples.

Obviously, the colonial authorities were not slow in making use of disharmony among the natives, and Indian power was steadily undermined. The defeat of the Pequot had "strook a trembling terror into all the Indians around about" and several Indian chiefs, formerly tributive to the Pequot, voluntarily offered to pay tribute to the English from then on. Surprised, the latter willingly accepted, later even insisting upon it, but they were not able to render the expected protection in return. Soon it became clear that with the defeat of the Pequot the balance of power between the Indian tribes had also been crushed. Moreover, the whites undermined the position of the tribal chief sachems by dealing with the subject local chiefs. In vain the Narragansett chief sachem begged the English that these upstarts "be as your little dogs, but not as your confederates, which . . . is unworthy." The native political shell that protected the social whole was slowly breaking down.

With the captives taken in the Pequot War, the English took the lead in enslaving the Indians. Throughout the colonial period New England held more Indians in slavery than any of the other Colonies except South Carolina. Aware of these developments the Dutch on Manhattan in 1639 also resolved to exact tribute from the local Indians, stating that they were under Dutch protection. In 1640 the New Amsterdam Council sent an armed force to Long Island in order to "reduce the Indians to obedience and to levy a contribution on them." Captives were given to the Dutch soldiers. During the Esopus Wars many Indians were shipped to Curaçao as slaves.

Miantonomo's conspiracy was an important stimulus to the founding of the United Colonies of New England and the initiation of a less clement Indian policy. From the Merrimack River down to Long Island Indian chiefs submitted to colonial authority. In some parts the county courts were invested with jurisdiction over the Indians as individuals, but in practice the local tribe was held liable for damage; tribal property was seized to force the tribe to discover the culprit. With too heavy a burden of responsibility placed upon the sachem by the expectations of the whites, requiring him to exercise an authority that custom did not recognize, the sachem was caught between two fires and lost prestige both among his own people and with the foreigners. The whites, however, attempted to maintain the Indians as semi-independent groups with a chief as the responsible officer. Lacking a chief, the Nipmucks were divided among the Mohegans and Narragansetts; Indian governors were appointed for the Pequot remnants. By 1670 the election of any new chief was under colonial supervision, and superior sachems were no longer recognized by the whites.

Friction and open warfare between the Dutch and the Indians continued until 1663, and the next year the English captured New Netherland, in the Hudson River region. Indians of Long Island wrote a letter to the new rulers, stating that they "acknowledge ye Governor of New Yorke as our Chiefest Sachem." To the local natives English rule probably meant more legal security than they had experienced under the Dutch; but although regulations increased in number, both parties did not necessarily follow the rules. Indian complaints in all Colonies were usually settled by informal agreement outside court. Imperfect control of the individual on both sides remained a source of friction for a long time.

Unceasing encroachments of the New England colonists and their double-standard treatment of the Indians brought the relationship between both parties to a breaking point in 1675. A series of battles known as King Philip's War culminated in a serious defeat for the Indians. When the smoke had cleared away, southern New England contained only what might be called reservation Indians, insofar as they were not mere slaves. Many of the survivors had moved out of the area to join the Mahicans or the French on the St. Lawrence River, or they had gone as far as the Illinois country.

Finally, the settlers' frontier began to expand gradually. The coastal Indians were left to make a living and to manage their affairs as best they could, so long as they did not work to the disadvantage of the whites. For the land they lived on, some groups now had to pay an annual rent to the white owner. It took another half-century before the settlers reached the upper courses of the rivers, by which time Indians like the Mahicans had either moved away or settled down upon their last landholdings. By a combination of many remnant groups, the historic Delaware tribe was emerging by 1740.

Characteristic of the Settlers Phase is a marked increase in the amount of recorded contact with the Indians, contacts that were often of a coercive type. These records are apt to obscure the fact that for a long time these contacts were highly localized and often interspaced by long periods in which the native society was able to adjust somewhat to the effected change. Certainly, it must have been a period of crisis and stress, but there is no evidence of wholesale cultural disintegration. Indian adjustment to European civilization continued to be of a selective character; if possible they refused anything that might impair essential elements of the native culture. It is an indication that the basic value system withstood all strain and stress; without real understanding, the Indians continued to view the changing world from the frame of logic of their own cultures. By the end of this period tribal names like Narragansett, Delaware, and Nanticoke covered heterogeneous populations consisting of several remnant groups clustering around a well-governed core. The Shantok culture of eastern Long Island, for example, represents the fusion of Pequot refugees with the local Metoac. Other tribes emerged by separation from the main body, like the Catskill of Mahican origin.

Intertribal political relationships, developed during the Traders Phase, were intentionally undermined by the colonial government in accord with the concept "divide and rule." Colonial interference with the native political organization subjected the office of chief to a strain that tended to weaken its original influence. Apparently, however, the office remained hereditary within a traditional line of descent recognized as that of the old leading family. Marriage relations of chiefs remained restricted to comparable families among neighboring tribes and usually had political implications. Apart from polygynous marriages, which were on the wane, all other features of chieftainship were maintained. Possibly the institution of chief's assistants developed during this period. A speaker for the chief usually addressed the common people, whether Indians or whites. Beaver skins thrown down during such speeches as a confirmation of what was said slowly gave way to wampum belts by the end of the century. The symbolic function of wampum belts in political and ceremonial affairs that developed among the Iroquois eventually spread throughout the eastern woodlands.

Artifacts, particularly dress and tools, showed a rapid decrease in the use of traditional materials. European influence, however, was no longer restricted to the import of goods. Frequenting the Colonies, the Indians rapidly mastered new techniques. The easy relationship between Scandinavians and Indians on the Delaware River seems to have made that area a particular center of technological and decorative developments, which were to be of more widespread importance in the eighteenth century. Acculturation in this area was voluntary, and the new materials, techniques, and decorative inspirations gave rise to several adaptive innovations, foreign to both Indian and European culture.

By the end of this period the annual cycle of economic activities of the Mahican and related tribes began around March, when the Indians moved to the woods to make sugar from the sap of maple trees. This activity was not mentioned in the early sources, probably because maple sugar became an important food only after the introduction and wide use of steel axes and knives to cut the trees and metal kettles to boil the maple sap. While the upstream "River Indians" went sugaring, many coastal natives arrived at the beaches to spend the summer there as of old. Dugouts, used for fishing and transport, now often were fitted with sails. Many dugouts were made for white clients. Planting and tending the traditional crops remained a female activity. The women also made rope and bags of Indian hemp, which they traded to the colonists. Of European origin were the peach trees growing near the scattered longhouses and the pigs and chickens foraging in the surrounding forests.

Many an Indian was able to repair his gun, but the bow and arrow did not disappear, since the use of such hunting gear saved powder. Besides hunting and fishing, by this time often for a colonial market, the men found an increasing variety of jobs among white employers. They served as interpreters and postmen for the local authorities, made wampum during the winter months, tended cattle, and by the end of the century, the Mahicans helped the Dutch farmers to bring in the harvest. Most important, however, was the Indians' engagement in the whaling industry, beginning on Long Island about 1650. Although most of the local Indians were thus employed, from 1672 Indians from southern New England also had to be hired due to the rapid development of offshore whaling.

The early white settler in the New World has been compared with Adam in paradise, in his giving of names to the details of his new environment. But the Indians were also giving names to the new things from the whites. Moreover, many Indians mastered the English or Dutch language. Mahican vocabularies collected in the early twentieth century still preserved several Dutch words.

Both the languages and their speakers intermingled to some extent. The Dutch particularly availed themselves of the situation and cohabited with Indian women. The English, bringing their own families and their rigid social controls, for the most part seem not to have done so. Among the English, apprenticed servants occasionally fled to the Indians, but among the Dutch even a provincial secretary "has run about the same as an Indian, with a little covering and a small patch in front."

Behind the Frontier: The Integrative Phase (*c.* 1650–1800)

North and east of the Delaware River a third phase of historical Indian culture change was characterized by the introduction of Protestant Christianity. It is not surprising that most of the early missionary activities failed, the native cultures being as yet wholly intact and the

Indians assured of their own beliefs. At least in these regions the conventional accusation that the missionaries destroyed the (romanticized) aboriginal cultures does not hold. Members of undamaged cultural wholes usually are too provincial to have any interest in useless novelties. Only in those areas where earlier contacts had undermined native life were the missionaries successful.

All colonial charters of the early seventeenth century expressed the desire to introduce a Christian way of life among the Indians; the Massachusetts Bay Colony even adopted a seal, picturing an Indian with his hands spread out, saying "Come over and help us." Conversion of the Indians was stimulated by the popular belief that they were descendants of the ten lost tribes of Israel.

By a stroke of luck the Puritans had settled in a region where recent epidemics had wiped out the greater part of the native population. The remainder was powerless against both the colonists and strong Indian neighbors. More than anything else this was a promising factor when John Eliot started his missionary work in the 1640s. The Puritans as well as the Virginian colonists agreed on the necessity of "civilizing" the natives before conversion to Christianity would be possible. Hence, from the very start of colonization Indian children were placed in English households. "Civilizing" amounted to becoming Anglicized Puritans and to identifying completely with the English society. Humane fervor of the colonists was, as usual, stimulated by material benefit, that is, the cheap acquisition of house servants. Indian women and children taken captive in war were distributed among the colonists with the same mixture of intentions. At a later time native children were apprenticed by law to the English.

Mission activities really started when people such as John Eliot and Thomas Mayhew learned a native language and went among the Indians. To finance such activities, the Society for the Propagation of the Gospel in New England was founded in 1649, followed by other organizations. Protection from the assumed temptations to sin was given to the "Praying Indians" by the establishment of separate villages on lands acquired by the missionary society. However, the conscious efforts to create a distinct society made them an easy target for both whites and other Indians. Internal government of these mission villages was in the hands of a village chief elected by the Indians; the religious teacher, usually also an Indian; and a native constable. To secure a "well principled people," the Indians were daily catechized in Christian know-how, schools were established, and the people were instructed in diverse trades. Moreover, Puritan ideas of "right walking" were made understood by a series of prohibitions against idleness, fornication, women with loose hair or with uncovered breasts, the killing of lice between one's teeth, and a range of other niceties. Their village chiefs were empowered to hold monthly courts to decide small civil cases; all other matters were treated by the colonial magistrates in quarterly courts. By 1674 fourteen of such Praying Indian Towns were founded in the Nipmuck-Massachusetts area besides a number among the Nauset on Cape Cod and the nearby islands. Thirty-six books were translated into the local Indian language and published between 1653 and 1721, all of a religious nature.

Even in the high days of these mission settlements, however, the neighboring colonists distrusted their quiet inhabitants. The too close association between the colony and mission made paternalism inevitable. Approached from the colonial side with often harsh control, the Praying Indians were despised and hated by the other natives. The tribal chiefs were especially opposed to missionary activity, since it deprived them of their subjects and, thereby, of their tribute and power. King Philip's War dealt a devastating blow to the Praying Indians; of the 4,000 converts in 1674, only 2,500 were left in 1698. Many had died but, of course, as many had joined the hostile Indians, whether eagerly or forced to the decision by the embittered whites.

By the end of the seventeenth century the attitude of the colonial governments toward the Indians was changing from fear of a power to charity for a minority. The coastal Indians were wards and dependents of the governments, which began taking measures to protect them. The colonial records become strewn with annulments of sales of reservation lands, new allotments, appointments of white overseers for each reservation, and other protective decrees.

The colonists, however, were less sympathetic than their high authorities, which resulted in continuous loss of land and prestige for the Indians. During the eighteenth century the reservation system degenerated, and the governments contented themselves with the support of missionary work and the provision of minimum protection to prevent conflicts. In the latter case the Indians usually paid the piper. A growing number of regulations restricted them in their social and economic activities. Another consistent trend was population decline. Nevertheless, instead of seeking assimilation, the Indians attempted to find isolation, and to continue a life as nearly as possible like that in former times. This led to the rise of reservation cultures and to continuous removals.

King Philip's War has often been viewed as the end of the first mission period in New England, marking these missionary activities as a failure. Four Praying Indian Towns survived, however, and continued for a long time in Massachusetts. More important is the fact that the mission settlements on Cape Cod and the islands had hardly felt the

Chief Etowwaghaum, alias Nicholas, Mahikan, 1710. Engraving by John Simon after original painting by John Verelst.
(Courtesy of the New-York Historical Society.)

impact of the war. In several respects this area constituted the link between the Praying Indians and the missionary expansion caused by the Great Awakening, a religious revival among whites, beginning about 1734. The Cape Cod missions absorbed many Praying Indians during, and long after, King Philip's War. Due to the high death rate among the local Indians, missionaries from this area explored southern New England in the early eighteenth century with the view of establishing new missions.

The Mohegans excepted, the Indians in New England reacted favorably to these contacts, and missionary work started in Rhode Island and Connecticut. Here, again, the negative in respect to the positive reaction of the Indians was directly related to their socioeconomic condition. Through the skillful manipulations by their chief, the Mohegans succeeded in retaining their traditional way of life up to the 1740s. Most of the other tribes, on the contrary, were exposed to all the destructive and disintegrative forces that combined against the Indians in those days.

Attention was also directed to the Mahicans and Mohawk Iroquois, who were approached by French Roman Catholic missionaries, thereby endangering their alliance with the English. Mission work among these tribes still living on the frontier was unsuccessful until the 1730s.

The new missionary and philanthropic fervor that originated with the Great Awakening was probably related to similar movements that swept all of Western Europe between 1730 and 1760. The missionaries of this period were powerful preachers who were able to get the whole congregation weeping and crying for remission of sins. The astounding fact is that they were able to produce this "experimental religion" even among the Indians. One of their famous Indian converts was the Mohegan Samson Occom. Trained as a missionary, his success inspired the founding of Eleazar Wheelock's School, forerunner of Dartmouth College. Pupils of this school were sent out far and wide; Occom himself worked among the Long Island Indians.

By this time whaling was of primary importance to the coastal natives, though many of them had to be forced into debt to make them willing to go to sea. The other Indians were subject to indentured and forced labor on farms and large estates. Their fellow workers were Negro slaves. The Negroes and the Indians were treated identically by the whites, which instigated their interracial mixing. This was further stimulated by a scarcity of women among the Negroes. Portuguese and other "foreigners" returned with the Indian sailors and settled among the Indians. Miscegenation laws enacted by the government took a race-classification form and became discriminatory to both Negroes and Indians.

The Reverend Occom realized that the social environment of the

coastal Indians was increasingly unfavorable to mission work and that it
could only lead to the further disintegration of their communities. Together with several other native missionaries he propagandized removal
to the West. Some 250 Connecticut, Rhode Island, and Long Island
Indians reacted to an invitation of the Oneida Iroquois in 1775 and
founded a settlement called Brothertown in the latter's territory. The
Revolutionary War forced them to take refuge with the Stockbridge Indians in western Massachusetts.

The Stockbridge tribe was the result of Mahican policy and mission
interests since 1734. Increasing settlement in the Hudson River valley
and the loss of manpower by removals had forced the remaining Mahicans, in 1675, to consolidate with the Wappingers and Housatonics.
The Mahican chief acted as Chief Sachem of this late confederacy. In
1734 the Reverend John Sergeant contacted the Housatonic remnant, a
group of around fifty Indians in all. When the Mahican chief reluctantly
consented to it, a mission post, called Stockbridge, was founded. The
Indians, living widely scattered, were settled at this place to facilitate
mission work. Sergeant preached in the local Indian language and translated several devotional works. Among his first converts were the local
chiefs with their families, and special attention was given to the educa-
tions of their sons. Other children were also gathered, and a white
teacher was appointed for them. Moreover, some English families acted
as examples of civilized behavior and instructed the Indians in diverse
trades and crafts. As with most other mission projects in this area, the
greatest opposition and obstruction were experienced from neighboring
whites. A Moravian mission started among the Hudson River Mahicans
had to be abandoned for this reason; as a result, many Indians followed
the Moravian brothers to Pennsylvania in 1746. Others joined the Stockbridge group, particularly after the old Mahican chief sachem had died
and leadership had devolved on a converted lineage at Stockbridge. The
extra attention given by the missionaries to the leading families now
paid off; all successive chiefs were leaders in Church affairs and religious
life.

In 1750 the Stockbridge population had increased to 250, among
them Mahicans, Wappingers, Mattabesecs, Wyantonocs. Under the guidance of white teachers, the Indians started farming and built simple
houses. Originally held in common, the land was divided among the
family heads. Farming, however, was not a success, the Indians preferring
their traditional economy. Land allotment resulted in land loss, due to
the increasing white population in the neighborhood. During the French
and Indian Wars, and again during the Revolution, the greater part of
the Indian men were recruited by the Army, and many were killed.
Growing demoralization faded the once bright mission prospects. White

settlers crowded the Indians first out of the town's government and, ultimately, out of Stockbridge itself. Together with the Brothertown Indians, the approximately 420 Stockbridge Indians settled among the Oneida Iroquois in 1785, later removing to Wisconsin in the early nineteenth century.

There were several other mission groups along the coast in the eighteenth century, and their history paralleled that of Stockbridge to a great extent. For a long time native missionaries still worked among the Indians who remained behind, but religious fervor slowly decreased. By 1800 there were no more than around 3,500 Indians in New England south of the Merrimack River and around 550 Indians in coastal New York and New Jersey. Pure Indians among these groups were rapidly disappearing.

It should be obvious that Indian culture change during this phase was most intense. With the impact of a new religion the whole value system and all related patterns of the native culture were under attack. Traditional norms and beliefs, however, had already been weakened by the failure to maintain cultural and political independence. Ongoing population decline brought about a simplification of native ceremonial structures, the more elaborate rituals disappearing first. As soon as a tribe included Christians and traditionalists among its population, the effectiveness of religious sanctions on social behavior broke down. The loss of confidence in the old religion manifested itself in the neglect of ceremonial observances, which even more tended to disappear from view because of the withdrawal into secrecy of the conservative core. Some native religious traits got a place in the new context. Converted chiefs, as of old, took the lead in the imported rituals. During their services, they, as well as their enthusiastic audience, described religious experiences of a visionlike character. Most important, however, are data indicating that Christianity was viewed by many Indians as an anti-white messianism, offering magical knowledge to meet the threat to their existence. Missionary work among the Delawares preceded their more nativistic religious modifications. Many traditional customs slipped away as their meaning was gone or persisted as "empty" forms. Witchcraft beliefs became mixed with similar ideas of European and African origin.

The acceptance of Christianity also meant a thoroughgoing reorganization of native leadership and community life. Scattered extended family longhouses gave way to clusters of nuclear family wigwams. The position of converted chiefs was strengthened by support of the mission, several of his traditional functions being integrated into the new organization. Marital relations of the chiefs remained restricted to the old elite group; the giving of tribute to the chief diminished, but did not disappear. The chief also led the way in agricultural activity and the knowledge of reading and writing, though his people were slow in following his example. If possible, the Indians preferred to hunt and fish and to lease their lands to white farmers. The women maintained their power in internal affairs. Matri-descent and inheritance of land were strengthened by the fear of losing birthright title to reservation occupation through marriage with, or descent from, incorporated outsiders. Besides intermarriage with Negro slaves, mixture with whites also took place; in both cases usually male non-Indians married female Indians.

Missionary influence was also felt in the native languages. The widespread use of religious literature published in the Massachuset dialect as well as the conscious efforts on the part of the missionaries to "perfect" the native languages became noticeable, particularly in writing by the Indians. A great many Indians were bilingual to some extent, and many foreign words were assimilated into the native tongues. Among the coastal groups the native language was rapidly disappearing by the end of the eighteenth century.

Economic activities on the reservations were practiced mainly by women, since many men were employed by the whites and were often away for long periods of time. The women took care of small gardens and a few cows. Most important, however, was their craftwork with which they turned gypsy every summer, selling their wares to the whites. Their splint baskets particularly attest to their industriousness. Most probably this craft was learned from Scandinavians on the Delaware River about 1700 and introduced by Moravian Indians to the Indians in the Hudson River region and in Connecticut some fifty years later. From that time on it rapidly spread throughout the coastal Algonkian area. Much ornamental art applied to craftwork and dress clearly betrayed its derivation from European folk art. The Indians roamed the countryside not only with baskets, but with wooden bowls and spoons, brooms and dugouts. Indian herb doctors became popular among the whites, who, in their turn, added several European plant remedies to the Indian's medicine bag.

The Nonvanishing: The Modern Phase (*c.* 1800–)

About the turn of the eighteenth century the Indians of the Middle Atlantic seaboard were socially and culturally at their lowest point. Their recent history is one of slow and painful emergence of racial consciousness as a reaction to the attitude of the dominant whites, of the birth of a race as hybrid and as assured of its historical myths as any other race. The significant difference, however, is provided by the skepticism of the others about the ancestry claimed by this new group.

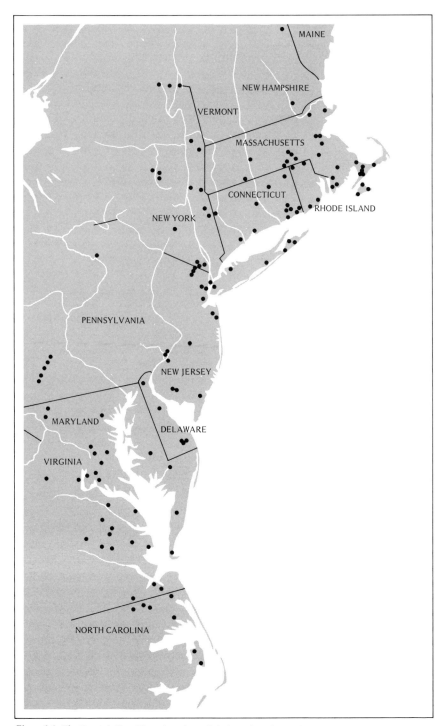

Figure 3.2. The Coastal Algonkians: locations of their modern descendants.

Widely scattered in a world of industrious villages, farms, and estates, the Indians lived a shabby life around 1800. Their wigwams and small "squaw patches" were to be found in isolated places shunned by the whites. Some of these locations were recognized as state reservations, others were considered worthless spots inhabited by small groups of squatters. The Indians in the latter areas began disappearing from the records, losing their identity when Negroes and poor whites settled among them. In addition, there were the Indians who had left their communities and roamed the countryside. Whatever income these groups and detribalized tramps had was earned by irregular work in the whaling industry, on white-owned farms or estates, and from the production of splint baskets, brooms, scrubs, and a number of other things. A source of more regular income was provided by the lease of reservation land to white farmers, as the Indians were not themselves interested in farming. If possible they hunted a little, fished a little, and drank a little too much. The traditional socioeconomic role of the Indian male proved difficult to change and provided the persistent stereotype of the lazy Indian man and his drudging wife. Religious fervor and the interest in education, characteristic of the mid-eighteenth century, was on the wane, and a feeling of inferiority was taking their place. After the greater part of the tribes had removed to the West, community life was weakened by factionalism. The factions consisted of a central "Indian" group and a marginal mestizo group. The Indian core included the old leading families, relatively pure Indians due to their traditionally restricted marital customs, besides those families whose African ancestors came in long ago and the Indian-white mixed-bloods. This inner group tended, not always successfully, to conform to the restricted marriage pattern of the leading families, even preferring endogamy above relations with the mestizo group, not to speak of the Negroes. Around 1800 hereditary chieftainship gave way to annually elected trustees, but leadership remained within the Indian faction. The mission culture and aboriginal crafts and customs lived on and died off with this faction, and after that no population increase could restore what had been lost.

The mestizo faction took care of that increase. After the Revolutionary War, New England Negroes had escaped from transport to the South by hiding among the Indians. Many Negroes joined the Indians between 1820 and 1860, as a result of the abolition of slavery in the North and because the Underground Railroad had several of its terminal stations at, or near, Indian reservations.

About 1830 the picture of a rural slum was being completed by the replacement of wigwams with draughty and squalid shacks. The last of the truly aboriginal crafts were disappearing. The only outlets left for aesthetic vigor were the gaily painted and stamped decorations on basketry, whereas the Indian whalers contributed to the variety of scrimshaw work. Splint basketry became so important in New England that labor-saving tools were developed for it. The narrow splints produced by these tools, however, slowly replaced the broad splints on which the decorative patterns were possible. A decline of this colorful art set in between 1850 and 1870.

The decline of the whaling industry about 1860 coincided with the expansion of the white population, railways, better roads, and the start of tourism. Suburbanization around the larger cities and the development of summer resorts increased the value of land and initiated the continuous efforts to oust the Indians from their last landholdings. These activities of real-estate speculators are still going on. The triracial composition of the Indian groups was seized upon by such people as a proof that the Indians were extinct or at least that they had not abided by the old miscegenation laws. On the other hand, groups like the Montauk on eastern Long Island, who to a great extent had complied with those discriminatory regulations, had become so small and inbred that they, too, were declared extinct. Of course, such nonreservation groups as yet extant were broken up or forced to remove to even more inaccessible locations. Due to these inhumane attitudes of the whites, friction between the Indian and mestizo factions increased on the reservations.

Both the resultant status struggles and the development of tourism gave rise to the birth of a neo-Indian culture and intertribal activities that are currently characteristic of the coastal groups. This modern Indianism is at best remotely connected with the aboriginal culture. The immaterial world of ancient times was lost together with the language; traditions preserved among the present older generations mainly consist of some hunting, fishing, and weather lore of colonial derivation. The new development was clearly a revitalization after a period of cultural distortion. Neo-Indianism made use of intertribal relations developed by the Indian whalers and wandering basket vendors and of hazy memories romanticized by literary fashions of the period. The urban whites, creators of this romanticism, now came as tourists, more than willing to believe in the survival of the heroic Indians of the first frontiers.

Early indications of this conscious Indianism were the "longhairs" about 1880 and the revival of Indian first names (Tecumseh Cook, Pocahontas Pharaoh, etc.), followed by the appearance of Indian dress obtained through Wisconsin Brothertown relations and the St. Regis Mohawk Iroquois. Impetus to these developments was given by ethnologists like James Mooney and Frank Speck, working among these groups around 1900. They, as well as other white friends, stimulated the organization of "powwows" and other Indian pageants. The annual powwows took over several of the social functions of religious June Meetings, which were slowly disappearing. An important role has been played by the Iroquois and western Indians living in New York City since around 1930. They attend and dance at the coastal powwows, and the local Indians are eager pupils. Thus, the means by which the coastal Indians assert their identity are of foreign origin. Connected to this movement are the efforts of several nonreservation groups to obtain official recognition as Indians; attempts to attend federal Indian schools in the western states; and submittal of claims for payment for lost lands, even for Manhattan Island.

In view of the racist attitudes of the local whites, there is no denying that this Indianism has done much good to the individuals and to the social life of these Indians. Self-respect and group spirit have reasserted themselves, and the relations between the Indian and mestizo factions have, among many groups, lost much of the old bitterness. Since World War II the trustees have usually been progressive younger men, and they no longer come exclusively from the old core families. Moreover, the present-day old core is composed mainly of families that a century ago still belonged to the marginal group. Usually they trace their relation to the extinct Indian families via a mother or grandmother. In fact, most of the coastal groups remember some old woman as the last "full-blooded" Indian, and their daughters or granddaughters play an important role in conserving and transmitting basic group values. The few remaining direct descendants of the really old families are recognizable by their undersized stature and occasional physical defects, indications of endogamy and of the wretched conditions of life in the past.

Recognition of the Indian status of the coastal remnant groups is growing but very slowly among the local whites and is next to absent among the Negroes and Iroquois. Extreme anti-Negro sentiments expressed by the frustrated mixed-breed groups are the result. Intermarriages with Negroes and even with relatively darker "Indian" groups has rapidly decreased.

Though not wholly disappearing, the reservations have become less isolated with the growth of the tourist industry and the increase of suburbanization during the last decades. These developments also brought new sources of income to the Indians. Land leasing declined with the decline of farming among the whites, but seasonal work in the vacation resorts increased as well as employment in the expanding industries. Relief is necessary for many families during the winter period. Improved means of transport and rising costs of living increased the population resident on the tax-free reservations. Education improved when poorly equipped reservation schools on Long Island were closed and the children sent to integrated schools in the nearby towns. Better education may seem to catch up with the lag in socioeconomic improvement, but the world of poverty cannot be destroyed by education alone.

There are exceptions to this generalized review. The very light-skinned Gay Head Indians on Martha's Vineyard are rather well-to-do; they keep away from "Indian doings." Among several groups color factionalism is still destructive to any cooperative activity. Small nonreservation groups are currently being assimilated into the general population, yet the core families tend to remain in or near their old locations. The population numbers of reservation groups and the larger nonreservation groups, however, have been on the increase since the turn of the century. The fertility of these Indian-mestizo groups is—and probably was for a long time—higher than any other racial or ethnic group in the United States. Thanks to better medical facilities and the resultant lowering death rates, the population increase is enormous. In 1960 the descendants of the coastal Algonkians numbered at least 4,165 in southern New England, 2,000 in New York State, 1,699 in New Jersey, 2,135 in Delaware and Maryland, and 2,155 in Virginia. These groups will probably remain socially distinct from the larger society for a long time to come.

BIBLIOGRAPHY

This chapter is based on material to be included in a doctoral thesis I am presently preparing. This is a partial listing of published and manuscript sources on which I have drawn; space would not permit a complete listing. In addition to the works cited, I have also drawn on my field notes from research among the Long Island Indians and the Wisconsin Stockbridges in 1964–1965.

Most important for the section on the proto-history are:

BYERS, D. S.

1946 The environment of the Northeast. *In* Man in Northeastern North America. Fr. Johnson, ed. Andover.

FLANNERY, R.

1939 An analysis of coastal Algonquian culture. Washington.

KROEBER, A. L.

1953 Cultural and natural areas of native North America, 3rd ed. Berkeley: University of California Press.

RITCHIE, W. A.

1965 The archaeology of New York State. New York: Natural History Press.

TRIGGER, B. G.

1962 Trade and tribal warfare on the St. Lawrence in the sixteenth century. Ethnohistory, Vol. 9.

Some of the most important seventeenth-century sources have been reprinted in:

JAMESON, J. F., ed.
1909 Narratives of New Netherland 1609–1664. New York: Barnes & Noble.

O'CALLAGHAN, E. B., AND B. FERNOW
1853–1887 Documents relative to the colonial history of the state of New York. Albany.

The last two mentioned and the following publications are of value for the traders and settlers phases:

DAY, G. M.
1965 The Identity of the Sokokis. Ethnohistory, Vol. 12.

DE FOREST, J. W.
1964 History of the Indians of Connecticut from the earliest period to 1850. Hamden, Conn.: Shoe String Press.

FENTON, W. N.
1940 Problems arising from the historic northeastern position of the Iroquois. Washington.

HUNT, G. T.
1960 The wars of the Iroquois, 2nd ed. Madison: University of Wisconsin Press.

LEDER, L. H., ed.
1956 The Livingston Indian records. Gettysburg.

NEWCOMB, W. W., JR.
1956 The culture and acculturation of the Delaware Indians. Ann Arbor.

RUTTENBER, E. M.
1872 History of the Indian tribes of Hudson's River. Albany.

TRELEASE, A. W.
1960 Indian affairs in colonial New York. Ithaca: Cornell University Press.

VAN LAER, A. J. F.
1908 Van Rensselaer Bowier manuscripts. Albany.

VAUGHAN, ALDEN T.
1965 New England frontier: Indians and Puritans 1620–1675. Boston: Little, Brown.

Sources concerning the period of Indian missions include:

BRAINERD, D.
1746 The rise and progress of a remarkable work of grace . . . Philadelphia.

DE LOSS LOVE, W.
1899 Samson Occom and the Christian Indians . . . Boston.

DODGE, E. S.
1951 Some thoughts on the historic art of the Indians . . . Bulletin of Massachusetts Archaeological Society, Vol. 13.

HOPKINS, S.
1753 Historical memoirs relating to the Housatonic Indians. Boston.

HORTON, A.
1744 Journals. Christian Monthly History. Edinburgh.

JONES, E. F.
1854 Stockbridge, past and present. Springfield.

LOSKIEL, G. H.
1789 Geschichte der Mission der Evangelischen Brüder. Barby.

ROOY, S. H.
1965 The theology of missions in the Puritan tradition. Delft.

SPECK, F. G. AND E. L. BUTLER
1947 Eastern Algonkian block-stamp decoration. Trenton.

Important on "memory cultures" and modern conditions are:

BERRY, BIEWTON
1963 Almost white. New York: Macmillan.

BOISSEVAIN, E.
1963 Detribalization and Group Identity. . . . Transactions of the New York Academy of Sciences, Ser. II, Vol. 25.

BRASSER, T. J.
1964 An outline of Long Island Indian culture change. Leiden. mimeographed.

GILBERT, W. H.
1948 Surviving Indian groups of the eastern United States. Annual Reports of the Board of Regents. Washington: Smithsonian Institution.

HARRINGTON, M. R.
1942 An ancient village site of the Shinnecock Indians. Anthropological Papers of the American Museum of Natural History, Vol. 22. New York.

SCHUSKY, E.
1957 Pan-Indianism in the eastern United States. Anthropology Tomorrow, Vol. 6.

SPECK, F. G.
1928 Native tribes and dialects of Connecticut. Washington.

4   *Creek into Seminole*[1]

WILLIAM C. STURTEVANT

The ethnogenesis and history of the Florida Seminole epitomize both the tremendous effects of European settlement and warfare on North American Indian societies and the contrary remarkable persistence of Indian social identity and distinct cultural tradition.

Particularly in the eastern part of the continent, intense and violent European-Indian relations resulted in major fissions, fusions, movements, and extinctions of Indian ethnic groups. The Seminole provide a striking instance of these transformations of Indian society and polity in response to European pressures, for the tribe is an entirely post-European phenomenon, a replacement by Creek settlers of the Florida aborigines whom they eliminated in frontier military campaigns growing out of antagonisms between European powers. Furthermore, at both ends of Seminole history we find demonstrations of the importance of what we may term *ethnonymy;* that is, the naming of sociopolitical ("tribal" or "ethnic") groups by their own members and by outsiders. This has been important for ethnogenesis, or the establishment of group distinctness. It was especially useful in facilitating the recognition of this group distinctness by the literate foreigners on whom we are largely dependent for information on Indian history beyond the range of our modern informants' memories.

In another way the Seminole (and to a lesser extent the Cherokee in the mountains of western North Carolina) are atypical of eastern Indians but similar to many groups in the western and extreme northern parts of the continent, for once established in their south Florida refuge, the Seminole occupied an ecological niche that non-Indian settlers have been unwilling and unable to exploit until very recent years. Thus, there was a long period for adjustment to the new natural and social environment before the country began filling up with settlers of European origin. The Everglades in the interior of the tip of the Florida peninsula are a vast, flat, open, grassy marsh, so wet that houses and fields can only be located on the isolated "hammocks" (small islands of trees and shrubs only slightly higher than the surrounding marsh) or on similar small areas of higher ground in the wet, densely wooded Big Cypress Swamp on the western edge of the Everglades.[2] This interior is still largely free of non-Indian occupation, even though only a few miles away Miami and neighboring towns have grown over the last fifty years into a practically continuous metropolis lining the lower east coast, while similar urbanization is now rapidly spreading down the west coast from the older towns of Tampa and Fort Myers.

The Indians occupying this region, like most peoples anywhere, trace their own history back to the original creation in a quite direct line. In a discussion of Seminole history it might make sense to borrow from this Seminole point of view and to begin with the Paleo Indian hunters in the Southeast, and then proceed through later archeological phases and the earliest identifiable historic societies to the Creek and their later settlements in northern Florida and to their modern descendants in south Florida. This chapter will follow the preceding route to the extent of ignoring those Creek and Seminole who were deported to Oklahoma in the nineteenth century, concentrating on the small minority who survived in Florida. However, we will begin not with prehistory, but rather with an exploration of Seminole "origins" as colonies that gradually became distinct and independent as communication with their relatives was severed.

Creek Background[3]

Whichever was trunk or branch, mainstream or tributary, before the division the history of the Seminole and Creek is unitary, according to both Seminole and ethnohistorian. Thus to understand the fission, we must begin with the Creek of the seventeenth and early eighteenth centuries.

In the early seventeenth century the central Georgia and Alabama region was occupied by a dozen or two dozen named Creek towns. These basic units of Creek sociopolitical organization were (and still are) "towns" in a special sense. In Muskogee, the majority language of the Creek, they are referred to by the term (*i*)*tálwa,* meaning the group of people associated with a particular ceremonial center (often called a "square grounds" in the literature, and known in modern Oklahoma English as a "stomp ground") at which their major annual religious ceremony, the "busk," is held. The word *itálwa* does not imply a physical group of residences (which is called by a related, but different, term, *taló·fa*), for the members of a "town" often lived in several settlements and also, at least in later times, in scattered family homesteads. Each *itálwa* was a separate "tribe" in the special sense of that ambiguous concept that Fried (1966, 531–532) ascribes to Lewis Henry Morgan: a specifically named group of affinally interconnected kin units (here matrilineal sibs) governed by a supreme authority embodying the popular will

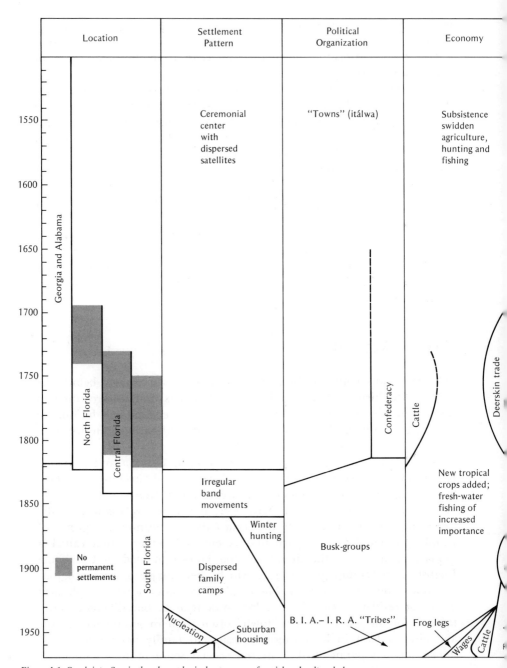

Figure 4.1. Creek into Seminole: chronological summary of social and cultural change.

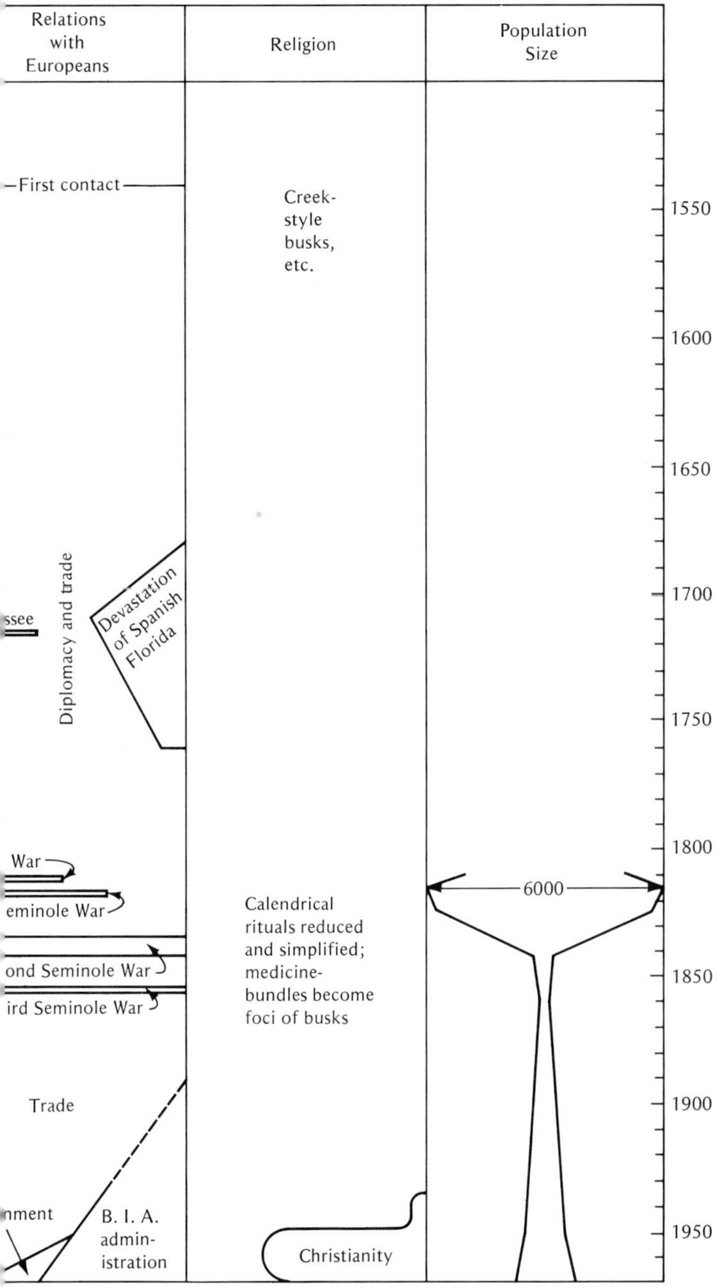

Relations with Europeans	Religion	Population Size

-First contact-

Creek-
style
busks,
etc.

1550

1600

1650

Diplomacy and trade

ssee

Devastation of Spanish Florida

1700

1750

1800

War

eminole War

ond Seminole War

ird Seminole War

Calendrical
rituals reduced
and simplified;
medicine-
bundles become
foci of busks

←——6000——→

1850

Trade

1900

nment

B. I. A.
admin-
istration

Christianity

1950

(the *mi·kko* or "chief" and other town officials), who own and defend a territory and possess a common language.

The different Creek towns were quite similar in culture and probably felt closer to each other than to their non-Creek neighbors. They shared theories and traditions, which derived various towns from common ancestral towns (perhaps ultimately all from one), which classified and ranked them in a moiety system of "red," "war" towns versus "white," "peace" towns with a gradually shifting membership (since a town switched sides after a series of defeats in the ball games played between towns of opposite moieties), and which assigned cooperative roles in peace and war. Muskogee was the internal language of the majority of towns and the lingua franca between towns. But there was a large minority of towns whose internal language was Hitchiti (in the same family, but not mutually intelligible with Muskogee). There were also Alabama- and Koasati-speaking towns (two more Muskogean languages, or perhaps two quite distinct dialects of one language), and, at least in late times, towns of languages whose other speakers were outside the Creek orbit (including some non-Muskogean languages). Because of the preponderance of Muskogee-speaking towns and the use of this language for inter-town communication, there was a tendency for non-Muskogee-speaking towns to replace their distinctive languages with Muskogee. This happened in many Hitchiti towns, and the town of Tukabahchee, for example, may originally have spoken Shawnee, an Algonkian language. Undoubtedly, assimilation to Muskogee models occurred also in aspects of culture other than language.

Whether it is appropriate to speak of a Creek "confederacy" linking these towns together in the seventeenth and early eighteenth centuries is uncertain. Late nineteenth- and early twentieth-century anthropological field work tapped the results of far-reaching changes in Creek political organization under European pressure and following European models. Eighteenth- and early nineteenth-century observers' reports reflect heavy European biases as to the nature of Indian ethnic, social, and political units. The two biases coincide, so that twentieth-century attempts to describe an "aboriginal" confederate political organization by synthesizing data from these two sources have very likely gone astray. If Opler (1952) is right, the whole late nineteenth-century "national" and "confederate" governmental structure, with many of its forms modeled on the United States federal government system, was a shallow overlay imposed by a powerful European-oriented minority, largely mixed-blood (but, importantly, matrilineally Creek), often Western-educated, and given to collaboration with external American power groups. The mass of the Creek people, however, maintained their primary town loyalties and scarcely participated in "confederacy" affairs. For their data and interpretations on Creek political institutions, John R. Swanton and Albert S. Gatschet (the principal anthropological synthesizers of data on Creek culture and society) relied heavily on literate informants, chiefly sophisticated Confederacy officials and delegates to Washington, who as experts on the subject were logical sources for the information but who belonged precisely to this probably unrepresentative minority.

The superficiality and the non-Muskogee orientation of the Confederacy governmental structure is illustrated by a comparison of some of its terminology in English and in Muskogee. The earliest surviving version of the Laws of the Confederacy (Waring, 1960) was written in English by Chilly McIntosh, the Clerk of the National Council, in 1825. The document is titled "Laws of Muscogee Nation," and in the body of the text the Confederacy is referred to as "the Nation" (usually) or "the Creek Nation" (three times). But the terminological distinction made in English between the traditional "towns" and the later "Nation" or "Confederacy" was evidently not made in the Muskogee language. Thus, a vocabulary compiled in the 1930s (Haas, 1940b) glosses the Muskogee word *itálwa* as both "tribal town" and "nation," and the latter usage appears in four official collections of laws published in the late nineteenth century by the Confederacy government in parallel English and Muskogee versions (Hargrett, 1947, 83–87). Where the English titles of these read "Muskogee Nation," the equivalent Muskogee says either *ísti ma·skó·ki,* "Muskogee people," or *ísti ma·skó·ki itálwa.* Standing opposite the phrase "National Council of the Muskogee Nation" is simply *ma·skó·ki itálwa talwa-álki* (where the last word is merely (*i*)*tálwa* again, plus the plural suffix used for people).

Recent anthropological usage, which I follow, has tended to distinguish between "Muskogee" (from *ma·skó·ki*) as the name of a specific language and "Creek" as the label for the Confederacy and the ethnic or cultural grouping that included speakers of other languages in addition to Muskogee. But the preceding examples demonstrate that normal Indian usage does not make this distinction. In Muskogee, *ma·skó·ki* refers both to the language and to the Confederacy, including speakers of other languages; in Indian English, "Muskogee" and "Creek" are used synonymously for the same two meanings. This implies that the larger grouping, which I call "Creek," is a foreign concept, or at least is symptomatic of European pressures toward the formation or recognition of ethnic and political units larger than the towns. The etymology and history of the English ethnonym "Creek" point in the same direction. In the late seventeenth century the English referred to some of the Indians beyond the South Carolina frontiers by the names of specific towns such as Kasihta, Coweta, and Okmulgee—variously spelled and often loosely applied—and with a derivative of the Indian term *òci·siˀ,* which is the

Hitchiti name for the Muskogee-speaking people (and is also the source of the ethnonym variously spelled Uchises, Uchizes, Ochizes, and so forth, used in eighteenth-century Spanish documents for the Creek as a whole and for a subdivision thereof). Originally, the Carolinians applied the term "Ocheese" to the towns on the stream they then called the "Ochese creek"—the upper Ocmulgee River. This region became a center for the South Carolina Indian trade, an important way point on the trading path to Indian groups farther on, and a defensive outpost for the colonial frontier. Because the area was an important one, the name "Ochese Creek Indians"—soon abbreviated to simply "Creeks"—replaced the other loosely applied designations. At first merely a cover label for the eastern Muskogee towns, the term was extended as Carolinian interests expanded; by about 1710 it referred to all the Muskogee and the associated Hitchiti towns. At about the same time the terms "Upper Creeks" versus "Lower Creeks" began to be used to distinguish between, respectively, the western and eastern towns (Crane, 1918; Swanton, 1922, 215, 226).

Creek Expansion

In aboriginal times the area to the south of the Creek—the present state of Florida—was an integral part of the Southeastern culture area. (The southern half of the peninsula was a deviant nonagricultural region.) But the situation changed with the arrival of the Spanish, who began explorations in Florida at least as early as 1513 and established themselves firmly in the region with the founding of Saint Augustine in 1565. Beginning in 1573 a Franciscan mission system was introduced among the Timucua and Guale in northern peninsular Florida and along the Georgia coast, following abortive attempts by the Jesuits in these regions, in south Florida, and on the South Carolina and Virginia coasts. In 1633 the missions were extended westward to the Apalachee and by about 1675 still farther west to Pensacola. These missions were strictly controlled by the Spanish crown, from whose point of view the region was important only strategically, as an outpost protecting the Spanish New World empire against English and French incursions from the north. The area was of no economic importance to the Spanish, civilian settlements were not established, and the military and religious personnel were severely limited in number and often starved of administrative and economic support. Occasional attempts to expand northward into the Creek country consistently failed, at first because they were not necessary for Spanish strategic interests and later because of English activities in the region.

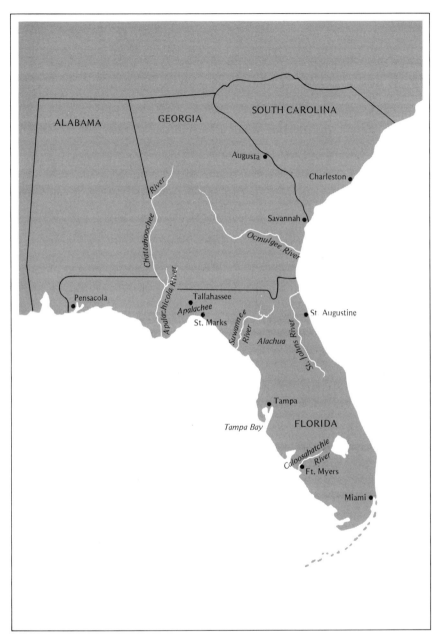

Figure 4.2. Southeastern states.

Among the Timucua, Guale, and Apalachee Indians the missionaries introduced major cultural changes, almost entirely by peaceful means. In religion a syncretistic system typical of other Spanish mission areas seems to have become well established. Very likely some aspects of social and political organization underwent marked changes, but the Indian economy and technology remained almost entirely untouched. Although the Spanish used very little military force in this region, there are records of severe population decline due to introduced diseases (one epidemic in 1613 is said to have halved the Timucua population). The nonagricultural aborigines of south Florida were not under Spanish administration, but the fort at Saint Augustine and the missions and small Spanish posts stretching west from there sealed them off from northern contacts.

This stable situation was radically changed by the encroaching English settlements, especially after the founding of Charleston in 1670. The rapidity and completeness of the ensuing genocide in Florida are almost unbelievable. The Spanish military presence in Florida was extremely weak, and firm Spanish policy there, as elsewhere, forbade guns in Indian hands. In contrast to the Spanish holding operation, the Carolina colony was actively expansionist, was much interested in the Indian trade, and readily supplied guns to the Indians. Especially when rice agriculture began in Carolina, plantation slavery was introduced, at first using Indians, and later, Africans. The colonists obtained Indian slaves by direct capture and by encouraging Indian warfare and raiding, subsequently purchasing the captives. With the rise of African slavery Spanish territory became a refuge area for runaway Negro slaves, but Indian slaving continued, now for export to the West Indies and New England.

Destruction of the mission population in north Florida began about 1680 with raiding by Creek and Yamasee Indians who used English weapons and sometimes had a small core of Carolinian leadership. The culmination was a raid in 1704 by 1,000 Creek warriors under Colonel Moore and fifty Carolinians into Apalachee and similar incursions into the peninsula under Thomas Nairne soon thereafter. The colorful, yet hardly exaggerated, reports by Nairne in about 1710 are indicative:

> Your Lordship may preceive by the map that the garrison of St. Augustine is by this warr Reduced to the bare walls their Casle and Indian towns all consumed Either by us in our Invasion of that place or by our Indian subjects, since who in quest of Booty are now obliged to goe down as farr as the point of Florida as the firm land will permit they have drove the Floridians to the Islands of the Cape, have brought in and sold many Hundreds of them, and Dayly now continue that trade so that in some few years thay'le Reduce these Barbarians to a farr less number.
>
> ·　　　·　　　·
>
> There remains not now, so much as one Village with ten Houses in it, in all Florida, that is subject to the Spaniards; nor have they any houses or

cattle left, but such as they can protect by the Guns of their Castle of St. Augustine, that alone being now in their hands and which is continually infested by the perpetual Incursions of the Indians, subject to this Province [Fairbanks, 1957, 95–96, 98].

In 1708 the Spanish governor at Saint Augustine reported that he had withdrawn all his outposts and that all the aborigines left consisted of some 300 refugees at Saint Augustine; some 10,000 to 12,000 had been enslaved by the Creek, Yamasee, and Carolinians (Boyd, Smith, and Griffin, 1951, 90). This hardly sounds like an "Effectual way of Civilizing and Instructing" the Indians, which Nairne claimed it to be (Fairbanks, 1957, 96).

In 1715 the Creek leader Brim of Coweta conceived a general plan to drive the English, French, and Spanish out of the Southeast. The first move was an attack by the Yamasee on the South Carolina colony. The effects were nearly disastrous for the colony. Other Indian groups joined in, but the Carolinians succeeded in preventing the Cherokee from participating in the attack, and the move collapsed. Many Yamasee fled to the Saint Augustine region, where they were largely destroyed by subsequent Carolinian raids.

As a result of this war and because of dissatisfaction with the English trade, in 1717 several Lower Creek towns that had moved away from the Spanish to the Ocmulgee after 1685 returned to their old locations on the Chattahoochee River. They were soon followed by other Lower Creek towns in a general withdrawal from the English frontier. Brim's aggressive moves having failed, he fell back on a policy of neutrality and diplomatic negotiation with both the English and the Spanish. The Creek leadership continued this balance-of-power game for the rest of the century, bringing it to perfection under Alexander McGillivray, who skillfully vacillated between the English, Spanish, and Americans. One result was the origin and growth of pro-English and pro-Spanish factions among the Lower Creek.

A significant Spanish diplomatic move after the Yamasee War was the sending of emissaries to the Lower Creek in 1716, 1717, and 1718 in an attempt to persuade them to resettle the now vacant Apalachee region to serve as a buffer against English expansion. While no direct evidence of the outcome of these efforts has come to light, indirect evidence points to their success. The towns of Apalachicola, Oconee, Hitchiti, Sawokli, and Yuchi were reported as agreeing to move, and all of them are identifiable later as components of the early Seminole. It is not certain when the first permanent settlements were made in the Apalachee region, but there are hints of Creek groups there as early as 1727. The Cherokee raids of the 1720s and the increased English penetration that followed James Oglethorpe's founding of the colony of

Georgia in 1732 provided further impetus for southward movements of the Creek. By the early 1740s the Apalachee region was clearly serving as a winter hunting territory for the Creek towns on the lower Chattahoochee River that were engaged in the deerskin trade. The Spanish again attempted to attract the Creek by opening a trading store at Saint Marks in 1738. But Cline (1964) finds no clear evidence for permanent Creek settlements in that area before about 1755. A conference at Saint Marks in 1764 listed five Creek villages in the neighborhood—evidently Tallahassee (led by Tonaby of Coweta), Mikasuki, Chiskataloofa, Tamathli, and Ocklocknee; in addition, there may have been a few Apalachee and even Timucua refugees incorporated into these settlements. These "Western Proto-Seminole" (as Cline dubs them) tended to be pro-Spanish and anti-English.

The early history of the Eastern Proto-Seminole of the Alachua region south of what is presently Gainesville is similar. By the 1730s there are references to pro-English Creek in the region between the Saint Johns River and Alachua. When Oglethorpe laid siege to Saint Augustine in 1740, among his many Creek warriors was a group led by Cowkeeper, a chief from Oconee, who was either already, or soon to become, the leader of the settlement at Alachua. Many Creek undoubtedly gained familiarity with the area while accompanying Oglethorpe on this expe-

Billy Bowlegs (second from right) and his suite in New York, 1852.
(Engraving after a daguerreotype, from Illustrated London News, *May 21, 1853, page 396. By courtesy of the Trustees of the British Museum.)*

dition and another in 1743. At any rate, by 1764 the Alachua region included settlers from at least the Creek towns Oconee, Apalachicola, Sawokli, and Chiaha, as well as some Yamasee.

A colony from Eufaula was established in central Florida well south of Alachua by 1767, and in 1778 there is a reference to settlers from three additional Muskogee-speaking towns as well as from two Alabama-speaking towns (Swanton, 1922, 403; Cline, 1964). Hawkins in 1799 listed seven Seminole towns—"they are Creeks," he explained—and said that "they are made from the towns" Oconee, Sawokli, Eufaula, Tamathli, Apalachicola, and Hitchiti (1848, 24–25). From these lists of towns it is quite clear that at this period the dominant language of the Creek settlements in Florida was Hitchiti, while Muskogee formed a strong minority, and that there were also speakers of Yuchi, Alabama, and probably other languages.[4]

In a sense these were the beginnings of the Seminole. Creek individuals, families, groups, and perhaps small towns began moving from Georgia and Alabama south into north Florida after they and the English had destroyed the aborigines and limited the area of Spanish control to the immediate environs of Saint Augustine. But crossing over the international boundary was of no significance for the Indians. The actual frontier was fluid and not under the direct control of either English or Spanish authorities. The Creek movements into Florida were only part of the complex fissions and migrations of Creek towns before and after this period, both north and south of the European-drawn line, in a period of rapid change of Creek culture and society, under heavy military and economic pressures and influences from the English. The deerskin trade, the introduction of guns, and the increase of warfare all encouraged increased mobility and the breakup of the old settled agricultural villages; and the new diplomatic negotiations with Europeans undoubtedly affected the Creek political system.

Florida passed under British dominion and remained so for twenty years, between 1763 and 1783. British methods for dealing with Indians spread into Florida, where the Spanish techniques had never succeeded with these northern-derived Indians. When Florida returned to Spanish dominion for the period between 1783 and 1819, the Spanish were forced to continue these British methods, even to continuing the use of a British trading company as their main point of contact with the Creek in Florida as well as to the north. For the Indians the change back to Spanish sovereignty made little difference.

After 1763 British trade goods and quantities of diplomatic gifts were available through Saint Augustine, Saint Marks, and Pensacola, as well as from Carolina and Georgia traders. Creek expansion into the region continued, until by 1783 they had towns scattered from the Apalachicola

River nearly to the Saint Johns and from Georgia south to the Caloosa-hatchie River. Between the widely separated towns were hunting terri-tories under Creek control. The south Florida aborigines had been en-tirely destroyed by Creek raids, and the few pitiful remnants had left with the withdrawing Spanish administrators and garrisons in 1763.

The British divide-and-rule policy for dealing with the southern In-dians, including those in Florida, was clearly expressed by John Stuart, Indian Agent for the Southern District, in 1764:

> It will undoubtedly be detrimental to His Majesties service, that too strict a friendship and union subsist between the different Indian nations within this department; it is therefore incumbent upon us by all means in our power to foment any jealousy or division that may subsist between them. But this must be done with great delicacy, and in such a manner as not to awaken the least suspicion in them that we have any end of view to answer by it [Fairbanks, 1957, 146].

This policy, as applied in treaty negotiations, diplomatic gifts, and the organization of the Indian trade, furthered a tendency toward sepa-ratism, which was also inherent in the Creek situation. The Confederacy, insofar as it existed at all, was not firmly organized and effective through-out Creek territory. The Creek pioneers in Florida began as hunters, traders, and warriors and then gradually established more permanent settlements of growing size and stability at increasing distances from the old towns in the north. Independent action was also no doubt facilitated by the conglomerate origins of these settlements. Segments of the Creek that had established organizational connections with other towns rarely, if ever, moved as units. Rather, new towns were established by emigrants from various sources, and new patterns of town organization and rela-tions with other settlements must have had to grow up, rather than being simply transplanted.

Evidence of the gradually increasing autonomy of the Florida settle-ments appears in the documents. In 1756 the Alachua settlements held aloof from an anti-English outbreak of the Chattahoochee Lower Creek. In 1757 Cowkeeper visited Savannah and reported "that he had not been in the [Creek] Nation These four Years, nor had he received any Instruc-tions from thence whereon to Talk" (Fairbanks, 1957, 134)—an indica-tion both that a relationship was assumed and that it was not very effective. In 1763 at the time of the Treaty of Augusta the Creek dele-gates, none of them from Florida, claimed "jurisdiction" over that area. For the Treaty of Picolata in 1765 the Florida Indians acted independ-ently of the Lower Creek, but for the Treaty of Pensacola in the same year Creek representatives again spoke for the Florida region without the presence of delegates from there. By the end of the British period in Florida it seems clear that the Florida Indians, although often treated

independently and acting independently, were still considered by themselves, by the rest of the Creek, and by the English, Spanish, and Americans as part of the Creek Confederacy. McGillivray, negotiating for the
Confederacy, often claimed to speak for the Florida settlements in international affairs, but he also complained of his lack of knowledge and
control of their activities. With his death in 1793 separatism accelerated,
and negotiations in 1804 over land cessions and debt payments show
the Seminole acting almost entirely independently of the Creek.

It was during this period that the term "Seminole" came into use by
Europeans. The earliest occurrence so far found is in an English document of 1765 (Cline, 1964), where the label is applied to Cowkeeper's
Alachua group without either explanation or definition (implying that
it was a term already in general use). At first the name was apparently
restricted to this Alachua group, but by the mid-1770s it was extended
to include the settlements in the Apalachee region. Until about 1860 the
ethnonym continued to be used on two levels: as a general term for all
the Florida Indians and, particularly by those with a more intimate
acquaintance with the situation, as a specific label for the component
deriving from the Alachua settlements.

The ethnonym is of Muskogee origin: *simanó·li* (earlier *simaló·ni,*
surviving in some dialects) means "wild, runaway," as applied to animals
and plants. It was originally borrowed by Muskogee from the Spanish
word *cimarrón,* which has the same meaning. A more appropriate translation of the Muskogee word in its extended, perhaps metaphorical, use
as an ethnonym is probably "emigrants," "pioneers," or "frontiersmen."

The borrowing of the ethnonym into English and Spanish, early reports of its meaning as "wild, runaway," and its growing application
toward the end of the eighteenth century all emphasize the tendency
toward independence of the Florida Creek settlements.

Warfare and Separation

A major change in the composition of the Florida settlements and in
their relationship with the rest of the Creek was introduced by the
Creek War of 1813–1814. Up to this point these were largely offshoots
of the Lower Creek towns, which latter had a relatively long history of
acculturative relations with the European outposts and settlements.
These Lower Creek towns had served as a buffer against intensive European contacts with the Upper Creek of central Alabama. But after the
American Revolution this frontier was ruptured, and the Upper Creek
region was flooded with American colonists and traders. In 1796 Benjamin Hawkins began a long career as American agent among the Creek.

He strongly encouraged economic acculturation, with consequent changes that undermined the traditional male roles, and he pressed for reorganization and increased centralization of political forms. A strong opposition to these changes arose among the Upper Creek; this opposition was strengthened by the visit in 1811 of the Shawnee chief Tecumseh, who preached nativism and anti-Americanism. Numerous Creek prophets took up his call, and their faction finally, in 1813, attacked a fort of the pro-American group, killing many Americans. The Georgians and Tennesseans under Andrew Jackson quickly struck back, soon defeating the conservative Upper Creek (see Nunez, 1958). These nativistic "Red Stick" Creek, mostly from Muskogee-speaking towns, streamed into Florida, away from the Americans and their Creek allies, partly as individual refugees and partly as whole towns. Many of them joined existing Florida settlements, while others moved beyond them to establish new towns in their hunting territories to the south and west toward Tampa Bay. Fairbanks (1957, 208, 211) estimates the Creek population of Florida before this influx at 3,500 to 4,000 and immediately afterward at about 6,000. He has also provided some striking archeological evidence of the nativistic conservatism of the Red Sticks, who had "divested themselves of their European animals and much of their European trade materials" (Fairbanks, 1962, 48). Florida separatism was intensified by the influx of defeated conservatives antagonistic toward the Lower Creek, who had remained neutral or had aided Jackson, while the Creek to the north had still more justification for considering their Florida relatives to be "runaways" and "outlaws."

In 1812–1813 the Alachua groups had supported the British and Spanish in British-Spanish-American difficulties in East Florida, drawing a counterattack by Georgia and Tennessee militia in which they lost much livestock and crops and in which two towns were burned. As a result they moved their settlements south. The western Seminole, including Red Stick and Negro refugees, were armed and supported by the British in 1814 during the War of 1812. In 1817 the British were encouraging them to raid across the border, and the Georgians were retaliating by stealing livestock and Negroes. Finally, in 1818 Andrew Jackson with 2,000 men, many of them Creek, crossed into Spanish Florida in what is called the First Seminole War (1817–1818). He destroyed the Seminole and Negro forts on the Apalachicola River and moved east to the Suwannee River, burning the villages of the Seminole in the old Apalachee region and around Tallahassee. Many of the occupants fled as he approached, but they suffered massive losses of crops, livestock, and houses. As a result, the Mikasuki and others moved east, some into the Alachua region and many southward into the peninsula, while some moved west toward Pensacola. Reports resulting from this foray list twenty towns and describe the main ones with square grounds, councils, and officials, and with outlying fields and associated smaller settlements—very clearly towns of the regular Creek pattern (Fairbanks, 1957, 212–240).

The accession of the Red Stick refugees, Creek collaboration on the American side in the First Seminole War, and the eastward and southward movements of the Seminole settlements combined to establish firmly Seminole independence from the Creek Confederacy.

The First Seminole War amounted to the American conquest of Spanish Florida. The final transfer took place in 1821, and almost immediately the Americans entered negotiations with the Seminole. From the initial American explorations of the new territory and from the negotiations and signatories for the 1823 Treaty of Moultrie Creek, we have a good deal of data on the Seminole situation, which is well summarized by Fairbanks (1957, 239–267). His analysis of several lists of Seminole towns at this time shows seventeen deriving from the settlements predating the Creek War, eight of Red Stick refugees, two of Yuchi (properly part of the first category), three of Negroes, and two of unknown derivation. These settlements were spread over most of peninsula Florida, from the Apalachicola River east and south. In south Florida, the Everglades and perhaps the Big Cypress Swamp were not occupied but were in use for hunting, fishing, and gathering. Exploitative techniques suitable for the subtropical South were being developed, but the Indian occupation still concentrated in more northern regions, where the Creek agricultural, hunting, and (recently developed) herding practices were more readily applicable. The Creek-style town organization persisted, with centers of concentrated settlement and outlying satellite villages. There was evidently no overall political organization—a head spokesman had to be appointed specifically for the Moultrie Creek treaty negotiations.

Fairbanks attempts to find in this period the origins of the dichotomy among the modern Seminole between a larger, Mikasuki-speaking group and a smaller, Muskogee-speaking one—but with little success, for the old divisions between Creeks and Seminoles or (western) Mikasukis and (eastern) Seminoles do not seem to have coincided with a division between Mikasuki (Hitchiti)-speaking and Muskogee-speaking groups. One of the difficulties is that nearly all the direct linguistic data in the documents for the eighteenth and nineteenth centuries are Muskogee, no matter what the town or the presumed intratown language. The Florida Indians quite obviously carried over the Creek custom of using Muskogee in extra-community dealings, with Europeans as well as with Indians.

In the Treaty of Moultrie Creek the thirty-two signatories gave up all claim to Florida territory except for a reservation to be designated in the central part of the state. They also submitted a census, which totaled 4,883. The decrease from the estimate of 6,000 for about five years earlier is accounted for by Fairbanks by losses caused by the First Seminole War and by the return to Alabama of some of the Red Stick refugees after the war; but this 1823 figure is surely too low by at least 600. It proved difficult to carry out the treaty terms, including locating the reservation, moving the Seminole within it, and protecting the Indians against the incursions of rapidly increasing American settlement. Local American sentiment opposed the agreement, coveting both the set-aside territory and the Negroes associated with the Seminole.

Finally, in 1835 the seven-year Second Seminole War began. It is reputed to have been one of the most costly Indian wars ever fought by the United States Army; nevertheless, it ended in a truce rather than with a treaty (this is the basis for the modern claim that the Seminole "have never signed a treaty"). A few summary statements on this complex and poorly studied war must suffice here, even though from most points of view—Seminole included—this was the most significant event (or series of events) in Seminole history.

The most readily noted effects were the massive population loss and the territorial dislocations. One firm measure of the decline in population is the total of 4,420 captured and surrendered Seminole who were counted as they were deported to Indian Territory (present Oklahoma) during the war. To these must be added an unknown, but surely large, number killed during the fighting. The number of survivors left in Florida in 1842 cannot be accurately given. General Worth, who succeeded in declaring a draw in that year, reported to the War Department an estimate of 300 Seminole remaining in Florida (Coe, 1898, 158), but his interest in ending the fighting may well have resulted in an underestimate. In round numbers, 500 survivors in 1842 from 5,500 Seminole seven years before cannot be far wrong.

The losses on the other side were also high, for reasons pointed out by a German officer who fought on the Russian front in World War II:

> Practically the identical shortsighted attitude as that of the German General Staff during World War II [in regard to the Russian campaign] was displayed by the U.S. military command during the Seminole Indian War in Florida under Jackson's and Van Buren's administration. The government troops dispatched to pacify the Indians were certainly sufficiently trained for orthodox battle but, not being familiar with Indian fighting in the woods, they paid a terrible toll in blood for their eventual success [Dohnanyi, 1962, 201–202].

As this remark indicates, this was a guerrilla war. In its length, severity, disparity of forces, strategy and tactics, and in the total involvement of the native population, it resembled modern guerrilla campaigns more than much of the warfare on the American frontiers did. The Indians suffered constant losses through death, capture, surrender, and (according to vivid modern Seminole traditions) the hardships attendant on continual movement, lack of food, and the warriors' efforts to conceal themselves and their families from the troops. Fields and stored food were systematically destroyed by the Army. Settled life became impossible, and the Indians were forced to divide into small bands subsisting largely by hunting and gathering.

The long, costly fighting was unpopular with the American public in the North. But the interests of the white settlers in Florida and the Jackson administration's firm policy for "Removal" of eastern Indians west of the Mississippi sustained the war in the face of its political unpopularity until the actual aims had been met, although the vigor of the Seminole resistance forced some compromises with the theoretical aims. In the end it proved too costly to remove all the Indians. Here, too, there are obvious parallels with some more modern wars.

One aim of the war had been to "recover" from the Seminole the Negroes who were associated with them. These were escaped slaves and their descendants, many of whom played a major role in the fighting since their interests in resistance were at least as strong as the Indians' and since many Negroes were bilingual and more familiar than the Indians with European behavior (actually, this biculturality made Negroes very important to both sides as interpreters, guides, and tactical advisers). In some ways, in fact, the Second Seminole War was more a Negro insurrection than an Indian war. Contemporary documents contain some evidence of the independence of the Seminole Negroes from their Indian associates (Porter, 1932, 323–348; 1943), and this is also indicated by the survival of two communities of Seminole Negroes, separate from Indians, founded during this period: one in Coahuila, Mexico, whose ancestors went there from Indian Territory in the 1850s, accompanied by a Seminole Indian group that soon returned; and the other on Andros Island in the Bahamas, whose ancestors reached there via English ships and perhaps their own canoes from the Miami region at the beginning of the nineteenth century (Porter, 1945; Goggin, 1946). There is much evidence of military cooperation between the Seminole and Negroes during the wars; but there is also evidence of social separateness in the fact that blood-group frequencies prove that the modern Florida Seminole have almost no Negro ancestry. Yet the Army and the Floridians were not able, in general, to separate the Negroes from their Seminole associates during the war. When Indians and Negroes surrendered or were captured in Florida, the Army found that the Indians could not be kept under control for deportation unless the Seminole Negroes were allowed to accompany them to Indian Territory. Nevertheless, at the end only a small handful of Negroes remained in south Florida with the Seminole who evaded capture, and these free Indians in the far South no longer provided a significant refuge for escaped Negro slaves. Most of the peninsula had been cleared of the Indians who were in the path of American settlement, and those remaining in the Everglades and the Big Cypress Swamp were in country very difficult for the Army to scour out and were too far away, too few, and too weak to pose any threat.

Despite the dislocations and realignments of population groups during the war, ethnonyms indicative of origins in the North continued to be applied to various bands by close observers, presumably reflecting Indian usage (although the terms used in the Indian languages are unknown). The two-level use of the term "Seminole" continued: it was the ethnonym for all Florida Indians; and it was the specific ethnonym for the band derived ultimately from Alachua, as opposed to other bands called Mikasuki, Creek, Tallahassee, Yuchi, Choctaw, Hitchiti, Spanish Indians, and, occasionally, by other ethnonyms.[5]

But Florida Seminole contacts with their Creek relatives, and, in fact, with all other Indians, had been decisively severed by the southward movement and by the removal during the 1830s of the Creek and other southern Indians to Indian Territory west of the Mississippi. There the great majority of the Seminole joined the Creek in exile, where they maintained—or adopted—Creek social, political, and cultural patterns and became one of the "Five Civilized Tribes." From 1842 on Seminole culture in Florida evolved entirely independently.

A rough sketch map prepared about eight years after the war (Casey, 1850–1856) shows the Seminole survivors in perhaps ten settlements (probably now best called "camps," following modern usage) in six rough groupings within an area about 40 miles in diameter on the northern edge of the Big Cypress Swamp and south of the Caloosahatchie River. There may have been a few other camps farther south, to judge by events of 1855–1858.

One final spasm remained before the Seminole were left in peace. In 1849 and 1850 minor troubles broke out between Indians and whites. The Seminole surrendered six or seven supposedly guilty men, but Florida agitation for removal was aroused. The federal government hired a "removal expert," who brought to Florida a delegation of Seminole from the West and took them, with Billy Bowlegs, the principal Florida leader of the Seminole, and some of his followers, on a grand tour of Washington, Baltimore, Philadelphia, and New York in 1852. By various means, thirty-six Seminole were persuaded to emigrate, at a cost to the government of over $50,000 (Coe, 1898, 191–209; Porter, 1967). The expert was discharged. Finally the Third Seminole War broke out in 1855. During the ensuing three years Florida militia and a few federal troops killed perhaps twenty Indians in the Big Cypress Swamp area and finally managed, in 1858 and 1859, to deport 240, including Billy Bowlegs. In 1860 there remained fewer than 200 Seminole in Florida.[6]

Isolation

For nearly twenty years after the end of the Third Seminole War in 1858 the survivors in their refuge within the Everglades and Big Cypress Swamp kept away from the very few non-Indians who were then in southern Florida. As one result, we have practically no contemporary published or manuscript data on the Indians during these years. Not only are documents lacking, but the time is also just beyond the range of personal recall by the elderly informants I encountered in the early 1950s. Yet it was undoubtedly an extremely important period of cultural and social adjustment to radically new ecological and demographic conditions. We can only see the results of the changes in the 1870s and 1880s, when documentary data are again available and my own informants' earliest memories begin.

The Seminole appear in these new sources as though discovered afresh, the continuity of tradition and documents stretching from the eighteenth century into the 1850s having broken off. The old ethnonymy, with its references to towns and bands in north Florida and among the Creek, is replaced by a new one. The label "Seminole" is regularly applied in English to all Florida Indians. But modern informants reject the translation "runaway" for *simano·li·* (in Mikasuki) and *simanó·li* (in Muskogee); in Florida these terms mean simply "wild" and are used to refer to naturally wild animals and plants in contrast to tame or domesticated ones. The Indians recognize the derivation of the English word "Seminole" from these Indian words, but at least in the 1950s they disliked being called "wild" and did not use *simano·li·* or *simanó·li* as ethnonyms in their own languages. In 1881 MacCauley made "several efforts to discover the tribal name by which these Indians now designate themselves"; his principal informant rejected the label "Seminole" and instead provided the Muskogee expression *kanyóksa isticá·ti,* literally "peninsula Indians" (1887, 509). I know of no other occurrence of this term and suspect that it was invented to satisfy MacCauley's persistent questioning. The usual inclusive term in the Indian languages was simply the word for "Indian": *yá·tkitisci·* in Mikasuki and *isticá·ti* in Muskogee, both meaning literally "red person" and paralleling terms meaning "white person" and "black person" applied to whites and Negroes. The lack of an ethnonym to distinguish the Seminole as a whole from other Indians is symptomatic of the long period of Seminole isolation.

Of course there were, and still are, specific labels for the two languages spoken by the Florida Seminole. In Mikasuki, the Mikasuki language is called *i·làponki·* and the Muskogee language *ci·sàponki·*. In Florida Muskogee, the Mikasuki language is called *cilo·kkitá* and the Muskogee language *oci·sopónaka*. The etymologies of these terms are interesting; in addition to stems meaning "language," they contain *i·l-*, of unknown etymology; *oci·s-* and a shortened derivative *ci·s-*, which I was told refers to a river to the north that is mentioned in the Seminole migration legend and is clearly the Hitchiti term for the Muskogee language (and the source of the "Ochese Creek" lying behind the ethnonym "Creek"); and *cilo·kkitá*, which contains the stem sometimes translated as "different speech," which is well known as a Muskogee term for their Red moiety (Swanton, 1928a; 1946, 664). Here we do have some continuity with the Creek ancestors of the Seminole.

The term "Mikasuki" was known to some of my Seminole informants, but not much used in their English and not at all in Mikasuki, except rarely as a conscious borrowing from English (and, occasionally, perhaps from Oklahoma Muskogee by those few individuals with knowledge of usage there). This and some other examples of the older ethnonymy for Seminole bands occur only rarely in modern English literature, and then, I think, are learned from the Indians who recalled some traces of the earlier English usage. Thus, MacCauley heard the term "Tallahassee Indians" (1887, 509) but applied it to two groups of families whose distinct identity is denied by recent genealogical and traditional evidence. He also recorded the cryptic note "Fragments of Mikosuki— O-ko-ni—in Florida" (MacCauley, 1881) but did not apply these terms to any social group.

An occasional attentive observer recognized that the Seminole spoke Muskogee or "Creek" (e.g., Pratt, in Sturtevant, 1956a; MacCauley, 1887; Cory, 1896, 35). But hardly any outsider was aware until well into the twentieth century that another language was also spoken—when in fact, some two-thirds of the Florida Indians speak the dialect of Hitchiti, which, by a transferral of the Oklahoma terminology, has been called "Mikasuki" in English since about 1920 (e.g., Spencer, 1921; Nash, 1931; Stirling, 1936; and, subsequently, in anthropological sources). Even Mac-Cauley, the first ethnographer of the Florida Seminole, did not discover this; his Mikasuki linguistic and ethnographic informant gave him only Muskogee forms. The Mikasuki, even though they were now in the majority, maintained the old Creek convention of using Muskogee for communicating with outsiders. Good evidence for this is the incipient jargon that was used between Indians and non-Indians in Florida until about 1920. All the Indian terms in this jargon were of Muskogee origin, despite the fact that the majority of its Indian users were native speakers of Mikasuki. But by the 1950s the situation had changed. In most of the cases I observed of conversations between Mikasuki and Muskogee speakers, the language used was Mikasuki. The jargon had died, and one Mikasuki word had even been borrowed into local south Florida English: "chikee," meaning "Seminole house" (from *ciki·*, meaning "house"). This is in contrast to the two earlier local borrowings from Muskogee, "sofkee," meaning "Seminole corn soup," from *sá·fki;* and "coontie," a wild cycad, genus *Zamia,* locally used for starch by both Indians and non-Indians, from *konti·*.

But even in the 1950s Muskogee maintained a status advantage over Mikasuki in at least some contexts for Mikasuki speakers. One occasionally heard comparisons invidious to Mikasuki of the advantages or capacities of the two languages, comparisons reminiscent of attitudes elsewhere of native speakers of a nonstandard dialect or language toward the standard language of their region. These attitudes presumably derived from the traditional use of Muskogee for extra-community communication, from the fact that nearly all personal names and the words of nearly all curing songs of the Mikasuki are in Muskogee, and from the fact that Christianity was first effectively introduced to the Mikasuki in the 1930s and 1940s by missionaries from Oklahoma who spoke Muskogee and used the Muskogee New Testament and other Christian literature in that language, translating orally into Mikasuki.

Although the distribution of a few other traits does coincide with the linguistic difference, in most respects Florida Seminole culture is shared by speakers of both languages. Sociopolitical subdivisions over the last century, as well as earlier, are only partially congruent with the Mikasuki-Muskogee difference. Beginning in the 1870s both contemporary documents and modern reminiscences distinguish groups of families associated with regional locations in south Florida, with ethnonyms in English and the Indian languages referring to these places with varying specificity and changing quite quickly over time. About 1880 there were three "settlements" of Muskogee-speaking families immediately east, north, and west of Lake Okeechobee. Some twenty years later these had coalesced on Cow Creek north of the lake, from which came the common name "Cow Creek Seminole" for the Muskogee-speaking element. Another label, "cabbage palm Indians," points to the ecological difference between this region and that occupied by the "Big Cypress Indians," the Mikasuki speakers who in the earliest part of this period were localized on the northern edge of the Big Cypress Swamp and on the rim of the Everglades just within the coastal ridge between Fort Lauderdale and Miami. The largest settlement was on Pine Island southwest of Fort Lauderdale, where until about 1900 there were some twenty-five houses (i.e., probably eight to ten families), a busk ground, and nearby fields. But this was an unusual situation. In other regions the settlement pattern was very dis-

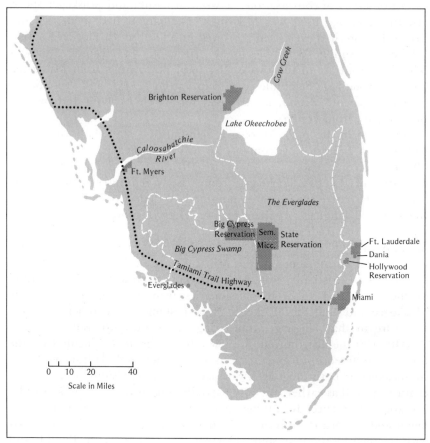

Figure 4.3. South Florida.

persed, with the "camps" of matrilocal extended families often miles
apart. A very large area of interior southern Florida was exploited.
Suitable locations for the shifting fields of swidden agriculture tended
to be small and widely scattered; here, fields were made, tended, and
harvested during spring and summer. In the winter hunting for hides,
skins, and meat was important, and families often shifted to temporary
camps for this purpose. Visits were made, often over great distances in
dugout canoes, to the small coastal towns to exchange hides and skins
for cloth, metal tools and utensils, guns and ammunition, and sugar,
salt, and coffee.

   It is clear from modern reminiscences that many locations were
abandoned after a few years, especially in reaction to encroaching non-
Indian settlements, railroads, and farming and cattle raising (Sturtevant,

1956a, 1956b). Trading patterns shifted also. Hunting became less profitable with the decline in game populations and increasing application of game laws (especially those prohibiting the sale of feathers and alligator hides). Major ecological changes were introduced by the draining of the eastern and northern Everglades by canals dredged between 1906 and 1913. The Florida real-estate boom of the 1920s pushed the Miami–Fort Lauderdale groups off their land; some of them moved into the Everglades west of Miami, and others onto the small federal reservation at Dania between Miami and Fort Lauderdale. On the other hand, the 1928 opening of the Tamiami Trail highway running west from Miami directly across the Everglades increased Seminole contacts with the outside world. From 1928 to the present there has been a steady movement of camps from the hammocks in the open Everglades to locations along the highway. One result of the Tamiami Trail has been a realignment and overlapping of groups that were previously geographically more distinct. The region toward the town of Everglades at the south end of the Big Cypress Swamp began to be occupied by families from the northern Big Cypress about 1882 (Tebeau, 1957, 53). Later these moved north to the Trail, while others who had remained in the Big Cypress moved south to the highway, both meeting those who had moved west from the Miami–Fort Lauderdale region. The occupants of these "Trail" camps have gained a significant portion of their income from selling souvenirs to passing tourists (and charging them admission to the camps) and from selling frogs' legs to wholesale houses in Miami.

Seminole social and political organization during this period correlated only partially with settlement areas. There were three fundamental types of units: matrilocal extended families, matrilineal sibs, and busk groups. The families, of course, were localized in "camps." The matrilineal core of each camp belonged to one sib, so that the women and the unmarried men of a sib lived in a series of scattered camps, which could be viewed as the residential manifestations of the sib. These scattered camps drew together for a few days on two occasions during each year: for the busk in the early summer and the Hunting Dance in the fall. At these times the people gathered at the busk grounds, each sib living together for the duration of the ceremonies in its own large camp, the larger sibs in two camps (see Spoehr, 1941, 1944; his descriptions will also serve in most respects for the Mikasuki). Otherwise the sibs were geographically localized only in that the lists of sibs of the Mikasuki speakers and of the Muskogee speakers are not identical, although they are similar—a situation comparable to the one Swanton (1928a) described as between various Creek towns. Some sibs occur in both groups, having equivalent names in the two languages and being considered the "same" by their members; but several sibs occur only

Little Billie and his family, Big Cypress, 1910.
(Photo by Alanson Skinner; courtesy, Museum of the American Indian, Heye Foundation.)

in one or the other of the two groups (although there are then customary equations that serve for such purposes as residence and hospitality when visiting a busk of the other group). This difference between the two linguistic groups has been maintained by the strong tendency toward matrilocality, for linguistic affiliation is determined by propinquity rather than by descent. Genealogies and tradition do show intermarriage between the two linguistic groups. Occasionally a woman moved across to take up residence with the other group; after a generation or two her descendants grew up speaking the language of their neighbors and were no longer considered to be immigrants from the other language group. If the original immigrant belonged to a foreign sib (or subsib), her descendants added this to the list of the linguistic group with which they were now affiliated. That the lists of sibs of the two language groups are not now identical shows that such instances were quite exceptional.

There has never been any overall Seminole political organization. The largest political units until very recent times were the busk groups. Each of these groups was affiliated with a medicine bundle (a collection of magical objects) on which the annual busk ceremony was focused— a non-Creek feature that evidently developed after the Second Seminole War (Sturtevant, 1954). Every Seminole "belonged to" one of the medicine bundles, attended its busk (although he could also attend others as a visitor), and fell under the jurisdiction of the judicial and political council meeting of that busk. Until about 1890 there were nine of these medicine bundles; two were destroyed in a fire soon thereafter, and another about 1910. The rest survive and are still in use. One of these, and the associated busk, has always belonged to the Muskogee-speaking Seminole. The other five are Mikasuki; but within living memory there have been a maximum of four separate Mikasuki busks in any one year rather than the possible five (or eight, before 1890). Much more normal is the situation of the past thirty or forty years, when there have been only three busks each year, one "Cow Creek" (Muskogee), and two Mikasuki. The Mikasuki medicine bundles have been grouped, with several bundle-holders ("medicine men") putting on a single busk cooperatively or with one medicine man holding more than a single bundle. But the busks have also been more or less regional (the locations persist often for many years, but they, too, may shift). For example, around 1900 there were usually four, one on the East coast (probably at Pine Island near the present Hollywood Reservation), one near the northern edge of the present Big Cypress Reservation, one in the Big Cypress Swamp southwest of there (these three Mikasuki), and the last at Cow Creek. Although visiting occurred, the relative isolation is indicated by the fact that in the mid-1880s two teen-age boys were inadvertently given identical adult names (contrary to the rule limiting the holding of a name to one living person), one at the eastern busk and the other at Big Cypress (Sturtevant, 1956b, 60).

New Ethnogenesis

The Bureau of Indian Affairs made a slow start in Florida in the 1870s and 1880s, assigning temporary agents, arranging for occasional investigative trips, and at first still attempting to arrange for removal to Indian Territory. Land acquisition for reservations began in 1891, but the plots were scattered and often changed, and the Indians seemingly ignored them. Even by 1930 only three or four of thirty-nine Seminole camps known to the Bureau, containing less than 10 percent of the population, were on the reservations (Glenn, 1931; Nash, 1931). But during the 1930s reservation lands were consolidated, forming three reservations that exist today: Brighton near the west shore of Lake Okeechobee, Dania (recently renamed Hollywood) on the lower east coast, and Big Cypress on the northeastern edge of the Big Cypress Swamp. Social services, roads, a cattle-raising program, and schools were gradually introduced. While the jobs and welfare services, combined with economic difficulties off the reservations, induced an increasing number of Indians to move to the reservations, the Seminole were very cautious about participating in the schools. In other ways also acculturation proceeded very slowly until the mid-1940s. Even by 1953 there were only three or four high school graduates.

The real cause and symptom of change was the sudden success of Christian missionizing, which had continued intermittently with no discernible effects since the 1890s. In 1943 the Reverend Stanley Smith, a dynamic Muskogee-speaking preacher (a member of the Creek town of Arbika in Oklahoma), was sent to Florida by the Muskogee, Wichita, and Seminole Baptist Association, an Oklahoma Indian religious organization. When he arrived, the total church membership among the Seminole was eleven—mostly converts made by another Oklahoma Creek missionary who arrived in the 1930s. Smith preached in Muskogee, using Seminole interpreters to translate into Mikasuki when necessary. He made his first converts in 1944. In 1947, quite suddenly, a flood of conversions began—there were 197 in that year, and many others subsequently. Very soon Florida Seminole men were being trained as Southern Baptist preachers, the small church at Dania was reactivated and enlarged, and new churches opened on the Big Cypress and Brighton Reservations.

Conversion meant severing connections with the busk organization, which made it nearly impossible to continue living among the off-reservation people who maintained the traditional political and religious procedures. There was a sudden increase in the Big Cypress and Dania populations. Among the Cow Creek the pace of conversion lagged at first and, perhaps for that reason, seems to have caused less friction; at any rate, the sharp division between off-reservation non-Christians and on-reservation Christians that characterized the Mikasuki did not obtain among the Cow Creek on and off the Brighton Reservation. By 1950 Seminole religiopolitical organization and communication networks had been transformed. The three busk groups remained, but with lessened membership. About half of the population were Christians, organized into four churches—one on each reservation affiliated with the Southern Baptist Home Missions Board and informally cooperating with each other, plus a small schismatic "Mekusukey Independent Seminole Indian Mission" on the Dania Reservation.

The Bureau of Indian Affairs was beginning to succeed in promoting a formal political and business association on each reservation, with a representative Indian "advisory" body over all three—but attempts to persuade the off-reservation "Trail" Mikasuki to participate consistently failed. The Trail people had split into two or three political factions with membership that was shifting but that somewhat corresponded to the two Mikasuki busk groups.

Then began a series of federal and state investigations, with meetings and hearings in Florida and Washington that brought attendant publicity. A case was prepared for submission to the Indian Claims Commission, with disagreements between reservation and off-reservation factions as to whether to participate in the suit at all and, if so, which lawyers to hire. In 1954 the Florida Seminole were one of the groups chosen by the Bureau of Indian Affairs for "termination" of federal activities. I suspect that they appeared on the list in an effort at bureaucratic sabotage of the congressional order—certainly no objective observer would have placed the Florida Seminole among the first small number of tribes most prepared for "termination," and in the end Congress did not do so. The political agitation and publicity aroused by this proposed termination and the congressional hearings on it (U.S. Congress, 1954) were very likely useful. At any rate, the state of Florida began taking official notice of the Seminole; and the Bureau of Indian Affairs markedly stepped up its activities, transferring the Seminole Agency from the Muskogee Area Office to a direct dependence on the Washington office, increasing expenditures in Florida, and making some changes in the Agency personnel. Attempts to introduce an all-Seminole organization were dropped, and soon thereafter the reservation communities, plus a few off-reservation individuals, voted to organize as the "Seminole Tribe of Florida" under the Indian Reorganization Act (see Seminole Tribe of Florida, 1958a, b). At first the new tribal government was more or less a puppet of the agency. But very recently an election has brought in a new set of officers, and there are indications of a new political militancy, which may well be a symptom of truly representative government among this group.

Political turmoil among the Trail factions continued throughout the 1950s. In 1959 Mad Bear (Wallace Anderson), a Tuscarora Indian nationalist, visited the Trail factions and promoted a trip with some Trail representatives to visit Fidel Castro in Havana (Wilson, 1960, 270–272). The next year the state of Florida turned over to the Seminole year-round hunting, fishing, and frogging rights to 143,620 acres of

Everglades north of the Trail, and there was considerable argument over which factions would accept this in what manner. In 1961 the Bureau of Indian Affairs established a separate Miccosukee Agency on the Trail, directly dependent administratively on the Washington office. In the same year a large proportion of the Trail Indians adopted a constitution and bylaws under the Indian Reorganization Act, constituting themselves as the Miccosukee Tribe of Indians of Florida (Miccosukee Tribe, 1965). Soon thereafter the Miccosukee Tribe acquired what amounts to a reservation in five separate parts, under the administration of the Miccosukee Agency. First, a large part of the (used but still not inhabited) State Indian Reservation just east of the Big Cypress Reservation was transferred from the Seminole Tribe to the Miccosukee Tribe. In 1962, the Miccosukee Tribe was given use rights to a narrow strip of the Everglades National Park, just south of the Tamiami Trail Highway, and the state of Florida deeded to the tribe three small tracts of land just north of the highway. These last four pieces are all located about forty miles west of Miami.

A rough estimate of the political divisions and their membership in 1967 is the following:

SEMINOLE TRIBE OF FLORIDA	
Hollywood Reservation	275
Big Cypress Reservation	335
Brighton Reservation	250
off-reservation	140
Total	1000
MICCOSUKEE TRIBE OF INDIANS OF FLORIDA	150
UNORGANIZED TRAIL MIKASUKI	200
Grand Total	1350

Religious differences have become less significant. Church participation and membership on the reservations have markedly declined; Christians (or ex-Christians) from the reservations have begun attending busks again; there are more individuals who moved from the Trail to the reservations without joining churches; and there is a Christian missionary effort from the reservations at work among the Trail people. The major division is along more strictly political lines; the three groups have different attitudes toward assimilation and different techniques for dealing with the outside world. Yet there is a fair amount of movement of individuals and families between the two formally organized groups (and it is said that the rolls of each are not kept up by the dropping of those who switch membership)—probably more such movement than in the 1950s between the reservations and the Trail.

The Trail population is nearly 100 percent Mikasuki-speaking, both those organized as the Miccosukee Tribe and those not formally organized and maintaining only the traditional busk officials and procedures. But a majority of the members of the Seminole Tribe are also speakers of Mikasuki. Furthermore, because of the recency of the split and the continuing movement between the divisions, there are close ties of consanguinity and affinity between all the Seminole groups.

But the Miccosukee Tribe is engaged in a conscious attempt—dating from the mid-1950s—to establish a separate identity complete with a distinct history. I do not know the modern Mikasuki and Muskogee ethnonymy, but there is a tendency for the more vocal Miccosukee spokesmen to deny, in English, that they are Seminole and to insist that the Miccosukee have always been a separate unit. Some have claimed that the Miccosukee are aboriginal to Florida whereas the Seminole are immigrants from the Creek of Georgia and Alabama. I think this derives from the research of a Miami lawyer, who noticed that the term "Mikasuki" does not seem to appear in the historical record before the settlement (by Creek emigrants, of course) of the town of that name in northwest Florida. I heard a rumor, also, that the Miccosukee Tribe plans to use Community Action Program funds to have written, under the direction of the Miccosukee General Council, a history that will validate this claim to distinct identity. The confusion and complexity of the terminology and of residence, language, and political affiliation may permit the success of this attempt to create a charter and an ethnonymy to further a new ethnogenesis.

At any rate, acculturation and assimilation are proceeding rapidly. Although the economic development schemes supported by the federal government are not all successful or even at the takeoff point, there is the possibility of a more or less stable symbiosis (or mutual exploitation) between Seminole society and the larger surrounding dominant population. The Indians are an important asset to a state heavily dependent on tourism (especially in the southern area where they are concentrated). Thus, publicity often proves an effective weapon for gaining recognition, support, and assistance. For many decades Seminole families have successfully exploited the tourist market, in large part on their own initiative, with the production of craft goods and the operation of souvenir stores and "exhibition villages" and by a type of theatrical performance called "alligator wrestling." New ventures, such as the offering of short, expensive "airboat rides" (on the shallow-draft craft driven by airplane propellers, which have almost entirely replaced dugout canoes) into the Everglades, are readily begun. The Bureau of Indian Affairs has recently invested heavily in a showplace souvenir store and exhibition village at the Hollywood Reservation, in an excellent restaurant and gasoline station in the Miccosukee area on the Trail, and in more mechanized and assembly-line style souvenir production at the isolated Big Cypress Reservation. These efforts are geared to the Florida economic situation. Although it is not yet clear that they will be successful, they do not represent a sentimental preservation and isolation of the Seminole as zoo or museum exhibits. The zoolike exhibition villages operated by non-Indians in Miami now have great difficulty in recruiting Seminole to live in them and have much reduced stocks of Seminole handicraft. The competition offered by Indian-owned and Indian-operated enterprises, on- and off-reservation, is too great, and the general economic situation is such that few Indians need to fall back on these "villages" when they run into economic difficulties (which was the pattern during the 1940s and 1950s).

Nearly all school-age children, on and off the reservations, attend school, and by now there are many high-school graduates and one graduate of a regular four-year college. Because of this education and the increase in wage labor there has been a striking increase in the ability to use English, and this language has become the lingua franca between the Muskogee and Mikasuki groups. Occupations have diversified. A suburban-style housing development has been constructed on the Hollywood Reservation, nearly entirely replacing the palm-thatched, open-sided chikees that were the only Seminole houses fifteen years ago; and a similar but smaller housing development has been built on the Big Cypress Reservation, while new houses of a different style have been developed in the Miccosukee strip of the Everglades National Park. Land on the Hollywood Reservation has been leased to a plastics factory that agreed to hire Indian workers. Recently the Seminole won their case before the Indian Claims Commission. The amount they will receive in compensation for unfair treatment with regard to their Florida land holdings in the early nineteenth century remains to be determined, but in a few years there will surely be a sudden influx of a large amount of dollars from this source—creating the usual problem of deciding how it will be allocated. The disproportionate amount of funds and effort expended by the Bureau of Indian Affairs in Florida over the past few years seems to have come at the right moment in Seminole history.

The Florida Indians are not yet participants in Pan-Indian political and cultural developments, partly because of their geographical separation from all other Indians. However, there are indications that education, acculturation, and political changes have moved them sufficiently away from their traditional ethnocentric isolation so that the geographical distance will be overcome and their leaders, at least, will soon enter the mainstream of modern Indian politics.

NOTES

[1] This chapter is based on (1) approximately eighteen months' field work among the Mikasuki Seminole in Florida in 1950–1953 and 1959, plus four days in June 1967, (2) intermittent research since 1950 on (in order of decreasing thoroughness) museum, library, and archival materials on the Florida Seminole of all periods, and (3) the major published anthropological and historical literature on the Creek (I have done no field work and very little archival work relating to the Creek).

The orthography used here for Indian words is phonemic. That for Mikasuki (and Hitchiti) is West's (1962), except that the mid tone is indicated by the absence of a diacritic over the vowel symbol rather than by West's macron. I am also directly indebted to West for correcting my spelling of the terms *i·làponki*⸲ and *ci·sàponki*⸲ and for providing a morphological analysis of them. For Muskogee I use Haas' (e.g., 1941) orthography, in the earlier form with /o/ rather than her later /u/.

Because this chapter was completed in England in the fall of 1967, I was unable to use three recent sources that I now know to be relevant: Garbarino, 1966; Mahon, 1967; Pollitzer *et al.*, 1970.

[2] The "sawgrass" that is the dominant plant of the Everglades is technically a large sedge rather than a true grass; the dominant tree of the Big Cypress Swamp is classified by botanists as a taxodium rather than a cypress.

[3] For data on Creek culture I rely largely on Swanton's compendia of historical and ethnographic material (1922; 1928a; 1928b; 1929; 1946), plus an important paper by Haas (1940a) and one by Opler (1952). Stern (1965) has recently provided a good brief summary of seventeenth- and early eighteenth-century Creek culture, better rounded than is attempted here. For the history of Creek expansion and of the Seminole up to 1823, I rely heavily on an excellent semi-published monograph by Charles H. Fairbanks (1957). I have elsewhere used this and other sources for a survey of pre-Seminole Florida Indian history (Sturtevant, 1962). Some of the material on the early Seminole comes from a manuscript by Howard F. Cline (1964), which in turn makes much use of Fairbanks' report.

[4] The towns mentioned classify into language groups as follows (Swanton, 1922; Fairbanks, 1957):

Muskogee: Coweta; Eufaula; three others.
Hitchiti: Hitchiti; Chiaha; Oconee; Mikasuki (perhaps settled from Chiaha); probably Tamathli, Sawokli, and Apalachicola; perhaps Yamasee.
Mixed Muskogee and Hitchiti: Tallahassee (?).
Yuchi: Yuchi; probably Chiska Taloofa.
Alabama: two towns.

[5] This series of ethnonyms was collected by Porter (1949, 365, n. 8) from ten listings of three or more Seminole components in the standard published account of the war, which is largely a collection of contemporary documents. Seminole and Mikasuki appear in all ten lists; Creek occurs nine times; Tallahassee six; Yuchi five; and Choctaw, Hitchiti, and Spanish Indians once each. An as yet unpublished, detailed "Roll of the Seminole Nation in Florida in October 1850—verified by Wm Bowlegs" (Casey, 1850–1856) still specifies the traditional affiliations of most men. The heading versus the listing illustrates the continuing two-level use of the ethnonym "Seminole," for sixty-two men are specified as "Seminole" in contrast to thirty-two Mikasuki, ten Tallahassee, eight unknown, six Creek, and one Yuchi (the last annotated, "Emigrated 1852").

[6] The population estimates here and above require some substantiation, dubious as they certainly are. The bases for my calculations are the following figures:

1823	Total Seminole population (cited above after Fairbanks, 1957)	4,883
1835–1842	Deported to the West during the Second Seminole War (Coe, 1898, 161)	4,420
1850	Census listed 119 men by name, age, sib, band, and often relationship (Casey, 1850–1856); total estimated by applying the ratio of 39 to 126 in the 1858 entry below	502
1852–1854	Sent West by the "removal expert" (Porter, 1967, 236)	36
1855–1858	Killed during the Third Seminole War (rough estimate deduced from Coe, 1898, 210–221, and Covington, 1966)	20
1858	Sent West as a result of the war (Porter, 1967, 239) —39 warriors and 126 women and children	165
1859	Sent West as a result of the war (Porter, 1967, 241)	75

Even if these figures are accepted as accurate, we lack totals of those killed during the 1835–1842 war and data on the natural increase in population between 1823 and 1860. I have assumed that under the difficult circumstances of the period, deaths other than in warfare must have at least balanced out births. My guess of less than 200 surviving in Florida in 1860 assumes Casey's 1850 total of 119 men to be accurate, which seems reasonable since it derives from an enumeration rather than an estimate and because he clearly had an intimate acquaintance with the Seminole and at least a rudimentary knowledge of the Muskogee language. But it also assumes the representativeness of the 1858 ratio of 39 warriors to 126 women and children, which is less safe, especially since it is reasonable to assume that a higher proportion of men than women and children were killed during the Third Seminole War. But increasing the estimated proportion of women and children would raise the total, whereas after twenty years of peace the Florida Seminole population was estimated at only 292 in 1879 and 208 in 1880 (Sturtevant, 1956a, 13, 20). The first of these figures is clearly unreliable, because it is a totaling of guesses by local non-Indian "experts"; but the second is based on a careful census enumeration. I presume that (1) the 1880 total is too low, the census probably having missed younger children and others concealed by Seminole secretiveness; but even so, (2) the 1860 estimate of 200 may well be too high.

REFERENCES

BOYD, MARK F., HALE G. SMITH, AND JOHN W. GRIFFIN
1951 Here they once stood: the tragic end of the Apalachee missions. Gainesville: University of Florida Press.

CASEY, JOHN C.
1850–1856 [Notebook of 110 pp., 49 left blank.] Manuscript, Folder 155, Casey Papers. Tulsa: Gilcrease Institute.

CLINE, HOWARD F.
1964 Colonial Indians in Florida, 1700–1823. Manuscript in its author's possession.

COE, CHARLES H.
1898 Red patriots: the story of the Seminoles. Cincinnati: The Editor Publishing Company.

CORY, CHARLES B.
1896 Hunting and fishing in Florida . . . 2nd ed. Boston: Estes & Lauriat.

COVINGTON, JAMES W.
1966 An episode in the Third Seminole War. Florida Historical Quarterly 45 (1):45–59.

CRANE, VERNER W.
1918 The origin of the name of the Creek Indians. Mississippi Valley Historical Review 5 (3):339–342.

DOHNANYI, ERNST VON
1962 Combating Soviet guerrillas. *In* The guerrilla—and how to fight him; selections from the Marine Corps Gazette. T. N. Greene, ed. New York and London: Frederick A. Praeger. pp. 201–217.

FAIRBANKS, CHARLES H.
[1957] Ethnohistorical report of the Florida Indians. Defendant's Exhibit No. 141, Before the Indian Claims Commission, Docket Nos. 73 and 151 (mimeographed).
1962 Excavations at Horseshoe Bend, Alabama. Florida Anthropologist 15 (2):41–56.

FRIED, MORTON H.
1966 On the concepts of "tribe" and "tribal society." Transactions of the New York Academy of Sciences, Ser. II, 28 (4):527–540.

GARBARINO, MERWYN S.

1966 Economic development and decision making process on Big Cypress Indian Reservation, Florida. Manuscript Ph.D. dissertation in anthropology. Northwestern University.

GLENN, J. L.

1931 Annual report, fiscal year 1931, Seminoles in Florida; narrative section. Seventeen-page typed manuscript; carbon copy in the files of the Seminole Agency, Dania, in 1951.

GOGGIN, JOHN M.

1946 The Seminole Negroes of Andros Island, Bahamas. Florida Historical Quarterly 24 (3):201–206.

HAAS, MARY R.

1940a Creek inter-town relations. American Anthropologist 42 (3):479–489.

[c. 1940b] Creek vocabulary. Manuscript in author's possession.

1941 The classification of the Muskogean languages. In Language, culture, and personality: essays in memory of Edward Sapir. Leslie Spier et al., eds. Menasha, Wisconsin: Sapir Memorial Publication Fund. pp. 41–56.

HARGRETT, LESTER

1947 A bibliography of the constitutions and laws of the American Indians. Cambridge: Harvard University Press.

HAWKINS, BENJAMIN

1848 A sketch of the Creek country, in the years 1798 and 1799. Collections of the Georgia Historical Society 3 (1):19–85.

MACCAULEY, CLAY

1881 [Muskogee vocabulary collected from a Florida Mikasuki Seminole informant.] Manuscript 589, B.A.E. Collection. Washington, D.C.: Smithsonian National Anthropological Archives.

1887 The Seminole Indians of Florida. In Bureau of American Ethnology 5th Annual Report. pp. 469–531.

MAHON, JOHN K.

1967 History of the Second Seminole War: 1835–1842. Gainesville: University of Florida Press.

MICCOSUKEE TRIBE OF INDIANS OF FLORIDA

1965 Constitution [and bylaws] of the Miccosukee Tribe of Indians of Florida [ratified December 17, 1961, with amendments adopted 1964 and 1965]. [Washington, D.C.: Bureau of Indian Affairs, U.S. Department of the Interior.]

NASH, ROY

1931 Survey of the Seminole Indians of Florida. 71st Congress, 3d. Session, Senate Document 314 [serial 9347].

NUNEZ, THERON A., JR.

1958 Creek nativism and the Creek War of 1813–1814. Ethnohistory 5 (1):1–17.

OPLER, MORRIS EDWARD

1952 The Creek "town" and the problem of Creek Indian political reorganization. *In* Human problems in technological change: a casebook. Edward H. Spicer, ed. New York: Russell Sage Foundation [reprinted 1965. Science Editions. New York: Wiley]. pp. 165–180.

POLLITZER, WILLIAM S., *et al.*

1970 The Seminole Indians of Florida: morphology and serology. American Journal of Physical Anthropology 32 (1):65–81.

PORTER, KENNETH W.

1932 Relations between Negroes and Indians within the present limits of the United States. Journal of Negro History 17 (3):287–367.

1943 Florida slaves and free Negroes in the Seminole War, 1835–1842. Journal of Negro History 28 (4):390–421.

1945 Notes on Seminole Negroes in the Bahamas. Florida Historical Quarterly 24 (1):56–60.

1949 The founder of the "Seminole Nation": Secoffee or Cowkeeper. Florida Historical Quarterly 27 (4):362–384.

1967 Billy Bowlegs (Holata Micco) in the Seminole Wars. Florida Historical Quarterly 45 (3):219–242.

SEMINOLE TRIBE OF FLORIDA

1958a Constitution and bylaws of the Seminole Tribe of Florida, ratified August 21, 1957. Washington, D.C.: Bureau of Indian Affairs, U.S. Department of the Interior.

1958b Corporate charter of the Seminole Tribe of Florida, ratified August 21, 1957. Washington, D.C.: Bureau of Indian Affairs, U.S. Department of the Interior.

SPENCER, LUCIEN A.

1921 Special report of the Florida Seminole Agency. 67th Congress, 2d. Session, Senate Document 102.

SPOEHR, ALEXANDER

1941 Camp, clan, and kin among the Cow Creek Seminole of Florida. Field Museum of Natural History, Anthropological Series 33 (1):1–27.

1944 The Florida Seminole camp. Field Museum of Natural History, Anthropological Series 33 (3):115–150.

STERN, THEODORE C.

1965 The Southeast. *In* The native Americans: prehistory and ethnology of the North American Indians. Robert F. Spencer, Jesse D. Jennings, *et al.* New York: Harper & Row. chap. 10, pp. 402–434.

STIRLING, GENE

1936 Report on the Seminole Indians of Florida. Washington, D.C.: Applied Anthropology Unit, Office of Indian Affairs [document 126567] (mimeographed).

STURTEVANT, WILLIAM C.

1954 The medicine bundles and busks of the Florida Seminole. Florida Anthropologist 7 (2):31–70.

1956a R. H. Pratt's report on the Seminole in 1879. Florida Anthropologist 9 (1):1–24.

1956b A Seminole personal document. Tequesta 16:54–75.

1962 Spanish-Indian relations in southeastern North America. Ethnohistory 9 (1):41–94.

SWANTON, JOHN R.

1922 Early history of the Creek Indians and their neighbors. Bureau of American Ethnology Bulletin 73.

1928a Social organization and social usages of the Indians of the Creek Confederacy. *In* Bureau of American Ethnology 42nd Annual Report. pp. 23–472.

1928b Religious beliefs and medical practices of the Creek Indians. *In* Bureau of American Ethnology 42nd Annual Report. pp. 473–672.

1929 Myths and tales of the Southeastern Indians. Bureau of American Ethnology Bulletin 88.

1946 The Indians of the southeastern United States. Bureau of American Ethnology Bulletin 137.

TEBEAU, CHARLTON W.

1957 Florida's last frontier: the history of Collier county. [Coral Gables]: University of Miami Press.

UNITED STATES CONGRESS

1954 Termination of federal supervision over certain tribes of Indians: joint hearing before the Subcommittees on Interior and Insular Affairs, Congress of the United States, 83rd Congress, Second Session, on S. 2747 and H.R. 7321. . . . Part 8. Seminole Indians, Florida. March 1 and 2, 1954. Washington, D.C.: U.S. Government Printing Office.

WARING, ANTONIO J., ED.

1960 Laws of the Creek nation. Libraries Miscellanea Publications (1). Athens: University of Georgia.

WEST, JOHN DAVID

1962 The phonology of Mikasuki. Studies in Linguistics 16 (3–4):77–91.

WILSON, EDMUND

1960 Apologies to the Iroquois. New York: Farrar, Straus and Cudahy.

5   *The Iroquois in History*[1]

WILLIAM N. FENTON

The Era of the Formation of the League: Precontact Period

The aboriginal inhabitants of the lands bordering the lower Great Lakes—Lakes Huron, Erie, and Ontario—and the St. Lawrence River, in what are now parts of Ontario and Quebec in Canada, upstate New York, and adjacent Pennsylvania, spoke languages of the Iroquoian family, of whom the most important ethnic entities were the Huron of Ontario and the Iroquois of New York. The peoples of Huronia, as the Jesuit scholars named them, referred to their country as *Wendat E'hen,* "This Old Island," because they conceived of the world as resting on the back of a turtle swimming in the primal sea; and what the French termed Iroquoia, the Iroquois themselves called *Wi:s Nihwendjiadage:,* "Five Native Lands," or "Five Nations" of the English. The Huron dominate the literature of discovery; but after their dispersion and incorporation by the Iroquois in the mid-seventeenth century, the colonial records are filled with the doings of the Five Nations (Figures 5.1 and 5.2). They became Six Nations when the Tuscarora from North Carolina joined them early in the eighteenth century (Figure 5.3). For purposes of this paper Huronia and Iroquoia are considered as one cultural province (Figure 5.1).

The Iroquois annalists periodize their cultural history by the achievements of prophets. Native theory speaks of a time of Sapling, who brought cultural benefits to the people after the formation of the earth; the period of Sapling precedes that of Deganawidah, who founded the League of the Longhouse, initiating the period of confederacy; and it speaks of the present period since Handsome Lake, the Seneca prophet. Each period comprises the subject and content of a myth about the doings of the prophet, which are recited by their learned men at informal gatherings or formal rituals. Great heed is paid to verbatim recall; virtuoso performers are honored; and learned arguments vie over variant versions. The myths and accompanying rituals are thought to be so powerful that recitals occur only after the first frost when the Earth sleeps.

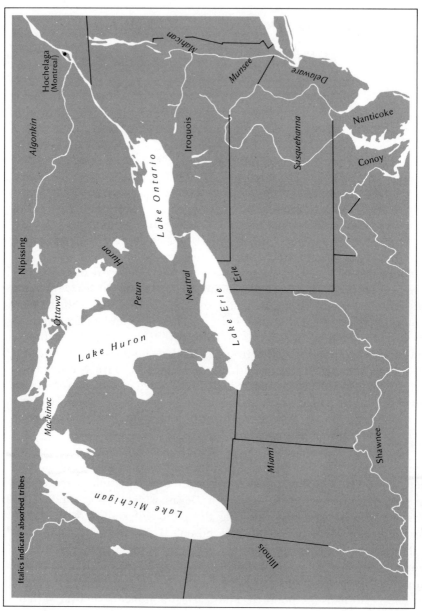

Figure 5.1. "Knocked in the head"—nations destroyed or displaced by the Iroquois in the Beaver Wars. (Map prepared by Gwyneth Y. Gillette.)

The cosmological myth of the Earth-grasper, or the World on the
Turtle's Back, tells how the earth, various plants and animals, and the
several celestial bodies and forces were created and put into operation;
it tells how the first human beings on the earth learned to adjust to this
situation and how they coped with emergencies as they arose. Projected
into this formative period are the paradigm for returning thanks to the
spirit-forces from earth to sky (Chafe, 1961) and the creation of clans
and moieties. These latter embellishments are ascribed to a fatherless
boy from the fringe of the bush who arises to define the situation, pro-
pose a solution, and lead the community out of its dilemma. The Iroquois say that whenever man is up against it a prophet will emerge and
society is attuned by tradition to listen. The prophet who would succeed
among the Iroquois must speak in ancient tongues, he must use the
old words, and he must relate his program to the old ways. He is a
conservator at the same time that he is a reformer. All of the Iroquois
reformers have been traditionalists. This is one of the reasons that
Iroquois culture has endured so long (Fenton, 1962, 283–286 *passim*).

The second of the great public utterances by which the old men of
Iroquoia marked their cultural history is the so-called Deganawidah
legend, a tradition of the founding of the League of Five Iroquois tribes
who are the People of the Longhouse. The tradition tells how the
"People of the Flint" (now called Mohawk), the "People of the Stone"
(Oneida), the "People on the Mountain" (Onondaga), the "People at
the Landing" (Cayuga), and the "Great Hill People" (now called
Seneca) were persuaded to stop feuding, grasped Deganawidah's message,
and joined in the Great Peace; it constitutes a myth of epic proportions.
Although never published in its entirety, the myth of confederation
has been known for a century (Morgan, 1851; Hale, 1883; Hewitt, 1892).
It was first noted in 1743, a century after contact, but it is doubtful
how much of it was known for another hundred years, even though
it underlies an understanding of Iroquois political institutions. It mo-
tivates and rationalizes their political behavior, and the Iroquois in
history acted as if it were true, often when they could not make public
policy follow its ideal principles. A knowledge of the teaching imputed
to Deganawidah goes far to explain Iroquois self-confidence, their
superiority to their neighbors, and at times their polite arrogance to
representatives of European governments. Louis XIV was to read, "The
Iroquois are the only people on earth who do not know the grandeur of
your Majesty" (Parkman, 1899, 87).

How it happened that something so basic to political philosophy
escaped the notice of early writers on Iroquois manners and usages is
a problem in intellectual history that cannot be considered here. Suffice
it to say that what we know of its symbolism from seventeenth-century

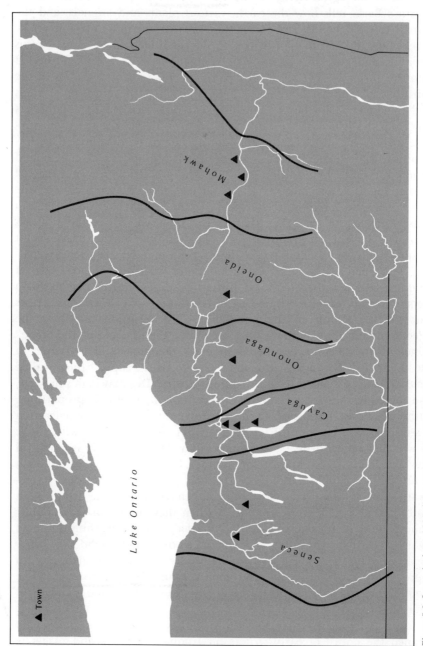

Figure 5.2. Iroquoia about 1600. (Map prepared by Gwyneth Y. Gillette.)

writers and of its plot from eighteenth-century sources enables us to speak of its existence for two centuries before it was recorded. Its chroniclers were native scribes who by the nineteenth century had an interest in communicating the origins of their government to the powers that might abolish it. Victorians were intellectually unprepared to handle a body of customs or to interpret myths. They were accustomed to reading Scripture and took history literally. In their view, either Deganawidah and Hiawatha were historical personages or they were fictitious. Exceptionally gifted for his day, the pioneer ethnologist Horatio Hale (1817–1896) analyzed the literary content of the myth and approached the problems of internal dating, glottochronology, and the origin of the confederacy in a remarkably sophisticated way (Fenton, Introduction to Hale, 1963). Hale and Morgan put the date of confederation at the middle of the fifteenth century; Beauchamp and Hewitt later favored the close of the next century. The historical and economic conditions at the opening of the contact period support the latter view, although modern archeology moves increasingly toward a permissible earlier date.

Precise dates for complicated social institutions are at best spurious. The myth relates a long struggle involving internal strife and external threats. The League was a confederacy of independent but related tribes; and confederacies, as political institutions, usually owe their rise to the need to compose internal hostilities in order to meet the threat of common enemies. Most confederacies begin this way but gradually develop organization tending toward strong central government according to necessity (Linton, 1936, 341). Such makeshift states leave local government largely intact; they co-opt unequal representation of preexisting sovereignties; unanimity is therefore the rule; and they never quite achieve central stability nor communication to the margins. Such governments are peculiarly at home in aboriginal America; their success requires extremely democratic societies, and the Iroquois made of its forms a ritual and enduring myth. Their widespread distribution supports an earlier date. Indeed, the Iroquois confederacy was a long in the making (Linton, 1955, 125, 601–607; Hoebel, 1949, 380).

No amount of argumentation will resolve such historical enigmas; they can only be examined in the light of new theory that has been tested with verifiable historical data. We have such information for the third period of Iroquois cultural history, from the vision of the Seneca prophet Handsome Lake to the present. It is now 172 years since Handsome Lake began to utter "the Good Message," or *Gaíhwi:yo:h* at Cornplanter. He foretold the path that the Senecas should follow to escape the evils of white civilization and reach the heavenly road. The

Code of the prophet's utterances, as they are now recalled and preached on public occasions, says that his vision occurred during the Berry Moon (June) of the year 1799, a fact which is substantiated by the journals of Quaker missionaries who were present (Deardorff, 1951; Wallace, 1970). If an oral tradition can persist for nearly two centuries, maintaining its essential historical accuracy by public recitation and constant criticism from appointed Keepers of the Faith, it stands to reason that other similarly kept and validated traditions in the same culture merit consideration as oral history.

The archeological record showing gradual cultural development during 5,000 years in New York is most convincing. Iroquois comes late in the cultural sequence and chronology of eastern North America, during the Late Woodland period after A.D. 1300, preceded by the great flowering of Hopewell cultures and societies in Ohio, which barely reached them (Ritchie, 1965, 1969; White, 1961; Wright, 1966; and Griffin, 1967, 189). The triad of maize-beans-squash horticulture, which is so typical of Iroquois culture and is so thoroughly integrated with their religious thinking, is considerably older than the material culture that can be ascribed to them with certainty, and it goes back through the Owasco to Middle Woodlands times, to well before A.D. 1000. Its introduction, therefore, cannot be ascribed to the Iroquois, and their own origin now seems to lie in the area of their historic seats where their culture evolved.

Although one cannot link Iroquois to Hopewell, Iroquois culture perpetuates at least two symbolic elements of a ritual complex for which Hopewell affords striking artifacts. Antlers are a metaphor for chiefly office throughout the literature of the Condolence Council, although antlers have not been worn in historic times as emblems of office by Iroquois chiefs; yet the copper headdresses in the form of antlers found in Hopewell graves are striking fulfillments of this symbolism. Processions of chiefs going between villages to lament the dead and install their successors are a feature of the condolence ritual and treaty making; the formal walkways from river landings to ceremonial centers containing burial mounds perhaps had a similar purpose. Moreover, the weeping-eye motif of the southeastern ceremonial climax bears a logical if not historical relationship to the wiping away of tears in the same ceremony. Similarly, the Iroquois Eagle Dance as a surviving example of the widespread Calumet Dance of historic times affords a realistic basis for interpreting the eagle dancers engraved on large *Buscyon* shells during the Mississippian period (Griffin, 1967, fig. 7r, s; Fenton, 1953).

The Deganawidah epic speaks of clearings scattered here and there in the forest. Until the Late Woodland stage of the culture sequence none of these was of a size comparable to the settlements of the historic period. Settlements of 250 people were not possible before Owasco times (*c.* A.D. 1000), and their size increased rapidly with the development of horticulture, which freed men from hunting pursuits throughout the year (Ritchie, 1965, 280 ff., 309). The late Prehistoric Iroquois phase (1450–1600) saw the flowering of Iroquois culture as we know it archeologically with corresponding increase in number and size of communities (Ritchie, 1965, 316). By this time the Iroquois were confederated and living in longhouses, of which some were of prodigious size, notably at Onondaga. Towns were palisaded. The Five Nations were a league of a dozen villages, averaging perhaps 500 persons, some having less, and few counting 1,000 souls. They could muster 2,000 warriors, half of whom were Seneca, and estimates of the total population vary from 4,500 to 15,000 (Snyderman, 1948, 41). Today they number 10,000 in New York alone, with a corresponding number in Canada, being twice their original size, and yet they are a small minority in a population of 20 million.

The size of Iroquois society depended on an economy that was attuned to ecology in the northeastern forest. Avoiding the coniferous forest of the Adirondacks, the Iroquois settled on hilltops adjacent to glaciated valleys in central New York. In the prevailing deciduous forest, interspersed with stands of white pine and hemlock, maple, beech, hickory, and elm were the predominant hardwoods of interest to the Iroquois. Living south of the distribution of the white birch, a line that corresponds roughly with the northern extension of maize horticulture, the Iroquois relied on elm bark for housing, vessels, and transportation, whereas the Algonkians to the north used birch bark. The rough and ready elm bark technology of the Iroquois was no match for the beautiful and efficient birch bark vessels of the Algonkian.

Ecological time was comprised of a yearly round of activities that synchronized a hunting and gathering cycle with a maize cycle. These activities were keyed to a lunar calendar divided into four seasons and marked by a calendric cycle of ceremonies, with the great ceremonial mark at midwinter and a lesser climax at late summer for the ingathering of crops. It is apparent that the Iroquois had been primarily hunters and gatherers, like the cultural predecessors in the Northeast, but they had been more or less freed of dependency on meat, greens, berries, roots, and nuts by the surplus of maize, beans, and squash grown by the women with increasing productivity into the historic period. When the Seven Dancing Boys (the Pleiades) reached the zenith at dusk, families returned from the winter hunt to subsist on these stores and to celebrate the renewal of all ceremonial obligations revealed through dreams. For a time they were hungry as the days grew longer; two moons later they repaired to maple groves to gather and boil sap and to return thanks to the forest. Next came flights of millions of passenger pigeons to roost in beechwoods, where they were netted on the hillsides, and the squabs were poked out of the nest with long poles, to be tried into oil and packed in bark tuns. These forays were interspersed with removals to fishing stations, where weirs of converging stones directed the fish under the spears of waiting men or into splint basket traps. Prodigious runs of fish ascended the Mohawk, the outlets of Oneida, and the Finger Lakes, and the quantity of bone harpoon and spear points found on sites there attest to the importance of fisheries to the subsistence economy. Meanwhile, women gathered spring greens, such as skunk cabbage, poke, milkweed, leek, and so forth (Waugh, 1916, 117–118).

When the white oak leaves are the size of a red squirrel's foot, the old people said, it is time to plant, and they blessed the seed of the Three Sisters (corn, beans, squash) before returning them to the earth. Men assisted in clearing the fields, but the stirring of the corn hills with wooden spades and planting was done under a matron's supervision by a work party of women. The Berry Moon is yet remembered fondly for the strawberry, the first fruit to ripen on the earth; and the Strawberry Festival calls for the preaching of Handsome Lake's message in commemoration of his vision. The Medicine Society still meets on the fifth night of the new moon to sing over the bundles and renew its strength. This is also the season when the bark peels readily and men formerly were busy building houses, repairing stockades, and working elm bark into bark utensils and canoes. It is the season of the long days.

The Thunder rite addresses the most important hazard of the growing season. The invocation asks the sun, the elder brother and patron of war, not to scorch the earth; men dance the war dance in his honor, play the hoop and pole game—the rolling sun being snared by the spear; and the prayer pleads for the thunders, "our grandfathers of the rumbling voices who come from toward the sunset" to water the Three Sisters. There was a second and third hoeing of the corn, again by a work party of primarily women and a few old men.

When the corn is adjudged ready, even today the officials gather the community to celebrate the ingathering of the crops in honor of the Three Sisters coming to maturity. At the next moon they dance in honor of the bread, returning thanks that the cycle is complete, that the maize is husked, strung, shelled, and put away in the barns. The women's song says, "The Three Sisters are happy because they are home again from their summer in the fields." Formerly husking bees were the main autumn activity (Fenton, 1963b).

The leaves now turn red and fall, marking the season when, as the old saying runs, the hunter with his dogs (Ursa Minor) rounds Polaris, overtakes the bear (Ursa Major), and slays him. It is then that families separated from the communal longhouses and went hunting in the deep woods for venison. Deer was thus the paramount item of subsistence and also the symbol of men's labor and of the authority of chiefs. Hard cold is followed by the short days. Men were still hunting and dressing meat in shanty camps, jerking it over the fire, to be packed home, when the deer yarded up and hunting became difficult, save on snowshoes. So the cycle ends.

Autumn was the great season for councils. It was also a time when men were free to go on the warpath.

The Iroquois moved easily in his environment and did little to alter it. He would clear and burn and then plant his crops between the stumps. When the soil was exhausted and fire wood became scarce, which occurred twice in a generation, he would move on (Ritchie, 1955–1956). The places where he stopped to smoke were soon overgrown with brush, and the grass overgrew the graves of his ancestors.

Of the preceding reconstructed annual cycle only the agricultural festivals are still observed, even though the Iroquois have largely abandoned farming. And these owe their perpetuation, along with supporting music and the dance, to the Handsome Lake Religion.

Iroquois technology is not remarkable in itself, but it does demonstrate great facility in utilizing whatever comes to hand. Botanical knowledge is still extensive. Besides eating everything that is edible, they know and employ some 200 or more medicinal plants (Fenton, 1942), and their understanding of the properties of woods and fibers is astonishing. Besides the inner bast of hickory, basswood, and slippery elm, which can be used as peeled in June, they leached the fibers of nettle, milkweed, and Indian hemp to braid into rope, burden straps, and prisoner ties. Specimens in museum collections are frequently embroidered with dyed moose or deer hair and porcupine quill. Besides the understanding of how to bend wood to make house frames, pack frames, snowshoes, toboggans, and so forth, the principle of the spring is recognized in the bow and the twitchup snare; the principle of gravity in the deadfall and the corn pounder; centrifugal force in the war club and pump drill; and the lever in a number of devices. Motor habits persist. Javelin, fish spear, and snowsnake are alike propelled with the right index finger from the proximal end, which is the motor principle of the spear thrower. The principle of torque facilitated the penetrating power of the arrow. The blow gun and dart for small game and birds utilizes the principle of the piston (Morgan, 1851).

A wide variety of splint baskets are still made by women, although the origin of the technique appears to be post-Columbian. They formerly did finer weaving of belts, garters, and sashes in several media. More impressive than a list of utensils used in food preparation—kettle, washing baskets, sieves, bread bowls, nested eating dishes of bark, spoons with crests, and paddles for stirring—items that can be seen in museum collections, is the art of cookery that persists in the making of hulled corn soup by Iroquois women today under modern conditions in New York and Canada (see Fenton, 1953, plates; Waugh, 1916; and Parker, 1910). The kettle is still a symbol of hospitality. They still parch corn to make mush for the Society of False Faces—a medicine society whose members wear wooden masks and impersonate the supernatural shamans whom the masks represent—and two generations ago hunters still carried it. This was the food of hunters, warriors, and ambassadors. It is light and nourishing and can be eaten cooked or raw, and it can be mixed with meat to make a savory stew.

The Iroquois were essentially landsmen, and they produced some great runners. In contrast, the Huron were traders and canoemen. A good case exists for the Huron's having acquired the birch bark canoe and the technique of paddling, running rapids, and portage from northern Algonkian neighbors in exchange for surplus maize. By contrast, the Iroquois elm bark canoe was a clumsy craft not amenable to long voyages, to crossing lakes, or running white water (Fenton and Dodge, 1949). The disadvantages of ecology, which equipped the Iroquois poorly for travel and trade by comparison with the Huron and Algonkian, when contact began, were far outweighed by geography.

Whether the League was a response to a perceived threat, as the economic historians would have us believe, or whether its previous existence enabled the Five Nations to take advantage of the situation when it arose, it soon made them a formidable power that had to be reckoned with by Indian neighbors and colonial powers alike. Indian warfare was not new in the woodlands, nor was the structure of Iroquois polity; but no other groups combined structural principles with policy as effectively. Deganawidah's League for Peace enlisted existing village chiefs to accept the principles of peace, justice, and civil authority, which combined to make up the Great Law, or Commonwealth. Civil or peace chiefs, the so-called *rotiyanehr,* sat in village councils of the old men; they were elected by the women of their sibs; and succession of titles passed in the matrilineage. Incumbents were men of middle age who had first made a name on the warpath. On assuming office, they forsook the warpath for the council fire, an act that, to a degree, confirmed graduation to the next age grade. They served for life on good behavior, subject to the trusteeship of the eldest matron in the sib, and on death their tribe and sib were condoled and a successor was installed in the title. Besides, men of unusual merit were elevated to the rank of Pine Tree chief, a rank that died with the incumbent, when the tree fell. Pine Tree chiefs were orators for the council or they spoke for the women, and they went on embassies. By contrast, war chief was a role and an achieved status, and although there tended to be a ranking war chief in each sib, their number was unlimited.

Woodland peoples generally recognized the distinction between civil and war chiefs. But the Iroquois League structured this relationship so as to accord prestige to the former and reduce conflict between the offices and the generations. The civil chiefs were the fire keepers, with a concentric ring of warriors, women, and the general public around them. Unequal representation among the tribes was not a problem, although there were nine Mohawk, nine Oneida, fourteen Onondaga, ten Cayuga, and eight Seneca titles in the League council, because each tribe or nation voted as one. Moiety and tripartite arrangements for counseling extended from sib, to tribe, to league councils, and there were devices for gaining unanimity at each level and for reporting up and down the chain. Village, tribal, and national autonomy were not abridged. What made the League effective was not its ability to centralize power and communicate authority to the margins, in which it failed miserably, but the consensus not to feud among the Five Nations and to compound such infractions by ritual payments of wampum. Iroquoia was a kinship state. The image of the Longhouse, as they saw themselves, as one united house, with its central fire at Onondaga and its doors fronting on the Hudson and Niagara, was clearly intelligible to every Iroquois person, and it made their 2,200 warriors appear even more formidable when they went out to enforce the Pax Iroquoia.

More frequently discussed by historians than the kinship state, which Hunt decried as an argument for their superior organization (Hunt, 1940), is their geographical position astride the height of land dominating four river systems. Their interior position placed them once removed from contact with European traders. At first disadvantaged by being deprived of direct access to trade goods and then beset by enemies armed with iron tools, they were in the long run better able to withstand the shock of culture contact than were the Algonkian coastal peoples, who were disorganized and decimated.

The Impact of Colonial Civilization: The Seventeenth Century

Whoever came to Iroquoia came on their terms. Iroquoia felt the impact of colonial civilization early in the seventeenth century, when the French established Montreal and the Dutch built Fort Orange. In the competition for furs between the two centers, first among the River Indians, then among the Iroquois, the Huron, and the Far Indians, the free Dutch trader enjoyed the advantages of cheaper goods over the royal monopoly.

"Trade and Peace we take to be one thing." This affirmation of Iroquois policy in 1735, by the spokesman of the Six Nations to the Governor of New York, epitomizes a relationship of Indian dependency on the trade that was already long established. Its beginning on the St. Lawrence had been friendly, but the Iroquoian-speaking people whom Jacques Cartier met at Stadacona (Quebec) and Hochelaga (Montreal) were neither the Five Nations nor the Huron. In the next century Algonkian-speaking peoples were in possession of the valley, leaving the Iroquois at one remove from goods, and both towns had disappeared by the time of Champlain's second voyage (1603). Thereafter the French image of the Iroquois is of fiends, not friends. However ill-advised it may be to revive the controversy over the consequences of Champlain's skirmish at Ticonderoga with a Mohawk war party and his siege of an unidentified Iroquois town in central Iroquoia some years later, the essential point is that he employed surprise and superior weaponry. In the second instance, these advantages failed to overcome a vigorous defense; and military logic bowed to Indian impatience with a siege when his allied Indian reinforcements failed to show. Champlain went home on a pack frame with an arrow in his knee. His colony identified with the Algonkian and Huron as allies. Iroquois resentment was bitter, and they never forgot it. Whether these actions represent a turning point in history, as the older historians maintained and moderns deny, they did affect French relations with the Iroquois and color the images that each side held of the other.

Historical causation is always complicated, and in the absence of written records it is difficult to establish. Within a decade of withstanding Champlain, the Iroquois made their first peace with the French, presumably to trade, in 1624, the year Fort Orange was reestablished. It took nearly twenty years to formalize relations between the Iroquois and the Dutch, who were afterward their traditional friends. French and Dutch motivations in these relations are easy to understand. They were primarily economic, as Hunt (1940) maintains. The Dutch wanted the furs, and they would subsidize the Mohawk to get them, even if this meant hijacking the western fur fleets on the Ottawa River. Maintaining alliances with the sources of the furs was in the French interest to insure that the furs came to the St. Lawrence. Such a policy would include the Iroquois in the network of alliances, for their trade was valuable to the French; even though they had no beaver to sell after 1640, without raiding the western fur fleets or extending their hunting territories at the expense of the western tribes. And only when Iroquois war parties proved incorrigible did the French sanction punitive measures. The Dutch, after a few misadventures, wanted no trouble with the Indians or between the Indians nearest Fort Orange and the

Tee Yee Neen Ho Ga Row ("Doorkeeper") *known as Hendrick to the English, was billed in London as "Emperour of the Six Nations." In this engraving by John Simon after the painting by John Verelst, he is petitioning Queen Anne to send Anglican missionaries to his people, as the crosses in the wampum belt imply. His ax lies at his feet in peace, and behind him is the wolf, his clan totem. (Courtesy of the New-York Historical Society.)*

Mohawk to the west, because it interfered with the trade, and although they were in no position to push the Indians around, geography and prices were on their side. They had to compromise (Trelease, 1960).

The image of the Iroquois as "economic man" or even as "middleman" has never appealed to me as being at all consistent with his character or his culture. To be certain, his culture was changing rapidly. He could trade beaver and maize for items of white man's material culture that made his own tools, weapons, and clothing obsolete. Indeed, he must have these improved items to increase his productivity and to enable him to bring in more furs and corn in the trade on which he was now dependent. To supplement the bow, the war club, the flint knife, the warrior wanted a gun, iron axe, and steel knife; his squaw stopped making pottery and using bone awls in skin work, demanding a kettle, a needle, and an iron hoe. Everyone liked the new cloth and coats with sleeves, and both sexes and all ages developed an insatiable thirst for rum.

But the Iroquois wars were not fought entirely to satisfy these cultural demands. The Iroquois warrior could be a homicidal maniac and the old men of Onondaga were capable of intrigue and duplicity when it suited their ends. For the Iroquois wars had gone on for a century before the French and Dutch arrived in force, and there were elements of prestige and personal glory, of revenge and self-preservation, that impelled them to maintain old feuds that they had only checked among themselves by the formation of the League, with all its supporting ritual sanctions and symbolic metaphors. The man hunt and the cannibal reformed were too recent in their cultural memories to shock anyone who heard the central plot of the Deganawidah epic. Cannibalism was something they knew and practiced on their enemies; shamanism was all around. What was shocking was the possibility of either's being abolished.

The early sources agree that Iroquois war parties were volunteer affairs, motivated by revenge or self-glorification, to bring back scalps, or better, prisoners who could be tortured for the amusement of the village or adopted to replace relatives lost in similar engagements. As the beaver became scarce in Iroquoia, by the middle of the seventeenth century, these war parties assumed the character of raids to secure plunder or, with sanction of the council, to knock on the head those nations that hunted on lands taken in previous conquests. In the process the Iroquois confederation, which had responded to outside aggression, itself became a conquest state. Warriors of several nations combined to destroy within a decade the Huron, Neutral, and Erie—all Iroquoians —and to disperse the Mascouten, Miami, Illinois, and others who fled westward. These punitive expeditions had economic motivation, but

* Iroquois: "a conquest state"

they also yielded large numbers of captives, who were adopted wholesale into the Seneca, Onondaga, and Oneida tribes as new sibs or communities. By the end of the seventeenth century the adoptees or their offspring outnumbered the Iroquois proper. They became thoroughly acculturated and acted more like the Iroquois than the Iroquois themselves. Chieftainship titles were even conferred on adoptees. This regenerative power of the People of the Longhouse amazed everyone who wrote about them.

The French image of the Iroquois was built out of the wreckage of the fur trade and the failure of the Jesuit missions. Mindful of the Jesuit martyrs, it mirrored the views of the friendly Huron. Gabriel Sagard, Champlain, and Jesuit writers had described the culture of Huronia to the delight of French readers. By comparison Jesuit writers slighted Iroquois culture except to refer to the League and its grand council at Onondaga as something ancient and powerful to be reckoned with, to give some vivid descriptions of diplomatic receptions and councils and performances of the rituals of condolence, and to dwell on the Dream Feast, the predecessor of the Midwinter Festival. In sum, the Iroquois were powerful politicians, they were compulsives in ritual and in the fulfillment of dreams, and they showed remarkable regenerative powers. The Jesuit writers make it clear that the restorative powers of the Iroquois population and the persistence of their culture rested on two facts: the custom of "drawing a name from the bottom of the Kettle," or adoption into a maternal family, and the organization of their confederacy. Because the old men were unable to control the young people at home and abroad, one of the main purposes of the annual meetings of the general assembly at Onondaga was to "make their complaints and receive the necessary compensation in mutual gifts" in the presence of deputies of all the nations. I know of no better exemplification of Malinowski's theory of reciprocity: reciprocal gift giving, supported by ritual sanctions having the force of law, cements the ties of mutuality. The beauty of Jesuit observations on the character and customs of the Iroquois is that they afford repeated instances of the same behavior independently observed, as well as general statements. One can read these accounts and find almost the same language as occurs in texts that Hale and Hewitt recorded in the last century at Grand River and that I have edited with living informants (Hale, 1883; Hewitt, 1944; Fenton, 1946, 1950). But the existence of this liturgical literature did not help the image of the Iroquois in New France.

As the witty Baron de Lahontan put it, the French trembled with the "Savage Nations in *Canada* . . . at the very Name . . ."; and though they attributed to them the glory ". . . they purchased on several occasions, . . . at the same time [they hated] the Rascally People, as much as Horns

Fenton an Jesuit anthropology — VALUABLE

and Law-Suits . . .!" (Thwaites, 1905, 6, 498). Lahontan, a seventeenth-century social critic, might revel at the humbling of an imprudent governor by an Onondaga orator who spoke in the name of the Five Nations, but the French colonists would recall the nights of horror following the massacre at La Chine, which nearly brought the colony to its knees. Small wonder that Iroquois is still a name of infamy in French-Canadian textbooks.

The Dutch at Fort Orange had no particular love for the Indians. The sources support the view that the Dutch were mainly interested in the trade, less so in politics, and that the Indians were a necessary evil that had to be tolerated like cold winters and hot summers in the Hudson valley. Lacking in civic consciousness, the Dutch traders contributed to the delinquency of their savage neighbors (see Trelease, 1960). For all their tradition of literacy in Holland, the Dutch at Fort Orange, with one or two exceptions, were surprisingly uninterested in the Indians as a phenomenon. Only Van den Bogaert's journal of his visit to the Mohawks (1634–1635) and Dominie Johannes Megapolensis' (1603–1670) "Brief Sketch of the Maquas" speak with authority (Jameson, 1909). The former covers a trading mission to the Mohawk towns and to Oneida made in winter when the Iroquois threatened a second peace with the French, and it contains some nice ethnographic detail. They found people at home in the third Mohawk "Castle," and they "were much looked at by both the old and the young . . . [so that] we could hardly pass through. They pushed each other into the fire to see us, and it was most midnight before their departure. We could not absent ourselves to go to stool; even then they crawled around us without feeling any shame." The visitors got lice, ate venison, and traded. They were entertained with a military exercise, announced by a caller through the houses, a sham fight between participants clad in reed armor who contended with clubs. The guests were chided when one lost his temper in council. As ambassadors to Oneida they were lodged as distinguished guests in the house of the chief, and they participated in a feast. The pattern of the feast, which is still followed, entails cooking in a separate building in common kettles; carrying the kettles into the banquet hall; ladling a basinful of food for everyone present, starting with guests and chiefs; and procuring dishes and spoons for those who have not brought them. Guests sing at will, and all present thank the host before they return home. The visitors observed two instances of shamanism. And they were given a lesson in geography: "They showed us with stones and maize grains [names of castles and distances traversed], and Jeronimus then made a chart of it." (Jameson, 1909, 145 ff., 150.)

The three clans of the Mohawk—Bear, Turtle, and Wolf—are associated with particular towns. Of these the Turtles boast that they are most numerous, most eminent, being descended from the Woman Who Fell from the Sky, in the cosmology; and the Wolf clan are the descendants of the first two. The totems appear as emblems in warfare, as personal medicine, and in tatoos. The character of the council is described, but there are no hints of the League. Chiefs characteristically impoverish themselves by generosity.

The Iroquois could never understand why hospitality was not accorded them in Albany. Complaints of the meagerness of Dutch hospitality, of the shortage of gunpowder, and of having to pay wampum to get their guns repaired are interwoven with remarks that the chain of friendship "lasts only so long as we have beavers." Indians tell of being robbed of their furs after having been enticed by calls from a stoop or beaten and forcibly driven into a particular trader's house or after having been waylaid and made drunk on the Schenectady road. All of these practices that commenced during the Dutch regime were continued into the English reign, and all were subject to regulations that were promptly ignored. Civil disobedience in Albany began before 1664. English writers constantly inveigh against the "Albanian spirit."

It seems appropriate to let an English garrison officer, Captain William Hyde, put a tail piece to the seventeenth century:

> I have seen Seaven or Eight of these fellowes sitt Round upon the Ground all drunke, and to maintaine fair Justice among them in drinking a young handsom Squa Sate in the middle with a Cagg of Rum, & measur'd Each man's due proportions with her mouth into a dish and so it went Round [Fenton, 1966].

Forest Diplomacy: The Eighteenth Century (1701–1776)

If the great issue of the seventeenth century was who should sell rum to the "Farr Indians" of Green Bay, Wisconsin, to get their furs, land was the issue of Indian and white relations in the eighteenth century. Since in Indian polity land titles reposed in the tribe and the sachems, or peace chiefs, were the trustees, if not the owners of the land, Indian leaders perforce became politicians to be courted and heard. Men who were knowledgeable about Indian affairs knew that Indian leaders were of at least two kinds: war chiefs, who organized and led parties of volunteer raiders and traders; and sachems, or peace chiefs, whose attention was confined to civil affairs. What further complicated Indian affairs was that the speakers at conferences with the whites were often appointed for the purpose by principals who remained silent, unless these principals could themselves double as orators, in which case their names are recorded. There were also the interpreters to be reckoned with, and they had the last say in building the image in the minds of colonial officials and in the minds of ministers who read their reports. Joncaire, who had been captured and raised among the Senecas, was bilingual as were some of the Jesuits; but with the exception of George Croghan and Sir William Johnson, none of the English officials was bilingual or knew any smattering of Iroquoian language. Small wonder that chiefs were at first confused with "kings" and that deals were consummated with Indians who had no right to sell. It is amazing how good the colonial records are, considering that for the most part the interpreters were illiterate or were prisoners who learned an Indian language during captivity. But a few were scholars, and even they struggled for words, without infusing the fire of Indian oratory into the treaty proceedings (Clinton, 1812).

Of the writers on forest diplomacy during the eighteenth century, two are French and two are English. Bacqueville de la Potherie, who was in New France as a Royal Commissioner during the proceedings attending the Grand Settlement of 1701 between the Iroquois and the tribes of the Upper Lakes, supplements nicely Lafitau's contemporary systematic treatment of the Iroquois society (La Potherie, 1722, III, IV; Lafitau, 1724).

The protocol of forest diplomacy demanded the use of metaphor, timing, manipulation of space, and reciprocal action by both parties. The kettle, the hatchet, the road, the fire, the mat, the sun, and the Tree of Peace were each subject to qualifiers appropriate to the mood or intent. Leading or receiving a procession at the wood's edge, taking guests by the arm to the main fire, arranging the council grounds, seating delegates, allowing them to withdraw to consider and to return to reply were aspects of spatial arrangements. Wiping away the tears, opening the ears, and clearing the throat, exchanging greetings of condolence and songs, passing the pipe, throwing wampum belts, returning prisoners, distributing presents, and apportioning the feast were expected alike of host and guest. All of this was comprised in a ritual paradigm that was widely shared in the Lower Lakes by Iroquoian and Algonkian speakers alike, and it survives today (Fenton, 1946, 1950, 1967; Hale, 1963).

The discovery that the proceedings of Indian treaties contained the seeds of a native species of American literature belongs to Cadwallader Colden, Lieutenant Governor of New-York, who found so much else of interest in the New World. Of Indian orators he says:

> . . . I am ignorant of their Language; but the Speakers whom I have heard, had all a great Fluency of Words, and much more Grace in their Manner, than any Man could expect, among a People intirely ignorant of all the liberal Arts and Sciences. I am informed . . . They have . . . a certain *Urbanitas,* or *Atticism,* in their Language, of which the common ears are

very sensible, though only their great Speakers attain to it. . . . They have some Kind of Elegancy in varying and compounding their Words, to which, not many of themselves attain, and this principally distinguishes their best Speakers. . . . [Colden, 1750, 14]

Others in the English colonies besides Colden admired the genius of the Five Nations. Indeed, all the best minds of the day had their first brush at diplomatic negotiation in the conduct of Indian affairs. There were Peter Schuyler (1657–1724), first mayor of Albany, who accompanied the Four Indian Kings to the court of Queen Anne (Bond, 1952); Conrad Weiser (1696–1760), the Pennsylvania Indian interpreter, whom the Iroquois claimed belonged one-half to them (Wallace, 1945); Sir William Johnson (1715–1774), who walked in their moccasins, conducted their affairs, and slept in their beds; and Samuel Kirkland (1741–1808), New England missionary to the Oneida, who first enumerated the Six Nations by town and clan.

The Iroquois of the eighteenth century were already transformed. Economically dependent on the Albany traders, they were now Six Nations. Having made peace with the French, neutrality was their policy. But they wanted Anglican missionaries to offset the French Jesuits. They were at war with southeastern tribes; although reduced in manpower, they were still a force to be reckoned with. And although the Mohawks would deed their best lands, the rest were still largely intact. But their culture was changing rapidly from East to West.

All who described them spoke of this change, including Colden, who was adopted into the Bear Clan and to whom a sachem gave a distinguished name that "would echo from Hill to Hill all over the Five Nations." Colden noted that their hospitality declined after they learned not to expect it from whites and that they no longer offered their young girls to visiting Christians. He observed: "This Nation indeed has laid aside many of its ancient Customs, and so likewise have the other Nations . . . and have adopted many of ours; so that it is not easy now to distinguish their original and genuine Manners, from those which they have lately acquired . . ." (Colden, 1750, 11). Johnson was to repeat this observation later.

The Iroquois were still the buffer between the expanding English colony of New York and the French. But governors of New York regularly were unable to raise troops and fulfill their promises to the Six Nations or to mount an attack against Canada. And to offset such attack, during the periods of warfare and between, the French Jesuits at Oneida encouraged the Iroquois to take up arms against the Indians of the Southeast, who lived at the back of the English colonies. The Oneida especially went out repeatedly against the Catawba and their allies, and later in the century the Seneca went against the Cherokee. It is difficult to explain these campaigns in other terms than the traditional drive for honors, scalps, and, above all, captives. There was certainly no economic motive of the fur trade in them for the Iroquois; no one packed home deerskins that far overland. But the embarrassment to the English was considerable, and the problem created by these incursions brought the colonies together, first in a series of Indian conferences and ultimately in the Albany Congress.

From the Siouan and Muskogean peoples of the Southeast came a steady flow of captives, displaced tribes, and culture traits. With the reduction of manpower through the wars and the adoption of alien captives, the power of men declined and the power of Iroquois matrons was enhanced. Richards has recently made a case for this, questioning the matrilocal, matri-centered picture of Lafitau, although the evidence can be read either way (Richards, 1967). It was the women who stayed home; descent, inheritance and succession passed in the female line; and it is likely that they became the conservators of the old culture. We do not know, because women seldom enter the literature until Mary Jemison's captivity.

The Tuscarora, an Iroquoian-speaking people of tidewater Carolina, were defeated and displaced in a war with the whites in 1712. Bands of Tuscarora began to drift northward through Maryland and Pennsylvania, until they were made a prop to the Longhouse at Oneida a decade later. Similarly, Siouan-speaking bands known as Saponi and Tutelo came as minorities under the wing of the Cayuga at mid-century, as did part of the Delaware somewhat later. Thus, what had been the junior side of the Longhouse became known as the Four Brothers.

After the gun displaced the bow and the tomahawk made in Sheffield supplanted the ball-headed war club inlaid with wampum and fashioned like a human leg, there was a corresponding change in tactics away from massing warriors under strict leadership to forming small guerrilla bands. The number of volunteer leaders increased, competition for prestige was enhanced, and status of the war chief declined. Not until the Mohawk Christian leader Joseph Brant became Captain of the Six Nations for putting together large raiding parties that ranged far out of Niagara during the American Revolution did the war chief's position improve. The multiplication of the number of war chiefs during the century also eroded the office of the peace chief, because the unemployed veterans of former status insisted on being heard in council. The power of the Pine Tree chiefs increased in direct proportion to their involvement in negotiations with the whites, as witness the rise of Red Jacket, the Seneca orator at the close of the period.

These circumstances and the fact that peace chiefs were heard through appointed speakers explain why the names of the fifty titles of the

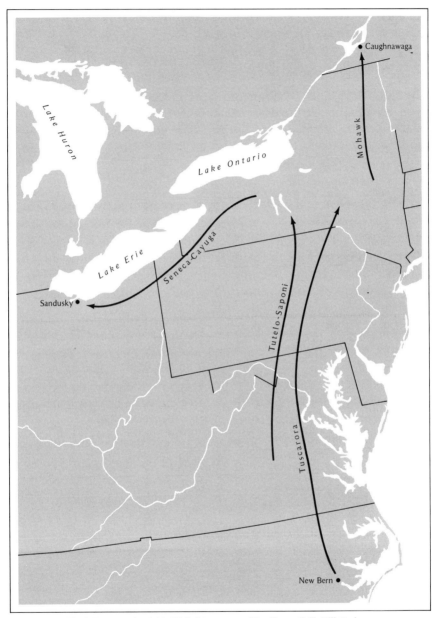

Figure 5.3. Drift of the Iroquois, 1700-1784. (Map prepared by Gwyneth Y. Gillette.)

founders, which were passed along within matrilineages as ascribed statuses, appear so infrequently in the literature. The names of the leading titles for each tribal delegation occur more frequently, both by the force of incumbents and the custom of referring to the tribes by these titles.

Through such adopted intermediaries as Conrad Weiser and Sir William Johnson, the civil chiefs communicated their ceremony to the colonial powers. Whoever in the colonies would deal with the Iroquois must do it on the Indian's time, using his metaphors, following the sequence of his ritual, "as it was laid down by our grandfathers when they founded the Great Law." He must document his words with attestations of wampum, beaver skins, or presents, which became known as "Indian goods."

Concepts of time are among the most difficult understandings to communicate between cultures. All Europeans who did business with the Indians suffered from the delays of Indians arriving for a meeting in their own time and chafed at the deliberateness with which they conducted business. Indians were never in a hurry. They would arrive "in so many moons, when the corn is knee high, when the bark is ready to peel for canoes, when the corn is in the milk, or when they get done hunting"—concepts that were important to them, but all too vague and uncertain for gentlemen attuned to a calendar. To this day, in my experience, Indian time is an hour after prevailing time, and meetings are called "when we turn the lamps up" or "when we get done eating." No Iroquois to this day will answer to a proposition on the same day, nor will he press another party for a reply until the latter is ready. One listens carefully, repeats the main points of what he hears, and then takes the message home and puts it under his head for the night as a pillow. One never interrupts another. Indeed, this bit of forest protocol is sanctioned by ritual. In the invocation to the founders of the League, it says:

> Oh my grandsires!
> Even now that has become old which you established,
>   —the Great League.
> You have it as a pillow under your heads in
>   the ground where you are lying,
> this Great League which you established;
> although you said that far away in the future
> the Great League would endure. [Hale, 1883, 125.]

The metaphors of the path, the fire, the column of smoke, the tree with the white roots of peace extending in cardinal directions, and the chain of friendship run through speeches that comprise the treaty literature. And these metaphors must be said in a particular way. Preliminary to any negotiation is the reciprocal condoling of the dead on both sides and the filling up of the empty places in the council. The Iroquois always expected to devote the first day or so at any public council to reciting the laws of their ancient government before moving to the conduct of public business. Similarly, they were concerned and made appropriate gestures at the death and replacement of governors and agents. They expected the same of others.

So in time Englishmen learned from experienced interpreters to say "the three rare words of requickening—to wipe away tears, open the ears, and clear the throat—to cleanse the house, wipe the bloody mat, cover the grave, bind up the bones and restore the sun to the sky." This bit of ritual business was done at Albany, Montreal, Philadelphia, and elsewhere, often enough so that men of imagination were impressed by its dramatic quality and by its style and were aroused afterward to inquire about its content. Although the United States Constitution was not modeled on the League, its authors, particularly Franklin, were aware of the existence of the Iroquois Confederacy and used it to whip their fellow countrymen into line (Boyd, 1938, 78; Van Doren, 1938, 209). On the eve of the American Revolution both the representatives of the Continental Congress and the Iroquois recalled the connection. Indeed, the League was an image to be reckoned with. It did not prevent feuds between members, and it often failed to act; but acts of unanimity are recalled and recorded, no nation ever seceded, and it was not until the American Revolution involved in civil war. The symbol of the League itself was the most powerful image operating in its preservation during the eighteenth century. Beneath the extended rafters of the Longhouse were sheltered five tribes at as many fires, united as one family of kindred. Like all families, they had their fallings-out, but they patched them up ritually so that society could continue.

It was the custom of the Iroquois to document their words with wampum beads, made of the shell of *Venus mercenarius* L., that they got from the Mahican, Hudson River people, and their congeners living on Long Island. When the Dutch came to Manhattan, they introduced steel drills and hired Indian wampum makers to turn out beads on grindstones, until the wampum industry flourished at Albany and wampum became a kind of money in the trade. It was a natural transition from the Indian custom of the exchange of gifts to the trade and payment of presents in European goods. Long lists were prepared of those items wanted by the Indians and sent back for manufacture on the Continent and in Britain. Such lists mirror the changing culture of the Iroquois (Jacobs, 1950; Johnson, 1921–1966, *passim*).

Iroquois culture change reflected conditions of daily contact on the frontier as well as forces far-removed, on the Ohio River and in Europe. Having displaced the occupants of the Ohio valley themselves during the previous century, and commanding access to the valley from both the

French and the English, the old men of Onondaga were aware that the
back country was being infiltrated by other Indians like the Delaware
and Shawnee and behind them by settlers from Virginia, during what
is now known as the westward movement. At the eastern door Palatine
Germans were pushing up the Mohawk valley. In Albany and Whitehall
the game was to keep the French out of Iroquoia and the Ohio country
by persuading the Iroquois to let them fortify Oswego; by sending Anglican missionaries among them; by gaining trusteeship, if not title, to their
lands in return for protection; and by replacing the Albany Commissioners of Indian Affairs, who were losing control of the trade, by a single
head appointed by the Crown. In short, the missions, the westward movement, land cessions, the trade, politics, and war were one package called
Anglo-French rivalry, and the Iroquois were the string around it.

No Englishman understood the languages of the Five Nations during
the first quarter of the eighteenth century. The Albany commissioners
were Dutch traders, and they themselves depended upon a bilingual
Dutch woman who knew Mohawk; she in turn was translated by a Scot
named Robert Livingston (1654–1728). The English governors, Lord
Bellamont and Lord Cornbury, represented to Whitehall the want of
ministers of the Church of England to counteract Jesuit teaching and
French propaganda among the Five Nations, and the Indians themselves
expressed an interest in hearing their views. And Livingston, who was in
England to collect an expense account, petitioned the newly founded
Society for the Propagation of the Gospel (S.P.G.) to send out two clergy-
men. The delays and frustrations these first Anglican missionaries experienced in making contact with the Mohawks were augmented by the
dislike that the Indians were developing for Englishmen generally, dislike based on the feeling that the New Englanders took their lands without purchase and on continual misrepresentation of the English by the
Dutch. The difficulties of the Anglicans underscore how poorly prepared
they were in contrast with the Jesuits.

A more favorable situation would arise following the embassy of four
sachems to the court of Queen Anne. Ostensibly they enlisted the royal
favor for the missions; but their real purpose was political, and their
visit was one slick public relations scheme. For the first half of Queen
Anne's War (1702–1713) New York remained neutral, mainly because the
Albany traders wished to continue the black market traffic with Canada,
and the New England frontier suffered Indian raids. Then Governor
Dudley and others cooked up the scheme of sending Indian sachems
abroad to plead for men, money, missionaries, and ships to reduce
Canada. Going via Boston, three Mohawks and one Mahican, or "River
Indian," from near Albany made the voyage, under the care of Peter and
John Schuyler of Albany, arriving in London, tatooed and befeathered,

armed with clubs and wampum belts, and wearing matchcoats girded with burden straps. They were received in court; made their plea; ran down a stag in the Queen's park; saw the sights of London; appeared at the theater, where they were billed as "the Four Kings of Canada" and stopped the show; attended a cockfight; and witnessed various military exercises. They traded their gear to Sir Hans Sloane, and it is now in the British Museum. Returning home safely, one of the "Kings" was "put out of his honor" for being too clubby with the English.

The enduring results of the visit were the establishment at Fort Hunter of Her Majesty's Chapel, equipped with communion plate, Bibles, and prayer books, and the dispatching of missionaries from the S.P.G. The great fault of the Anglican mission to the Mohawks and the reason it got nowhere for thirty years was its institutionalized nature, linked as it was to the established Church, to the army, and to the Crown. It had two bright moments at mid-century when Barclay and John Ogilvie (1724–1774), both educated at Yale (still today the seat of Iroquoian studies), started schools and translated the Scriptures into Mohawk. There were some Indians who wanted to learn English and to write their own language. Hendrick (c. 1680–1755) as the Dutch named him, or properly, Tiyanoga, now an elderly veteran of the journey, was the confidant of William Johnson, the rising Irish trader and Superintendent of Indian Affairs, and both were pro-Anglican. And Joseph Brant, or Thayendanegea, descendant of one of the four, as Johnson's protégé became at home in two cultures and assisted in translating the Gospel into Mohawk. David of Schoharie wrote down the ritual of the Condolence Council (Hale, 1883).

During Johnson's long charge of their affairs the Mohawks remained faithful to the English, and the confederates kept one ear in Johnson Hall, as Sir William called his eighteenth-century mansion at what is today Johnstown. They were willing to leave affairs in his hands because they knew that, having acquired a barony of his own, he was interested in keeping other land speculators out. And in 1763 he was instrumental in obtaining a Royal Proclamation that for a time stemmed the tide of westward movement beyond the line of 1768 drawn between their lands in the Ohio country and the expanding colonies.

These concerns kept Johnson too busy for philosophical reflection or for systematically recording his considerable knowledge of Iroquois political structure. He was aware of the defects in general works on the American Indian, and he answered an inquiry from Arthur Lee of Virginia by commenting that they failed to take into account changes in the manners and customs, so that a "description of them at a particular period must be insufficient." (O'Callaghan, 1849–1851, IV, 430–437; Johnson, XII, 950.) He distinguished near and remote tribes as to their degree of acculturation and noted that those Indians having most contact with traders had altered their system of politics while retaining ancient customs that they were unable to account for. While those farthest removed from contact retained "the greatest part of their primitive usages . . . [but could] give no satisfactory account of their original signification . . ." (Johnson, XII, 950). He also noted a tendency for the Iroquois to cloak political tradition with mythology, and he observed that it was more than a century since the Jesuits who were first among the Iroquois introduced "some of their own inventions which the present generation confound with their ancient ceremonies" (Johnson, XII, 950).

The structure of the League, as we know it from nineteenth-century sources, and the duties of chiefs, their manner of election, and installation, as spelled out in the ritual of the Condolence ceremony, are not discussed in Johnson's papers. Each of the Six Nations, however, is characterized and its symbol given: Flint (Mohawk), Stone (Oneida), Great Mountain (Onondaga), Pipe (Cayuga), and several unexplained symbols for the Seneca. The latter were remote, and Johnson knew them least. He was certain that the authority of the chiefs was waning; he notes that there was formerly one person of each nation who appeared to have more authority than the rest, but that in general, and especially near the settlements, humility was the best policy for their survival. The chiefs were chosen by public assembly, presumably by men; nothing is said about the role of women in the nomination of chiefs, although "she-sachems" are mentioned by some writers. That "some families have a kind of inheritance in the office and are called to this station from their infancy" is recognized by some writers. By this time it is evident that superior ability and tacit consent counted for more than inheritance of office in determining which officer mediated between the cultures. In cases where the office descends, Johnson says, "should the successor appear unequal to the task, some other sachem is sure to possess himself of the power and the duties of the office" (Johnson, XII, 433). Although the introduction of firearms changed tactics and lessened the power of chiefs, the duties of chief sachem comprised custody of the wampum belts, keeping the records of public transactions, prompting speakers at all public treaties, and attending the grand council. Tribal councils included a variety of officers; but regularity, decorum, and avoidance of interrupting the speaker marked all their proceedings.

One further accommodation to change is noted in the power structure. Johnson comments that the Indians formerly lived under "more Order & Government" than at present; but their intercourse has been with the lower classes of colonial society from whom they learn only vices, and their long wars and immoderate use of liquor have so reduced them that they cannot maintain policy and order. There was a further change in their system of politics since the reduction of Canada: "Their Eyes are upon us . . . and much of their Time is spent in Intrigues of State . . ." (Johnson, XII, 436). Factionalism, which is characteristic of the Reservation Period, was on the rise. Witchcraft is noted, and thievery is described as on the increase. But Johnson manifests no doubts about the capacity of the Indians for learning. In his opinion they were put to the English schools too late and then sent back to their own people unprepared to cope with the demands of a hunting, warring society.

Johnson's views on education were to be taken up by Samuel Kirkland (1741–1808), as champion of the day school. Having first visited the Seneca in 1765, Kirkland spent the remainder of his life at Oneida. A Dissenter from New England, he was at odds with Johnson politically, but they respected each other's understandings of the Indians. Kirkland studied the languages, kept journals, and took a census. He was keen, systematic, and thorough, and his record is ethnologically superior to Johnson's. To live in the woods, to know the etiquette of campfire and council, and to speak an Iroquoian language, even though imperfectly, were what counted among Indians and what distinguished Kirkland from his contemporaries. While knowing Oneida best, Kirkland understood the workings of the League Council at Onondaga well enough to discuss its mechanisms with returning delegates. On one occasion he says that the council severely censured the Cayuga Nation for releasing their warriors before the League had met to determine a policy. It was then that the "governesses or she-sachems," through their speaker, lectured the assembly on the matter. This was a month-long meeting, which had been opened by rehearsing "their traditionary system of politics and counsel of the ancients . . ." (Kirkland, manuscript).

The fact of cultural change is nowhere better recorded nor the hope of future success in the education of Indians better postulated than in Kirkland's later writings. Past failures rested on faulty premises that need not apply in the future, because "The whole face of things throughout the country of the Six Nations is of late years very greatly changed." He finds four factors at work: (1) their former attachment to their own culture, which engendered contempt for our society, (2) their present desire for introduction of manners and arts of civilized society, (3) the economic transition from a hunter society to an agricultural society, and (4) the abatement of their deep anti-white prejudice. Kirkland had made a significant discovery: that cultural differences are due to differences in education and are not owing to race, and that cultures change (Kirkland, manuscript).

The Father and Son Quarrel: The American Revolution (1774–1783)

The differences between the views of Johnson and Kirkland appeared to the Iroquois as "a father and son quarrel." They would have no part in such an argument, and as faithful Mohawks they would remain loyal to the Crown. Johnson died on the eve of this struggle in July 1774, and his office, at the urgent request of the Six Nations, passed to his nephew Guy, whom they condoled at the loss of his uncle. But the faction that favored Kirkland at Oneida had grown tired of being manipulated by the Establishment. Their services were no longer to be had for presents, and their sympathies were with their German farming neighbors to whom they could sell venison in return for produce. Several of their leaders were now Christians. When they carried their view to the Onondaga council, objecting to English pressures to take up the hatchet for the King, they were accused of "throwing ashes in the eyes" of the confederates. Indeed there was pressure from Congress as well, and Kirkland was their agent. In the summer of 1776 a conference was held in Albany on the eve of the hostilities to get the Six Nations to remain neutral; it was promptly followed by a British-inspired meeting at Oswego, pulling the tie to the Crown. Torn between these forces it is said that the Grand Council of the League met at Onondaga and, finding itself unable to maintain a policy of neutrality between the generations and unable to reach unanimity on what policy to follow, the Lords of the League covered the fire for the duration. This meeting, which proved the culminating session of the League, left affairs in the hands of the war chiefs.

Brant, having been to England, returned with a commission. But Cornplanter, Blacksnake, Little Beard, Fish Carrier, and others among the Seneca and Cayuga also led raiding parties. And not all the leaders were Indians: prominent Tories like Walter Butler, having fled estates in the Mohawk valley, raised ranger companies, who on occasion proved more vicious than the Iroquois from whom they learned the crafts of warpath and ambush.

In reprisal General Washington sent General Sullivan of New Hampshire with largely New England troops to burn their towns and cut their cornfields. This expedition ended their means of subsistence and emptied the granary of Fort Niagara. The journals of Sullivan's Army record the number and distribution of Cayuga and Seneca towns around the Finger Lakes, note the presence of orchards of peach and apple trees, and mention extensive fields growing several varieties of maize, beans, squash, and melons. The soldiers found bark houses, as expected, but the number of frame and log houses encountered was surprising. Among the relics of Indian customs collected were several wooden False Faces from one town, which were brought back to Philadelphia and which once hung in Du Simitière's museum. Soldiers from Massachusetts returned home with ears of white corn that developed into a famous domestic variety of "evergreen." But the memory of rich farmlands in the Genesee country would lure New Englanders from stone-strewn hill farms to western New York within a few years.

For a season the war out of Niagara increased in intensity, but the stocks of provisions were gone from the Seneca towns, and a hard winter sent refugees streaming toward the escarpment to live in miserable squalor on the bounty of the British. There might have been a few strings of corn at Buffalo Creek and along Cattaraugus Creek, but there was not an ear to be had at Allegheny, Geneseo, or Canandaigua. Onondaga was a wasteland, and the Oneida with their Algonkian allies, the Stockbridge Mahikan, withdrew to Schenectady. The memory of that year of starvation was vividly recalled by Seneca informants thirty years ago.

When the last smoke of hostilities vanished, the embers of the fire that had burned from time immemorial at Onondaga were cold. Families gradually drifted back to their old settlement sites but found nowhere to lay their heads, and they had little will to build new housing. The refugees at Niagara removed to Buffalo Creek, which became the largest post-Revolutionary settlement of the Six Nations. Their lands were now in jeopardy, and they were living as displaced people, threatened by land speculators and agitation for their removal to the westward.

The Reservation Period (1784–1967)

Three "times of trouble" have marked the history of Indian and white relations in western New York since the American Revolution. Each has involved major land cessions and has been followed by cultural reintegration. Two major treaties were signed by the Six Nations and the growing new republic of the United States, a decade apart, first with commissioners of the Congress at Fort Stanwix (1784) and then with a sole commissioner appointed by the President at Canandaigua (1794), the last for peace and friendship and to patch up the rusty spots in the chain of friendship left by the first. Colonel Timothy Pickering, arch-federalist of Salem, and fifty chiefs and sachems of the Six Nations concluded a just and equitable peace, which provided a charter for all subsequent Indian and white relations and which was to endure, as the

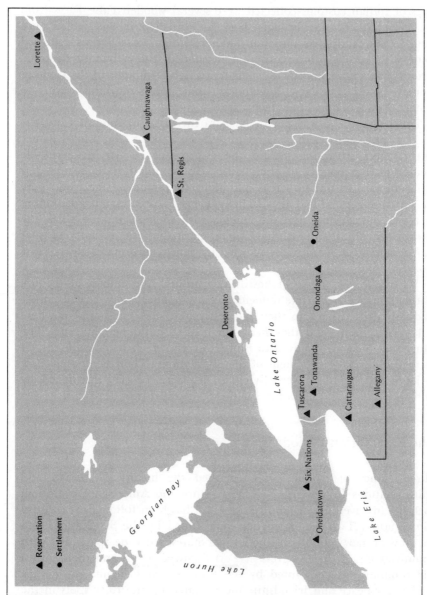

Figure 5.4. Modern reservations and settlements of Iroquois descendants. (Map prepared by Gwyneth Y. Gillette.)

Indian line runs: "as long as the sun shines, waters flow and the grass grows . . ." It endured until Congress, by a process of legislative erosion, appropriated moneys for building the Kinzua Dam, thereby setting the treaty aside.

Four issues were at work in this decade. There was first the question of lands, which was manifest in continual disputes over boundaries; there were fraudulent land sales without consent or supervision of governments, and the whites made incursions on Indian hunting territories. Joseph Brant and the British insisted on the Ohio line of 1768. The Cayuga wanted to sell and emigrate to Canada. Incursions led to murders, and murders to war. Second was the ever-present danger of an Indian war involving 1,000 veterans of the Six Nations, which no one in Congress wanted let loose on the border settlements. It was in the federal interest to keep the Six Nations quiet, and this was a major purpose of a series of conferences. Third, British Loyalists nurtured hopes that with Canada as a base they might recover the Northwest, and they refused to give up the forts at Niagara, Detroit, and Michilimackinac until 1796. The fourth issue was the gradual civilization of the Indian, a purpose with which all agreed, but with differing plans for achieving it.

From the Iroquois viewpoint Fort Stanwix was bitter medicine. New York, Pennsylvania, and Congress sent commissioners, each with different purposes, and they tried to get the tribes to sign separately out of deference to the Oneida and Tuscarora, who had assisted in the Revolution. Brant and Cornplanter were there as war chiefs, and Cornplanter, hoping to save a portion of the Seneca lands, signed; for the rest of his days he regretted it, for Red Jacket and the Buffalo Creek faction never let him forget that peace was the business of sachems. Out of this treaty grew the conflict between the state of New York and the federal government regarding control over the conduct of Indian affairs. Control was later given by the Constitution to the federal government, although federal jurisdiction has never been acknowledged by the state.

In this confused situation the land speculators were active. The Stanwix treaty had conveyed all the Six Nations lands in New York and Pennsylvania east of a meridian running south at Geneva, New York. In 1788 Oliver Phelps (1749–1809) and Nathaniel Gorham (1738–1796) purchased the Massachusetts preemption right to everything west of the line; they subsequently sold to Robert Morris of Philadelphia, who sold to the Holland Land Company. In these transfers the Seneca, at the Treaty of Big Tree (1797), reserved certain parcels that comprise their present reservations. Of the other lands, east of the Genesee, which remained from prior sales, the Cayugas sold their reservation and removed to Canada or to Buffalo Creek (Figure 5.4).

The Crown forgot the faithful Mohawks and their allies in the peace settlement and left them to their own devices. For a while Joseph Brant was extending the principles of confederation to a coalition of western tribes who were trying to hold their lands north of the Ohio with the open assistance of the British. He was also much concerned about getting them grants of land, especially for the 1,600 who had settled along the Grand River since 1784. These lands were allotted to them by proclamation and deed, over which there has been a long and bitter controversy, and originally they held everything from its mouth to its source and six miles on either bank. One can still sense the spirit of living history there as the old chiefs recount the removal of their great-grandfathers from New York State, how they looked around and discovered that they had a majority of the League chieftainships, and how they rekindled their fire and reconstituted their confederacy as local government on the reserve (Fenton, 1949, 1965a; Shimony, 1961; Johnston, 1964).

The generation between the Treaty of Big Tree and the onset of trouble at Buffalo Creek (1797–1836) saw the beginnings of reservation culture and was the first generation to speak English. From living on rations and cooking out of iron kettles at Niagara, they had resumed farming in the bottom lands, although they were still dependent on the Niagara garrison and the traders for powder and ball for the autumn and spring hunt. Dependency is never good for any people, and they resented those who fed them. And it was not easy for warriors to adapt to farming, which they refused to do within sight of neighbors who ridiculed them. Unemployed warriors frequented the taverns that sprang up at Buffalo, nearly everyone drank to excess when he could obtain spirits, and the disorganization of the culture was apparent to Indian and white observers alike.

The situation was particularly bad in the Allegheny settlements, where after the sale of pelts at Pittsburgh, drunken frolics lasted for days and not infrequently people were killed. To solve the problem, the chiefs instituted reforms. They appointed two men to keep whiskey out of town, and all miscellaneous dances and feasts were prohibited as invitations to drinking parties, especially fiddle dances attended by whites, although the main religious festivals were retained as native rites. These were the circumstances in which Handsome Lake had his vision in June 1799 and began to reveal the Good Message of the Creator. The revitalization movement that followed was the product of cultural forces already at work, and in its long course it has provided the focus for the retention of the old culture (Parker, 1913; Deardorff, 1951; Wallace, 1958, 1970; Shimony, 1961).

The Quakers found Handsome Lake preaching to a ragged band of hunters who were finding the deer scarce and were subsisting on the gardens of Three Sisters, in striking contrast to the social and political life of the seventeenth and eighteenth centuries, when game was plentiful and plantings more extensive. The Friends of Philadelphia, at the suggestion of President Washington, had devised a plan of aid, which must have been the first such effort, and sent some of their young men to live with the Senecas. They found them still living in bark houses clustered in settlements. By teaching the Senecas how to build log and shingle houses of lumber sawed in their own mills and by persuading them to spread out on fenced farmsteads along the river, the Friends produced a housing revolution that altered the settlement pattern and social organization. Now warriors could farm beyond ridicule, plowing with oxen and horses, fencing their lands, and sowing and reaping cereal crops. Within twenty years they had cleared 440 acres of land and owned 26 horses and 22 yoke of oxen. The close relationship of house-type to family structure that Morgan posited on theoretical grounds is substantiated by history (Morgan, 1881). The importance of the clan and the *decline* lineage have declined steadily since the abandonment of the joint-family *of clan* longhouse. *and family*

Certainly the best observer of Iroquois society immediately before Morgan was Asher Wright (1803–1875), who had unusual gifts in linguistics. Asher and Laura Wright came out to Buffalo Creek in 1831, the year after Red Jacket died, stuck out the time of trouble, and retired with the Senecas to Cattaraugus for the remainder of their lives. Wright devised an orthography and published a Seneca speller, a newsletter, and other tracts. Unusually perceptive, Wright analysed the causes attending the disorganization that he found.

When a pattern of culture is shattered, the people lose their vital spark. The Iroquois had long done things in common and with unanimity, and it was the abandoning of this principle, Wright thought, that led directly to the loss of their lands. Scattered on reservations, they were dealt with separately and were forced to act independently of each other. Reduction in size of territory increased population density, so that formerly autonomous tribes were thrown together on reservations, where the old lines of tribal distinction were soon obliterated. It was a new ball game with new rules. White farmers were settled among them, impeding communication further between scattered Indian homesteads. The felling of the forests spoiled the hunting of the warriors; their sport ruined, they turned reluctantly to farming, which was traditionally women's work. The paths to self-respect were closed. There was no way that the young men could answer their elders, who had achieved distinction in the war out of Niagara. The body politic, moreover, was loaded with war chiefs, who, unable to validate their prestige on the warpath, became the frustrated leaders of factions. Factionalism, as is well known, is characteristic of societies in transition.

The issues were land sales, substitution of majority rule for unanimity, election of chiefs versus the Condolence Council, the extension of white man's law to the reservations, schools, and the new Christian mission versus the "New Religion" of Handsome Lake. These issues polarized around a "Pagan party" versus a "Christian party," or "emigration party," who for a time thought that the best way to escape the white man's encroachments was to remove to Green Bay, Wisconsin, or to Kansas.

Faced with the agents of eastern land speculators, who could bribe chiefs with cheap whiskey at waterfront taverns, Wright was unable alone, funded only by moral suasion, to head off the sale of Buffalo; but he did educate the new leaders, who afterward brought off the revolution of 1848 that led to the founding of the Seneca Nation, a republic. In the upheaval, the life chiefs and war chiefs who were bribed individually to sign their reservation away to the Ogden Land Company were put out of office, and their old ceremony was supplanted by a constitution, stipulating elective officers, which was printed at first in Seneca on Wright's own press. The new government was ratified by the laws of New York, and it persists to the present day (Fenton, 1956; 1965a).

The third time of trouble is so recent that its effects cannot yet be known. But out of it the Seneca Nation has already been transformed into a corporation having assets of over $15 million. For 150 years after the Friends came to hear Handsome Lake, the prevailing settlement pattern of the Allegany Reservation, which stretches some 40 miles around an oxbow in the river, was aptly characterized by a theme in the Medicine Song, "The houses of my grandchildren stretch in a long line." This was until 1938, when the United States Corps of Army Engineers decided that the best place to dam the Allegheny River and impound its waters for flood control was Kinzua narrows, or "Fish on spear," to slake the thirsty boilers of Pittsburgh's steel mills. The project has taken by condemnation some 9,000 acres of bottom lands and dispossessed the Senecas of their homes.

These lands were thought to be protected by the so-called Pickering treaty. But the courts have held that Congress has the unilateral right to set aside treaties with Indians, and the Senecas have been compensated. Without entering into the merits of the controversy, I shall dwell on what the Senecas have done by their own efforts to regain themselves after a disaster.

What I term the second housing revolution is the name of a social revolution. From hemlock-board shanties and frame houses built in the last fifty years, they have planned, built, moved into, and furnished houses of the most modern type that the American economy affords. I have described elsewhere how this was accomplished (Fenton, 1967). The two new communities are of the nucleated suburban type, each surrounding a courthouse or community building, in this respect not unlike the aboriginal settlement pattern without the stockade.

For a time a major threat unified the Seneca Nation. They reorganized their government to meet the threat, forming business corporations to carry out enterprises. But once the threat subsided and they found themselves living in their new houses near a major tourist attraction, old issues attending factionalism returned to plague them. They voted their leaders out of office and installed a moderately conservative government. They have money in banks, and one of the issues is what to do with it.

Life in three Seneca communities of western New York and at the Six Nations Reserve in Ontario west of Niagara Falls does not differ superficially from that of the surrounding population. One approaches these Iroquois communities on paved highways. Although much of the housing is poor, some residences are the equal of any outside. The architecture mirrors that of their neighbors' houses; only at Tonawanda and in parts of Six Nations are log houses yet to be seen. There are the usual churches and community buildings. The Iroquois love motor cars, and they frequently own tractors and trucks. Every house, even the most humble, has its television antenna. Farming has declined, and the reservations have become bedroom communities for workers commuting to factories, gypsum mines, and service occupations in the neighboring cities of Brantford, Hamilton, Buffalo, Salamanca, and Syracuse.

Although the modern Iroquois works at the white man's occupations, he has specialties in which he excels. For example, he has a passion for dangerous occupations. He builds our bridges, erects our skyscrapers, and in general walks where the earth is narrow. When one scrutinizes the brown, canvas-clad iron worker, beneath the steel helmet one often discerns mongoloid physical features. Caughnawaga and Saint Regis Mohawk communities are the traditional nests of these migrant workers. Nominally they are Roman Catholics, but they cling tenaciously to the Mohawk language. There is a Longhouse of the Handsome Lake religion at Caughnawaga and one at Saint Regis, both recent developments.

Those Iroquois who are nominally Onondaga, Cayuga, and Seneca have kept up the ceremonial obligations of the Handsome Lake religion, which depends for its communication upon the native languages, but its adherents are losing their language rapidly. Governments are both elective, with parliamentary procedure, and traditional, dependent on life chiefs installed by ritual. The latter, though losing out, show amazing persistence in the face of change and command the respect of faithful adherents, who must one day realize that the old forms are no longer viable. Such paradoxes of acculturation await further research (see Fenton, 1965a, 1967; Shimony, 1961).

NOTE

[1] The writer is Research Professor of Anthropology at the State University of New York at Albany. Throughout his professional life he has engaged in field work among the Iroquois, most actively from 1933 to 1951, a period which included a stint for the United States Indian Service at Tonawanda, and thirteen years for the Bureau of American Ethnology at the Smithsonian Institution. Then for fifteen years he was preoccupied with the organization and administration of research, first briefly at the National Academy of Sciences–National Research Council, and then for thirteen years as the Assistant Commissioner for the New York State Museum and Science Service in Albany, which limited his contacts with the Iroquois to official visits. All this time he hunted sources on the "redskins" in archives, libraries, and museums here and abroad. Historical documentation of the Iroquoian peoples is quite rich, but ethnology began only a century ago; consequently, one may not expect earlier writers to anticipate current scientific interests. One learns to make do with what he finds. The orthography of Iroquoian terms acknowledges the recent work on Seneca by Wallace Chafe (1963). The material presented here was originally written for, and will appear as a chapter in, a book entitled *The People of the Longhouse,* to be published by Farrar, Straus & Giroux, Inc.

REFERENCES

BOND, RICHMOND P.

1952 Queen Anne's American kings. Oxford: the Clarendon Press.

BOYD, JULIAN, AND CARL VAN DOREN, EDS.

1938 Indian treaties printed by Benjamin Franklin, 1736–1762. Philadelphia: Historical Society of Pennsylvania.

CHAFE, WALLACE L.

1961 Seneca Thanksgiving rituals. Bureau of American Ethnology Bulletin 183.

1963 Handbook of the Seneca language. Albany, New York: State Museum and Science Service, Bulletin No. 388.

CLINTON, DE WITT

1812 A discourse [on the Iroquois or Six Nations] delivered before the New-York Historical Society. Dec. 6, 1811. New-York Historical Society Collections, Ser. 1, II:37–116.

COLDEN, CADWALLADER

1750 The history of the five nations of Canada. London.

DEARDORFF, M. H.

1951 The religion of Handsome Lake: its origin and development. *In* Symposium on Local Diversity in Iroquois Culture, no. 5. William N. Fenton, ed. Bureau of American Ethnology Bulletin 149:77–107.

FENTON, W. N.

1942 Contacts between Iroquois herbalism and colonial medicine. Washington, D.C.: Smithsonian Institution, Annual Report, 1941. pp. 503–526.

1946 An Iroquois condolence council for installing Cayuga chiefs in 1945. Journal of the Washington Academy of Sciences XXXVI (4):110–127.

1949 Seth Newhouse's traditional history and constitution of the Iroquois confederacy. Proceedings of the American Philosophical Society. 93:141–158.

1950 The roll call of the Iroquois chiefs: a study of a mnemonic cane from the Six Nations Reserve. Washington, D.C.: Miscellaneous Collection. Smithsonian CXI (15).

1953 The Iroquois eagle dance: an offshoot of the calumet dance . . . Bureau of American Ethnology Bulletin 156.

1956 Asher Wright's Seneca mission. Proceedings of the American Philosophical Society 100 (6):567–581.

1957 Indian and white relations in eastern North America: a common ground for history and ethnology. With a bibliography by L. H. Butterfield, Wilcomb E. Washburn, and William N. Fenton. Chapel Hill: The University of North Carolina Press.

1962 This island, the world on the turtle's back. Journal of American Folklore 75 (298):283–300.

1963a Horatio Hale (1817–1896): introduction to the Iroquois book of rites, vii–xxvii. Toronto: University of Toronto Press.

1963b The Seneca green corn ceremony. The Conservationist XVIII (2):20–22, 27–28.

1965a The Iroquois confederacy in the twentieth century: a case study of the theory of Lewis H. Morgan in "Ancient society." Ethnology IV (3):251–265.

1965b Captain Hyde's observations on the five nations of Indians at New-Yorke. American Scene Magazine: Gilcrease Institute of American History and Art, Tulsa, Oklahoma. 1–20.

1966 Field work, museum studies, and ethnohistorical research. Ethnohistory XIII (1–2):71–85.

1967 From longhouse to ranch-type house: the second housing revolution of the Seneca nation. *In* Iroquois culture, history, and prehistory. Elisabeth Tooker, ed. Albany: N.Y. State Museum and Science Service. pp. 7–22.

FENTON, W. N., AND ERNEST STANLEY DODGE

1949 An elm bark canoe in the Peabody Museum of Salem. American Neptune IX (3):185–206.

GRIFFIN, J. B.

1967 Eastern North American archeology: a summary. Science 156 (3772):175–191.

HALE, H.

1883 The Iroquois book of rites. Philadelphia. [Reprinted with an Introduction by W. N. Fenton. Toronto: University of Toronto Press, 1963.]

HEWITT, J. N. B.

1892 Legend of the founding of the Iroquois league. American Anthropologist V:131–148.

1944 The requickening address of the Iroquois Condolence Council. W. N. Fenton, ed. Journal of the Washington Academy of Sciences XXXIV:65–85.

HOEBEL, E. A.

1949 Man in the primitive world. New York: McGraw-Hill.

HUNT, GEORGE T.

1940 The wars of the Iroquois. Madison: University of Wisconsin Press.

HICKERSON, H.

1966 Review of Saum: the fur trader and the Indian. American Anthropologist 68:822.

JACOBS, WILBUR R.

1950 Diplomacy and Indian gifts: Anglo-French rivalry along the Ohio and northwest frontiers, 1748–1763. Stanford, Calif.: Stanford University Press.

JAMESON, J. FRANKLIN, ED.

1909 [Van den Bogaert's] Narrative of a journey into the Mohawk and Oneida country, 1634–1635. Rev. Johannes Megapolensis, Jr. A short account of the Mohawk Indians, 1644. Both in Narratives of New Netherland, 1609–1664. New York: Scribner, pp. 135–180.

JOHNSON, SIR WILLIAM

1921–1966 Papers, James Sullivan et al., eds. 13 vols. Albany: University of the State of New York.

JOHNSTON, CHARLES M.

1964 The valley of the six nations: a collection of documents on the Indian lands of the Grand River. Toronto: The Champlain Society.

KIRKLAND, SAMUEL

Papers. Manuscript, Hamilton College Library.

LAFITAU, JOSEPH-FRANÇOIS

1724 Moeurs des sauvages amériquains, comparées aux moeurs des premiers temps. 2 vols. Paris: Saugrain l'Ainé.

LA POTHERIE, BAQUEVILLE [LE ROY] DE

1722 Histoire de l'Amérique septentrionale. 4 vols. Paris.

LINTON, RALPH

1936 The study of man. New York: Appleton-Century-Crofts.

1955 The tree of culture. New York: Knopf.

MEGAPOLENSIS, see JAMESON

MORGAN, L. H.

1851 The league of the Ho-de-no-sau-nee, or Iroquois. Rochester: Sage. [Reprinted with an Introduction by William N. Fenton. New York: Corinth Paper Backs, American Experience Series, 1962.]

1877 Ancient society. New York.

1881 House and house-life of the American aborigines. Washington. [Reprinted, Chicago: University of Chicago Press, 1966.]

NAMMACK, GEORGIANA C.

1969 Fraud, politics, and the dispossession of the Indians: the Iroquois land frontier in the colonial period. Norman, Okla.: University of Oklahoma Press.

O'CALLAGHAN, E. B., ED.

1849–1851 The documentary history of the state of New York. Albany: State of New York.

PARKER, A. C.

1910 Iroquois uses of maize and other food plants. New York State Museum Bulletin 144.

1913 The code of Handsome Lake, the Seneca prophet. New York State Museum Bulletin 163.

PARKMAN, FRANCIS

1899 Count Frontenac and New France under Louis XIV. Boston: Little, Brown.

RANDLE, MARTHA C.

1953 The Waugh collection of Iroquois folktales. Proceedings of the American Philosophical Society XCVII:629.

RICHARDS, CARA E.

1967 Huron and Iroquois residence patterns, 1600–1650. *In* Iroquois culture, history and prehistory. Elisabeth Tooker ed. Albany: N.Y. State Museum and Science Service.

RITCHIE, W. A.

1955–1956 The Indian and his environment. The Conservationist. Dec.–Jan.

1965 The Archaeology of New York State. Garden City, New York: Natural History Press. [Revised edition, 1969.]

SAGARD, GABRIEL, O. F. M.

Long journey to the Huron country. G. M. Wrong, ed. Toronto: The Champlain Society.

SHIMONY, A. A.

1961 Conservatism among the Iroquois at Six Nations reserve. Yale University Publications in Anthropology 65:1–302.

SNYDERMAN, GEORGE S.

1948 Behind the tree of peace: a sociological analysis of Iroquois warfare. Pennsylvania Archaeologist XVIII:2–93.

STEWARD, J. H.

1942 The direct approach to archaeology. American Antiquity VII:337–343.

THWAITES, R. G., ED.

1905 New voyages to North-America by the Baron de Lahontan. 2 vols. Chicago.

TOOKER, ELISABETH

1964 An ethnography of the Huron Indians, 1615–1649. Bureau of American Ethnology Bulletin 190.

TRELEASE, ALLEN W.

1960 Indian affairs in colonial New York: the seventeenth century. Ithaca, N.Y.: Cornell University Press.

VAN DEN BOGAERT, *see* JAMESON

VAN DOREN, CARL

1938 Benjamin Franklin. New York: Viking.

WALLACE, A. F. C.

1958 The Dekanawidah myth analysed as the record of a revitalization myth. Ethnohistory V:118–130.

WALLACE, A. F. C., AND R. FOGELSON

1962 Culture and personality. Biennial Review of Anthropology, 1961. Bernard Siegel, ed. Palo Alto, Calif.: Stanford University Press.

1970 The death and rebirth of the Seneca. New York: Knopf.

WALLACE, PAUL A. W.

1945 Conrad Weiser: friend of colonist and Mohawk. Philadelphia: University of Pennsylvania Press.

WAUGH, F. W.

1916 Iroquois foods and food preparation. Ottawa, Canada: Geological Survey, Anthropological Series XII, Memoir (86).

WHITE, MARIAN E.

1961 Iroquois culture history in the Niagara frontier area of New York State. Anthropological Papers, Museum of Anthropology, University of Michigan No. 16. Ann Arbor: The University of Michigan.

WRIGHT, JAMES V.

1966 The Ontario Iroquois tradition. National Museum of Canada Bulletin 210, Anthropological Series (75).

WROTH, LAWRENCE C.

1928 The Indian treaty as literature. The Yale Review, ser. 2, vol. 36, pt. 2, p. 17; pt. 2, pp. 750–766.

6

The Chippewa of the Upper Great Lakes: A Study in Sociopolitical Change HAROLD HICKERSON

Very little is known about the Chippewa[1] before European contact. It is known that they had a stone age culture adapted to a mixed deciduous-coniferous forest region with many lakes and streams. This region is centered in the northern upper Great Lakes. They lived in groups of perhaps 100 to 150 related persons, and these made their living chiefly by fishing and hunting. Their manufactures were simple and based upon materials they took from their immediate environment, such as containers and utensils fashioned from bark, stone, and animal horn and a goodly amount of crude ceramic ware; they made spears and arrows tipped with flint or bone to catch fish and game, and they made fishing nets from plant fibers; and they made scrapers and knives of flint, bone awls, and other equally simple items to process hides.

They wore skins of various kinds of deer, including moose and caribou, and pelts of beaver and otter, roughly tanned and tailored. Their houses were built by covering sticks and small poles bent to form a dome, or arc, with birch bark and matted grass. These could house a domestic family or be large enough to accommodate several families. They made canoes of birch bark reinforced with the gum of spruce or pine, and in these they navigated the Great Lakes and tributary waters in the summertime. For winter they buried their canoes so that they would not snap in the intense cold. In winter they crossed the snow to reach their hunting grounds and to track game on raquettes whose frames were usually white birch, laced with moose-hide thongs. To transport heavy goods, including animals they killed, they dragged wooden toboggans across the snow. They carried their infants in wooden cradle boards strapped to the back of the mother or an older child.

All the essential articles they used they made themselves, and all adult members of the group could perform most of the required tasks. Although they perhaps carried on some formal trade with neighboring peoples like the Iroquoian Huron, exchanging hides of moose and caribou for corn, they were primarily self-sufficient and self-contained, each group avoiding close contacts with all but near neighbors to whom they were related by marriage and with whom they shared traditions, myths, and ceremonies.

In their ceremonial and religious life, insofar as it is known, they emphasized direct relations with objects in their immediate surroundings. Religious leaders, shamans, were men and women who had magical ways to ensure that game animals and fish would be available to the people. In return for the animals making themselves vulnerable, they did not overexploit them, and they performed certain ceremonies of thanksgiving that would ensure their future supply. The shamans also had special medicines, mainly herbs and poultices of various kinds, and employed these with other procedures to prevent and cure sickness and repair wounds.

Their belief system centered in establishing and maintaining close and friendly relations with spirits investing and giving form to the animals and plants upon which they subsisted and even to such nonanimate things as stars, stones, storms, hills, and lakes.

The technological and ideological systems, then, were geared to the simple needs of small communities whose members exploited a difficult environment without using artificial means to produce animal or plant food.

Artifactual and belief systems are known in general through cultural data garnered through archeological and ethnographic field work not only on Chippewa, but on contiguous and even distant cultures on a similar level of development. But what of the social system and the polity that gave the technological system form and the ideological system birth? Little is known about this from historical research. We can assume minimally that the prehistorical Chippewa peoples had an egalitarian political system founded in kin relations. Each group of relatives comprised a corporate unit tied to a territory and maintained ties of hospitality with similar neighboring units to whom they were related through marriage. We will have more to say on this later.

The Chippewa, like other peoples of the upper Great Lakes and neighboring areas, by the end of the seventeenth century had come to place great dependence on European trade goods, in fact could not survive without them. Although certain items continued to be manufactured in the local area, particularly those that were specially adapted to the subboreal climate, like toboggans, canoes, and snowshoes, the importation of metal wares and textiles, as well as objects of art and decoration like the famed Venetian glass beads, placed them in an inseparable relationship with Europeans. But despite their reliance on the importation of new commodities from Europe, they tried to preserve social and political autonomy, although the *degree* of autonomy was ever a matter of debate, the issue around which factions could readily form.

A problem faced by the Chippewa throughout contact history, then, has been how to preserve sociopolitical autonomy while depending upon Euro-American trade goods for survival.

Despite universal acceptance of European goods, which in most respects represented a marked increase in efficiency and comfort over aboriginal goods, each tribe in the area of the upper Great Lakes responded differently to European inroads. We have, for example, the career of the Fox Indians. Without access to fur grounds except as middlemen to other Indian groups, and because of French and Indian opposition unable to solidify that position, the Fox not only exacted toll from Mississippi-bound French traders at the portage between the Fox and Wisconsin rivers in central Wisconsin, but plotted with the Iroquois and Albany English to expand the latter's influence and interest to the west. So "troublesome" were the Fox during the last part of the seventeenth century and the first part of the eighteenth that they became subject to a policy of genocide exerted against them by the French and the Indians of the northern Great Lakes. The historical movement of the main body of Fox was ever westward, first, in earliest trade days from lower Michigan to Wisconsin, thence, after defeats at the hands of the French, to the Mississippi, thence into central Iowa, and finally into Indian Territory. Except for the final stage in this movement, it was normally one that involved the displacement of entire clusters of population, village populations, and not fragmented villages remaining as residual groups in old areas. Moreover, in the 1730s the Fox were joined by their close relatives, the Sauk, and after that date their history is virtually a single history. Such movements, of course, involved altering subsistence and trade patterns to adapt to changing environments.

This contrasts with the migrations of the Chippewa against whom no conscious policy of attrition was ever developed by Europeans. The character of their migrations was that of old villages giving birth to new, involving pioneer groups opening up frontier areas in defiance of Indian hostility or in ecozones that once were inhospitable but had become desirable because they provided fur. Unlike the Fox, Chippewa invariably left residual populations in the parent communities to which the members of the daughter groups remained attached until strong enough or scattered enough to follow their own paths.

By the beginning of the nineteenth century, Chippewa groups had expanded from a narrow area around eastern Lake Superior and northern Lake Huron in all directions through a vast region in the center of the continent, stretching from the lower peninsula of Ontario through both peninsulas of Michigan, through the northern parts of the North tier states as far as eastern Montana, and through contiguous regions of

Canada including most of the western part of the southern drainage area of Hudson Bay.

The Fox and Sauk were agriculturalists and were tied to semi-permanent villages vulnerable to spoliation by vengeful French and later by American settlers (as in the Black Hawk War in 1832) expanding the frontier. Partial reliance on field produce in combination with a weak geographical and political position forced the abandonment of such villages, and this to a great degree determined the character of their migrations. This is not to say that the Fox, cooperating among several village groups, could not at times assemble a formidable force; it was indeed their very strength and cohesion in military activity that proved their greatest weakness, for it permitted them to become at various times combatants against the French, later, the Americans, and hence, vulnerable to reprisal and defeat.

Chippewa, on the other hand, by the late seventeenth century were no longer tied to Great Lakes fisheries, where they had been living from time immemorial; because of their ready access to trade goods including firearms in a relatively productive region, they could fragment to seek new fur, fish, and game grounds. The populations left behind were of a size suited to local subsistence and trade provisions. Not having been subject to the hostility of Europeans, trading and living as they were in a region not suitable for European settlers, and having little cohesion among their own settlements, their migrations could take an expansionist form. *Their* overall weakness, then, proved to be an advantage. Other peoples, Menominee, Kickapoo, Winnebago, Sioux, and still others, followed different patterns of movement. Some, like the Menominee, remained in traditional areas until the reservation period; others like the Kickapoo underwent constant relocations. Movements of the various peoples comprise part of the history of the upper Great Lakes and connect the lakes with areas beyond. Culture change among such groups and factors of acculturation involving ceremonial as well as sociopolitical aspects of organization cannot be understood without reference to these events. What has been accomplished with this history, however, are but pages scattered thinly in a volume that is yet to be written, indeed for which the basic research has scarcely begun.

General Aspects of Chippewa Sociopolitical History

In the following I attempt to reconstruct the history of Chippewa sociopolitical institutions to bring some pages of the Chippewa chapter together. I emphasize early phases in the contact history of the Chippewa and how relations with Europeans affected important aspects of tribal and local organization. For the Chippewa the period of contact and intensification of relations of trade, first with Indian middlemen, then with Europeans, occurred between *c.* 1615 and 1850.[2]

Let us first set forth briefly four stages of sociopolitical development among Chippewa, before elaborating on aspects of the sociopolitical organization. These stages we look upon as representing adaptations to the imposition of external economic and political systems congruent with the availability of raw resources. These stages should not be viewed in terms of the total replacement of past systems, but rather as shifts to new norms while keeping much traditional material.

First, there were *autonomous patrilineal descent groups,* or local clans, of which there were about twenty-five. Such clans appear to have characterized proto-contact[3] Chippewa organization. This stage, under the impact of direct trade, first with Huron middlemen, later with French, gave way in early historical times to the *political village.* The village, incorporating under a single political authority several descent groups, arose and flowered under conditions of peaceful trade and amity with Sioux neighbors living to the south and west.

Village organization began to break down as its trade channels were taken over by the French and survived only in limited areas where Chippewa were frequently at war with their former allies, the Sioux, who continued to occupy adjacent territory. Upon the collapse of the village the *composite hunting band* assumed the role of the basic socio-economic unit.

The *composite hunting-trapping band,* the third stage, was adapted to relations demanding the primary production of fur and subsistence. This organization, representing a more or less stable adjustment to the fur trade and relations with French, then British, and finally American, garrisons and agencies, lasted among southwestern Chippewa from about 1730 to 1850.

The composite band as a viable unit in turn disappeared as game areas became depleted due to the plunder required by the trade and encroaching American settlement. Depletion of game and advancing settlement coincided with the land cession treaty period, which in upper Michigan, Wisconsin, and Minnesota after some minor cessions during the second and third decades of the nineteenth century, got well under way in 1837 and continued until the 1880s, by which time all Chippewa communities were located on reservations.

Among Chippewa north of the international boundary the village stage did not last as long as among southwestern Chippewa or, for reasons that will be given, did not exist to any degree at all. Also, due to more rigorous conditions of life in the North, the bands tended to be smaller and more sparsely distributed than in the Southwest, but they were equally composite (Bishop, n.d.) despite agnatic tendencies related to frequent instances of virilocal residence. *Agnatic filiation* does not mean the exclusion of members allied through *cognatic relationship,* but constitutes merely a style, or pattern, of affiliation. Particularization of social life in the North did not result, as it did in the South during the reservation period, in the virtual *autonomy of the nuclear family,* as long as fur trapping continued to be the mainstay of the economy. Trapping and related pursuits require the cooperation of at least two men, and hunting of large game as well as fishing was best pursued by more men than would comprise a trapping partnership. Such activities coordinating the efforts of several mature men and their youthful followers persist here and there in Canada even today.

Recent clustering of members of small multifamily bands at lake sites around stores and schools in the North has not resulted as yet in cohesive village organization, even though councils are elected under government supervision to represent the communities in internal and external affairs (cf. Dunning, 1959a, 1959b). If such cohesion does occur, it will not depend upon the extention of kin ties, but rather on the development of enterprises demanding the cooperation of related and nonrelated village members. The status of American reservation Chippewa communities is discussed at somewhat greater length below.

In sum, then, the four stages of sociopolitical development are: (1) patrilineal descent groups (proto-contact), (2) multi-descent group villages (early contact), (3) composite hunting bands (pre-reservation contact), and (4) nuclear or small extended families (reservation). The village stage may be missing in specific areas due to local conditions making large population clusters nonadaptive. We now turn to a more detailed examination of general processes of change.

Precontact and Proto-contact Organization

The precontact organization was communal and based entirely upon relations of kinship. The notion of the autonomous familistic patrilocal band (Service, 1962) fits postcontact society but does not illuminate pre- or proto-contact Chippewa groups. Proto-contact Chippewa local groups were territorial-based descent groups related one to another across contiguous territories through marriage. Such groups maintained ties of cordiality through exchange of access to fish and game areas. Such groups had interlocking and complementary ceremonials and beliefs. Ties among such groups, then, developed from direct economic, social, and ideological relations.

I have indicated elsewhere that the shape of such proto-contact groups was the patrilineal clan, thus stressing factors of *descent* and *territory* rather than *residence*. The population of such groups ranged in many instances well upward of one hundred, at least in the eastern Lake Superior region, where we hear of concentrations of population from the first French to enter the region. The clans, of which there were about twenty-five, grouped in five exogamous phratries, or brotherhoods, of linked clans, were *totemic;* that is, the members believed themselves descendants of an animal ancestor, such as a beaver, sturgeon, loon, marten, and so forth. By maintaining strict observance of restrictions on marriage within these totemic groups, clans and phratries, orderly social and economic relations were maintained over broad areas of the Chippewa domain through intermarriage and the exchange of courtesies among the many local groups.

Did this organization characterize Chippewa before *any* trade with European or Indian middlemen? Prehistoric middens and hunting sites in the upper Great Lakes in and near historical Chippewa areas indicate the existence of villages, implying regular relations among populations that were sedentary for at least part of the year. If we presume organization based on kinship in *proto*-contact times, we must infer such organization in *pre*contact times, because society based on kinship cannot arise (but can only disappear) as the result of intensive trade relations.

Were these societies in precontact times patrilineal or matrilineal? The widespread distribution of culture traits throughout the entire American subarctic indicating matrilineal norms (see Hickerson, 1967b) might suggest prior existence of matrilineal organization everywhere. Among the Chippewa such traits as temporary uxorilocal residence, bride service, and sororal polygyny look like survivals from matrilineal systems. Trade relations with Europeans in the East and with East Asians and, later, Russians, in the West could have led in some instances to the dispersal of communities and the concentration of wealth in the hands of leaders of small emergent patriarchates, in others to the preemption of rights to trading regions by leaders of larger patrilineal or composite groups acting in concert. However, there is a lack of ethnohistorical evidence from which such a historical stage could be deduced on any more than a highly speculative basis, and the weight of testimony by present American anthropologists, theoretical and historical, would be away from such an inference.

If a change from matriliny to patriliny *did* occur, it would represent the first significant change in community organization among northern collectors. Not only that, but concentration of trade wealth in the hands of petty patriarchs or agnatic or cognatic partners in larger groups would lay the basis for the intensification of socioeconomic individualism and the further establishment of competitive norms as trade and other relations with more advanced economic systems outside increased. Among the Chippewa, middleman trade during the seventeenth and early eighteenth centuries appears to have been an enterprise summoning the joint efforts of most, or all, of the men of large village communities. Chippewa were never exclusively traders, however; in later times, when their trade with the Sioux was disrupted, small bands headed by one or more skilled trappers emerged. These were adapted to the primary production of fur, a pursuit that did not involve uneven accumulation of wealth. This is elaborated below.

The major change we have been discussing, the change from matriliny to patriliny, if it took place, did so before the coming of Europeans literate or sophisticated enough to describe it. Hypotheses for such reconstructions totter on a very weak empirical base.

The Political Village

We first see the Chippewa in history (cf. Hickerson, 1960; 1962; 1966) divided into several groups with animal names living in the area where Lake Huron and Lake Superior join. In the 1640s and for a generation after, they and other Algonkians, closely related by language and culture, congregated in numbers upward of 1,000 during the summer at Sault Ste. Marie. There they fished, traded, and carried on ceremonials, the most striking of which was the Feast of the Dead, a ceremony for the renewal of alliances. In winter they dispersed over a broad area in smaller groups to hunt and trap. Some were middlemen who carried the fur trade to hinterland peoples. The activities concentrated in this region, and warfare with Indian competitors, chiefly the Iroquois from the lower Lakes, added to the ferment. The old autonomous kin units were not adapted to new conditions involving (1) the occupation and utilization of vast extents of territory demanded by the search for fur, (2) the maintenance of trading entrepôts common to a variety of tribal groups, and (3) defense against economic and military inroads, potential or realized, of Indian and European competitors. Such factors underlay the redistribution of political authority over wider groupings; hence, the concentration of populations in larger and more elastic settlements.

The first fruit of these factors was the clustering of Algonkians in large, permanent villages at such places as Sault Ste. Marie, Mackinac, Arbre Croche, Green Bay, and the Chequamegon and Keweenaw peninsulas of western Lake Superior. The Chippewa, first centered in historical times at Sault Ste. Marie, and later (1680–1736) in the Chequamegon-Keweenaw area, now incorporated within single tribal-village aggregate populations of former independent territorial clan segments. This is not to say that all members of all related clans placed themselves under the political authority of the tribal village; indeed, small Chippewa, or Chippewa-like, populations at the same time were scattering into the region north of Lake Superior to get fur as trappers or petty traders (cf. Masson, 1890, II, 241–242), and these may at that time have represented clan fragments detaching themselves from the greater clans of which they had been part, perhaps as "conservatives" separating from their "progressive" brothers (Masson, 1890, II, 246–247). Others, like some of the Amikwa, remained in their original clan villages and seem to have maintained local autonomy for a while, until finally absorbed by larger and more diversified populations. Still, we can for this period typify Chippewa as living in multi-clan villages much larger than the unilineal local groups of former times.

The large Chippewa settlements incorporating members of the old clans were founded on trade relations with contiguous Sioux (and perhaps to a certain extent with Cree) and on subsistence gleaned from Lake Superior and from open woodland areas in the Sioux country. Their relations with the French were for the most part stable and remained so as long as direct French trade in their area was confined to the Great Lakes depots. Between the early 1680s, when Daniel Greysolon, Sieur Duluth, found his trading endeavors arrested by the French policy of restriction of the movements of the *coureurs de bois,* and the early 1720s, when this policy was changed to one of exploration and trade toward the west, the Chippewa settlements along the south shore of Lake Superior appear to have flourished.

There is unfortunately no contemporary description of the large Chippewa villages. We know only that over 1,000 persons lived at Chequamegon, and a small French garrison under a commandant who also had rights to the trade of the region was close by. However, we can with a certain sense of confidence infer from later sources (cf. Hickerson, 1963) the *tribal* character of the Chequamegon settlement, indicated by a thriving Midewiwin cult, a religious and medicine society that incorporated old practices of curing, a tribal mythology including migration myths, and regular ceremonies of initiation conducted by a large and apparently duosexual priesthood.

We do not know if the smaller settlement at Keweenaw had its own cult and its own trade and, thus, a separate political existence. The status of the residual settlement of Chippewa at Sault Ste. Marie is also not known, except that population there had shrunk drastically from the peak it had reached in the mid-seventeenth century.

On the north shore the situation is clouded by lack of continuous data. However, a report for 1736 (NYCD, IX, 1054) indicates a population of over 300 persons at the mouth of the Kaministiquia River (the present Fort William, Ontario). It is known that later this was an important trading center for Indians and Europeans. Aside from Kaministiquia, there was a small settlement of about one hundred persons at the Michipicoton River on the north shore to the east. These together may well have represented the entire Chippewa population north of Lake Superior at that time; there was no ecological base for a much greater population, even if the inhabitants of Kaministiquia had middleman trading rights over much of the vast region to the north. We know nothing, however, about the principles of organization of the Kaministiquia settlement, not even whether its members were mainly traders or trappers. Such a population concentration might indicate that they carried some trade to small Algonkian groups scattered in the hinterland north of the international boundary.

We have, then, manifested first in the embryonic tribal community at Sault Ste. Marie, and later in the developed Chequamegon settlement, and possibly in other smaller settlements as well, a form of organization new to Chippewa, that of the *village* incorporating a number of related groups. If we postulate precontact change from matrilineal to patrilineal organization among archetypical Chippewa, then this represents the second significant change in Chippewa society, that of the local kin group, or clan, transformed to the political multi-clan village.

This did not involve the decay of communal organization, which is to say, kin-based organization. In fact, proscription of cross-cousin marriage, which I have inferred took place at Chequamegon at the end of the seventeenth century (Hickerson, 1962, chap. 4), served to extend kin ties and cooperation among village inhabitants. Organization of social units was on its way to becoming "composite," or bilateral, and this manifested itself, as we will see, more strongly in the next stage of development. Patrilineal clan ties persisted, and clan-mates continued to call each other "brother." But the clan, now engulfed by the village, served less and less as the unit of authority and control, surviving in technonymy, as a unit of exogamy, and perhaps in certain rituals, especially those of mourning.

We know nothing of intra-village conflict during this period. Stable relations with the French and with Indian allies like the Sioux permitting the development of communal norms on a broader base than formerly, and employing ceremonials and myths to reinforce extended social ties, may have mitigated strife within the village. Having access to trade goods and preserving a degree of autonomy in trade and political organization, these Chippewa may well have been in a state of general florescence. It is perhaps significant in this regard that the Chippewa historian of the mid-nineteenth century William Whipple Warren referred to the Chequamegon period as a golden age (MHC, V, 95–108).

The Composite Band

The 1730s saw the end of this period, the decline of the Chequamegon settlement and the formation of a large number of villages smaller than the Chequamegon village. The period of the fragmentation of southwestern Chippewa society we call the *pre-reservation period,* for the entire period that saw the deterioration of communities was a direct consequence of Euro-American expansion leading to engulfment and final confinement of surviving groups to reservations.

The dismemberment of the Chequamegon village occurred as a result of the expansionist policy of the French in Canada to oppose the expansion of French from Louisiana northward along the Mississippi, a movement that threatened to drain away trade in the upper reaches of the great river. This threat was early realized, for in 1700, at about the time of the founding of Louisiana, the trader and prospector Charles Pierre Le Sueur traded with Sioux along the Blue Earth branch of the Minnesota River, using Louisiana as his base of operations (WHC, XVI, 168 ff.). To thwart this expansion, and incidentally to oppose the expansion of British trade southwestward from Hudson Bay via Cree middlemen, the Canadians outfitted expeditions to establish trading posts in areas like Lake Winnipeg where only Indians had been before, or, as in the case of the upper Mississippi River, where there had been only sporadic French occupancy. The best known figure in this exploration and trade was Pierre Gaultier, Sieur de La Vérendrye (cf. Burpee, 1927), who over a period of twenty years was able, with the cooperation of Cree and Assiniboin, whom he weaned away from the British, to extend a series of posts along what is now the international boundary region west of Lake Superior and northwest as far as the Saskatchewan River.

Such expansion could only be carried out with the help of the Indians of the country, secured through granting trading privileges, that is, through trading with them at specified points and leaving to them the role of middlemen to interior groups. In historical perspective such relations were the first step in a process that saw Europeans usurp these privileges, as the first probings led to the establishment of regular posts, in many cases fortresses, then settlements or agencies from which authority could be extended.

One effect of trade with the Cree, which of course involved traffic in firearms, was the need to mollify Sioux of the Mississippi headwaters region, who held the Cree in bitter enmity. To accomplish this, the French attempted and to some degree succeeded in establishing direct trade with Sioux at posts on the Mississippi where it forms the boundary between the present states of Minnesota and Wisconsin. This post was founded in 1727, abandoned due to Fox hostility in 1729, reestablished in 1731, and again abandoned in 1737 due to general warfare among tribes in the region (Charlevoix, 1902, 277; WHC, X, 302; WHC, XVII, 11 ff).

The French traders took cognizance of the presence of Chippewa contiguous to their trading area by agreeing in a charter drawn up with the Canadian government "not to trade nor hunt in the direction of Point Chagouamigon, elsewhere than in the hunting grounds whither the Sioux go . . ." (WHC, XVII, 11). Despite this injunction to avoid Chippewa trading and hunting areas, the Chippewa of Chequamegon, as middlemen to the very Sioux with whom these French were now carrying direct trade, were by-passed, hence placed in a position of competition with the French as carriers of commodities and also with the Sioux upon whom they had come to rely not only as a source of fur, but for access to hunting grounds from which they harvested game for subsistence.

The warfare that erupted between Chippewa and Sioux in the late 1730s (cf. Hickerson, 1962, chap. 2) was a direct consequence of Canadian expansionist policy, a policy that was not relinquished until the loss of Canada by the French in 1760 and that was continued by the British when they took control. As a result of their need to get fur and food, the Chippewa waged relentless war against their erstwhile allies, the Sioux. At first they succeeded in reducing a large area south and west of Lake Superior to a buffer zone, entering it only to hunt game and kill Sioux (cf. Carver, 1779, 102–103, map facing xvi); then, as Sioux began moving westward in large numbers drawn by the Plains horse culture, which was reaching the northeastern Plains in the mid-eighteenth century, Chippewa began to occupy permanently lake and river sites in northern Wisconsin and later (1780) lake sites in northern Minnesota, including the entire region of the headwaters of the Mississippi. As they did so, Sioux who remained in the East, their ranks thinned by the westward movement of substantial numbers of them, fell back to the Minnesota River and the Mississippi south of the present Minneapolis–St. Paul area, where they established villages and opposed successfully further inroads by their enemies to the north.

Major results of these movements for the Chippewa were (1) the destruction for all time of their status as middleman traders between French distributors and Indian producers, (2) their participation in constant abrasive warfare with contiguous Sioux who had not adopted the Plains horse culture, and (3) their fragmentation into numerous villages, large and small, distributed over so broad an area that economic, ceremonial, and political cooperation and communication were not maintained among them.

The effect of these events was to place the Chippewa in direct relation with Euro-American traders as primary producers of fur, and to enhance the status of younger men in the village as warriors, often in opposition, especially in the more populous villages, to the older civil leadership. Perhaps, most important, the *hunting band*, the largest numbering under a score of men and their dependents, the smallest a few related families, became the basic socioeconomic unit, even in those places near the Sioux frontier where several bands resided together in single villages during the summer season, when trapping was not carried on.

These bands were bilateral, or "composite," in overall membership and tended to split away from village bodies when conditions of war and ecology permitted; thus, there was a proliferation of residential units throughout Wisconsin and Minnesota during the pre-reservation period (cf. Hickerson, 1962, chap. 3). Throughout the first half of the nineteenth century there were more than a score of Chippewa settlements, most of them with a trading post or fort. But again, during the 1780–1850 period among the southwestern Chippewa, communal norms persisted, and this is reflected in the total absence of the development of family hunting territories and other forms of property vested in individuals or small clusters of agnates. However, the absence of such forms of tenure must have related chiefly to the state of warfare. This is so because in contiguous areas where warfare was not important, including the wooded sections of the international boundary region east of the Red River of the North, during the same period there was a nascent movement toward family or small-band proprietorship over trapping grounds, encouraged by the fur traders, a form of tenure that became fully developed during the reservation era (cf. Hickerson, 1967a).

Despite the adherence to communal norms in the frontier Chippewa villages (the largest of which, Leech Lake, maintained a population of about 800 divided in three or four settlements), symptoms of decay are seen in such events as the development of factions along the military-civil axis in the larger villages and of intracommunity and even intra band brawling resulting frequently in serious injuries and at times even in death. These brawls occurred chiefly during periods of orgiastic drunkenness in the vicinity of the trading posts. Drunkenness itself was symptomatic of the decay of old mechanisms enforcing hospitality; the distribution of liquor fell to the lot of successful trappers, perhaps at times to shamans, and this enabled them to assume the guise of "chiefs." Under the fur trade, provisions were only sporadically available for distribution; such items as venison and wild rice were traded in large amounts to the traders, and trade goods were consumed within small extended family units. The function of the distribution of liquor to be consumed communally within the band, then, was the assertion and maintenance of leadership.

Among Chippewa north of the international boundary it is clear (cf. Hickerson, 1967a; Bishop, n.d.) that during the last part of the eighteenth century and the first part of the nineteenth, composite bands formed the basic economic and social units, but the village, or a broader entity coordinating the activities of several such, was entirely absent. Such bands were trapping and hunting units, and although several of them might have come together for fishing at appropriate seasons, the village as a political unit would have been superfluous. I am of the opinion now, although I have not stated so explicitly in the past, that the village among southwestern Chippewa continued in existence right up to the reservation period only because conditions of war persisted. In the case of certain fairly large settlements on the south shore of Lake Superior, away from the war zones, located at places where there was a great abundance of fish, especially sturgeon, large numbers of people came together for the express purpose of fishing; but such settlements were without political or military organization. These settlements were somewhat like those north of the Great Lakes, where members of scattered trapping units came together at favored fishing spots, only to disband when the fishing was over. The communal habits of such people, north and south, were manifested in their erection of weirs used to trap great numbers of fish, which were then distributed among all those who participated.

Indeed, the development at Leech Lake and other large villages of a volatile "warrior" sodality, with its own rules, chiefs, ceremonies, and policies, was symptomatic of the decay of organization based upon kinship alone. Upon the commencement of the reservation period through cession treaties with the United States during the last half of the nineteenth century, when warfare ended and external matters relating to the political life of the reservations were mediated through the Indian agencies, the warrior groups disappeared, leaving a few songs and drums to faintly echo past wellsprings of action. Factions crystallized around other groupings: medicine cult groups, drum societies, church groups, local and tribal councils, and so on. Disputes were fought out in narrower arenas, once the land base and social autonomy were lost. The reservation, of course, put an end to the land base, the village, and the composite band; and social and economic life became so particularistic, or "atomistic," as to convince observers of the present, even professional anthropologists (cf. Hallowell, 1955; Barnouw, 1950; Landes, 1937), that "atomism" had always typified Chippewa social relations.

The Particularization of Social Relations

We began this essay by discussing the germination of factions pivoting in early times around the question of the degree of participation and cooperation with Europeans. In the Great Lakes region this could involve a high degree of complexity in intertribal relations. At the same time that commodities could be obtained more cheaply through direct trade with Europeans, it was not necessarily advantageous in the long run for Indians to allow Europeans free run of the country. Those Indians who avidly sought direct trade in a strong sense were seeking political extinction. This essential contradiction is one that is reminiscent of certain types of imperial-colonial relations where those native to the country are producers or, as local middlemen, procurers of raw products to be exchanged for commodities over whose source of manufacture and supply they have no control. Europeans, whether traders, missionaries, or agents, in the final analysis could and did in times of stress hold withdrawal of trade as the ultimate threat in bending Indians to their will. Was this contradiction understood by Indians?

Certainly, by the time of the land cession treaty era of the nineteenth century, Chippewa spokesmen had no illusions concerning the implications of sale of lands, but it was too late to assert strong claims to fruitful occupation due to a general depletion of resources. This was true especially where trapping, hunting, and fishing had been the mainstays; these activities demanded free roving within large extents of ground, and game of all kinds, even fish, became depleted through over-exploitation by Indians and traders or disappeared in the wake of American settlement. Indian leaders were unable to press successfully the interests of their groups in negotiations, no matter how sophisticated their appraisal of treaty transactions. Factional divisions occurred within local groups when the full impact of ill-made treaties became felt.

In gross form, then, I am suggesting: (1) changes in social norms over the historical period related directly to the imposition of outside socio-economic and ideological systems that everywhere gathered momentum; (2) such outside systems were in their nature exploitative and continue to be so; and (3) changes in organization, if for a while adapted to specific conditions within local environments, in the long run did not result in accommodation to real relations, that is, relations of exploitation.

What has been the effect of these factors on community life? Again, we cannot discuss here at any length the specific effects of such broad historical events on the local community, except to indicate variability, as we have done, within certain broad frameworks.

But an issue arises that does not at first blush appear to lend itself to analysis, the issue of the increasing individualization and nucleation of social and economic relations. It would be meaningless to deny that interpersonal hostilities existed among Chippewa in olden times, when kinship was the determinant for the shape of social groups. But differences and antagonisms of the kind that occur in any group of people could be resolved without violence through structured relations: the distribution of food, joking, dances, games, and the giving of gifts. Hostilities, then, could be suppressed in the context of a variety of behavior sanctioned as custom, integral to the foundation and continuation of local groups.

Agencies of control, channels through which interpersonal and broader relations, hostile and otherwise, could be expressed in acceptable ways, were worn away under the unceasing impact of the trade and other relations in which Euro-Americans played a leading role. But not only did such media as we have mentioned lose their function of supporting the solidarity of the groups, whether in prosperity or adversity, or decay altogether; so did other formal mechanisms relating directly to the business of getting a living and keeping the community going.

I should like to focus attention on the question of leadership. Certain historical data seem to indicate that Europeans filled positions of leadership within social groups that in other more cohesive societies fell to "chiefs" (cf. Barnouw, 1950, 44–46). Such functionaries—fur traders, missionaries, agents—appear to have filled a void, the implication being that leadership was absent from aboriginal groups. There is admittedly a superficial basis for such an assumption; indeed, under certain circumstances, especially in times of turmoil, Euro-Americans were able to momentarily assume and assert leadership. Thus, during times of warfare among Europeans when trade goods were scarce, certain traders could assume authority within a band or village by distributing trade goods in exchange for military help or the promise of noninterference in military affairs. As I have pointed out elsewhere (1967a), actual leadership[4] by Europeans was rare, although it is abundantly evident in numerous sources throughout the historical literature that once trade had become established, Europeans inevitably played an important role in the affairs of local groups and to some degree dictated the policies and movements of such groups. How did this come about?

Patterns of trade and trade relations set the style for other relations involving not the assertion by Euro-Americans of leadership of communities, but rather the assumption by them of the role of intermediaries in community life. This mediatory role could in particular instances lead to the assumption of a dictatorial pose. Agents were able to mediate affairs within local groups with varying degrees of success, even during the pre-reservation period. For example, the journals of Lawrence Talia-ferro (Minnesota Historical Society ms.), who served as agent for the Sioux and Chippewa of Minnesota and Wisconsin during the period 1819–1839, are full of allusions to complaints made by Chippewa civil leaders of the usurpation of their obligations by young men whose great skill in trapping resulted in their being invested with the "chief's coat" by traders. But the agent himself issued medals and flags as part of the duties of his office to certain civil leaders. And although Taliaferro, for one, was sympathetic to the older civil leadership insofar as it continued to exist, he in effect became another channel through which conflict be-tween the "old-and-wise" men and the "young-and-foolish" men was expressed.

Leadership within the local group arising from trade relations was often ephemeral. But it must be mentioned that in certain areas, par-ticularly where social units were small and discrete, the traders were forced to recognize men who preserved their leadership over many years, perhaps in their capacity as shamans, certainly not because they were rich, as could conceivably have been the case. Such men wore the chief's coat on ceremonial occasions and had the prerogative of distributing liquor, but such riches accrued from status, not status from riches. Need-less to say, such leadership continued only as long as the man retained powers of curing and the ability to find subsistence for the people.

Still keeping in mind the idea that relations of trade established the pattern of the Euro-American acting as *intermediary* and not *leader,* we are able, through canvassing the journals of missionaries among the Chippewa in Minnesota during the pre-treaty 1830s, to see how they tried to take over leadership and how they failed. One of the most articu-late and least successful of the missionaries of the American Board, Wil-liam T. Boutwell (cf. Hickerson, 1965; Minnesota Historical Society ms.), described Chippewa in Minnesota as communal and without any concept of private ownership (Neill, 1891, 437–438). He wrote of the necessity to break habits so "inveterate." This was to be done by issuing food and clothing to persons who would work as individuals and cease sharing with their fellows.

Over a period of four years Boutwell tried to introduce practices in harmony with his ideas. He even "purchased" from an old woman, the sister of a prominent civil leader, a sugar maple grove upon which he established his mission and farm. Despite early successes in attracting into his house some of the older civil leaders, his every effort was met in the long run with frustration, and he was finally ejected from Leech Lake by the "young men" who resented his meddling in their affairs without contributing to their well-being.

The attempt to exert direct leadership through a mission during a period when there was still fur and forage to be taken was an error. Actually, during certain seasons when the Chippewa found it hard to get food, they tried to make a leader of Boutwell by raiding his stores of potatoes and dried fish, an overture he met by protesting their actions informally and also formally in council. Had he been able to give freely of his abundance of food and clothing, without the burden of an ideology that led him to restrict their distribution to hypothetical Chippewa already becoming rich through individual exertions, he might well have fared better. On one occasion in council a Chippewa compared him unfavorably with traders.

How did the traders, then, who were in a sense more *Indian* than missionaries, contribute to the decay of social groups? Frank G. Speck and others have emphasized that traders, thinly distributed throughout the vast Algonkian subarctic, could scarcely have affected Indian ways to the extent, for example, of introducing such an important norm as the *family hunting territory system*. Leacock (1954) has concurred in this and sees familistic tenure as a less direct response to conditions engendered by the fur trade. I will not detail her arguments: they are well known. But one factor seems to me of overriding importance and must apply at one time or another everywhere the trade was instituted. This was a factor growing out of the very conditions of trade, at the same time generating its social relations. This is the factor of the *individualization of the distribution of food* (cf. Hickerson, 1967a).

There are one or two matters of primary importance that must be understood before this principle is understood. Once the fur trade was introduced in a region, it affected *all* persons in reach of the posts. Trading forts with their outposts encompassed areas of great extent. Before the beginning of the nineteenth century there were no Algonkians in the subarctic living outside of the area of direct trade with Europeans. In another article (1967b) I quoted a relevant journal entry by a Hudson's Bay Company trader. A Mr. Sutherland in 1780 reported a conversation he had with a clerk who had sent a post employee to the area between the Albany and Severn rivers to see if he could contact Indians to drum up trade:[5]

> Mr. Solomon asked him very foolishly if he had any Indians that had never seen White people yet, the man assured him very prettily—o yes Says he I did indeed Sir, Lord Says Solomon can't we get among them, to be shour you can what is to hinder you, well done my lade, I will double you your wages for this lucky jaunt of yours. Oh Sir, I am afeared you will not because those Indians that I saw never killed any thing in their Lives. What the divel kind of Indians are they says Solomon. why says he I never saw any but two small children and I thought they had never seen white people because they seemed to be afraid of me—Is this the wisdom of Solomon to

Winnebago camp in Wisconsin, early twentieth century, typical of dwellings still in use in many Great Lakes Indian communities at that time.
(Courtesy of the Jackson County Historical Society, Black River Falls, Wisconsin.)

imagine that there was Indians within three or four hundred miles of hudsons bay had never seen white people. Oh thou foolish blockhead change they name [HBC, 1780].

It is true that traders and Indian agents "made chiefs" and interceded in the social and political life of communities. But Indians, as we have seen, were chained to the trade system once it was introduced, and this system affected all persons (not even excepting the smallest children). Entrapment in the fur trade system did not result in any disproportionate distribution of wealth among members of local groups or even between neighboring groups, only in gross distinctions between Indians and whites. The missionaries and government officials during the pre-reservation and treaty periods never ceased reminding the Indians of this as a general phenomenon, in distinction to the traders who preferred to emphasize *trade* and not *status;* hence, the *Indianness* of traders.

But it was the traders, paradoxically, who served chiefly to erode the communal system by taking over, not political leadership, but the mode of the distribution of food. They did this by enforcing upon the Indians through controlled scarcity of goods the specialized role of trappers. Quite simply, this meant that in post-trade times Chippewa and other fishermen and hunters of the North were partially neglecting traditional means of getting a livelihood, especially the fall fishery and the communal fall hunts, in order to trap to pay their debts. In pre-trade times they had been devoting their energies to gaining subsistence from land and lake in ways appropriate to seasonal changes. The loss in direct subsistence was to some degree made up for by improved material equipment enabling more intensive exploitation of certain kinds of subsistence: large copper kettles for preparing maple sugar, firearms permitting individual hunting of large cervines, steel traps for taking fur game, even gill nets for individual fishing.

It is graphically portrayed in Boutwell's journals, for example, that the traders at Leech Lake employed themselves in the fall fishery, which provided a great abundance of whitefish for their own consumption, *after* the Indians were in the trapping grounds. Again, the Northwest Company trader Duncan Cameron (Masson, 1890, II, 254) remarked that he refused to give gill nets to able hunters because then they would live on fish and not trap.

It is equally clearly stated in the journals of the traders of the Hudson's Bay Company and other companies, American and British, extending back into the late eighteenth century, how the Indians of the upper Great Lakes and interior regions supplied them with provisions during the fall, when they were coming into the wilderness areas to begin the season's business. The kind of provisions varied with place, but Chippewa here and there gave great amounts of wild rice, venison, grease, fish (including chiefly sturgeon and whitefish), and even corn in the few places where it was grown. In addition to these supplies the traders also cultivated gardens in which vegetables, mainly potatoes, were grown, the harvest providing some of their winter's food.

At times the distribution of food by Indians to traders was referred to as "presents." These presents were reciprocated by the distribution of liquor and other trivia to leaders, who in turn distributed them to their followers. These exchanges, for that is what they actually were, were nominally distinct from those that involved fur and useful commodities, the latter being expressed as "trade." Such habits of exchange, apart from the formal trade, must have characterized Indian-European relations way back in French times, indeed must have been established as soon as trade began, fitting *Indian* rather than *European* patterns of exchange.

The liquor, chiefly rum produced in the West Indies by slaves and, therefore, very cheap, was quickly exhausted by the Indians, but the provisions were stored by the traders.

What did this entail? It was the custom in much of the northern fur-trading country for Indians to come in to the posts at various times during the winter to bring fur, to replenish their supplies by taking new debts, and to *eat*. References in traders' and missionaries' journals, as well as those of Indian agents, to Indians *starving* in the trapping grounds are legion, and although some subsistence hunting was done, this was discouraged by traders because hunting, like fishing, interfered with trapping.

Indians without food, but with fur (in most cases they had consumed the food they found within the fur), came to the posts in family units or in groups of a few related families or as individuals on behalf of trapping units. They were given food, and this food was none other than the produce of the harvest and the hunt they had given the traders in the fall according to rules of reciprocity.

In aboriginal times, before trade, food was produced and distributed within local Indian groups. Some of it was consumed at the moment by great companies of people, some laid away for later distribution in caches under the ground or above the ground in trees. It was the prerogative and the obligation of local group leaders—clan leaders—to supervise the production and distribution of such food, hence, to assume the responsibility for the survival and welfare of the clan.

How had this system of local cooperation been transformed? Indians still produced subsistence communally during the summer and early fall when the traders were settling their accounts at distant entrepôts. But these same traders, by seizing provisions in exchange for baubles, achieved control of distribution. They took on some of the prerogatives and obligations of leadership, but they were incapable of assuming the one obligation that would have made them chiefs—the obligation of purposeful self-impoverishment. In breaking the cohesion of local groups, they had no leadership to supply in return.

Chippewa Today[6]

There are at present approximately 10,000 Chippewa living on reservations in northern Minnesota and probably as many as 5,000 more living in off-reservation communities, the bulk in the Twin Cities. These are some of the descendants of the historical peoples discussed in this paper, others living on reservations scattered through Ontario, Manitoba, Saskatchewan, Michigan, Wisconsin, North Dakota, and Montana. This number represents a very sharp increase over the total number of Chippewa in Minnesota at the time of the establishment of the reservations starting in the mid-nineteenth century. At that time the population could not have been more than 2,500.

According to the reports of Minnesota anthropologists, conditions among the Minnesota Chippewa are highly variable. Without detailing circumstances of life in specific reservations and other communities, it still can be seen from published and unpublished reports that life in certain communities is much more marginal with respect to economic and social opportunities than in others; also the amount and nature of retention of the traditional culture varies. In some places the people constituting the Indian population, whether exclusive or intermingled with whites, are highly factionalized, individualistic in outlook, and seemingly unable to initiate and develop programs for economc and social development. In other places, reservation, town, and village, factionalism seems minimal, the standard of living is reasonably high, and community activity is not inhibited significantly by an individualistic orientation.

There seems to be a direct relationship between such economic factors as job opportunities and occupancy of good farming land, and communal participation. The one reservation community that appears to be able through its tribal council to promote general welfare is the only closed reservation of the seven in the state: at "Deer Lake," unlike the other reservations, the General Allotment Act of 1887 was never applied. Reservation land has remained intact and is communal land. Here (Miller, 1967, 264; 1967a) the elective tribal council, after some difficulties over the question of hereditary succession in the late 1950s, has initiated far-reaching programs aided by federal and state grants to develop existing resources like lumbering, commercial fishing, and tourism and also has initiated new programs for economic development. Although their efforts have met with only a modicum of success, Miller states that the council, supported by the community, is proceeding with tenacity to bring about implementation of their programs.

Contrasting with this, the Chippewa living in a town on the "Broken Reed" reservation had not until recently been able to secure funds due them as compensation under the Indian Claims Commission Act because they could not decide upon any other disposition than a straight per capita split. The federal government would not release such funds until some community disposition affecting part of the money was promised. Recently, however, a disposition of the funds has been made, with the bulk of the money being distributed on a per capita basis, presumably other proceeds going into community funds (Paredes, 1967). In this town Chippewa express hostility not only toward whites, who comprise half the population, but also toward various local and state Indian organizations. In this town employment and the standard of living are low.

By and large in areas where there is no work to be had in farming or mining, industrial and commercial development is needed because old subsistence bases, including the technology to exploit resources, play only a minor role in the economy. Hunting and fishing, which are pursued on the reservations without a permit, still provide some food, but most food is purchased in shops. The wild rice harvest, an activity saturated with nostalgia, provides a very enjoyable social occasion for many Chippewa, many of whom return to the reservation from towns and cities for the event. However, the wild rice is sold to processors, and very little is kept for domestic use. The proceeds from the harvest are used to pay debts and to buy school clothing and for other immediate needs. This is reminiscent of the later days of the fur trade, when wild rice was traded in large quantity to traders in exchange for equipment for the winter trapping and hunting.

The great majority of Chippewa in Minnesota belong to the Roman Catholic and Episcopalian churches. There is a high degree of retention, however, of "native" beliefs and practices concerning the supernatural. In at least one community the Midewiwin continues strong, and in another the Native American Church is well established.

There is an increasing tendency for Chippewa from the reservation to move to urban centers and towns where they hope to find wage work. Although there has thus far been little research on this, it is apparent that at least in the smaller centers, even where Chippewa form distinctive minority groups, discrimination and prejudice on the part of whites is a factor, although this has not developed ghetto life. In the Twin Cities, however, there is a tendency for part of the Chippewa population to form ghettos and avail themselves of state social and welfare services. The Chippewa who move to urban and town centers return frequently to the reservation to visit relatives, hunt and fish, and harvest wild rice. Chippewa who migrate to the cities tend not to play a role in the political life of the reservation from which they come.

Indians in towns, on the basis of Guttman scale analysis and field observation, occupy on the average a significantly lower economic range than the whites among whom they live, despite the fact, however, that Chippewa families are found scattered as well in the upper range. In general, Chippewa, where they live as neighbors of whites, do not participate in the political and club life of the town, even where they comprise a substantial proportion of the population. Thus, Chippewa occupy a marginal position not only with respect to the white population as a whole, but also in specific communities where they coexist with whites.

Until very recently the Chippewa involvement in Pan-Indian movements has been slight, although one Chippewa from Minnesota is active in the National Congress of American Indians.[7] The chief ways in which Chippewa have participated in Pan-Indianism are powwows and peyote meetings. There has been increasing interest in recent years in holding powwows, and these attract not only tourists, but Indians from all the states around, Canada, and as far away as Montana, Oklahoma, and

New Mexico. Chippewa in increasing numbers attend powwows given by other tribes in places near and far. The powwow serves as a means to exchange dances, songs, and ideas. Information of a more explicit kind on the effect of this with respect to participation in Pan-Indian organizations is not available.

Another possible source of Pan-Indianism is the Native American Church. Peyotism does not appear to be widespread among Chippewa in Minnesota, but in at least one small community, comprising related families descended from a single founder, everyone belongs to the Church. Apparently these Chippewa confine peyotism to their own community and do not go elsewhere to join in ceremonies.

As to termination, the policy as established in 1953 was extremely unpopular among Chippewa in Minnesota, and the idea remains so. Although many Chippewa leave the reservation, a few of them permanently, most maintain ties. Only in this generation are numbers of Chippewa beginning to locate more or less permanently in centers away from the reservation, but even they return for visits.

In sum, the picture regarding reservation and non-reservation Chippewa in Minnesota is not as yet clear-cut. Current research is bringing to light a wide variety of behaviors, broad differences in community morale, significant differences in such factors as income and standard of living, and also differences in the degree of adherence to traditional norms including religious practice. All in all, the picture is not one of an apathetic people resigned to its fate, but rather one of a people emerging on various levels into an arena of struggle to break down certain barriers, while maintaining others. We see in their efforts a continuation of an age-old conflict, the establishment, with respect to the world outside, of a balance between participation and withdrawal, between dependency and autonomy. The resolution of this conflict apparently lies within the capacity of the Chippewa to develop economic means affording income while maintaining the land base, permitting continuing status as a distinctive people. This will be most successful where communal norms have best persisted, as at the closed reservation of "Deer Lake" and in the small communities where farming and mining work makes viable the local economy.

Epilogue

Despite individualization, it is remarkable the degree to which groups of Indians, including Chippewa and others of the upper Great Lakes, have in some areas retained vestiges of communal norms, despite all the pressures exerted toward individualization of activities and interests.

Such retentions have, in fact, been reinforced by the monumental inability of North American governments and the peripheral society at large to understand, first, social structuring in societies whose relations were based wholly or partially on kinship and, second, the social and economic attributes of leadership in such societies. Emphasis placed by scholars on facets of behavior expressed in "psychological" or "personality structure" terms have served only to obscure fundamental areas of contradiction and to reinforce the misconceptions of government bureaucracies.

Analysis of socioeconomic changes closely related to modes of production and distribution of articles of subsistence and trade, uncluttered by ideas concerning the importance of individualistic norms in societies only recently transformed from kin-based societies, lays bare stages, first, of development, then, of decay. These have been set forth for the Chippewa here, but in the spirit that they have a much broader application.

In no case does movement from stage to stage involve the obliteration of older norms, economic, social, or ideological. In total perspective, however, changes that have occurred over the entire historical period have resulted in a profound reorientation of social life, from the intensively discrete communal kinship groups of prehistory to the loosely aggregated small-family clusters of the recent past. In fact, it is noteworthy that changes in Chippewa social organization over the past four centuries seem to recapitulate in a superficial and minuscular way the broad sweep of *evolutionary* change in human society, or at least that part of it which lies between developed clan society and society characterized by the nucleation of social units and the particularization of property. That some Chippewa groups still maintain vestiges of corporate organization only attests the strength of the old norms. Among Algonkians these changes were dictated by the need for small groups to adapt to ever-shifting economic relations imposed upon momentarily existing social orders; they did not, in other words, occur as the result of relations within broad cultural systems developing their own antithetic and progressive forms. In short, individualization has come to characterize Chippewa relationships, but largely outside of the context of the political superstructure of those superordinate societies with which the Chippewa have been in contact. Nor has a political superstructure supporting nuclear tendencies arisen to any great degree within Chippewa society itself. Thus, we refer to the latter stages of Chippewa society in terms of the *decay of social life,* rather than the *evolution of individualistic norms.*

Economic and political relations with exploitative Euro-American systems have resulted, then, in geo-cultural marginality promoting further the decay of internal social and psychological relations. That is why Chippewa and their congeners have at times exhibited traits of personality indicating apathy and the suppression of creativity. In this they have more or less resembled certain colonial peoples in other areas, who for historical reasons have been unable to assert self-determination.

The work of the Minnesota anthropologists seems to indicate a reversal in some local areas of the individualistic trend. Perhaps it has run its course. Spirited attempts to revive communal interest in work and community projects on the part of Indians and interested agencies building on surviving cooperative patterns perhaps foretoken better times. Whether this is accomplished within or outside the Pan-Indian movement or Civil Rights movements will be interesting to see. Whatever internal and external factors exist, it is clear that there will be a distinctive Chippewa culture for many years to come, but this culture is not that of 100, 200, or 500 years ago, nor will it continue to be the culture of today.

NOTES

[1] Alternatively "Ojibwa" or, in Canada, "Saulteaux," "Chippewa" is most widely used, not only by anthropologists and others, but, at least in the United States, by Chippewa themselves.

[2] We refer chiefly to the southwestern Chippewa and their Great Lakes ancestors who lived in the area now comprising the northern portions of Michigan, Wisconsin, and Minnesota. It is these Chippewa who form the main subject material of this report, although reference will be made also to Chippewa living in Canada. In parts of Canada the 1850 date would be thirty to fifty years later, depending upon the remoteness of the region. According to the general chart of historical periods, relations of the Chippewa during the contact period show general stability, but with brief periods of conflict. These conflicts took the form of several local hostile incidents, in one case with the French in about 1680, in another with the British during the general Pontiac uprising in the 1760s. In each case stable relations were quickly restored.

[3] Proto-contact means the period of first contacts with European goods in the fur trade, and later, the very earliest direct contacts with Europeans. I would guess the first date at *c.* 1600, the second at *c.* 1635. I would suggest the possibility of a prior matrilineal stage changing to patriliny as trade relations began affecting local community life. If such was the case, this shift took place before the coming of the Europeans, or at least before there were witnesses to describe indigenous social systems.

[4] *Authority* and *leadership* are separate concepts, especially in intensely democratic societies where public opinion and consensus are the only sanctions for sociopolitical action and decision making.

[5] I wish to thank the governor and committee of the Hudson's Bay Company, who have kindly extended permission to quote this passage. The Archives

of the company, which contain rich cultural material on North American subarctic peoples, are available in Ottawa and London to interested scholars. Exploitation of this incalculably valuable resource by anthropologists is long overdue.

6 This entire section is written on the basis of articles, reports, and correspondence by anthropologists from various Minnesota institutions working with Chippewa of several communities in Minnesota. Much of this material has been gathered by the Upper Mississippi Research Project, funded by the George W. Nielson Foundation of Minneapolis, Minnesota. The coordinator of the project, which lasted from 1964 to 1966, was Anthony Paredes of Bemidji State College, Bemidji, Minnesota. Professors Paredes, Frank C. Miller, and Pertti J. Pelto of the University of Minnesota have been most kind in sending published and unpublished manuscripts by them and their students on various phases of contemporary Chippewa life. Unpublished material comprises papers read at the Central States Anthropological Society meetings in Chicago during May 1967 and a Symposium on Minnesota Indians held March 11, 1967, at Bemidji State College, under the direction of Mr. Paredes. Authors whom I have drawn upon are Paredes, Miller, Mathew Starke, Pelto, Gretel Hoffman Whitaker (unpublished Masters Thesis entitled *People and Politics in a Chippewa Community*, 1967), Michael Rynkiewich, Barbara Simon, and Timothy Roufs. Space limitation forbids a more extensive use of these materials. I hope I have encapsulated accurately and also look forward to seeing much of the material now unpublished in print.

7 In the short time since mid-1968 the Twin Cities has become a major center for Indian militancy through the activities of the American Indian Movement (AIM), in which many Chippewa participate. The organization has had recent success in union activities, collective bargaining, and so on. Space and time limitations prevent a more detailed summary of these new developments. The reader is also directed to Nancy Lurie's remarks on powwows in this volume.

BIBLIOGRAPHICAL NOTES

There is very little archeological information on the precontact and proto-contact Chippewa of the upper Great Lakes. Available material is summarized in George Quimby, *Indian Culture and European Trade Goods* (Madison: The University of Wisconsin Press, 1966), and in various publications of James V. Wright, including *An Archaeological Survey Along the North Shore of Lake Superior* (Ottawa: National Museum of Canada, Anthropology Papers, No. 3, 1963), and *The Pic River Site* (Ottawa: National Museum of Canada, Bulletin 206, Contributions to Anthropology 1963–1964, pt. 1, 1966). Wright and some of his colleagues will soon be issuing more material as the result of archeological surveys of Chippewa-like prehistoric cultures in the western Great Lakes region.

There is extensive data on the early contact period, especially after the first

Jesuit probes to the upper Great Lakes in 1640. One of the best sources for this period is R. G. Thwaites, *The Jesuit Relations and Allied Documents* (73 vols., New York: Pageant, 1959). Other sources are various state historical society collections, especially the *Collections of the State Historical Society of Wisconsin* (WHC), *Historical Collections of the Michigan Pioneer and Historical Society, and Documents Relating to the Colonial History of the State of New York* (NYCD). Other outstanding sources on French trade and missionary contacts with the Chippewa and their neighbors are P. Margry, *Découvertes et établissements des Français dans l'ouest et dans le sud de l'Amérique septentrionale (1614–1754): Mémoires et documents originaux* (6 vols., Paris, 1876–1886), especially vol. 6; and E. H. Blair (tr. and ed.), *The Indian Tribes of the Upper Mississippi Valley and the Region of the Great Lakes as Described by Nicolas Perrot, French Commandant in the Northwest; Bacqueville de la Potherie . . .* (2 vols., Cleveland: Arthur H. Clark Co., 1911).

Another source that may be consulted profitably for the early French period is R. G. Thwaites (ed.), *A New Discovery of a Vast Country in America by Father Louis Hennepin* (2 vols., Chicago: A. C. McClurg & Co., 1903).

Excellent references to trade, warfare, and diplomacy involving Chippewa in their relations with the French and also with other Indians, especially the Sioux, are vols. 16, 17, and 18 of the *Collections of the State Historical Society of Wisconsin;* L. J. Burpee (ed.), *Journals and Letters of Pierre Gaultier de Varennes de la Vérendrye and His Sons* (Toronto: The Champlain Society, 1927); and P. F. X. de Charlevoix, *History and General Description of New France* (6 vols., New York: J. G. Shea, 1866–1872), especially vol. 2.

For the British period, which lasted among the Chippewa of the upper Great Lakes from *c.* 1763 to the close of the War of 1812, excellent descriptions of trade and intertribal relations are found in A. Henry, *Travels and Adventures in Canada and the Indian Territories Between the Years 1760 and 1776* (Boston: Little, Brown, 1901), and J. Carver, *Travels Through the Interior Parts of North America in the Years 1766, 1767, and 1768* (London: W. Richardson, 1779). An account of the advance of the Chippewa into the country west of Lake Superior at the expense of the Sioux, based largely on oral tradition long after the event, but not entirely unreliable in general outline, is W. W. Warren, *History of the Ojibway Nation, Based upon Traditions and Oral Statements* (St. Paul: Minnesota Historical Collections, 1885) vol. 5, pp. 21–394. Again, various volumes published by historical societies in Michigan, Wisconsin, and Minnesota provide valuable sources of information on the British period.

For the terminal British period and the American pre-reservation period (*c.* 1795–1850) there are many excellent accounts, some published and some unpublished, on trade, mission activities, and government relations. Some of these are the trade journals of the younger Alexander Henry—E. Coues (ed.), *New Light on the Early History of the Greater Northwest . . .* (3 vols., New York: F. P. Harper, 1897); J. B. Tyrrell (ed.), *David Thompson's Narrative of His Explorations in Western America 1784–1812* (Toronto: The Champlain Society, 1916); various trade journals published in C. M. Gates (ed.), *Five Fur Traders of the Northwest . . .* (Minneapolis: University of Minnesota Press,

1933); the journals of F. V. Malhiot for 1804–1805 in *Collections of the State Historical Society of Wisconsin,* vol. 19, pp. 163–233; the journals of M. Curot for 1803–1804 in the *Collections of the State Historical Society of Wisconsin* (1911) vol. 20, pp. 396–471; and the journals of C. J. B. Chaboillez for 1897, H. Hickerson (ed.), *Ethnohistory* (1959) vol. 6, no. 3, pp. 265–316, and no. 4, pp. 363–427. Other valuable sources for trade during this period are L. R. Masson, *Les Bourgeois de la compagnie du nord-ouest, récits de voyages, lettres et rapports inédits relatifs au nord-ouest Canadien* (2 vols., Quebec: Impr. générale A. Coté et Cte, 1889–1890), especially the descriptions and journals of D. Cameron, vol. 2, pp. 231–265. A most invaluable record of trade for the Chippewa of the international boundary region and north is the extensive archival collections of the Hudson's Bay Company, which are now available on microfilm in the Public Archives of Canada, in Ottawa. Another excellent source of data relating to the western Great Lakes fur trade is Grace Lee Nute (ed.), *The American Fur Company Papers* (3 vols., New York State Historical Society mss. 1831–1849, 1944), also available on microfilm.

Other excellent sources for the American period during the nineteenth century are the unpublished journals of L. Taliaferro, Indian Agent in southern Minnesota, 1819–1839, and the Reverends James T. Boutwell and Edmund F. Ely, missionaries of the American Board at Leech and Sandy Lakes, respectively, during the 1830s (St. Paul: Minnesota Historical Society). A good summary of Boutwell's activities at Leech Lake and elsewhere, cited in this paper, is found in E. D. Neill, *Memoir of W. T. Boutwell* . . . (St. Paul: Macalester College Contributions, Department of History, Literature, and Political Science, 1891), ser. 2, no. 1. Outstanding published sources for this period are: the account of the Lewis Cass expedition to the sources of the Mississippi in 1820, including journals kept by several members and a lengthy narrative account by H. R. Schoolcraft, published in M. L. Williams (ed.), *Narrative Journal of Travels Through the Northwestern Regions of the United States Extending from Detroit Through the Great Chain of American Lakes to the Sources of the Mississippi River in the Year 1820, Henry R. Schoolcraft* (East Lansing: Michigan State College Press, 1953). Other writings by Schoolcraft, who was Indian Agent for the Chippewa at Sault Ste. Marie between 1821 and 1840, including especially *Discovery of the Sources of the Mississippi, or Narrative of an Expedition Through the Upper Mississippi to Itasca Lake, the Actual Source of This River; Embracing an Exploratory Trip Through the St. Croix and Bruntwood (or Broule) Rivers; in 1832* (New York: Harper & Brothers, 1834), provide important sources of data on the Chippewa of the period.

For the early and later reservation period the best sources of information are the various agency reports on file in the National Archives in Washington, D.C., and also unpublished manuscript material in the state historical societies at Madison, Wisconsin, and St. Paul, Minnesota (MHC).

As far as the present-day Chippewa are concerned, I have noted in note 6 the extensive survey of Minnesota Chippewa made by faculty members and students at the University of Minnesota and Bemidji State College.

Much of the ethnohistorical material on the Chippewa has been summarized and appears in various publications of mine (1960, 1962, 1963, 1965, 1966, 1967a, and 1967b). Additional references can be found in a volume by W. V. Kinietz on the *Indians of the Great Lakes* (Ann Arbor: University of Michigan Press, 1940). Excellent sources for the present-day Chippewa, and relating to some degree to forerunners, are the extensive writings of A. I. Hallowell, R. W. Dunning, E. S. Rogers, R. Landes and V. Barnouw. For a list of cogent contemporary sources on the Chippewa see the Bibliography to this chapter.

BIBLIOGRAPHY

BARNOUW, VICTOR W.

1950 Acculturation and personality among the Wisconsin Chippewa. American Anthropological Association Memoir 72.

1961 Chippewa social atomism. American Anthropologist 63:1006–1013.

BISHOP, CHARLES A.

n.d. [Unpublished doctoral dissertation on the Ojibwa of the Lake St. Joseph region]. State University of New York at Buffalo.

BOUTWELL, WILLIAM

1832–1837 Minnesota Historical Society manuscript. St. Paul.

BURPEE, L. J.

1927 Journals and letters of Pierre Gaultier de Varennes de la Vérendrye and his sons. Toronto: The Champlain Society.

CARVER, J.

1779 Travels through the interior parts of North America in the years 1766, 1767, and 1768. London.

CHARLEVOIX, P. F. X. DE

1866–1872 History and general description of New France. 6 vols. New York: J. G. Shea.

DUNNING, ROBERT W.

1959a Social and economic change among the northern Ojibwa. Toronto: University of Toronto Press.

1959b Rules of residence and ecology among the northern Ojibwa. American Anthropologist 61:806–816.

HALLOWELL, A. IRVING

1937 Cross-cousin marriage in the Lake Winnipeg area. Publications of the Philadelphia Anthropological Society 1:95–110.

1955 Culture and experience. Philadelphia: University of Pennsylvania Press.

HICKERSON, HAROLD

1960 The feast of the dead among the 17th-century Algonkians of the upper Great Lakes. American Anthropologist 62:81–107.

1962 The southwestern Chippewa: an ethnohistorical study. American Anthropological Association Memoir 92.

1963 The sociohistorical significance of two Chippewa ceremonials. American Anthropologist 65:67–85.

1965 The Virginia deer and intertribal buffer zones in the upper Mississippi valley. Washington, D.C.: American Association for the Advancement of Science, no. 78. pp. 43–46.

1966 The genesis of bilaterality among two divisions of Chippewa. American Anthropologist 68:1–26.

1967a Land tenure of the Rainy Lake Chippewa at the beginning of the 19th century. Washington, D.C.: Smithsonian Contributions to Anthropology 2 (4).

1967b Some implications of the theory of particularity, or "atomism," of northern Algonkians. Current Anthropology 8:313–343.

KINIETZ, W. VERNON

1940 The Indians of the western Great Lakes, 1615–1760. Ann Arbor: Occasional Contributions from the Museum of Anthropology of the University of Michigan, no. 10.

LANDES, RUTH

1937 Ojibwa sociology. Columbia University Contributions to Anthropology 29. New York: Columbia University Press.

LEACOCK, ELEANOR

1954 The Montagnais "hunting territory" and the fur trade. American Anthropological Association Memoir 78.

MASSON, L. R.

1889–1890 Les Bourgeois de la compagnie du nord-ouest, récits de voyages, lettres et rapports inédits relatifs au nord-ouest Canadien. 2 vols. Quebec: Impr. générale A. Coté et Cte.

MILLER, FRANK C.

1966 Problems of succession in a Chippewa council. *In* Marc J. Swartz, Victor W. Turner, and Arthur Tuden, eds. Political Anthropology. Chicago: Aldine Publishing Company.

1967a Humor in a Chippewa tribal council. Ethnology 6:263–271.

1967b [Unpublished manuscript.]

NEILL, E. D.

1891 Memoir of W. T. Boutwell. St. Paul: Macalester College Contributions, Department of History, Literature, and Political Science, ser. 2, no. 1.

PAREDES, ANTHONY

1967 [Private communication.]

ROGERS, E. S.

1962 The Round Lake Ojibwa. Toronto: Royal Ontario Museum, Art and Archaeological Division, Occasional Papers, no. 5.

SERVICE, ELMAN R.

1962 Primitive social organization: An evolutionary perspective. New York: Random House.

TALIAFERRO, LAWRENCE

1819–1839 Minnesota Historical Society manuscripts. St. Paul.

7 The Plains Indians: Their Continuity in History and Their Indian Identity GENE WELTFISH

Into the Great Plains of North America peoples migrated from all directions.. The first pioneers came onto the continent out of Asia as big game hunters, a way of life that prevailed all over the world from 15,000 to 20,000 years ago. Food gathering of seeds and small animals succeeded this way of life, possibly with the onset of drought, warmer climate, and the diminution of the large animal population, roughly about 7,000 years ago. It is likely that some of the big game hunters of the Plains had to adopt this way of life out of necessity. A third changeover beginning with the Christian Era can be attributed to immigrant peoples from east of the Mississippi, the Woodland peoples of Hopewellian derivation, who planted some crops, made pottery, and constructed rather flimsy houses. Their scattered settlements clustered along the riverbanks to which the wooded areas of the Plains are confined. The several rivers rise in the foothills of the Rockies, flowing eastward across the Plains to join the Missouri or the Mississippi. Woodland settlements were scattered throughout the area up to the Rockies themselves. The woodland peoples were deer hunters, as they had been in their old home to the east, hunting buffalo only occasionally (Wedel, 1965; Griffin, 1965).

About A.D. 1000 the Woodland people were succeeded by a new set of immigrants from east of the Mississippi River, the Mississippian mound-builder peoples of Caddoan tradition, more advanced in their dependence upon maize agriculture, with more substantial dwellings of logs and thatch covered with earth and an economic regime that combined full-scale buffalo hunting with more plentiful horticultural production and a food storage complex based on a drying process to preserve both meat and vegetables, which were kept in large grass-lined pits (Wedel, 1965). Archeologically, the Caddoan Complex from which they were derived parallels the Gulf from the Appalachians to the Mississippi with evidence of a structured religious ideology that has obvious ties with the more advanced cultural center in Mexico (Sears, 1965).

There is good reason to believe that these latest immigrants moved onto the Plains from south to north in the "Caddoan Corridor," settling in the middle courses of the rivers and giving rise to the Caddoan-speaking peoples first contacted by the Spaniards in the sixteenth century. The Spaniards came from two directions simultaneously, Coronado from the Southwest and de Soto from the Southeast, both around 1540. De Soto met the Tula, a southern Caddoan people near Hot Springs, Arkansas, and was offered a quantity of soft buffalo robes as a tribute, which they had in commercial quantities; they also had turquoise and cotton, and the people indicated to him that they had trade relations with the Southwest (Swanton, 1942, 1946).

The Caddoans known to history were a numerous people of one large language family, distinguished into four clusters of tribes by linguistic differentiation. The southernmost were the Caddo peoples of Texas and Louisiana, further north the Wichita of Oklahoma and Kansas, and still further north the Pawnee of Nebraska and the Arikara of North Dakota. By the eighteenth century these long-settled Plains peoples came under heavy pressure from displaced tribes coming onto the Plains from east of the Mississippi. With the increasing immigration and settlement of the European on the East coast, the Indian populations that lived there were displaced and began to move westward, in turn pushing the indigenous people further westward in a kind of chain reaction. About the time of the American Revolution the peoples closest to the Mississippi were driven across the river into the already heavily populated Plains (Secoy, 1953).

Up to this time none of these Indian peoples had been nomads. All came from settled villages, where horticulture provided their basic food supply. Now driven onto the Plains, they attacked the settled Plains villages in an unsuccessful attempt to displace them, a goal that was eventually realized, but too late to benefit the displaced Indian immigrant, who had now to contend with his final successor, the European settler.

That Amerindian history in and of itself did not stand still is eminently clear, but with the incursion of the European, historical events led toward a crescendo of disaster that brought the Indian peoples to the brink of extermination. In different parts of the continent the process was more or less accelerated in its pace, but the Plains were the scene of its most dramatic expression.

In the pre-European period, with the prevailing Indian methods of exploiting the resources, a delicate balance between population and resources was maintained. There is evidence that intertribal raiding did occur with a consequent disruption, and sometimes displacement, of tribes. Population increase and migration also brought contests for land

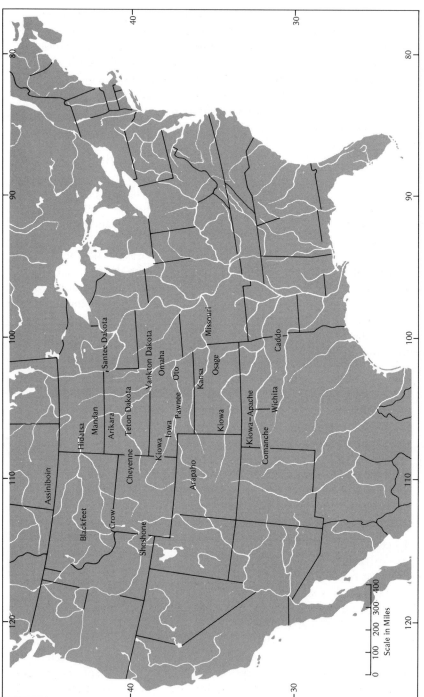

Figure 7.1. Location of Plains Indian tribes at the time of the Lewis and Clark expedition, 1804–1806. (Compiled according to the original journals of Lewis and Clark by Sharon McConnell, July 18, 1968.)

and resources in its wake. Thus, military power was not new to native Amerindian life, but the introduction of European facilities added a new dimension to the older balance of power. Two features serve as an index of this process, the gun and the horse, spreading almost simultaneously, the gun from the Northeast and the horse from the Southwest. The first acquisition of the gun in the Northeast was a function of the fur trade. The whole eastern area was the territory of the Algonkian-speaking peoples reaching down along the Atlantic to Virginia and inland in Canada north of the Great Lakes. South of the Great Lakes and inland were the Siouan-speaking peoples. The contest between these two groups impelled their final displacement across the Mississippi into the Plains and the forced adoption of a defensive nomadism. Backed up against the Rockies with no further area of escape, it was the last stand against extermination of the remnant tribes of these two groups that has furnished the world with its "typical" picture of the American Indian. This is not without reason, as it was a heroic defense that stands as a lasting tribute to the courage and determination of the American Indian will to live. The tribes that have most actively reached attention are the Cheyenne and Arapaho, Algonkian-speaking peoples, and the Dakota and Teton Sioux and the Crow of the Siouan-speaking family. In 1766 eight of eleven Dakota bands had moved westward onto the Plains, the Crow between 1795 and 1804, and the Cheyenne and Arapaho were completely nomadic by 1830 (Lowie, 1954). Most ethnological accounts as well as popular renditions have carried over the "settler" image of these peoples as Stone Age Plainsmen who lived as nomadic hunters and warriors since the beginning of time, thus freezing them out of the stream of history and giving a static and distorted picture of the significance of their lives in the normal continental historical setting. In point of fact the major form of their Plains way of life is a function of the origin, growth, and emergence of the American nation as it grew and expanded from the Atlantic westward. They belong in the mainstream of Euro-American and New World continental history, not beyond the pale, like frozen museum pieces.

The typical nomadism of the Plains way of life was especially fostered by the acquisition of the horse. There were no horses when man entered the New World in the sixteenth century. Before the Spaniards came, there were some foot nomads living in the Plains west of the settled Caddoan peoples and north of the Pueblos—Athapaskan peoples—who had come down from interior northwest Canada, entering the area about a hundred years before the Spaniards arrived. Conditions in their barren area of origin were extremely hard, and as they arrived in the Plains, they attacked the "Pre-Pawnee" villages of western Nebraska (Champe, 1949), continuing southward. A small band of them

joined the Kiowa at some juncture and were known historically as the
"Kiowa Apache," or as the Pawnee referred to them, "White Faces,"
tska-taka. Entering the Plains from the West were the Shoshonean-
speaking peoples of the Great Basin and the Rocky Mountains, the
Shoshoni prominently noted in later history as traders in horses in the
northern region, the Ute who settled north of the Pueblo peoples, and
the Kiowa and Comanche, who moved aggressively into the southern
Plains in the eighteenth and nineteenth centuries (Hoebel and Wallace,
1952).

The first to adopt the Spanish horses were the former foot nomads,
the Athapaskan Apache, the bulk of whom were settled around the
Pueblos by the time the Spaniards arrived. Some Apache had settled
into partial agricultural settlements and others were leading a Plains
nomadic life, hunting the buffalo in the high Plains west of the settled
Caddoan peoples. Apache prosperity and its ensuing population increase brought on a confrontation with the western Caddoan peoples
for their lands, and the horse became a major advantage against the
highly organized, but unmounted, Caddoans. By 1690, through their
own trade channels, the Caddoans of east Texas and Oklahoma were
mounted and provided with leather armor and metal-tipped lances
equivalent to those of the Apache. In addition to acquiring land, the
Apache took captives to sell to the Spaniards as slaves (1659), since they
had little else to trade with the Spanish conquerors. By this time the
Shoshonean Ute had moved out of the Great Basin and camped as
mendicants outside the Pueblo villages. But soon they became powerful
enough to challenge the Apaches and the Pueblo peoples, establishing
a well-organized cavalry by the end of the seventeenth century and
then drawing in their Shoshonean-speaking kinsmen, the Comanche,
into the southern Plains as horse traders and as a powerful force. Meanwhile horses were few in the northern country at the opening of the
eighteenth century.

The northern Shoshoni, who had given up food gathering for a
nomadic buffalo-hunting way of life, reserved their horses for buffalo
hunting rather than expend them on warfare with neighboring peoples.
The Pawnee of Kansas, on the other hand, in 1719, confronted by
mounted Indians and having long hunted buffalo on foot, felt it necessary to reserve the few horses they had for fighting, and they had barely
enough. In 1742–1743 the Shoshoni are reported to have developed the
full military cavalry pattern. The Caddoans, however, never had as
many horses as the nomadic tribes at any time. In the mid-eighteenth
century the Caddoan Wichita had handled the situation by allying
themselves with the Comanche, in this way obtaining both horsepower
and horsemen in their attack on their powerful enemies, the southern

Siouan Osages. In the northern Caddoan region in North Dakota it is reported that the Caddoan Arikara began to trade horses to the Sioux between 1750 and 1770.

> During the period before 1670, the Sioux lived mainly in scattered villages throughout the lake-studded woodlands of northern and eastern Minnesota. They practised a mixed economy of horticulture, hunting and wild rice gathering. Seasonally, many of the groups made bison-hunting expeditions out on the adjacent prairie lands [Secoy, 1953, 66].

After 1680 the French decided to by-pass their eastern Indian middlemen in the fur trade, the Cree, Huron and Ottawa, who had previously blocked their contact, and they dealt directly with the western Sioux, who had more immediate access to new and undepleted hunting grounds (Brebner, 1966), supplying them with guns. From the 1680s to the 1760s the Sioux hunted and sold furs to the French. They were well equipped with guns. In the mid-eighteenth century the Sioux began encountering cavalry among their enemies, such as the Missouri River village tribes. At this time they managed to hold their own as their war parties were large and well organized, and they did have guns, which the western people lacked. An equilibrium was established between the gun-owning Sioux and the horse-owning Missouri village tribes, who also had some metal weapons acquired from the Kiowa, who got them from the Spanish Southwest.

During this phase, from around 1750–1770, the Sioux got their first horses from the Caddoan Arikara and began to develop horse nomadism and cavalry warfare. Later they swept West and South across much of the Central Plains in a spectacular invasion and developed one of the most mobile and effective Indian armies in the Plains.

Limitation in the distribution of guns ended once and for all after the War of 1812 when steam navigation carried trade along the whole length of the Missouri River and points west. Guns became available to anyone who had the price.

If European facilities had a major effect on Amerindian life, the relationship was not entirely one-sided. Two gifts among many deserve special mention: Corn had been raised in the Plains for 2,000 years, and the proverbial plough that broke the Plains had long been preceded by the Indian hoe. Corn raised by the old Caddoan settlers and stored in their huge 10-foot pits must have supported many a party wandering onto the Plains in the time of initial contact, just as it did the well-documented Atlantic Colonies and the long overland journeys of De Soto (Swanton, 1946). For their own part the supplies of dried corn that the village Indians carried out into the buffalo-hunting grounds made it possible to bring the whole migrating tribe to bear in the strategic attack against the herds. Due to the dried foods they carried, they could also hold out as they dried and processed the buffalo meat to take home for future use (Weltfish, 1965a). The European settler in the Plains planted corn as his first crop before wheat became available. Today we count among our blessings popcorn, syrup, corn-fed meat, and corn oil products. It is not entirely accidental that corn is the major product of Nebraska, the Cornhusker State, and that Iowa raises some of the best corn-fed pigs in the world. Yankee beans are, of course, an adaptation by a North Dakota agronomist, George Will, of local Indian beans.

The concept of the Pipe of Peace is a unique gift not readily assessed. The real story of its origin among the Plains Indians and of its function in the earliest contact period is almost entirely unknown. The making and the keeping of peace is an old Indian hope, as it is the hope of all peoples on earth. Perhaps knowledge of its true place in Indian life may somehow help us to think through some of our own problems. The legendary efforts of the Iroquois Hiawatha to form a political league was emulated in our century in the attempted League of Nations. The basic idea behind the ceremony of the Pipe of Peace was the equivalence in the Indian mind of Peace with Trade. In their thinking, however, trade is not a contest of wits. The resources of an Indian tribe depended both upon its detailed environment and its stock of technical knowledge. In the nature of the case the intimacy of each individual tribe with its surroundings was much more profound than we would be likely to conceive. For this reason each tribe was more varied from the next than any of the peoples we ordinarily deal with. The uniqueness of what each people had and produced had great value to other peoples much more in our sense of a work of art than a standardized industrial product. Trade meant bringing to one the uniqueness of the other. It was this implicit value, rather than profit, that was involved.

In 1673, Father Marquette, exploring the Mississippi, describes the "calumet," as he calls the peace pipe, in the following terms:

> There remains no more except to speak of the Calumet. There is nothing more mysterious or more respected among them. Less honor is paid to the Crowns and scepters of Kings than the Savages bestow upon this. It seems to be the God of peace and of war, the Arbiter of life and of death. It has but to be carried upon one's person, and displayed, to enable one to walk safely through the midst of enemies—who, in the hottest of the Fight, lay down their arms when it is shown. For that reason, the Illinois gave me one, to serve as a safeguard among all Nations through whom I had to pass during my voyage. . . . They also use it to put an end to their disputes, to strengthen Their alliances and to speak to strangers [Thwaites, 1900, 129–131].

In 1687, Joutel, companion of La Salle, witnessed the ceremony among the Caddo in the southern Mississippi area. The word *calumet,* which is sometimes used as an alternative term, refers in old French to a tube, reed, or flute, especially to a shepherd's pipe, preserving the correct understanding of the old explorers that it was the pipestem, not the bowl, that carried the sacred significance. This involved the association of the breath, the windpipe, and the voice with the life principle. This ceremony had its most intense development among the Caddoan peoples, especially the Pawnee, among whom the sacred pipestem symbolized the eagle; the stem was decorated with a pendant fan of eagle feathers, one stem representing the male and the other the female, the female pipe representing the affairs of the home, the male, those of the world outside (Weltfish, 1965a). The pipe with some of its ceremonial implications was adopted by many tribes, reaching as far as the Iroquois, whose Eagle Dance is an example (Fenton, 1953).

In the Pawnee version the peace pipe ceremony had its inception in the enterprise of a prominent man. It usually began with a supernatural revelation from the cosmic powers, whereupon he called upon the assistance of a holy man to conduct the ceremony. On his own part he enlisted the help of his influential friends and relatives to provide material support. He then sent a messenger to a man of equal prominence in a distant tribe, apprising him of his intention. This man now began his efforts to collect the appropriate return gifts when the visiting party should appear. These efforts would consume a year or more. The instigator and his party were designated as "the Fathers" and the tribe that was being visited, "the Sons." The Fathers comprised a party numbering twenty to a hundred people. They brought with them everything necessary for their own support, including fine tents, food supplies, and all other domestic paraphernalia. They brought fine clothing and ceremonial materials, including the pipes themselves. The party had to include representatives of what they considered their essential officers—two chiefs (representing administration), braves (representing law and order), holy men (representing religion). When they arrived, after the initial ceremonies, they assisted their hosts in their regular round of work and finally, upon leaving, presented them with everything they had brought along—tents, dishes, clothing, holy objects. The "Sons," in turn, made a substantial gift of as many horses as they could, elaborately decorated; in pre-horse days they gave highly decorated rawhide packages containing quantities of dried buffalo meat (Weltfish, 1965a). Was it a good will mission, a cultural exchange? It was long remembered by both tribes. But peace was not to come to the Indians of America, despite the exchange of unique gifts.

The Beginning of the End: The Clash of Tradition

The whole confrontation of European and Indian, given the physical circumstances and even more particularly the profound divergence of backgrounds, was bound to generate an extreme conflict of interests. But wide as was the gulf between material values, it was even wider in the realm of religion. In the depth of his belief, wherever he has gone, the European has tried to impose his religion. Indian religion, with its strong involvement in the ideology of man's integral place within the system of the universe, found antithetical to it the idea of a world ruled by humans alone or by a deity that was a large extrapolation of the human personality as conceived. Religion for the American Indian validated his place in the natural order and its rhythms. Communion for the Plains Indian was with the universe itself. It was on the open plain that each man sought the vision that gave direction to his life. The vision that came to him with its offer of personal help and salvation was from the cosmos, the animals, the winds, and the storms (Benedict, 1922, 1923).

Of the various peoples that inhabited the Plains area, the Pawnee Indians were the longest resident. They had one of the most highly integrated theological systems and were little affected by missionary activity even in the nineteenth century. Their systematic approach has considerable aesthetic appeal, and it has drawn the admiration of ethnologists and others who have come to know it. However, it can readily be understood that their practice of sacrificing a young girl to the Morning Star could hardly be condoned by the Euro-American community on any level. The chiefs were actively in touch with Merriwether Lewis and William Clark when they came through in 1804 and later with Clark when he became Indian Agent in St. Louis. The chiefs were well aware that this sort of religious practice would have to come to an end.

For the Pawnee priests and the populace, however, their theology was as binding as that of the European. The Pawnees had a cosmic religion in which all power and life continued to stream down from the cosmos. In the dream of creation, *Tirawahat,* The Vault of the Heavens, was the first cause, producing the world in a series of violent storms and then creating the star gods, who in turn were to create humanity in their image. The two most prominent star powers were the Evening Star, goddess of darkness and fertility, who held sway in the western skies, and the Morning Star, god of fire and light in the eastern skies. Evening Star guarded her realm with four fierce animals stationed at the semi-cardinal gateways. Morning Star sent numbers of emissaries, but they never reached her, as they were all swallowed up while trying to pass through her hazardous terrain. Then Morning Star decided to go himself, and he took with him his assistant, the Sun; together they conquered each of the four fierce animals in turn and finally reached Evening Star as she sat in her garden of life, attended by her assistant, the Moon. After further hardships Morning Star managed to mate with Evening Star, and a girl was born of the union; then the Sun and the Moon mated and produced a boy. First the girl and then the boy were sent to earth on a whirlwind by the Vault of the Heavens and taught by the supreme power to mate and to populate the earth. Morning Star did not forget the struggle this process had cost him. He expected that the human beings of earth would sacrifice a virgin girl to him on his command to compensate him for his part in the creation of humanity. He would come in a dream-vision to a noted warrior, who was thus charged with capturing the girl in a war party that he would lead so that she might be sacrificed in an appropriate ceremony. The warrior would run crying through the village at dawn to the home of the priest, who would then comfort and instruct him in the proceedings and pray to the Morning Star on his behalf. These visions came in the early spring before the corn was planted and were intimately connected with the success of the crops.

After extensive spiritual and ceremonial preparation the visionary gathered a party of the most experienced warriors, and after an arduous journey replete with ceremonial procedures, an enemy village was surrounded and a young virgin captured and brought back to the village, where she was placed in the charge of the Wolf Priest, who represented the Southeast Star of Death. A summer and a winter passed and the young girl was finally sacrificed in the early spring. A scaffold of two uprights planted in the ground, joined by cross sticks, one at the top and four near the lower end, was erected. The girl was tied to the scaffold by the wrists, one at each corner, her feet resting on the cross poles below. She was shot through the heart with a sacred arrow by the Wolf Priest, who had concealed himself in a gully; the priest then made an incision below her heart, letting the blood drip onto a rectangular trench below the scaffold, lined with white down feathers that symbolized the sacred bed and garden of the Evening Star. All the men and boys of the tribe then shot at the body with arrows, even the smallest of them. The body was cut down by the priest and left lying face down on the earth at some distance from the village so that all life would multiply.

In 1817 there entered upon this solemn scene a young man known as Man Chief, son of Knife Chief, as the Comanche girl who had been captured for sacrifice stood tied to the scaffold. To the awe and fear of the assembled worshipers, he rode up to the scaffold and addressed them all, stating that his father disapproved of what they were about to do, and he had come to rescue the girl or die right there. The significance of this act can only be understood in terms of the historical events that immediately preceded it.

At the beginning of the nineteenth century there were four villages in the Skidi Band of the Pawnees. The sacred bundle of the Morning Star was owned by the chief of one of the villages known as Village Across a Ridge, *tuwahukasa*. In 1816 the Comanche girl was captured to be sacrificed in the spring of 1817. The leading chief of the entire Skidi Band was Knife Chief, whose own village was Pumpkin Vine, *pahukstatu*. His son or possibly nephew, Man Chief, *pita-risaru,* was his protégé. It is not known whether he was Knife Chief's son or maternal nephew, as in the Pawnee system of family organization the same kin term is applied to both. Man Chief was a young warrior highly regarded for his bravery. In 1811 at the invitation of William Clark, Knife Chief, accompanied by Man Chief, went to St. Louis for a consultation on behalf of the Pawnees. Clark had a long and frank talk with Knife Chief and impressed him with the fact that the white people were coming "like the waves of the ocean—in, in, in—."

In 1817, as preparations for the ceremony of sacrifice were being made, Knife Chief, who knew of the depth of hostility that was generated by their practice, tried to convince the people to abandon it. But the warriors and priests were always suspicious of the political motives of the chiefs in their dealing with the European powers, and they proceeded with their ceremony. The Pawnee believed that anyone who touched the girl upon the scaffold would be taken by the Morning Star in her stead. What went through the minds of the crowd and even more of Man Chief himself as he rode up to the scaffold is hard for us to imagine. He was a brave warrior standing before Morning Star, who was the god of war. He cut down the girl and rode with her to the outskirts of the village, where he placed her on a horse and directed her southward so that she succeeded in reaching her own people.

Convinced that the crops would cease to grow and all living things wither, the priests and warriors were not ready to give up the ceremony, and they were apparently desperate enough to accept a somewhat inappropriate substitute, for in the following year a Spanish boy of ten was captured in Oklahoma and dedicated by the warrior who was his captor to the Morning Star. Knife Chief then called together a council of chiefs, and with his own property and that of a French trader, Louis Papin, and the assistance of Manuel Lisa, trader in St. Louis, they ransomed the boy from the warrior who had captured him and he was placed in Lisa's charge. Throughout the nineteenth century and in the early part of the twentieth, there was a persistent rumor in Nebraska that warriors and priests took any captives they could get, including adults, and sacrificed them to the Morning Star in secret.

In mid-June 1818 the sensational rescue of the boy by Knife Chief and the story of Man Chief's previous exploit appeared in *The Missouri Gazette* of St. Louis, and during 1820–1821 it came to the attention of Edwin James and Jedidiah Morse. James was a member of Major S. A. Long's expedition that wintered on the Missouri in 1820, and Morse was a Congregational clergyman from Connecticut who had a humane interest in the Indians and submitted a "Report to the Secretary of War" in 1822; his other works were widely read (Morse, 1822). Through them the story became widely known, and Knife Chief and Man Chief became national heroes. In the fall of 1821 Major O'Fallon was commissioned to lead a delegation of Pawnee chiefs, including Knife Chief and Man Chief, to Washington. The purpose was to impress them with the might and majesty of the new nation. Man Chief, especially, was singled out for public attention. In addition to other events, the girls of Miss White's Select Seminary had pooled their money and had a special silver medal cast "To the Bravest of the Brave," with the picture of the warrior leading the young girl to her escape on one side and the sacrificial scaffold and the crowd of priests on the other. At the presentation the handsome young hero said, "When I did this thing I did not know it was brave, but now that you have called me brave and given me this medal I thank you and I will always think of you" (McKenney and Hall, 1842, 101–106). Man Chief's portrait was painted in Washington by Charles Bird King and has been reproduced a number of times. He was dressed in a beautiful feather war bonnet and white fur robe (McKenney and Hall, 1842, opposite page 101 and in Folio volume, picture 17). The medal was excavated by Alonzo Thompson in 1883 in an Indian grave near Fullerton, Nebraska, on the Loup Fork at the location of a Skidi village built around 1830, where Man Chief must have died. (A drawing of the medal from the original can be seen in Hyde, 1951, opposite page 83.)

After a triumphal tour of Washington the Pawnee delegation was taken on to Baltimore, Philadelphia, and New York, everywhere greeted by large crowds and showered with gifts.

The ritual of the Pawnee Indian human sacrifice has deep roots in American Indian religion. Its form is so similar in its detail to a specific type of Aztec sacrifice, the scaffold sacrifice of Guerrero in Mexico, that it furnishes additional evidence of the close connection of the Plains Pawnee with the complex religious center of Mexico. Wissler and Spinden feel that circumstances place the probable date of this specific transfer between 1506 and 1519, which indicates that the route must have been through the plains (Weltfish, 1965a).

The Signing of Treaties and the Increase of Travelers and Settlements

The formal relations with the Plains Indians by the United States began with the Lewis and Clark expedition of 1804. From this time until 1833 treaties of peace and friendship were signed with the purpose of cutting off the Indian trade with agents of other nations and directing it toward the United States exclusively; there was an attempt to keep down hostilities toward United States nationals.

By 1833 a new set of treaties was concluded with the purpose of acquiring land upon which to settle tribes to be transposed from east of the Mississippi. This was according to Andrew Jackson's plan in which all lands east of the Mississippi would belong exclusively to the Euro-American population and those to the west of the Mississippi would be of a generalized Indian nation, with only a few white officials living there.

By 1850 the utter unfeasibility of this plan was realized, and the government responded to the demand for opening Indian lands to public settlement (Hyde, 1951). Each Indian group was confined to a separate limited area surrounded by white settlers eager to acquire more land. By this move, the Indian groups were not only separated from each other, but they had little access to any food supplies, except those shipped in by the United States Government. As pressures on the natural food sources increased, Indian hostilities among the tribes as well as to the surrounding people increased.

With the Civil War the United States found it hard to honor its obligations toward the Indians in terms of food and protection. With the total extermination of the buffalo in the 1870s and 1880s, Indian hunger became endemic and their social and physical isolation even more acute.

The following are some examples of kinds of treaties that were signed between the United States and Plains tribes, showing the changing character of the relationship and United States needs (Source: "Statutes at Large").

Sioux: 1816 friendship (VII, 143); 1837 land cession and movement west of the Mississippi (VII, 250–251); 1858 reservation (XI, 743, 744, 745).

Crow Indians of Montana: 1882 sale of reservation lands individual allotments (XXII, 42, 43).

Cheyenne and Arapaho: 1825 (VII, 265–266); 1861 (XII, 1163–1165); 1868 (XV, 656, 657); 1877 (XIX, 254, 255).

A modern leader of the Blackfeet Indians of Montana, whose lifetime spanned the transition from buffalo hunting to modern cattle raising.
(Courtesy, United States Bureau of Indian Affairs.)

Kiowa and Comanche: 1867 Treaty of Medicine Lodge, agree not to attack white workers, to stay on reservation, to have hunting rights on ceded lands as long as the buffalo last (XV, 581, 584).

SIOUX

A Treaty of Peace and Friendship, June 1, 1816. Proclamation, December 30, 1816 ("Statutes at Large," VII, 143).

Made and concluded between William Clark, Ninian Edwards, and Auguste Chouteau, commissioners plenipotentiary of the United States of America, on the part and behalf of the said states of the one part, and the undersigned chiefs and warriors, representing eight bands of the Siouxs, composing the three tribes called the Siouxs of the Leaf, the Siouxs of the Broad Leaf, and the Siouxs Who Shoot in the Pine Tops, on the part and behalf of their said tribes, of the other part.

The parties being desirous of establishing peace and friendship between the United States and the said tribes, and of being placed in all things, and in every respect, on the same footing upon which they stood before the late war between the United States and Great Britain, have agreed to the following articles:

Art. 1. Every injury or act of hostility, committed by one or either of the contracting parties against the other, shall be mutually forgiven and forgot.

Art. 2. There shall be perpetual peace and friendship between all the citizens of the United States, and all the individuals composing the aforesaid tribes; and all the friendly relations that existed between them before the war shall be, and the same are hereby, renewed.

Art. 3. The undersigned chiefs and warriors, for themselves and their tribes respectively, do, by these presents, confirm to the United States all and every cession, or cessions, of land heretofore made by their tribes to the British, French, or Spanish government, within the limites of the United States or their territories; and the parties here contracting do, moreover, in the sincerity of mutual friendship recognize, re-establish and confirm all and every treaty, contract and agreement, heretofore concluded between the United States and the said tribes or nations.

Art. 4. The undersigned chiefs and warriors as aforesaid, for themselves and their said tribes, do hereby acknowledge themselves to be under the protection of the United States, and of no other nation, power, or sovereign, whatsoever.

In witness whereof, the commissioners aforesaid, and the undersigned chiefs and warriors as aforesaid, have hereunto subscribed their names and affixed their seals this first day of June, in the year of our Lord one thousand eight hundred and sixteen, and of the independence of the United States the fortieth.

WILLIAM CLARK
NINIAN EDWARDS
AUGUSTE CHOUTEAU

By 1825 the chief concern was conditions of trade:

Treaty with the Teton, Yancton and Yanctonies bands of the Sioux tribes of Indians. June 27, 1825 ("Statutes at Large," VII, 250–251).

For the purposes of perpetuating the friendship which has heretofore existed, as also to remove all future causes of discussion and dissention, as it respects *trade and friendship* between the United States and their citizens, and the Teton, Yancton, and Yanctonies bands of the Sioux tribe of Indians, the President of the United States of America, by Brigadier-General Henry Atkinson, of the United States' army, and Major Benjamin O'Fallon, Indian Agent, with full powers and authority, specially appointed and commissioned for that purpose of the one part, and the undersigned Chiefs, head men and Warriors of the Teton, Yancton, and Yanctonies bands of the Sioux tribe of Indians, on behalf of the said bands or tribe of the other part, have made and entered into the following Articles and Conditions; which, when ratified by the President of the United States, by and with the advice and consent of the Senate; shall be binding on both parties,—to wit:

[In Article I] In addition to acknowledging the supremacy of the United States and claiming its protection, the bands also admit the right of the United States to regulate all trade and intercourse with them.

[In Article III] A place for trade selected by the President is to be designated through his agents and none but U.S. citizens, duly authorized shall be admitted to trade with said bands of Indians.

Other conditions include the obligation of chiefs to exert themselves to recover stolen property, and a proviso that no arms shall be provided to any nation or tribe of Indians not in amity with the United States.

By 1837 the treaty concerned the cession of land east of the Mississippi, from which the Indians had moved, to the United States, and the compensation to be paid ("Statutes at Large," VII, 538–539):

Sept. 29, 1837. Made at the City of Washington, between Joel R. Poinsett, thereto specially authorised by the President of the United States, and certain chiefs and braves of the Sioux nation of Indians.

Article 1st. The chiefs and braves representing the parties having an interest therein, cede to the United States all their land, east of the Mississippi river, and all their islands in the said river.

Article 2d. In consideration of the cession contained in the preceding article, the United States agree to the following stipulations on their part.

First. To invest the sum of $300,000 (three hundred thousand dollars) in such safe and profitable State stocks as the President may direct, and to pay to the chiefs and braves as aforesaid, annually, forever, an income of not less than five per cent thereon; a portion of said interest, not exceeding one third, to be applied in such manner as the President may direct, and the residue to be paid in specie, or in such other manner and for such objects, as the proper authorities of the tribe may designate.

A sum was designated for persons of mixed blood.

A sum was designated for the payment of Indian debts.

Annuities were to be paid, agricultural implements provided, mechanics' tools, implements and stock and support of a physician and a blacksmith.

For twenty years a certain amount of provisions to be supplied.

Compensation to the interpreter for 20 years in recognition of his valuable services.

On April 19, 1858, land was relinquished and the boundaries of the reservation sharply delimited ("*Statutes at Large,*" *XI, 743, 744, 745*).

Article I. The said chiefs and delegates of said tribe of Indians do hereby cede and relinquish to the United States all lands now owned, possessed or claimed by them, wherever situated except four hundred thousand acres thereof, situated and described as follows: . . .

Article II. The land so ceded and relinquished by the said chiefs and delegates of the said tribe of Yanctons is and shall be known and described as follows, . . . And they also cede and relinquish to the United States all their right and title to and in all the islands of the Missouri River, from the mouth of the Big Sioux to the mouth of the Medicine Knoll River.

Article III. . . . And the said Yanctons hereby agree to *remove and settle and reside* on said reservation within one year from this date, and until they do so remove, (if within said year,) the United States guarantee them in the quiet and undisturbed possession of their present settlements.

Article IV. . . . 1st. To protect the said Yanctons in the quiet and peaceable possession of the said tract of four hundred thousand acres of land so reserved for their future home, and also their persons and property thereon during good behavior on their part.

Payment and annuities are then designated.

Subsistence, schools and school-houses, instruction in agricultural milling and mechanic shops for which the Indians are to furnish apprentices.

CROW INDIANS OF MONTANA

April 11, 1882, a treaty with the Crow Indians of Montana now concerns the sale of some of their reservation lands to the United States and arrangements for their settlement on lands in severalty outside the tribal boundaries.

Annuities are provided for twenty-five years in consideration of the cession of lands to be made to the United States (*"Statutes at Large," XXII, 42–43*).

CHEYENNE AND ARAPAHO

Treaties with the Cheyenne and Arapaho follow a completely parallel course to those with the Siouan peoples: July 6, 1825, trade ("Statutes at Large," VII, 255–256); February 18, 1861, cession of land, delimitation of boundaries ("Statutes at Large," XII, 1,163–1,165). This treaty was authorized by Abraham Lincoln, then President of the United States.

May 10, 1868 ("Statutes at Large," XV, 656–657).

. . . the Northern Cheyenne and Arapahoe Indians do hereby relinquish, release, and surrender to the United States all right, claim, and interest in and to all territory outside the two reservations above mentioned, except the right to roam and hunt while game shall be found in sufficient quantities to justify the chase.

The following includes the Northern Cheyenne and Arapaho among those sending a delegation to select land in Indian Territory.

Feb. 28, 1877 ("Statutes at Large," XIX, 254–255).

If such delegates shall make a selection which shall be satisfactory to themselves, the people whom they represent and to the United States, then said Indians agree to remove to the country so selected within one year from this date.

KIOWA AND COMANCHE

The so-called Treaty of Medicine Lodge, October 21, 1867, made between the United States and the Kiowa and Comanche tribes, was particularly concerned with protecting our citizens from armed attacks by the Indians.

Article I.   From this day forward all war between the parties to this agreement shall forever cease.

The government of the United States pledged itself to prosecute "bad men among the whites" who commit wrong upon the person or property of the Indians, while the Indians in their turn pledged punishment upon Indians who commit a wrong or depredation upon the person of property of anyone, white, Black, or Indian, subject to the authority of the United States and at peace therewith, to be turned over to the United States authorities for punishment.

. . . the tribes who are parties to this agreement hereby stipulate that they will relinquish all right to occupy permanently the territory outside of their reservation as herein defined, but they yet reserve the right to hunt on any lands south of the Arkansas (river) so long as the buffalo may range thereon in such numbers as to justify the chase (and no white settlements shall be permitted on any part of the lands contained in the old reservation as defined by the treaty made between the United States and the Cheyenne, Arapahoe, and Apache tribes of Indians at the mouth of the Little Arkansas, under date of October fourteenth, one thousand eight hundred and sixty-five, within three years from this date . . . ["Statutes at Large," XV, 581, 584]

The locality of Medicine Lodge was seventy miles south of Fort Larned in the State of Kansas.

The treaties were indeed an important index of United States good intentions, but economic developments proved too drastic and rapid to allow these provisions to be carried out.

A Hundred Million Buffaloes and Then a Sea of Carcasses (1867–1876)

The buffalo was a major target of the industrializing East. Persons seeking adventure and many who could find no work came in large numbers to make use of what they thought was an inexhaustible supply of meat to sustain them and hides to enrich them. The crowded, penned up Indians, in the face of this massive pressure, had little chance to survive. During the Civil War buffalo robes and leather had military uses and by 1864 over a hundred buffalo hunters, including Wild Bill Hickock, were in Kansas with a similar number of camps among other trails. The United States government hoped that by sharply defining the territories of the Indians and supplying them with agricultural implements and other materials, they would settle down to marginal farming and keep out of the way of the white migrants to the Plains. The kind of agriculture that was being prescribed was already obsolescent as a viable method of subsistence in a rapidly industrializing society. The Indians needed the buffalo and anything else they could get from the natural resources to compensate for the inadequacy of what they could produce with the means they had.

Meanwhile the soldiers in the small garrisons that guarded the frontier who had charge of the forts were alike in their eagerness to speed the day when the Indians would be compelled to stay in their own confines; they had the feeling that the best means of accomplishing this was the rapid extermination of the buffalo. These sentiments, diametrically opposed to the stated intent of the treaties, could hardly bring good faith into Indian-white relations. In 1867, when Colonel R. I. Dodge received the regrets of Sir W. F. Butler that his party had killed thirty bulls in a hunt at Fort McPherson below the forks of the Platte, Dodge replied, "Kill every buffalo you can. Every buffalo dead is an Indian gone." Colonel Dodge reiterated his advice to professional buffalo hunters in the 1870s concerning the Indian-restricted Texas herd after the northern herds had become extinct. When the Texas legislature was about to pass a bill outlawing the hide hunter, General Phil Sheridan hurried to Austin to protest, stating that they were about to make a sentimental mistake—they should give the white hunters a unanimous vote of thanks and appropriate sufficient funds to present a bronze medal to each one, with a dead buffalo on one side and a discouraged Indian on the other.

With these sentiments so generally held, the young Indian warriors were unwilling to be restrained by their chiefs, whom they felt had betrayed them, and they proceeded to raid hide camps, the Kansas Pacific Railroad builders, and particularly the settlers as they expanded westward to occupy the Indians' last refuge.

Confusion multiplied when the Kansas Pacific Railroad ran out of money in 1868 and laid off 1,200 laborers indefinitely, while at the same time the Santa Fe Railroad was coming up the Arkansas River, drawing thousands of hopeful laborers from the unemployed in the East. Some of these unemployed workers came intending to become buffalo hunters, but in a few weeks, or even days, they turned to outlawry, sometimes poorly disguised as Indians. The death toll from all sources, including Indian attack, was, of course, considerable.

The saloon became the focus of life for experienced hunters as well as others in the face of rumors that the bottom had dropped out of the hide market. Too frequently fights and shooting up the streets were their only outlet. Meanwhile attacks by Indians on the settlements resulted in complaints to Washington. In addition to private militias that the settlers organized, Washington responded by sending Army men, who quickly assembled, and armed companies of civilians, a plentiful supply of idlers being readily available. Besides their government pay, they were offered all the plunder they could get. The fact was readily lost sight of that a force of civilians was going to attack all Indians on their legal hunting grounds because a few young men of one tribe or another had committed depredations. Indian raids in reprisal, particularly on helpless civilians in the settlements, were bound to be intensified (Sandoz, 1954).

Until 1871 the fur buffalo robe was the main marketable item, the leather being a far more limited commodity. Leather was used by the British Army in the Crimean War (1854–1856), but only after 1871 did an English firm provide a mass market for the buffalo hides. Previously, when the robes were the main item of value, commercial hunting was confined mainly to the winter when the fur was thick, but with leather as the mass product, the buffalo hunter could kill with profit all year round (Vestal, 1952, 40). The railroads, too, were glad to have the business. Their progress westward had been stopped by the long depression of the 1870s; with almost no traffic, carrying buffalo meat, hides, and bones to eastern markets was a valued business opportunity. Merchants and freighters welcomed the business that came from buffalo hunting (Vestal, 1952, 38).

> Hardly had the market for buffalo hides become widely known than the panic of 1873 began which lasted for five years. During those years most of the buffalo on the southern plains were destroyed [Vestal, 1952, 45].

In 1871 the buffalo were estimated in the millions. Many of the hunters entered the profession expecting it to prove a life work and despaired of killing off more than the annual increase of the herd. Hunters encamped by water holes and rivers where the animals came to drink, built watch fires at night so that the slaughter could go on for twenty-four hours a day [Vestal, 1952, 46].

For maximum efficiency some hunters used the Big Fifty, a gun produced by Sharps to the hunter's specifications, made to load and fire eight times a minute (Sandoz, 1954, 97; Vestal, 1952, 41). "In a brief two years (1873–1875), where there had been myriads of buffalo, there were only myriads of rotting carcasses. The air was filled with the sickening stench of death. . . ." [Vestal, 1952, 46].

The meat rotted, the bones remained, and then they, too, became a source of commercial profit. They were used in making fertilizer or in making bone china. They brought good prices. A man driving to town to trade would fill his wagon bed with bones and sell them on Front Street, Dodge City (Kansas). There were bones piled up as high as a man's head, extending all along the track for many yards awaiting shipment. Many of the settlers managed to keep going by selling bones when drought and depression again struck the plains and destroyed their corn crop (Vestal, 1952, 50), before wheat had become a major crop of the area. One bone-buying firm estimated that over seven years (1884–1891) they bought the bones of approximately 5,950,000 buffalo skeletons. This firm was only one of many (Sandoz, 1954, 358).

Plains Indians on Reservations: Rural Isolation Within an Obsolescing Industrial Complex (1969)

Today, as the once mobile Plains Indians remain isolated in their enclaves, they are in still a further danger—that of becoming rootless. In the face of typical rural poverty that besets Indian and non-Indian in outlying regions, attempts are being made to introduce small industries on the reservations. There is no possibility of producing a reasonable living out of such means, while automation and the computer demand increasingly mammoth operation and require fewer laborers on all levels (Davis, 1967). There is surprise that the magic of industry, any industry, does not today bring occupation or even a modest living (Mizen, 1966; 1967), any more than in the past, the obsolescent marginal farm in an industrializing nation, which was so universally held up as the Indian's solution, could bring even a meager subsistence. These are sorry attempts to dole out simple pieces of our complex society deemed suitable for simple people.

The second attempt to handle the problem is to move the Indians off the reservation, encouraging further encroachment of the surrounding populations on the Indians' family estate. If it is of advantage for the rural poverty-stricken non-Indian to urbanize, there are elements that further complicate the problem for the Indian. As it is, the city is not a haven for the untrained person, Indian or non-Indian. But, in addition, for the Indian his land is not only real estate but still stands as a memorial of his family past and of the past of the continent and its Indian developers. The psychosocial value of the Indians' lands cannot be dismissed.

There is a dilemma to be faced that is certainly not impossible to resolve. Today none of us can live without intensive training for life, both in work and leisure and on all levels, training that can only be offered in large centers and requiring constant renewal. There is certainly a way of establishing Indian areas as centers of public education and recreation on the significance of our Indian heritage, while at the same time releasing most of the people for other participations, along with whatever part they may choose to take in the educational work at the home base. This could be developed by a combination of Indian initiative and national effort, as it is very much in the national interest that we all understand our continental roots. To some extent our extreme exploitation of the environment may, in part, be due to a continuing "settler" mentality. Most of us are still oriented toward European origins and lands.

Pan-Indianism and the Plains Indian Stereotype as Its Symbol

The Indian community certainly cannot afford to disregard the material and social effects of the popular view of the American Indian. A crude representation of the recent horse nomadism phase of Plains Indian life has come to permeate most people's representation of general Indianness. The costuming, the horses, the tipis, the cavalry war formation, have come to symbolize "Indian" *par excellence*. In a sense these visual symbols of the Indian spirit do represent something very important. This "nomadic" Plains pattern has such a profound appeal because it is an enactment of resistance as it was played out on the Plains, the theater of the heroic last stand of uprooted Indians displaced from their European-occupied homes. As such it belongs to all American Indians and is rightly a symbol of a resistance movement of the whole people.

But on a deeper level the long Indian presence on the continent is of even more significance for Pan-Indian identity. Hopefully we will be able to bring it to the consciousness of every schoolchild, so that he grows up with a sense of appreciation and understanding of the land he stands on and its real human history, the 15,000-year panorama in which Indian ancestors enacted the whole human drama evolving from the big game hunter to the empire builder. There was a parallel growth in both the New World and the Old, the Mexican–Central American–Peruvian heartland compared with that of the Tigris-Euphrates, radiating their advanced knowledge to the outlying areas. Archeology is bringing light and refinement to these aspects of Indian identity—no longer a vague speculation, but a history pinned down to reality by the archeological artifact. Newer archeological work that is growing fast is historic archeology, finding expression in a newly founded Society for Historical Archeology, covering the common life of both populations in addition to Indian prehistory. This work will be the wellspring of a much more, and constantly enriched, version of the European invasion and the Indian resistance. It is largely from this source that the true nature of Plains Indian nomadism as a reaction and resistance to conquest has been revealed, as against the notion that the Plains Indian was a rootless nomad, a backward survivor of Stone Age man—a cultural fossil. This general idea manifests itself in the attitude toward Indian property, continuing into our time from the age of the Pilgrims. In this view Indian property rights to their legally assigned family estates are somehow not owned in the sense of other United States landed properties. It is the general feeling on the part of the white population that the Indian owners are not making use of the land as they should, that they should be squeezing certain quick profits from the use and possibly final drainage of natural resources— a right of judgment not applied to any other class of landowners. The universality of the Plains Indian nomadic stereotype as a function of the natural order of things gives active support to this ideology. A few quotations from a time span of three centuries of American history may clarify the character of this implicit attitude (Forbes, 1964).

Quoting William Bradford, 1617, on the outlook of the English Puritans in the Netherlands as they were deciding to leave that country:

> The place they had thoughts on was some of those fruitfull and fitt for habitation, being devoid of all civill inhabitants, wher ther are only salvage and brutish men, which range up and down, little otherwise then the wild beasts of the same. . . . [Forbes, 1964, 14, 15].

And from Father Luis Velarde, c. 1716, a Jesuit missionary in northern Sonora:

> And truly it has been due to the particular providence of our Lord, that this nation [friendly Pimas of Arizona-Sonora] has been diminished due to con-

tinuous epidemics; for because of their pride they are not lacking among them people who are restless and troublesome [Forbes, 1964, 15].

From Captain J. Lee Humfreville, an officer of the United States Army, 1897:

Our savage Indians had no idea of the ownership of land either individually or collectively. . . . The idea propagated by some modern sentimentalists that in resisting the march of civilization the wild Indians were fighting for their homes and firesides belongs to fiction rather than to fact. . . . they have no home and no fireside in the civilized sense of these terms [Forbes, 1964, 18].

It is only possible to maintain such a view if we continue to keep the American Indian out of the stream of history. The Sioux Indian, for example, viewed as a culture fossil, a nomadic Stone Age hunter, attacking settlements and wearing a war bonnet as part of his primitive aboriginal nature is readily open to the above interpretations. But the Sioux Indian tracing his ancestry to the Mound Builder civilization of the Southeast (Wedel, 1965), his pioneering migration and settlement to a new frontier home in the Great Lakes area, his fight to maintain himself against the onrush of the displaced European coming across the ocean and then inland from the Atlantic seaboard where no industry could offer him a place, the organized Sioux army finally acquiring horses and moving as a cavalry into the Plains frontier during our Revolutionary period to make a stand for the survival of his people and his family—a dynamic image validated and progressively strengthened by the science of history and archeology—this is an Indian identity well worth memorializing to all that can listen.

REFERENCES

ALLIS, SAMUEL
1887 Forty years among the Indians and on the eastern borders of Nebraska. Proceedings and Collections of the Nebraska State Historical Society 2:133–196.
1918 *See* Dunbar, John B., 1918.

BENEDICT, RUTH F.
1922 The vision in Plains culture. American Anthropologist 22, 1 (January-March), 1–23.
1923 The concept of the guardian spirit in North America. Memoirs of the American Anthropological Association 29.

BREBNER, JOHN B.
1966 Explorers of North America, 1492–1806. Cleveland: The World Publishing Company.

CHAMPE, JOHN L.

1949 White Cat village. American Antiquity XIV:285–292.

DAVIS, ROBERT

1967 The advance of cybernation: 1965–85. *In* The guaranteed income. Robert Theobald, ed. Garden City: Doubleday. pp. 39–68.

DUNBAR, REVEREND JOHN B., AND SAMUEL ALLIS

1918 Letters concerning the Presbyterian mission in The Pawnee Country near Bellevue, Nebraska, 1831–1849. Collections of the Kansas State Historical Society, XIV:570–689, 690–741. Topeka, Kansas.

EWERS, JOHN C.

1955 The horse in Blackfoot Indian culture. Bureau of American Ethnology Bulletin 159.

1958 The Blackfeet. Norman, Okla.: University of Oklahoma Press.

1960 Selected references on the Plains Indians. Smithsonian Anthropological Bibliographies (1). Smithsonian Institution.

FENTON, WILLIAM N.

1953 The Iroquois eagle dance: an offshoot of the calumet dance. Bureau of American Ethnology Bulletin 156.

FORBES, JACK D. ED.

1964 The Indian in America's past. Englewood Cliffs: Prentice-Hall.

FORDE, C. DARYLL

1963 Habitat, economy and society. New York: E. P. Dutton.

GRIFFIN, JAMES B.

1965 The Northwest woodlands area. *In* Prehistoric man in the new world. Jesse D. Jennings and Edward Norbeck, eds. Chicago: University of Chicago Press. pp. 223–258.

1967 Eastern North American archeology. Science 3772 (April 14, 1967), 175–191.

HAGAN, WILLIAM T.

1964 American Indians. Chicago: University of Chicago Press.

HODGE, FREDERICK WEBB, ED.

1912 Handbook of American Indians north of Mexico. Bureau of American Ethnology Bulletin 30.

HOEBEL, EDWARD

1960 The Cheyenne. New York: Holt, Rinehart & Winston.

HOEBEL, EDWARD, AND ERNEST WALLACE

1952 The Comanches: lords of the southern Plains. Norman, Okla.: University of Oklahoma Press.

HYDE, GEORGE E.

1951 Pawnee Indians. Denver: University of Denver Press.

IRVING, JOHN TREAT, JR.

1955 Indian sketches. John Francis McDermott, ed. Norman, Okla.: University of Oklahoma Press.

JENNINGS, JESSE D., AND EDWARD NORBECK, EDS.
1965 Prehistoric man in the new world. Chicago: University of Chicago Press.

KRIEGER, ALEX D.
1965 Early Man in the new world. *In* Prehistoric man in the new world. Jesse D. Jennings and Edward Norbeck, eds. Chicago: University of Chicago Press.

LÉVI-STRAUSS, CLAUDE
1967 Structural anthropology. Garden City: Doubleday.

LOWIE, ROBERT H.
1935 The Crow Indians. New York: Farrar and Rinehart.
1954 Indians of the Plains. New York: McGraw-Hill.

MACDERMOTT, JOHN FRANCIS *see* IRVING

MCKENNEY, THOMAS L., AND JAMES HALL
1842 History of the Indian tribes of North America. "With Biographical Sketches and anecdotes of the Principal Chiefs." vol. I. Philadelphia: Daniel Rice and James G. Clark.

MCNICKLE, D'ARCY
1962 The Indian tribes of the United States. London: Oxford University Press.

MIZEN, MAMIE L.
1966, 1967 Federal facilities for Indians, tribal relations with the federal government. Committee on Appropriations, United States Senate. Report, 1965–66; Report, 1967. Washington, D.C.: U.S. Government Printing Office.

MORSE, JEDIDIAH
1822 A report to the secretary of war of the United States, on Indian affairs, comprising a narrative of a tour performed in summer of 1820. New Haven: S. Converse.

ROE, FRANK G.
1951 The North American buffalo. Toronto: Toronto University Press.

ROSS, MARVIN C.
1951 The west of Alfred Jacob Miller (1837). Norman, Okla.: University of Oklahoma Press.

SANDOZ, MARI
1954 The buffalo hunters. New York: Hastings House.

SCHULTZ, J. W.
1935 My life as an Indian. Greenwich, Conn.: Fawcett.

SEARS, WILLIAM H.
1965 The southeastern United States. *In* Prehistoric man in the new world. Jesse L. Jennings and Edward Norbeck, eds. Chicago: University of Chicago Press. pp. 259–287.

SECOY, FRANK R.
1953 Changing military patterns on the Great Plains. American Ethnological Society Monographs XXI.

STRONG, WILLIAM DUNCAN
1940 From history to prehistory in the northern Great Plains. *In* Essays in

historical anthropology of North America. [Published in Honor of John R. Swanton.] Smithsonian Miscellaneous Collections 100:353–394.

SWANTON, JOHN R.

1942 Source material on the history and ethnology of the Caddo Indians. Bureau of American Ethnology Bulletin 132.

1946 The Indians of southeastern United States. Bureau of American Ethnology Bulletin 137.

THWAITES, REUBEN GOLD

1900 Travels and explorations of Jesuit missionaries in New France 1610–1791. Cleveland: The Burrows Bros. Co. vol. 59, pp. 129–131.

UNITED STATES STATUTES

"Statutes at Large." Published by Little, Brown, Boston, until 1873; since then by the Government Printing Office, Washington, D.C.

VESTAL, STANLEY

1952 Queen of the Cowtowns, Dodge City. New York: Harper.

WEDEL, WALDO

1936 An introduction to Pawnee archeology. Bureau of American Ethnology Bulletin 122.

1965 The Great Plains. In Prehistoric man in the new world. Jesse L. Jennings and Edward Norbeck, eds. Chicago: University of Chicago Press. pp. 193–220.

WELTFISH, GENE

1936 The vision of fox boy, a South Band Pawnee text, with translation and grammatical analysis. International Journal of American Linguistics IX (1):44–75.

1937 Caddoan texts, Pawnee South Band dialect. Publications of the American Ethnological Society XVII.

1965a The lost universe. New York: Basic Books.

1965b The music of the Pawnee. New York: Folkways Record (FE 4334).

WINSHIP, GEORGE PARKER

1896 The Coronado expedition, 1540–1542. 14th Annual Report, Bureau of American Ethnology, pt. I (1892–1893).

WISSLER, CLARK

1917 Comparative study of Pawnee and Blackfoot rituals. Proceedings of the 19th International Congress of Americanists. Washington, D.C., December 1915. pp. 335–339.

References for Figure 7.1

COUES, ELLIOTT, ED.

1965 History of the expedition under the command of Lewis and Clark. vols. I, II, III. New York: Dover Publications, Inc.

GALLATIN, ALBERT

Map of the Indian tribes of North America, about A.D. 1600 along the Atlantic, and about A.D. 1800 westwardly. Published by American Antiquity Society. Boston: Heliotype Printing Co.

LEWIS, MERIWETHER

1902 History of the expedition of Captain Lewis and Clark 1804–6. Reprinted from the edition of 1814; with introduction and index by James K. Hosmer. A. C. McClurg & Co. c. 1902; reprint 1924.

STURTEVANT, WILLIAM C.

1958 (Compiler.) Selected bibliography of maps relating to the American Indian. Washington, D.C.: Bureau of American Ethnology, Smithsonian Institution.

WILLEY, GORDON R.

1966 An introduction to American archaeology. vol. I. Englewood Cliffs, N.J.: Prentice Hall.

8   *The American Southwest*[1]

EDWARD P. DOZIER

     The term "American Southwest culture area," as a device for classifying and delimiting the indigenous populations of the area, has been the subject of scholarly controversy for a long time. Its very name, "Southwest," indicates that the area has been proposed by United States scholars or scholars whose reference point was the United States. If Mexican anthropologists were setting up the area with the high cultures of Mexico as a focal point, they might very appropriately have termed the area the "Northwest" or the "Peripheral North" or some such designation. The early classifications typically stopped at the international border of the United States and Mexico and included primarily the indigenous peoples of New Mexico and Arizona. Later scholars have retained the ethnocentric designation but have gotten away from the national bias by expanding the geographical boundaries of the area. These scholars were concerned with the appropriateness of the term for designating an area roughly similar in geographical features and containing peoples exhibiting shared cultural characteristics. Wissler (1917) in his classification gave cognizance to the concept of "culture area" in the sense of including historically related cultural groups with a focal center representing the cultural characteristics of the area in heightened form. Kroeber (1928, 1939, 1948) and Beals (1943), following the lead of Wissler, crossed the international border and included larger parts of the states bordering New Mexico and Arizona. Perhaps the most generally accepted classification at present is that of Kirchhoff (1954, 533); also compare Haury (1962, 106–107). Kirchhoff, designating the area the "Greater Southwest," includes central, southern, and Baja California; the Great Basin, Arizona, New Mexico, southern coastal Texas; and northern Mexico south to the Sinaloa and Panuco rivers. In the more recent classifications such factors as the subsistence economies of the people and the ecological environment features of the area become the principles of classification.

     The present paper will be concerned with the broad geographical area delimited by Kirchhoff, whose classification has the advantage of presenting an area characterized by generally arid conditions, interspersed with desert and mountainous terrain, and containing historically related cultural groups. Materials are presented in five sections: The first section surveys the prehistoric peopling of the area; the second presents the continuity of prehistoric traditions to the present; the third details some of the salient features of the ethnography; the fourth discusses the changes that the indigenous people have undergone as the result of Western European contacts; and the fifth and final section is one of perspective and outlook.

Prehistoric and Historic Periods[2]

The earliest people in the area, dating back to about 10,000 B.C., lived contemporaneously with now extinct forms of the sloth, horse, elephant, and great bison. These early peoples hunted some of those animals, and two distinct patterns are identified on the basis of projectile points and plant extraction tools. In the eastern part of the area, extending into the Great Plains country, were the *Paleo-Indians,* or big game hunters. A second cultural pattern, the *Desert Cultures,* extended southward from the Great Basin and covered most of the Southwest. Apparently also, hunters of big game in the earlier periods, carriers of the Desert Cultures, appear to have adapted to the hunting of smaller game and to the gathering of plants as the large game animals disappeared.

The eastern expression of the Desert cultural pattern is important for the early elaboration of plant extracting techniques. Grinding implements like the *metate* and the *mano* are numerous in sites of the Cochise tradition, attesting to the extensive use of wild vegetable foods by these Indians. Corncobs from as early as 3000 B.C. have been found in east-central Arizona and west-central New Mexico. The occurrence of cultivated corn indicates diffusion of the technique of maize cultivation from Mexico, presumably along the corridor of the Sierra Madre. The maize appears to be a variety adapted to high altitudes; the sites in which it is found are all in elevations of 6,000 feet. By 1000 B.C. squash and beans were added to the diet, yet curiously these foods made no profound changes in the lifeway of these people; there are no permanent habitations or other indications of a settled life until about 300 B.C.

With the advent of pottery, about 300 B.C., archeologists recognize a new tradition, the *Mogollon*. This tradition reveals the earliest settled life in the Southwest. Mogollon peoples, about A.D. 1, erected quadrangular and rounded pit houses grouped into clusters of tiny villages. Shortly after A.D. 1, the bow and arrow makes its first appearance, and to this must be added a complex of *manos, metates;* mortars

and pestles; and implements made of stone, bone, and shell. Five periods are recognized by pottery types extending to about A.D. 1100, when
the area becomes substantially reduced and acculturated to another
tradition, the *Anasazi*. The Anasazi tradition begins later in what is
now the four states' corner area of Colorado, New Mexico, Arizona,
and Utah. This tradition exists parallel to the Mogollon tradition for
many years and eventually absorbs the latter. We will return to a fuller
discussion of the Anasazi after presenting the development of another
important prehistoric tradition, the *Hohokam,* whose beginnings are
later than the Mogollon, but earlier than the Anasazi.

The Hohokam appears to have also stemmed from the closing periods
of the Cochise (about A.D. 1), but its locale was the desert regions of central and southern Arizona. The Hohokam culture developed rapidly
into a complex irrigation society along the lower reaches of the Gila
River, where long and elaborate irrigation canals were constructed.
These water-control achievements imply a well-developed sociopolitical
organization, perhaps more complex than that achieved anywhere in the
Southwest among the indigenous populations. Toward the end of the
period strong influences of the Anasazi tradition from the North are evident, and the culture disappears abruptly about A.D. 1400 for reasons not
yet solved by archeologists. Influences of the Hohokam are also evident
northwestward in the lower Colorado River area in a sub-tradition
known as the *Patayan,* or *Hakataya*. Whether the Patayan developed out
of the Hohokam or directly out of the Desert cultural pattern is not
clear. The tradition, although sedentary, lacked permanent dwellings.
The Indians built brush huts, cooked in stone-lined pits, and like the
Hohokam Indians, cremated their dead. Flood farming, rather than irrigation, was employed. The Patayan never achieved the architectural or
technological complexity of any of the other Southwestern sedentary
traditions.

Still another sub-tradition, the *Sinagua,* is recognized by archeologists
in the area between the northernmost reaches of the Hohokam and the
Anasazi on the northeast. The tradition was short-lived, beginning about
A.D. 400 and ending by A.D. 1100. Influence from the Hohokam is evident
in dwellings and ball courts, but like the Mogollon, it, too, acculturated
to the Anasazi by A.D. 1100.

We may now return to the Anasazi. In prehistoric times the Anasazi
covered the San Juan River and Little Colorado River drainages as well
as the northern Rio Grande region. Its most complex development was
concentrated, however, in the four corners area of Arizona, New Mexico,
Utah, and Colorado where the tradition reached a cultural florescence
in the twelfth century. During the final phases of the tradition it absorbed the other traditions adjacent to it and, indeed, continued in re-

cessed form in northern Arizona, western New Mexico, and the northern Rio Grande valley until historic times. It may have developed independently from the Desert Culture, but it undoubtedly borrowed agriculture from the Mogollon. The beginnings of the Anasazi were at least 300 to 700 years later than the Mogollon or Hohokam, but it surpassed both of these earlier traditions in architectural excellence. While lacking the complex water control achievements of the Hohokam, the Anasazi nevertheless practiced intensive agriculture by exploiting flood-water farming and a simple stream-diversion type of irrigation. The potential development of another cultural peak characterized by irrigation in the Rio Grande valley was arrested by Spanish conquest in the sixteenth century. A study of the contemporary Pueblos indicates that the Rio Grande villages differ from the flood-farming Pueblos farther west in possessing institutions that give former villages central sociopolitical control and direction. The beginning in the Rio Grande valley of a miniature waterworks society that demanded more centralized control of the population probably reflects these institutional differences. This subject will receive additional attention in the ethnological section.

The prehistory of the southern portion of the Southwest is imperfectly known; extensive archeological investigations have been concentrated in the northern and central portions of the area. It is clear from the few excavations and surveys that have been made, however, that Cochise and its later manifestations, Mogollon and Hohokam, reach back into the Mexican states of Sonora and Chihuahua. Influences from Meso-America are also strong in the Hohokam, and such traits can be expected to be stronger in the South. Other traditions may be eventually discovered in this portion of the Southwest, but such discoveries can only come with further investigations.

Ethnological Continuities

Contemporary survivals of the carriers of the archeological traditions surveyed above cannot be determined with certainty. Anasazi and Mogollon traits are obvious in the social and cultural inventory of the present-day Pueblos. The present Yuman-speaking populations along the lower Colorado—the Havasupai, Yavapai, Walapai, and the Yuman proper—are also believed to demonstrate a continuity of Patayan cultural characteristics; but not all authorities are agreed. Similarly, the contemporary Pima and Papago of southern Arizona are said to be cultural descendants of the ancient Hohokam. If Spanish influences on the surviving northern Mexican tribal peoples, like the Tarahumara, Opata, Yaqui, and Mayo, can be separated, these tribes may be linked to the Hohokam or Mogollon. But this may not be possible, for the imprint of Hispanic and Catholic patterns is extremely heavy on these groups. The fact that all of these northern Mexican tribal peoples speak Uto-Aztecan languages might be used as evidence that they stem from a single tradition or related traditions, yet linguistic unity is not always prerequisite to cultural relatedness. The Pueblos of Arizona and New Mexico are a case in point. All authorities appear to be agreed that these Pueblos are the cultural descendants of the Anasazi tradition, with marked Mogollon characteristics; yet these Pueblos fall into four distinct language stocks: Uto-Aztecan, Tanoan, Keresan, and Zunian. It is important, therefore, to proceed with caution when we seek connections between contemporary language cultural groups and prehistoric cultural traditions.

In the northern periphery are the Paiutes and the Utes—nomadic peoples who may be considered continuities of the Desert cultural pattern or who may have reverted back to a hunting and foraging life after experiencing an early Anasazi sedentary life. During the historic period these people maintained a nomadic existence and, indeed, preyed on the settled farmers.

Another nomadic people who now comprise a majority in the population of the Southwest are obviously newcomers. The Apachean, or Southern Athapaskan, peoples surrounded the Pueblo and the southern Uto-Aztecan peoples in late prehistoric and historic times. These Southern Athapaskans are closely related linguistically to the Athapaskans of interior Alaska and the Canadian northwest. The earliest dependable archeological evidence places the Southern Athapaskans in the Chacra Mesa and Governador regions of northern New Mexico early in the sixteenth century. The Southern Athapaskans are divided at present into seven tribes: (1) Navaho, (2) Western Apache, (3) Chiricahua Apache, (4) Jicarilla Apache, (5) Mescalero, (6) Lipan, and (7) Kiowa Apache. The Navaho and the Jicarilla Apache are nearest the Pueblos, and both have absorbed many Puebloan traits. Such traits were obviously borrowed in the sixteenth and seventeenth centuries from Pueblo Indian refugees who joined them to escape Spanish oppression, particularly after the Pueblo Indian revolt of 1680 and the subsequent reconquest period of 1693–1696. Some of these Puebloan traits among the Navaho will be described in our survey of the historic and contemporary Indian tribes.

Ethnology[3]

In discussing the ethnology of the historic and contemporary indigenous peoples of the Southwest, we have grouped the southwestern tribes into broad subsistence categories. Subsistence patterns and cultural affinities correspond roughly to environmental factors, but except in the southern portion of the area, they do not always correlate with linguistic affiliations. A fourfold subsistence classification is employed: simple gatherers, advanced gatherers and hunters, part-time agriculturists, and agriculturists. The fourfold classification does not constitute exclusive categories, for there is some overlap of shared traits. This is natural, since, obviously, the more complex subsistence groups have evolved from the others; and since the groups are in touch with one another, considerable borrowing and exchange of traits have gone on.

SIMPLE GATHERERS

Of the simple gatherers, the Great Basin Paiutes of the Uto-Aztecan linguistic stock are perhaps the most typical. But shared characteristics extend to the north-central California Penutians, the Miwok and Yokuts, and the Washo and Pomo of Hokan stock. In northwestern Arizona the Yuman, Walapai, and Yavapai, and in southern California, other Uto-Aztecan speaking groups like the Luiseño, Cupeño, and Serrano can also be included in this group. Here, too, belong the Seri, a Hokan-speaking group in mid-coastal Sonora.

The gathering of a wide range of food plants comprises the basic subsistence of these peoples, with the fruit of one basic tree serving as a food staple: the piñon, the acorn, or the mesquite bean. Plant foods may be supplemented at times by rabbits and other small rodents and, in season, by locusts. These gatherers exhibit a form of life that is probably little removed from the basic prehistoric Desert Culture pattern once characteristic of the whole of the Southwestern area.

The basic social group of the simple gatherers is the nuclear family, comprising a husband, wife, and children and perhaps an unattached relative, such as a widowed grandfather or grandmother or an unmarried brother, sister, nephew, or niece. Such a family occupies a simple brush shelter clearly set apart from other structures. In earlier times little clothing was worn: Men often went naked; women wore simple aprons, one in front and one in back. The shaman is the only specialist, and the position in the meager economy is by necessity only part-time. He is both a healer and a diviner, obtaining his power through dreams. Ceremonies involve rites for the three events in the life cycle: birth, puberty, and death. The most elaborate of these ceremonies is the girls' puberty rite.

GATHERERS AND HUNTERS

Somewhat more complex in technology and social structure are the eastern gatherers and hunters—the early Uto-Aztecan speaking Utes and the Jicarilla of Athapaskan speech. The greater complexity of the social and cultural life of these gatherers can be attributed to more abundant

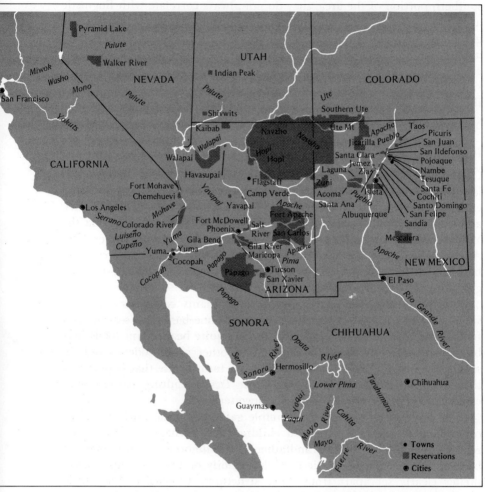

Figure 8.1. Historic and present locations of Indian groups in the North American Southwest.

and larger game. Band organization is a more frequent expression of their social life, as are extended family groupings. These groups constructed more permanent and substantial dwellings: the buffalo skin tipi and earth-covered structures. Clothing was also more substantial: the loin cloth for men and full-bodied tanned buckskin for women. The characteristics of the simple gatherers of the West, already described, also exist among these tribes, albeit in more elaborate form. The shaman, band chiefs, and puberty rites, particularly for girls, are highly complex; indeed, among the Apache groups the girls' adolescent rites are the central feature of their ceremonial and social life.

During the historic period, with the acquisition of the horse, the Ute and Apache groups became part-time buffalo hunters and raiders of sedentary Pueblos, Spanish-American settlements, and American caravans. If the southwestern area were extended, the Comanche, Kiowa, and Kiowa Apache might also be included; but these groups fall more properly in the Plains buffalo-hunting complex.

PART-TIME AGRICULTURISTS

Our category of part-time agriculturists is a transitional group. It is difficult to assign some groups into the category of gatherers or full-time agriculturists. The Western Apache and Jicarilla, for example, engaged in some farming activities, particularly the cultivation of maize, or corn. On the other hand, all intensive farmers also gathered and hunted wild game to some extent. Representatives of this category, like the Navaho, Western Apache, and the Upland Yumans (Walapai and Havasupai) have borrowed heavily from their neighbors: the Athapaskans from the Pueblos and the Upland Yumans from the River Yumans; but otherwise they retain many of the traits indicated for the gatherers.

The cultural inventory of the Upland Yumans, except for farming, is very much like that of the Great Basin; the only differences appear to be the practice of cremation and warlike tendencies, both of which they share with their linguistic relatives, the River Yumans. The Navaho, Western Apache, and Jicarilla have borrowed a number of Pueblo traits. Maize is a central part of their subsistence economy, and among the Navaho and Jicarilla there are fully developed matrilineal clans and linked clan organizations. With the Navaho, less applicable to the Western Apache, religious leaders are priests rather than simple shamans. While the girls' puberty rites are still important, elaborate ceremonies revolving around these rites are conducted by trained ritualists. In addition are a number of curing and purificatory rites which enrich the ceremonial life of these Athapaskan peoples to a degree that almost equals that of the Pueblos. Dwellings are more substantial than any of those of the simple and advanced gatherers and hunters or of the Yumans. Such a thorough reworking of the sociocultural traits of these people indicates a rather long and intimate contact with Pueblo neighbors. For the Navaho we have ample documentary evidence of intensive relations after the Pueblo revolt, and during the whole of the eighteenth century large numbers of refugees from the Pueblos fled Spanish oppression and eventually became absorbed in the population. Undoubtedly, from this period the Navahos learned agricultural techniques as well as skills that the Pueblos had acquired from the Spanish, such as weaving, animal husbandry, and silverwork.

AGRICULTURISTS

Our final category, agriculturists, includes indigenous farming peoples whose social and cultural activities are intricately bound with this form of subsistence. As might be expected, these are the groups in which Meso-American traits appear. Past explanations for such traits have been generally attributed to diffusion or migration; but the independent development of these traits as a response to similar environmental conditions and a level of subsistence and technological organization comparable, or nearly comparable, with those of Meso-America also deserve careful consideration. Even if Meso-American traits were borrowed, such traits could only have been accepted by the northern groups when the latter had developed an agriculturally based society.

True farmers in the greater Southwest during the historic period are the following: the Pueblos, including the "Western Pueblos"—Hopi, Zuni, Acoma, and Laguna—and the "Eastern" Pueblos—the Keresan and Tanoan; the Pima-Papago of central and southern Arizona; the River Yumans of the lower Colorado and Gila; the lower Pimans of Sonora, Mexico, and their neighbors; the Opata and Tarahumara; and the Yaqui-Mayo. While groups like the Papago do farm less intensively and have many characteristics in common with the gatherers, agriculture deeply pervades their socio-ceremonial culture and deserves to be included in our category of agriculturists. The fact that the Pima and Papago appear to be the genetic and cultural descendants of the Hohokam seems to be another good reason for including them in this category. On the other hand, the Navaho, among whom farming is quantitatively important, appear to have acquired agricultural techniques and other traits from the Pueblos in historic times. Their basic culture actually stems from the wider-spread hunting and gathering Apachean cultural complex. For these reasons the Navaho have been placed in the category of advanced gatherers and hunters, despite the reservations noted.

The Pueblos occupy a central position in the Southwest in the opinion of anthropologists. Wissler (1917, 244) considered the Pueblos typical of the Southwest culture area, exemplifying the traits that were shared by other southwestern tribes but which had attained complex development in the Pueblos. As a settled, farming folk, the Pueblos were also set apart from other groups during the Spanish and Mexican periods. For the Spanish settlers the Pueblos were considered to be "almost civilized" and distinguished from barbaric raiders who preyed on them. Because of this conception of the Pueblos as being different from other Indians, the Spanish Crown early assigned land grants to the Pueblos, but not to the other Indians. Under Mexican rule the Pueblos became citizens with all the rights and privileges of citizens; they could, therefore, sell or otherwise dispose of their land as they saw fit.

The Pueblos are not linguistically uniform. At least three distinct stocks, or phyla, are represented among them. Hopi has been placed in the Shoshonean branch of the widespread Uto-Aztecan stock (Sapir, 1913–1915). The Eastern Pueblos, speaking Tiwa, Tewa, and Towa, have been grouped along with Plains Indian Kiowa into Tanoan (Harrington, 1909, 1910; cf. also Trager, 1942; Miller, 1959; Trager and Trager, 1959; Hale, 1962). In 1937 Whorf and Trager linked Uto-Aztecan with Tanoan in a super-stock, or phyla, known as Aztec-Tanoan. Keresan, the language spoken by the western New Mexico Pueblos of Acoma and Laguna and by the Rio Grande Pueblos of Zia, Santa Ana, Cochiti, Santo Domingo, and San Felipe, seems to be a distinct language with no clear relations outside the area, although Sapir (1929) placed it tentatively in his Hokan-Siouan super-stock. In a recent comparative study of Zuni, Newman (1964) suggested a remote relationship of Zuni to Californian Penutian. Thus, the Pueblos speak highly diversified languages; while the relationship of the languages of the Tanoan branch appears to be fairly close, they are not mutually intelligible. Indeed, within the Tiwa family, members of Taos, Picuris, and Isleta pueblos have difficulty communicating with one another in the native language. Rio Grande Tewa speakers of San Juan, Santa Clara, Nambe, San Ildefonso, and Tesuque do, however, converse freely in native Tewa; but the language of the Tewa village of Hano on the Hopi reservation is divergent, and members of the two groups require a period of adjustment and familiarity with one another's linguistic differences before conversing in the native language.

The early work among the Pueblos was carried out in the western pueblos of Hopi and Zuni, and it was generally assumed that the characteristics noted in these pueblos were shared by other Pueblo communities as well. It was not until Parsons' (1939) investigations among the Keresan and Tanoan Pueblos that anthropologists became aware of important differences between the pueblos along the Rio Grande drainage and those of Zuni and Hopi. Recent investigators have made either a two- or threefold division. These divisions have been made because of important social structural differences. The kinship system of the Hopi, Zuni, Acoma, and Laguna is known as the "Crow type." It is matrilineal and its household organization is based on the lineage and clan. Associational structures, ceremonies, and the symbolic system are also related to the lineage, or clan, principle. Thus, these Pueblos are lineage- or clan-centered (Eggan, 1950, 291). The Rio Grande Keresan Pueblos and Jemez, while also organized on a lineage principle, are dependent as well on a number of non-kin associations that are independent of lineage or clan control. The Tanoan-speaking Pueblos, despite considerable minor variations, have a social structure of quite another type. The Tanoan Pueblo kinship system is bilateral. The household either is of the nuclear type or is extended to include relatives of one or both parents, often forming a kind of minor bilateral descent group. There is no hint of a lineage principle in the organization of the terms, the family structures, or the behavior of its members. Beyond the household is a dual division of the community, usually referred to as a moiety, whose functions are governmental and ceremonial. Other related structures include three types of sodalities, or associations: (1) those with governmental and religious functions associated with the dual divisions; (2) medicine associations embodying curing and exorcising practices; and (3) associations with special functions, such as those for war, hunting, and social control.

Ceremonial organizational differences are also pronounced between the major Pueblo divisions. The Western Pueblo ceremonials revolve around the Kachina cult. The Kachina are supernatural beings impersonated in ceremonies by men elaborately costumed and masked. Kachina ceremonies are performed to minimize the difficulties of temporal life; the Western Pueblos perform them particularly to induce rainfall. The cult is less important among the Keresans and Tanoans, and, indeed, the Tiwa Pueblos do not impersonate Kachina supernaturals. The Keresans emphasize curing rituals conducted by curing associations, while the Tanoans highlight performances of associations specifically devoted to hunting, warfare, and social control. Ritualistic events among the Eastern Pueblos are also marked by the cleaning and opening of irrigation ditches in the spring. Typical of both Keresan and Tanoan Pueblos are large group dances performed by men and women, colorfully costumed but unmasked. These dances involve the whole village and are performed in a gay atmosphere of social and festive activity.

The non-kin-based associations charged with governmental and religious functions among Tanoan Pueblos give these pueblos greater unity and central direction. The Rio Grande Keresan Pueblos also have centralized village control for village affairs and the responsibility of non-kin associations; Keresan matrilineages lack the sociopolitical and ceremonial functions of Western Pueblo counterparts. The importance of river irrigation among the Eastern Pueblos has been suggested by some authorities for these differences in social institutions between the Eastern and Western Pueblos (Wittfogel and Goldfrank, 1943; Dozier, 1960). Other authorities have attempted to explain the differences as being due to diverse origins, diffusion or borrowing from distant indigenous neighbors, or Spanish contact influences (Hawley, 1937; Parsons, 1939; Underhill, 1954).

We now move to the extreme southern part of the Southwest area, to tribes speaking languages of the Cahita branch of the Uto-Aztecan stock. Like the Pueblos, the economy of the Cahitans is based on intensive farming. Virtually no archeological work has been done in the area, and the prehistory of these people is unknown. The indigenous characteristics of their culture are also obscure; for the group came under intensive Christian influence early in the seventeenth century, resulting in a rapid syncretization of Spanish-Catholic and indigenous elements in their culture. So thorough is this fusion at present that it is almost impossible to separate the indigenous characteristics of Cahitan culture. Information gleaned from early Spanish reports gives some notion, however, of indigenous Cahitan society and culture.

The Cahitan tribes lived along the bottom lands of the Sinaloa, Fuerte, Mayo, and Yaqui rivers. All spoke dialects of the same language and had a combined population somewhat in excess of 100,000. At the time of Spanish contact, these tribes occupied a series of villages where dwellings were distributed in a scattered pattern, quite unlike the compact Pueblo villages. Extensive farming of rich bottom lands provided the primary subsistence needs. Floods periodically inundated the flood

Navaho silversmith with improvised forge and anvil.
(Courtesy, United States Bureau of Indian Affairs. Photo by Milton Snow.)

plains and thus provided the moisture needed to grow corn, beans, and squash. Those villages that bordered the gulf supplemented their diet with fish and shellfish, and all Cahitans also hunted game and gathered wild food plants and fruits. Despite the importance of these subsidiary foods, the mainstay of Cahitan subsistence was farming.

Early missionary accounts make no mention of extensive differences in the lifeways of the various Cahitan peoples; we may, therefore, assume that a summary description of Yaqui indigenous cultural elements may apply in general to all of them. The Yaqui are the most northern and the most populous of the Cahitan peoples, and at the time of Spanish contact they had a population of 30,000. The following sketch has been summarized from Spicer's account of Yaqui aboriginal culture (Spicer, 1961, 14–19).

Yaqui villages were exogamous. The kinship terminology is bilaterally arranged and, hence, indicates the probable importance of bilateral extended families and the absence of lineal organizations. Although the villages were independent units, there was a far greater sense of tribal unity among the Yaqui than among the Pueblos. This unity was demonstrated during the initial period of Spanish contact when the Yaqui periodically defeated Spanish soldiers with a fighting force of 5,000 to 7,000 warriors. Spicer believed that the tribal organization was based on a system of military associations with ranked offices. There was no development of markets or extensive individual or regional specialization, although ceremonial participation and visiting patterns on a tribal level may be inferred from contemporary practices. The major ceremonial orientation of the Yaqui consisted of warfare, initiation rites, hunting, and curing; judging again by contemporary Yaqui ceremonial organization, such rituals were very likely managed by specific associations similar to the ones among the Tanoan Pueblos. Ritual techniques emphasized the individual vision as a source of supernatural power, and typical ceremonials depicted animal representations either in the dance or in ground paintings.

The River Yumans of the Hokan linguistic stock and the Cheme-huevi, closely linked in language to the Uto-Aztecan Paiutes, settled the rich bottom lands of the lower Colorado. These people are an interesting group, for although located in rich agricultural lands with great potential for developing food surpluses and a complex society, they retained the social and cultural characteristics that typify their neighbors, the simple gathering peoples of the Great Basin. Underhill, who made a study of the social organization of the Mohave, a River Yuman tribe, has characterized the River Yumans as an intrusive people who did not take advantage of the possibilities afforded them by a rich natural environment (1954, 653).

River Yumans lived in non-centralized, loosely integrated villages. Like the Cahitans, they are reported to have had a strong tribal consciousness (Spier, 1936, 154). Tribal solidarity was expressed by their having only one chief for the whole tribe; by the absence of internecine feuds; and by their presenting a united front against enemies, whether in attack or defense. But there was no formal organization on a tribal level, and "the functions of a chief seem to have been slight, his authority more admonitory than coercive" (Spier, 1936, 158). River Yumans also had patrilineal unlocalized clans, but lineages or clan segments did not function as corporate groups on either the tribal or village level.

Between the River Yumans and the Cahitans live tribal peoples whose society and culture differ hardly at all from those of the simple gathering people, yet who are primarily sedentary folk. Among them farming is quantitatively more important than gathering or hunting. Except for the Tarahumara and Opata, these people occupy an arid desert environment that is remarkably uniform from the Gila River to the Yaqui River. They belong to the Uto-Aztecan linguistic stock except for one small pocket of Hokan speakers, the Seri, along the Gulf Coast in northwestern Sonora. The Piman are all fairly uniform from the Pima-Papago of Arizona to the Lower Pima of southern Sonora, while the Tarahumara and Opata are closely related to the Cahitan speakers.

Studies of Piman, Tarahumara, and Opata are meager and for many subgroups nonexistent. The Tarahumara and the Opata have experienced considerable influence from contact with early Jesuit missionaries, and it is not easy to distinguish aboriginal elements and patterns. The Tarahumara share a number of traits with Cahitans, and Beals (1932, 145, 149) has suggested that the latter may have moved to their present location from the Tarahumara area. Curiously, however, some of the traits the two groups share are also those found among the simple gatherers: life cycle ceremonies, shamans, vision, and some notion of the guardian spirit. Other Tarahumara and Cahitan ceremonial organizations and functions are suggestive of the Pueblos, particularly Tanoans: men's and women's societies with hereditary leaders and rituals for curing, weather control, hunting, and war (Beals, 1943, 69). Tarahumara alternated living in cave dwellings in winter and on the plateau during the summer, where they carried on farming activities. No irrigation was practiced; the growth of corn, beans, and squash was dependent on natural rainfall.

The best known of the Piman peoples are the Papago, and their social and cultural characteristics may apply in general to the others. The Papago, and perhaps the Pima, appear to have had main villages with surrounding "daughter villages." These daughter villages were apparently founded by members of the main village who needed new farm land, and they remained ceremonially dependent on the mother village (Underhill, 1956, 193). Four or five patrilineal but non-exogamous clan-like structures have been reported for the Pima and Papago. In addition, a patrilineal moiety system, also non-exogamous, operated on the village level. The Papago-Pima moiety organization may have been, like the Keresan dual divisions, a division primarily to afford opposing groups for dances and games. The villages, including daughter villages, are also reported to have been exogamous. The data are ambiguous, however, and it is impossible to achieve a satisfactory reconstruction of early Pima-Papago social organization (Russell, 1908, 196–197; Parsons, 1928, 448–458; Spier, 1936, 10–11; Underhill, 1939).

The ceremonial picture of the Pima-Papago is also unclear. Strong (1927, 45) characterized the Pima and Papago as having a "clan house–priest–fetish complex," similar to the western Pueblos, but this is doubted by Spier (1936, 11), who suggests that ceremonial paraphernalia included individual, rather than clan-owned, equipment. The Vikita-Navitco ceremony of the Papago and Pima, which was associated with masked dancers, curing sickness, and bringing rain, may have been performed by a curing association. But there is no evidence for other social and ceremonial organizations of the kind reported for the Pueblos.

In summary, the Pueblos and the Cahitans exemplify our most complex social and cultural groups in the Southwest. These groups exploited the agricultural potential of the ecological environment to the limits possible by a primitive technology. Following in descending order of complexity are the River Yumans, the Pima-Papago, and the Tarahumara-Opata tribes. None of these peoples farmed as intensively as the Pueblos and Cahitans, and their social and ceremonial institutions are correspondingly simpler. Of the gatherers and hunters, the Athapaskans and Utes exploited a more productive ecological environment and, therefore, produced a richer social and cultural inventory and organization than the Great Basin foragers. The latter lived in the most inhospitable natural environment of the Southwest, and understandably their lives exhibit the least social and cultural elaboration.

The Southwest affords an excellent laboratory for the study of the interplay of ecological environment and subsistence economies. While a beginning has been made in these studies, as is evident in the references cited in this paper, more work is needed. These studies may be integrated with historical ones of diffusion, borrowing, and cultural contacts to give us a more reliable and more complete picture of social and cultural development in the Southwest.

Response to Western European Cultural Contact[4]

Most of the Indians of the Southwest have experienced the impact of three major representatives of Western European culture: Spanish, Mexican, and Anglo-American. These contacts brought about revolutionary changes unknown in contact relations involving Indians and other Indians. The character of the organization and technological skills of Western European powers was beyond the comprehension of most of the Indian groups. Another revolutionary factor in European contact had never been encountered in Indian-Indian contacts: Europeans had definite plans and programs for modifying the Indian groups they invaded and eventually dominated. The goals and the objectives of each of the three powers changed through time, but there were always definite plans and policies, often explicitly stated in writing, as to how the Indian was to be brought into the dominant culture.

It is possible in a brief paper to sketch only the bare outlines of the contact circumstances and the patterns of adjustment worked out by the Indians. We shall focus on the three major groups for whom the most information is available and who seem to illustrate the most typical reactions to Western European contact. These three are the Cahitan Yaqui-Mayo, the Pueblos, and the Athapaskans. (Important Indian-white contact dates for the Yaqui-Mayo and the Pueblo are given in the table on page 244.) Effects of the Mexican regime will be considered for the Yaqui-Mayo only, for the Athapaskans and Pueblos scarcely experienced Mexican rule. The new nation of Mexico was born in 1823, when Anglo-Americans were beginning to penetrate the northern Southwest area as traders and fortune seekers. Finally, in 1846, following the United States–Mexican war, the entire northern area became officially a part of the United States. After the mid-nineteenth century, Anglo-American influences and policies came to dominate in the North. The southern tribes were affected in different ways by Mexican policies and programs, which changed from those under Spain and also differed from those of the United States.

THE CAHITAN YAQUI-MAYO

Initial contact with Cahitans and Spaniards occurred in the mid-sixteenth century and was characterized by military encounters that continued for almost a century. The Mayos accepted the Spaniards as allies against Indian enemies toward the end of the period, but the Yaquis were never conquered and in all engagements defeated the Spaniards.

Important Indian-White Contact Dates for the Yaqui-Mayo and the Pueblos

YAQUI-MAYO		PUEBLOS	
1533	First contact with Spanish slave raiders under Diego de Guzman	1540	Coronado expedition—first intensive contact with Spaniards
1609–1610	Defeat of Captain Hurdaide by Yaqui and establishment of peace between Yaqui-Mayo and Spaniards	1580–1592	Contact with three exploring Spanish expeditions
1684	Encroachment of non-Indians on Yaqui-Mayo lands	1598	First Spanish settlement in New Mexico by Oñate
1740	First major Yaqui-Mayo revolt to rid aliens from agricultural land base	1630	The Benavide's report—relates the establishment of ninety missions and chapels in as many villages
1767–1771	Expulsion of Jesuits by Roman Catholic Church and the secularization of Yaqui-Mayo missions	1680	Pueblo Indian revolt—expulsion of Spanish settlers from the Pueblo country
1824–1875	Series of Yaqui revolts against non-Indian settlers	1693	Reconquest of Pueblos by Diego de Vargas
1877–1910	Mexican government embarks on extermination program; numerous massacres; Yaqui-Mayos deported to work in mines outside homeland; hundreds of Yaqui families escape to United States	1776	Fray Dominguez's visitation—detailed report of missionary activity and description of Pueblo life
		1821	Anglo-American trade with New Mexico
1920–	Social and cultural reintegration of Sonoran and Arizona Yaqui-Mayo communities. Tribal title to land by presidential decree in 1939 for Sonoran Yaqui-Mayos. Arizona communities shift to wage-work economy, but continue to practice traditional syncretized Catholic-Indian religion	1846	U.S. occupation of New Mexico
		1850–1900	Conflict over land between Pueblos and non-Indian settlers
		1924–1936	Pueblo Lands Act (1924)—Squatters on Pueblo lands removed or Pueblos compensated for lands lost
		1940–	Pueblos enter wage-work economy; are nominally Catholic, but retain indigenous religious beliefs and practices—the two religious systems are "compartmentalized"

Eventually, through the intermediary efforts of Mayo leaders, peace was established between the Yaqui and the Spaniards. Both groups of Indians voluntarily accepted Jesuit missionaries early in the seventeenth century. The relation between the Jesuits and the Yaquis and Mayos was from the beginning a friendly and intimate one. Directed cultural change occurred, mainly at the hands of those priests who entered the area without military escort. There is also evidence that the missionaries protected their Indian charges against wholesale exploitation by secular authorities. The Jesuits learned the native language and translated prayers and Catholic ritual into Cahitan, which exists today as an important part of the ceremonial ritual. Although the Jesuits apparently compelled Indians to attend mass, there is no evidence that they suppressed native ceremonies or destroyed ceremonial paraphernalia. Indeed, that they permitted the Indians to rework native ceremonial practices and beliefs is indicated by the present hybridized nature of Yaqui-Mayo religion. The result of this permissive situation was that in a little more than a century the syncretized character of the culture had been established.

Encroachment of non-Indians on Yaqui-Mayo lands, which began during the late Spanish period, intensified during the succeeding Mexican period, changing the favorable conditions for cultural exchange that had lasted for over a century. During this period, roughly from 1740 to 1877, the Yaquis and Mayos participated in a series of rebellions to rid their land of non-Indians. The autonomous character of Indian life in the area became heightened when Jesuit missionaries were removed as the result of the expulsion of these missionaries from the New World in 1767. The Franciscans who took the place of the Jesuits were never able to establish the good working and personal relations that the Indians had had with Jesuit missionaries.

Following a decisive military defeat of the Yaquis and Mayos in 1877, the Mexican government embarked on a program of deporting the rebellious Indians to work in mines many miles outside their homeland. Hundreds of Yaqui families, forced out of their land and threatened with removal to forced labor camps, escaped across the international border into Arizona. Those who remained in Sonora took refuge in the mountains and raided the Mexican settlements. It was not until after the Mexican Revolution of 1910 that the Yaquis were permitted to reoccupy their old tribal lands, and then only a portion of them; Mexican settlers had moved into most of the former Yaqui land and converted it into rich, irrigated farmlands. The Mayos, however, had made peace with the Spanish earlier and remained essentially on friendly terms with their non-Indian Mexican neighbors.

Many of the Yaquis who left their homeland have not returned, but in Arizona and Sonora, where small Yaqui colonies have appeared, Yaqui identity is strong. The Mayo, too, consider themselves a distinct people and have not become assimilated to Mexican society and culture. In both the Yaqui and Mayo societies a culture that is non-Spanish and non-Indian persists. This culture may be characterized as a fusion of European and indigenous traditions—an amalgam achieved during the permissive period of relations with Jesuit missionaries. During the later periods of unrest and dispersal, borrowing of new cultural elements was resisted, particularly in aspects of ceremonial organization. Yaqui-Mayo religious beliefs and practices today thus represent a kind of crystallization of the earlier amalgam—a fusion of preconquest Indian elements and sixteenth- and seventeenth-century Spanish-Catholic cultural traits.

THE PUEBLOS

During the early contact period, Spanish-Pueblo relations were completely the reverse of those experienced by the Yaquis and Mayos. The first century and a half of contact with the Spaniards was a most unfavorable one and ended in the bloody revolt of 1680. The expedition of Francisco Vasquez de Coronado in 1540 was the Pueblos' first experience with Europeans. Coronado entered the Pueblo area with a party of five Franciscan missionaries and several hundred mailed and armed horsemen accompanied by Indian servants. The party established headquarters at Tiguex, a large Tiwa pueblo near the present site of Bernalillo in the heart of the Pueblo country. The expedition was supported by provisions supplied by the pueblo and probably by neighboring pueblos for a period of two years. Coronado and his party established a reputation for brutality and ruthlessness that later generations of Spaniards were to continue. For a minor rebellion, brought on by the incessant demands for provisions made by Coronado's party, the pueblo of Tiguex was "punished" by the execution of several hundred of its inhabitants. This news spread rapidly throughout the Pueblo country and laid the foundation for bitter and antagonistic relations between the two peoples that were to last throughout the period of Spanish and Mexican political control.

Other exploratory expeditions followed, and finally, in 1598, the Pueblo area received its first colonists. Under the command of Juan de Oñate arrived several hundred settlers. Church, civil, and military authorities immediately set about "civilizing" the Indians and making demands for labor and tribute from them. The Franciscan priests were unlike the considerate and understanding Jesuits who had brought Christianity to the Yaquis and Mayos. The Franciscans did not learn the native languages or bother to learn about native customs. They were concerned primarily in stamping out all vestige of the native religion and substituting by force Catholic doctrine and practices. In these efforts they were aided by both the civil authorities and the military. The ceremonial chambers known today as *kivas* were raided periodically, and masks and ceremonial paraphernalia of all kinds were burned and destroyed. Those Indian leaders who persisted in conducting ceremonies were executed or punished in a variety of ways. To supplant native

Young Navaho wearing jewelry of silver, turquoise, and shell beads made by tribal craftsmen.
(Courtesy, United States Bureau of Indian Affairs.)

ceremonial patterns and beliefs, missionaries baptized Indians, forced attendance at mass, and made instruction in Catholic doctrine compulsory in missionary establishments. A Spanish decree in 1620 permitted the creation of native officers among the Pueblos (Bandelier, 1890–1892, 200). These officers were expected to cooperate with Spanish civil and church officials in compelling their members to comply with the civilizing and Christianizing efforts of the Spaniards. But the Indians turned the new governmental system to meet their own ends. They filled the positions with native priests who owed primary allegiance to native ceremonial life.

As the abuses went on unabated, resentment toward Spanish domination mounted, and a number of minor rebellions beginning about 1650 culminated in the successful revolt of 1680. The revolt was planned by a Tewa Indian of San Juan Pueblo, Popé, who had been one of forty-seven Pueblo religious leaders who in 1675 had been subjected to a public whipping in Santa Fe for practicing native religious rites. While the Tanoans were most active in the revolt, the other Pueblos cooperated by killing their resident missionaries and other Spanish officials. At the end of the revolt, 33 missionaries and 380 colonists out of a total of 2,500 non-Pueblo settlers were dead. The rest of the alien population fled southward to the El Paso area, well out of the Pueblo country. All missions were destroyed, together with furnishings and records. Only a few Southern Tiwa and Piro Indians failed to support the uprising; these joined the retreating colonists and established the pueblos of Senecu and Isleta del Sur below El Paso.

The Pueblos were not reconquered until 1693, when Don Diego de Vargas marched into the Pueblo country with a well-armed force of several hundred soldiers. Anticipating a reconquest attempt or punitive expeditions, the Indians had abandoned most of the pueblos and had established themselves in mountain strongholds. But few resisted when De Vargas' formidable army was sighted. De Vargas persuaded the Indians to return to their villages, and in a few months settlers, missionaries, and the Indians had resumed a relationship similar to that of the prerevolt period. Yet not all was serene, and there were a number of minor, abortive revolts, while large numbers of Pueblos, seeking asylum from Spanish oppression, fled to the Hopis, Apaches, and Navahos.

After the seventeenth century the Pueblos settled down into outwardly peaceful relations with the Spaniards. The Western Pueblos— Hopi and Zuni—were rarely visited after the Pueblo revolt. While an attempt was made to reestablish the Hopi and Zuni missions, destroyed during the revolt, these efforts were finally abandoned, and Spanish missionary activity stopped altogether. The many miles of rough terrain between Santa Fe and the Hopi country and the constant threat of

Navaho and Apache attacks en route discouraged the establishment of effective lines of communication. For the Rio Grande Pueblos, change in Spanish attitudes and policies made for at least tolerance of Spanish neighbors.

The *encomienda* system, which perhaps more than any other factor had helped bring about the revolt, was discontinued after the revolt. An encomienda, given to prominent colonists by the Spanish Crown, entitled the recipient to the services of a number of Indians. Some of these Indians were household servants, but the main service they performed was the maintenance of farms and livestock for the benefit of the *encomenderos*. The Spaniards or their heirs who lost encomiendas in 1680 never regained the traditional right to collect tribute from the Indians. There was only one exception: De Vargas, the reconqueror of New Mexico, was granted a large encomienda; but the encomienda was never put into operation, and De Vargas' heirs had it changed into a pension.

Distrust and suspicion continued to characterize Pueblo and Spanish relations, but the policies of force gradually gave way to less brutal treatment of the Pueblos in the succeeding generations. The Pueblos, to appease the missionaries, adopted the externals of the new faith and conformed to other demands, but they continued to practice their own indigenous religion in secret. In time, with succeeding generations who were brought up completely under the new order, the externally practiced Catholic religion and other Spanish patterns also became an important part of the Pueblo culture. But the two traditions were kept distinct, partly because they had been learned in this manner, but also because of the fear of reprisals.

The changed policies of missionaries and Spanish colonial officials in the eighteenth and early nineteenth centuries permitted the Pueblo Indians to revive and reorganize their ceremonial patterns. Some of the more secret dances began to be practiced in the open again, apparently without opposition (Adams and Chavez, 1956, 256–258).

The advent of Anglo-Americans in the middle of the nineteenth century resulted in a return to the earlier conditions of suspicion and mistrust. American Protestant missionaries and United States Indian Service officials were openly critical of the "obscene" and "immoral" practices of the Indians, and they took steps to stop them. Indian children were enrolled in boarding schools at considerable distances from the reservations, in order to wean them from their traditional culture. In these schools the use of the Indian language and all other "Indian" ways were prohibited. Infractions were countered by a variety of physical punishments. During the early 1900s investigators were sent to the pueblos to study reported immoral and anti-Christian practices of the

Indians. Under the Religious Crimes Code, Indian Service officials were instructed to stop ceremonial practices that might be contrary to accepted Christian standards. The Pueblos reverted to secrecy in their native ceremonial system, and the pattern of compartmentalization achieved during the early years of Spanish oppression was again reinforced.

Criticism from Indian leaders and white friends eventually brought about a more humane treatment of Indian children and lifted the restrictions on speaking the native language and the ban on holding Indian rites. Before the mid-twenties, federal policy toward Indians generally was committed to transforming Indian communities into variants of the dominant American culture as quickly as possible. An investigation of Indian–United States government relations was authorized by Congress, and its findings were reported in the Meriam Report of 1928. This report was instrumental in bringing about revolutionary changes in American Indian policy. Indian administrators were instructed to respect Indian ways of life, but to assist the Indian to achieve equality with whites in economy, education, and health.

Among the Pueblos the new regime permitted traditional authorities to relax controls that safeguard Pueblo ceremonial life. But the Pueblos have not abandoned these controls. The Pueblos are prepared to tighten social control mechanisms in the event that outside agencies threaten traditional patterns of life. Thus, the Pueblos continue to exist as social and cultural enclaves surrounded by the dominant Anglo-American society and culture. They have improved health conditions and have accommodated to the economy and educational requirements of the dominant society, but within the confines of their communities they cling tenaciously to their own language and ceremonial organization. While individuals move out occasionally to disappear into the general Anglo-American society and culture, and others participate in Pan-Indian activities in off-reservation towns or in the more distant urban areas, the majority prefer to live within pueblo walls, enjoying the rewards of a rich social and ceremonial life.

THE SOUTHWESTERN ATHAPASKANS

The response of the Navaho and the various Apache groups to white contact contrasts in many important respects with those of the Pueblos and Yaqui-Mayos. The Athapaskans were never conquered or militarily dominated by the Spaniards or Mexicans. Their culture was, however, redirected in orientation and given a different emphasis by contact with the agents and products of Spanish culture. The Catholic religion as either a belief or a ceremonial system made no appreciable impression on the Athapaskans. This was true also of the Spanish governmental system and community organization. But the acquisition of Spanish material items, particularly livestock, brought about a complete reorientation of the Athapaskan economy and social life. The Navaho adopted a sheep-herding complex; and for both the Navaho and the Apache, the horse made possible a raiding life. Livestock also became integrated into the prestige and social structure of both groups. Raids on Spanish, Mexican, Pueblo, and later, Anglo-American settlements added to the material cultural complex and frequently brought in captives who, adopted and humanely treated, further enriched the indigenous cultural inventory. For the Navaho, silversmithing and Navaho blanket and rug weaving were skills acquired during this period. Experiencing neither political domination nor forceful coercion to accept aspects of Spanish, Mexican, and Pueblo culture, the Athapaskans could afford to be selective, adding what they desired, rejecting what they did not want, and most important of all, not having to give up what they already possessed and valued.

The later military conquest of the Navaho and Apache eliminated the raiding complex and brought about, at least temporarily, deprivation and demoralization. The Apaches were rounded up by United States soldiers and placed in virtual concentration camps for a period of several years in the late nineteenth century. The Navaho roundup and removal to Fort Sumner in eastern New Mexico likewise resulted in defeat and demoralization. But before the end of the century, the Apache and Navaho were placed in large reservations in their own familiar homeland, where they were able to reintegrate cultural patterns.

Throughout their history in the Southwest, southern Athapaskans, or Apacheans, have been characterized by receptivity to change and borrowing. Vogt (1961, 325) describes the Apacheans as an opportunistic folk who made the most of their contacts with socially and culturally more sophisticated groups:

> The enormous economic differential between the hunting and gathering Apacheans and the Pueblo, Spanish, and American cultures was undoubtedly a crucial factor in their cultural development. To put it simply, the Apacheans arrived in the Southwest with little to lose and almost everything to gain by borrowing economic and technological patterns they successively came into contact with in the Southwest. Economic advantage was to become an outstanding case of an "absorbing" or "borrowing" culture [Kluckhohn, 1942; Adair and Vogt, 1949].

While the label of an "absorbing" or "borrowing" culture more appropriately fits the Navaho, the other Apachean groups have also followed the same pattern, although perhaps less spectacularly. Today, these Athapaskans are the most rapidly growing group of Americans. Birth rate is two to three times the national average; despite a fairly high mortality rate, they are experiencing a population boom. The Navaho and Apache groups have absorbed a tremendous infusion of Anglo-American cultural patterns, particularly the economic and technological aspects, but the core of their culture is still oriented along traditional lines.

The Present and Prospects for the Future

The largest concentration and most conservative of North American Indians are to be found in the Southwest. Their population is about 250,000, with the highest densities in the northern and southern extremities of the area. This figure is approximately half of the total United States American Indian population. Far from being a group on the verge of extinction or absorption into the dominant population, the rate of increase is higher among these native Americans than among the dominant Anglo-American population. The cultures of the American Indians everywhere exhibit vitality and persistence, with no signs of eventual assimilation into some dominant homogeneous culture. As is capably demonstrated by Nancy Lurie in her chapter in this volume American Indians are experiencing a renaissance. This renaissance exhibits itself no less strongly in those individuals and groups whose indigenous patterns have been drastically modified or replaced or have even disappeared altogether.

Among these latter groups the movement that has been adopted is Pan-Indianism. Pan-Indianism is characterized by social and cultural patterns synthesized from elements derived from a variety of Indian cultures. Some traits are not Indian at all, but are taken from white American culture, although the majority are of Indian origin and drawn primarily from Great Plains Indian culture. Pan-Indianism is, at least partially if not wholly, a rebellion against the white American culture that assigns Indians and other minority groups a subordinate status. Unlike American Negroes, Indians who are critical of white American society and culture have not yet achieved enough of a collective voice to be politically effective in national affairs. Indians who participate in Pan-Indian activities and espouse a concern over issues that affect general welfare of all American Indians are still in a minority. The majority of the southwestern Indians, for example, are still preoccupied with local, particularistic problems that affect their own specific reservations or groups. Most Navahos, Pueblos, and Yaqui-Mayos are still primarily involved with their own social and ceremonial life, which is often as unfamiliar and exotic to Pan-Indian adherents as it is to the general non-Indian population.

Yet one thing is clear: The vast majority of Indians do not want to lose their identity, which they proclaim stems from their own native land. American Indians want full equality in health services, in educational, political, and economic opportunity, but they are strongly opposed to programs that will integrate them forcefully into the dominant society and culture.

NOTES

[1] This paper has drawn from field notes collected among the Pueblo Indians of New Mexico and Arizona. I am grateful to a Social Science Research Council Faculty Grant-in-aid, to a National Science Foundation Institutional Grant (to the University of Arizona), and to Miss Doris Duke and the American Indian Oral History Project for the support of my research.

[2] This section has been summarized from a number of recent archeological surveys: Haury, 1962; Jennings *et al.*, 1956; Rouse, 1962; and Willey, 1966.

[3] Besides the sources noted in this section, the following references dealing with Southwestern ethnology have been used to write this section: Beals, 1932, 1943; Kirchhoff, 1954; Russell, 1908; Spier, 1936; Underhill, 1954.

[4] The following sources summarize the nature and results of Euro-American and Indian culture contact in the Southwest: Dozier, 1961; Spicer, 1954, 1961, 1962; Vogt, 1961.

REFERENCES

ADAIR, JOHN, AND EVON Z. VOGT
1949 Navaho and Zuni veterans: A study of contrasting modes of culture change. American Anthropologist LI:547–562.

ADAMS, ELEANOR B., AND ANGELICO CHAVEZ, EDS.
1956 The missions of New Mexico, 1776. Albuquerque: University of New Mexico Press.

BANDELIER, A. F.
1890–1892 Final report of investigations among the Indians of the southwestern United States. Cambridge: Archaeological Institute of America, Papers. American Series, vol. III, pt. 1; vol. IV, pt. 2.

BEALS, RALPH L.
1932 The comparative ethnology of northern Mexico before 1750. Ibero-Americana II:93–225.

1943 Northern Mexico and the southwest, *El Norte de Mexico y el sur de Estados Unidos*. Mexico, D.F.: Tercera Reunion de Mesa Redondo Sobre Problemas Anthropologicas de Mexico y Central America.

DOZIER, EDWARD P.

1960 The Pueblos of the southwestern United States. The Journal of the Royal Anthropological Institute XC: 146–160.

1961 Rio Grande Pueblos. *In* Perspectives in American Indian culture change. Edward H. Spicer, ed. Chicago: University of Chicago Press. pp. 94–186.

EGGAN, FRED

1950 Social organization of the western Pueblos. Chicago: University of Chicago Press.

HALE, KENNETH

1962 Jemez and Kiowa correspondence in reference to Kiowa-Tanoan. International Journal of American Linguistics XXVIII: 1–5.

HARRINGTON, JOHN P.

1909 Notes on the Piro Language. American Anthropologist XI: 563–594.

1910 On phonetic and lexical resemblances between Kiowa and Tanoan. Papers of the School of American Archaeology, no. 12.

HAURY, EMIL W.

1962 The greater American southwest. *In* Courses toward urban life. Robert J. Braidwood and Gordon R. Willey, eds. New York: Viking Fund Publications. no. 32, pp. 106–131.

HAWLEY, FLORENCE M.

1937 Pueblo social organization as a lead to Pueblo history. American Anthropologist XXXIV: 504–522.

JENNINGS, JESSE D., *et al.*

1955 The American southwest: a problem in cultural isolation. *In* Seminars in archaeology. Robert Wauchope, ed. Memoirs of the Society for American Archaeology, no. 11.

KIRCHHOFF, PAUL

1954 Gatherers and farmers in the greater southwest: a problem in classification. American Anthropologist LVI: 529–550.

KLUCKHOHN, CLYDE

1942 The Navahos in the machine age. Technology Review XLIV: 2–6.

KROEBER, ALFRED L.

1928 Native cultures of the southwest. University of California Publications in American Archaeology and Ethnology XXIII: 375–398.

1939 Cultural and natural areas of native North America. University of California Publications in American Archaeology and Ethnology XXXVIII: 1–242.

1948 Anthropology. New York: Harcourt, Brace.

MILLER, WICK R.

1959 A note on Kiowa linguistic affiliations. American Anthropologist LXI: 102–105.

NEWMAN, STANLEY
1964 Comparison of Zuni and California Penutian. International Journal of American Linguistics XXX:1–13.

PARSONS, ELSIE CLEWS
1928 Notes on the Pima, 1926. American Anthropologist XXX:445–464.
1939 Pueblo Indian religion. 2 vols. Chicago: University of Chicago Press.

ROUSE, IRVING
1962 Southwestern archaeology today. *In* Kidder, A. V. An introduction to the study of southwestern archaeology with a preliminary account of the excavation at Pecos. New Haven: Yale University Press. pp. 1–53.

RUSSELL, FRANK
1908 The Pima Indians. Washington, D.C.: Twenty-sixth Annual Report of the Bureau of American Ethnology.

SAPIR, EDWARD
1913–1915 Southern Paiute and Nahuatl, a study in Uto-Aztekan. Journal de la Société des Américanistes de Paris X:379–425; XI:443–488. American Anthropologist XVII:98–120, 306–328.
1929 Central and North American languages. Encyclopaedia Britannica, 14th ed. V (1929):138–141.

SPICER, EDWARD H.
1954 Spanish-Indian acculturation in the southwest. American Anthropologist LVI:663–678.
1961 Yaqui. *In* Perspectives in American Indian culture change. Edward H. Spicer, ed. Chicago: University of Chicago Press. pp. 7–93.
1962 Cycles of conquest. Tucson: University of Arizona Press.

SPIER, LESLIE
1936 Cultural relations of the Gila River and lower Colorado tribes. Yale University Publications in Anthropology, no. 3.

STRONG, WILLIAM DUNCAN
1927 An analysis of southwestern society. American Anthropologist XXIX:1–61.

TRAGER, GEORGE L.
1942 The comparative phonology of the Tiwa languages. Studies in Linguistics I:1–10.

TRAGER, GEORGE L., AND EDITH CROWELL TRAGER
1959 Kiowa and Tanoan. American Anthropologist LXI:1078–1083.

UNDERHILL, RUTH M.
1939 Social organization of the Papago Indians. New York: Columbia University Press.
1954 Inter-cultural relations in the greater southwest. American Anthropologist LVI:645–656.

VOGT, EVON Z.
1961 Navaho. *In* Perspectives in American Indian culture change. Edward H. Spicer, ed. Chicago: University of Chicago Press. pp. 278–336.

WHORF, B. L., AND GEORGE L. TRAGER

1937 The relationship of Uto-Aztecan and Tanoan. American Anthropologist XXXIX:609–624.

WILLEY, GORDON R.

1966 An introduction to American archaeology volume one: north and middle America. Englewood Cliffs: Prentice-Hall.

WISSLER, CLARK

1917 The American Indian. New York: Oxford University Press.

WITTFOGEL, K. A., AND ESTHER GOLDFRANK

1943 Some aspects of Pueblo mythology and society. Journal of American Folklore LVI:17–30.

9 The Ute and Paiute Indians of the Great Basin Southern Rim[1]

MARVIN K. OPLER

The Precontact Culture: Before 1540

The Ute and Paiute Indians occupy a pivotal position in the history of the entire southwestern region of the United States. Their early contacts with Mexicans above and below the border, their possible primacy in acquiring the horse and transmitting its use to Plains tribes like the Comanche, and the reports of such enlightened agents as Kit Carson all point to beginnings of contact with Spanish frontiersmen around 1540 followed by a period of band consolidation in the following century and a later period of decisive United States contacts, beginning in the eighteenth century and extending into the twentieth.

The Southern Ute tribe represents a culturally intermediate position in the evolution of Uto-Aztecan peoples. The strictly hunting and gathering Paiute (or "Water Ute," in translation) and Western Shoshone were to the west and north, with settled agricultural village dwellers like the Hopi further west in Arizona. To the south, across the Mexican border, were the Aztecs, who represented around 1540 a more dominating and conquering agricultural civilization.

Most of the writings on Great Basin sociopolitical groups dealing with tribes north and west of the Continental Divide emphasize band or village consolidations in the colder seasons of the year. But the Southern Ute and Paiute, both before the acquisition of the horse and after, attempted their population consolidations in the spring and summer. In the fall and winter, snow locked the passes even in the foothills of the Rockies. Before the horse the Ute were unable to live in villages as did the Hopi and the settled Plains tribes, both of whom possessed an agricultural base for consolidation.

The Southern Ute occupied the terrain below the Gunnison River in a seasonal circuit of extended families traveling separately. Only in the spring, when the mountain passes were free of snow, could they find a safe haven in larger band encampments in the foothills of the mountains. The fall and winter seasons, because of snowfall in the Rockies, forced them south to the borders of Comanche, Apache, and Navaho country and, in early times, down into Mexican borderlands.

The Southwest and the Great Basin southern rim are connected in cultural evolution. The Pima and Papago to the south of Athapaskan-speaking Navahos and Apaches speak languages remotely related to Hopi and Basin Shoshonean, on the one hand, and to the Aztecan groups of Mexico, on the other. The Hopi of Arizona conform to a pattern of the western Pueblos, which according to Fred Eggan (1966) also includes Hano, Zuni, Acoma, and Laguna. All of these have matrilineal exoga-mous clans, a lineage type of kinship system, and extended matrilocal households, in contrast to the eastern Pueblos of the Rio Grande, like the Tewa, who are bilateral, with a dual division of society and with a kinship system in which relative age is emphasized. While the Hopi have a relatively strong political organization and ceremonial societies con-cerned with rain, the eastern Pueblos are more diffuse in organization, and they more greatly emphasize the curing of illness. Yet, according to Eggan, there is a gradual variation in these respects from East to West, which gives the Pueblos as a whole a kind of cultural and psychological unity. One can even find certain linguistic continuities. The Hopi, whose closest relations are with the Shoshonean-speaking groups of the Basin, are also distantly related to the Tewa and other Tanoan-speaking peoples of the Rio Grande. Conversely, Hano represents a Tewa-speaking group that settled in Hopi country following the Pueblo Rebellion of 1680. From that date to the present they resided with the Hopi of the First Mesa.

Linguistics, therefore, suggests an earlier unity of hunting and gath-ering peoples, followed by a cultural differentiation into Great Basin hunters and gatherers contrasted with the eastern and western Pueblo horticulturists. The further extension to Pima-Papago and even Aztec creators of specialized agricultural civilizations climaxes this evolutionary process. E. W. Haury (1950, 1954) and others have indicated that modern Pima and Papago peoples are probably descendants of the Hohokam, who had extensive irrigation projects in the Gila River and Salt River drainages, but who declined as complex cultures around A.D. 1300. J. D. Jennings (1957) at Danger Cave excavations in western Utah in 1957 disclosed the picture of the Great Basin 10,000 years ago. At the close of the Pleistocene a disappearance of lakes and larger mammals neces-sitated the gathering of wild seeds and piñon nuts and a nomadism that, on this food-gathering level, could support only small groups. In the marginal regions the development of agriculture from wild-seed gathering and the development of techniques for grinding seeds and other foods gradually led to the agriculture and settled village life characteristic of Pueblo and Hohokam cultures.

Earlier, by 1927, A. V. Kidder (1924) and others established a series of stages of development from Basket Maker beginnings to the modern Pueblos. Hohokam and Mogollon cultures were differentiated and seemed even older than the Pueblo developments to the north. A fusion in the thirteenth and fourteenth centuries in the Little Colorado region gave rise to the modern western Pueblos of which Hopi and Hano were a part. Kidder also notes the abandonment of the San Juan–Mesa Verde region during the thirteenth century. Droughts, and possibly depredations by Navaho and Apache marauders, resulted in wholesale movements of population to the Rio Grande. The Tewa and other Tanoan-speaking peoples were among those who left.

It is interesting to note that while Uto-Aztecan-speaking peoples took part in all these cultural evolutionary movements, a core of Utes, Paiutes, and Western Shoshone aboriginally retained their basic hunting and gathering style of culture. These tribes are characteristic of the Great Basin as a whole. In southern Mexico, according to R. S. MacNeish (1964), this food gathering had changed to agriculture with the gradual development of corn, beans, and squash beginning about 5000 B.C. and with the later addition of cotton. The evolution of the high civilizations of Mexico influenced a slow diffusion of this agricultural complex northward, since it is found in the Southwest and Great Basin rim at least by 1000 B.C. At first agriculture supplemented food gathering and hunting in early Pueblo developments, as it does among Western Apache and Navaho. In the cultures developing irrigation, even the agricultural occupation of desert regions became possible. As Pueblo population grew, it spread as far north into the Basin heartland as the Great Salt Lake of Utah. The Pueblo domain contracted only with the conditions of drought previously mentioned and the incursions of Utes and Athapaskans. By the thirteenth and fourteenth centuries, the Pueblo tribes were in modern settings. Two centuries later they were to suffer military defeats at the hands of the Spaniards, beginning with Coronado's expedition of 1540–1542. Zuni and other tribes having been defeated, Juan de Oñate by the end of that century established the first Spanish province on the Rio Grande. Its food and forced-labor requisitions were to lead to the 1680 Pueblo revolt. For twelve years the Spaniards were driven from New Mexico, but they finally prevailed, especially along the Rio Grande. The Hopi were not subject to heavy reprisals. Athapaskans and Comanche played variable roles throughout this period. But the Ute, who had enjoyed long periods of peaceful contact with early Mexican settlements, were the least affected. They even adopted Mexican children; Mexicans adopted Utes; and occasionally there were intermarriages. No doubt such relationships facilitated the acquisition of the horse by the Ute Indians on the Spanish border and involved them less in the turbulence of border warfare. While the Apache and Navaho raided Spanish settlements and Indian pueblos, forcing the Pueblos from areas of northern New Mexico, the Southern Ute and Paiute retained the whole Basin rim of the corners of four adjoining areas (today, Colorado, New Mexico, Utah, and Arizona), which was Ute and Paiute hunting terrain.

The increased mobility afforded by widespread acquisition of the horse caused greater difficulty for the Ute on their southeast border. There the Comanche, who originally had acquired horses from both Mexicans and Utes but chiefly from the latter, bred the animals to increase herds. Their pressure on the border was felt through deep and warlike incursion. By the end of the seventeenth century the Comanche not only had forced the abandonment of Pecos but, from the Ute point of view, were the chief raiders in the southern plains and the most constant enemy. Even following independence from Spain in 1822, the New Mexican colonists listed the Comanche along with the Apache and Navaho as marauders; but they used the Ute to arrange truces in either direction. After the Mexican War of 1846 the United States utilized agents like John Greiner and Kit Carson for liaison. And the precontact patterns of peaceful trade continued.

We shall deal later with the Ute Indian and Southern Paiute contact continuum during the period when the United States controlled their destinies. Here it suffices to note that the precontact patterns of peaceful relations beginning on the Mexican border were maintained almost without interruption through the nineteenth and twentieth centuries. Together with the equally peaceful Hopi and certain other Pueblos, Southern Ute served as scouts and guides when Carson in 1864 rounded up the Navaho. Because of the Ute intermarriage and close cultural contacts with Jicarilla Apache, the Ute were not involved when Generals Miles and Crook captured Geronimo and certain other Chiricahua local group leaders about twenty years later. The one exceptional circumstance involving the Ute Indians of Colorado is known as the Meeker Massacre, or the Ute Indian War of 1879 (Opler, 1939c). A parallel circumstance was the still more recent Allen Canyon massacre of Paiutes from that district.

Both the author and J. Steward, writing independently in 1938, showed how the horse enabled small groups of extended families in the Great Basin to come together into larger band groupings. But this pattern had always existed for the Southern Ute, who gathered for brief periods in the spring of every year in the safe haven of mountain camps located in the foothills of the Rockies. During the summer such cohesion could not be sustained because of the limited food supply. Ecologically, the Ute were not typically in buffalo-hunting territory; so having horses and hunting buffalo could not become the basis for a relatively more fixed form of pastoral nomadism. At best, segments of a band, that is, only the merest precursor of a true band organization, could emerge. The Great Basin form of social structure throughout Ute terrain remained the seasonal circuit of extended family groups. The pattern of movement was mythologically likened to the circular trek of the wolf; and Wolf, rather than Coyote, is the Ute culture hero. For people in this tribe the usual pattern of movement, besides being orbital, was South in winter to lowlands and North in late spring to the then unlocked mountain camps familiar to members of a band.

The Ute have a large body of oral literature, some of which describes in mythological terms the creation, shamanism, and practices, or customs. Parallel to this is their Wolf Cycle, since Sunavawi (Wolf), as previously mentioned, was the culture hero. Besides this magico-religious literature, they have an extensive series of accounts, called "true stories," which are passed down from generation to generation. These latter are historical narratives that deal with real ancestors by name. One hears of a famous Ute wrestler whose first encounters with Mexican villagers included beating an able Mexican wrestler in a peacefully staged match. Or one may learn of leading shamans and their ability to cure ailing members of the band group. For more recent times there are accounts of Utes visiting Washington and negotiating with a named representative of Abraham Lincoln's government. Accounts of Kit Carson are prominent. Stories of Buckskin Charlie, told not only by his family members and descendants when he was one hundred years old in the 1930s but checked, as were all these stories, by band groups, describe his life and times. By dating techniques the "true stories" become vivid pictures of both precontact culture and the contact continuum. Some of these stories apparently date back three centuries to when the Ute ranged on foot near the Continental Divide or over more level land in southern Colorado, southeastern Utah, and northern New Mexico. With the coming of horses and communal buffalo hunts, the range extended to a corner of Oklahoma and sometimes, although rarely, to the Texas Panhandle. The southern Rockies are a tangled crisscross of mountainous spurs, with narrow passes, rock pockets, and swift streams flattening out to plateau and desert country to the south and west and into dreary plains and prairies to the southeast. The Ute were never strong in number and before the advent of the horse they were a defensive and peaceful people whose extended family groups moved in orbital circuits.

No doubt the southern Plains tribes, such as the Comanche of western Texas or the Arapaho and Cheyenne, surged along the eastern edge of the Ute terrain and even into the mountains around Denver deep in Ute country. Ralph Linton reported that Comanche were in fact intruders into the southern Plains. They initially received horses, as did Arapaho and Cheyenne, from Ute sources. Before the horse, Ute families located as segments of a band in favorite mountain camps near springs or rivers in the springtime. Limitations of food supply forced them to split again into extended family camps, and by fall the early snowfalls forced them South. By this migration the hunters followed a southward path of antelope, which provided them with winter supplies of meat. Deer were also accessible. The Ute were constantly on the move, foraging in the South during winter. The danger of enemies and even the migration patterns of buffalo forced them back to mountain camps in the spring season of each year. This annual circuit of families was a function of a struggle for existence, with a more pressing need for food in winter and a desire for protection from alien tribal marauders in the spring and summer. Extended families moved within known circuits according to dictates of older and more experienced family members.

Ute kinship distinguishes older siblings and cousins from younger ones as well as older from younger uncles and aunts. Older relatives, men or women, are believed to have better knowledge of the conditions of existence and the problems of hunting and gathering. Rights to territory were not vested in land, but were rather the habitual hunting and gathering places where an extended family group typically moved. One might simply send an emissary to call a shaman from another family; or one might come to know the accustomed places where a certain family hunted or the women gathered wild plant foods. A family pitched camp in the northward-southward circuit wherever the elders chose familiar sites. Consequently, though there was no fixed property in land nor its resources, no one seriously challenged the right of an extended family group to hunting grounds or berry patches established by long usage or seasonal occupancy.

There were no techniques of agriculture. On rare occasions corn, beans, or squash were obtained by peaceful and direct trade with Pueblo Indians to the south. For example, the author has described the peaceful transmission of the Ute Dog Dance to the Pueblo of Taos on such occasions (Opler, 1939b). Since the winter supply of meat and hides in the South was rarely sufficient, a Ute family could spare little from their own possessions, and such trade lagged. Yet the Ute practice of wintering in the South, a fact noted by early Spanish explorers, did occasionally lead to such barter.

The total lack of emphasis on property in land, together with the rigors of a hunting and gathering economy, accounts for population scattering and mobility. The Ute had no concept of trespass and never hunted by setting individual trap lines. Segments of the band gathered in the spring camps for the annual Bear Dance, which ushered in a brief period of other social dances, games, courtships, and curing ceremonies. In aboriginal times this was the only consolidation of band groups, except when terrain was invaded by the encroaching Plains tribes and word went out for mutual protection. Before white contact it is doubtful whether Southern Ute population ever exceeded 1,000. The Gunnison River served to separate northern and southern divisions of the tribe with no break in cultural and linguistic homogeneity. All Ute, North and South, were called by the term *nutc,* or The People. This word in the early English literature was recorded in several spellings, such as: *Yutah, Utah* (after which the western state has been named), *Eutaws,* and so forth.

The bands existed only in a rather formal and abstract sense. Like the southern and northern divisions of the tribe, the band names simply pointed to geographical positions. West of the Continental Divide, below the Gunnison, and down as far as Navaho and Jicarilla Apache country to the south lived the Weminutc, who pitched summer camps in the La Plata and San Miguel ranges or on the western slopes of the San Juan mountains around Pagosa Springs. To the east across the Divide lived the Kapota band, who occupied the region around the San Juan and the Sangre de Cristo ranges in the warmer seasons. Farther to the east lived the Mowatsi, occupying the territory from the Sangre de Cristo and the Culebra ranges on the west to the present sites of Denver, Colorado Springs, Raton, and Trinidad. The bands, therefore, had their ranges marked off by mountain barriers. The Weminutc, separated from the others by the Divide, were at all times the most isolated. The Mowatsi and Kapota, facing the more warlike eastern enemies, tended toward greater unity when threatened by the Comanche, Arapaho, Cheyenne, and even the Kiowa. Messengers could gather the camps for defense or warn them of impending danger. But leadership in such defensive warfare was casual and temporary, with participants as often as not representing persons from the two bands, rather than from one alone. The early band had no political cohesion nor centralized authority.

The social groupings just described did not loom large in the life of precontact times. The tribe was more conceptual than real. Warfare was defensive of invaded localities, not of band territory. In spring parts of a band gathered for Bear Dance. A few extended families, related by marriage or by blood ties reckoned to fourth cousins, sometimes assembled at favorite summer camps near springs and along rivers. But gatherings of extended families never survived the winter season.

Ute social and religious horizons intensified as their scope narrowed. It was the extended family group to which one belonged by birth or marriage. A married couple called each other by the term *piwan.* Their residence was with the parents of either husband or wife, the parents who either most needed their aid or with whom their relationship was most congenial. Sometimes they camped alone, although the presence of children made this arrangement inconvenient for hunting and gathering. Their first household was most often matrilocal and grew out of court-ship that culminated in trial marriage. The girl's female relatives erected a tipi, because women always tended the camp equipment. The marriage ceremony involved keeping the couple within a closed tipi where a smoking fire was used symbolically to test their compatibility under adverse conditions. On occasion, though less frequently, it was agreed by the families of the marrying couple that the residence be patrilocal, if the boy's parents or relatives needed his help or his wife's. Throughout the kinship system connected with such extended family group alliances sex and age distinctions were the chief means of differentiating relatives. The Ute group, all consanguineous relatives on their own generation level—siblings, parallel cousins, and cross cousins—were divided into four categories: the older, the younger, the male, and the female relatives of one's generation. The same sex and age distinctions applied to uncles and aunts, distinguished according to whether one was related to them through a mother or father, whether older or younger than the respective parent, and whether they were male or female.

Nepotic-avuncular terminology was verbally reciprocal. Great-grand-parent and great-grandchild employed a single reciprocal term, irrespec-tive of sex. The four grandparental terms, referring to mother's and father's parents, were likewise verbally reciprocal. While the consanguine-ous system bears out at almost all points the social importance of age and sex distinctions, the affinal system recognizes only a difference in sex; one term classified male in-laws and another female affinals.

The emphasis on age implied the authority of wisdom or greater knowledge of hunting, gathering, custom, and religious lore. Etiquette required the eldest to take the seat of honor opposite the tipi door or to be the first to speak, to be served, or to drink. To precede an elder in such things or even to light a cigarette from his firebrand made one old before his time. Yet children, despite tacit deference to authority, were at the same time indulged and spoiled from the earliest years. Breast feeding could continue episodically to ages like four or six, long after solid food intake began. Female breasts were regarded as feeding instruments rather than sexual objects, and a child might try a wet nurse at such an age. Babies were taken from cradleboards for demand feedings, fondling, and changing. Children were never bodily punished. Toys were leaf cutouts, cat's cradles, and replicas of adult tools. Brief references to mythic ogres, reputed to kidnap the young, were enough to instill obedience. The lip kiss, rare among nonliterate peoples generally, was limited to small children as an adult or public display of affection.

Not only parents but grandparents and older siblings tended the young; a child's training was begun by the older relatives.

At around age six the child's training became imitative of the sexual division of labor in the adult world. Girls tanned hides, made baskets and clay pipes, pitch-lined basketry jugs, dried meat, sewed clothing, and helped in preparing camp sites. Before puberty there was often baby tending. Women and girls made cradleboards, baby bags, wooden cups, and ladles. Men instructed the boys in male occupations such as hunting, chiefly by the stalking or tracking methods; fishing; clearing camp sites and gathering tipi poles; butchering; and making rope, bows, arrows, shields, and spears. The aboriginal extended family made every effort to develop children into industrious and useful members.

The Ute and Southern Paiute vocabulary is rich in a variety of terms for stages of infancy and childhood, with special terms for the newborn infant, the small baby, the toddler, and the little child before puberty. Special terms also exist for pubescence and full maturity.

While age determined authority in a general sense, both mythology and everyday humor provided safety valves for laughing at impositions of family authority. Thus, a joking statement could be, "Don't point at that rainbow, or you'll lose your finger." In the long winter months both the Wolf story cycle and the true stories about heroic exploits extended the horizons of a Ute's training. The family functioned in promoting marital choice, determining postmarital residence, and guiding one through crisis ceremonials.

Supernaturalism centered in curing rituals to maintain life, vigor, and mobility and also in ceremonies at birth, puberty, and death, the events of natural biological significance. Three to four months before childbirth, the prospective parents observed rules of continence that were expected to continue after the birth of the child, ideally for about a year. This birth control measure insured spacing of children. Social and religious dances were banned for pregnant women. Prospective fathers were expected to refrain from gambling games, and they believed that their luck would fail them anyway at such a serious time. The Ute believed that semen produced the baby. A child could be produced by filling the amniotic sac, either in a single intercourse or over a protracted period of time. Inferior semen explained childlessness. This theory of conception through biological accretion related to the belief that the child belonged not only to the immediate parents who produced it but to all consanguine relatives who helped in the survival of the nuclear family over time. If, therefore, a girl had a baby immediately following her husband's death, the dead man's mother could demand the child according to common Ute practice of placing it in the grandparents' household when so requested. The request could equally imply that the mother was to remain with her child at the grandparents' camp, contributing to economic support and help for the older generation. If the girl opposed this plan and had another lover before the birth of the child, she could claim that the baby had two fathers, and she might even prefer to make her life with the relatives of her second "husband." In such cases either family needs or personal attachments could prevail.

Personal property was the only kind of ownership the Ute recognized. Food, tipis made by joint family efforts, and even clothing that might be passed down were regarded as essentials of life for the extended family group. Bows, arrows, weapons, and baskets were individually owned by those who made them and could not be disposed of by another, even a spouse. The right to use what one made gave one the right to dispose of it by gift or by verbal testament. At time of death there was a distribution of such items to members of the bilateral family, and personal effects or cherished belongings of the deceased not so willed were destroyed. Finally, since bequeathed property could remind one all too often of the deceased himself and thereby entail the danger of ghost sickness through such remembrances, highly personalized objects were usually traded beyond the confines of the family circle for other things of a similar nature. Later, following the introduction of the horse on the Mexican frontier, the favorite horse of the deceased was usually killed at his grave; any additional mounts that were bequeathed were traded for horses from another band.

In Ute and Southern Paiute cosmology the sun travels clockwise around a flat earth. The stars move in a circle with the seasons. An animistic universe contains a Milky Way and Big Dipper, used for getting one's bearings, with the former being the earth's "backbone" or strewn ashes of a campfire and the Big Dipper being either Jackrabbit or a mythic wooden ladle. The Pleiades in the Wolf cycle explain the Basin rule prohibiting incest, for the largest star, Eta or Alcyone, is none other than Wolf's enraged wife surrounded by her children. A cyclone occurred because of sorcery sent in a cloud; a black obsidian knife was a common protective amulet that turned cyclones from their sporadic strikes. The whole world was charged with supernatural power, but shamans in diagnoses identified troubles within the individual as well as outside evil wishes. Death through sorcery led to vengeance by kin, including even fourth cousins (classificatory brothers). Murder, whether real or imagined, caused feuds between family groups.

The Great Basin birth ceremonies included a most elaborate couvade, or lying-in ceremony for the father of the child. For Ute women about to give birth, or even during menses, segregation was practiced. For birth, however, the entire family moved camp to a separate place. Either the mother's blood or menstrual flow caused illness, especially to unrelated men or sick individuals. The prospective father called one or two experienced women as midwives and took over his wife's work, such as hauling wood and fetching water. He and the midwife dug two pits of adult body length and almost 2 feet deep, one on either side of the fireplace. Hot ash with cedar bark and green brush for insulation and a rawhide covering made what the Ute called a "hot bed," one for the husband and one for the wife. For thirty days after birth the mother remained in the bed, attended by several female relatives. For four days the father also remained in his bed and observed the same taboos as his wife. She drank only warm water, said to clean out the bad blood that had accumulated in the baby sac since the time of conception; cold water would coagulate such blood. Meat and fish were taboo lest harm come to the husband's luck in hunting or fishing. The midwife remade the "hot beds" each evening before supper was given to her. Both parents used scratching sticks lest their nails leave welts on the skin. The Basin couvade signalizes an event of future importance. If parents scratched ears, deafness would result; if they laughed immoderately, their faces would become old and wrinkled; forgetfulness foretold a future poor memory. Indeed, family well-being was determined at this time.

The Ute father's couvade lasted four days and was followed on the fifth by his eating meat or fish and receiving clothing from the grandfather, at whose camp the couvade was staged. The meat was a token of hunting prowess bestowed upon the young man. The older relative painted his face with red ocher and deer fat during prayers for hunting and family welfare. Following this the father went on a ritual hunt alone, running tirelessly along trails and breaking twigs from trees marking animal paths, thereby assuring himself both speed and endurance as well as a deer or antelope for each broken twig. The baby, meanwhile, was tenderly molded by the grandmother, who "shaped" its nose or pressed in ears or stroked the face to round it handsomely. Prayers for straight growth and good looks insured these benefits.

Basin life-cycle ceremonies also included a girl's adolescence rite at the onset of menses and segregation in a separate brush wickiup at this and subsequent times. Avoidance of blood contact with males and meat and fish taboos protected the hunting and fishing ability of male kin as in the couvade segregation. After the horse was acquired in the Basin, such taboos were extended to male horses, and menstruating women rode mares to protect male animals. Either at birth or first menses prayers by a grandmother, special baths, and, at the end of a couvade, a gift of clothes from an older woman ensured long life and vigor.

The adolescent boy, in a parallel ceremony, was taken on a hunt by an older male relative, who killed a large game animal and daubed its blood on the boy's body. He received characteristics of the animal, such as the strength of a mountain lion or the cleverness of a coyote. Both boys receiving this rite and adolescent girls taken on plant-gathering expeditions were ritually bathed and blessed.

Dreams of a magical sort by children or youth also represented visitations of the animistic power of the heavenly bodies or animals that appeared in the dream sequence. Thus, individual supernatural power and even the curing ability from such agencies in nature came from Creator-of-Humans through such phenomena as the moon, stars, lightning, cyclone or from specific birds and animals. By late adolescence, a Ute or Southern Paiute had been through protective ceremonials and had usually learned the rules, rituals, and paraphernalia governing his own shamanistic power.

Shamanism in the Basin combined dream interpretations with individual songs, rituals, and spirited attacks on illness. To summon a shaman relatives would approach him with a gift of eagle tail feathers; a painted stick; or after the introduction of the horse, the almost standard payment of a mount. The shaman then visited the afflicted family and dramatized in songs and rituals, sleight of hand, and through extraction of the evil substance, the power of his inner spirit (represented by a manikin within) to swallow down the sickness. Besides power for good, power for evil or witchcraft occurred if the shaman's ability was weakened by overuse or old age or even by the power's itself becoming enraged. A shaman answered any call, no matter how far away, except when power was thus weakened. His younger relatives might fear his power and thereby express unconscious or repressed resentment against his authority, making bleak allusions to a family shaman's overtaxed ability. Dead relatives could inflict ghost sickness upon a victim through visitations in dreams of the animal or titular power after whom the relative had been named. This theory, suggestive of E. B. Tylor's on the origin of religion, likewise represented a reaction to the Basin conception of a linked age and authority pattern within the family circle.

The Great Basin customs and beliefs concerning death remind one of conceptions that are widespread in nonliterate societies concerning the importance of breath as a symbol of living. When a person was deathly ill, the Utes said that his heart was leaving his body. They believed that breath, or *suapun,* also left the organism and could only be recalled by the shaman as returned breath, or *suapits.* The shaman had songs to restore the weakening heart. By sleight of hand tricks he might have sent a light downy feather after the heart or might have pleaded with his power to make it catch on rocks or bushes. In the total drama relatives rushed from the tipi to recall the heart. If death came, the deceased was quickly buried under rocks or burned on a pyre. The camp then moved hastily, and the family made efforts, after a brief period of mourning, to avoid the burial place and to forget the deceased who otherwise might return in ghostly dreams. Close relatives cut their hair, and those in the immediate family even donned old clothes and for four days remained quiet with taboos against singing or laughter.

Having dealt with Basin rites of birth, adolescence, and death, it remains to deal with courtship, often conducted near the girl's seclusion camp. Each boy made a four-holed flageolet, which he fashioned to fit his voice range, to use in serenading. In social dances the woman took the initiative by throwing a small stone or stick into the youth's lap as an invitation to a clandestine visit to her family camp. These "girl-hunting" (*naqwitpaqwi*) expeditions involved the creeping lover at night in a risky and possibly abruptly ended courtship, since if he was caught, the family might press for marriage. Elopements were also practiced, though they were not socially approved because they conflicted with parental authority in arranging marriages. If a boy was shy, an older male relative might be the go-between to plead the case for matrimony. Sexual intimacy usually preceded marriage, and early adolescence was a period of philandering, during which parents often feebly protested. When two compatible individuals settled down, it was called trial marriage, and they used the term sweetheart (*piwanapun*), signifying becoming spouse.

Ute and Allen Canyon Paiute sex egalitarianism is a cultural theme that continues unchanged from earliest times to the present. The creeping lover, the flageolet serenade, the women's initiative at dances, grandparental adoptions, and even instruction in abortion techniques freed girls as well as boys for sexual exploration leading to trial marriages. There were no affinal gift exchanges or avoidances, but rather fluidity in postmarital residence. Divorce was effected simply by returning to the parental camp. In the case of adultery either spouse physically accosted the adulterer, and the contest of strength could settle matters. Both levirate and sororate could bind widow or widower to affinal relatives wishing to retain an industrious relative. Sororal polygyny with a sister or wife's cousin did occur, albeit rarely. Still more rarely, unrelated wives occupied separate tipis in less stable arrangements, as when one wife was ill. Polyandry did not occur. Aggrieved spouses might destroy possessions of the rival and then separate. When a man complained pettishly to a girl's parents, the Ute might joke about it, saying, "He's going to marry her younger sister!" Finally, in tribes of the southern rim there were cases of marriage to both a mother and her stepdaughter; this custom, also, is found as far north as the Western Shoshone.

In summary, aboriginal cultures of the Great Basin southern rim, Ute and Southern Paiute showed various common features that can be regarded as the early Uto-Aztecan pattern, so widespread are they, in

An aged Paiute woman of the Fort McDermitt Indian Reservation, Nevada,
wears rabbit skin blanket, an artifact of the ancient Desert Culture.
(Courtesy, United States Bureau of Indian Affairs.)

their detailed working out, among Shoshonean-speaking peoples in general. These include: sparse population moving in extended family
groups in large and seasonal orbits or circuits; short periods of band
segment consolidations followed by dispersal; a hunting and gathering
economy; shamanistic religion; life-cycle ceremonials emphasizing birth,
youth, and death; and the typical preoccupations of a nomadic people
with health, vigor, and economic skills. This pattern, with its typical
Great Basin elaborations, continued, with some modifications in both
economics and sociopolitical structuring throughout the period of early
contact. The modifications, in the absence of agriculture or real animal
breeding, were really microevolutionary in character, as we shall see, so
that the Great Basin culture of the southern rim as described above
largely survived and persists in the American Southwest even today.

Early Contacts and Culture Change: 1540–1800

The characteristics of Ute culture before the horse are closely related to those of other Great Basin societies. Loose patterns of authority by virtue of age and experience were reflected in kinship terminology. Bands were solely territorial groupings with occasional communal gatherings of parts of the band for the spring Bear Dance, for winter rabbit hunts, or for fall antelope drives. The animistic concept of supernatural power, with a creator or sun deity, plus a "trickster cycle" of stories, led to notions of power offered in dreams, to ideas of the spirit wandering during sleep, and to animistic birth and adolescence ceremonies, with little emphasis on tribal or band rituals. Even the initial matrilocal residence followed by shifting family alliances, the menstrual taboos, and modes of courtship, or such minor arrangements as the ceremonial hunt following a couvade give a clear impression of a unity of pattern that is typically Basin Shoshonean.

J. Steward (1938) has noted that throughout the Humboldt River drainage system band organization and war chieftainship followed close upon the introduction of the horse around the middle of the nineteenth century. We have stated that the horse allowed for the transporting of food to central campsites. However, the author has also noted that the common Western Shoshonean pattern of winter consolidation into small villages and a summer scattering of population in extended family groups was seasonally reversed among the Southern Ute and Allen Canyon Paiute prior to the band-camp organization and the introduction of the horse. This seasonal reversal of population concentration and dispersal is best understood as a result of the ecology of the Rockies and especially the pressure of Plains invasions in the spring and summer seasons. The Ute could not gather in the Rockies in the winter season. Colonel R. I. Dodge noted in the 1880s that Utes were "the Switzers of America." The Ute bands, numbering less than 500, were held in utter contempt by powerful Plains tribes but nevertheless were respected for their advantage in the mountains.

In addition to being locked out of mountain camps in winter, the Ute were lured South for fall antelope drives, since it was then that the great herds gathered on the southern foothills. Winter supplies of meat were stored in pit caches. The southern range in northern New Mexico and adjoining states was the scene of only occasional consolidations of extended family groups for communal rabbit hunts or trading expeditions to the Pueblos. The proximity to warlike Plains tribes, especially the Comanche, Arapaho, and Cheyenne, deterred Southern Ute society from following the typical Shoshonean patterns of winter consolidation.

Compared with Western Shoshone, the Ute lacked fertility cere-monies other than those found in the context of their life-cycle rites of passage. There are traces, however, of such rituals. The bulk of Ute prayers are addressed to the sun, and each family head begins the day by invoking this central deity. One dance, the Deer Hoof Rattle Dance, or *tasutcinqap,* recalled as a very ancient dance, was reported in the 1930s only by informants over eighty years old. In it willows 3 feet long, covered with buckskin and having deer hoof rattles at the top, were shaken by single files of dancers of each sex, facing the East. A feather from an eagle or a brightly colored bird topped the dancing staff, which was stamped on the ground in time to songs. The dancers' faces and hair were painted in red and yellow streaks that represented the sundown. Dances and prayers called for the sun's rejuvenation; and final prayers to the East appealed for multiplication of plant and animal life and for food, health, and vigor.

The Spanish governor Otermin was the first to enter into treaties with the Ute. This was around the year 1675, according to R. E. Twitchell (1914). Yet all the explorers' accounts by this time picture the Ute as being already equestrian and also organized into band camps with camp leaders. The total shift involved extensions of former customs. In place of the exclusive use of family hunting and foraging units, a new cooperative group emerged in the band, or parts of a band called a band camp. In the group food was shared through such instruments as the buffalo hunt, which became a communal enterprise overshadowing the earlier antelope drives and rabbit hunts, now secondary in im-portance. Before the horse there had been rare expeditions on foot of small family groups to the Plains in quest of buffalo. The Ute, living to the north of Spanish settlements, were unlike the Apache, who re-garded the centers of Spanish influence as encroachments upon their own territorial rights. Early Ute relations with the Spaniards, con-sequently, were generally as peaceful as the contacts with the Pueblos had been.

Oñate's settlements are still remembered in historical or true stories among the Ute. The region around Santa Fe, a southern limit of their former winter range, is mentioned by the Ute as the place where the horse was acquired from Spaniards. Their own equestrian accouterments, such as the saddle, quirt, stirrups, and saddlebags, are all replicas of early Spanish models, both traded and imitated around 1640. Various accounts of the Ute identify a former Southern Ute leader, Maiyoar, as a tall, thin man important in solidifying such trade. There are also widespread stories of Yoa, a Kapota chief, who lived at the time when the Ute were still under Mexican jurisdiction and when Santa Fe was the oldest town. In Yoa's story it is told how a group of Mexicans traveling West tried to purchase Indian children for purposes of herding sheep. On occasion Mexicans unceremoniously captured Paiute or Ute children.

In earlier contacts with the Rio Grande Pueblos, the Ute typically supplied meat and hides in exchange for agricultural products. In subsequent trade from the latter half of the seventeenth century into the early 1700s a constant item for barter was the horse. The Southern Ute were undoubtedly the major transmission belt for the introduction of the horse from the Spanish frontier.

Not only did Mexicans barter for Indian children or capture them, but the Southern Ute practices of adoption were also known to the Mexicans. Both child adoption and child barter were justified by the older Ute custom of giving children to an older grandparental generation so that the young people could maintain the mobility demanded by the exigencies of hunting and gathering. In the case of twins, the Ute had formerly promoted the adoption of one child of the pair by an unrelated family in a different locality. Illegitimate children, if not adopted by the extended family in name-giving ceremonies, were sometimes bartered for horses from the Spaniards. In return the early Spanish settlers, normally relying upon sheep and cattle raising, brought up the Ute shepherds and cowherds within their own families. Even such a famous Ute Indian as Chief Ouray was adopted by Mexican settlers and spent his early years among them employed as a shepherd. The payment to his Ute relatives was, of course, in horses. The friendly and peaceful Ute were sought, in 1675, as allies against the traditionally hostile Apache. As we have noted, they were also used to quell recurring Pueblo outbreaks and, still later, were allies of the Spanish in wars against invading Comanche.

Throughout this early period of contact Ute culture shifted somewhat to band organization in microevolutionary change. The Ute never became complete pastoral nomads, nor did they develop clan organization like the settled Hopi. Rather, as trade in horses flourished, larger band camps came into existence. Ute accounts now speak of occasional, though rare, expeditions to the plains for buffalo, even into borderlands of adjoining states, such as Texas and Oklahoma. A buffalo hunt, under the authority of a band leader, was preceded by two scouts and cautiously directed. It might occur in the fall hunting season in order to lay in winter supplies of meat. Not only were pit caches filled, but also the buffalo provided tipi covers and buffalo robes, sinew-thread, bowstrings, horn glue, skin bags, and, of course, meat in greater abundance than before. The horse and the travois allowed transport of supplies back to central campsites.

As Alfred B. Thomas (1932b) and Rupert N. Richardson (1933)

point out, the appearance of the Comanche in the region around west Texas around the beginning of the 1700s intensified raiding for horses and also the need for protective functions among the Ute. Both Comanche and Ute claimed that the raids were retaliatory. But the Ute, who had originally obtained horses on the Spanish frontier by such painful methods as child barter, tended to develop strong defensive patterns for the guarding of camps. Once in Plains country, however, mechanisms for turning a hunting party into a war party or retaliatory raiding expedition were necessary. After 1706 the Ute occasionally joined Apache, Navaho, or even Comanche in raids on the Spanish frontier for livestock and horses. The Ute, however, are the least identified with depredations of this period. The Spanish governor's declaration of war upon the Comanche in 1719 included the Ute solely on the basis of vague reports from places like Taos and Cochiti that some Utes had participated in hostilities there. In the period following and up to 1786 there is no evidence of a Comanche-Ute alliance. The Jicarilla Apache, who had borrowed such cultural items from the Ute as the Bear Dance, moved westward at this time and no longer formed a barrier between the two hostile tribes. Warfare flared on the southern Plains as raiding and hunting progressed. A Spanish-Ute alliance was again solidified, and Utes became the scouts of Spanish punitive expeditions against invading Comanche.

The Ute were poorer in horses than the Comanche and, unlike the Comanche, did not make a practice of breeding horses. Warfare was more a result of buffalo hunting and raiding or stealing horses than any desire of the Ute to win prestige by bravado or valor. The Ute had no war honors institutionalized. Whether one captured a horse or stripped an enemy of possessions was solely a matter of expediency. Standing fights were avoided. If a Ute leader in warfare caused a foolhardy shedding of blood by his men, he risked a flogging at their hands.

The famous Ute capture of the Kiowa sun-dance doll occurred accidentally when some Ute met a party of Comanche and Kiowa bent on trouble. After the leaders parleyed together and the Ute proclaimed their peaceful intentions, the others became threatening, causing the Ute to scatter and flee in small groups in order to divide the superior enemy force. In the skirmish that followed, one Kiowa was caught alone at the top of an arroyo, and the Utes who shot and stripped him discovered the famous sun-dance–doll bundle on his person. In their haste to escape from the enemy, they carried the bundle along and examined it only much later when they were in safe terrain. Then, thinking it to be ritually dangerous, they stuffed it into a gopher hole. The Ute remained a Great Basin culture in which war honors had no formalized role and bravery was not worshiped for its own sake.

The Ute band camp in pre-Reservation days was composed of extended-family camps spread out for about half a mile along a stream or river in a sheltered location. The games, dances and visiting that once marked the brief period of early spring were now a year-long interest made possible by horses, organized buffalo-hunting expeditions, and the fuller pit caches storing food products. A band or part of a band now camped together, with the tipi of the camp leader slightly larger than the rest to accommodate meetings of the older, more experienced persons. From this center of activity a band leader each morning announced to his followers his suggestions for the day. If he were aged or his voice too low, the news was broadcast through a camp crier.

The chiefs themselves were variously called by such titles as *nimwi tawav* (band chief), *tawats* (the man), *tavanamum* (leader, or head man in the camp), and *nagotu tawats* (man of war, or war leader). Only respected camp leaders were qualified to call out for organized buffalo hunts or raids. They were men who had proved their worth as daring scouts and wise counselors and who had been publicly chosen for such office. Such leadership required the sanction of followers and held only so long as one led wisely and well.

There were economic gains involved in raiding, and a leader might announce that tonight the camp would dance and tomorrow raid. Informal gift exchanges were made possible through such expeditions. But equally, organized hunts, camp movements, or dances were prized, and a balance existed between the authority of older relatives in the extended family and the achieved status of band leaders. In warfare the chief interest of the Southern Ute band centered on loot. One tried to dismount the enemy and make off with his horse. The Ute trained their mounts to respond to knee movements so that, commonly, bridles were not necessary and the rider's hands were free to unhorse the enemy. Ambush was also used. And stories tell of stealthy intrusions into enemy camps at night to cut away horses. After such a raid a Ute gave away all the horses he did not need, or he traded them for buckskin and meat. One sent a child over when meat arrived to stand by expectantly for portions of the animal. A returning war party was preceded by scouts riding ahead and notifying of success or failure. Then, others might ride out of camp singing the praises of the lucky men returning. Those honored were expected to give reciprocal gifts of loot, or distributions might be made at a public scalp dance. As a third, and final, method of sharing loot, poorer people went to the tipis of returned warriors to dance and honor them, with a view to presents. The benefits of raids in horses, enemy clothing, pipes, weapons, and other booty were spread evenly throughout the band.

Ute women of active age also participated in raids, following the men into battle and stripping the enemy. Their war dance regalia was ornate, and the step they danced included a lame dragging of one foot to symbolize the heavy burden of loot they had taken.

The band, however, mainly organized protective mechanisms, rather than offensive ones. When a camp was pitched, the leader appointed scouts to post themselves on high ground or at lookouts in order to protect the people from enemies. The scouts, called *saridzka,* or Dog Company, were youth of the camp. They included younger relatives of leaders, who were being trained for future positions of importance in either families or bands; recruits; orphans of war; and sometimes unadopted child captives. They camped with small parfleches of dried meat and jugs of water, and with them lived one older woman, called *bia* (mother) honorifically by the boys. The *bia* also acted as go-between with people in the camp below. If enemies were sighted, the company of boys ran their horses back and forth as a signal. Another signal system consisted of the young "male dogs" trotting after the *bia*. The Dog Company might also camp with the band, or else separately a short distance from the main group. Then, as camp watchmen, they were expected to run up into the hills in "watchdog fashion." When the camp moved, the Dog Company lagged behind as a rear guard. Thus, they notified the camp at all times of enemy marauders.

The combinations of scouts who were appointed and the small Dog Company that was recruited from among the youth constituted both a warfare training apparatus and the young men's elite. Their only peculiar mark of distinction, however, was a necklace of slit wolfskin. Not all youth chose to join, nor could all families spare active young men from their ranks. Indeed, the boys were said to be without families or family obligations throughout the training period. Hence, the pseudonym *bia* for the woman in their ranks. Occasionally, the *bia* cooked stews of dog meat for them to impart the agility and alertness of the "watchdog" function.

The Dog Company channelized social functions. Boys who had been out with girls of the camp romantically were publicly prohibited from the next day's feast. Their own patterns of institutionalized philandering included outright rape. The youth indulged in provocative antics to attract the girls of the main camp; girls who laughed or flirted with them were then promptly spirited away to the hillside camp of the Dog Company for purposes of sexual diversion. Girls in menstrual lodges were, of course, not molested. The *bia* could not be molested; and she herself warned women and girls not to laugh at the boys' provocative antics. The *bia* acted as formal go-between in arranging social dances and also in connection with ripening romances that could not be curbed.

The Dog Company also resorted to a kidnap method of recruiting boys who had already undergone puberty hunting rituals. In this way their numbers were replenished as older members dropped out. The image fostered of *saridzka* was one of hardened and impetuous manhood, whether on raids, living in seclusion for protection of the camp, or protecting groups on larger communal buffalo hunts. In fact, the *saridzka* is the clearest example of a correlated social change occasioned by the horse complex, the buffalo hunt, and the protective warfare involvements of the band camp.

To illustrate the tenuous authority of camp leaders, Ute punishment of crime can serve as an example. Thievery within the band, though rare, was solely a family matter. Often the object was returned and the thief flogged by his own relatives. Yet, with economic sharing and gift giving forming a cooperative foundation, gangs of hungry boys or girls were as often as not allowed to rifle pit caches for private feasts. Murder or witchcraft again mobilized the family as the sole avenging unit. Adultery led the aggrieved husband or wife to seize a horse or buffalo robe from the intrusive person or, if philandering continued, to require the rival to fight it out. Chiefly authority stopped at each tipi door, and chiefs were powerless to control feuds or marital disputes.

The traditional tactics of ostracism and gossip, or "reputation," were major methods of social and legal control. *The* man, or the band leader, as he was called, often relied on counsels of older men, and both the chief and his crier, or talking chief, were sensitive to orally disseminated public opinion. When Buckskin Charlie (approximately one hundred years old during our initial field work in 1936–1938) was chosen to be a chief in his band during his late teens, this was formally signalized by his being given a scrap of scalp tissue to swallow after a certain brave exploit. But it was preceded by several occasions when note was taken of his abilities in public speeches of various elders. The shout of acclaim that greeted the presentation of the scalp meat was simply a climaxing expression of approval.

In the final stages of early contact Buckskin Charlie's band, the Mowatsi, joined with the Jicarilla in evening the score through retaliatory raids on Plains enemies, usually to the exclusion of other Ute bands. Similarly, the western band, the Weminutc, called on the Jicarilla in their war with the Navaho. During this period, which marked a fluid or expansive period of the Ute band, the total range extended from the borders of Utah and Arizona down to northern New Mexico and east to Texas and Oklahoma. Contacts with white traders and settlers were generally peaceful at this time of maximum territorial expansion in the eighteenth century. The century that followed brought the full impact of white contact, ushering in long years of defeat, territorial loss, and disillusion. Indeed, the shrinkage of range is the major theme running throughout recent Ute history to the present.

We learn from Spanish sources that the Ute borrowed the game

Canute and possibly a number of Spanish folk tales, revised in terms of animal characters, water spirits, and ogres.

The move north from Santa Fe was bitterly opposed by the Ute, but stories of their livestock depredations are more than matched by historical accounts of the white capture of Ute women. In 1778 a decree was issued from Chihuahua prohibiting settlers and allied Indians from visiting Utes for purposes of trade and barter. In the war on the Comanche (1786) the Ute allies showed a characteristic disinterest in conquest, which was clearly the Spanish motive. Ute desertions in the Spanish campaigns are matched by evidences of the desolation they felt at loss of territory suffered during their Mexican alliance. Antonio de Bonilla tersely noted, "They do not consider being converted." By the time of Zebulon Pike's expedition in 1805–1807 and in Jacob Fowler's Journal less than two decades later they are described as already being pressed back toward the mountains, as living there without "any settled home," and as having receded from previously broader territories.

The Contact Continuum: Period of Land Sales: 1800–1895

The United States conquest of New Mexico did not change the generally peaceful disposition of the Ute toward white neighbors. J. T. Hughes (1848), reporting on Doniphan's march of 1846, noted that the Ute did not combine with the Pueblos and New Mexicans in opposition, as had been alleged. He wrote also that Major Gilpin, returning to Abiquiu, described "an utmost tranquility amongst the Mexicans, Pueblos and Yutas." Josiah Gregg (1850), in this same period, pictures the Ute as wintering "in the mountain valleys northward" and spending summer seasons "generally in the prairie plains to the east, hunting buffalo." But he adds to this description of prevailingly peaceful hunting their need occasionally to take some cattle for food as required. With General Kearney's arrival in the region they are rather fancifully described, in army parlance, as "suing for peace." By the close of the Mexican campaign the United States government had negotiated a Ute treaty, at Abiquiu on December 30, 1849. The Indian Agent, James S. Calhoun, through letters, described them as more frequently the victims in New Mexican border incidents than the aggressors.

The 1850 decade brought the spread of more effective firearms, the dollar-a-hide slaughter of buffalo herds, and the arming of Plains Indian enemies. In 1851–1853 John Greiner was stationed at Taos, and in 1853–1859 Kit Carson had charge of this regional agency. The last feeble stand was taken by the Ute in 1853, when they joined the Jicarilla against Governor Merriwether. Colonel Fauntleroy "defeated" them in 1855.

R. E. Twitchell (1911–1917) pictures the Mowatsi Ute as being the chief allies of the Jicarilla during this last defiant period, the alliance marked by intermarriage as well as by a mutual interest in survival. He states that the Ute frequently asserted their rights to broad tracts of land over which they had ranged and with equal vehemence stated their firm opposition to farming and reservation life. In his words, "Their ideal was to retain their hunting grounds." The *Report of the Commissioner of Indian Affairs* (1854) describes the Ute in a similar vein as now being at the mercy of Plains Indian tribes of Oklahoma and Texas, which were amply supplied with new arms and ammunition. This forced the Ute again to recede both in territory and, consequently, in resources. The same report pictures parties of Ute coming to white settlements for short periods of labor in threshing grain after harvest. While Governor Merriwether, in 1856, eulogizes the Ute as peacefully "professing a willingness to commence farming next spring," Kit Carson, in 1857, after similarly complimenting the Mowatsi on being free of all "vices, prostitution and drunkenness," continues to suggest that they be removed from white settlements entirely and furnished with their own farming and mechanics staff. Carson reported that game supplies were now so depleted that the Ute in the southern winter range must otherwise subsist by raiding and thievery.

Carson's reports are studded with accounts of Utes being subjected to violence and injustice. In one incident that he relates, a Ute man and woman were killed and the relatives were denied restitution in payment, the mildest form of legal settlement according to Ute custom. In another instance, a Ute at Taos was soaked with turpentine and burned alive. The outcome of such events was the removal of the agency center to Maxwell's ranch. In 1861 the new Agency Superintendent, Collins, complained that the Utes lacked reservation land, though they received gifts of rations at Abiquiu. He, too, eulogized them as being "loyal, and intelligent," since they "tendered their services for the protection of white settlers" against border "rebels as well as savage foes."

The entire decade of the 1860s, including Lincoln's administration, had the same character. There were Ute agencies in the Cimarron Valley and at Conejos. In one battle 12 Ute were pitted against and fought off about 300 Plains warriors with 9 of the Utes killed, 1 wounded, and 2 remaining unscathed. These two seized their wounded chief, Sesareva, and a dead leader named Benita and stood off the whole band of Plains Indians from a hiding place in the brush. In 1863 an entire band of Arapaho descended on the Cimarron Agency to wipe out all of the Utes in the neighborhood. The Indian Agent at the time refused to extend any support to the Indians under his charge, while in the same year, the white settlement at Tierra Amarilla was using Ute men of the neighborhood to protect the local white citizenry. Since agency

centers of this period afforded the Ute little protection during Plains
Indian border incidents, certain leaders of parts of a band group broke
away. In 1866 a part of the Mowatsi band turned to rebellion, and in
1868, Chavves, a renegade Kapota, led a guerilla band of sixty-one
men.

Wars of suppression by white troops were punctuated by assaults
of Plains enemies, again leading to treaties with the United States government. The Ute accounts of negotiations with officials of the Lincoln
administration contain the usual stories of lavish promises to pay for
lost territory "as long as grass grows and the rivers flow." But they
include, also, bitter detail about intoxicating the signers with whiskey
and then obtaining signatures (actually marked by crosses) to cede lands
that were not even properly defined in Ute terms. By 1868 the *Reports
of the Commissioner of Indian Affairs* had begun to describe the
Cimarron Agency Mowatsi Ute and Jicarilla as being fed by white
soldiers, because they were by now unable to live by means of hunting
and gathering. The Kapota and Weminutc of Abiquiu were already
asking to pursue their old life on a reservation in the San Juan valley.
However, a treaty dated March 2, 1868, located their reservation entirely within the confines of western Colorado and ordered that any
reserves previously established be vacated and sold.

It is well to look at the policy of the United States in this period.
After 1871 it became the common practice to institute general agreements
with Indian tribes that sounded very much like the preexistent treaties,
but that did not require legislative ratifications. For many of these
arrangements a presidential executive order sufficed. The Ute Indians,
looking back on the previous treaties and the subsequent presidential
orders, regarded them all as initiating what they called, thinking retro-
spectively no doubt, "the period of land sales." The reserves, previously
established and now ordered vacated and sold, were put on public auc-
tion in 1873, 1878, and 1880. In the first instance, a portion of the
newly established reservation (containing the entire San Juan mining
area) was ceded to the United States for a small sum. The remaining
land, merely a strip about 15 miles wide and approximately 100 miles
long, came to be known as the Southern Ute Reservation. The treaty of
November 9, 1878, reduced rights to Confederate Ute land, except those
that "might be allotted to them in severalty." The 1880 treaty contained
agreement to settle down on unoccupied agricultural lands bordering
Colorado's La Plata River.

The intention of the United States government at this time was
signalized by the Allotment Act of 1887. Intended to allot farms to
Indians "in severalty," the act was also passed with the notion of eliminating the need for an Indian Bureau in due course. Against the back-

ground of land loss among the Ute in the sense of broad hunting
terrain, this legislation could not help but be viewed with suspicion.
By 1895 the government was allotting individual farms along the Pine,
Animas, and Piedras rivers. In the years immediately following, such
allotments, the Ute claim, were opened up for sale in a way that involved
collusion between ambitious white farmers of the neighborhood around
Ignacio and Durango and agency superintendents. Thus, in the Ute
viewpoint the shrinking of reservation land resulted both from earlier
treaties establishing a long and narrow reserve and from subsequent
arranged sales of land held in severalty.

Stock belonging to Indians grazed out of bounds, and cattle belonging to whites broke into the poorly demarcated reservation. The Ute
constantly requested territory having better boundaries. Instead, the
"time of land sales" continued, during which families were actively
encouraged by agents to exchange lands for cash payment. As was common elsewhere, white settlers and traders quickly converted any such
cash payments into inferior trade goods and horses. Since the white
homesteaders epitomized farming, and since their trading practices
were often dishonest, the Ute complained of further inroads upon the
land remaining to them in the Southern Ute Reservation near Ignacio.
Agricultural experts, with whom we have carefully surveyed the former
reservation lands in some detail, assure us that the best farmlands in
Colorado went to the white homesteaders, leaving the Ute on poorer
land, which was threaded through by that now owned by white farmers.

The decrease in land and economic resources led to the adoption
of different positions among the Ute bands, which were now housed
side by side on the reservations. A split occurred, with the Weminutc
band later settling at the Towaoc Subagency near Ute Mountain in
southwestern Colorado, a desert region within sight of the arid Navaho
lands around Shiprock. The two eastern bands, Mowatsi and Kapota,
remained in the East and now live at the Consolidated Ute Agency near
Ignacio. Decisions within the Weminutc band, in response to the loss
of farmlands during the period of land sales, led to their determination to
settle down in the arid region around Towaoc. Because of Ute band
autonomy, the two eastern bands at Ignacio regarded themselves as
living under a single "reservation chieftain." Buckskin Charlie, the
former Mowatsi leader, became the nominal tribal head, and certain
Kapota leaders were influential at Ignacio in various ceremonial dances,
such as the Sun Dance.

The Split Reservation (After 1895): Revitalization or Loss?

A cultural dichotomy in the split between the two southern reservations now became apparent in the greater degree of cultural conservatism at Towaoc. Actually, this is curious, because it was persons of the Weminutc band who first began farming on the original reservation and who claim they were induced to sell better lands to white settlers. Now these Indians prefer to stay on arid lands far from white neighbors in order to follow the old Ute practices of seasonal circuit in the microcosm. In summer their camps were moved up into the Ute Mountain. In winter they pitched camp down below, often using Ute wickiups rather than the clapboard houses that came to be built around Ignacio, side by side with the tipi or the wickiup. The separation occurred in 1895, at the height of the period known as "land sale." When we remember that it was the men of the Weminutc band who were the first to farm, around the turn of the century, and who were also among the first to suffer the disillusionments occasioned by relinquishing land for cash payments, it is clear that the opening of reservations to allotment procedures backfired in the Ute case. At any rate, the Weminutc were the most alienated from "the White Man's ways" and determined to avoid farming among white neighbors in an effort to return to "the old ways."

The recoil from white contact occurred not only among those who moved to Ute Mountain but also at Ignacio. However, the choice was implemented for the Weminutc band at Towaoc by their leaders, while the two bands at Ignacio continued on allotted lands among white farmers. While Buckskin Charlie hoped to interest the Mowatsi and Kapota seriously in education, and a school was formed on the eastern Consolidated Ute Reservation for both Ute and Paiute children, the remaining crop lands on which the two bands he led settled were poor pickings. And although the Ute Mountain Reservation, with its headquarters at Towaoc, afforded a cool mountain habitat for summer camps, its terrain included some of the poorest land in the southwest. Consequently, both band groups, east and west, felt aggrieved and despoiled.

If one looks back in time, the introduction of the horse allowed Ute bands to consolidate, to expand their resource utilization, to establish political leadership, to develop such society organizations as the Dog Company, and to form social mechanisms for protection. Now the Dog Company degenerated into a singing group and soon passed away. The old dances and horse parades became mere reminders of better times, soon used as spectacles at Mexican fiestas and, later, as pageants in the town of Ignacio. The Sun Dance, the Ghost Dance, and the Peyote Cult were the last attempts at cultural revitalization, and of these, the Ghost Dance, as the movement symbolizing the greatest degree of cultural resistance and "nativistic feeling," was the specific ritual that entirely disappeared.

To compare the cultural differential between the two groupings of bands, the Ute Mountain band at Towaoc lead the most nomadic existence, living in movable tents, occasionally owning flocks of sheep. In superficial aspects like dress, they held the longest to Ute standards, wrapping their braids, and wearing native garb in celebrating the Bear Dance. They have suffered from poverty, and until 1931 cash, clothing, and food from the government were rationed. Disease was greater at Ute Mountain; in the 1930s syphilis claimed a quarter of the population, and gonorrheal arthritis and trachoma assumed epidemic proportions. Five deaths from tuberculosis occurred in one family within three years during our Ute Mountain field work in that period.

On the other hand, it was around Towaoc that one could best study the old Ute ways, including gerontocratic family organization, band chieftainship, gambling games, and the more typically Ute form of Peyote Cult. A Weminutc band group, then having a population of only 450, had only half a dozen Utes who could speak English and even fewer who had the benefits of secondary school education. The "community farm," located on Mancos Creek, was then run by Navaho farmers. A brick hospital was unused because menstruating women and women in childbirth had been known to be confined there.

Looking more closely at Ignacio, where 72,508 acres originally allotted in 1895 had dwindled to 33,202, one found that almost all mature Utes had come to possess farms and homes through inheritance. Rationing had existed here, too, but by 1931 it was stopped. Tribal council meetings became prominent in the period of John Collier's administration of the Bureau of Indian Affairs. (Under Collier, too, reservation lands were closed to further attrition.) The meetings were resplendent with Ute oratory and attended more frequently by younger men who groped for Ute words, but who often won by sheer weight of numbers. In fact, Ignacio soon had its conservative older element and also its younger progressive one. Ute and Southern Paiute children learned English in the Consolidated Ute School on the reservation. In spring and throughout the warmer seasons the flageolet courtship serenades could be heard at either Ignacio or Towaoc.

Early in the reservation period, before the split and around 1888, dances were introduced by a Weminutc who had traveled westward to the Paiute. He had received songs, power, and messages prophesying the spiritual return of the dead. This was the Ute Ghost Dance, in which the living were enjoined to prepare themselves by returning to the old ways. When this prophet died, Jack Wilson, a Paiute leader of the new cult, sent his personal messenger to teach the Ghost Dance religion to the Utes. The Paiute's prophecy stated that the Ute ancestors would return from the West in real bodily form and that there would be a great cyclone in which the whites would perish. Interestingly enough, the prophet set the time within the next year so that the Ute waited expectantly, though many doubted the possibility. Although the prophecy was brought in from the outside, the Ute utilized an older dance in which musicians stamped their feet and the men and women danced clockwise, crossing the right foot in front and dragging the left behind. The dance leader would call out after a dancer fell in the center of the circle in a trance. The words were a prayer for messages to come from the ancestors through the person in the trance. Actually, the Ute feared the appearance of the dead, because they feared ghosts; consequently, they were relieved when the dire events failed to transpire.

Both the Sun Dance and the Peyote Cult have had greater vitality, lasting down to the present in both Southern Ute reservations. These rituals in both their eastern and western group settings have been discussed earlier; consequently, there is no need to expand upon their strength as vehicles of cultural revitalization. Suffice it to say that the Ute also pooled individual shamanistic powers in a similar way up to the 1940s in their own indigenous Round Dance ceremony, which they continued as a method of combating illness and in which the eagle tail feather wand was used as in the Sun Dance to ward off "white man's plagues" in addition. The chief point in all these revivalistic rites was that the "Indian answer" pertained to attempts of Christian missions to convert them. Missions had both a Roman Catholic and a Protestant form at Towaoc. But there the Ute Mountain people even preferred Navaho curing practices to the intrusive Christian forms of doctrine. On the other hand, at Ignacio some Utes became regular churchgoers at the Mexican Catholic Church.

Gradually, these later attempts to revitalize Ute Indian culture shifted to a general awareness of being Indians with the same necessities of promoting Indian rights as existed in other tribes. The Navaho neighbors of the Towaoc, or Ute Mountain, people became highly sophisticated in reservation politics. It was a Navaho who first ran the community farm at Towaoc. Similarly, at Ignacio, where a somewhat unified conception of chieftainship emerged, at first in the person of Buckskin Charlie, the Tribal Council established during the Collier administration and reorganization gradually tended to take over in matters of leadership and decision making. At first, younger leaders struggled against the older Ute conceptions of age being linked to authority. Nevertheless, it must be remembered that all matters of leadership and decision making had always been regulated by such general social sanctions as group consensus, public discussion of an informal sort, and the social control mechanisms of gossip and ostracism. During the 1950s the three Southern Ute bands, led by people at Ignacio, began to launch legal cases for restitution in the form of payment for earlier land losses. A private legal firm in Washington was hired, and a Southern Ute tribal payment of $10 million was obtained.

If one constructed a scale of organization referring to larger tribal units of social decision making, such as tribal councils, and applied this to the two Southern Ute reservations as well as to the Allen Canyon Paiute to the west in Utah, one would discover that Ignacio, largely because of allotment in severalty, first began to accept modernization; they were followed by Towaoc in the 1950s decade and by the Allen Canyon Paiutes thereafter. Movements from multiple family camps to single family dwellings, notions of a legal or strictly territorial group right to land, and the gradual impact of a new bilingualism and education mark these inevitable trends. On the other hand, most Southern Utes take intense satisfaction in the idea that their Indian religion, their Peyote Cult, Sun Dance, and shamanistic cures are inviolable retreats where their white neighbors cannot interfere. At Towaoc peyote at first provided a stronger rallying point for Indian belief than individualistic shamanism did. There in the 1940s every tent was provided with a peyote gourd rattle and the appropriate canes and drumsticks. Sun Dance and Bear Dance were prominent on both sides of the reservation. As if to mark a gradation, this was the time when individual shamanism best flourished among the Allen Canyon people. In the 1940s decade, the Allen Canyon Paiute were still located in isolated camps throughout the remote country to which they had fled following the Paiute Massacre at the hands of whites in Utah not too much earlier than that date in the twentieth century.

We can state that the Southern Ute and Southern Paiute had few choices open, other than a defiant cultural revivalism or a gradual accommodation to "white ways." The Southern Ute located on the Consolidated Ute Reservation of Colorado took the latter path without fully relinquishing their culture, first at Ignacio and next at Towaoc. Two World Wars brought many veteran's status without political autonomy or control. After World War II the finding of uranium deposits in their former terrain swept them again into public notice and stimulated federal cases for restitution—again in cash—for long since lost land. As a tribe of the southwestern frontier, they are as culturally retentive basically as any Pueblo or Great Basin people. They were among the earliest in contact with surrounding white cultures, Mexican and American, but they have been less vitally involved in the American political and social scene than their neighbors on the Plains or their linguistic relatives in Mexico. Lacking a viable economic base, their culture changed as territory shrank and old resources disappeared. Yet culture was their chief weapon, and even today it is their major source of pride.

NOTE

[1] The field work on the Southern Ute and Allen Canyon Paiute was conducted for a two-year period in 1936 and 1937 and was continued in 1938. There have been subsequent trips of shorter duration to Ute and Paiute territory. The author also, without recompense, aided in the Southern Ute claims case mentioned in the chapter.

This chapter is a completely condensed and rewritten account of the field work materials that were first published by the author in "The Southern Ute of Colorado" in *Acculturation in Seven American Indian Tribes,* Ralph Linton (ed.) (New York: Appleton-Century-Crofts, 1940). New materials have been added in the revision, so it is not a reprint. The total theoretical emphasis on cultural evolution is also new, as are several of the points now made. However, reprinting permission was granted by Appleton-Century-Crofts, Division of Meredith Corporation, when the present work, totally rewritten, was undertaken. The reader is encouraged to read the earlier account, pages 119–203, of that book.

REFERENCES

DODGE, RICHARD I.
1877 The Plains of the great west. New York: Putnam.
1882 Our wild Indians. Hartford: A. B. Worthington.

EGGAN, FRED
1966 The American Indian: perspectives for the study of social change. Chicago: Aldine Publishing Company.

FOWLER, JACOB
1898 Journal. Elliott Coues, ed. New York: F. P. Harper.

GREGG, JOSIAH
1850 Commerce of the prairies, 4th ed. Philadelphia: J. W. Moore.

HAINES, FRANCIS
1938 Where did the Plains Indians get their horses? American Anthropologist, New Series 40 (1).

HAURY, E. W.

1950 The stratigraphy and archaeology of Ventana Cave, Arizona. Albuquerque and Tucson: University of New Mexico Press and University of Arizona Press.

1954 The Southwest issue. American Anthropologist 56:529–731.

HUGHES, JOHN T.

1848 Doniphan's expedition. Cincinnati: J. A. and U. P. James.

JENNINGS, J. D.

1957 Danger cave. Salt Lake City: University of Utah Anthropological Papers, no. 27.

KIDDER, A. V.

1924 An introduction to the study of Southwestern archaeology. Andover, Mass.: Phillips Academy.

LESSER, ALEXANDER

1933 Cultural significance of the ghost dance. American Anthropologist, New Series 35 (1).

MACNEISH, R. S.

1964 Ancient Mesoamerican civilization. Science 143 (3606):531–537.

OPLER, MARVIN K.

1939a Southern Ute pottery types. The Masterkey XIII (5):161–163.

1939b The Southern Ute dog-dance and its reported transmission to Taos. New Mexico Anthropologist III (5):66–72.

1939c The Ute Indian war of 1879. El Palacio XLVI (11):255–262.

1940a The Southern Ute of Colorado. *In* Acculturation in seven American Indian tribes. R. Linton, ed. New York: Appleton-Century.

1940b The character and history of the Southern Ute peyote rite. American Anthropologist 42 (3):463–478.

1941a The integration of the sun dance in Ute religion. American Anthropologist 43 (4):550–572.

1941b A Colorado Ute Indian bear dance. Southwestern Lore (September): 21–30.

OPLER, MARVIN K., with W. Z. PARK *et al.*

1938 Tribal distribution in the Great Basin. American Anthropologist 40 (4):622–638.

PARSONS, ELSIE C.

1936 Taos Pueblo. *In* General series in anthropology, no. 2. Menasha, Wisc.: George Banta Publishing Company.

PIKE, ZEBULON M.

1895 Expedition of, to the headwaters of the Mississippi River, etc., 1805–07, vol. 1–2. Elliott Coues, ed. New York: F. P. Harper.

REPORTS OF THE COMMISSIONER OF INDIAN AFFAIRS

1854, 1857, 1861–1863, 1868 Reports to the secretary of the interior. Washington, D.C.: Government Printing Office.

RICHARDSON, RUPERT N.

1933 The Comanche barrier to south Plains settlement. Glendale, Calif.: The Arthur H. Clark Company.

RUXTON, GEORGE F.

1847 Adventures in New Mexico and the Rocky Mountains. London: John Murray.

STEWARD, J.

1938 Basin-Plateau aboriginal sociopolitical groups. Bureau of American Ethnology Bulletin 120.

THOMAS, ALFRED B.

1932a Antonio de Bonilla's Spanish plans for defense of New Mexico, New Spain and the Anglo-American west. *In* H. E. Bolton, ed. New Spain, vol. I, pp. 183–209. Private Printing, Los Angeles.

1932b Forgotten frontiers. Norman, Okla.: University of Oklahoma Press.

1935 After Coronado. Norman, Okla.: University of Oklahoma Press.

TWITCHELL, RALPH E.

1911–1917 Leading facts of New Mexico history, Volume I. Cedar Rapids, Iowa: The Torch Press.

1914 Spanish archives of New Mexico, Volume 2. Cedar Rapids, Iowa: The Torch Press.

UNITED STATES STATUTES

1873–1875 "Statutes at Large," Vol. 18, pt. 3. Washington, D.C.: Government Printing Office.

10   *California* JAMES F. DOWNS

    The American Indian populations of California have been in various degrees of contact with Euro-American culture since the early sixteenth century. Some aboriginal groups remained virtually unaware of non-Indian peoples until the 1850s. Others experienced such complete and intense contact after the third quarter of the eighteenth century that their aboriginal culture has totally disappeared, leaving little or no record. Their very existence verges on the conjectural.

    Any attempt to draw a picture of a California "culture area" would either fall well within the political bounds of the state or extend well beyond them. As a result of the work of A. L. Kroeber and his students and colleagues at the University of California at Berkeley, we have been presented with some of the richest sources of ethnographic detail ever assembled. In addition, their work has frequently attempted a synthesis of these details. Both the detail and the synthesis are maddeningly frustrating for anyone attempting to present California Indian life in a relatively brief paper. One is confronted with a general sameness of culture influenced by the obvious forces of environment while at the same time being presented with rich and infinitely varying detail of custom and practice from tribelet to tribelet, almost from village to village.

    Within the boundaries of the state, representatives of every major language stock spoken in North America (save Eskimo-Aleut) are to be found. These often fragment into dozens, perhaps hundreds, of dialects and even separate languages. There is, however, only the most general correspondence between culture type or environment and language. Perhaps no other area in the world illustrates so clearly that language and culture are two distinct, and not necessarily related, phenomena.

    A general understanding of California geography and environment is essential. The state forms an arc some 1,500 miles long from latitude 33°30′N. to latitude 42°N. In width it is from 200 to 400 miles from the Pacific Ocean to the eastern boundary, which roughly parallels the crest of the Sierra in the north and extends southeast to the Colorado River south of Lake Tahoe.

    The gross geography of the region is dominated by a huge interior valley stretching from the Tehachapi Mountains, scarcely 100 miles above the Mexican border in the south, to Mount Shasta and the sur-

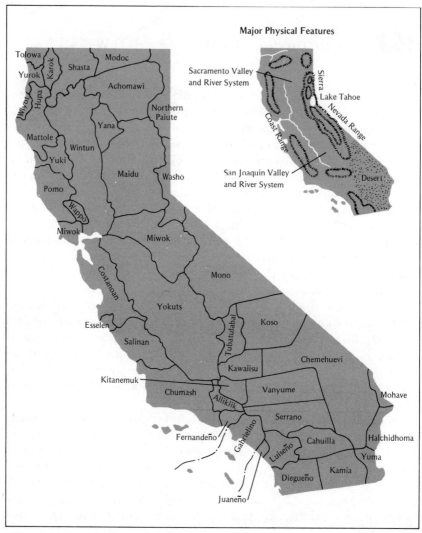

Figure 10.1. Major tribes and stocks of California.

rounding high country to the north. To the west it is separated from
the coast by a series of relatively low, but extremely rugged, mountain
ranges. In the south these are exceedingly arid with few water courses
into the sea and none flowing east into the valley. From the Sierra
flow into this valley the two great river systems of the state, after which
the two sections of the basin are named. The Sacramento and its tribu-

taries run from Shasta to the San Francisco Bay area. The San Joaquin, directly draining the Kern and Stanislaus and indirectly the Kings River, flows north where both rivers join and flow into San Pablo Bay, the northern extension of San Francisco Bay proper. Through the less than two-mile opening of the Golden Gate drains the entire interior watershed of California. And through the same opening come the ocean-going salmon seeking spawning grounds often hundreds of miles from the sea. Both these valleys were intersected with hundreds of small creeks and sloughs and spotted with perennial swamps. Except for low-lying islands surrounded by marshes and wet prairies, much of the low country was uninhabitable most of the year. And during the hottest part of the year the islands were often malarial.

East of these valleys the Sierra mounts in a series of rolling foothills, gradually giving way to pine and fir forests, mountain lakes, and meadows, and eventually to the alpine and arctic environments above timberline, often rising to 13,000 or more feet above sea level. To the east the Sierra drops away in a dramatic escarpment that forms a gigantic wall, pierced only by high passes. In the north the steppe country east of the Sierra is broken by low rugged ranges of mountains and covered with xerophytic plants, such as pig weed, various grasses, and sage. In the south the altitude lowers and the environment changes to true desert, dotted with smaller, utterly dry, mountain ranges. This region is sparsely supplied with flora and fauna. It is scarcely watered, the dryness only occasionally relieved by short seasonal waterways, springs, and oases, usually tucked into canyons on the eastern slope of the mountains.

To the west the Coast Range rises between the Central Valley and the sea. In the south the Coast Range virtually isolated peoples of the coast from the San Joaquin valley. To the north, above Monterey, the Coast Range hugs the coast closely but is much less arid, catching the ocean-born rains and fog that nourish the dense cover of cedar, fir, pine, and redwood for which the region is noted. The mountains are pierced by several short rivers and many streams flowing year-round into the sea and forming lagoons. In the extreme north the coastal plain broadens somewhat with the Klamath and Trinity river system, which rises in southern Oregon and flows north of the Central Valley and debouches into the Pacific. The most serious barrier to human communication in much of this region are the nearly impenetrable redwood forests, which produce few vegetable or animal foods and do not encourage travel.

The extreme south of the state presents a rather different picture. From the Tehachapis, which in a sense link the Sierra and the Coast Range, the state is divided into two parts by a single confused range. These mountains are often exceedingly arid, supporting pine forests and boasting streams only in the highest regions. The streams that tend to flow west into the ocean are usually seasonal. A narrow coastal plain, varying in width, from less than a mile in places to the vast basin of Los Angeles, extends from San Diego to above Santa Barbara. Above Santa Barbara the Coast Range is broken by a number of intermediate valleys as well as a narrow coastal plain. The valleys tend to open into the sea in a northern direction but to be blocked from the central basin of the San Joaquin, save where they and the great valley approach the San Francisco Bay. East of the southern range is the great desert zone of the Colorado Basin, broken only by the course of the river itself.

Over most of the state the weather is mild. Even the rainy and foggy north coast seldom experiences freezing weather or snow. Snow is a novelty except in the higher mountain ranges. Rains most generally fall in the winter, except in the extreme northwest. Only the northeastern corner of the state and the Great Basin immediately east of the Sierra served as a year-round habitat for men who had to cope with extremely cold winters.

All the people of California except the Yuman tribes of the Colorado were hunters and gatherers. Significant environmental differences appear to have been those of altitude. The general environmental conditions of the southwest, central, and northern interior area were very much the same, perhaps accounting for much of the uniformity of culture through these areas. The northwest, the northeast, the desert southwest, and the east side of the Sierra present us with either markedly different cultures or signficantly different cultural variations.

The coastal and riverine peoples of the northwest corner of the state are best seen as the southernmost extension of the classic Northwest Coast complex of Washington, British Columbia, and Canada, influenced by contact with California peoples and the specifics of their environment. In general when compared with the northerners their culture is simpler, although by California standards it is complex. The northeasterners reflect Basin and Plains influences as well as patterns from California and are on the whole simpler than any of the three sources from which they draw inspiration. The central area, although infinitely varied in detail, seems to reflect general patterns that extend from the Pacific Coast to the Great Basin. In this area the relatively more hospitable and provident environment of California, coupled with more extensive contacts with peoples of other cultural traditions, allowed the Great Basin pattern to reach its greatest degree of elaboration. South of the Tehachapis, from the coast to the Colorado River, the Shoshonean- and Yuman-speaking peoples display strong influences from the Southwest and from the Great Basin, developed on a fairly adequate gathering subsistence base but without the added complexities of an agricultural technology and the social structural adjustments that agriculture makes necessary.

Food Resources

Despite the fact that almost no agriculture was practiced within the present boundaries of California, the aboriginal systems based on hunting and gathering supported the greatest density of population found anywhere in North America north of Mexico, not excluding the eastern and southwestern agricultural regions.

Throughout the state, except on the desert proper, parts of the immediate seacoast and the higher elevations of the Sierra and the Coast Range grow numerous varieties of acorn-bearing oaks. For the most part these occur most densely in the savannah and rolling open foothills countries at the base of mountain ranges, but smaller coastal valleys and the coastal plains, such as those where Los Angeles is now located, also boast growths of oak. Acorns constitute the universal food source of most of the California tribes. The development of distinctly "Californian" cultures might be suggested, with some reservations, to coincide with the distribution of acorn-bearing oaks. Although the details of gathering, leaching, grinding, and storing differed throughout the state, a basic California food was acorn mush, stone boiled in a basket. Tribes located outside the area of the natural distribution of the acorn often made journeys into the area to collect them, and acorn flour was also an item of trade between interior and coastal tribes. This food source was virtually inexhaustible. Even if conditions occasionally prevented the collection of acorns in customary groves, there was seldom a problem of finding another productive grove within convenient distance. This natural crop above all others probably contributed to the fact that California peoples did not experience annual famine months or develop traditions or legends dealing with famine.

In addition to the oak there were virtually hundreds of other plant foods. In the north at Klamath Lake, the Modoc collected *wonkas,* the seed pod of the water lily. Mesquite beans were collected in the deserts, piñon nuts on the eastern slope of the Sierra, and seeds of the digger pine and manzanita throughout the state. A number of natural grasses also supplied seeds in abundance. The more northerly and higher environments produced root and bulb crops of value.

Rivers and the seashore were zones of great food production potential. Clams, mussels, and abalone were plentiful on the littoral, not to mention crabs, seaweed, and water creatures such as the sea lion. At least some surf fishing and some maritime fishing produced more food. The large migrating population of whales, which in aboriginal times came far inshore, regularly left stranded members on the beaches to be consumed by man. The river systems of the north coast as well as the double complex of systems in the interior valley were well supplied with salmon. In addition, fresh-water fish, suckers, trout, sturgeon, and catfish, were plentiful.

California is on the western flyway and serves as a winter nesting ground for many species of waterfowl and as a summer habitat for others. The great marsh areas were sources of duck, goose, swan, crane, coots, and loon, which nested there in the millions. Several varieties of dove and quail were to be found through the state, as well as numbers of other native upland game birds.

Mammalian food sources included the cottontail and jack rabbit, deer, elk, and antelope, and numerous rodents, such as chipmunks and ground and tree squirrels. Of large North American game, only the moose appears not to have had a foothold in California. In the extreme northeast the buffalo was probably found in small numbers, until perhaps as late as the sixteenth and seventeenth centuries. Caterpillars, grasshoppers, locusts, and the like were regularly eaten. Only reptiles, some amphibians, and the dog were regularly, and almost universally, rejected as food. The coyote was avoided in part for ritual or religious reasons, as was the grizzly bear and to a lesser extent the black bear.

In general these food resources occurred regularly and plentifully so that the problem of obtaining food for most of the peoples of California was not a pressing one. A rather constant application of effort was required, though, with peaks of effort at the times of acorn or seed harvest.

The availability of food and the relative productivity in the several food categories, within small areas, may be one of the main underlying causes of an almost universal California pattern of social atomism, with little organization beyond the village level and few structural links with other such units. Subsistence activities did not require that the aboriginal Californian expand his social horizons much beyond the zone in which he dwelt and found his food. In the areas where social expansion was necessary, the environmental situation was generally so unproductive that no social or political elaboration could be expected, despite an almost infinite extension of kinship ties of reciprocity and obligation.

The Northwest

The most distinct area of culture in California was in the Northwest, centered on the Klamath and Trinity river systems, which do not connect with the great river systems of interior California. Although the sea produced some food, the focus of these cultures was along the rivers. Only one notable settlement fronted directly on the sea, that of Trinidad Head, which faced the well-sheltered bay behind the Head. Various settlements claimed sections of shoreline but appear to have exercised the claim only in the event of a whale stranding.

Like most other Californians, these peoples usually went nude or almost so, save for festive occasions, when a great deal of decoration was worn. They lived in houses fashioned of redwood planks, which in general followed the pattern of the northern Northwest Coast cultures. They did not, however, develop the elaborate symbolic art of crests and totem poles or carved doorposts that added so much to the color of the northern peoples. In this complete lack of representative or symbolic art, they most closely approached the general pattern of California culture. Redwood and cedar were easily worked into serviceable canoes, primarily designed for river travel, although used in inshore waters, lagoons, and Humboldt Bay. Although the culture was so much the same that it must be considered virtually homogeneous, it was shared by representatives of three language families, Algonkian, Athapaskan and Hokan, spoken by the Yurok, Hupa, and Karok, respectively.

The most distinctive feature of these people, who produced in a material sense a much richer and more complex culture than any other California group, was the lack of complex social institutions. Defined roles of headman, chief, herald, councilman, or elder were absent, as was any real consciousness of community continuity even on the settlement or "village" level. Concurrent with this was an elaboration of the concept of personal wealth and the use of wealth to direct and guide social behavior in almost every conceivable situation.

Wealth was kept in the form of strings of dentalium shells, obtained by trade from the north. The accumulation of large numbers of dentalium was the primary goal of every person, and status was directly determined by the possession of these shells. The lifelong status of a child was determined by the bride price in shells paid for its mother. This not only determined the social position of her offspring but also determined the minimal acceptable price of her girl children and in all probability the minimum price offered for brides by her sons. Young men sought to marry girls of a high, rather than low, price because of the subsequent social benefits that would accrue to him and his children. Every act of commission or omission was rated with a customary price in shells, ranging from a number of strings for taking a life to a few shells for mentioning the name of a dead man in the presence of his family. The concept of negligence was carried to an almost fantastic extreme. A person unable to pay the claimed damages became the "slave" of the claimant. In feuds and inter-village fighting, the individual deaths and injuries were totaled, and dentalium and other valuables changed hands without reference to who won or lost the fight. This meant that the "victor" always paid more damages to the "loser" than he received. This

Yuma mother and baby.
(Photograph courtesy of Museum of the American Indian, Heye Foundation.)

must have inevitably worked to restrain warlike and bellicose impulses within the society. After payment of blood money, the matter was considered absolutely closed, and any expression of resentment after receiving payment was itself considered an offense and therefore subject to damage payments.

Ceremonies among the northwestern peoples were tied to certain specific spots and had little communal content. Dances were viewed as opportunities to display valuable objects and reinforce public acceptance of one's importance due to this wealth. Favorite objects were large, carefully wrought, obsidian blades, objects decorated with woodpecker scalps, shell beads, and deerskins—particularly white deerskins, which were priceless.

As one moves away from the confluence of the Klamath and the Trinity, various other groups display a decreasingly intense northwest culture making gradual adjustments to upriver environment and greater contacts with tribes of the interior. Far to the northeast, on the rugged plateau where California joins Oregon, the Achomowi and the now extinct Atsugewi represent an adaption to an interior hunting and gathering way of life. Although the horse was not adopted by these peoples until the 1860s, they display some traits of clearly Plains origin, particularly the wearing of a variation of tailored buckskin clothing and decorations of porcupine quills. Minor ritual and material traits originating on the northern coast and in California proper were also present, but in essence these people were best classified as within the Great Basin–Plateau culture area. On the borders of California and southern Oregon, the Modoc shared something of California but partook greatly of patterns and styles developed farther north by the Klamath and other tribes of southern Oregon.

North Central Tribes

South of these groups, inhabiting the Sacramento valley and the adjacent mountains, are a number of peoples displaying what might be called a more distinctly "Californian" way of life. These tribes are, from west to east, the Pomo, Wintun, Yana, and Maidu. Just north of San Francisco Bay we also encounter the northern fringes of the Miwok, which can be divided into Coast, Plains, Lake, and Mountain divisions.

The Pomo can serve as an illustration of the culture of this region, keeping in mind that variations in environment influence the details of culture even between villages of the same tribes. The Pomo occupied the region from the eastern foothills of the Coast Range to the Coast, with a center on a large fresh-water lake, Clear Lake. Their habitat extended into the Sacramento valley, but the bulk of that basin was occupied on the west by the Wintun and on the east by the Maidu. To the north between these two groups were the Yana, divided into northern, southern, and Yahi divisions. Another group in this area to the south were the Wappo.

These gross divisions of tribal occupation do not reflect the reality of the situation. Settlements, both permanent and temporary, were oriented to food sources, particularly watercourses. The ranges between watercourses were traversed in search of game and in food collecting and in traveling from summer to winter settlements, but relatively little concern was evidenced for any truly national region.

Among these North Central peoples, the village appears to have been the primary unit of society. Within these relatively small settlements— made up of semi-subterranean houses of bark, tule, or earth and often containing a large semi-subterranean dance or sweat house—there were headmen with little more than admonitory authority. The individual's consciousness centered on his family, usually patrilineally defined, but with rather strong matrilineal elements among the Pomo, and his village. Other villages, speaking the same dialect and sharing the same general culture, were not considered any closer than were villages of peoples speaking other languages. Traditional reports suggest that fighting between Pomo-speaking villages, over slights or in competition for resources, were as common as fights against foreigners. In general all strangers were met with suspicion and might well be killed out of hand if it did not seem that such an act might lead to retaliatory raids. Villages appear to have been permanent, with long histories of continuous occupation. In the various seasons the entire village might travel into the valley to hunt, fish, or collect plant foods or to the seashore to gather shellfish and seaweed. These trips were, however, always viewed as temporary.

Among the Pomo we see the highest development of basket weaving, a craft that appears to have reached its epitome in California. All California groups made baskets, but none were so expert in fashioning them or used so many and various techniques. Receptacles with as many as sixty stitches per inch are reported, as well as baskets lavishly decorated with bird feathers and beads. Neighboring groups are also reported to have made baskets, but none equaled the Pomo in skill.

Among these tribes we see the dentalium money of the north give way to the clam-shell beads common to the rest of the state. Money was used here in much the same way as we see among the northerners. The difference was in emphasis. Many slights and offenses considered worthy of payment by the Hupa or Yurok were ignored by the Pomo and their neighbors or were resolved in other ways. In short, wealth was important but not overwhelmingly so.

From the Pomo almost to the crest of the Sierra, covering all of the Sacramento valley, extending down the coast from San Francisco west of the Coast Range and the upper portions of the San Joaquin, we find the Kuksu Cult. It was a distinctive religious system built around secret societies that occurred in each village in generally similar form. The religion found public expression in communal ceremonies featuring elaborately costumed and partially disguised, but not masked, dancers. Curing centered on the shaman, as it did throughout California. Shamanism in California was often exceedingly elaborate in practice. Both men and women might become shamans, although the role was sex-exclusive in some groups. Contests of shamanistic power were also common.

The Pomo and others built serviceable canoe-shaped balsas made of tules (which must have been what Francis Drake saw when he visited the Coast Miwok at Drake's Bay in the mid-sixteenth century). They also built log rafts, used to paddle to offshore rocks to take shellfish or sea mammals.

In this area we find what is common to all of California, a contrast of degree of development between lowlanders and highlanders. In the valleys and foothills settlements were larger, social and political institutions more developed, religious systems more complex, arts and crafts more expert than those found among the peoples of the mountains. And correlated with relative complexity of culture and society was a decreasing emphasis on girl's puberty ceremonies in favor of more complex communal ceremonies, secret societies, and initiation rituals centered on the male.

Central Interior

The immediate San Francisco Bay area and the coast to the south were peopled in aboriginal times, but subsequent events so thoroughly dispersed the Indians that we have little firm knowledge of their specific ways of life. In the San Joaquin valley itself, although depopulation occurred on a large scale in very recent times, we have adequate descriptions of the Yokuts and Miwok who occupied all of Central California from the Coast Range to the crest of the Sierra.

The contrast between the Yokuts and Miwok is the same one to be found everywhere in California: The generally less complex culture is found at higher elevation and the richer and more elaborate in the lowlands.

Among the Yokuts we find social systems that can be described as tribal, albeit almost microscopic in nature. Throughout the area several villages occupying a single limited region offered allegiance and subordination to a chief, who was usually the headman of one of the villages. These tiny tribelets differed from each other very little, and all displayed a further elaboration, a division into moieties. The moiety systems, with some minor differences from place to place, extended from the northern reaches of the Yokuts country throughout Southern California, save among the Luiseño and Diegueño. Most generally the moieties were divided into "land" and "water" groups, with many animals and plants having association with one or the other of the divisions. To a degree, then, these were also totemic. The moieties were generally exogamous. A suitor might choose a wife from another tribe and from the opposite moiety from his own just as if his bride were from his own tribe. Inter-moiety obligations included funeral and mourning services and apparently some ritualized rivalry.

The Miwok appear to have also had some forms of lineages in addition to the moiety system. As everywhere else in California the Yokuts and Miwok reckoned descent patrilineally.

The most notable difference in material culture is the appearance of pottery among the latest phases of the Yokuts' culture in the extreme south. This ware is exceedingly crude with no standardization of style or techniques and, as Kroeber has said, looks very much like the work of experimenters.

Among both Yokuts and Miwok clothing was scanty even by California standards. Children wore nothing until puberty, at which time women donned a small fore-and-aft apron. Men on the other hand went nude or occasionally donned a deerskin kilt.

The Yokuts practiced large-scale mourning ceremonies common in Southern California. And at least some of the Yokuts' groups participated in the ingestion of jimson weed during male initiation rites.

OTHER TRIBES

This general outline of the culture of Central California excludes the Washo of the Lake Tahoe region, who are properly described in the context of the Great Basin, along with the Paiute and Shoshoneans east of the Sierra and the coastal tribes between San Francisco and Santa Barbara. Of these latter we can say little. Almost totally absorbed or dispersed, they have left little direct ethnographic evidence and only a handful of survivors. There is nothing to suggest any major departures from the general patterns of California culture among these peoples, however.

Southern: Coast Foothills and Desert

To the east and south of the Yokuts area the extensive area of Sho-shonean speech that originates in the Great Basin begins. Shoshonean dominates almost all of Southern California save the southern border area and the Colorado River region and extends to the west as far as San Nicholas Island, the most westerly representative of Uto-Aztecan.

The groups in the Sierra east of the San Joaquin valley displayed a generalized California hill and mountain culture changing into a more and more Basin-oriented system on the eastern slopes of the Sierra. Of these the Mono were the most numerous, a position they retain today among California's aboriginal populations.

In Southern California proper, distinctions in life-style can be made in terms of habitat and whether the desert, the coastal plain, or the intervening mountain system was the main focus of the various peoples. Rather complete ethnographies have been obtained from some of the groups that existed beyond the zones of influence of the coastal missions; of these, the Cahuilla are probably best known. For the other Southern California groups we are, and have long been, isolated from the truly aboriginal conditions. In general, Indian groups are defined in terms of orientations around various missions. While this convenience does repre-sent the real situation after 1769, it does not represent the sociopolitical situation prior to that time.

Some of the aboriginal groups were so thoroughly absorbed by mission life and exposure to other Indians that aboriginal culture re-mains no more than a memory, a series of inferences drawn from histori-cal documents and few surviving material artifacts. The most notable Southern Californian group are the Chumash of Santa Barbara and the offshore islands. This was a truly maritime culture, utilizing sewn plank canoes to travel between the mainland and the channel islands for fish-ing, trading, and in pursuit of seal, sea lion, and sea otter. Almost com-pletely obliterated by history, the Chumash and their distinctive canoe, made in the manner of many Polynesian canoes, have left little more than an intriguing footnote for those interested in possible trans-Pacific contacts.

The Southern California environment is generally arid, but exceed-ingly mild, with a more than adequate supply of the California staples, acorns and seeds. It is fairly well supplied with game in the form of deer, rabbits, and various rodents, as well as bighorn sheep of the mountain and desert varieties. The river systems, being primarily short and seasonal, did not provide fish. They did, however, provide willows and other plant life useful in material culture and with seasonal value as food.

The patterns of moieties first found in the San Joaquin extends throughout Southern California. In all likelihood aboriginal political life was based on small tribelets of the Yokuts type, each occupying a fairly well-defined territory, but sharing language and culture. In the post-mission period the Indians in this area can be divided into five major groups, which refer to the missions that influenced them: the Fernandonos, the Gabriliennos, the Juanaos, the Liuseños, and the Diegueños, centered in San Fernando, San Gabriel, San Juan Capistrano, San Luis Reyes, and San Diego.

Two distinctly Southern California complexes should be noted in comparison with the more northerly groups. The Southern Californians were, of course, basket makers, but they also used two other materials for containers. From the northern island and coastal regions we obtain beautiful bowls made of carved soapstone, much of it quarried on the offshore islands. Elsewhere in Southern California pottery was made. Unlike the crude pots found to the north, these were well-formed and expertly made containers. Although they must stem from some connection with the Southwest, the connection is by no means clear. Another Southwestern element prominent in Southern California is the use of sand painting, albeit comparatively crude and nonrepresentational. Nonrepresentational art is characteristic of California as a whole.

Religious and ritual activities also set the southerner apart from the northerner. Here was the center of the use of jimson weed, or *totlache,* an emetic and hallucinogen, in initiation and other religious rites. This practice extended over the Tehachapi, but its most elaborate form and center of origin was in the south.

In clothing, house styles, and so forth, Southern California conforms to the general California patterns. The elaborateness of annual, or at least periodic, mourning ceremonies that included the destruction of much pottery is distinctively Southern California. It also suggests that the material life of these people, often thought of as relatively poor and crude, was actually quite rich and could support large-scale property destruction. There is no suggestion of the formation of classes, although it does appear that the authority of the chief was somewhat higher than in the north. Some degree of deference was shown to him and his close relatives.

In the extreme south the Diegueño were a Yuman-speaking extension to the sea, but in all essentials save one they were basically similar to other southerners. Here we do not find totemism or moieties, but rather localized patrilineal clans.

In general, then, California was a provident environment in which indigenous peoples with relatively simple technologies were able to develop rather elaborate religious and ritual systems based on relatively simple social and technical systems. Some of the native California communities may have, indeed, been the largest ever supported by non-agricultural technologies, with perhaps as many as 2,000 persons in semi-permanent residence.

Contact Developments

The significant contact developments in California history are outlined in the accompanying table. When Juan Rodríguez Cabrillo and Francis Drake came into contact with California people in the sixteenth century, they were favorably impressed. Extended contact, however, did not begin until the end of the third quarter of the eighteenth century, when the Franciscans began to establish missions. The first was built in San Diego, followed rather quickly by missions at San Luis Reyes, Capistrano, San Gabriel, San Fernando, San Buena Ventura, and Santa Barbara. The chain eventually extended to the north of San Francisco and included twenty-one main missions plus their outstations.

The Spanish generally settled on the coastal plain and the intermediate valleys of the Coast Range and seldom penetrated the interior. Much of the subsequent history of California Indians is influenced by this pattern of colonization.

Significant Periods and Events in California History

1539–1769   Exploration period: voyages of Cabrillo, Ullos, Drake; expedition of Portola; discovery of San Francisco Bay

1769–1832   Spanish colonial period: establishment of all missions and outstations (1769–1821) and of all major Spanish settlements and cities, including San Diego, Los Angeles, Santa Barbara, Monterey, San Francisco

1812   Establishment of Fort Ross by Russians

1832–1846   Mexican period: revolution; secularization of missions; dispersement of Indians

1841   Establishment of enterprise by Sutter at confluence of American and Sacramento rivers

1846   Founding of California Republic; annexation by United States

1848   Sale of Fort Ross to Sutter by Russians, who withdraw from California; discovery of gold on American River

1849–1851   Gold rush period: general contact made between Indians and prospectors

1851–1870s Statehood (1851); general persecution of Indians by prospectors and settlers; anti-Chinese hysteria sweeps northern California; treaty signed in Sacramento (1851), not ratified by Senate; Ghost Dance in northern and central California

1870s–1900s Period of disorganization and adjustment

1900–1952 Assumption of responsibility by federal government; establishment of reservations and *rancherias*

1953 "Termination Act"

1954 Withdrawal of federal responsibility

In this narrow strip the indigenous patterns of social organization and culture were drastically altered. California missions were designed to be self-supporting vehicles of conversion. Indians were induced and coerced into resettlement near the mission, acceptance of clothing, a nominal conversion to the faith, at least a partial suppression of native religious activities, and partial bilingualism. They were taught various arts and crafts of civilization, including riding and stock work, carpentry, masonry, and agriculture. In addition to the missions, secular land grants were also made by the Spanish king, and they formed the basis of an extensive cattle industry specializing in the production of hides and tallow for export. Although basic domestic arts were cultivated, the area was dependent on the outside for much of its manufactured needs. The number of Spanish or Mexican colonists of the lower, or artisan, class was relatively small. In essence, the society was one of an upper civil-clerical and governmental strata resting on a foundation of servile Indians. The productivity of the land appears to have produced plenty for even the poorest, although the disparity between life-styles was great.

Living in close proximity in mission settlements, wearing clothing, lacking bathing facilities, and being exposed to new diseases brought about a high mortality rate among the mission Indians. To recruit neophytes, the missions went further and further afield. This drew the more interior tribes into the colonial area; on the other hand, it sent some tribes further into the interior to escape the attentions of the missions. Throughout Southern and Central California there was a general displacement of tribes and individuals to the east toward the interior valleys and the foothills of the Sierra. One of the results of this was an increased rate of diffusion of religious and material traits between tribes and a readjustment of social systems to fit the new environmental settings. As seems inevitable in this situation, the zone of biological influence of the newcomers extended far beyond the political or cultural influences. Disease spread widely over the San Joaquin valley and brought about a drastic reduction in populations that had had no direct contact with the Spanish. This last may have contributed to a flight to the eastern slope of the Sierra in an attempt to escape the rampant epidemics of the valleys.

We know virtually nothing, save by inference and tantalizingly incomplete remarks in contemporary documents, about the post-colonization societies of these "wild," but no longer aboriginal, Indian groups. Many of them quickly adopted the horse, both for riding and eating. Wild horses and cattle flourished beyond the rim of colonial influence. There are suggestions that the eastern slope of the Sierra from 1769 through 1849 was seeing the development of what Steward (1955) has called mounted composite raiding bands. In the upper San Joaquin a number of groups appear to have developed into horse-raiding and -eating societies, living in large part by raiding Spanish livestock and fleeing into the interior beyond the reach of colonial vengeance, which was generally weak and ineffective. Although details are lacking, there is every reason to believe that for a few decades at least totally horse-oriented pastoral societies, subsisting largely on the meat of horse herds that were constantly replaced by raiding, existed in the swampy plains of the central basin. Robert Heizer (personal communication) has conjectured that had the development not been interrupted, the reorganized tribes of the western slope and the interior valleys might have driven the increasingly ineffective and weakened Spanish-Mexican colonists from California.

The stage for such a revolution was certainly set after the Mexican revolution in 1832. The missions were secularized by the Republic and in theory turned over to the resident Indians. Actually they were expropriated by large landholders, the Indians either remaining as peons or removing themselves to their traditional lands or to new lands in the interior. These removals did not constitute a reversion to indigenous culture, however, and the new communities developed an entirely new culture, which was a combination of Indian and European traits and languages.

The problems of contact that beset the Indians of the south and central portions of the state did not affect the northeastern portions. Spanish-Mexican influence was limited to the narrow coastal strip and for the most part went no further than San Francisco. However, the establishment of a Russian outpost on the coast north of San Francisco at Fort Ross in 1812 encouraged the Spanish to attempt to counterbalance this presence by setting up missions as far north as Sonoma. In addition, the California authorities themselves, without real resources or energies to meet what they saw as a threat, permitted the Swiss adventurer John Sutter to establish a colony, New Helvetia, at the confluence of the Sacramento and American rivers. This enterprise was complete with what was the best fortification in California and was largely self-

Scar-faced Charlie, Modoc tribe.
(Photograph courtesy of Museum of the American Indian, Heye Foundation.)

supporting, with successful farming and manufacturing enterprises run by Euro-American employees. Local Indian tribes often provided the labor for this ambitious scheme. It was at a lumber mill being constructed on the American River that one of Sutter's employees, John Marshall, discovered gold and set off the rush that overwhelmed Sutter and totally changed the direction of California history.

Fort Ross had been established as a logistical support for the Russian operations in Alaska and as a center for the collection of sea otter skins.

Its first goal was never achieved. The damp, windswept shelf overlooking the sea where the colony was located produced few crops and never succeeded in becoming the bread basket of Alaska. For a number of years Fort Ross was the center of an aggressive program of sea otter taking, which affected, often quite adversely, the condition of the tribes of the offshore islands. However, the colony was not profitable, and the entire operation was eventually sold to Sutter, leaving little imprint on the native life of California, save perhaps the introduction of some Russian and Aleut genetic materials and loan words to the Pomo populations (Oswalt, 1958).

In 1846, as a consequence of the Mexican war and the Treaty of Guadalupe Hidalgo, California became part of the United States. The discovery of gold soon brought hundreds of thousands of adventurers, particularly into the San Francisco region and the western foothills of the Sierra. Although little gold was found in the Coast Range, miners and prospectors probed through most of this region as well. For many of the tribes in the area this was the first contact, perhaps even the first knowledge of non-Indian peoples.

The history of White-Indian contacts during the Gold Rush period is tragic. The miners were oblivious to the rights of either previous settlers or Indians. Sutter's land, for instance, was simply overrun, crops burned or stolen, livestock run off, and entire cities built without the slightest question of establishing any legal claim. Indian tribes fared even worse. All during the period 1850–1880 a series of Indian "wars" were recorded. For the most part these were simply sadistic massacres of inoffensive Indians guilty of little more than offending the rapacious miners or at the worst trying to defend themselves or their women against assault and rape. High pressure placer-mining hoses were frequently used to wash away entire Indian villages as a sport. There sprung up in the towns of the Sacramento valley a class of Indian hunters, who pursued virtually unarmed and inoffensive Indians as a sport. One such man decorated a tree in front of his house with Indian scalps. Not one of these "wars" was dignified as such by the War Department. In the Northwest the coastal tribes did resist the white man. Hostilities often broke out over claims for damage made against the whites by the Indians. Outraged and uncomprehending, the whites refused to pay and were, in keeping with native custom, killed. Revenge brought revenge, and eventually a military outpost was established at Humboldt Bay to attempt to keep the peace in the northern country. These desperate conditions led the Mill Creek band of the Yahi (Yana) to go into hiding, avoiding all contact with whites and living a furtive, modified aboriginal life until the last survivor, Ishi, surrendered in Oroville, California, in 1911 (T. Kroeber, 1961).

Attempts to regularize the chaotic conditions came to nought. A meeting of all the California tribes (which did not represent all the tribes, but did provide a forum for tribes of the northern and central region) established a price for the land that had been expropriated and other conditions to establish relations between Indians and Whites. It was signed by many Indian leaders but never ratified by the Senate. Subsequent attempts to regularize Indian life were equally haphazard and unsuccessful. All during the late 1800s reservations were set aside for various groups, but generally no consideration was given to the desires or needs of the Indians. Often the relocated population simply melted away, returning to their original homelands. Throughout much of northern California, "Indian towns" often developed on the outskirts of white communities. The inhabitants eked out an existence by scavenging, begging, agricultural labor, prostitution. These communities usually developed in areas less favorably located for farming. As the Gold Rush subsided, the lush valleys of the interior were quickly settled and put under the plow. The more numerous and prosperous valley tribes were the most quickly displaced or absorbed. Remnants of these groups drifted into the mountains or foothills or remained in obscurity in tiny *rancherias* on the outskirts of white towns. Perhaps because aboriginal patterns stressed small and flexible social groups, many Indians were able to make individual adjustments to the new situation. Learning skills needed by whites, adapting to immediate social and economic conditions, they frequently disappeared into the general population or mixed with other Indians, losing old tribal identities. In the early 1870s a nativistic movement, originated in Nevada (by the grandfather of Wovoka, who founded the Ghost Dance of 1890–1891), swept through the demoralized peoples of North and Central California. Many aboriginal practices, especially the Kuksu Cult, were greatly altered by this movement.

The Gold Rush period saw the introduction into California of two additional cultural traditions, about which relatively little is known. Men from Polynesia, "Kanakas" in the vernacular of the period, were often recruited as seamen. Like other sailors, they frequently deserted in San Francisco to seek their fortunes in the goldfields. Their impact on California Indians has been virtually ignored. My own subjective impressions are that intermarriage has left its stamp on the Pomo physical type and that certain Polynesian elements have been adopted into Pomo vocal music.

Even more obscure is the effect of the hundreds of thousands of Chinese males imported to work on railroads. There can be little doubt that the prostitution of Indian women led to the introduction of new genetic materials into Indian populations. The Chinese belief that wildcat meat enhanced virility provided a ready market for Indian hunters. My own research has revealed one borrowed Chinese term in Washo. Beyond that virtually no information is available.

The northern peoples, who had fought the whites, were more fortunate. Placed on reservations within their old homeland, they made fair adjustment to a greatly modified way of life in which lumbering, dairying, and farming became important without total loss of language and culture to date. All through the interior valley, groups of people survive who are identified as "Indians" or given tribal designations such as "Shasta" or "Mariposa," which have no ethnic meaning at all. Often without memory of the old culture save for perhaps a few traditions or a smattering of language, they continue to exist, sometimes successfully and sometimes in complete poverty.

In Southern California the Mission Indians melded with the population, often being identified as Mexicans by the increasingly dominating Anglo-American. Until the second quarter of the twentieth century most Southern California towns had one or more families identified and identifying themselves as "Indians."

After the publication of the great dramatic novel *Ramona* and the factual report "Century of Dishonor," which called attention to the plight of California Indians, efforts were made to stabilize their lives. There were few areas of any size available for setting aside as reservations. Instead, Indian claims as homesteaders or squatters on public lands were confirmed and smaller plots were purchased and held in trust. The Cahuilla of Southern California received a sizable grant, as did the Mohave tribes of the Colorado and the northwestern tribes. In general, "reservations" were at the most only a few thousand acres, often a few hundred, and not infrequently no more than ten or a dozen acres. In many cases this was initially satisfactory, inasmuch as it simply confirmed existing situations and required no removal of population.

Such a situation was exceedingly difficult to administer, however. Over one hundred separate parcels of land were designated as reservations but after called *rancherias*. The Bureau of Indian Affairs, organized primarily to administer the large reservations of the Plains and Southwest, was not prepared to handle the California situation. Indian lands for which the government now was responsible were difficult to improve and develop because of their size and wide dispersion. Bureau offices were established in Sacramento and Riverside, and a special Indian school was built at Riverside. However, the presence of the bureau was often more a curse than a blessing. State and local government tended to ignore Indian problems because they were officially under federal jurisdiction. On the other hand, the federal government was never completely able to devise a system whereby it could properly administer to Indian needs. Some pieces of Indian land proved to be exceedingly valuable. One such is the area around Palm Springs, which became a world-famous vacation resort almost entirely on land owned by Indians, who eventually profited greatly. Other areas, however, were too remote, too arid, and too small for any real development and were abandoned or, at best, served as the site of poverty communities. Others were traditional communities of long standing, related to missions, such as Pala and Pauma valley, where life was little affected by either the presence or the absence of the federal government. As compared to Indians on the Great Plains and in the Southwest, California Indians frequently had greater opportunity to associate with whites and to learn Anglo culture; they went to integrated schools and saw themselves more as another ethnic group within the complex American society than as a special aboriginal isolate. Such people often abandoned the reservation and *rancheria* and made their own way into the modern life. Others remained on the extreme outskirts of modern society, dependent on federal support in some way or, once off their tiny reservations, becoming public charges or working at the lowest paid unskilled employment.

With the establishment of the policy to terminate the federal responsibility for Indians, House Concurrent Resolution 108 in 1953 singled out the Indians of California, among other groups from which federal supervision should be withdrawn. For the most part it would seem that most California Indian groups were, in fact, capable of managing their own affairs, at least as well as they had been managed in the past. However, the real reason for termination may well have been that it provided a way out of a dilemma that the Bureau of Indian Affairs had failed to solve.

Termination was not popular with California Indians for two reasons. Some of the communities that had retained something of aboriginal culture and organization reacted to what they saw as a removal of federal services on which they had come to depend. The majority, however, objected, not to the loss of services, which were minimal at best, but to the fact that the government was leaving them with problems it should have solved. They argued that in the period when the government had been responsible, it should have made improvements and developments on Indian lands, as it had elsewhere, and they argued that as trustee the government should not be relieved of this responsibility until it had fulfilled its obligations.

For all Indians there remained the century-old question of compensation for expropriated lands. For many, those who had made an adequate adjustment to modern life and who retained only a slight identification as Indians, this was the only question.

Because of the chaotic past, the bureau and federal government were faced with an almost insoluble problem of distribution of monies that were awarded by the U.S. Indian Claims Commission (which is distinct from the Termination Resolution) to the Indians of California. Tribal rolls had to be established, some definition of "Indian" created, rules of eligibility made. For nearly a decade meetings were held throughout the state. The solutions reached were seldom satisfactory to either the government or the Indians, and Indian opinion was always widely divided.

Meanwhile, state and local authorities took over administration of Indian affairs, accepting Indians within their jurisdiction as citizens without special status. Because of poverty and lack of education, many of these people were eligible for welfare support and public health treatment. For the vast majority of California Indians the situation was incomparably better than it had been in the past. The federal government had generally been a distant and ineffective presence. The county social worker or health officer was a real person who responded to immediate problems. However, the old problems of government trusteeship and the settling of claims remained and have not yet been resolved fully. Indians now regularly attend California schools and are eligible for welfare payments, pensions for the aged and blind, unemployment insurance, and public health and other services. However, many Indian communities remain at the bottom of the socioeconomic ladder and cannot boast having received the benefits of the affluence of modern American life.

There are today, officially, 40,000 Indians indigenous to California among the state's population of nearly 18,000,000. This covers most of the inhabitants of reservations, *rancherias,* and traditional Indian communities. It is impossible to estimate how many Indians live in the cities and rural communities of California in complete adjustment to modern society. At least another 40,000 work in all fields of endeavor, not in any way discriminated against or inconvenienced by their Indian background. Some of these retain enough identification with the past to serve as articulate and effective spokesmen for their people. Others are scarcely aware of an Indian heritage. The possibility that this heritage might make them eligible for payments of land claims has brought forth thousands of people claiming Indian ancestry. The Gabrillenos, for instance, are culturally extinct. But some 1,500 people claiming to be Gabrilleno have filed for a share of land claims.

In reaction to the Termination act, the state of California established a commission on Indian affairs, composed of legislators, appointed officials in the welfare and education field, and prominent Indians. To date the commission has done little more than attempt to collect information on the needs of the Indian population. Disagreements among the Indians themselves have made it difficult to fill the Indian positions on the commission.

Yet another problem has developed that is unique to California. In

addition to indigenous Indians, there are an undetermined number of
Indians who have migrated to California, particularly to Los Angeles
and the San Francisco Bay area. Estimates range from 40,000 to over
100,000. These people argue that their voluntary removal from reservations does not relieve the federal government of responsibility for
financial and educational assistance. They also claim a special voice in
the State Indian Affairs structure. Once again, the contrast in condition
among these Indians is vast. Some are exceedingly successful in law, the
motion picture industry, and skilled trades. On the other hand, many
people coming from reservation backgrounds are totally unprepared for
urban life and have drifted into the lowest and most disorganized strata
of society. Because of the almost nationwide provenience of these visiting
Indians and the connections they maintain with home reservations,
events in California are increasingly important in the remote plains of
South Dakota and the mesa country of the Southwest.

It is impossible at this time to predict the future course of Indian life
in California. With few exceptions, however, it would seem that on one
level or another Indians will assimilate into general California life.

BIBLIOGRAPHY

ABLON, J.
1964 Relocated Indians in the San Francisco Bay area: social interaction and
Indian identity. Human Organization XXII (4):296–304.

ANTEVS, E.
1952 Climatic history and the antiquity of man in California. Reports of the
University of California Archaeological Survey 16:23–31.

BARRETT, S. A.
1910 The material culture of the Klamath Lake and Modoc Indians of northeastern California and southern Oregon. University of California Publications
in American Archaeology and Ethnology 5:230–292.
1963 In Washo Indians of California and Nevada. W. L. De Azevedo, ed. University of Utah Anthropological Papers, no. 67.

BARRETT, S. A., AND E. W. GIFFORD
1933 Miwok material culture. Bulletins of the Public Museum of the City of
Milwaukee 2:117–376.

BAUMHOFF, M. A.
1958 California Athabascan groups. Anthropological Records 16:157–237.

BEALS, R. L.
1933 Ethnology of the Nisenan. University of California Publications in
American Archaeology and Ethnology 31:335–410.

BEARDSLEY, R. K.
1948 Culture sequences in central California. American Antiquity 14:1–28.

CASTETTER, E. F., AND W. H. BELL
1942 Pima and Papago Indian agriculture. Albuquerque: Inter-American Studies, no. 1.

COOK, S. F.
1941 The mechanism and extent of dietary adaptation among certain groups of California and Nevada Indians. Ibero-Americana 18:1–59.
1960 Colonial expeditions to the interior of California: Central Valley 1800–1820. University of California Anthropological Records 16 (6).

DAVIS, J. T.
1961 Trade routes and economic exchange among the Indians of California. University of California Archaeological Survey, Reports, no. 54.

DE AZEVEDO, W. L., ED.
1963 Washo Indians of California and Nevada. University of Utah Anthropological Papers, no. 67.

DIXON, R. B.
1905 The Northern Maidu. Bulletin of the American Museum of Natural History 17:119–346.
1907 The Shasta. Bulletin of the American Museum of Natural History 17:381–498.
1911 Maidu. Bureau of American Ethnology Bulletin 40:679–734.

DIXON, R. B., AND A. L. KROEBER
1913 New linguistic families in California. American Anthropologist 15:647–655.
1919 Linguistic families of California. University of California Publications in American Archaeology and Ethnology 11:47–188.

DOWNS, J. F.
1961 Washo religion. University of California Anthropological Records 16 (9).
1963a Washo response to animal husbandry. In Washo Indians of California and Nevada. W. L. De Azevedo, ed. University of Utah Anthropological Papers, no. 67.
1963b Differential response to white contact: Paiute and Washo. In Washo Indians of California and Nevada. W. L. De Azevedo, ed. University of Utah Anthropological Papers, no. 67.
1965 Two worlds of the Washo: Case studies in cultural anthropology. New York: Holt, Rinehart and Winston.

DRIVER, H. E.
1936 Wappo ethnography. University of California Publications in American Archaeology and Ethnology 36:179–220.
1961 Indians of North America. Chicago: University of Chicago Press.

DRUCKER, P.
1936 The Tolowa and their southwest Oregon kin. University of California

Publications in American Archaeology and Ethnology 36:221–300.
1941 Culture element distributions: Yuma-Pima. Anthropological Records 6.

DU BOIS, C.

1935 Wintu ethnography. University of California Publications in American Archaeology and Ethnology 36:1–148.
1939 The 1870 ghost dance. University of California Anthropological Record 3 (1):1–151.

FREED, S. A., AND R. S. FREED

1963a The persistence of aboriginal ceremonies among the Washo Indians. *In* Washo Indians of California and Nevada. W. L. De Azevedo, ed. University of Utah Anthropological Papers, no. 67.

FREED, S. A.

1963b A reconstruction of aboriginal social organization. *In* Washo Indians of California and Nevada. W. L. De Azevedo, ed. University of Utah Anthropological Papers, no. 67.

GARTH, T. R.

1953 Atsugewi ethnography. Anthropological Records 14:123–212.

GAYTON, A. H.

1948a Northern Foothills Yokuts and Western Mono. Anthropological Records 10:143–302.
1948b. Tulare Lake, Southern Valley, and Central Foothills Yokuts. Anthropological Records 10:1–140.

GIFFORD, E. W.

1916 Miwok moieties. University of California Publications in American Archaeology and Ethnology 12:139–194.
1931 The Kamia of Imperial Valley. Bureau of American Ethnology Bulletin 97.
1932 The Northfork Mono. University of California Publications in American Archaeology and Ethnology 31:15–65.
1933 The Cocopa. University of California Publications in American Archaeology and Ethnology 31:257–334.
1936 Northeastern and Western Yavapai. University of California Publications in American Archaeology and Ethnology 34:247–354.
1939 The Coast Yuki. Anthropos 34:292–275.
1955 Central Miwok ceremonies. Anthropological Records 14:261–318.

GODDARD, P. E.

1903 Life and culture of the Hupa. University of California Publications in American Archaeology and Ethnology 1:1–88.

HOOPER, L.

1920 The Cahuilla Indians. University of California Publications in American Archaeology and Ethnology 16:316–380.

JOHNSTON, B. J.

1955–1956 The Gabrieleno Indians of southern California. Masterkey 29:180–191; 30:6–21, 44–56, 76–89, 125–132, 146–156.

KELLY, I. T.

1932 Ethnography of the Surprise Valley Paiute. University of California Publications in American Archaeology and Ethnology 31:67–210.

KROEBER, A. L.

1908 Ethnography of the Cahuilla Indians. University of California Publications in American Archaeology and Ethnology 8:29–68.

1925 Handbook of the Indians of California. Bureau of American Ethnology Bulletin 78.

1928 Native culture of the southwest. University of California Publications in American Archaeology and Ethnology 33:375–398.

1932 The Patwin and their neighbors. University of California Publications in American Archaeology and Ethnology 29:253–364.

1935 Walapai ethnography. American Anthropological Association memoir 42.

KROEBER, T.

1961 Ishi in two worlds. Berkeley: University of California Press.

LEIS, P. E.

1963 Washo witchcraft: a test of the frustration-aggressions hypothesis. *In* Washo Indians of California and Nevada. W. L. De Azevedo, ed. University of Utah Anthropological Papers, no. 67.

LOWIE, R. H.

1923 Culture connection of California and Plateau Shoshonean tribes. University of California Publications in Archaeology and Ethnology 20:145–156.

1939 Ethnographic notes on the Washo. University of California Publications in American Archaeology and Ethnology 36:301–352.

MASON, J. A.

1912 The ethnology of the Salinan Indians. University of California Publications in American Archaeology and Ethnology 10:97–240.

MEIGHAN, C. W.

1959 Californian cultures and the concept of an archaic stage. American Antiquity 24:289–318.

OLSON, R. L.

1933 Clan and moiety in native America. University of California Publications in American Archaeology and Ethnology 33:351–422.

OSWALT, R. L.

1958 Russian loan words in Southwestern Pomo. International Journal of American Linguistics XXIV:245–247.

RAY, V. F., *et al.*

1964 Primitive pragmatists, the Modoc. University of Washington Press: Publications of the American Ethnographic Society.

REID, H.

1885 Account of the Indians of Los Angeles County. Bulletin of the Essex Institute 17:1–33.

SCOTT, N. A., AND F. L. SCOTT

1963 Social factors in hypertension among the Washo. *In* Washo Indians of

California and Nevada. W. L. De Azevedo, ed. University of Utah Anthropological Papers, no. 67.

SPARKMAN, P. S.

1908 The culture of the Luiseño Indians. University of California Publications in Archaeology and Ethnology 8:187–234.

SPIER, L.

1923 Southern Diegueño customs. University of California Publications in American Archaeology and Ethnology 20:297–358.

1930 Klamath ethnography. University of California Publications in American Archaeology and Ethnology 30.

STEWARD, J. H.

1933 Ethnography of the Owens Valley Paiute. University of California Publications in American Archaeology and Ethnology 33:233–350.

1937 Ecological aspects of southwestern society. Anthropos 32:87–104.

1938 Basin-Plateau aboriginal socio-political groups. Bureau of American Ethnology Bulletin 120.

1955 Theory of culture change.

STEWART, O. C.

1941 Northern Paiute. Anthropological Records 4:362–446.

1942 Culture element distributions: Ute-Southern Paiute. Anthropological Records 6:231–355.

STRONG, W. D.

1929 Aboriginal society in southern California. University of California Publications in American Archaeology and Ethnology 26:36–273.

WHITING, B. B.

1950 Paiute sorcery. Viking Fund Publications in Anthropology 15.

11 The Tlingit Indians

JULIA AVERKIEVA

The Northwest Coast

On the Pacific coast of North America from the Bering Strait on the north to the Juan de Fuca Strait to the south, millennia before European discovery, a unique Indian culture of fishermen, hunters and gatherers was developing. The Pacific coast consists of a broken coastline and countless islands, separated from each other and the mainland by narrow channels. The largest of these is Vancouver Island, 300 miles long, with Queen Charlotte Strait separating it on the north from the islands of the same name. Dixon Strait separates the latter in the north from such Alaskan islands as Baranof, Chichagof, Admiralty, Kupreanof, and others. A chain of high mountain ranges isolates the coastal strip from the interior.

Due to the mild climate and heavy precipitation the vegetation of the coastal area is unusually abundant, and deep forests cover the mountains' slopes. Animal life was rich and varied and sea mammals were plentiful, with whales, porpoises, hair seals, sea lions, sea otters, and fur seals frequenting the coast. Migrating salmon annually appeared in immense schools and filled the inlets on their way to breeding grounds up the rivers. In the early spring olachens, a special variety of candlefish rich in oil, visited certain of the larger rivers, the Fraser, Kitimat, Nass, and Chilkat.

The abundant food resources made the area especially favorable for the development of a coast-oriented culture, and for a period of nine millennia (Borden, 1962, 19) it was the setting for the development of a unique Indian culture based upon salmon fishing and the hunting of water and land animals (Borden, 1962, 11). On the basis of archeological explorations in the delta of the Fraser River, Borden concluded:

> These delta cultures of the first millennium B.C. loom up before us with the Northwest Coast culture patterns well blocked out: maritime orientation, highly developed woodworking, large villages with commodious houses along the shore, and so forth. . . . Exploitation of the rich fish resources, which started more than 7,000 years earlier, is still the economic basis, supplemented by fowling and some hunting of land animals. But in addition

shellfish is extensively eaten, and numerous harpoons . . . as well as the bones of seal, sea lion, and porpoise, attest to the importance of sea mammal hunting [1962, 12].

The linguistic investigations of Swadesh seem to corroborate the time depth of the Northwest coast culture indicated by archeology. His lexico-statistical data suggest that the Indians of the Mosan phylum, ancestors of Wakash-Chimakuam-Salish, were present on the Pacific Northwest in the seventh or eighth millennia B.C., that Wakashan existed as a separate stock by at least the fifth millennium, and that Wakashan separated into two main divisions, Nootkan and Kwakiutl, at approximately 1000 B.C. (Swadesh, 1954, 362). Swadesh agrees with Borden that the Tlingit, Haida, and Tsimshian appeared on the Pacific seaboard about 1,000 years ago, probably moving from the interior. Their intrusion was followed by extensive population shifts, and it curtailed the cultural contacts between Wakashan speakers and the Eskimos.

By the time Europeans first appeared in the region, the Indians of the coast lived in permanent winter villages of large wood-plank communal houses, which they left for summer camps during the fishing season. Summer fishing provided the Indians with a staple food supply. Salmon, which could be caught in great numbers during the fish runs, was the mainstay of the Pacific coast Indians, but they also caught large quantities of cod, halibut, and olachen. The oil extracted from the last was the main oil product in their diet. The hunting of sea and land animals and the gathering of berries and roots, while important, were supplementary. The yearly calendar of the Indians was determined by the fish runs. It was divided into two main seasons: the summer season of active work, producing the means of subsistence, and the winter season of handicraft, trade, and ceremonial activities.

The Indians of the Northwest coast attained a high level of technological development. They adapted a wide variety of fishing techniques— weirs, traps, nets, hooks, spears, rakes, and hoop nets—to the habits and routes of the salmon and the ecology of the region. The Indians also attained a fine mastery in the art of constructing large dugout canoes from big cedar trees. Canoes were essential for trade and travel, and varying sizes were made to accommodate to use in rivers, shallow bays, and channels, and in the open sea.

Early explorers of the coast reported fish to be taken in vast quantities. Actual estimates of the size of the salmon catch are lacking, but given the numbers of fish visiting the rivers and coastal banks, the efficiency of the fishing technology, and the experience of the fishermen themselves, one can assume that the catch was heavy and that a surplus was produced. Evidently here was an example of the conditions of production referred to by Engels when he pointed out that "at a fairly early stage in the development of production, human labor-power obtains the capacity of producing a considerably greater product than is required for the maintenance of the producers" (Engels, 1963, 160). The possibility of producing a surplus product had fundamental social implications, for thereby was created the basis for the development of crafts, barter, accumulation of wealth, and the exploitation of man by man.

The production of surplus is usually connected with the development of horticulture. However, the level of socioeconomic development of the Northwest coast Indians is comparable to that of horticultural tribes. As "sedentary gatherers" the Northwest coast Indians present an example of another line of the evolutionary process. On the basis of developing a highly specialized fishing-hunting (so-called gathering) economy they approached the stage of transition from primitive communism to a society based on exploitation of man by man.

The same was true of the fishing-hunting tribes of northern Eurasia, of the people of Keltelminar culture of the Aral sea region in middle Asia in the fourth century B.C., and of some fishing tribes of Africa. All these peoples reached the last stage of primitive communal organization on the basis of a "gathering economy." By this it is meant that the norms of a clan community were being dissolved and incipient norms of class society were maturing. Summing up the general characteristics of this stage of primitive communal society, Engels wrote:

> . . . within this structure of society based on kinship groups the productivity of labour increasingly develops, and with it private property and exchange, differences of wealth, the possibility of utilising the labour power of others and hence the basis of class antagonisms . . . [Engels, 1963, 6].

This statement characterizes well the society of the Northwest coast Indians of the precontact and early contact periods. On the basis of existing knowledge about these tribes one can trace the processes whereby economic inequalities within an as yet clan-organized society were yielding to the norms of a class society.

The study of this transition is of great theoretical importance, because the concrete historical investigation of the processes characteristic of that period in human history disproves any conception that classes, private property, exploitation of man by man, or acquisitive individualism and competition have always existed. Instead, the data support Marx's contention that "The *existence of classes* is only bound up with *particular historical phases in the development of production*" (Marx and Engels, 1968, 679).

By the time of colonization, Northwest coast society was no longer a clan society, and clan organization already belonged to a former period in the history of these peoples. By the end of the eighteenth century the matrilineal clan as the economic unit had already given way to the big family community and, together with the appearance of private wealth and slavery, patriarchal forms were developing. Patrilocal marriage was already common, coexisting with matrilocality and avunculocality. The tendency to patrilineality was also well defined (Averkieva, 1960). Territorial ties were becoming important. First disguised as fictitious kin relationships, they later appeared in their pure form. Multi-clan village communities appeared, the structure of which can be compared to the village communities of horticulturalists. However, the society of the Northwest coast Indians was not yet a class society as such. Private property was developing within a society where communal ownership of the main means of production predominated.

Internal contradictions were characteristic of all social institutions during the period of transformation of clan to class society. That it was a prolonged period is attested to by the fact that slavery, a direct negation of the norms of clan society, had existed long enough to become hereditary. Following Marx and Engels, one can define the type of slavery found in the Northwest coast as "patriarchal slavery," as distinguished from slavery as the basic mode of production and plantation slavery (Marx, 1962, 326). Appearing within the limits of clan society during the last stage of its existence, patriarchal slavery was the earliest form of social cleavage along class lines. Widespread ethnographic data indicate it to be universal during the transitional stage from pre-class to class society. Commencing with the temporary enslavement of war captives, patriarchal slavery slowly became transformed into hereditary slavery, its most developed form.

There are few known instances where patriarchal slavery grew into slavery as the basic mode of production as it did in ancient Greece and Rome. In the majority of cases patriarchal slavery existed parallel to the transformation of common people into a lower class, but the slaves did not become the principal source of labor. Patriarchal slavery is found in economic systems where the ownership of resources is basically communal in character and where the activity of the slaves is mainly "devoted to the production of immediate means of subsistence," by contrast with slavery as the basic mode of production, where it is aimed at creating surplus value (Marx, 1962, 326–327).

The colonization of the Northwest coast, which drew the Indians into the sphere of capitalistic productive modes, put an end to their independent historical development. It is hard to say what course they would have followed without European intrusion. In any case, the patriarchal slavery they practiced was altogether different from plantation slavery, which was part of a capitalistic system oriented toward a world market.

Such were the general trends in the development of Northwest coast Indian society. However, while sharing these fundamental aspects of technology and social life, each tribe had unique cultural traits. These distinguishing traits were due to diversities in the natural environment and to a tribe's origins, its specific history of contacts with other peoples, and elaboration of its own cultural traditions. On the basis of these differences, the Northwest coast tribes form three distinct cultural groups: northern (Tlingit, Tsimsian, and Haida), central (Kwakiutl, Nootka, and Bella-Coola), and southern (Coast Salish and Chinook). At the time of colonization general socioeconomic trends were at different stages of development among these groups. This has led some investigators to the conclusion that, although their economic basis was similar, the social relations of the three groups were developing along different lines, and the tribes of this small region therefore give a vivid picture of "multi-linear evolution," or the lack of general or consistent trends in man's history. The tribes of the northern group (which includes the Tlingit) were considered to be developing along the lines of matrilineal clan organization; the southern tribes were said to have always had clanless patriarchal institutions; while the central group was seen as an example of a transitional stage from patriarchal family organization to matrilineality. Since slavery and the potlatch, or giveaway feast, were recognized as common to all three groups, it seemed that matrilineal clan organization coexisted with slavery and economic inequality (Swanton, 1905). The present author disagrees with this position and feels Lewis Henry Morgan was correct in positing matrilineal clan organization as early in human social life and as coordinate with communal forms.

Let us make an attempt to trace the above-mentioned trends of socioeconomic development in the concrete history of a Northwest coast tribe, the Tlingit. Were they really, as has been claimed, a matrilineal clan-organized society at the end of the eighteenth century?

Early Explorations and Contact History

At the time of the first European contacts, the Tlingit inhabited the southeastern coast of Alaska and the adjoining islands of Baranof, Chichagof, Admiralty, Kupreanof, among others. In addition, a small group of inland Tlingit lived around Lake Teslin. The Tlingit comprised the largest Indian tribe of Russian America, numbering around 12,000.

Historically traceable contacts between Tlingit and Europeans began in the middle of the eighteenth century. Sporadic early expeditions to the coast—beginning with Gabriello's of 1542, followed by those of Francisco Gali (1582), Lorenzo Ferrer de Maldonado (1588), Juan de Fuca (1592), and Bartolomew de Fonte (1640)—do not seem to have made contact with the natives.

The first definite information on Tlingit life was brought back by the Berings-Chiricov expedition of 1741, which was followed by many others during the eighteenth century.[1] The early descriptions characterize the Tlingit as fishermen, hunters and gatherers, and as woodworkers, living in wooden plank houses, and using tools of stone and copper. They were reported to be a warlike people and shrewd tradesmen. The items most desired in barter with the whites were iron and copper, with which they were already acquainted. By the time of Cook's voyage of 1778 they were carrying on a lively sea otter trade with China via the

Drawing of a Nootka man from a plate entitled "Macuina Xefe de Nutka," in Viage al Estrecho de Fuca, *1802.*
(Photograph courtesy of Museum of the American Indian, Heye Foundation.)

Russians and other Europeans visiting their area. Tens of thousands of sea otter furs were being traded by Indians at the end of the eighteenth century.

More extended accounts of Tlingit life come from early nineteenth-century records of various sorts, such as ships' logs; diaries; descriptions of voyages; and accounts of Russian explorers, traders, and missionaries. The establishment of the Russian-American Company at the end of the eighteenth century resulted in systematic investigations of native life, which laid the foundation for later ethnographic research on the Tlingit. The first attempt to describe Tlingit society as a whole was made by Lisianski [1803–1806] (1812), whose materials were further enlarged by the surveys of Chwostov and Davidov (Davidov, 1810–1812), and Lütke [1826–1829] (1834). Valuable materials on the Tlingit were also gathered by people in the service of the Russian-American Company, such as Chlebnikof, Wrangel, and Tichmenief. Particularly noteworthy is the work of Veniaminov (1840), whose book on the Tlingit was the first descriptive monograph on a North American Indian tribe. The extensive documents of the Russian-American Company also contain materials of ethnographic value.

In the latter part of the nineteenth century, accounts of the Tlingit were made by Krause [1881–1882] (1885), Niblack [1885–1887] (1890), Petroff (1881), and Anatoli (1906). Further studies of this people are connected with the names of the American anthropologists Boas, Swanton, Drucker, Barnett, Garfield, McClellan, de Laguna, and the Canadians Barbeau and Jenness.

It is on the basis of these data that we can assess the character and level of economic development of the Tlingit when the first contacts by Europeans were made.

Technology and Economy

Although the Tlingit originally did not practice agriculture, and their economic life, like that of the other Northwest coast tribes, was founded on fishing and hunting along with the collection of berries and shellfish, they had attained a relatively high stage of development. The efficiency of their techniques, like those of the other Northwest coast Indians, followed from the specialization of their fishing gear and its adaptation to a wide variety of conditions. These techniques persisted long after colonization, the only innovation being the replacement of bone and stone points with iron (de Laguna, 1960; Averkieva, 1959).

The waters of the Tlingit lands yielded plentiful catches of different kinds of fish, but especially of salmon, the main food. During the summer season thousands of salmon were cut and smoke dried in special smokehouses for winter use. Another valuable item of food for the Tlingit themselves, and one in great demand among other tribes, was the oil rendered from olachen. As to the amount of oil rendered in one season, Krause states that the Chilkats made 40 to 60 gallons of fish oil per person in 1882 (Krause, 1885, 178).

Hunting in aboriginal times was carried on for meat and for skins with which to make clothing, but with the development of the fur trade and the advent of whites its aims as well as the equipment used were changed completely. The old hunting gear was replaced by flintlock rifles, and other types of guns, as well as by steel traps, and the main aim of the occupation became the procurement of furs for exchange with white traders.

The division of labor in Tlingit society originally developed along sex lines. Men did the fishing and hunting, and women did the work of processing and preserving the catch. However, specialists were already appearing in wood carving, copper working, and later, in iron and silver working. Women were the blanket weavers, basket makers, and leather workers, and some became highly respected specialists in their crafts. The handicrafts of both sexes were valuable as commodities in the intertribal market, especially copper plates and Chilkat blankets, for the production of which a particular skill was needed. Specialists in these crafts held a prominent position in Tlingit society, as did the professions of shaman and trader.

Trade

The efficiency of productive methods plus the natural riches of the country permitted the Indians to produce a surplus product that could be exchanged on the intertribal market. As a result of certain differences in the distribution of natural products, a lively intertribal trade was carried on along the Northwest coast and between the coastal and interior tribes long before the coming of the Europeans. This trade was stimulated by developing specialization in particular handicrafts and arts among the different peoples of the coast and among the Tlingit themselves. Chilkat blankets were famous all through the area, while the Yakutat, Sitka, and Huna Tlingit made the finest basketry. The largest and best canoes were made by the Haida, while the Kwakiutl were famous for their wooden utensils and the Tsimshian for their carved horn spoons and dance headdresses. From Copper River came native copper, which was worked by Indian coppersmiths into arrow points, lance points, daggers, rings, bracelets, and the famous copper plates. From the southern coastal tribes the Tlingit traded slaves, dentalium shells, and shark teeth.

At the time of the first contacts with whites Tlingits were already avid traders. There were regular trade routes reaching from the coast into the interior of Alaska through mountain passes. Using these, the Tlingit traded with Athapaskan peoples, exchanging products of the sea for caribou and moose skins. By the early 1800s fur trade with Europe was well established. It stimulated the Tlingit to devote more energy both to their own hunting and to trading for skins with interior Athapaskans. The Tlingit played the role of middleman between Athapaskan tribes and the white traders on the coast, and they tried to block the Athapaskans from direct contact with the whites. A special class of traders began to appear in Tlingit society.

Slaves, dentalia, and abalone shells formerly served as standards of value and units of wealth. However, the development of the fur trade enormously increased the value of otter and beaver skins, which, together with slaves and copper plates, had become the units of Indian wealth by the beginning of the nineteenth century. However, after the middle of the nineteenth century these items were replaced by woolen blankets of European manufacture, and the wealth of the rich Tlingit was amassed in the form of these blankets.

Clan Organization

Tlingit social organization was usually described in terms of typical matrilineal clan structure. The Tlingit were divided into two totemic phratries or moieties—the Raven and the Wolf (or, among the northern Tlingit, the Raven and the Eagle). Relations between the two moieties involved the obligation of mutual help at births, funerals, and ear- and lip-piercing ceremonies. According to tradition, only artists of the opposite moiety could carve the totem poles of a given clan and build their houses. Each phratry consisted of several clans with animal names, as noted by early Russian observers (Lisianski, 1812; Lütke, 1834; Veniaminov, 1840; Anatoli, 1906). Veniaminov counted twelve totemic clan names among the Tlingit, and Lisianski wrote that the same animals after which the clans were named were carved over the Tlingit houses (1812, 216).

The American anthropologist Swanton noted fourteen named groups, which he considered to be the original Tlingit clans. But he saw the difference between clan names and clan crests and, while recognizing the animal character of the crests, interpreted the clan names as having reference to locale (Swanton, 1908). Veniaminov's analysis (1840) of the suffixes attached to clan names clarifies what was actually the twofold nature of their origin. Clan names that refer to animals end in *kujadi* or *edi,* which connote stock or generation. Other clan names end in *it* or *ittan.* Veniaminov explains that *it* means "house" and *tan* means "inhabitant." Thus these endings denote groups of secondary origin, that is, of the big house communities; and only those clans that have names ending with *kujadi* or *edi* can be viewed as the original ones. It is interesting to note that in 1947 Garfield wrote about the two Tlingit clans of Angoon-Decitan and Angakitan, "These are not strictly clans but descendants of houses, as their names clearly show. According to tradition their ancestors were T'lene'di, Dog-Salmon-People" (1947, 438).

Clans and moieties were both exogamous and matrilineal in descent. However, according to early nineteenth-century sources, patrilocal residence, with the wife joining the man's household, was practiced, and it predominated among the chiefs. When a woman joined a man's household, her children, particularly her sons, when they were about ten years old, were sent to the household of her brothers. Thus the *avunculate* was a developed institution. The hereditary office and all rights and prerogatives of the clan chief were passed to his sister's son. According to Anatoli (1906, 18–19), it was the youngest nephew who was his recognized heir.

Moiety and clan affiliations were significant in relation to questions of land tenure. The right of a clan group to a certain tract of land was substantiated by the clan legends that were incorporated into clan rituals and costumes, and were also symbolically represented on the clan totem poles.

Clans were so scattered and intermixed that families of each, Lisianski wrote, "are found in the same settlement. These families, however, always live apart; and to distinguish the cast[e] to which they belong, they place on the top of their houses, carved in wood or painted, the bird or beast that represents it" (1812, 216). Nonetheless, the members of a given clan recognized their common origin. "All members of a given sib," wrote McClellan, "wherever they may be, share with fierce pride the ownership of a certain crest, stories, songs and other prerogatives, as well as a pool of personal names, house names . . ." (1964, 77).

Territorial Subdivisions

All Tlingit people were divided into thirteen territorial groups called *qwans.* Each *qwan* had fairly well-defined borders, and a particular name, such as Yakutat-qwan, Chilkat-qwan, Hoonah-qwan, Sitka-qwan, Aukqwan, Taku-qwan, Tongass-qwan, and so forth (Swanton, 1908). The population of a *qwan* varied from about 100 to 1,000 individuals, who inhabited one, two, or three permanent winter villages. Fishing, hunting, and gathering grounds belonged to the different clans represented in the *qwan*.

In each *qwan*, clans or lineages of both moieties were represented. For instance, the Hutsnuwu-qwan consisted of Wuckitan, Daqlawedi, and Tlokwedi clans of the Wolf moiety and Decitan and Anqakitan of the Raven moiety. The general tendency in aboriginal times was to contain an equal representation from each moiety (Veniaminov, 1840; Swanton, 1908, 398–400). This tendency was related to reciprocal marriages and matrilineal inheritance (Krause, 1885, 77).

The archeological investigations of de Laguna at Yakutat and Hutsnuwu suggest that aboriginal settlements were neither large nor numerous and that clans were originally resident in "separate but affiliated villages." Even now, when descendants of those clans live in one village, for instance in Angoon, "people recognize that they form a local community, but express this by saying that they are a group of 'tribes,' or 'nations,' that is, a group of sibs" (de Laguna, 1960, 26). Larger settlements developed after contact. This was also true elsewhere on the coast, as in the case of the Kwakiutl Fort Rupert and the Tsimshian Fort Simpson. The members of one clan settled in different *qwans* recognized blood ties and common territorial rights. When a local subsib or lineage died off in one *qwan* "their relatives in other *qwans* have claimed or used their hunting and fishing places" (de Laguna, 1960, 26).

The *qwans* have sometimes been referred to as "tribes" (Swanton, 1908, 397), but they appear rather to have been emergent neighborhood communities analogous to the village communities of agricultural peoples, in which territorial bonds were originally cemented through ties of marriage, but gradually developed and replaced the clan bonds of blood relationship as the primary organizing principle.

The Household—The Economic Unit

Although delocalized Tlingit clans had lost their economic importance, the former economic unity of clan members was recognized by the theoretical right of a person to the use of clan property in any village where fellow clan members resided. In practice, however, it was necessary for him to have a special invitation from the local village clan or lineage. The localized lineage of a clan was composed of a man, his brothers and sisters, his sisters' children, and his sisters' daughters' children. They did not share a common residence.

The main economic unit in Tlingit society by the end of the eighteenth century was the house group, usually composed of a core of brothers with their nephews (sisters' children) and the wives of these males, their sons under ten years of age, unmarried daughters, and often some married daughters as well. Members of the house group, numbering from ten to forty individuals, lived in one large wooden plank house. Each house had its traditional name, by which its inhabitants were known. The majority of these names were derived from the animal totems of the clans. In each *qwan* one of the clan's houses carried the name of the clan totem. For instance, members of the Bear clan (Téqoedi) had a "Bear house" in each village where they were represented. Where several households in a village belonged to the same clan, one bore the clan totem name, while the names of others either indicated parts of the totemic animal or referred to the material, form, or location of the house. For instance, in Angoon members of the Daqlawedi clan (or Killer Whale people) lived in three houses, the names of which were Killer Whale House, Killer Whale's Tooth House, and Killer Whale's Dorsal Fin House (Garfield, 1947, 448).

The property of the house group consisted of the house itself, big canoes, important tools, big food boxes, important weapons, food products resulting from collective work, ceremonial gear, names, crests, house posts, and myths. All the clan lands in a given *qwan* were divided among households, and each house group had usufructuary rights to its lands. The activities and properties of the household were managed by its head, whose position was hereditary.

Forms of Property

It is a truism that the nature of property corresponds to the stage of development attained by a given society and that the definition of property relations in a society means describing the basis of all social relations in that society. What forms of property were characteristic of Tlingit society of the precontact and early contact periods?

The earliest data on the Tlingit indicates coexistence among them of both communal and private property. Fishing and hunting territories, berry- and root-gathering patches, houses, and big canoes were considered communal property of the clan to which the totemic crests on the homes and canoes attested. Slaves, coppers, weapons, and valuable shells were privately owned. Thus, private property was developing on the basis of using communally owned resources. This situation slowed down the emerging importance of private property relations. But probably by the end of the eighteenth century, limits on the fully collective use of communally owned resources were already taking place. Surplus clan lands could be used by members of other clans, but only with the permission of a given clan head and for "a tribute paid to the clan owning the area in the form of a percentage of the harvest" (Rogers, 1960, 277). In this practice one can see an incipient form of land rent.

Titles to clan lands were included in the hereditary names of the lineage of clan chiefs. As the carriers of clan ownership rights, the chiefs received part of each clan member's catch, a practice that can be considered the earliest form of rent. Gradually it became possible for the surplus produce that followed improvements in fishing and other techniques to be individually appropriated and bartered. Part of it, however, had to be given to the clan chiefs as a vestige of the former collectivism in the distribution of goods and as a recognition of clan ownership of lands. The generous distribution of products accumulated in this way was expected from the chiefs. Thus the economic basis was laid for the appearance of exploitation and the appropriation by the clan nobility of the surplus produced by clan members and by slaves.

Slavery

All investigators since the end of the eighteenth century describe Tlingit society as divided into three social groups: chiefs, commoners, and slaves. By the time of the first European contacts, slavery was hereditary, which evidences its long aboriginal history among the Tlingit. Here, as among Northwest coast tribes generally, it has left a deep impression on the ideology of the people.

Slavery among the Tlingit was mentioned by the early Russian explorers, who reported slaves to be owned by clan chiefs and lineage and household heads. Slaves were at the complete disposal of their masters; some were killed at the funeral of their owner to attend him in the other world. Slave labor was used in fishing, hunting, transportation, house and canoe building, domestic service, and even in war. As Romanov wrote, Tlingits "exhaust their slaves with hard labour" (Averkieva, 1966). Wives and children of chiefs are described in Tlingit legends as always chaperoned and attended by slaves. As to the number of slaves, there are different estimates. In the early nineteenth century Lütke wrote that the rich Tlingit had thirty to forty slaves (1834, 150). According to Simpson's estimate in the middle of the century, slaves composed one-third of the Tlingit population (1847, 211). Somewhat later, however, Petroff reported that Tlingit slaves composed 10 percent of the total population (1881, 38).

Slaves were prisoners of war and their descendants. Special war expeditions, sometimes for long distances, were undertaken for the capture of slaves. Comparing the Tlingit with ancient vikings, Anatoli wrote that their war expeditions usually consisted of several big war canoes manned with forty warriors each (1906, 5). The warriors would stealthily approach an enemy village at night and attack the sleeping people. Early Russian reports, as well as Tlingit traditions of warfare and museum collections of Tlingit armor, all testify to the efficiency of Tlingit military organization and equipment. In a letter describing the first Tlingit attack on a Russian camp in 1792, Baranoff emphasized the orderly behavior of the warriors under the command of one person. He wrote that the armor of wooden planks and moose hides, and the head masks, were so thick that they were impenetrable to bullets (Anatoli, 1906, 6–7). War among the Tlingit had become a regular means of obtaining booty, and the best warriors of the clan were always at the disposal of the chief, whose nephews formed the bodyguard that regularly accompanied him to feasts and to war (Anatoli, 1906, 29).

Slaves were bought as well as captured. In the beginning of the nineteenth century a lively slave trade was carried on along the coast. "Though under the Russian rule wars among the Tlingit tribes became of rare occurrence, the number of slaves did not diminish," wrote Petroff. "The supply was kept up by barter with the more southern tribes, and at that time a majority of the slaves belonged to the Flathead Indians of the British possessions" (1881, 172). According to Wrangel's data, the price of a slave in the first decades of the nineteenth century was fifteen to twenty deer skins, twenty-five beaver skins, or two sea otter skins (1839, 64). Slaves could also be bartered for precious shells, copper, canoes, and Chilkat blankets. From the middle of the nineteenth century they could be bought for European woolen blankets, the price being from 60 to 200 blankets.

According to Indian tradition, they once practiced the killing of slaves at the potlatches connected with the building of a new house or with a funeral. At other potlatches, slaves, as units of wealth, were given away. Slaves were also given as a dowry to daughters and used for paying the shaman or in payment of an indemnity incurred by injury to another's person or possessions. However, by the second half of the nineteenth century, slaves were more often given freedom at their master's funeral or commemorative potlatch instead of being given away or killed (Anatoli, 1906, 23). At house-building potlatches they were ordered to climb into each hole dug for a house post and then were given their freedom (Garfield, 1947, 439). Tlingit slaves were part of the household of their master and worked together with the free members of this household. As was the case among other tribes of the coast, slaves had not yet become the main productive force in society, and their labor was subordinate to the labor of the free. The institution grew along with the development of the fur trade among the Tlingit. The number of slaves increased; they became more widely distributed among the rich and the nobility; and their labor became more extensively exploited. However, after its prohibition by the Russian government in the middle of the nineteenth century, slavery began to pass away. In 1867 it was once more outlawed by the United States, and in 1898 the last Tlingit slave was killed.

Stratification Among the Free

Along with the social division of society into free men and slaves, social stratification was developing among the free Tlingits. Wealth was of great importance in the society and laid the basis for the social status of an individual. "In highest esteem among the Tlingits," wrote Lütke, "is the person who has more relations, more wealth and more slaves" (1834, 73).

Clan chiefs and hereditary heads of communal house groups made up the ruling group in the Tlingit communities, but since the households were unequal economically, the influence held by their heads varied. The head of the wealthiest household was a recognized chief of a clan lineage, or *ankau*. The most influential among these was called *atlan ankau,* and his power went beyond his clan and moiety mates and was recognized by the *qwan,* or village, as a whole. His house was built in the middle of the village and was fronted by magnificent and beautifully carved totem poles. The chief was able to pay liberally for the best wood carvers to make totem poles, ceremonial masks, and headdresses (see album of these masks in Siebert and Forman, 1967). The chief was considered the representative of the clan ancestors, and all clan regalia and totemic signs were in his possession, serving as the signs of clan landownership. Hereditary chiefs comprised the Tlingit nobility, who made every endeavor to underline their differences from the commoners. Most of them were occupied only with the noble tasks of war, trade, and hunting. Legends say that their wives and daughters worked much less than common people. Their sons are mostly described as hunters. But legendary heroes are described as persons of such noble origin that they did not even know how to hunt (Swanton, 1909).

In early Russian descriptions, Tlingit chiefs appear as petty princes, proud of their eminence and their noble heredity. Lisianski wrote that the chief of Sitka was "so elated . . . with pride, that he made no use of his legs for walking, but was invariably carried on the shoulders of his attendants, even on the most trifling occasions" (1812, 205). Some of them were even carried from one place to another on litters (Anatoli, 1906, 29–30). Clan chiefs are described by Anatoli as always surrounded by a crowd of slaves and war captives. Only chiefs had jewelry of precious shells and copper, and their dress was made from the best materials. Only they could wear replicas of the clan totems on their dress and body. The copper plates belonging to the clan were in their private possession and were given as a dowry to their daughters. Their hereditary names were connected with clan origin legends and clan totems and served as titles to the possessions of the clan. However, their obligation to feed clansmen in times of need was the other side of their rights to clan property. Chiefs had to be generous. But a clear distinction was developing between their rights and their duties. Thus, toward the end of the eighteenth century Tlingit clans consisted of noble slave-owning chiefs and their families as well as commoners.

Socioeconomic inequality existed not only inside the clan, but between clans. Some clans were rich and claimed possessory rights to the lands surrounding a village. Others were poor and had to have permission for the use of these lands.

Potlatches

In the ethnological literature, wealth on the Northwest coast, whether amassed in the form of blankets, copper plates, valuable shells or slaves, is often conceptualized as "prestige wealth," or wealth of a distinctly noneconomic character. According to this view, the only use of such wealth was for validating titles of nobility, for heightening prestige, and for contests between rival chiefs who lavishly gave away and destroyed hoarded riches at the potlatch feasts.

The extreme interpretation of the noneconomic character of Indian wealth and of the potlatch was given by Ruth Benedict, who saw the potlatch as the means for realizing the inherent desire of the Northwest coast Indians for superiority and for expressing their "unabashed megalomania" (1955, 175).[2] Other authors did not go so far in psychological interpretations of the Indian potlatch, but still saw the emotional striving for incorporeal prestige as the mainspring in the Indian game with wealth. They saw the manipulation of wealth as noneconomical in that property was not used for the extension of production, as it is in capitalist society (Rogers, 1960, 191). Boas, on the contrary, gave an economic interpretation of potlatch as an institution of capital investment (Boas, 1897, 341). Thus, the social role of Indian property and potlatch was evaluated according to standards of capitalist social relations. Such an approach to the understanding of a social system, which was quite

Kwakiutl woman in traditional dress.
(Photograph courtesy of Museum of the American Indian, Heye Foundation.)

different, not only from capitalism, but also from precapitalistic class systems, naturally led to many misconceptions about Northwest coast Indian society and to conclusions that in this society there existed capital interest and a complex monetary system.

The analysis of property, potlatching, and the unequal distribution of wealth in Indian society in terms of its own social level of development at the time of colonization permits a more profound understanding of the system in its entirety. First, it is evident that some of the hoarded wealth—the slaves—was used for the extension of production. The wealthy could buy better canoes and better fishing and hunting gear than the poor, so these, too, were used for obtaining greater returns.

Of course, this part of an Indian's wealth was not boasted of at a potlatch, where the riches prepared for giving away were exhibited. The desire for prestige not only was a psychological drive of a Northwest coast Indian but also had a deep economic sense, as pointed out in the work of Goldschmidt and Haas, who stated:

> . . . the potlatch and totem pole, both served to substantiate the claim of the individual clan head to the territory which that clan claimed . . . The fact of ownership is publicly announced at the dramatic potlatches in which the new owner—whether by inheritance or other legal means—establishes his title [1946, 14–17].

The new wealth created by the fur trade sharpened the contradictions inherent in Tlingit society. Before the period of the fur trade, wealth could be acquired primarily by clan chiefs and heads of lineages, in their position as slave owners and supervisors of clan and household property. However, the trading of furs with Europeans gave individual hunters the opportunity to acquire riches. By obtaining furs, they could buy slaves, copper plates, and other native valuables, and they could accumulate considerable wealth, despite the fact that they had to give the chief some share of their gain. At this time the term "chief" became synonymous with "owner of wealth," and the *nouveaux riches* became a growing menace to the power of the hereditary clan chiefs. Rich but untitled Indians tried to gain social recognition and rights through giving a house-building potlatch, which earned them the title of household head. To save their rights and bolster their prestige, the hereditary chiefs had to boast of their noble ancestry, names, totems, and crests, all of which had to be validated with wealth given away at great potlatches. The competition between heads of the households for clan chieftainship sharpened, which along with the growth of new wealth led to ever more lavish potlatches. Here was the main cause of the rivalry between the chiefs and of the "waste" of wealth. In the last instance the potlatch was an institution for validating claims to resources, land titles, and the right to acquire surplus products from the use of clan lands.

Moiety and clan affiliations figured importantly in the distribution of wealth associated with the potlatch. The most important potlatches and related ceremonies were given to the people of the opposite moiety and particularly to the clan of one's father or one's wife in that moiety. Thus the potlatch helped reinforce the moiety division of Tlingit society. The earliest description of the Tlingit potlatch was given by Lütke, who mentions feasting, dancing, and giving away of wealth as the main features of the ceremony. Lütke writes about two forms of pot-latching: "domestic" and "social." The first was held by a clan leader who invited other clans in the vicinity. To the "social potlatches are invited wealthy people from far away places." They were given not by a family, but by a whole "tribe," and invited guests stayed about a month. Presents were given according to a guest's status and with the hopes of receiving similar presents in the future (1834, 79). The pretexts for the giveaway were many, according to Lütke: "new alliances, new acquaintances, peace and war, all noteworthy events, funerals, etc.—all these can be a pretext for making these ceremonies" (1834, 79).

The fullest description of Tlingit potlatching in the first decades of the nineteenth century is given by Veniaminov. He writes in detail about three main potlatches of the tribe: (1) *Ukesh-atashich*—commemoration of the dead, (2) *Kchatashi*—given in connection with the building of a new house and the erection of a totem pole, and (3) *Gishtashigi*—given for one's children. Veniaminov notes that only members of another phratry, called *achkani*, meaning "affines" (sons-in-law and brothers-in-law), were invited (1840, 99). Presents were distributed among them, and they very jealously watched to see that all the riches of their brother-in-law were distributed. Thus the wealth of the potlatch-giver went to the clans of his wife and children. In a way potlatch was a mechanism for transmitting private property from the father to his children's uncles and, consequently, to his children.

The accumulated data on the Tlingit potlatch reveal the institutionalization of new social and property relations within the framework of norms derived from clan society. Since the privately owned riches were made on lands that were still communally held, they had, in a sense, a tinge of communal property about them and had to be distributed. They were distributed among the members of the opposite moiety having some relation with totemic ideology (McClellan, 1964, 89–90; Averkieva, 1960, 61). This distribution of private riches had the appearance of eliminating inequality, but in fact it was an affirmation of inequality and the public recognition of the high social standing of a man who was able to gather great riches and lavishly give them away. The important feature of the potlatch was that the richest presents were given to a man's wealthiest guests.

The potlatch of the Northwest coast Indians, like similar institutions among Indians in other parts of North America (such as "giving-away dances" among the Plains Indians and feasts of the dead among the Iroquois and Algonkians), is an institution characteristic of a transitional stage between the communal property relations of clan society and the development of society based upon private property. Such institutions originate when there are already possibilities for producing and accumulating surplus products in the form of natural riches, as yet without ways of using them, besides the previously existing pattern of reciprocal exchange between moieties. The vestiges of totemic ideology in the ceremonialism connected with the potlatch permit us to trace its roots in the institution of mutual gift giving in a dually organized society, similar to the *intichiuma* ceremony of Australian aborigines. However, the meaning of these persisting traits had changed completely. In place of reciprocal exchange, the distribution of riches in the opposite moiety to the clan of a wealthy man's wife and, consequently, his children, meant that the potlatch was becoming an institution whereby property was being indirectly transferred to a man's own sons and daughters. It is worthwhile to note in this connection that Anatoli identified the potlatch as a "division of inheritance" (1906, 46).

The efficiency of productive forces, developed trade, hereditary slavery, social differentiation, and assertion of wealth and status through the potlatch—all these traits found in Tlingit society at the end of the eighteenth century indicate that their egalitarian matrilineal clan organization had long ceased to function. The clan as the primary basis of the social structure was in the past, although vestiges of clan organization persisted in relation to landownership, marriage, descent, inheritance, and participation in the potlatch and in religious life. The basis for their persistence was conceptualized by Engels when he referred to "new social elements which in the course of generations strive to adapt the old social order to the new conditions, until at last their incompatibility brings about a complete upheaval" (Engels, 1963). The incompatibility between older norms and arising new forms was demonstrated most vividly in the conflict between the principle of matrilineal descent and inheritance by a nephew, and the desire of a wealthy Tlingit to make his son the heir to his private riches. Other contradictions arose in connection with the persistence of matrilocality and the avunculate and the practice of patrilocality. Wealthy Tlingits tried to overcome these difficulties by appealing to the ancient custom of adoption into the clan and by giving their clan names to sons and even to wives through the potlatch.

Recent Changes in Tlingit Economic and Social Life

The sale of Alaska to the United States, which coincided with the decline in the fur trade, was a turning point in the history of the Tlingit people. The active colonization of Alaska by the United States after the 1880s and the development there of capitalistic enterprises, especially the fishing industry, changed the status of the Tlingit, who under Russian rule were considered "an independent nation." The main fishing grounds of the Tlingit were expropriated by fishing companies, and the Indians have become a source of cheap labor. Paid work has become the only source of income for Indians; the men fish and the women work in the canneries. The growth of the white population resulted in further expropriation of many family trapping, gathering, and fishing resources by individual settlers.

The native economic system collapsed as the Indians became discriminated against as a cheap labor force in a capitalistic economy. These changes in the economic life of the Indians were followed by fundamental transformations in their social relations. Paid work stimulated the stabilization of the nuclear family, and missionaries encouraged the nuclear family living pattern. The growth of a half-breed population and adoption of a white father's surname also greatly undermined the matrilineal inheritance pattern. These trends caused many profound changes in kinship relations and many disputes around questions of matrilineal inheritance, the avunculate, and marriage rules. The old house groups lost their importance as economic units and disintegrated into individual families, living separately. However, the members of such groups still consider their obligation to help each other in times of stress, and communal houses, clan crests, names, myths, and ceremonial gear are still considered the property of the house group. Communal houses still stand in several villages. Some of them are unoccupied and used only on ceremonial occasions, while in others live a nuclear family, considered the keeper of the old heirlooms.

The present-day Tlingit live in three types of settlements. Six traditionally Indian villages are still situated on the territories of their old *qwans* (Rogers, 1960, 206–207; Stanley, 1965, 18). Some Indians live in settlements originally established by whites, but now with a predominantly native population. The third group live in white towns where they are a minority, either settled together at the outskirts of town or intermingled with the white population.

The old communal right of clans and lineages to lands has persisted as the corporate right to village communities. Lands unexpropriated as yet by capitalist enterprises can be used by everyone in the village, although the Indians still remember what lands belonged to what clan (Goldschmidt and Haas, 1946, 42). However, "American law has refused to recognize that any Tlingit individual or corporate group has exclusive right to exploit salmon streams, hunting grounds, fishing grounds or other types of natural resources" (Stanley, 1965, 4). In traditional native villages there is more survival of old-time practices. However, attempts have been made to organize such communities on the basis of United States territorial law, and courts have been established that greatly undermine the old social controls and the authority of the old chiefs (Stanley, 1965). Also weakened are the nonmaterial aspects of

Tlingit culture, such as shamanism, potlatching, dancing, singing, carving, and storytelling, which were intimately connected with the clan organization of their past.

The oldest Christian church in Tlingit communities is the Russian Orthodox Church with its center at Sitka. Its influence remains stronger in the northern Tlingit communities than the newer Presbyterian Church now found in almost every village. There are Salvation Army units in many Tlingit settlements, although their influence is weak (Stanley, 1965, 15).

The growth of the Indian population in modern Alaskan white towns is accompanied by two main processes: the weakening of old native institutions and the integration of Indians into the larger society. However, the latter process is slow and painful because of racial discrimination. Jim Crowism exists in Alaska in relation to work, pay, and social services. The natives of Alaska are not socially accepted by whites and do not share equal economic opportunities in the country of their ancestors (Rogers, 1960, 258).

The acquisition of Alaska by the United States drastically changed the status of people of mixed Indian and white parentage. In Russian America they were on equal grounds with Russian workers, but the American authorities have declared that the "status given to these people by the imperial *ukase* is not binding upon the United States." It was officially stated that "persons of mixed white and nonwhite parentage are classified according to the race of the nonwhite parent" (Rogers, 1960, 197). In the census after 1929 half-breeds were not distinguished from full-blood Indians, and persons of minimal Indian heritage were counted as natives. As Rogers states, the number of mixed-bloods has increased, and "these people are more indigenous in their orientation today than they probably were one hundred years ago" (Rogers, 1960, 198). They are the most active sector of the Indian population today and are largely responsible for a new phenomenon in Tlingit Indian life, which is the emergence of a political and national self-consciousness. The Indian organization established in 1912, the Alaskan Native Brotherhood, affiliated with the Alaskan Sisterhood, has chapters in every Tlingit settlement. The Indians are becoming more and more resolute in the fight for fishing and other rights, for job opportunities, and against all kinds of discrimination.

Starting in the early 1940s, a crisis in the fishing industry due to the decline of the salmon population has meant tragedy for the Tlingit people. The drastic loss of their main source of income has led to a heavy migration from the villages to the towns in the hope of making a living there. However, they find severe poverty and experience race prejudice and disorganization more sharply. The Indians' standard of living was going down so rapidly that in 1953–1954 the President of the United States declared southeastern Alaska as a disaster area. "The natives of Alaska are a depressed class, one of the poorest under the American flag," writes Rogers (1960, 152). As a solution he feels Indians should be drawn into the developing Alaskan lumber industry as well as into other industrial enterprises. For the Indians, Rogers points out, this would mean the acquisition of new skills and habits and the basically new way of life entailed by the organization of labor in industrial plants. However, he sees the main difficulty in achieving this reorientation to be the white discrimination against Indians as reflected in governmental policies concerning them (Rogers, 1960, 215–217).

NOTES

[1] The observation of Steller, the physician of the expedition, and steersman Chytrov, characterized the people of the region as fishermen and hunters and as woodworkers using tools of stone and copper. They reported seeing stores of smoked salmon and wooden plank houses. Further explorations of Tlingit life were made by Russian traders (Andreev, 1948). Ethnographic data on the Tlingit were brought back by the expeditions of Juan Perez (1774), Juan Francisco de la Bodega y Quadra with Maurelle (1775), James Cook (1778), La-Perouse (1786), George Dixon and Portlock (1787), Robert Gray and John Kendrick (1788), Etienne Marchand (1790), and G. Vancouver (1792–1794).

[2] See criticism of R. Benedict's "megalomaniac paranoid" characterization of the Northwest coast Indians in the works of Helen Codere, "The Amiable Side of Kwakiutl Life," *American Anthropologist*, 58, No. 2 (1956), p. 347, and Clellan S. Ford, *Smoke from Their Fires: The Life of a Kwakiutl Chief* (New Haven and London, 1941), p. 2.

REFERENCES

ANATOLI, KAMENSKIY ALEXEI
1906 V strane shamanov indiane Alaski. Odessa.

ANDREEV, A. I.
1948 Russkie otkrytija v Tichom Okeane u Severnoi Ameriki. Moscow.

AVERKIEVA, J. P.
1959 K istorii metallurgii u indeitsev Severnoi Ameriki. Sovietskaja Ethnographia no. 2.
1960 Rod i potlatch u Tlingitov, Haida i Tsimshian. Trudi Instituta Ethnographii Academii Nauk SSSR. t. 58. Moscow.
1962 Rasloshenie rodovoi obschiny i formirovanie ranneclassovych otnosheniy

u indeitsev severo-zapadnogo pobereshija Severnoi Ameriki. Trudi Instituta Ethnographii Academii Nauk SSSR. t. 70. Moscow.
1966 Slavery among the North American Indians. G. R. Elliot, tr. Victoria, B.C.: Victoria College.

BENEDICT, RUTH
1955 Patterns of culture. New York: New American Library.

BOAS, FRANZ
1897 The social organization and the secret societies of the Kwakiutl Indians, based on personal observations and on notes made by George Hunt. U.S. National Museum Report for 1895. Washington, D.C.

BORDEN, CHARLES E.
1962 West coast cross ties with Alaska. Arctic Institute of North America Technical Paper, no. 11.

CHLEBNIKOF, CIRILL
1861 Essays on America: Materials on the history of Russian settlements on the coast of Eastern Ocean. Supplement to Morskoy Sbornik, no. 3. St. Petersbourg.

COHEN, YEHUDI, ED.
1968 Man in adaption. The cultural present. Chicago: Aldine.

COOK, JAMES
1961–1967 The journals of Captain James Cook. J. G. Beaglehole, ed. 3 vols. Cambridge, England: Cambridge University Press.

DAVIDOV, I.
1810–1812 Twofold travel of naval officers Chwostov and Davidov to America. 2 vols. St. Petersbourg.

DRUCKER, PHILIP
1965 Cultures of the North Pacific coast. San Francisco: Chandler.

ENGELS, FRIEDRICH
1963 The origin of the family, private property and the state. New York: International Publishers.

GARFIELD, VIOLA E.
1947 Historical aspects of Tlingit clans in Angoon, Alaska. American Anthropologist 49 (3).

GOLDSCHMIDT, W., AND T. H. HAAS
1946 Possessory rights of the natives of southeastern Alaska: a report to the commissioner of Indian affairs. October, 1946. Our citations are taken from G. Rogers. Alaska in transition. Baltimore: Johns Hopkins Press.

KRAUSE, AUREL
1885 Die Tlinkit-Indianer. Jena, Germany. (The Tlingit Indians. Erna Gunther, tr. Published for the American Ethnological Society. Seattle: University of Washington Press, 1956.)

LAGUNA, FREDERICA DE
1960 The story of a Tlingit community: a problem in the relationship between

archeological, ethnological, and historical methods. Bulletin 172, B.A.E. Collection. Washington, D.C.: Smithsonian Office of Anthropological Archives.
1964 Archeology of the Jakutat Bay, Alaska. Bulletin 192. B.A.E. Collection. Washington, D.C.: Smithsonian Office of Anthropological Archives.

LANGSDORF, G. H.
1803–1807 Voyages and travels in various parts of the world during the years 1803–1807. 2 vols. London.

LISIANSKI, U.
1812 Voyage round the world on the ship "Neva" in 1803–1806. St. Petersbourg. (English tr., London, 1814.)

LÜTKE, F.
1834 Voyage round the world in the war sloop "Seniavin" in 1826–1829. 2 vols. St. Petersbourg.

MARX, KARL
1962 Capital, vol. III. Moscow: Foreign Languages Publishing House.

MARX, KARL, AND FRIEDRICH ENGELS
1968 Selected Works. New York: International Publishers.

MCCLELLAN, CATHARINE
1964 Culture contacts in the early historic period in the northwest. Arctic Anthropology 2 (2).

NIBLACK, ALBERT P.
1890 The coast Indians of southern Alaska and northern British Columbia. Washington, D.C.: U.S. National Museum Report.

PALLAS, P. S.
1782 Erläuterungen über die in östlichen Ocean zwischen Sibirien und Amerika geschehenen Entdeckungen. Magazin für die neue Historie und Geographie. Halle.

PETROFF, IVAN
1881 Report on the population, industries and resources of Alaska. Tenth census, VIII, 165–177. Washington, D.C.: U.S. Department of the Interior.

ROGERS, GEORGE
1960 Alaska in transition. The southeast region. Baltimore: Johns Hopkins Press.

ROMANOV, VASILY
1825 On the Koluzhs or Koloshs in general. Severniy Archiv, pt. XVII. St. Petersbourg.

SHABELSKY, A.
1826 Voyage aux colonies russes de l'Amerique. St. Petersbourg.

SIEBERT, ERNA, AND WERNER FORMAN
1967 Indianerkunst der amerikanische Nordwestküste. Prague: Polygraphia.

SIMPSON, GEORGE
1847 Narrative of a journey round the world during the years 1841–1842. London: H. Culburn.

STANLEY, SAMUEL

1965 Changes in Tlingit social organization. (Mimeographed.) Los Angeles: Los Angeles State College.

STELLER, G. W.

1793 Tagebuch seiner Reise aus dem Petripauls Hafen in Kamchatka bis an die westlichen Küsten von Amerika und seiner Begebenheiten auf der Rückreise. Neue Nordische Beiträge, t. V. St. Petersbourg.

SWADESH, M.

1954 Time depths of American linguistic groupings. American Anthropologist 56 (3).

SWANTON, JOHN

1905 The social organization of American tribes. American Anthropologist VIII (3).

1908 Social conditions, beliefs and linguistic relationship of the Tlingit Indians. 26th Annual Report, B.A.E. Collection. Washington, D.C.: Smithsonian Office of Anthropological Archives.

1909 Tlingit myths and texts. Bulletin 39, B.A.E. Collection. Washington, D.C.: Smithsonian Office of Anthropological Archives.

TICHMENIEF, P.

1861 Historical survey of the organization of the Russian American Company. Parts I and II. St. Petersbourg.

VENIAMINOV, I.

1840 Zapiski ob ostrovach Unalaskinskogo otdiela, pt. III, St. Petersbourg.

WAXEL, VITUS

1940 The second Kamchatka expedition of Vitus Bering. Translated into Russian from manuscript in German by U. P. Bronschtein. A. I. Andreev, ed. Moscow.

WRANGEL, FERDINAND

1839 Statistische und ethnographische Nachrichten über die russischen Besitzungen an der N-W Küste von Amerika. Beiträge zur Kenntniss des Russischen Reichs, herausgegeben von C. E. Baer und G. Helmer. Bd. 1. St. Petersbourg.

12 The Hunting Tribes of

Subarctic Canada[1] JUNE HELM &

ELEANOR BURKE LEACOCK

Background

LAND AND PEOPLES

The subarctic forest of Canada is the homeland of Athapaskan and Algonkian hunters. Although these Indian peoples comprise two separate language families, they share fundamental similarities in their adaptation to the northern forest and in their recent history and fortunes.

The subarctic forest zone[2] extends over 2,500 miles across Canada: from Labrador on the North Atlantic, along the southern shores of Hudson Bay, following the Mackenzie River lowlands north past the Arctic Circle. It forms a crescent cupping Hudson Bay and the Arctic tundra that flanks the bay's northern shores. In terms of the political divisions of Canada, the subarctic forest zone includes, from east to west, the Labrador division of Newfoundland and most of Quebec, which together make up the Labrador Peninsula; Northern Ontario, Manitoba, Saskatchewan, and Alberta; and the District of Mackenzie of the Northwest Territories.

In this great arc of Canadian taiga, winters are long and severe, summers short and mild. It is a land of lakes and streams. The forest cover is of conifers, interspersed with stands of birch and willow.

The Indians of the subarctic forest comprise several major groupings. On the east side of Hudson Bay live the Algonkian-speaking Montagnais-Naskapi. Aboriginally, they inhabited all of the Labrador Peninsula except the coastal Eskimo areas. In the region of James Bay, the southeasternmost extension of Hudson Bay, the designation of the Algonkian-speaking inhabitants changes from Montagnais to Cree. This Central zone of the Canadian subarctic forest, draining through marshy lowlands into Hudson Bay, was the Cree homeland. Even as Ojibwa impinged on the southern Cree territory in early historic times, some of the Cree

· 343 ·

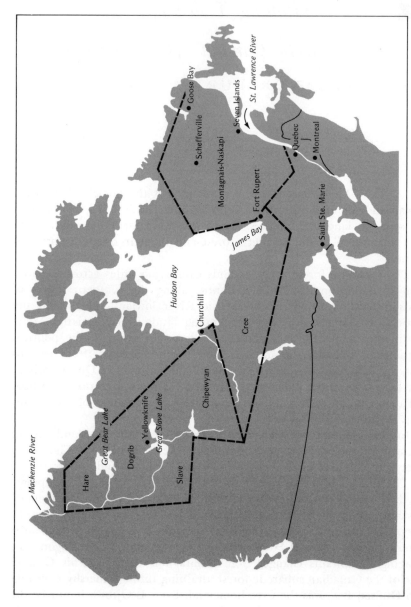

Figure 12.1. Subarctic Canada: The three ethnographic zones treated in this chapter are bounded by broken lines. Major Indian populations, principal settlements, and geographic features are also indicated.

thrust west as far as the Peace River in western Alberta. Others spilled out of the forest to become Plains Cree.

North of the western Cree lands lies the Athapaskan domain. Immediately contiguous to the Cree are the Chipewyan.[3] Northwest of the Chipewyan are the Athapaskans of the Mackenzie basin, known today as Dogrib, Slave, Mountain, Bear Lake, and Hare Indians.

For present purposes, the Canadian subarctic forest is divided into three ethnographic zones (see Figure 12.1): the northeastern lands of the Montagnais-Naskapi; the Central zone, occupied by the Cree; and the Northwest, occupied by the Athapaskan tribes. The southern Montagnais of the Northeast and the Dogrib, Slave, and Hare Indians of the Northwest are peoples known to the authors through their field work. Accordingly, in this study we draw more heavily on the Northeast and the Northwest zones for particular examples and illustrations. For documentation on various Cree groups of the Central subarctic zone we have relied especially on the studies of Honigmann (1962), Rogers (1963, 1965, 1966, 1967), Mason (1967), and Knight (1968).

The tundra, or barren grounds, that flanks the forest on the north has served as an ecological buffer zone between the Indians of the subarctic and the coast-dwelling Eskimos. To the south, the environmental and cultural contrasts between the subarctic Indians and adjacent tribes are less marked. The southern edges of the boreal forest and the plains adjoining it in the west were exploited by other Algonkian and Athapaskan groups. These include, from east to west, the Micmac, Algonkin proper, Northern Ojibwa, Plains Cree, Sarsi, and Beaver. The westernmost reaches of the Canadian boreal forest mount the flanks of the Cordillera and are inhabited by other Athapaskan speakers—Kaska, Sekani, and Kutchin. Posing certain distinct questions of ecology, social organization, and culture history, these adjacent Indian peoples are not considered here.

THE ABORIGINAL BASELINE: SUBSISTENCE AND SOCIETY

Indian groups inhabiting lands adjacent to the tundra seasonally penetrated the barrens, but it was the animals in or of the forest upon which the northern Indian hunters relied. Large game animals, principally the caribou but also the moose, were of prime importance. In parts of the Algonkian area there were deer. In the west, woods bison were to be found as far north as Great Slave Lake, and musk ox were occasionally exploited by those Athapaskans who inhabited the edge of the woods. Throughout the north, Indians killed bear, beaver, and porcupine and fell back on hares, snared by the women, when the hunt was unsuccessful. Fish were important; for some groups they were a vital reserve staple. Migratory waterfowl were a welcome supplement when in season, as well as seals and white whales along the southern Labrador coast. Plant foods were inconsequential in the diet, though blueberries, cranberries, and edible shoots and bulbs were collected in the summer.

Although the details of the methods of obtaining food varied regionally, tools and techniques were similar throughout the subarctic forest. Animals were hunted with bow and arrow or spear or were trapped with a variety of ingenious deadfalls and snares. In mating season moose were lured toward the hunters with calling devices. Caribou were sometimes driven toward long brush fences that forced the animals into defiles, where they could be snared or killed outright. When crossing lakes and rivers, caribou were easily speared from canoes.

Fish were caught with hooks and in gill nets laboriously woven by the women from rawhide or the tough bast (inner bark) of the willow.[4] In some areas fish weirs and traps were also used. In winter holes were chopped in the ice with horn chisels so that nets could be set or the hook and line used.

Methods of preparing and preserving food were also similar throughout the subarctic. Meat was either roasted or "stone boiled" in bark or leather containers. After a large hunt extra meat was dried and cached on platforms or in trees, or it was pounded into a flour, mixed with fat to become pemmican, and stored. Surplus fish were automatically preserved in cold weather by quick freezing in the open air. In summer they were sliced open into thin slabs for drying on racks with the aid of the sun and a smoky fire.

The hides of caribou and moose were cured by the women and sewn with sinew into tunics, leggings, moccasins, and mittens, as well as being used for tipi coverings. Rawhide was cut into long strips for snowshoe lacings. Strips of furred hide from small animals such as hare were netted to form tunics or capes. From the bones and antlers of caribou, moose, and deer were made various tools and utensils, such as needles, awls, chisels, ladles, and skin scrapers. With knives and shavers of stone, bone, and antler, or even of beaver teeth, split lengths of wood were whittled into snowshoe frames; bows, arrow shafts, and spear shafts; ribs, thwarts, gunwales, and bottom sheathing of bark-covered canoes; planks for the hand-pulled toboggans. (The dog team drawing a toboggan is apparently a postcontact development.)

Hide or bark-covered tipis served as shelters throughout the subarctic. In the east, dome-shaped or ridge-pole lodges were also used, and double brush-covered lean-tos were sometimes used in the west.

The arduousness of the tasks and the mobility demanded by the food quest meant few luxuries. Yet people always took time for elaboration of the beautiful, the meaningful, and the enjoyable. Tools and utensils were sometimes decorated. Clothing was adorned with dyed porcupine quills, and the Montagnais-Naskapi used paint as well. Decorative extras were often incorporated in the shaping of the snowshoe "tail," and here, as elsewhere, expert craftsmanship was appreciated and respected.

The people found great pleasure in games and dancing, particularly in the summer, when different groups might gather for courtship and festivities. Celebrations were held when a youth killed his first large game animal. Shamanistic performances, too, were occasions for relaxation and enjoyment. The Algonkians (but not the Athapaskans) enjoyed a good steam bath, produced by pouring cold water over hot stones in a small lodge set up for the purpose. The long northern evenings, spent sitting or reclining around the fire on a floor of spruce or hemlock boughs, were times for talk and storytelling.

Later in this chapter aboriginal social organization is considered in detail. Briefly, social arrangements and relations within and between groups were flexible and egalitarian. Men of wisdom, supernatural powers, and hunting ability attracted followers, but as "the first among equals." The gross "tribal" names by which the subarctic forest Indians are today known do not reflect the significant territorial entities of early times. Large areas were inhabited by small autonomous regional groups that commonly numbered a few score members each.[5] They were usually loosely related to surrounding groups through intermarriage, economic dependence in times of local scarcities, linguistic affinity, and some feeling of ethnic identity.

A large kill from a herd of migratory caribou or an extensive fish run enabled the regional group of one hundred or more to stay together for a period; but when game was scarce or scattered, the people separated into smaller groups of perhaps only three or four nuclear families and spread out to cover a larger area. Such groups were in touch with each other and ready to help one another in case of trouble. The shifting of "membership" between groups was apparently easy and common, and people felt free to hunt outside their usual areas in time of shortage.

Aboriginally, before the exacerbations of European contact, intergroup hostilities were apparently at a minimum. For the most part it was with alien language groups, such as the Eskimo, that occasional skirmishes occurred. The more usual practice, however, was for each group simply to keep its distance from the other.

The Course of Indian-European Relations

The hunters of the subarctic forest have not suffered armed coercion or forced removal by Europeans. The climate and physiography of subarctic Canada have frustrated the usual North American pattern of intrusion and takeover of the land by Europeans for livestock raising or farming. Instead, the greatest single product of the north has been fur, and the course of Indian relations with the Europeans, and later with Euro-Canadians, has in the main followed from the fur trade. Where whites have moved onto Indian lands, it has been primarily as competing trappers. Only on the southern margin have they preempted lands rich in fur-bearing animals, notably those lying close to Euro-Canadian fishing villages on the north shore of the St. Lawrence River in eastern Canada. Other Euro-Canadian economic activities—mainly mining, lumbering, fishing, and other extractive industries—have intruded only in limited portions of the northland, and only within the last few decades.

The history of Indian-European relations in boreal Canada has unrolled over four and a half centuries, and it is interwoven with the emergence of the western European nations as commercial, and then industrial, world powers. From the first exchanges between Algonkians and French fishermen near the mouth of the St. Lawrence River to the building of an enormous air base at Goose Bay and the opening of an iron mine in the heart of the interior, the Labrador Peninsula itself exemplifies what the course of history has meant to the Indian of the Canadian north. The main direction of the European penetration in Canada was westward. Thus, into the twentieth century most of the Labrador Peninsula remained as isolated from the mainstream of contact and change as any region below the Arctic. Not until the nineteenth century were permanent trading posts set up in the central and northeastern portions of the peninsula, the same period in which the first posts were being established along the Mackenzie River in the far Northwest. In 1926, when the ethnologist William Duncan Strong wintered with a northern Naskapi band, its members were less committed to a trapping and trading economy than were some of the Indians of the Northwest.

The fur-hungry Europeans followed three successive routes of access to the Indians of the subarctic: first, the St. Lawrence River; second, the northern sea passage into Hudson Bay and its southern extension, James Bay; and third, the continental river-lake-and-portage route into the interior Canadian northwest. The opening of each of these routes

Naskapi man mending a fishnet; Northwest River, Labrador
(photo by Richard Leacock).

serves to establish the date of the inception of early contacts in, respectively, the St. Lawrence region, the lands draining into Hudson Bay, and the Mackenzie River basin.

On the whole, conditions of life and culture contact for the Indians throughout Canada's boreal forest have changed slowly. Three major phases of contact relations and responses can be discerned: the era of early contacts, the stabilized fur and mission stage, and the government-industrial stage. The southern Montagnais situated along the northern shore of the St. Lawrence River were involved much earlier in the fur trade than were the rest of the peoples of the subarctic forest. For the former, face-to-face contact began around 1500, more than 250 years earlier than it did for Athapaskan groups of the farthest Northwest. For most parts of the north the beginning of the stabilized fur and mission stage can be placed about the time of the establishment of effective hegemony by the Hudson's Bay Company in 1821. In general, the inception of the present government-industrial stage can be dated about 1940, although again, the Montagnais of the upper St. Lawrence experienced the encroachment of Euro-Canadian populations and modern industry earlier than did the rest of the northern Indians.

ERA OF EARLY CONTACTS

The era of early contacts begins in the upper St. Lawrence valley in 1534 and, elsewhere, generally after 1670 up to 1789. The end date is around 1820.

> Without Iron, man is weak, very weak, but armed with Iron, he becomes the Lord of the Earth, no other metal can take its place.—David Thompson's Narrative, 1784–1812

For the Indians the labor saved by iron chisels, knives, and axes was vast, and the knowledge that fur gained iron sped ahead of the European's presence. In 1534 Cartier could not dispel with cannon shot the Micmac Indians, who waved furs on sticks to entice him ashore and who "showed marvelously great pleasure in possessing and obtaining these iron wares and other commodities." From the beginning the tenor of contact between Indian and European in the subarctic forest was one of mutual trade advantage.

Some difference in early contact conditions from the east to the far Northwest followed from the fact that the fur trade came later to the west. This meant not only that the imperial contest between France and England was no longer a significant factor in Indian-European relations but also that trading practices were fully regularized and that the period of entrepreneurial competition among traders was shorter. Furthermore, with the development of English commerce during the seventeenth century came the great royally chartered companies. One was the Hudson's Bay Company, which was granted by the British Crown trading monopoly and powers of war and peace over "Rupert's Land," all the territory draining into Hudson Bay.[6] "The Honourable Company" at once became a powerful protagonist in the history of the Canadian north.

At the beginning of the sixteenth century the first consequences of the European presence were already being felt by the Indians of the St. Lawrence valley. French fishing fleets were by then regularly working the Newfoundland banks, and they soon found their way into the St. Lawrence River. The fishermen habitually bartered furs with the Indians, and by mid-century there are references to vessels in the St. Lawrence River for the sole purpose of trading. During the latter part of the sixteenth century, competition for a monopoly of the fur trade developed, although no single company succeeded in maintaining it.

Around the turn of the seventeenth century the somewhat sporadic and uncertain trade of the St. Lawrence River region had shifted to a steady mutual involvement between the French and the Indians. Permanent French posts were established at Tadoussac in 1599, at Quebec in 1608, and farther up the St. Lawrence at Three Rivers, in order to reach the Hurons and Algonkins, in 1617. By the second decade some 1,000 ships in one year are estimated to have left Europe for trade and fishing along the American coasts, and accounts indicate that a considerable number were headed for the St. Lawrence. The Indians had learned to await the arrival of at least several ships before commencing to trade, in order to be in a stronger bargaining position. Montagnais summering on the St. Lawrence River traded with those Montagnais accustomed to summer at interior lakes, but some of the latter were beginning to make the trek to the river shore to obtain directly the tools, clothing, utensils, grain, and dried fruits offered in exchange for furs.

It was during this period, in 1610, that a lone Cree approached Henry Hudson's ice-locked ship in Hudson Bay with furs for trade, inaugurating the first direct contact in the Central zone of the subarctic (Mason, 1967, 6).

During most of the seventeenth century the fortunes of the fur trade and the warfare stemming from competition over it among the Iroquois, Algonkians, British, French, and Dutch dominated the history of the St. Lawrence River region. Algonkians' relations with Champlain, sent to establish a firm foothold in the upper St. Lawrence to assure the trade, were friendly, but measured. The Algonkin and Montagnais Indians persuaded him to accompany them on a retaliatory expedition against the Iroquois; yet his way was blocked by friendly but consistent noncooperation from the Algonkins and Hurons, who were protecting their position as middlemen in the trade with the westerly tribes.

The monopoly of the Indian middlemen over the Cree trade was finally broken through the efforts of two Frenchmen, Radisson and Grosseliers, but it was the English, as "the Governor and Company of Adventurers of England trading into Hudson's Bay," who reaped the benefits. In 1668, two years before the Hudson's Bay Company received its royal charter, Grosseliers had sailed to the southernmost waters of the Hudson Bay to build Fort Charles (now Fort Rupert, see map) for his English sponsors on the coast of James Bay. Other "factories" or "forts"[7] for the Northern Montagnais and Cree trade were soon established along the southern shores of Hudson Bay. The trading forts along the coast of Hudson Bay were year-round establishments. The governor of the post and two or three score workmen-artisan recruits from the British Isles formed a small community that was supplied by ship from England once a year.

By perhaps 1700 a few trade goods were reaching the Chipewyan through the Cree. In 1717 the Company built a log fort farther up the coast of Hudson Bay, in the mouth of the Churchill River, in an effort to provide a point of trade to which the "Northern Indians" (of the Chipewyan nation) might bring their furs safe from plunder by the Cree.

For almost one hundred years after founding, the Hudson's Bay Company maintained the policy of drawing inland Indians to its coastal forts to trade. By the last quarter of the eighteenth century, however, it was forced to establish inland posts to meet the competition of the Montreal "pedlars," entrepreneurial French and Scottish Canadians who followed the interior waterways by canoe to intercept the Cree and Chipewyan trade.

The Crees south and west of the Hudson Bay lowlands caught the brunt of the contest between "free traders" and the Hudson's Bay Company. The intense competition among these rivals brought about the debauching of these Cree groups with rum and, in some areas, the depletion of the beaver resources. The Athapaskans of the far Northwest were spared these tragic consequences of the fur rivalry, for north of Chipewyan lands there was little direct confrontation of rival traders.

Some of the most destructive consequences of the European presence in the era of early contacts were inadvertent; these were intertribal warfare and disease. The Iroquois, who first acted as middlemen in the fur trade, increasingly trespassed upon Montagnais territory, raiding villages and encampments. In conjunction with smallpox, they virtually wiped out some Indian bands, and any rumor that they were in the area caused terror and dispersal. Hostilities did not cease until the latter half of the seventeenth century. One hundred years later, first the Cree and then the Chipewyan played much the same role vis-à-vis the Northern Athapaskan peoples as had the Iroquois in the east. In the early 1780s smallpox swept the Cree groups and almost destroyed the Chipewyan who traded into the fort on the Churchill River. Influenza epidemics, tuberculosis, and other European-derived diseases also attacked northern Indian populations.

By the final quarter of the eighteenth century an enterprising group of Montrealers had joined together as the Northwest Company and were establishing inland trading posts the length of the overland waterway and portage route, through the Central zone into the Mackenzie drainage. In 1821 the Hudson's Bay Company absorbed the Northwest Company and established an effective trade monopoly over a newly enlarged domain.

THE STABILIZED FUR AND MISSION STAGE

The fur and mission stage is the longest era in the postcontact history of the subarctic Indians. In the upper St. Lawrence River valley it lasted from about 1670 to 1900, and in the rest of the northeast and in the central and northwest zones, from, roughly, 1820 to 1940. This stage lacks the dramatic upheavals in Indian life that characterize the preceding and following eras. It was a time of slow, relatively undisruptive change. The trends begun in early contact times were consolidated and routinized.

Two prime conditions of the contact situation in this era must be recognized. First, contact with the Western world was channeled preeminently through the few agents of the two major institutions: the church and the fur trade. Secondly, contact with these figures was infrequent, and most of the Indians most of the time pursued their activities apart from the presence of Europeans.

More indirect factors of change include nineteenth-century technological developments, increasing biological and cultural interpenetration between European and Indian peoples, and alterations in the formal political and legal relations between Indians and the Euro-Canadian governments. Even in the latter instance, however, formal change only slowly had consequences for Indian life.

The Fur Trade   By 1666 the disruption of Iroquois incursions into the southern part of the Labrador Peninsula was ended. The passage of the next 200 years was marked mainly by the slow extension of the fur trade east and north into remote parts of the peninsula.

From Labrador to the Rocky Mountains, the decade of the 1820s brought the effective monopoly of the fur trade by the Hudson's Bay Company. The liquor trade was ended, fur raiding had ceased, and the Indians entered into regularized relationships solely with the Company traders. In the days of fur competition, the giving of "credit," whereby the Indian is "grub-staked" for his winter trapping tour by the trader, had been an aggravation to The Honourable Company. Exploratory visits to rival posts, rum, or other persuasions often diverted the Indian's furs from the grub-staking trader. Now, with fifty years of complete monopoly, the Hudson's Bay Company was able to set prices and credit to its own advantage. Even after Rupert's Land and later territorial-commercial grants passed from the control of the Hudson's Bay Company to the Confederation of Canada after 1869, many large areas of the Northwest, the Central zone, and the Northeast saw no trading competition until after 1900. Revillon Frères in the James Bay region and

Northern Traders in the Northwest Territories were two large-scale competitors of the Bay that then entered the scene for a time.

Throughout the fur and mission period there was a continuing shift in the Indian standard of living toward greater and greater consumption of European commercial products. The pace of this changing standard of living was checked by two primary conditions: the price of furs,[8] which was in turn governed by the external market in combination with the amount of competition existent between traders in the different areas of the north; and the costs and energies involved in the transportation of goods from the European manufactories to the Indian lands. Especially in the Northwest the diversity of goods available for trade was limited by the high costs and slow methods of waterway transportation. As long as The Honourable Company controlled the fur trade of the Central zone and the Northwest, its goods were transported in the slow-moving York boats, towed by lines of Indian trackers. Renewed competition in the trade after 1870 was, Mason (1967, 8) suggests, a spur to the introduction of the steamboat in the waterways of the Central zone and the Northwest. In the later part of the era and up to the present only a very few roads and rail lines have penetrated northern Indian lands. It is the airplane, since World War II, that has more significantly affected transport of goods and persons.

Missionization   In the 1630s, with the arrival of the Jesuits, missionizing began on a large scale in the east. The Jesuit fathers made extensive trips into the interior, living and working with the Montagnais, who themselves took part in converting one another. In the early days missionary interest in the Indians was high, and attempts to transform the Indians of the St. Lawrence region into a settled agricultural population were strong. Convent schools were established, and zealous converts were taught a sense of guilt and sin that occasionally led to such extremes as self-flagellation and the beating of children. At the same time, however, there were conflicts between the priests and Indians over such things as traditional burial practices, and those Indians disposed to be suspicious of the new teachings questioned what relation they might have to the smallpox, which, it was aptly observed, followed the arrival of the Europeans and their alien beliefs (Bailey, 1937). As the French settlements grew, church interest waned in Indians who were committed to fur trapping and who were clearly not going to become agriculturalists. Over the years Indian culture developed a stable balance between aspects of Roman Catholic belief and ritual and traditional beliefs.

After 1641 roving Cree from the Central subarctic zone south of Hudson Bay were probably in occasional contact with the Jesuits of Sault Ste. Marie, where the waters of Lake Superior flow into the lower Great

Lakes. However, active missionization (by Catholics, Anglicans, and Wesleyans) did not encompass all the Cree until 200 years later (Mason, 1967, 6, 8).

Missionaries also entered the Mackenzie region in the middle of the nineteenth century. Anglican missionaries made some converts, but through the energetic proselytizing of the Oblate fathers, the Roman Catholic creed gained ascendancy among most of the Athapaskans. On the whole, Athapaskans quickly accepted formal conversion. The isolated Trout Lake band of Slave Indians was apparently the last group to convert in 1902 (Duchaussois, 1928, 326).

A few mission schools were established in the vast land. From each generation of Indian children a few were removed to mission school for years on end. For most the experience did little but give them a limited command of French or English before their inevitable return to the life of the "bush Indian."

Throughout the northern forest the interests of the church stood at variance with those of the traders. In the early days the position of the Jesuit fathers in the St. Lawrence area expressed certain contradictions besetting France herself, caught between short-range commercial interests and the interests of long-range colonization. The Jesuit desire to see their new "flock" settle in agricultural villages was contrary to the traders' desire for furs, and in particular the use of liquor as a trade-good was a bone of contention between the two. Later, in the Northwest, ethnic, occupational, and religious commitments combined to insure a lack of sympathy and, on occasion, overt antagonism between the Anglo-Protestant trader and the French Catholic missionary. Thus the two dominant forces in the north, the church and the fur trade, did not present a monolithic union, but rather two separate systems forced into uneasy association as each strove to manipulate the Indian for its own ends.

Interpenetration of Populations Throughout the fur and mission stage in the Labrador Peninsula, there was a gradual growth of coastal fishing settlements, peopled by the French along the St. Lawrence River and by British along the Atlantic coast. Frenchmen and Englishmen occasionally married Montagnais-Naskapi women, either then to join an Indian band or to remain with their Indian wives in one of the coastal villages. Thus, when a "color line" began to be drawn between peoples during the late nineteenth century, persons of common Indian and European descent were to be found on both sides.

In the lands south and west of Hudson Bay, the many unions between Indian women and Euro-Canadian workers in the fur trade created a culturally and ethnically distinct population, the métis. The Cree-

French métis of the Prairie Provinces became a political and cultural force that reached its denouement in the Riel rebellions of 1869–1870 and 1884–1885. The Athapaskan lands saw the creation of an indigenous métis from Scottish and Athapaskan unions, as well as penetration by Cree-French métis following the northward route of the fur trade. The trading settlements of the Northwest today include a distinguishable métis group, who have served for generations as cultural and linguistic middlemen between the European and the Indian (Slobodin, 1966).

Political Relations Between Indians and Government   The political events marking the emergence of Canada as a nation—the cession of French holdings to Great Britain in 1763, the union of Upper and Lower Canada in 1841, and the establishment of Canada as a federal union in 1867—did not markedly affect the Indians of the subarctic. However, at least two reserves were granted Montagnais of Quebec province in the

Naskapi man shaving planks for a canoe using a "crooked knife"; Northwest River, Labrador
(photo by Richard Leacock).

1850s before Confederation (Laviolette, 1955). Altogether four were established, all on the north shore of the St. Lawrence River. Portions of the reserve populations continued to move over the land as trappers, as do the Montagnais-Naskapi groups who do not hold reserves.

Soon after Confederation the government of Canada concluded the first of several treaties with the Indians of northern Ontario, the Prairie Provinces (Manitoba, Saskatchewan, and Alberta), and the Northwest Territories. By "taking treaty," the signatory Indian groups did thereby, in the usual parlance, "cede, release, surrender and yield up His [Her] Majesty . . . and successors forever all the lands" included within defined limits. The treaties included provisos for the establishment of reserves for the Indian bands involved. A "reserve" (as defined in the Canadian Indian Act of 1951) means "a tract of land, the legal title to which is vested in His [Her] Majesty, that has been set apart . . . for the use and benefit of a band." Except in the Northwest Territories, many forest Indian groups have "taken" reserves.

The last treaty involving major populations, the Athapaskan peoples north of Great Slave Lake, was made in 1921. Only after that date were the first representatives of governmental authority, in the form of the Royal Canadian Mounted Police (R.C.M.P.), established at the fourteen main trading settlements of the Mackenzie River region. Not until the late 1960s, as the government began to negotiate with the Indians of the Northwest Territories to accept reserves or other forms of compensation in return for the land they relinquished upon "taking treaty," were these Indians faced with the full implications of the act.

THE GOVERNMENT-INDUSTRIAL STAGE

In the upper St. Lawrence River area, the inception of the government-industrial stage can be set about 1900. In the rest of the north it has emerged since 1940. This stage is marked by the precedence of mining and other extractive industries over fur trapping as the major source of revenue in the subarctic and by the proliferation of governmental agencies and activities dealing with the health, education, and welfare of Indians. Both aspects of the new era carry profound implications for Indian life. As the monetary importance of fur production recedes, so does the Indian's "value" as the significant laborer in the land. As government in its many branches assumes responsibility for the alleviation of the poverty, illiteracy, and health problems of the Indian, it increasingly requires the involvement of the Indian—predominantly in the form of accommodation and submission to the Euro-Canadian sociocultural system.

In 1939, the value of other forms of production for the first time exceeded that of furs in the Northwest Territories. Limited industrial exploration and activity in the north had begun, of course, in earlier decades, especially along the St. Lawrence River valley. There, when lumber mills began to appear after 1900 at river mouths entering the St. Lawrence, spreading eastward from the city of Quebec, the majority of the Indians simply moved back to their traditional inland country. Occasional mineral exploration in the northern forests drew a few Indians into the orbit of the coming era as guides for white prospectors. Apparently no Indians gained lasting profit from such ventures.

In spite of the acceleration since 1940 the face of the land as yet bears only occasional marks of industrial development. But at scattered points large-scale enterprises promise to change increasingly the nature of northern life for both Indians and whites. In Labrador, for example, the air base at Goose Bay and, especially, the iron mine at Schefferville in the north-central interior are rapidly attracting immigrants, not only Euro-Canadians from urban centers and Labrador villages but Indians from the hinterland as well. Comparable settlements in the Northwest are Churchill, a port on Hudson Bay, and Yellowknife on Great Slave Lake. (See map.) Founded as a gold-strike boom-town in the mid-1930s, Yellowknife is today, with a population of 5,000, the largest town in the Northwest Territories and has recently become the seat of territorial government.

It has been more common, however, for sites of extractive industry —of precious and base metals, oil and pitchblende—to sustain only a small company of imported southern Canadians. Some such settlements may have only a brief life. Commercial fishing and small-scale lumbering for a local or regional market are the main sorts of nonmineral industries to be found in a few places in the north. On the whole, northern industrial enterprises are staffed overwhelmingly by transient white workers from southern Canada.

The Canadian government assumed almost no responsibility for the economic and physical well-being of the northern Indians or for their education and preparation for the modern world until after World War II. A very few mission "hospitals" (often lacking resident physicians) and church residential schools provided the scant services offered the Indian. The Grenfell Mission hospitals, first established in 1892 to service the English settlements in Newfoundland-Labrador, have recently received government aid to render minimal services to the Indians as well. Recently, too, a government nursing service has been set up for summer visitations and inoculations of the Indians in Quebec province.

As late as 1950 there were only eight physicians serving the far-flung populations of the entire Northwest Territories (Phillips, 1967, 156). The establishment of government nursing stations at some trading settlements and increments in government medical personnel are bringing more adequate prevention and treatment of disease and creating a substantial increase in the native populaton.

Federal social services and subsidies available to Indians, introduced mainly since World War II, include the Family Allowance, the old age pension, and welfare allotments to the indigent and ill. One of the most significant advances in governmental responsibility has been the founding of day schools and hostels. For the first time, in the decade of the 1960s the majority of northern Indian children were exposed to at least a few years of formal schooling, although language barriers between teachers and students, inappropriate curriculum, and other contingencies have inhibited the effectiveness of the experience.

In the trading-post communities, the number of Euro-Canadians, though in the minority, has grown significantly in the last ten to twenty years. For the most part, they are civil servants (and their families), whose jobs relate directly to Indians and Indian activities. Schoolteachers, welfare officers, Indian agents, doctors, nurses, R.C.M.P., game wardens, are usually given assignments for only one or a few years in any one community or area. Their level and style of living are geared to the standards of urban Canada. Well fed and housed, secure in income and future, and rich by Indian standards, these mentors and administrators live in daily contact with the Indians—and in another world.

Changes in Indian Life

ECONOMY

In the era of early contacts the occasional taking of fur-bearing animals sufficed to provide the Indians with more efficient tools and utensils than those they could produce themselves, as well as some luxury goods. In the seventeenth century, items in the St. Lawrence trade included iron arrowheads, bodkins, knives, picks, swords, hatchets, and kettles; various items of clothing; and foods such as raisins and prunes, Indian corn, biscuits, and tobacco. In the early Cree and Chipewyan trade, luxury items were more limited, and foodstuffs are missing from the trading indents of the early 1700s (Davies, 1965). In later times lard, flour, and tea became staples for all Indians of the north.

During the stabilized fur and mission era the Indians of the Canadian subarctic became more regularly committed to fur trapping as reliance on trade goods grew. Firearms were a more and more common acquisition, although some use of the bow and arrow for small game continued into the twentieth century. The steel trap largely replaced deadfalls in Indian commercial trapping only after 1900 (Knight, 1968, 20; Helm, field notes). Photographs show that by the 1890s the Indians of the Northwest wore European clothing except for their moccasins, mitts, and winter caribou parkas; but canvas had not yet replaced the bark covering on canoes or the caribou skins on the lodges. By this time a few Indian families had built log cabins at the trading post or at rich fishing sites.

In the government-industrial era dependence on manufactured goods is all but complete. Carpenter's tools, tin or iron stoves, outboard motors, gasoline lanterns, battery-powered radios, and hand-cranked sewing machines are standard household items, along with many lesser goods, such as plastic plates and oilcloth table covers. Permanent dwellings, including outbuildings for storage, house most families and their expanded inventory of possessions. But low income severely restricts acquisition of commercial products. Those families who continue to live in "the bush" most of the year rely heavily on fish and game. Their protein-rich diet is substantially more nutritious than that of post-dwelling Indians, who must spend much of their income for store food.

Industrial development has allowed a few Indians to become wage laborers for either a primary or supplementary source of income. On the north shore of the St. Lawrence River lumbering has become the mainstay for some 800 Indians. They live in permanent houses and have been given the title to their lands along the Bersimis River, although some still elect to work as trappers. In the rest of the Labrador Peninsula, the air base at Goose Bay and the interior iron mine at Schefferville (see map) afford new ways of earning a living for a small number. A few score Indians of the Northwest Territories work, or have worked, in the gold mines and similar industries, but in no numbers comparable to those in the lumbering industry of the St. Lawrence region. Recently janitorial jobs in government installations and unskilled or semiskilled seasonal labor on government road building or housing construction have become available for a few others, as is true throughout the north.

For the great majority of northern Indian families, _earned_ income is derived mainly from fur trapping. This is not a matter of choice. To the handicaps of illiteracy, inexperience, and, for many, monolingualism is added the fact that very few opportunities for wage work exist at the local level.

The general depression of fur prices, coupled in some areas with government restrictions on take, means that even the present low level of living of the northern Indian cannot be maintained without additional sources of income through wage work or government subsidy measures.

Most northern Indian families receive a significant percentage of total income from the federal welfare programs. For three neighboring trading-post communities on the east side of James Bay, Knight (1968, 101) records the per capita income for one year (1960–1961) within the narrow range of $207 to $225. The proportion of income in the same communities derived from wages versus trapping versus welfare was, in that order, 40 percent, 22 percent, 38 percent; 17 percent, 36 percent, 48 percent; and 7 percent, 50 percent, 42 percent (round figures). Probably the ratios at most northern posts fall within these ranges.

COMMUNITY AND KIN

Subsistence and Settlement Patterns It might seem that trapping fur-bearing animals for trade could readily be substituted for a self-sufficient hunting economy without affecting the deployment of people over the land. In fact, however, the two activities involve different animals (of the fur-bearing animals, only beaver was important aboriginally as a source of food and clothing) and call for different patterns of exploitation and settlement. For the mobile populations of the north, "settlement" is employed broadly, to comprise "any place occupied by one or more individuals for one or more nights, for any purpose that falls within the ordinary, expected and predictable round of activities for the society in question" (Campbell, 1968).[9]

Hunting and fishing for direct use and consumption can most effectively be done by free-ranging groups who gather together when they are able and spread out when they must and who share game animals within the group. Trapping at maximum efficiency, on the other hand, involves setting a line of 200 to 400 steel traps, with huts, or "tilts," at each day's journey along the line, and laying in a store of supplies at the beginning of the trapping season so that the trapper can work the line consistently. It means leaving one's family with sufficient store foods and other supplies at some permanent location and then trapping alone. Few Indians have wholly adopted this way of life, for they prefer to trap in pairs and to spend more time with their families.

The northern Indians have made various arrangements and compromises between their traditional hunters' way of life and the demands of trapping for trade.[10] These solutions derive from such considerations as the remoteness of the trapping ground from the trading post, the degree of commitment to trade goods and thereby to trapping, the plentifulness of fur-bearing animals, and the amount of credit that will be given by the trader. Moreover, in the last two decades two additional considerations have become increasingly important. The establishment of government winter day schools at trading communities necessitates that families stay in the village all winter if their children are to go to school. So, also, the post office in the trading community, from whence issues the monthly

Family Allowance checks and other subsidies, holds more and more families at the trading post.

Across subarctic Canada five main kinds of trapping-subsistence-settlement accommodations by Indian families can be identified:

1. A summer camp of tents at the trading-post site. The Indian families spend the winter in small groups in a number of trapping areas. Women and children may be left behind at a winter camp part way between the post (and its supply of staples) and the trapping area.
2. A permanent dwelling, usually a log cabin, maintained for summer occupation, at the point of trade. Winter dispersal is as in item 1.
3. A year-round base in an all-Indian hamlet occupied by several related families. From this base the men go out with their partners on trapping tours. The summer sojourn at the trading post tends to be brief; the women and children are usually left behind at the hamlet.
4. A year-round family residence at the trading post, from which male partners carry out a series of trapping tours.
5. A year-round post dwelling. Husband and wife do local subsistence snaring and fishing. The husband sets a few traps locally and seeks odd jobs, but usually the family is heavily dependent on welfare subsidies. For bilinguals a few relatively permanent jobs as store clerks or janitors may be available.

The first form of accommodation was typical for all Indians in earlier times. Continuing commitment to bush life and food and the remoteness of good trapping ground from the post encourage the first and second accommodations. The same considerations apply to the all-Indian bush hamlet, which has been a minority accommodation of the Athapaskans of the Mackenzie region for several decades.[11] Rogers (personal communication) reports that several all-Indian bush hamlets have been recently established in northern Ontario (Central zone).

The last two forms of settlement accommodation are emerging responses to the decline of the fur trade and to the government subsidies and services provided at the point of trade in recent years. They are being further encouraged in the 1960s by the accelerated federal housing program for Indians.

Within the total complement of Indians trading into some northern posts, all of these accommodations may be present. The fifth form is essentially an abandonment of trapping as a livelihood and, at most, is represented at any post by only a minority of the families that contain able-bodied males.

Finally, a sixth form of accommodation must be noted. It is represented by the few educated northern Indians who hold clerical jobs in white-dominant communities and by that small, but growing, number who are employed full time in mining or other industries. These Indians have moved beyond any involvement in trapping and the gaining of subsistence from the land. As Indian job seekers enter urban and industrial settings, they are apt to encounter discriminatory attitudes and practices from segments of the dominant white population.

Problems in Ethnological Reconstruction of Traditional Social Organization In the anthropological literature on northern Indian societies, questions have been raised about the degree and kinds of changes wrought on aboriginal social organization by conditions of culture contact.

Some, but by no means all, Algonkian groups recognize the exclusive use of trapping territories by family groups, ordinarily father and sons and/or sons-in-law. Some earlier investigators believed this so-called family hunting-territory system to be aboriginal, but contemporary ethnologists agree that it stems from postcontact alteration of the exploitative pattern, due primarily to commitment to fur trapping (Leacock, 1954; Rogers, 1963; for a variant interpretation, see Knight, 1965). In fact, the "territories" are, properly speaking, not *hunting* grounds, but areas surrounding traplines. All non-fur resources—meat, fish, berries, bark, and so forth—are available to anyone. The Mackenzie Athapaskans recognize no individual or family claim to any tract or resource, including fur animal locales.

The weight of evidence indicates that traditionally among the northern Indians all resources were available to anyone in need of them. When there was no game in one area, the people who had been hunting there felt no compunction in moving into an area hunted by a neighboring group. Nor did there seem to be any resentment or unwillingness on the part of the hosts to share the resources in the area they were hunting (Le Jeune [1632–33] in Thwaites, 1906; Fidler [1791–92] in Tyrrell, 1934).

We have spoken of "groups" hunting in "areas." But was there only one kind of socio-territorial group? What was the nature of the ties within and between groups that had some sort of socio-territorial identity? To what extent have such groups and the relations among them changed in historic times? Problems of the adequacy of the historical documentation and of allowable inference from the historic era into the aboriginal always render reconstruction problematic. But, working from the ethnographic and historical record and taking into account those factors in the contact situation known, or likely, to have induced changes, we find the following broad picture:

Northern Indians spent parts of the year, especially in late winter, in small groups of a few, perhaps three or four, nuclear families. No doubt in the past, as at present, primary kin ties ordinarily linked one conjugal

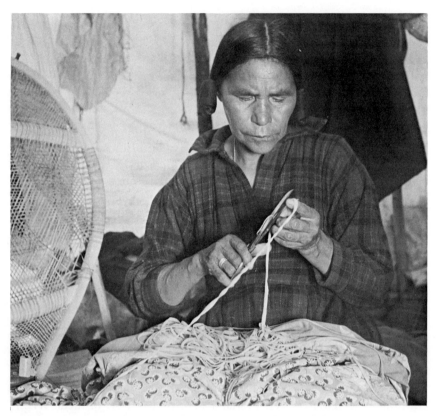

Naskapi woman cutting rawhide strips; Northwest River, Labrador
(photo by Richard Leacock).

pair in the group to another.[12] We may borrow Rogers' (1963) term
hunting group for such a collection of persons. Other terms that encompass this kind of arrangement are *task group* and *local band* (Helm,
1965), *lodge group* or *tent group* (Leacock, 1954, 1970), and *microcosmic
group* (Honigmann, 1946). In early times such small groupings may have
been more characteristic of the Montagnais-Naskapi of the Northeast.
According to the diary of Father Le Jeune, a Jesuit who spent the winter
of 1632–1633 with a group of Montagnais-Naskapi, in the difficult late
winter season larger groupings had to split up into single lodge groups.
This meant that three or four nuclear families lived together in one
large tipi. The historical record suggests that other peoples, such as the
Chipewyans described by Samuel Hearne in the 1770s, who could rely
heavily on great herds of caribou, spent less of the winter season in small
hunting groups. Evidence assembled by Rogers (1966) and Knight (1965)
indicates that in the Central zone the shifting game cover within historic

times, notably the lessening of the caribou population and incursion of moose, has encouraged the smaller hunting group as the effective exploitative unit. Finally, as we have seen, the introduction of commercial trapping has throughout the north encouraged fragmentation of the people into small groups over the land beyond the necessities of subsistence hunting.

As the ecology of the seasons permitted, several such small hunting groups came together to form what may be called a *band* (Rogers, 1963), *regional band* (Helm, 1965), or *macrocosmic group* (Honigmann, 1946). Summer fish runs and spring and fall caribou migrations, for example, provided ecological opportunity for gathering. Characteristically, the band region was shaped by the drainage pattern of the land, as the summer canoe routes and winter trails alike followed lakes and streams. Extrapolating from the composition of such regional bands today, we can say that the relations between the smaller hunting groups within the regional band involved many ties of blood and marriage; when the small local groups gathered together, they met not only as neighbors but as kinsmen. Both early and contemporary accounts record the shifting of some families from "residence" in one small hunting group to another when the band broke into smaller units again.

Early documentation on the Montagnais-Naskapi reveals summer meetings of two regional bands, at which time there would also be interchanges of members. Dogribs recount how, a few generations ago, Dogribs from other regions, even Indians from other "tribes," assembled in the traditional lands of the Edge-of-the-Woods Dogrib to exploit the great caribou herd during its spring retreat to the barrens.

Within the historic era several bands converged upon a single point of trade. These aggregations, unfortunately, are also usually called *bands* in the literature. It is impossible to determine with precision what the broadest extent of societal identity and named identification may have been prior to the advent of the trading post, as it has so heavily influenced territorial orientations and alignments. Some of the trading post aggregates of today are large—500 persons or more. The group known today as the "Dogrib Rae Band" is one of the largest, numbering over 1,200 in 1967.

It has been proposed on theoretical grounds that northern Indian social organization was more narrowly structured in aboriginal times, that the combined practices of virilocality and reciprocal band exogamy, resulting in cross-cousin marriage (at first or several removes) between two bands, were the norm, and that these practices were attenuated or destroyed by disruptions following from European contact (Service, 1962, 66–68, 84–89). It cannot be gainsaid that early warfare and continuing disease created crises, depopulation, and dislocations in the various groups over the centuries. Nevertheless, such data as there are for the past and present indicate that considerable flexibility in social organization always existed.

The practice of first cross-cousin marriage has been reported for the remote Barren Ground Naskapi of northeastern Labrador (Strong, 1929) and also for the Mistassini (a Montagnais group) of south-central Quebec (Speck, 1931; Rogers, 1960, 28). A high incidence of first and second cross-cousin marriage is well documented for neighboring Northern Ojibwa groups (Dunning, 1959; Hallowell, 1937). There is, however, no convincing historical or ethnographic evidence of the preference for or regular practice of cross-cousin marriage among the Athapaskans of the Mackenzie drainage.[13]

Today both virilocal and uxorilocal forms of residence are present among the Northern Algonkians and Athapaskans. That is, a married couple resides with a group containing members of the husband's natal family and/or of the wife's, but seldom stays apart from both. Traditionally, temporary uxorilocality as a part of bride service was widely practiced. It is with regard to an "ideal" of residence (after bride service) that the ethnographic data or, at least, ethnographers' assessments vary from one area to another. Leacock (1955, 1970) sees uxorilocality dominant in preference and practice among the Montagnais of earlier times, with a shift in practice toward virilocality in response to the growing importance of the fur trade and other acculturative pressures. Rogers (1963, 56) states that virilocal composition (father and married sons) of the hunting group is the Mistassini ideal, but that it is rarely achieved. Helm's Athapaskan informants cite bride service (involving temporary uxorilocality) as proper and traditional, but go no further in espousing residence norms. We have already noted that nuclear families may shift from one hunting group or regional band to another. For all areas ethnographers agree that de facto decisions and trends regarding uxorilocal versus virilocal residence are overwhelmingly governed by the immediate demographic and ecologic situation. In the northern Indian case, "residence rules" loom much larger for anthropological theorists than they do for the Indians.

Yet another dimension of the question of unilocal residence norms brings in the related problem of imputed *band exogamy*. A meaningful application of the concept of band exogamy (the practice of which would naturally occur under a unilocal band residence rule) depends upon being able to distinguish "the band" in northern Indian society. As previously indicated, the band is an exceedingly slippery entity. Is it the small hunting group of a few families who, being closely related, often offer no potential spouse for a marriageable member? Or is it the larger, more enduring but often dispersed regional group? By present evidence, the larger the group—as, for example, regional bands and the bigger bush hamlets—the greater the amount of marriage within the group. This seems to be a simple consequence of the larger number of potential spouses available within larger socio-territorial units (Rogers, 1963; Helm, 1965). In such cases, the preponderance of in-marriage within larger units obviates the question of unilocal residence.

Residence alternatives, including the option of changing hunting groups and regional band affiliation, and a wide choice of marriage partners (including cross-cousins) promote far-flung societal connections. Such multiple affiliations radiating out from each immediate local group would seem an efficient solution toward physical and social survival in the subarctic forest, where under aboriginal conditions small-group crises, such as the threat of starvation, might occur every several years.

Leadership Within the northern Indian group—be it hunting group, regional band, or trading-post assemblage—there is little role differentiation involved in the process of making and implementing decisions. This holds equally for Algonkians and Athapaskans. It is through the achievement of consensus that the body of responsible adult males functions as the policy-making group. By traditional standards a few men attain a position of influence and prestige among their fellows and are accorded a title designating leadership. Such leadership rests solely on realistic appraisal of, and deference to, their wisdom and judgment and their ability as providers for the group (MacNeish, 1956; Rogers, 1965).

In the early days, traders attempted to appoint a prestigious hunter as "captain," in the hope that he would exert pressure upon his followers to produce more furs. However, in Hearne's opinion of the Chipewyan and Cree captains in 1776:

> . . . the authority of these great men, when absent from the Company's Factory, never extends beyond their own family; and the trifling respect which is shown them by their countrymen during their residence at the Factory, proceeds only from motives of interest, . . . [1958, 186]

The Canadian government has by fiat established political administrative units among the northern peoples. A set of peoples, usually those trading into the same post, are designated a band by the government. Each band chooses by ballot or consensus a head chief and councillors to represent the people to the government. The chief, or councillor, is given no effective power by the government, and native tradition accords him no authority beyond that flowing from his character and ability. Where government impositions have crosscut traditional patterns of leadership, as in sections of the Northeast (Leacock, 1958), the Indians explicitly distinguish between "outside chiefs" and "inside chiefs."

Among the northern peoples the ethic of intra-community and interpersonal relations is "every man his own boss." Even the recognized leader does not presume the right to dominate others. Rather, there is a feeling-out of one another's wishes and needs, and an assessment of group requirements and possibilities, in order to arrive at consensus when action must be taken. Concordance of interest and the assumption that the right thing for the group will not be in conflict with what is right for the individual mean that the practice of "democracy" as an explicit majority rule is alien to the northern Indians.

Religion   Northern Algonkians and Athapaskans alike lacked church or cult. They shared belief in guardian spirits that gave "power" to men and aided adepts in curing, weather and game control, and divination. The Athapaskans, however, lacked the Algonkian belief in anthropomorphic gods and the Windigo, or cannibal monster, and did not share the complexities of Algonkian "bear ceremonialism" (see Hallowell, 1926) and the practice of the "shaking tent rite."

Missionization of generations of Indians has attenuated the aboriginal magico-religious system; but many beliefs are still firmly held, and the performance of shamanistic marvels is not entirely a thing of the past. In the shaking tent rite of the Montagnais-Naskapi an older man (occasionally it used to be a woman) discourses in the dark with supernaturals while his audience sits quietly around him in a specially constructed lodge. Although the rite was optimistically reported by a Jesuit missionary to have disappeared in the seventeenth century, in 1951 Leacock lay in her shelter listening to Indians leaving the shaking tent. Hearing them murmur and laugh about what the various gods had said (Djokobish had been very witty that evening), it struck her how similar they sounded to the people coming out of a rural theater and repeating the interesting and enjoyable parts of the film they had just seen.

The ceremonies of Christianity equally engage the Indian community. Sunday services or Mass are enjoyable social occasions. In the bush many groups hold their own Sunday prayer services, led by a respected man. In Protestant Indian groups, an Indian may hold the post of deacon as well.

Commitment to aspects of two belief systems, traditional and Christian, poses no problem for most northern Indians, who see them as complementary rather then conflicting. In any case, the northern Indians are not a people whose lives are pervaded by religious anxieties and moral perplexities. The ethics of the northern Indians have remained grounded in the pragmatic and cooperative mores of the traditional life.

Among the Athapaskans, prophet movements, syncretizing aspects of native and Christian belief, ritual, and morals, emerge from time to time. Within the last few years a vigorous movement has spread from Beaver-Slave populations in the province of Alberta to Dogrib and Great

Bear Lake Indians farther north. Each group has a major prophet who commands a set of adherents. And among the Dogrib, at least, those skeptical of the personal claims of the prophet nonetheless enjoy the group events he has introduced. The current Athapaskan prophet movement has striking correspondences to the movements that swept the Indian tribes of the American West in the last century. The Dogrib prophet, for example, has been to heaven and spoken with God. He has taken as his charge the regeneration of his people through public preaching and exhortation to virtue (notably, abstention from alcohol), and the leading of group religious ceremonies of prayer, offerings, and dancing.

Outside of the realm of religious belief and practice, the impact of Christianity has probably been strongest on the institution of marriage, by abolishing the practice of polygyny. Although full conformity to the restrictive sexual standards of official Christianity is often lacking, virtually all Indians of today recognize monogamous marriage in the church as the only valid union.

Prospects

In the course of contact all northern Indian groups have sustained blows to their social and cultural fabric. Yet some, the Rae Dogribs for example, have to the present day largely escaped demoralization. At the other extreme is a group such as the Duck Lake band of Chipewyan, removed from their hunting grounds to the town of Churchill. Apathy, drunkenness, intergenerational hostility, petty crime, and abject poverty have in a short fifteen years been the fruits of well-meaning but catastrophic government intervention in the lives of a hunting and trapping band (Koolage, 1968).

At the local level, then, the Indians of the north face the future with varying degrees of ethnic morale and integrity. But in terms of the economics of contemporary life, for all northern Indians "the government-industrial stage" might better be called the "the welfare era." Neither government nor Indian wants increasing dependency on the part of the native population, but the trend is clear. Above all else, the basic problem is that the Canadian subarctic is not self-supporting.[14] Decades of verbiage about the tremendous economic potential of northern Canada have not changed the fact that it is a subsidized land, whose resources have provided extremely few Indians or whites with an adequate living by modern standards. The fur trade can no longer meet the Indian's rising economic aspirations. And if the Indian is fully encouraged to participate in industrial developments of the future, it would seem likely to be at the price of his local and ethnic identity.

It is through political mobilization that the Indian has the best chance to hold to his ethnic integrity and to foster his economic well-being. Here, the concerns of the northern Indians are at one with those of the Indians of all of Canada. In recent years a few of the more politically oriented Indians across the Canadian north have begun to phrase their common identity in social and political terms. But, even for these concerned Indians, barriers of isolation, poverty, and, for the older generation, illiteracy combine to block intertribal communication of mutual problems and goals and the development of strategies. Without the growing activism and strength of sophisticated, bicultural Indians of southern Canada, there would be little hope that the isolated people of the north could withstand the juggernaut of the Euro-Canadian world. Such recent developments as the establishment of the Canadian Indian Brotherhood may for the first time create an effective Pan-Indian political force for the benefit of northern and southern Indians alike.

NOTES

[1] The authors are indebted to Edward S. Rogers of the Royal Ontario Museum for his critical commentary on a draft of this paper. Our grateful acknowledgment of his help should not imply that Dr. Rogers is in full accord with all emphases, summations, and judgments offered in this paper.

[2] The boundaries of the "Sub-Arctic Forest" on Kroeber's (1939) Map 4, "Vegetation Areas after Shantz-Zon (1924) and Dominion of Canada Map (1930)," most nearly approximate the "tribal" boundaries of the peoples treated in this paper. In their most southerly extensions, the Montagnais, Cree, and Chipewyan penetrate the "Eastern Coniferous Forest" and the "Northwestern Coniferous Forest," which rim the southern flanks of the "Sub-Arctic Forest" as delimited in Map 4. All three of these vegetational zones, and others, are comprised under the major northern forest region defined as "Boreal" in a more recent publication of the Canadian Forestry Branch (Rowe, 1959, 9, 12–35).

[3] Two groups of Chipewyan affinities that are described in the early literature are the Caribou Eaters and the Yellowknives.

[4] Hearne (1958, 170) provides an early description of rawhide and bast gill nets in use among, respectively, the Chipewyan and Dogrib in the 1770s. Rogers (1966, 111) questions whether the gill net was aboriginal among the subarctic Algonkians.

[5] The population density for the boreal forest area as a whole is the lowest in the New World. It is even lower than in the Eskimo area, where, forbidding as the Arctic may look to the city dweller, the supply of sea mammals is more plentiful and reliable than the supply of forest animals of the taiga. The aboriginal population density among Canadian hunters is estimated at 1.35 per

100 square kilometers; for the Eskimo it was 4.02, and it reached 43.3 in aboriginal California (Kroeber, 1939, 143).

[6] MacKay reminds us that

> Several generations of fur traders toiled, sweated and froze in "the northwest part of America" before the geographical significance of this grant was comprehended, and even then dimly. . . . On a modern map the Company received those portions of the Provinces of Ontario and Quebec north of the Laurentian watershed and west of the Labrador boundary, the whole of Manitoba, most of Saskatchewan, the southern half of Alberta, and a large portion of the Northwest Territories; in all a great basin of one million, four hundred and eighty-six thousand square miles [1966, 38–39].

In 1821 the Company received "license to trade" over an even vaster territory. "It was, in effect, the control of nearly half a continent: today's Dominion of Canada, except the Great Lakes–St. Lawrence basin and the maritime provinces" (MacKay, 1966, 159).

[7] Trading posts established by the Hudson's Bay Company are commonly called "forts," even in the present day. Insofar as a "fort" had a military aspect in early times in the subarctic, it was more in anticipation of hostilities with the French than with Indians.

[8] The standard of value used in the exchange of furs for goods was in terms of beaver pelts, standardized as the Made Beaver (MB). Money was not used in trading.

[9] In anthropological discourse the term "residence" has been preempted to refer to the social directives, notably kin relationships, that determine the disposition of individuals or conjugal pairs among households or communities. For this reason the term "settlement," rather than "residence," is here employed to refer to spatial-ecological locus per se.

[10] The authors' assessments in this section agree closely with Van Stone's (1963) examination of "Changing Patterns of Indian Trapping in the Canadian Subarctic." See also Rogers (1963) and Knight (1968, 59).

[11] It may be that the particular ecology and terrain of the Northwest has encouraged this form of trapping–subsistence–settlement compromise. The Mackenzie River serves as an artery of easy travel to the post, and the several hamlets of the Slave Indians are situated on its banks. In Dogrib country the hamlets are found at shoreline locales on major lakes where there is a year-round fish supply.

[12] See Helm (1965) on contemporary Athapaskan groups. Leacock's (1955) and Knight's (1968) diagrams of such units among the Natashquan Montagnais and Rupert House Cree, respectively, also manifest, as the predominant structure, bilateral ties of sibling to sibling and son or daughter to parents between constituent conjugal pairs.

[13] In an earlier study (MacNeish, 1960) Helm suggested that the kin terminology systems of contemporary Athapaskans of the Arctic Drainage might reflect the former practice of cross-cousin marriage. Subsequent ethnographic work among the Dogrib and data on Hare marriages (Helm, 1968) analyzed since that study have not supported this interpretation.

14 "Mr. Chrétien [Minister of Indian Affairs and Northern Development] reminded the people of the North that the people of Canada provide 95 percent or more of the money that is spent in the North . . ." Item in *News of the North,* August 28, 1969.

REFERENCES

BAILEY, A. G.
1937 The conflict of European and eastern Algonkian cultures, 1504–1700. Publications of the New Brunswick Museum, Monographic Series no. 2.

CAMPBELL, JOHN M.
1968 Territoriality among ancient hunters: interpretations from ethnography and nature. *In* Anthropological archaeology in the Americas. Anthropological Society of Washington [D.C.]. pp. 1–21.

DAVIES, K. G.
1965 Letters from Hudson Bay, 1703–40. London: Publications of the Hudson's Bay Record Society XXV.

DUCHAUSSOIS, R. P.
1928 Aux glaces polaires. Paris: Éditions SPES.

DUNNING, R. W.
1959 Social and economic change among the northern Ojibwa. Toronto: University of Toronto Press.

HALLOWELL, A. I.
1926 Bear ceremonialism in the western hemisphere. American Anthropologist 28:1–175.
1937 Cross-cousin marriage in the Lake Winnipeg area. Philadelphia Anthropological Society 1:95–110.

HEARNE, SAMUEL
1958 A journey from Prince of Wales Fort in Hudson's Bay to the northern ocean . . . in the years 1769, 1770, 1771 and 1772. Richard Glover, ed. Toronto: Macmillan.

HELM, JUNE
1965 Bilaterality in the socio-territorial organization of the Arctic Drainage Dene. Ethnology 4:361–385.
1968 The statistics of kin marriage: a non-Australian example. *In* Man the hunter. I. Devore and R. Lee, eds. Chicago: Aldine. pp. 216–217.

HONIGMANN, JOHN J.
1946 Ethnology and acculturation of the Fort Nelson Slave. Yale University Publications in Anthropology, no. 51. New Haven: Yale University Press.
1962 Foodways in a muskeg community. Northern Coordination and Research Centre Publication NCRC-62-1. Ottawa: Department of Northern Affairs and National Resources.

KNIGHT, ROLF

1965 A re-examination of hunting, trapping and territoriality among the northeastern Algonkian Indians. *In* Man, culture and animals. A. P. Vayda and A. Leeds, eds. Washington, D.C.: AAAS Publication 78.

1968 Ecological factors in changing economy and social organization among the Rupert House Cree. Anthropology Papers of the National Museum of Canada, no. 15.

KOOLAGE, WILLIAM W., JR.

1968 Chipewyan Indians of Camp-10. *In* Ethnographic study of Churchill. John J. Honigmann, ed. Institute for Research in Social Science, University of North Carolina at Chapel Hill. pp. 61–127 (mimeographed).

KROEBER, A. L.

1939 Cultural and natural areas of native North America. Berkeley: University of California Press.

LAVIOLETTE, GONTRAN

1955 Notes on the aborigines of the province of Quebec. Anthropologica 1:198–212.

LEACOCK, ELEANOR

1954 The Montagnais "hunting territory" and the fur trade. American Anthropological Association, Memoir 78.

1955 Matrilocality in a simple hunting economy (Montagnais-Naskapi). Southwestern Journal of Anthropology 2:31–48.

1958 Status among the Montagnais-Naskapi of Labrador. Ethnohistory 2 (3).

1970 The Naskapi band. *In* Band societies: proceedings of the conference on band organization. David Damas, ed. National Museum of Canada, Bulletin 228.

MACKAY, DOUGLAS

1966 The Honourable Company (rev. ed.). Toronto: McClelland and Stewart.

MACNEISH, JUNE HELM

1956 Leadership among the northeastern Athabascans. Anthropologica 2:131–163.

1960 Kin terms of Arctic Drainage Dene: Hare, Slavey, Chipewyan. American Anthropologist 62:279–295.

MASON, LEONARD

1967 The swampy Cree: a study in acculturation. Anthropology Papers of the National Museum of Canada, no. 13.

PHILLIPS, R. A. J.

1967 Canada's north. Toronto: Macmillan.

ROGERS, EDWARD S.

1963 The hunting group–hunting territory complex among the Mistassini Indians. National Museum of Canada, Bulletin 195.

1965 Leadership among the Indians of eastern subarctic Canada. Anthropologica 7:263–284.

1966 Subsistence areas of the Cree-Ojibwa of the eastern subarctic: a preliminary study. National Museum of Canada, Bulletin 204. pp. 87–118.

1967 The material culture of the Mistassini. National Museum of Canada, Bulletin 218.

ROGERS, EDWARD S., AND JEAN H. ROGERS
1960 The individual in Mistassini society from birth to death. National Museum of Canada, Bulletin 190.

ROWE, J. S.
1959 Forest regions of Canada. Ottawa: Department of Northern Affairs and National Resources Forestry Branch, Bulletin 123.

SERVICE, ELMAN
1962 Primitive social organization. New York: Random House.

SLOBODIN, RICHARD
1966 Métis of the Mackenzie District. Ottawa: Canadian Research Centre for Anthropology, Saint-Paul University.

SPECK, FRANK G.
1931 Montagnais-Naskapi bands and early Eskimo distribution in the Labrador Peninsula. American Anthropologist 33:557–600.

STRONG, W. D.
1929 Cross-cousin marriage and the culture of the northeastern Algonkians. American Anthropologist 31:277–88.

THWAITES, R. G., ED.
1906 The Jesuit relations and allied documents. Cleveland: The Burrow Brothers Company. vol. 7.

TYRRELL, J. B., ED.
1934 Peter Fidler's journal of a journey with the Chepawyans or Northern Indians, to the Slave Lake, and to the east and west of the Slave River, in 1791 and 2. Toronto: Champlain Society 21:495–555.

VAN STONE, JAMES W.
1963 Changing patterns of Indian trapping in the Canadian subarctic. Arctic 16 (3):159–174.

13 *The Changing Eskimo World*

CHARLES C. HUGHES

No discussion of recent Eskimo ethnohistory can be seriously presented without placing it in the larger context of political relations between the major world powers that confront each other in the circumpolar region (Figure 13.1). While it is true that a number of critical trends in sociocultural change (both of a directed and of an inadvertent nature) were becoming apparent by the 1930s, it was the post–World War II differences between the Soviet Union and the United States (to speak only of the two principal parties to this confrontation) that provided the major impetus for the infusion into many areas of the north of huge quantities of material resources and large numbers of outsiders. In its functional effects this invasion marks a decisive turning point in the culture history of most aboriginal Eskimo groups of Canada and those in many areas of Alaska.

So decisive a turning point is not as clearly evident in the case of Greenland and that small corner of the Soviet Union inhabited by Eskimos, some coastline portions of the Chukotski Peninsula. In the two latter areas programs of directed socioeconomic development had begun much earlier than the mainly defense-inspired developments of the past twenty-five years or so in Canada and Alaska. In Greenland, the program of reconstruction of the aboriginal population can be said in some ways to have started over a century ago. In the Soviet Union major steps toward the reorganization of the indigenous culture and communities began in the 1920s and gathered momentum during the 1930s, reaching fruition in the last two decades.

The purpose of this paper is to review salient developments, particularly those of a socioeconomic nature, in the sociocultural life of Eskimo communities over the last generation—from the middle years of the 1930s to the mid-1960s. For even taking into consideration the above comments regarding Greenland and the Soviet Union, this has been the pivotal generation in the culture history of practically all Eskimos. Major socioeconomic, contact, governmental-administrative, and situational factors and trends in Greenland, Canada, and Alaska will be examined, and developments in the Soviet Union among that small fringe of the Eskimo population living in the Chukotski Peninsula will be briefly summarized.[1]

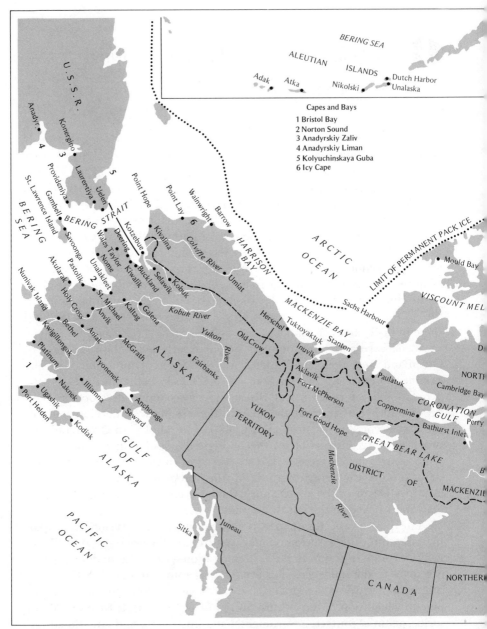

Figure 13.1. Major Eskimo and non-Eskimo settlements in Greenland, Canada, Alaska, and Northeastern Siberia. (Adapted from Arctic, vol. 7, 1954. The original map was prepared by the Surveys and Mapping Branch of the Canadian Department of Energy, Mines, and Resources.)

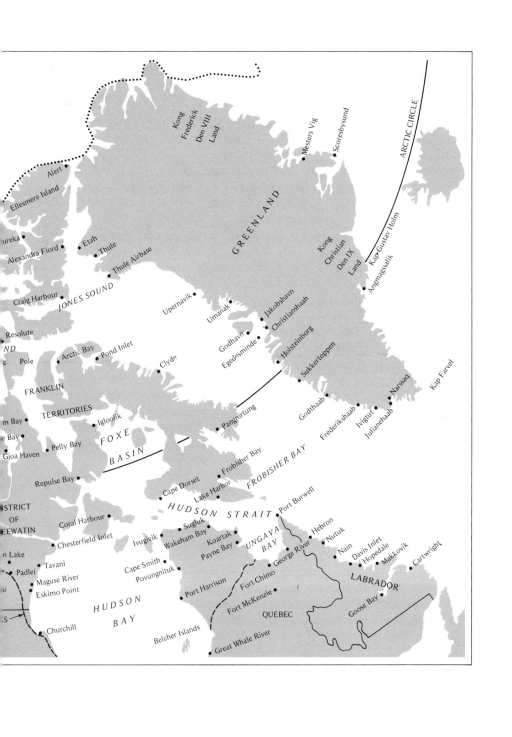

Greenland

If we are to understand the full sweep of Eskimo-white contacts and their functional aftermath, then with Greenland we must extend our purview back for one hundred years or more. Indeed, given some 400 years of settlement by Norsemen on Greenland's southwestern coast in the eleventh to fifteenth centuries, we would be justified in saying that "acculturational" influences were present 1,000 years ago. In fact, however, apparently little aside from contributions to the gene pool remains from that period of Eskimo-white relations; for by the sixteenth century, European explorers found only the weathered remains of Norse houses and farms. But in 1721 the permanence of the Danish presence was begun by the missionary Hans Egede, who had come to bring religion to his countrymen and who remained to plant the seeds of what we now rhetorically label "development"—that is, education, medical services, economic rationality, a stable social order—in an Eskimo population living under ecological and cultural conditions more similar to those in Alaska than in Canada. That is to say, there was a greater tendency toward permanent village locations, a relatively richer resource habitat, and probably a more complex ceremonial and ritual life. In social organization, however, the fairly typical picture seems to have prevailed —bilaterality, with extended families and loosely defined kindreds as the predominant forms of kin-based social units (although there are hints of at least an incipient unilineality in some areas).

By the middle of the nineteenth century there was a regularly published newspaper printed in the—by then transcribed—Eskimo language. Missions and trading stations had been established along the coasts, and from the early days there existed a firm government policy with respect to the types of materials and influences that would be allowed to enter the lives of Greenlanders. Through the government-controlled posts Eskimo material culture began to be markedly changed in weapons of the hunt, domestic and household equipment, and personal attire.

Concomitantly, governmental and political institutions were altered by the early contacts. Although the informal political structure remained the primary instrument of social control at the settlement level, by the 1860s there had been set up formal local, regional, and provincial representative governing councils. The local bodies consisted of the minister (as chairman), trading post manager, district medical officer (if there was one), post assistant, and a number of elected Greenlanders. The boards were responsible for maintaining law and order, providing leadership, administering relief, and making loans for housing (with funds for such activities financed by a tax on native products sold through the store). With some modifications in structure and scope of activity this basic pattern of governance and policy formation continued until the early 1950s, at which time a greater centralization of administration occurred throughout Greenland as a result of a Royal Commission study. With the creation of one governing body (the National Council) for the entire island, and thirteen local Municipal Councils, Greenland formally became a county, instead of a colony, of Denmark, represented in the Danish parliament by two elected Greenlanders.

Thus, while it is possible to discuss recent changes in the life situation and institutional forms of the Greenland Eskimos in recent times, it should be done only to give increased emphasis or saliency to one or another aspect of Eskimo relations with the European world. Contact relations have changed in degree and scope, not kind.

There is a point on a continuum of this nature, however, when differences in degree may, indeed, result in differences in kind; and it may well be that the total complex of activities and events occurring in Greenland during the past twenty years has begun to reach that point. Such a possibility can be seen in the widespread changes in the most basic subsistence activities—from a life dependent upon hunting to one dependent upon fishing, mining, farming, animal husbandry, or service occupations. The warming of the waters of the Labrador Sea and Davis Strait—a change in habitat that began a half-century ago—has resulted in a major shift in feeding areas of seals, to such an extent that they no longer frequent the southwestern coast of Greenland (the most populous section) as much as they did even until recent times. Along with this, there is an overall decline in absolute numbers of seals taken, even in outlying areas farther north. But it would seem that in this case, nature, which has taken away, has also provided; for cod and other types of fish have begun to appear in such quantity in the Davis Strait that during the last generation most southern Greenlanders have turned to being fishermen on the sea rather than hunters after the seal. By 1955 nearly 600 Greenlanders owned a motorboat of some type, most of them the 24-foot fishing craft, and purchase of fishing equipment is facilitated by government loan. The cod, halibut, salmon, and other varieties of fish caught with such craft are processed in some seventy to eighty landing depots and canneries.

For a people who throughout their culture history have excelled as hunters, the most drastic of all subsistence changes have been those toward farming, animal husbandry, and mining. In recent years the number of sheep in the more southerly districts has risen to 27,000, and farming— although posing difficult problems in that habitat due to the short growing season—has become an established activity of significant proportions. Greenlanders have also been involved as workers in the mining operations in the northwest and eastern areas of the island.

Both inadvertently and by design, the new subsistence activities have led to a greater concentration of population than had been the case with the scattered hunting population and to the development of urban, or, at least, semiurban, settlements. An explicit aim of recent government policy has been to bring together the scattered populations into larger communities of (eventually) 3,000 to 4,000 inhabitants, towns built upon fishing as the main economic base. One explicit reason for creating the larger communities was to allow easier provision of educational, medical, and governmental services. There are about a dozen such main population centers, all located in the southerly part of the western coastal areas. These settlements, termed "colonies," are visited regularly by supply and passenger vessels from Denmark; vary in size from 100 to 2,000 people; and are the sites of administrative, social, political, and economic institutions. From about 40 to 300 inhabitants is the range of population in the trading centers, of which there are over 50. Each of these communities receives supplies from the colonies, is the center for municipal activities, and has a church, school, and store. The smallest type of population unit is represented by the remaining 106 settlements, which are dependent upon the larger units for necessary economic and social services. An active voluntary associational life exists even in the villages, supported by extensive communicational contacts with the larger centers. Radios, movies, clubs, sports activities, study circles, and other activities fill the social scene.

In all these communities a full set of social, recreational, and welfare exists in addition to the formal governmental, political and economic infrastructure. In the area of social welfare, for example, old age assistance is available to all persons over fifty-five years old incapable of supporting themselves, and there is indigent relief and orphan assistance. A social security plan exists, and loans are made by the government for the building of houses. Medical facilities have existed for a long time, in the form of hospitals, sanatoriums, and, more recently, floating clinics to service outlying areas. Schooling, too, has long been a part of the Greenlanders' scene, and it is claimed that of the adult population everyone is literate in the Greenlandic language and some 10 to 15 percent speak Danish. A recent article by Hobart and Brant (1966) summarizes the changes since World War II in this key institutional area. The changes include importation of significantly more teachers from Denmark (rising from 1 in 1955 to 300 in 1965), a demographic change having many implications for the power structure; community segmentation; and the setting of role models in the small, outlying communities. In the following terms the authors summarize their principal conclusions as to the—on the whole—beneficent effects of the new educational developments:

> . . . education in Greenland is genuinely integrative and synthetic: students are taught to read and write in both Greenlandic and Danish; they study both Greenlandic and Western European geography, history, literature, art and music; vocational training includes both traditional Greenlandic and modern industrial skills; and instruction takes place in both languages. Thus in terms of language, attitudes, and skills, the education seeks to make available to the student two alternatives and two possible identities, the Greenlandic and the Danish. No doubt few are able to actualize both very fully, but the significant point is that the school does not prejudge the alternatives. Insofar as possible it makes both available to the student [1966, p. 56].

Thus, the general picture of recent change in Greenland (excepting Thule, in the northwest, and Angmagssalik, on the east coast, both of which present special cases)[2] is that of a more or less sustained supervisory control and guidance of development processes by the Danish government. This transition has been responsive to two basic types of ecologic imperatives: the restructuring of the psychocultural environment, whereby Greenlandic Eskimos have progressively internalized and acted in accord with sociocultural patterns adopted from the outside, primarily from Danish models; and secondly, the ecologic-geographic, whereby the natural resource environment has changed in some fundamental ways, and such changes, in turn, have had pervasive consequences for community organization and settlement patterns. It is apparent also, however, that transition to another life pattern has not come without dislocation and difficulty, for there are clear problems of social deviance and alcoholism, particularly among the young people, and a rise in the invidious use of Eskimo-Danish differences as the foci for crystallizing resentments and a vague sense of ethnic disparagement (see Hughes, 1965, 4–12).

Canada

Of all the Eskimos, those living in Canada have had their lives most changed in the shortest time by events of recent years. Their involvement with fox trapping (beginning around the turn of the century) had brought about decline in the degree of self-sufficiency that had characterized them when first contacted by Europeans (Jenness, 1964). It was not really until World War II, however, that most Canadian Eskimos had thrust upon them a sustained (if unbalanced) exposure to the dominant outside culture—material, social, and ideational. Of course, there had been contacts of one sort or another with the outside world for up to 300 years, especially by the coastal groups of Labrador, the Ungava Peninsula, and the eastern islands of the archipelago. But it can be asserted with a fair degree of applicability that among the Eskimos living in Canada there were more groups that had been little changed from precontact days than anywhere else, largely due to their extreme isolation from land and water transportation routes and to the resource poverty of their habitat. Some groups in the area around the Melville Peninsula, for example, had not even acquired rifles as late as the 1920s.

BACKGROUND[3]

With several important exceptions, all the principal elements of Pan-Eskimo culture were found in precontact Canada: a primary orientation to sea-mammal hunting, alternating, where conditions warranted, with inland caribou hunting; fishing as a seasonal pattern; collecting and gathering of various food items; migratory settlement patterns; ingenious technology, including the domed snow house, detachable harpoon, and so forth; highly animistic, relatively unformalized religious institutions, with many taboos and ritual prescriptions and with the shaman often the most important sociopolitical leader as well as the religious intermediary; relatively "loose" social organization in the sense of a few sharply specified behavior patterns or kinship-political social units; and the development of hunting and sharing partnerships of various types. There were, of course, local variations on these common elements. Examples were the greater focus of the Caribou Eskimos' economic life upon the migratory caribou herds in the Barren Grounds to the west of Hudson Bay, the almost complete dependence upon the seal as the principal winter game animal necessitated by the poorer habitat of the Netsilik and other groups in the central archipelago, and the greater dependence upon fishing than upon hunting seals in the Mackenzie Delta.

The main exceptions to the above outline of the "Eskimo culture pattern" lie in the area of social organization. For example, in precontact times in Canada there did not develop the permanent villages of the size and stability known on the Bering Sea coast of Alaska, Siberia, and, also apparently, in western Greenland. In these latter areas seasonal migration for fishing, caribou hunting, or pursuit of sea mammals occurred, but it did so from a central village of considerable size. In Canada there was far less development of permanency in any one locality for a relatively large group of people, "large" in this case being one hundred or so persons. The "villages" that have developed in the Canadian Eskimo north recently have been stimulated mainly by the building of a trading post, mission, or, in the past two decades, a defense or welfare installation as the core around which the population has settled in a framework of ecological relations rather different from the past.

Two other social organizational features of precontact times tended to be distinctive of Canada as compared to other areas. For one thing, Eskimo groups in Canada lacked the permanent men's house, or the community ceremonial house, found in Alaska. Nor in Canada were there clear instances, although intriguing hints exist, of the unilinear descent groups seen in some of the Bering coastal villages, both in Alaska and Siberia. Bilateral descent, reflected in a loosely structured personal kindred, and locality groups with the extended family as their core were the main features of traditional social organization among most Canadian Eskimos.

SETTLEMENT PATTERNS

The seemingly inexorable gathering of many of the approximately 12,000 Canadian Eskimos into more permanent villages and the attrition of outlying settlements has been going on to some extent for a generation, but it has become greatly accelerated in the years since World War II. Several factors are involved, but especially important have been better access to medical, mission, trading, and welfare services and opportunities for employment afforded by military construction. A number of small weather stations and airfields were built across the Canadian Arctic prior to the major construction activity—that of the Distant Early Warning (DEW) line of radar installations; and at least one of these, Frobisher Bay on Baffin Island, has continued as a principal governmental and commercial center (see Honigmann 1965 for a recent comprehensive study of Eskimos living in such quasi-urban conditions).

But several other population centers have also grown over the last decade and a half. In 1961 the Mackenzie Delta area was estimated to have a population of almost 1,800 Eskimos, and Eskimo Point, Churchill, Great Whale River, and other communities along the shoreline of Hudson Bay have similarly been foci for Eskimos moving in from outlying settlements. Although the populations involved are not large by outside standards, ranging from 100 to 300 in most cases, they are highly anomalous by traditional central Eskimo terms. There are, of course, still seasonally wandering bands that move about the hinterland and that are oriented to a trading and administrative center. But what has markedly changed is the degree of their dependence upon such centers and the increased tendency to establish permanent settlements at that point in search of wage opportunities or welfare assistance.

Elderly Eskimo hunter with seal he has just killed
(photo by Charles C. Hughes).

Noting this development, several investigators have spoken of the
evolving distinction between "camp" and "settlement" Eskimos—a distinction that it would have been impossible to make meaningfully on any
large scale a generation ago.

ECOLOGICAL AND ECONOMIC FEATURES

There had been, of course, some important changes in the Canadian
Eskimos' relationships to their environment prior to the most recent
period of intensive culture contact, World War II, changes induced

largely by technological factors. From the earliest appearance of whaling ships and commercial outposts (such as those of the Hudson's Bay Company), more efficient subsistence weapons and tools were eagerly sought and assiduously used—rifles, ammunition, steel fishhooks, knives, nets, and, more recently, boats and outboard motors. These technological items in themselves have had long-range ecological and social effects on the local scene. Some of the functional effects of widespread use of the rifle, for example, can be seen in greater slaughter of several animal species, sometimes reaching dangerous proportions insofar as overall resource depletion is concerned. This was especially true with regard to caribou herds, but it also applied to the sea mammals. With greatly increased fire power a single man could kill many more animals than could many men hunting together with more primitive weapons. And frequently such a single, rifle-equipped hunter could not retrieve the carcasses because the rifle had no harpoon line attached to it, thus further undercutting the animal resource base. Another concomitant of the enhancement of the individual hunter's capabilities brought about by the new technology was the decline in such cooperative hunting activities as the joint hunting at the seal-hole on the winter ice or at the caribou ambuscade.

Whereas the rifle and other hunting implements of this nature, as well as the boat and outboard motor, did not of themselves initiate basic changes in the use of environmental resources, other influences from the impinging dominant culture did. The most important of these in the early days (beginning at the turn of the century) has been the demand for arctic fox furs. When white commercial interests entered into the northland, trapping of this animal, originally a worthless scavenger in the eyes of the Eskimos, became the axis on which much of Eskimo life revolved. And establishment of permanent Hudson's Bay Company posts in Eskimo territory, beginning in the first years of this century, greatly increased the dependence of Eskimos on the outside world. It encouraged their use of imported foods, tools, and household and personal equipment; reliance on outside supply and administrative centers; concentration of population around trading posts; and commitment to a fluctuating, inconstant, and in recent years unrewarding economic base (due to the lowered market values of the product). Jenness (1964), in particular, has well documented—and deplored—the extent to which there was no control over how much Eskimo life was allowed to become pervasively dependent on such a whimsical resource base as the fur trade in the Canadian Arctic.

Another important effect of involvement in the fur trade insofar as traditional Eskimo social structure was concerned was, again, the enhancement of the socioeconomic position of the individual hunter-trapper. The basic activity did not require corporate effort—one man could set and tend a trapline—although sometimes there were overtones of this nature associated with it, such as father-son partnerships in ownership of the trapline. The subsistence imperatives did not therefore combine to produce joint social action upon which any sense of communal solidarity beyond the family might be based.

Although neither wage work nor the handling of money is new to the Canadian Eskimos, the extent to which both have become influential since the end of World War II is unprecedented and represents a critical aspect of change from the past. The first significant amount of wage work for Eskimos occurred during World War II, when some were hired as laborers on military defense base construction. And despite their employment in various other industrial developments since then (for example, in mines in Rankin inlet, the Ungava Bay, or Labrador areas), it is still military activities of the larger society that have provided much of the wage employment in postwar years. The most portentous of these activities was construction of the Distant Early Warning radar line (DEW), which, beginning in the mid-1950s, was built through the center of what were then some of the most isolated Eskimo regions in upper Canada. The building of this electronic network of about fifty stations, stretching from western Alaska to the eastern shore of Baffin Island, was the occasion for a massive display of the capabilities and wealth of industrial technology, for many stations were constructed under the most difficult weather and geographic conditions imaginable, at a total cost of $600,000,000.

It was stipulated by the Canadian government that the sites should disrupt Eskimo life as little as possible and be located out in the hinterland away from settlements. Some Eskimos, however, did work in various jobs, and the sites still provide a few maintenance jobs in various localities, in addition to the annual supply operations that give work in stevedoring, lightering, and similar activities. And the overall impact on Eskimo life could not so easily be controlled by administrative fiat, for certainly one telling effect of the DEW line activity was not so much in the actual jobs it gave as in the illustration it provided of the scope and capabilities of the technological culture of the outside world and of the measure of the dominant society's control over the environment demonstrated by the largely weather-immune housing, military facilities, and defense activities. In addition, the inevitable waste and by-products of such a large-scale operation enhanced the affluent image of the dominant culture and provided much material useful to the Eskimos—wood, for example, which had always been an exceedingly scarce and valuable item to groups living along the northern shores of Keewatin.

Much of this waste material is used in the construction of shanty-type houses in some of the larger centers, such as Frobisher Bay—an aspect of the technological invasion that has helped contribute to the much-increased public health problems in all Eskimo groups over the past two decades. The problems of inadequate housing in the wage centers are well recognized by responsible officials, and in some places attempts have been made to provide low-cost yet effective housing. Such attempts have included experimenting with unusual materials, such as styrofoam and corrugated aluminum, with the blubber lamp used for heating.

The most ambitious development along this line, however, has involved the construction not only of new houses but of an entirely new community. The relocation of a large part of the population of old Aklavik into the new town of Inuvik on the Mackenzie Delta began in the mid-1950s; the new town was planned and constructed to demonstrate the most recent engineering developments relevant to living in the north. Other recent relocation efforts have been directed at establishing small Eskimo groups from southerly regions in new locations in the northern archipelago at more favorable hunting and subsistence sites, such as Pond Inlet on Baffin Island. Earlier, during the 1930s, attempts at similar relocations were largely unsuccessful (Jenness, 1964).

Wages have provided only part—though an important part—of cash income in the past two decades. One of the principal dependable forms of government assistance has been through direct cash outlay. The family allowance, instituted in 1944, pays from $6 to $10 for each qualified child in a family. In addition, there is old-age and indigent support. In view of the highly fluctuating fox fur market, the importance of this dependable form of cash income cannot be underestimated. Further, in recent years there has been a great spurt in production and sale of Canadian Eskimo arts and crafts, particularly stone and ivory carving. Building on an older economic pattern, the greater exploitation of this activity was started in the early 1950s through outside stimulation of the soapstone carvers of Port Harrison and Povungnituk, on the eastern shore of Hudson Bay. Now a supervised program is found in many other places, such as Cape Dorset, and encouragement and sale of arts and crafts is a typical function of many of the recently formed community cooperatives.

These cooperatives in themselves are a dramatic example of some of the qualitatively different trends in socioeconomic change that have occurred among the Canadian Eskimos, and their development and florescence can be dated only from the early 1960s.[4] It was in 1959 that the first Eskimo cooperative was formed—at George River, on the eastern shore of Ungava Bay—and the success evident in that trial effort stimulated further deliberate activity by the Industrial Division of the Canadian Department of Northern Affairs and Natural Resources (now called the Department of Indian Affairs and Northern Development) toward establishment of production, marketing, and consumers' cooperatives in other Eskimo villages. By 1963 there were some eighteen such cooperatives in sixteen Eskimo communities across the Canadian north, dealing with such diverse activities and materials as the freezing or canning of native food, Arctic char, for example; the processing of lumber; and the marketing of arts and crafts. Since 1963 several other cooperatives have been added and other activities have been undertaken by the cooperatives: running a bakery, handling a tourist service, building houses, freighting, and boat building.[5] By March 1967, some twenty-five cooperatives and three cooperative credit organizations were operating in the Canadian north—twenty-one in the Northwest Territories and seven in the province of Quebec. The activities of these community organizations are supervised and facilitated by staff of the Cooperative Development Program of the Department of Indian Affairs. There is probably much truth in the statement made in a recent report:

> . . . there is strong evidence now that cooperatives have demonstrated themselves valuable tools for the people in the Canadian north. Through their participation in cooperative activities, the members of Arctic cooperatives now have many more opportunities to manage their own business matters than ever before. They have an opportunity to participate in decision-making concerning ordering their own supplies; in organizing production; in setting prices; and to play a more active and positive part in all aspects of their community [Sprudzs, 1967].

If, indeed, the Eskimos, through their actions in forming and participating in cooperatives, are becoming more adept in the arts of formal self-government and decision making with respect to the environing society, then another critical step will have been taken in terms of cultural change. The idea of a *formal* structure to which is assigned responsibility for debating, coordinating, and deciding community-wide issues of change and development is a new one in Canadian Eskimo culture history. All formal structures that have existed hitherto —church mission, Hudson's Bay Company post management, Royal Canadian Mounted Police—have been imposed from the outside. Any kind of formal indigenous sociopolitical development functioning successfully in response to the newer pressures was decidedly at a low ebb until the past decade.

Finally, along with the husbanding of traditional sources of food— the sea and land mammals—steps are being taken to initiate new industries in the north to obviate emigration southward. Based on the moderate success of Greenlanders in the raising of sheep, for example, attempts were made at one point to introduce animal husbandry in the Fort Chimo area. Also, experiments in domesticating the musk ox and introducing the yak were studied, and efforts have been made to develop the herding of reindeer as a reliable food supplement to replace dependence upon the unpredictable caribou herds.

EDUCATION AND HEALTH

After World War II the government began to establish schools throughout the north to replace or supplement the mission schools that had provided all education up to that point. In the 1950s a large number of schools were built in the bigger population centers—both day and boarding schools—and higher education facilities in the south were opened to Eskimo young people. In 1959 it was reported that of the Eskimo population outside the Mackenzie Delta there were 1,900 children from six to sixteen years old; of these, some 860 were registered in the twenty schools then operating.

Despite these developments, some contend that the formal aspects of the schooling experience may in certain respects militate against, rather than facilitate, an easier coping with the social and technical complexities of the dominant society. Focusing their comments vis-à-vis the Canadian scene on the western Arctic, but depicting a picture not seriously askew for the rest of the Canadian north, Hobart and Brant find major deficiencies in the communicational and overall coordinative aspects of the educational process:

> The educational system which has come into existence in the Western Arctic, at first under Mission auspices, and, since 1952, increasingly under Federal auspices, contrasts as sharply with the Greenland system as have the Danish and the Canadian Arctic administrative philosophies. The Educational system in the Western Arctic is characterized by these features: continuous use of non-native teachers, in the past dominantly clergy, changing to lay teachers today; throughout its history, instruction given wholly in English; establishment and heavy utilization, from the beginnings, of residential schools, with latter-day emphasis upon large units; curriculum almost entirely oriented to the southern Canadian culture and value system; and minimal attempts to produce text materials appropriate to the Arctic [1966, 57].

In addition to developments in educational programs, medical activities have been stepped up through more regular examinations and prompter treatment of diseases, particularly tuberculosis, and establishment of nursing stations and hospitals in the north. This aspect of the organizational response to problems and sociocultural integration and development is thus directed at one of the most critical threats to the native population, a threat—disease—that has always afflicted the Eskimos, but one that has been greatly exacerbated in the past two decades by the exposure of native groups to many outside populations.

SOCIAL ORGANIZATIONAL FEATURES

Traditionally, the nuclear family was residentially as well as socioeconomically embedded in the bilateral extended family. But in the past two decades, except perhaps for scattered groups such as the Iglulik Eskimos, the outstanding trend in family composition and functioning as a basic social and economic unit is the growing independence of the nuclear family as a unit of both production and consumption. The influence of the rifle, trapline, net, and other technological importations in increasing the adaptive capability of the individual hunter has contributed to the decline in the economic reliance of a man on his male patrilineal kinsmen. And it was these relatives who traditionally formed the core of the residential unit, which was also the principal kinship and economic unit. These patrilineal groups, although still common as the basis for the local residence group, are now much less often the interdependent, corporate production units that performed most of the subsistence activities in the past. The rifle made individual caribou and seal hunting possible; nets undercut the need for coordinated group fishing at stone weirs; and trapping gave the opportunity for independent acquisition of cash income.

Not all sense of corporateness is lost, however, for widespread distribution of the animal products from the hunt still occurs among the extended kin group in the small, outlying communities. As in the past, in times of scarcity the distribution patterns may extend to the entire community. This is highly unusual in the normal course of events, however, especially in those "amalgamated," quasi-urban communities composed basically of several discrete local bands, such as Port Harrison or Sugluk, not to mention the even larger community of Frobisher Bay. In those situations the sense of overall "ingroup" identification has not yet developed to the point of reciprocal exchange of animal flesh throughout the community at large.

And with the involvement in a money economy, another factor has entered the picture. Money tends to be treated differently from traditional economic items, quite aside from the modifications in traditional sharing patterns that have occurred in complex communities. It is evaluated in a very different framework. In most places money is not shared or distributed beyond the immediate nuclear family; and, through its transposable nature it has further increased the independence of the nuclear family.

Some counter-trends to this picture of growing nuclear family independence should be noted, aside from the flourishing development of community cooperatives previously noted. In a few instances there has been development of new forms of social organization (or revitalizing of old ones) centering around the acquisition and operation of a motorized whaleboat or a Peterhead craft. This new form of technology has made possible cooperative hunting patterns traditionally unknown in certain groups, such as open-water, summer hunting of walruses and seals among the Iglulik and Netsilik Eskimos. Drawing upon the increased purchasing power created by fox trapping, nuclear family heads now can contribute toward the purchase and maintenance of larger boats. Usually the core of the crew consists of brothers from the same residential band, with the father or oldest brother the acknowledged leader, but sometimes outsiders are taken into the group. Occasionally the boat is not purchased and owned cooperatively, but rather is the property of a single man, who then hires crew members. In any case, in this situation the otherwise autonomizing effects of fox trapping have contributed toward the development of new social forms or the strengthening of older structures that were passing into disuse.

Along with the changes in economic activities of the kindred grouping has grown the tendency, noted above, toward permanence of settlement throughout the year in one or more localities, even though there are still seasonal hunting or fishing trips to outlying camps. The tendency toward populational concentration is widespread, despite occasional exceptions and even administrative orders against it in some instances. Now within most of these larger and more permanent settlements, members of bands or localized kindreds who have moved there tend to live together in the same part of the community, thereby creating the basis for one type of segmentation of the overall community, that is, community of origin. This has occurred, for example, in Sugluk and Povungnituk. In other places religious affiliation has provided a basis for community segmentation.

Thus, there exist trends that may, with time, culminate in the congruence within one permanent settlement of what had formerly been the loose, extended "personal kindred" group—which did not have and could not have had any local base—and of the more immediate circle of bilateral relatives that composed the local group and that had social and economic interdependence. Rules of band exogamy supported the perpetuation of the extended kindred; economic interdependence and social support underlay the restricted kindred. Now, with more permanent year-round settlement of many of these formerly independent bands, there is a coming together into the same social arena of both types of relatives, and marriage and residence patterns are in process of redefinition. It is difficult, however, to generalize about marriage rules. A number of patterns seem to be evident, and these are based both on traditional considerations, such as consanguineal proximity or band affiliation, and on new factors, such as religious affiliation. Another feature relevant in some places is the presence of white men in the community, which has so disrupted relationships between the Eskimo young men and women that it becomes unwise to speak of "marriage rules." Some Eskimo young women have become unwilling to marry Eskimo men and constitute a "social problem" by their sexual promiscuity.

What is emerging in some areas, then, is a social unit with characteristics of the *deme,* in Murdock's usage (1949, 62–63)—that is, a group of people characterized by co-residentiality, endogamy (now sometimes on a religious basis), and bilateral descent and having a general feeling that they are all related somehow though they are unable to trace segmentalizing genealogical relations. This is not fully developed anywhere, but the germs of it are found in several communities that are characterized by fairly stable year-round residence, with band exogamy but settlement endogamy.

For the full development of the deme, however, there must be a "we-feeling" among all participants in the community. This may not occur for some time in communities such as Coral Harbour and Great Whale River, which are composed of groups of immigrants from widely different Eskimo "tribes." In these situations there may be, instead, community segmentation and/or—especially where there are white people in the community—a caste structure characterizing the community as a whole, with little ingroup feeling among the Eskimos. The division between white man and Eskimo is the major social parameter in many of these northern settlements. In the minds of many white Canadians the Eskimo has shifted from being a picturesque denizen of the north to being a "social problem," the representative of a deprived minority group that, by its very existence and condition, arouses guilt and perhaps hostility as a consequence of that guilt.

Another potential development arising from the conjunction of the local bands on a more or less permanent basis is the foreshadowing of a lineage structure. Given the focus around a corporate economic activity such as the operation of a Peterhead boat requiring several men as crew, exogamy with reference to the immediate kin group, and virilocal and common residence of the group within a particular neighborhood of the community, it is possible that with time there might evolve patterns of pronounced affiliation with the father's group. These would be sustained not only by sentiments of loyalty and familiarity but also by inheritance of property and the undertaking of joint subsistence tasks strong enough in their functional import to maintain separate group structures. This is speculation, however, and most likely the current subsistence patterns that could lead to this will be changed before they can help stabilize such types of kinship sentiments and structures.

SOCIAL CONTROL

Although the Canadian government had acquired formal control over the northland shortly after confederation in 1867, it did not seriously move into the Arctic until 1903, when it began to establish stations for the collection of customs duties and the administration of the legal codes of the Dominion. These posts were manned principally by the Northwest Mounted Police officers. Not until after World War I was there much further movement of government into the north; then the number of posts was increased and annual patrols and provisioning trips were begun. At that time administration of northern affairs was the responsibility of the Department of the Interior, on whose behalf the (by then) Royal Canadian Mounted Police (R.C.M.P.) worked. But the hand of authority (in both its positive and negative aspects) was light, indeed, and the social development of the Eskimo was, in reality, only minimally implemented. Matters of local life were still largely decided by the actions of traditional institutions.

But in recent years leadership of the local band and internal processes of social control have been critically affected by broad social environmental events. Traditionally, leadership was based on subsistence success and general good sense; and these qualities continue to be relevant for band and extended family groupings, although they are in competition with other criteria, such as education and English or French language skills. But to some extent the earlier criteria have had to be adjusted to different content in order to remain relevant. For example, skill in management and maintenance of the large, motorized hunting boat is still a demanding and respected capability. This quality is one of the several areas of competence evident when use is made of the traditional term for leader, a dialectical variant of which is *issumataq,* or "the one who thinks".

With the gathering together of formerly dispersed bands into a single community, problems of creating social order and control have emerged against the background of the lack of structural forms in Eskimo society for handling such unfamiliar relationships outside of the traditional kinship network. Since the coming in of alien legal authority having the sanctions of effective power (the R.C.M.P.), blood vengeance is no longer an acceptable method of social control and restitution. Further, with multiple kin- and locality-based segments comprising many communities, each segment with centrifugal loyalties, the coercive power of gossip and threat of ostracism often are no longer efficacious. In consequence, only rarely has there arisen a functionally effective sociopolitical mechanism, such as a village council, to integrate and express common concerns. In most places community integration is minimally or not at all developed, and nowhere is there a fully effective village council on an elective basis. Yet in some of the larger towns, such as Aklavik, problems of community integration and factionalism have arisen that require remedial action at the local community level, alcoholism and adolescent deviance and disruption, for example. The extent to which the community cooperatives (mentioned above), offering opportunities for social gathering, discussion, and development of a sense of the whole community, will serve as a foundation for community government remains to be seen; but such structures should prove to be effective in a number of cases.

Typically, in this recent contact and transitional situation, those who have moved into center stage and assumed control and leadership functions have been the traders, missionaries, R.C.M.P. officers, or, in later years, government officers of the several agencies concerned with the north. And their authority comes not just from filling a power vacuum in the absence of traditional structural forms. An important basis for their leadership lies in the fact that they provide access to, and have control over, many of the resources important to the community. Their basis of power is not subsistence or activity prestige but, rather, *access* and *informational* prestige. To them has been delegated from the outside, dominant society the power of refusal or facilitation of credit, hospitalization, local medical help, relief payments in money or goods, educational opportunities, punishment, and spiritual salvation—in short, of most of the range of needs in the new pattern of life that has become important.

Some of these contact agents have jealously guarded their prerogatives. Others have attempted to stimulate local self-government and instruct Eskimos in some of the complexities of self-decision and in the application of those decisions. But in general the picture is one of relatively little success in the development of local leadership and representative self-government. This is partly a consequence of the lack of concepts and of the lack of authority to implement decisions. But it would also seem due to a change in the character of the *relations* between a population and its environment and a change in magnitude of the problems with which local government has to contend. The problems now require an overall coordinated and many-faceted approach to questions of habitat as well as of human relations, for the psychosocial environment of these emergent communities is very different from that of a generation ago.[6]

Alaska

Several features of traditional Alaskan Eskimo culture especially stand out as contrasting with that of Canada.[7] One of the most obvious was the existence of widespread trading and exchange networks, particularly developed between coastal and hinterland peoples, and the existence of annual, or at least periodic, trading and recreational gatherings, such as those at Kotzebue. Another important sociocultural feature was the *kashgee* (or *kazigi,* or *karigi*—known dialectically by several terms), the ceremonial, work, and recreational house found in most Alaskan villages. Some of the larger communities had several such structures, which served as one basis for segmenting the population; conversely, as sites for communal ceremonies that at times involved the whole village, the kashgee helped to integrate the village and to create or maintain amicable ties with neighboring villages. Commonly this structure was also a *men's house,* where, in some of the more southerly villages, a teen-age boy would join his father and spend most of his time working, receiving instruction, discussing hunting and subsistence matters, even eating and sleeping. Women were allowed inside for observing performances of major ceremonies, although they did not normally spend much time there.

The more elaborate public ceremonial cycle of the Alaskan coastal Eskimos also contrasts with that of most groups to the east, in that it was more regularized and required a greater outlay of goods for performance (see Lantis, 1947). There were both "social" ceremonials (for example, the Messenger Feast) and more strictly religious ritual occasions, oriented to the ensuring of, or thanking the spirits for, good hunting (for example, the Spring Whaling Ceremony). These group rituals were in addition to religious activities involved in shamanistic practices, individual hunting prayers, rites, the wearing of amulets, and so forth. They were centered on the principal game animals and had multiple involvements with the social structural and prestige systems of the society.

Another distinctive aspect of Alaskan cultures was the greater elaboration and proliferation of art styles than in the eastern groups.

A final feature was the greater permanence and corporateness of the extended family unit throughout more of the year as compared to the shifting and somewhat evanescent bands of the central Canadian region. Especially in those areas where cooperative hunting activity for whales and walruses from a large open boat occurred—along the Bering Sea coast—the core of the hunting crew was usually drawn from a male sibling group. Even where walrus and whale hunting was not predominant, however, the extended family group with bilateral extensions was the basic unit of society, and in most communities there was no superordinate governing structure based on either kin or political criteria.

To say that bilateral extension of kinship affiliation was the norm, however, obscures what is perhaps the most interesting feature found in some Alaskan groups: the existence of numerous indicators of patri- lineality and in some instances of corporate kin groups. A full-fledged example of this was found on St. Lawrence Island (Hughes, 1958; 1960), and other indications are pointed out by Lantis (1946, 239) and Giddings (1952). In addition, unilineality appears to have been an integral feature of the Yuit living on the Siberian shore before the intensive social change of modern times (see Levin and Potov, 1956, or Hughes's translation, 1964; Fainberg, 1955; Menovshchikov, 1962; or Sergeev, 1962), indicating that the unilineality in Alaskan groups appears not to be adventitious. Birket-Smith (1959, 141 ff.) has a brief discussion of unilineality among the western Alaskan and Pacific Eskimos and the Aleuts, but his comments are not elaborated, nor are comparisons with other Eskimo groups sharply drawn. He also refers to indications of a moiety pattern among some groups. Judging from an earlier discussion of unilineality among the Eskimos, however (1924, 141–142), he probably would ascribe the presence of these phenomena to cultural borrowing from the northwest coast and not, as would I, to ecological and structural features inherent in the situation.

BACKGROUND

Of the Alaskan Eskimos the Aleuts were the first groups to be in close contact with Europeans. Russian fur hunters began to move east- ward along the Aleutian island in the middle of the eighteenth century. Although there was some Russian influence in the Yukon and Kusko- kwim River areas, the Eskimos farther north were relatively unaffected by Europeans until the middle of the nineteenth century, when com- mercial whaling activity brought an annual visitation by whaling crews. From that time on, for more than a generation, life in the coastal villages of the Bering and Beaufort seas was disrupted by lawless sailors, the disorganizing effect of whiskey, the introduction of many diseases to which the Eskimos had no immunity, and the diminution of game resources through excessive kills by the outsiders. The United States government attempted to regulate and control disruptive outside con- tact through its revenue cutters, but this was only partially successful.

The decline in subsistence resources—the killing off of whales, walruses, and seals—prompted a remedial action on the part of Dr.

Sheldon Jackson, a Presbyterian missionary who later became General Agent for Education. In the 1890s he began a program of importing reindeer from Asia, using at first Chuckchi and, later, Lapp herders to instruct the Alaskan Eskimos in methods of herd management. The purpose of this program was to provide a stable resource base to replace the declining sea mammal and caribou populations. The notable effort, although successful in its early years, has proved in the long run to be a failure.

A number of missions, often including a school, were established in the 1890s, particularly in the easily reached coastal villages. There were not only Protestant and Catholic missions but also, in the southwestern areas, Moravian, in addition to the earlier established Russian Orthodox influence. The government itself founded schools widely over the next two generations, taking most of the instructional matters out of the hands of the missions and making them the responsibility of the Bureau of Education (later the Bureau of Indian Affairs). By 1914 every sizable Eskimo community had such a school.

St. Lawrence Island Eskimo woman sewing sealskin parka (photo by Charles C. Hughes).

The economic history of the Alaskan Eskimos until recent times can be summarized by noting the movement from primarily subsistence hunting, fishing, and collecting activities to an increasing involvement with the money economy and production for sale. At first the latter was concerned with baleen, ivory, and sea mammal skin products. Then (as in Canada), when around the turn of the century these articles began to decline in value, income came largely from fox pelts, the sale of which reached its zenith in the late 1920s. In the 1930s—and especially following World War II—this source of cash also began to taper off markedly, until in recent years it has become only a secondary source of cash income. In some areas, however, trapping and sale of the pelts of animals other than the fox—such as muskrat and mink in Naspakiak and other villages of the Kuskokwim Delta—still provides a regular source of income. But nowhere in the Alaskan Eskimo communities did there develop a secure, dependable economic base free from the threat of sudden disappearance brought on either by a change in cold war policies, ecological cycles, or the whim of women's fashions.

Thus, up to World War II, the main effects of the preceding half-century of sustained contact between Alaskan Eskimos and outsiders had been the development of mixed subsistence and commodity economies in a number of places, with the traditional hunting ethos still clearly dominant; the failure of the reindeer herds as a subsidiary food resource, which added a measure of uncertainty and stress to the always potentially unreliable sea mammal hunt; gradual decline in fox trapping returns; for most communities relatively little intensive contact with outsiders beyond the usual trading post, school, mission, and perhaps a nursing station in the village; and, finally, widespread prevalence of diseases, particularly tuberculosis, against a backdrop of inadequate budgetary facilities and personnel on the part of the dominant society, making it difficult to provide curative health needs, much less preventive ones. The demographic picture was similar to that prevailing in all other Eskimo areas: high fertility but correlatively high infant and adult mortality.

With the coming of World War II many aspects of the picture changed. The most important development was much increased contact with a larger variety of people from the outside world. Included in this was military service by the Eskimos. There were also new opportunities for wage employment and other forms of cash income, combined with increased subsistence worries because of the virtually complete disappearance of the last remaining community reindeer herds and the probable overall decline in sea mammal populations. And there was intensification of worries over both disease and the inadequacy of government activities in doing something about the alarming health picture for this Eskimo population of about 23,000 people.

ECOLOGICAL AND ECONOMIC FEATURES

Much of the same effect as in Canada ensued from the introduction of firearms to the Alaskan Eskimos, who in many cases obtained the weaponry long before it was available to the Eskimos in Canada. The individual hunter's adaptive capabilities were enhanced; more seals, walruses, and caribou were killed; and more sea mammal carcasses were lost to the currents. But there was an important, habitat-based difference. Because of the unstable ice conditions, nowhere among the Alaskan Eskimos had there been the large winter settlement out on the ocean ice in which occurred the pattern of organized and cooperative hunting of seals found among the upper Central Canadian groups. The types of winter seal hunting that did take place in Alaska—the individual hunter standing over a breathing hole with harpoon, or employing a net at the hole—were, however, similarly undercut by the introduction of the rifle, so that in Alaska, as in Canada, open-lane hunting became the predominant type of winter sea mammal hunting. Thus there was little essential change in the patterns of social relations involved in winter hunting—only in the dominant type of equipment used.

The same is true of the boat crew, undoubtedly an ancient social form in the Bering coastal area. Introduction of the rifle merely gave a preexisting economic unit greater effectiveness in the hunting of seals and walruses and, with equipment adopted from commercial whalers, in whaling activities as well. The latter equipment consisted primarily of the combined darting gun and steel-headed harpoon, a device triggered so that a bomb explodes after the harpoon head has become firmly lodged in the flesh of the whale. Other items adopted from the white whalers were the wooden whaleboat, shoulder gun, manila rope, cutting tools, and, in the 1920s, the motor for the whaleboat, or umiak. Here again (as with the kayak) changes in equipment employed did not effect basic changes in social patterns, but tended only to make the hunter more effective.

As in Canada, formerly there was more or less regular hunting of caribou by some inland groups and, seasonally, by coastal dwellers. Before adoption of the rifle, for the same reasons as in Canada these hunts usually took the form of a communal activity—drives and surrounds—and, again, one of the principal effects of rifle power was to release the hunters from the imperatives of a corporate activity if game was to be obtained.

In the southwestern part of Alaska, where for inland groups the dominant subsistence pattern was riverine fishing, the fish wheel, introduced by whites in the latter part of the nineteenth century, was another technically more efficient device that replaced traditional patterns. In the middle reaches of the Kuskokwim River its adoption increased the salmon catch and thus to a certain degree stabilized the subsistence economy. Overuse of the device elsewhere in Alaska, however, especially by commercial interests, has apparently contributed to the diminishing of the fish resource, particularly salmon.

Although other skins—such as mink and muskrat—are sold on the market, the principal furbearer still trapped in the Alaskan Arctic as well as in Canada is the arctic fox. During the 1920s trappers in some villages could make several thousand dollars a year from this activity alone. However, the prime price declined through the 1930s, rose briefly during the war years, and since then fell to such a point that trapping has tended to become an unreliable, and often unproductive, source of income. As in Canada the unpredictable fluctuations in market demand, coupled with the natural cycles in the animal population itself, create a situation in which the trapper, upon whom such diverse cycles often converge, soon becomes dismayed at the seeming arbitrariness of the trader to whom he sells his furs.

By and large, however, the Alaskan Eskimos who have done fox trapping have been less tied to this as a principal subsistence activity than the Canadian groups have been. For one thing, there was not the same degree of monopolistic control of the market as in Canada. Also, they have had a richer natural habitat to exploit, as well as—in recent years —wage work of various types. In addition, however, the government early attempted to develop economic self-sufficiency and a full return by establishing cooperatives in native villages, which provided a central purchasing and marketing agency to handle furs and handicrafts.

The decline in population of various animal species upon which the Eskimos have been mainly dependent for their subsistence has been uneven and of differential importance. In the past, for example, there were fewer Alaskan Eskimos than Canadian who relied upon the caribou herds. Those who did subsist upon the caribou lived primarily in the Brooks Range and the Noatak-Kobuk river regions. But today all such groups have disappeared—merged and assimilated into coastal groups— except for two small bands. And yet in recent times there has not been the catastrophic decline in caribou characteristic of the Canadian scene; in fact, the herds are reported to have returned in greater numbers than a few years ago. The same cannot be said for the reindeer, upon which such great hopes at one time were placed as the bulwark of an Eskimo indigenous economy. In terms of its long-range effects on the continuance of a subsistence economy, undoubtedly the failure of the introduced reindeer herds among the Alaskan Eskimos is more critical than any depletion of the caribou population. Despite the fact that the herds were in decline (due to poor range management practices and other factors) and that the basic failure of the innovation was apparent during the 1930s, there still were enough animals available in that and the following decade to constitute a source of meat and skins. But the mid and late 1940s saw the general decline of reindeer as an economic resource. The herd on St. Lawrence Island, for example, estimated to number about 2,500 in 1946, had dropped to less than 100 by 1955. However, in the past decade there has been a revival of interest by the Bureau of Indian Affairs in the possibility of developing reindeer management as an indigenous resource base, and there are now sixteen herds under the Bureau's administrative purview.

There is also evidence of decline of other resources. A decrease in the numbers of whales and walruses is clearly seen in kill statistics, but it is also corroborated by zoological studies. Such apparently is not the case with respect to the population of seals of various types, although fluctuations in the number of animals taken from one year to the next do, of course, occur. There has been a clear lowering of resources in the salmon runs in recent years as well as a decrease in beluga in the east Bering Sea. There has also been a decrease in the number of polar bears—the latter a popular item for sport hunters, some of whom are now equipped with airplanes as an added item in the technological inventory.

WAGE WORK AND MONEY INCOME

Earning and handling money is nothing new to the Alaskan Eskimos; indeed, they have been at it for at least half a century. But there is no question that the great spurt in daily use of, acquaintance with, and dependence upon money as a basic standard for many activities and goals began with World War II. And with this there also ensued a change in the dominant activity through which money was acquired. Formerly obtained through sale of pelts or crafts, now increasingly it is obtained from wages, salaries, or welfare and aid payments. Only after World War II did the Eskimos become fully aware of their eligibility to receive support for dependent children, old age incapacitation, or disability. With the advent of wage labor there has also come the added boon of unemployment compensation as a widely used form of income. Various other types of episodic wage labor, such as unloading supply vessels and working as maintenance laborers on military or other types of sites, provide additional income for some workers. Still other wage opportunities—at greatly inflated wages, given the large proportion of overtime and double-time earnings—were found (as in Canada) in the construction of the DEW line and similar installations. And in the last decade such peripheral service activities as supplying the needs of tourism and petty shopkeeping have appeared in greater numbers.

In the meantime the traditional means of earning money continue—
the sale of fox and other pelts, ivory carving, and skin sewing—as well
as the collecting of bounties on wolves and occasionally other animals.
After World War II, indeed, the sale of handicrafts increased so much
that a fairly large-scale production and marketing organization grew up
in Nome, the Nome Skin Sewers, Incorporated. The Bureau of Indian
Affairs has encouraged other programs of this nature, such as the Alaska
Native Industries Cooperative Association, which, although they do not
fully solve the basic problem of economic insecurity for the Eskimo villages, do undoubtedly contribute in the short run to the viability of the
Eskimo mixed economy.

Thus, following World War II there occurred throughout Alaska a
significant increase in the amount of money coming into the villages
from various sources. In some places a relatively stable and successful
mixed economy was achieved, as at Point Hope. But in many other communities the picture was, rather, that of erratic and highly unpredictable
wage opportunities alternating with marked periods of unemployment.
Perhaps the most dramatic example of the building up of expectations
and orientations regarding money income, with a subsequent relatively
sudden disappearance of such opportunities, occurred at Barrow. In that
general area, beginning about 1944, the United States Navy conducted
petroleum explorations and undertook drilling of test wells, employing
in those activities upwards of one hundred local Eskimos. Ten years
later, however, the Navy stopped the operations and the jobs for local
Eskimos were done away with.

But to illustrate the unpredictable nature of the economy of Alaskan
natives in today's world, the most recent (and highly publicized) developments—again from the northern part of Alaska—may be cited. The discovery of vast oil reserves on the northern slope of the Brooks Range has
now raised hopes of great wealth to come to the Eskimos from oil royalties. The extent of such royalties, as well as a somewhat related question
of monetary payment for native land settlement claims all over Alaska,
is currently under negotiation; and the prospect of getting compensation
for what are conceived as aboriginal land and mineral rights gives the
Alaska Federation of Natives a meaningful and understandable basis
for political action at the present time.

The increase in income is turned mainly toward purchase of material
goods from the dominant culture, including adoption of housing forms
and furnishings. Relatively few "aboriginal" structures remain. The most
common dwelling is built of imported or scrap lumber; in some places
this is a makeshift building, utilizing discarded materials. The house is
no longer heated by a blubber lamp but by a stove that burns coal, fuel
oil, or wood. Constructed as they are, most of these houses create serious

public health hazards, a matter to which health authorities are turning much attention. An intensive program of improvement has been undertaken, directed not only at such background features as housing and diet but also at the obvious problems of disease control and prevention.

The extent to which Alaskan Eskimo material as well as social culture has been affected by sustained involvement with that of the dominant white society is illustrated by Kotzebue, a largely Eskimo semiurban town on the Bering coast north of Nome (V. L. Smith, 1966). The great majority of its inhabitants are Eskimos, mostly migrants from the hinterland and other Eskimo areas. The economic life of the town's approximately 2,000 inhabitants revolves around the provision of services mediated by a cash economy, rather than subsistence or production pursuits. Although the number of private commercial enterprises serving the town is larger than would be found anywhere else but in Nome, a listing of them (leaving aside the numerous federal and state offices) will help convey the range of cosmopolitan activities that now characterize Eskimo life in many parts of Alaska: two airlines (scheduled), one bank, one barge company, three charter flying services, five churches, two coffeehouses, three curio shops, one electric company, one fuel storage and gas station, three hotels, four household stores, two mercantile stores, one mining company, one movie house, one laundromat, one poultry farm, two restaurants, three taxi companies, one telephone company, and one water supply company.

The effect on native populations of the industrial development of the recently discovered oil fields in northern Alaska cannot be accurately predicted at this time. Given the technical skills involved, it is probable, however, that the Eskimos will form only a small portion of the total work force. But undoubtedly the side effects of such an extensive economic development will be pervasive throughout the entire northern territory—increased highway construction, expansion of towns and commercial services, and the like—and the Eskimos, like other Alaskans, will be involved in dealing with a markedly different world around them in the barren northern tundra.

CHANGING SOCIOPOLITICAL STRUCTURES

As in Canada there were missionaries and some governmental agencies operating in Alaskan Eskimo villages for many years prior to World War II. In Alaska, however, the difference between the degree and intensity of contact before and after the war is less than in Canada. For one thing, the influence of the missions goes back two centuries, for Orthodox missions were established in southwestern Alaska and on the Aleutian Islands by the Russians. With the purchase of Alaska in 1867 by the United States, other denominations entered the scene, and most coastal and some inland villages soon had a mission station. The functions performed by the missionaries were the common ones: They provided education and medical care, and they engaged in informal sociopolitical activities as well as in the formal religious ones. All schools, however, soon came under the authority of the Bureau of Education of the United States Department of the Interior; and after that the person of the teacher became important on the local scene as an agent of change more through his informal functions as an object of emulation and as a source of information about the dominant world than through his classroom activity.

As in so much of the rest of the world, World War II was a qualitative break with the past through the increased contact opportunities it afforded. Many Alaskan Eskimos (over 2,000) served in local home guard units, and others had some years in the Army. Defense and military activities brought outsiders into many until then relatively isolated communities. And the presence of armed invaders—in the Aleutian Islands and, by threat, portions of southwestern Alaska and some of the Bering Sea islands (such as St. Lawrence)—added a new dimension to the villagers' perceptions of the world they lived in and the degree to which they were involved with the fortunes of the dominant society.

Formal self-government in the pattern of a town council began in some villages during the 1920s and 1930s, usually initiated by a missionary teacher. In the late 1930s some of the existing councils were formally reconstituted under the Indian Reorganization Act when the communities themselves were incorporated, and by 1949 some thirty-two villages had thus organized themselves for representative self-government. They were often not very effective instruments of political integration and accomplishment, but they did exemplify a deliberate attempt at the development of a bridging institution that would articulate local-level structures with those of the national environment. By 1962 every Eskimo village was said to have a council of some type (although not all were organized under terms of the Indian Reorganization Act).

Although the institutional form has not changed since the war, the problems the councils have had to face are much more numerous as well as more varied. Because of increased contact with outside agents, there are more basic economic quandaries bearing down on the local community, conflicts between the generations as exponents of different ways of life, delinquency of the young, and a breakdown in aboriginal methods of social control. Without effective local enforcement powers the councils have an increasingly difficult role in maintaining social order.

Since the end of the war, also, the government has directed considerable attention—but in the view of some, not enough—to the problem of economic stabilization and the rehabilitation of community life. One of the first expressions of this was the formation of the Alaska Native Industries Cooperative Association, mentioned above, which was begun shortly after the war at the stimulation of the Alaska Native Service. A territory-wide consumer cooperative marketing and purchasing organization, its purpose was to bring the benefits of lower costs and better management to the village stores. By 1963, thirty-two Aleut and Eskimo communities belonged to the organization, and at the present time the stores are all said to be successful.

Another area in which government activity has increased in postwar years is welfare and emergency support. First the territorial and now the state department of welfare have attempted to alleviate cases of economic or other hardship, many times caused by hospitalization of the able-bodied male or the mother in the family. (This latter type of problem, however, has been somewhat in decline since 1955, when the intensive program aimed at controlling tuberculosis was initiated by the United States Public Health Service.) An inadvertent result of such welfare aid has been to increase the "social utility" of old age and to create a feeling of independence in elderly people by their receipt of welfare support. It may also influence marriage patterns (widows, for example, having less need to remarry to find support for their children). In any case, such income has become an important factor in helping stabilize the economic situation in many places, and dependence upon it has greatly increased since the war.

In 1948 there were fifty-five Alaska Native Service or territorial schools serving Eskimo communities, in addition to two high schools oriented especially to native students. At the present time education of the Eskimos has partially been turned over to the state of Alaska by the federal government, and about one hundred Eskimo communities have schools and teachers, some operated under the State Department of Education. Despite the frequent interruption in schooling occasioned by the subsistence activities of the children's families, no question exists of the desire of Eskimo children to receive an education. The most common educational objectives clearly reflect a strong economic purpose: immediate and continued employment, relatively high income, personal prestige and power.

Finally, although its forms are just beginning to be felt, mention must be made of the emerging sense of ethnic-racial nationalism. In sharp contrast to the inter-village hostility that used to characterize Alaskan Eskimo life, a sentiment of "Eskimo-ness," a reassertion of its legitimacy —and of its claims to property, mineral and land resources—is being fostered by a political movement in Alaska, the Alaska Federation of Natives, that is active in stressing civil and economic rights.

SOCIAL ORGANIZATIONAL FEATURES

In his definitive study of the north Alaskan Eskimos, Spencer (1959) lays great stress on the stability of the bilateral extended family group, both in past times and under modern conditions of change. In his view this is the cornerstone of village social structure, the principal locus of economic, social, and leadership functions. Indeed in the northern coastal area, the extended family in general continues to be the basic social, and to some extent the basic economic, unit, although it is not necessarily the basic residential unit. The same generally holds true for St. Lawrence Island, but there the extended families are themselves merged into larger lineage or clan groupings that function as corporate political and economic groups (Hughes, 1960).

But apparently a somewhat different situation prevails in many other villages, where the bilateral extended family has suffered attrition over the past generation and is being further subjected to shrinkage by extensive penetration from the outside world. Examples are Point Hope and Kotzebue. Kotzebue has major problems of social integration confronting it, with deep divisions existing not only between whites and Eskimos but also among the several groups of Eskimos, who identify with their place of origin rather than with the larger community. In addition there is the emerging gulf between the young and the old. This is a situation of relative, not absolute, restriction of scope in functioning of the extended bilateral family and one that, furthermore, has been going on for quite a while in some communities, although greatly intensified in postwar years.

Van Stone (1962) has indicated that, as elsewhere, the major bases of corporateness for extended families in the past were mutual protection of members and economic interdependence. But with the introduction of American legal institutions, the need for protection declined. With fox trapping and the use of the rifle and other modern subsistence equipment, the need for close ties of economic interdependence as a production unit has also somewhat declined, although it is still found to some extent in the operation of the boat crew. Greatly increased opportunities for wage employment further strategically undercut the extension of kinship relations, for money resources are not as widely distributed to kinsmen as are traditional economic goods. This shrinking in size of the effective functional family unit undoubtedly is the general trend in most Alaskan Eskimo villages, given the greatly changed ecologic, economic, and political circumstances.

Regarding marriage patterns, it is impossible to make comprehensive statements with respect to many aspects of recent changes, for the ethnographic background is not sufficiently well known to establish the base point for changes. About the only statement that can be made with assurance is that there was considerable diversity in choice of marriage partner at times, including a pattern of cousin preference. What is clear, however, is that in the past generation, regardless of former patterns, in most villages there is a strong tendency toward individual choice of spouse outside certain forbidden degrees of relationship (that is, the nuclear family). Such individualization of choice is still no doubt strongly influenced by parental desire in some cases, but with the increased emigration of young people for schooling or hospitalization or work, traditional sanctions are becoming far less effective. The same picture of change and flux in pattern is presented by residence after marriage. Traditionally, a variety of residence patterns was found: bilocal, neolocal, matrilocal, patrilocal, and even matri-patrilocal. Especially in those groups (such as Barrow) that had a well-developed bilateral extended family system, all of the first four alternatives were evident. Among the St. Lawrence Islanders and other Siberian groups, the fifth pattern was (and, to some extent, still is) characteristic. So, too, with regard to the question of exogamy and endogamy. With village boundaries somewhat amorphous and permeable, it is difficult to fix definite rules of ingroup versus outgroup marriage. In the past, however, there appeared to be a tendency toward village endogamy, at least in the larger communities. But with much more travel and exposure to the outside world now, this pattern is decidedly breaking down. For one thing, a considerable number of Eskimo girls have married white men and in most cases have then moved to cities in Alaska or other states.

The problem of clans and lineages among the Eskimos is of some theoretical importance. Did they or did they not have clans? Most of the smaller villages on the Alaskan mainland can be called (again in Murdock's term) demes, although traces of unilineality can be clearly seen. Point Hope is a good example. But several investigators have commented on the definite indicators of a unilineal structuring among groups farther south in Alaska than Point Hope, as well as on St. Lawrence Island. Such patrilineality is also indubitably found on the Siberian shore, among the Eskimos living in the Soviet Union.

Other social relationships and institutions have also declined in recent years. The whaling crew is one. Although in the past this corporate group was practically always composed of kinsmen, this is no longer the case. Indeed, in some places—Barrow, Point Hope, and Wainwright are examples—the shift to a universalistic, rational-economic basis for the work group has begun, with crew members being under informal contract for the season. Similarly, there has been marked decline in the number and variety of partnerships formerly so characteristic of the

Alaskan Eskimos. The most important basis of these relations was trade, but they also included mutual support and exchange of wives. Such relationships were functionally of great importance in extending outward to non-kinsmen the bonds of mutual aid and assistance characteristic of kinsmen; they thus provided a means whereby wider social integration and stability through multiple segmental relationships could be achieved. But these fictive kinship relations have practically disappeared.

The men's house, formerly so much the center of village life, has also gone the way of institutions under the pressure of multiple environmental influences—undercut by, among other things, disruptions of traditional occupational patterns resulting from new contact opportunities. Now the church, school, coffeehouse, and movie hall have effectively fractionated the integrative locus that was the *karigi*.

As elsewhere among the Eskimos, in Alaska leadership was always based on the combination of hunting prestige, wealth, respect, and awe. The whaling captain and the shaman were the traditional leaders. But for many years prior to World War II these two types had to contend with the missionary, teacher, or trader. And with the coming of the war, a wholly new set of influences entered the lists, the foremost of which was education and the ability to use the English language effectively in dealings with the many outsiders who came. Such younger aspirants to leadership do not, however, have a clear field, particularly in those coastal communities where whaling and walrus hunting are still major subsistence pursuits. The prestige of the successful hunter remains a bulwark of the leadership role. But in general the effectiveness of the indigenous leaders is being continually reduced because of the shrinking scope of the economic functions of the family units. Leader though he may be, the whaling captain is put in a position of seeing the number of his followers diminish if he bases his position of eminence solely on traditional skill criteria.

In many communities there are also other introduced institutions that in varying degrees serve leadership and coordinating functions. These range from the artificially imposed "chief" in Napaskiak (actually appointed by the Russian Orthodox missionary) to the voluntary religious, social, and educational organizations, such as (formerly) the men's "Brotherhood" or the women's "Sisterhood" (now superseded by the Alaska Federation of Natives). The importance of other types of new leaders should also be underscored: the lay preachers, ministers, National Guard noncommissioned officers, bosses of work crews, sanitation and health aides, and store managers. The types of people who serve leadership functions during transitional phases of culture contact are varied, spurred by the inventiveness of human adaptability in changed circumstances of life.

Siberia

The approximately 1,100 Eskimos living on the continent of Asia represent the westernmost extension of the Eskimos as a cultural group. They are also, however, an example of one of the classes into which the considerable homogeneity of Eskimo culture can be broken; for they are Yupik-speakers, as compared to the Inupik-speakers—Asiatic Eskimos as against many of the Alaskan and all of the Canadian and Greenland Eskimos. The Yupik language class includes the island groups in the Bering Sea and most of southwestern Alaska.

Characteristic also of some of the Yupik group (particularly the Siberians) is a more elaborate social organization, notably seen in the presence of clans or quasi-clan groups. The Siberian Eskimos, like those living on St. Lawrence Island, clearly had a clan system in precontact times, as evidenced by a number of indicators—the distinctive naming of "family" groups; probable exogamy; the reckoning of kinship from father to son; inheritance in the patrilineal line; patrilocal residence rules; corporate economic activities, such as organization of the boat crew along patrilineal kinship lines; territorial identification of the group; the former common residence of the extended family group within a single large structure; and distinctive religious rites. It is this feature of cultural life—the existence of strong, viable clan groupings—that, of all traits of Eskimo culture, was most distinctive of the Siberian villages.

The story of the intervention of the outside world into these communities perched on the easternmost edge of Eurasia can be briefly put, and it will be helpful to do so for comparative uses. It includes early contact by Russian explorers and fur hunters and traders; gradual outpost settlement after bloody clashes with the indigenous Paleo-Siberian people, the Chuckchis, and the Eskimos (who often live in the same villages); the strong influence of American commercial interests until well into the 1920s; and, finally, the establishment of firm Soviet control in the 1930s.

Details must be omitted here,[8] but the main events since the 1930s can be outlined. The Soviet government has made persistent and concentrated efforts to bring local community life under the aegis of a new cultural regime, one that rests primarily upon the collectivization of indigenous subsistence pursuits and that requires the dissemination of a new system of beliefs and values to make such economic forms legitimate and understandable. Such programs have been an aspect of overall Soviet national policy, directed at the integration of the minority groups into the environing society—a policy that has had to contend with and over-

Elders supervise while young Eskimos cut up whale tongue, St. Lawrence Island (photo by Charles C. Hughes).

come existing social institutions and vested interests, such as the shamans. (Indeed, the theme of doing battle with the *kulaks* and shamans is a frequent one in the literature on the problems of the Soviet development of northern Siberia.) In any case, the battles have been largely won and there has occurred the organization of collective work groups and brigades in reindeer herding, fishing, and hunting activities as well as in other production processes, such as skin sewing. This reorientation of economic institutions has been accompanied by the introduction of educational and medical programs and facilities as well as by political instruction and training at the local and higher levels of organization. Of special interest is the attempt in more recent years to encourage selected elements of the indigenous culture, such as artistic productions, so that they will be expressive of traditional cultural themes, but recast in an avowedly socialist mold to conform with national Soviet values.

In Review

Although the specific solutions may have varied, the general problem presented to Eskimo communities over the past generation has been that of trying to cope with an environment that, to some extent in its physical parameters and—much more critically—in its sociocultural ones, has been drastically altered. As Margaret Lantis once aptly remarked:

> The substance of the situation is that Eskimos are trying just as hard today to adapt as they did 500 or 900 years ago; the difficulty is that they are adapting not to the Arctic but to a Temperate Zone way of living. The people with their new standards have nearly overwhelmed the Eskimos, not in numbers but in wishes and wants [1957, 126].

The point is simply put, but is often obscured in the way various researchers approach study of the dynamics of the culture-contact situation. Any population, be it human or other, exists by virtue of varied and multiplex relations to a total environment; and when significant features of that milieu change in their functional import, so, too, must the behavioral response change if that population is to maintain a recognizable continuity with existent forms. The behavioral transactions carried out by Eskimo groups with their environments over the past thirty years must be viewed as of a fundamentally ecological character in the most pervasive sense, that is, as involving modes of mutual participation obtaining between an organism and the environment. This means much more than simply recording levels of caloric intake or unit of energy production or control per capita. Into such a comprehensive conceptual framework for viewing the cultural dynamics of a human population must also be incorporated a mode of such interrelation especially important in the conduct of human affairs: interpretive perception and the symbolic reworking of perceived environmental events under the press of a preexisting (or evolving) belief and normative system.

Obviously, even within a conventional ecological framework a number of features of the Eskimos' changing life situation can be fruitfully interpreted—such as those changes in subsistence institutions necessitated by modifications in animal migration routes; the decline in animal populations due to excessive predation or to cyclical, species-specific demographic control mechanisms; the rise in temperature of ocean water (as in the Labrador Sea around southwestern Greenland); or the befouling of waters with oil and other wastes discharged from vessels resupplying military outposts in the north, thus driving away maritime animals from their normal feeding areas. All of these instances are of a type that reflects primarily alterations in the materials and/or energy modes of interrelation between a population and its habitat—and, indeed, we need to know much more about both of these dimensions.

But another dimension of such multiplex relations—information— has received short shrift in ecological studies, no doubt largely because of the complexity of the processes and the overlapping problems involved. Yet this is equally crucial, perhaps in some instances most crucial, in accounting for much of the gross variability and the subtle phenomenology in human cultures. This is the mode that, it would seem, is expressed in the genesis of such concepts as "ethos," "value," "system of belief," and kindred terms (as contrasted to such notions as "levels of complexity"); the mode, in short, that is creative of man's profound capacity for cloaking the world and everything that happens to him with ideas and with affect-based perceptions.

Quite aside from content, some of the major difficulties for changing Eskimo populations have had to do with *form* insofar as informational relations with the environment are concerned. The *means* by which ideas, perceptions, and information about the world are acquired are, themselves, different from those of the immediate past. The *nature of knowing,* even as the nature of what is to be known, is also different. Now it is not manual skills that are solely important and adaptationally efficacious, not the honing of instinct and close observation of the hunter on the ice, nor the probabilistic reasoning process applied to empirical generalizations about natural events. Rather, another set of information-acquiring procedures have taken over much of the field. Examples range all the way from changes in (and needs for) foreign-language learning and reading and the use of mass media for communications (books, magazines, newspapers, movies) to conversational and observational contacts with outsiders and the outside world and travel to unfamiliar places. The ineptitude and incompetence, the lack of control over means, that many of today's Eskimos display with respect to such techniques for knowing are without question involved in the disappointment and bewilderment that so often accompanies the culture-contact situation.

But it is not simply the lack of techniques for knowing or coping with the new world that may create anxieties and stresses for persons upon whom impinge both demands from a traditional culture and inducements from a new one. Even with knowledge of how to deal with problems of that new environment, there is no guaranteed success in coping with the many contradictions and inconsistencies, the often unclear connections between means and goals, that are prominent features of the sociocultural content of that outside world. As a consequence, a great many Eskimos are caught in a situation of increased and variegated stresses, with increasingly fewer effective cultural mechanisms for alleviating those stresses and threats. For beyond the straightforward threats to physical survival—the disease, malnutrition and undernutrition, and poor housing widely found in Eskimo areas—there are the threats to self-esteem, to social acceptance and acceptability, to strivings for competing cultural versions of "success" and security. Indeed, given the more widespread and increased kinds of contact, it is even difficult to say that there is a stable and easily characterized environment to which the Eskimos can direct their efforts at adaptation.

The implications of the foregoing remarks for the study of recent Eskimo ethnohistory can, I think, be simply put: In a culture-change situation, it is people in their behavioral patterns who are changing, and only derivatively is it culture that changes. A great many factors, of course, enter into the changing of that behavior, and preexisting cultural structuring of perception, affect, and response is certainly one. But even the press of cultural structuring and, on the personality side, internalization of goals and means cannot foreordain the future. The accidents of history, the situational developments, the chaging tides of circumstance in greater or lesser degree may well change the environment toward which the behavioral response has been directed and in terms of which the culture has become more or less stabilized as an adaptational device. This is to say that human behavior must be seen within a dynamic framework, a framework that looks to the transactions and interchanges between persons and environment as providing the stuff of which meaningful conceptualizations of the direction of changes can be made. And such transactions involve a number of modes or areas of relationship, not only the gross ones such as exchanges of goods and energy but the complex forms of symbolization and affective loading of environmental events. The point can be made in simple language as well as more complex terms. In the words of one St. Lawrence Island Eskimo caught in the coming together of the world into which he had been born and the world that was his present reality, "People have more needs now. . . . There are new ideas coming in."

NOTES

1 Much of the discussion of these trends is taken from material and analyses that I previously brought together in the review article, published in February 1965, entitled "Four Flags: Recent Culture Change Among the Eskimos," *Current Anthropology* 6 (1):3–69. Many specific bibliographic citations found in that article have been omitted from this discussion, and the reader interested in more extensive documentation can consult the above-mentioned source. Supplementing the earlier review, however, I have also drawn on relevant materials

published since that review was drawn together, such as the valuable mono-graphs by Jenness concerned with governmental policies and programs in the Canadian Eskimo area, and recent community studies issued by the Canadian Department of Northern Affairs and Natural Resources (as it was then called). Even so, the reader will recognize that events of the past three or four years have quickly outstripped many features of the discussion contained herein, which was formulated originally for conference presentation in 1967. One might claim with justification that recent events are not sufficiently "history" to be included in a volume having the intent this one does; in actuality, of course, the sheer time required for scholarship and eventual publication is the more applicable response to such discomfiture.

2 For a recent assessment of the Angmagssalik Eskimos, see Gessain (1967).

3 The intensive exploration in the Canadian Arctic during the past century, including several expeditions sent out to look for Sir John Franklin, contributed greatly to popular knowledge of the Eskimos. More scholarly work began to appear in the 1870s and 1880s (e.g., Boas's study of the Baffin Island Eskimos), beginning a period of some fifty years of research, during which much basic ethnographic knowledge of many Canadian Eskimo groups west of Labrador was laid down. Perhaps the cornerstone of such work was the series of publica-tions emanating from the Fifth Thule Expedition, which included works by Rasmussen, Birket-Smith, Mathiassen, and Freuchen, published in the decade following Jenness's classic monograph on the Copper Eskimos, and the work of Stefansson in the Mackenzie Delta area.

4 See Iglauer (1966) for a general account of these recent developments.

5 Information was supplied by the kindness of Mr. A. Sprudzs, of the Cana-dian Department of Indian Affairs and Northern Development.

6 For a comprehensive and forthright discussion of the programs (and *lack* of programs) on the part of the Canadian government directed at improving the lot of its Eskimos over the past century, see Jenness's invaluable review published in 1964. Here I can only sketch the barest outline of this story of late-blooming recognition and action in regard to the need for "development" among Canada's Eskimos. Other highly useful reviews of administrative devel-opments and programmatic activities in the Canadian Arctic are found in the volume that MacDonald edited (1966), entitled *The Arctic Frontier,* especially chapters by Lantis, Jenness, Fingland.

7 Ethnographic knowledge of the Alaskan Eskimos is conspicuous by its uneven character. Following the several major early ethnographic compendia produced by Russian explorers, and then a couple of generations later, those published by the Bureau of American Ethnology (such as works by Nelson, Ray, and Murdoch), for three or four decades there was comparatively little written about these relatively settled, affluent, and socially complex Eskimos. Many basic studies of community life and organization, which should have been done a generation or two ago (i.e., before major alteration by outside forces), have been undertaken only within the past ten to fifteen years.

8 For such details, see references cited in Hughes (1965), or in an especially valuable later source, MacDonald (1966), which contains articles by Terence Armstrong and Neil C. Field dealing with the Soviet north.

REFERENCES

ARMSTRONG, TERENCE
1966 The administration of northern peoples: the USSR. *In* The Arctic frontier. R. MacDonald, ed. Toronto: University of Toronto Press.

BIRKET-SMITH, KAJ
1924 Ethnography of the Egedesminde district. Copenhagen: Meddelelser om Grønland 66:1–494.
1959 The Eskimos. London: Methuen.

FAINBERG, L.
1955 K voprosy o rodovom stroe u eskimosov. Sovietskaya Etnografiia 1:82–99.

FINGLAND, F. B.
1966 Administrative and constitutional changes in Arctic territories: Canada. *In* The Arctic frontier. R. MacDonald, ed. Toronto: University of Toronto Press.

GESSAIN, ROBERT
1967 Angmagssalik, trente ans après: evolution d'une tribu eskimo dans le monde modern. Objets et Mondes VII (2).

GIDDINGS, J. L.
1952 Observations on the "Eskimo type" of kinship and social structure. Anthropological Papers of the University of Alaska 1 (1):5–10.

HOBART, C. W., AND C. S. BRANT
1966 Eskimo education, Danish and Canadian: a comparison. The Canadian Review of Sociology and Anthropology 3 (2):47–66.

HONIGMANN, JOHN J., AND IRMA HONIGMANN
1965 Eskimo townsmen. Ottawa: University of Ottawa, Canadian Research Centre for Anthropology.

HUGHES, CHARLES C.
1958 An Eskimo deviant from the "Eskimo" type of social organization. American Anthropologist 60:1140–1147.
1960 An Eskimo village in the modern world. Ithaca: Cornell University Press.
1964 The Eskimos. *In* The peoples of Siberia (edited by M. G. Levin and L. P. Potov, Moscow, Academy of Sciences), translated by C. C. Hughes. Anthropological Papers of the University of Alaska, 12 (1):1–13.
1965 Under four flags: recent culture change among the Eskimos. Current Anthropology 6 (1):3–69.

IGLAUER, EDITH
1966 The new people. New York: Doubleday.

JENNESS, DIAMOND
1964 Eskimo administration: II. Canada. Arctic Institute of North America: Technical Paper no. 4.

1965 Eskimo administration: III. Labrador. Arctic Institute of North America: Technical Paper no. 16.
1966 The administration of northern peoples: America's Eskimos—pawns of history. *In* The Arctic frontier. R. MacDonald, ed. Toronto: University of Toronto Press.

LANTIS, MARGARET
1946 The social culture of the Nunivak Eskimo. Transactions of the American Philosophical Society, new series, 35(3):156–323.
1947 Alaskan Eskimo ceremonialism. Monographs of the American Ethnological Society 11.
1957 American Arctic populations: Their survival problems. *In* Arctic biology. Henry P. Hansen, ed. pp. 119–30. Eighteenth Annual Biology Colloquium, Oregon State College Chapter of Phi Kappa Phi. Corvallis: Oregon State College.
1966 The administration of northern peoples: Canada and Alaska. *In* The Arctic frontier. R. MacDonald, ed. Toronto: University of Toronto Press.

LEVIN, M. G., AND L. P. POTOV, EDS.
1956 Narody Sibiri. Moskow-Leningrad: Izdatel'stvo Academii Nauk S.S.S.R.

MACDONALD, R. ST. J., ED.
1966 The Arctic frontier. Toronto: University of Toronto Press.

MENOVSHCHIKOV, G. A.
1962 O perezhitochnykh iavleniyakh rodovoi organizatsii u asiatskikh eskimo-sov. Sovietskaya Etnografiia 6:29–34.

MURDOCK, GEORGE P.
1949 Social structure. New York: Macmillan.

MURDOCH, JOHN
1892 The Point Barrow expedition: Ethnological results of the Point Barrow expedition. Bureau of American Ethnology, 9th Annual Report.

NELSON, E. W.
1899 The Eskimo about Bering Strait. Bureau of American Ethnology, 18th Annual Report.

RAY, P. H.
1885 Report of the international polar expedition to Point Barrow, Alaska. Washington: U.S. Government Printing Office.

SERGEEV, D. A.
1962 Perezhitki otsovskogo roda u asiatskikh eskimosov. Sovietskaya Etnografiia 6:36–42.

SMITH, NEIL C.
1966 Administrative and constitutional changes in Arctic territories: the USSR. *In* The Arctic frontier. R. MacDonald, ed. Toronto: University of Toronto Press.

SMITH, VALENE LUCY
1966 Kotzebue: A modern Alaskan Eskimo community. Ph.D. dissertation. University of Utah, Department of Anthropology.

SPENCER, ROBERT F.

1959 The North Alaskan Eskimo: A study in ecology and society. Bureau of American Ethnology Bulletin 171.

SPRUDZS, A.

1967 Cooperatives in the Canadian north. Report to the Council of the North West Territories. March.

VAN STONE, JAMES W.

1962 Point Hope: An Eskimo village in transition. Publications of the American Ethnological Society. Seattle: University of Washington Press.

14   *The Contemporary American Indian Scene*

NANCY OESTREICH LURIE

General Considerations

A central issue in recent discussions of American Indians is that although for at least a century and a half their imminent disappearance has been confidently predicted, Indians have persisted as definable little communities and as an unassimilated minority (Provinse *et al.*, 1954).[1] A heightening of political activity has become evident among American Indian people since about the close of World War II both within tribes and among members of different tribes. The activity has been designed to promote common interests, including the assurance of their persistence.[2]

The present account is based on the proposition that the course and form of modern Indian activities may illustrate a distinctive phenomenon in the field of culture contact and culture change. This phenomenon, like revitalization movements, for example (Wallace, 1956), recurs with predictable characteristics depending on the presence and interplay of certain necessary variables within the movement and the larger social milieu.[3]

For present purposes, and with apologies for introducing a special term, the responses of what appears to be a significant proportion of the American Indian population in both Canada and the United States will be designated an *articulatory movement*. It is distinguished from movements such as the civil rights struggle of American Negroes seeking social and cultural acceptance within the total society on a par with other ethnic groups, and it differs from revitalization movements that focus primarily upon internal reforms. The established term *cultural pluralism* is not used, since pluralism often occurs without the positive effort and contractual features that seem to characterize the Indians' endeavors.[4] Pluralism is a basic goal of the articulatory movement, however.

A striking feature of the Indian movement, which may be an important criterion of articulatory movements as compared with more familiar types of social movements, is the lack of identifiable leadership and

spokesmen. There are widely embraced goals and a fair amount of patterned, predictable action, but there is no rallying around any particular
individual's banner. One can name persons who are active, informed,
and dedicated, but they are simply effective embodiments of the general
sentiment rather than well-springs of inspiration or direction.

The contemporary Indian scene, as it exemplifies the essentials of
articulatory behavior, can be described as follows. Indian communities
seek a way out of their historical dilemma posed by a dominant, encompassing society: the choice between economic marginality as Indian
communities and prosperity through individual assimilation. The solution is seen as successful redefinition of their socio-geographic environment from a condition of marginality to one of productivity in terms of
more or less formalized, interactive relationships with the larger socioeconomic system. Communities resist pressures to absorb and assimilate
them as part of the surrounding culture and society. The larger system
is recognized as inescapable and even necessary, but to be dealt with on
a contractual basis. Ideas and experiences are diffused among the different Indian communities in the search for successful models to articulate
the communities and the general Indian minority into the larger pattern. Such models assure a decent material foundation for existence, with
Indian identity maintained and actively utilized as an essential component of satisfactory community life.

Indian identity rests on traits of clearly local, tribal origin, such as
language or religion; on traits of white origin so markedly reinterpreted
in local terms as to be unique to the community and now part of its *own*
culture, such as styles of dress, diet, or specialized occupations; and on
traits of both kinds that have become widely diffused from tribe to tribe
so as to characterize virtually all Indian groups to some degree. The last
is usually designated as Pan-Indianism in the anthropological literature.
Indian identity as defined varies widely in kind and intensity among
the different tribes, permeating all aspects of life in some places and in
other places consciously exercised only on special occasions.

Articulatory responses have occurred spontaneously for a long time,
but what characterizes the contemporary scene and justifies speaking of
a movement is the development of a united Indian voice, even relating
Indians in Canada and the United States, able to verbalize its goals, and
stressing the sense of crisis for Indian people. The objectives are to
reach the larger public in order to win understanding of and support
for Indian goals and to counter policies and public attitudes that are
inimical to those goals.

Promotion of Indian causes by means of organized intertribal activities coupled with the increased diffusion of Pan-Indian traits can suggest
two quite different final results for the movement. First, it could be

self-defeating. Tribal distinctiveness may give way to a general Indian social identity, an "Indian nationality," as an adjustive way station to the long predicted assimilation of Indians into the general society. In large urban areas, for example, there are now people from many different tribes whose Indianness is necessarily expressed almost entirely in Pan-Indian terms. Intertribal organizations draw their membership from a tremendous diversity of tribal situations, and English is the lingua franca of their work.

On the other hand, there is the possibility that intertribal activities and even the urban situation are part of a complex whole making up articulatory adaptations. Local Indian communities may remain viable in part by maintaining and controlling their own channels of communication to urban centers for the selective adaptation of technological and other innovations. Although Indian populations in urban areas have increased markedly in size over the past twenty-five years, a large proportion of the people alternate residence according to a variety of patterns between the city and their tribal communities. Thus, it is also possible to argue that left to their own devices, tribal communities could persist indefinitely as distinctive and dynamic combinations of local tradition, Pan-Indian elements, and different selections from the larger society. Fundamentally, the present Indian movement is directed toward developing their own devices along these lines in the face of serious opposition.

There are several reasons why the larger system is reluctant to accommodate itself to the Indian minority, and these arguments are worth review. The point is often raised that Indians have not become assimilated because of special legislation, the reservation system usually being blamed for having isolated Indians and hampered the exercise of a free option to become assimilated. Unquestionably, reservation conditions must be taken into analytical account. However, Indian people consistently seek and use special legislation and statutory definitions to protect their lands and promote articulatory goals. That the reservation system has been helpful to articulatory attitudes but did not create them seems to be borne out by the fact that there are many distinctly Indian communities that were never under the federal jurisdiction or that sprang up where Indian people chose to live without benefit of reservations.

It is also argued that because assimilation is difficult in the face of racial barriers, Indian responses are a sorry alternative to the more desirable, but far more difficult, goal of availing oneself of the benefits of American society and culture in assimilative terms. This contention has greater merit as applied to such separatist groups as the Black Muslims or those who interpret Black Power as a self-contained Black society coming to terms of equal power with the now dominant white society. However, as a group, Indian people simply do not occupy the kind of ranking in the class system ascribed to Negroes on the basis of race. This is not to deny some serious instances of discrimination and prejudice against Indians in localized areas, but acceptance of individual Indians occurs and has always occurred in an atmosphere ranging from tolerant indifference to measures of outright force designed to lose them in the larger culture and society. No one seems to have worried that these efforts might lead to miscegenation, and, indeed, they have led to extensive miscegenation. Even in parts of Canada where liberal whites make the wry designation of Indians as "our Negroes" in deploring prejudice and discrimination, the ancestral *bois brûlé* is as much a point of pride as it is among whites in the United States. In neither country does a "white" ordinarily admit to a touch of the "tarbrush."

There is no question that Indians can become assimilated with relative ease; but this assimilation, termed *spin-off* by Philleo Nash, an anthropologist and former Commissioner of Indian Affairs, has usually occurred as the result of individual decisions. Despite regular spin-off, Indian communities persist and in many cases are actually increasing in size. Differential opportunities, particularly in education, doubtless explain why some people have followed the course of assimilation and others have been unable to do so. But even this situation is changing. Young Indian people today, who have clear alternatives, are opting in surprising numbers to remain Indian and promote Indian goals, using their educational advantages toward this end.

Without denying the contributory influences of the reservation system, racism, and educational and material deprivation, I believe that the fundamental reasons for Indians' preferences for articulation lie in the essential differences in white and Indian traditions and in the historical conditions of contact. Indian people are quick to point out that they are, in fact, different from all other Americans: they were here first. They speak of their right to endure as the "moral obligation" owed conquered aboriginal possessors of the land by invaders and usurpers. But this merely rationalizes the fact of their continuing distinctiveness from their own point of view, without explaining why they have chosen this course. From a historical perspective, however, it begins to appear that had they chosen any other course, it would have been much harder to explain. Modern Indian society derives directly and very recently from an antecedent condition of what can be broadly termed tribalism. This society under present conditions retains features that seem disharmonic and undesirable to the larger society, derived as it is from largely European traditions in a phase of transition from peasant to urban. Humankind has been tribal far longer than it has been peasant or urban, and the recently tribal peoples such as American Indians seem to be arguing that they have held fast to still valuable and adaptable social and cultural assets that others have lost in their more rapid pace toward technological improvement.[5]

If this is a romantic argument, it is no more romantic than the more acceptable emotional equation of the good life with technological complexity and material impedimenta. It is possible that our view as scholars has been obscured by the fact that ethnologists began studying Indian groups systematically and predicting their impending doom when the process of Indian retreat into marginal areas was still going on. Significantly, during this period of the mid-nineteenth century the industrial revolution was just getting into full swing in America. It apparently opened up new adaptive opportunities for Indians rather than betokening their inevitable demise. As hopeless as the Indians' situation appeared to ethnologists and other outsiders, and as great as the gap seemed to be between aboriginal lifeways and the burgeoning industrial nation, there is a strong suggestion that Indians did not accept defeat. They seem merely to have retrenched as communities still strongly committed to tribal attitudes, even when many aboriginal tribal institutions were destroyed. They did not view the industrial developments of the times with the awe expected of them by those who considered themselves the creators of the modern marvels (cf. Turner, 1951). Items were examined and adapted to acceptability on Indian terms or rejected. They were not seen as a complex entirety to which only a particular ideology could be attached.

At the beginning of contact, technological differences between Indians and isolated shiploads of Europeans were not very great. As the foregoing chapters illustrate, the earliest relationships were marked by egalitarianism and mutual benefit, and in many cases the Indians held the greater power in the relationships. For a long time Indian groups negotiated to their own advantage along tribal and intertribal lines with Europeans. A format became established that defined interdependent, but never totally merging, parties. Although spin-off of individuals occurred on both sides, contractual relationships were the only model Indians as groups really knew in dealing with whites, even after withdrawal to reservations or nonreservation settlements. Meanwhile, white society was being augmented constantly by the process of accommodation to alien, but still predominantly European, elements, resulting in their assimilation. Important ideological values—such as that of the "melting pot"—became attached to this process in the national interest.

As it became increasingly difficult for Indians to negotiate and enforce contracts because of economic pressures and disparity in numbers relative to the larger society, new adaptations were made to survive. By continuing to bring useful things selectively within their own socio-economic peripheries, Indians maintained their sense of boundaries. Many Indian people today have lived for extended periods entirely out-side their sociocultural peripheries; and upon thoughtful assessment of these experiences, they find them wanting as a satisfactory way of life. The movement that is underway among Indian people seeks to reor-ganize the total society to allow articulation into it on their own terms. The major problem is to find negotiable assets with which to bargain for survival in the larger system.

The following pages present a brief historical review of Indian-white relationships as necessary documentation in understanding the present Indian movement, which is covered in a final section.

European Contact and the Development of Contact-Traditional Cultures

The record of archeology makes abundantly clear that socioeconomic changes attendant upon the spread of agriculture, extensive trade, move-ments of populations, adaptations to different environments, and diffu-sion of cultural traits antedated the arrival of Europeans in North America (cf. McNickle, this text, Chapter 2). We can assume that the aboriginal people were not helplessly unprepared to meet and deal with strangers and incorporate innovations.

From the end of the fifteenth century, after John Cabot opened up the fishing-trading possibilities in New Foundland, to 1814, when the United States and Britain concluded their final war that established the Canadian boundary, and until 1848 in the Southwest, when the Mexican boundary was defined, Indian groups acted as autonomous political entities in encounters with Europeans. Actually, these formal dates only herald the close of eras that were not to end for the Indians until con-siderably later. In the northern Plains and the Southwest Indian groups were able to exploit still uncertain international relations and unsur-veyed boundaries to their own advantage up to the last decades of the nineteenth century. They crossed and recrossed borders to avoid punitive action and pursuit beyond what they knew were politically sensitive landmarks. For periods ranging from 100 to 300 years or more, different Indian societies traded, formed alliances, and entered into treaties and compacts among themselves, with different European groups including the French, Dutch, Spanish, and British, and eventually with the Mexi-cans, Americans, and Canadians.

Although some tribes succumbed completely in the course of white contact, for the majority there was a long period in which to adapt and enjoy material enrichment. The fur trade, beginning before the seventeenth century, spread from the eastern forests across the wooded northern boundary of the Plains into the Plateau country. By the beginning of the nineteenth century it brought new goods by ship to the Indians of the Northwest coast. Eventually, the trade was carried across the Arctic. Meanwhile, Spanish horses entered the Plains area to help produce a complex and highly mobile way of life dependent on the great herds of buffalo. In the Southeast and Southwest, new domesticated plants and animals of European origin as well as important material objects became firmly incorporated into the varying cultures of the resident Indian groups.

Today, when Indian people look back to a golden age, it is not to the period of pristine aboriginal conditions, but to the contact-traditional cultures. For some Indian groups, precontact conditions are all but forgotten. In only a few remote Eskimo communities were white men first encountered by the grandparents of living individuals.

The Disruption of Contact-Traditional Cultures

Although most tribes enjoyed a long contact-traditional phase, there were very early indications of the disruption that would eventually follow for all. A sequence of events occurring in New England and Virginia in the mid-seventeenth century was to be replicated time and again across the continent. These events also laid the foundations for American and Canadian Indian policy.

Upon their arrival, the British colonists encountered chiefdoms and nascent tribal confederacies. These became expanded and more effectively organized in resistance to the settlers' increasing need for land. Open hostilities followed upon a period of peaceful coexistence that had been beneficial to both Indians and whites. The Indians achieved some initial victories over the invaders but were ultimately brought to devastating defeat. This is hardly surprising; what is surprising is that the Indians held out as well as they did under the circumstances. The whites had better weapons, greater immunity to diseases that were new to the Indians, and a continual flow of adult migrants from Europe to augment their strength beyond the slow process of natural increase.

Some of the eastern tribes were either completely annihilated or so reduced in numbers that individual survivors were simply absorbed into the white population or neighboring tribes. However, where any significant tribal remnant remained, they regrouped and negotiated terms of peace. Today, few people even recognize the tragic names of King Philip of New England or Opechancanough of Virginia; from the

eighteenth century to the closing of the nineteenth century the followers of Pontiac, Tecumseh, Sitting Bull, and many others were to
experience a similar fate. As information diffused between tribes, some
saw earlier than others the wisdom of negotiating so as to avoid further
bloodshed or any bloodshed at all; but crisis was met generally by
attempts to negotiate in the group interest.

In the beginning, negotiation was also the most reasonable and
familiar course for Europeans to follow in dealing with Indians. Total
war was impossible as a technique for territorial expansion of isolated
colonies, and it remained impractical to the close of hostilities with the
Indians. It was easier to buy them out. Outnumbered and out-armed,
Indian groups could still bargain to some extent. In both New England
and Virginia the Indians gave up territory and pledged peaceful alliance
with the colonists against other enemies, European and Indian. In
exchange they received guarantees against encroachment on small re-

Powwow
(*courtesy*, Milwaukee Journal).

serves of land and the promise of assistance to overcome the disabilities of their drastically reduced circumstances (Underhill, 1953, 57–82; Lurie, 1959). By the mid-seventeenth century, treaties and similar compacts were already a standard feature of Indian-white relations. Such arrangements were not a European invention alone, but had clear analogies in the customs of the tribes for dealing with each other. However, in New England and Virginia these familiar patterns were expanded to introduce the precedent of reservations.

At the same time a second important precedent was set, one that was to underlie the continuing development of Indian policy for the governments of North America. Negotiation for Indian land was to be solely the prerogative of the crown acting through its designated representatives. Even when more authority was delegated to the colonies, shortly before the American Revolution, transactions were seen as involving societies rather than individuals. Among the Indians the landholding unit was understood to be the group, and individuals had no power to dispose of land except by common agreement voiced in negotiations through their recognized representatives. These ideals, at least, were mutually understood, even though exceptions occurred in practice. Treaties sometimes followed upon, rather than preceded, actual expropriation of land by whites; the Indians' representatives were sometimes managed, coerced, or bribed by the whites, particularly land speculators, to disregard the consensus of their people; the individual whites, usually traders, often paid for the privilege of building on Indian land and spoke of these transactions as deeds. In time, "the crown" became, in effect, the central governing bodies of the United States and Canada, but Indian people still speak of negotiations in terms of the American president or the reigning sovereign in England.

When the layman sentimentally deplores, or the historian objectively documents, the shortcomings in policy toward Indians, they single out the collusion and conniving that sometimes occurred in the course of treaty making. Naturally, the Indians resented a lack of fair play on the part of the governments. However, a deeper and continuing sense of bitterness relates to the constant governmental effort, particularly in the United States but recently also emphasized in Canada, to redefine the terms of transactions between "crown" and tribe to those involving individual citizens, white and Indian. For example, the policy of making formal treaties with Indians was abolished in the United States in 1871, and old treaties and later "agreements" remain in effect only as long as the government finds them expedient. Canada has tended toward the same sentiments as the United States but did not make its last Indian treaty until 1923. Treaty provisions remain an important consideration in the administration of Indian affairs,[6] and Indians in Canada have reacted strongly against the Trudeau government's recent efforts to negate treaties (cf. Cardinal, 1969).

Severe competition for land, open hostilities, loss of natural resources, and the effects of European diseases all contributed to the disorganization of contact-traditional cultures. In some places destruction was swift; elsewhere a slow attrition set in. The contact-traditional phase ended when a community could no longer make and carry out its own decisions freely and make its own selective adaptations from the inventory of white society. Generally this coincided with the establishment of reservations and equivalent settlements on both protected and unprotected lands. The reservation system, broadly defined, was as much a creation of the tribes as it was of the governments of Canada and the United States. For all that, both Indians and whites remained dissatisfied because of strikingly different perceptions of the objectives of the system.

The American and Canadian governments have generally operated under an assumption that the Indian treaty or comparable instrument is a kind of bill of sale for land. The bill can be marked paid in full when the governments' installments of education and material assistance result in the assimilation of Indians into the larger society and the abandonment of their distinctive communities. Until such time as Indians would master the white man's ways fully, reservations guaranteed protection from exploitation and unfair competition by members of the dominant society. They were also thought of as schools, places where Indians could be gathered and reeducated to become white Christians. Popular, and even official, self-righteousness sometimes is attached to these terms. Material assistance and protection of lands are seen as special privileges extended temporarily to Indians.

Apart from individual Indians who embrace this philosophy, Indians as local groups and a total minority have operated consistently under a very different assumption. For Indians, the treaty or similar contract is an enduring political compact, rather than a finite economic transaction. In exchange for occupying a great portion of the Indians' country, the white man would provide useful knowledge and new goods that would enable Indians to manage effectively as communities in the small areas still left to them. Their model was the contact-traditional culture in which mutually satisfactory and desirable relationships were regularly maintained between Indian and white societies. It was obvious that the buffalo, the fur-bearing animals, the Europeans' need for fighting men, and the natural resources of vast expanses of land could no longer figure in the Indians' reckoning. New and different adaptations would have to be made to restore community equilibrium and agreeable relationships with the surrounding white society.

The white man has grown increasingly impatient with the Indian's stubborn refusal to avail himself properly of the privileges extended by generous and benevolent governments to help him enter the white world. The Indian, in turn, has grown increasingly angry with the white man's willful refusal to honor governmental promises to provide meaningful wherewithal to build economically sound and socially comfortable communities to cope with the white world. Each has been disappointed by the other's apparent failure to live up to presumably mutually agreed-upon terms.

Generally, Canada has pursued a more gradualist and consistent course than the United States has in regard to assimilating Indians. Old organizational structures have been replaced with formally recognized chiefs and headmen elected or chosen by consensus, paralleling town council government. Canada has also tried to define religious changes as simply pagan to Christian by exercising some control over denominational competition among missions. For many years in the United States native leadership was discredited, and the government vigorously suppressed "heathen" practices with little concern for the confusion wrought by missions vying for the Indians' souls. Canadian patience with the persistence of Indian groups is probably consistent with national policy, which accommodates itself, despite some difficulties, to French- and English-speaking components in a bilingual and bi-cultural country. Certainly Canada was able to follow a more relaxed and humane policy for many years because competition for Indian land was not as crucial as in the United States. As Canadian population increases and natural resources are more intensively exploited, Canada is also reassessing its gradualist policy in favor of more forcible measures of assimilation.[7]

Because the majority of Indian people live in the United States and the present Indian social movement began largely in opposition to American policies, this study will concentrate on the American situation with comparative commentary regarding Canada. Greenland offers a special case, discussed in Chapter 13 by Charles Hughes.

The relationship between Indians and whites under contact-traditional conditions remained a significant model for all concerned at the time of American independence. The third article of the American Constitution empowers Congress to "regulate commerce with foreign nations, and among the several states, and with the Indian tribes." Government-tribal relationships were interpreted by Chief Justice John Marshall of the Supreme Court in two famous decisions that stressed the responsibility of the government to protect tribal land from illegal expropriation. In the earlier decision, *Cherokee Nation v. State of Georgia* (1831), Marshall noted that Indian tribes are neither foreign nations nor states, but that "the relation of the Indians to the United States is marked by peculiar and cardinal distinctions which exist nowhere else." He summed up their status as follows:

They may, more correctly, perhaps be denominated domestic foreign nations. . . . they are in a state of pupilage. Their relation to the United States
resembles that of a ward to his guardian.

Though equivocal in wording and relating to treaty obligations to
assist Indians, the concept of guardianship was increasingly interpreted
by the Indian Bureau and diffused to the general public as a specific
analogy to a guardian handling the affairs of individual minor children
until the children should come of age. However, contrary to popular
and even semiofficial opinion, Indians as persons are not and never were
"wards of the government" in any legal sense.

In the case of *Worcester v. Georgia* (1832), Marshall was much more
specific about the Indians' special status, suggesting no limits on its
duration but only defining the conditions under which it could be
terminated:

> . . . the universal conviction that the Indian nations possessed a full right to
> the lands they occupied, until that right should be extinguished by the
> United States *with their consent;* that their territory was separated from
> that of any State within whose chartered limits they might reside, by a
> boundary line, established by treaties; that within their boundary, they
> possessed the rights with which no State could interfere . . . [emphasis added.]

Further, in speaking of treaty provisions, Marshall commented on
recognition of the Indians' right to self-determination as groups:

> The very fact of repeated treaties with them recognizes it; and the settled
> doctrine of the law of nations is that a weaker power does not surrender its
> independence—its right to self-government, by associating with a stronger
> and taking its protection. A weak State in order to provide for its safety,
> may place itself under the protection of one more powerful without stripping
> itself of the right of government and ceasing to be a State.

Achievement of sovereignty over land by warlike or peaceful means
on the part of the United States and Canada was not construed as con-
ferring direct ownership of the areas held by particular tribes under a
previous sovereign or simple aboriginal title. Although Indians were
never paid more than an average of ten cents an acre, which usually
included the value of a guaranteed homeland in their original territory
or elsewhere, this amounted to millions of dollars pledged to Indians to
be paid over a number of years. Treaties contained other provisions:
blacksmiths, teachers, physicians, and other personnel to assist them in
adjusting to new circumstances and usually agricultural implements,
stock, and seed.

Frontier expansion soon engulfed the eastern reservations, and tribes
were moved on or their reservation acreage was reduced. The two terms
of office of Andrew Jackson (1828–1836) marked the removal of all but a

few eastern tribes to the Oklahoma area, known as the Indian Territory, west of the Mississippi River. Ideally Indians were to be welcome as part of the agrarian scene, but soon even the adaptable Cherokee, Creek, and others in the Southeast were pressured and harried into leaving prosperous farms and comfortable homes by means of federal measures whereby, Justice Marshall notwithstanding, local states managed to acquire Indian land.

A few eastern groups escaped or resisted removal. Some of them were simply ignored as Indians. These heterogeneous aggregates, the remnants of former southeastern tribes, often include a good deal of white and Negro ancestry. Through time, however, they have tended to reconstitute themselves as new "tribes."[8] On the other hand, a number of genuine old tribes can be found along the eastern seaboard from Maine to Virginia; but like the reconstituted tribes, they are not under federal jurisdiction. Early "pacified," in some instances they reside on reservations administered by local states as legacies of the colonial period. Segments of some of the larger tribes eluded removal in the nineteenth century or returned to their old homelands and remain there under a variety of official and informal arrangements. Where homesteads were granted to individuals, a nominal tie was usually retained between the Bureau and the group as a whole. Other communities simply sprang up on land purchased by individuals. The people are not recognized as Indians by the Indian Bureau, but some have been allowed to present claims before the Indian Claims Commission.

Except for bands of Ojibwa, the Menominee, and some of the Iroquois tribes, who negotiated successfully for reservations in their homelands in their treaty discussions, most of the Indian groups between the Appalachian Mountains and the Mississippi River are there because of strenuous resistance to government plans for them. After repeated failures to dislodge the Seminole bands in Florida by force of arms, the government finally granted them reservations or simply let them stay in the state. When the Cherokees were moved to the Indian Territory, a segment of fugitives and returnees reassembled in North Carolina and, through friendly white intermediaries, quietly bought some 40,000 acres. The tract was augmented by another 20,000 acres when the government finally granted reservation status to the Eastern Cherokee.

From the end of the American Revolution until well into the nineteenth century, Indian groups continued to employ old expedients, choosing among alternative political alliances. Segments of the League of the Iroquois who had been loyal to Britain decamped to Canada, as detailed in Chapter 5 by William Fenton. One band of Kickapoo, originally from the Illinois country, became so incensed by governmental interference with their customary practices after they were located on lands in Oklahoma that in the 1840s they sought sanctuary in Mexico. Indian and métis fugitives from Riel's Rebellion fled Canada after 1885 and were granted the right to remain among the American tribes who had accepted them. The Oneida and Stockbridge of New York negotiated privately through white agents with the Menominee and Winnebago for permission to settle in Wisconsin in 1821–1822. This "illegal" contract was eventually formalized by the government in the next decade. Many more examples of such tactics could be cited for Winnebago, Potawatomi, Choctaw, and others.

Although by 1880 systematic destruction of the buffalo had brought about the disruption of the contact-traditional culture of the Plains Indians, military encounters with these people led to a reevaluation of the policy to resettle all tribes in a general Indian Territory. It posed the danger of a coordinated intertribal uprising. By the 1840s the eastern tribes had all been "pacified," but there were still fresh memories among Americans that Tecumseh's intertribal followers at the side of Britain had posed a formidable threat during the War of 1812. The result was that except for establishing a few multi-tribal reservations and, as an extreme punitive measure, relocating some hostile bands, such as Geronimo's followers, the government granted most of the tribes west of the Mississippi reservations in or near their own homelands, safely isolated from one another.

At first, the western tribes were dealt with by treaties, but after 1871 the United States substituted "agreements." These resembled treaties and were often considered treaties by the Indians, but agreements did not require complicated legislative measures for ratification. Above all, the new measures represented an effort to erode the status of nations that was imputed to tribes by the Marshall interpretation of Indian treaties.

Some of the later reservations were created simply by executive orders of the President. The area most directly affected by discontinuation of treaties was Alaska, purchased from Russia in 1867. Unlike the situation in the Southwest, where Spanish recognition of Indian land title was respected in turn by Mexico and the United States and where treatylike contractual relationships were set up, the Russians passed on no such clear-cut precedents. Only the land rights of "civilized natives" around the Russian settlements were given explicit recognition in the negotiations, but Congress failed in its obligations to set clear policies to protect even these natives. Consequently, the land status of many Alaskan communities remains ill-defined.

In Canada, where competition for land was less acute, we do not find the familiar American pattern of making repeated treaties with the same tribe by which the tribe gave up more and more land or accepted a succession of ever more westerly reservations. Canada confined itself to making about a dozen major treaties, dealing in most instances with a number of tribes in a large district, and to occasionally revising details of treaties. By comparison, the United States entered into hundreds of Indian treaties (Kappler, 1904; Royce and Thomas, 1896–1897). Significantly, in Canada, the most complicated land issues arose and a disregard for treaty negotiations occurred in the rich fishing and timber area of the west coast, which was also a region of relatively heavy concentrations of native population.

As the nineteenth century wore on and tribes and alliances of tribes could no longer offer armed resistance, both Canadian and American policy conformed increasingly to actual guardianship over all aspects of life of childlike wards. Canada delegated much responsibility for Indian health, education, and welfare to Christian missions. This system promoted a certain consistency of programs and a reasonable continuity of dedicated personnel at the level of each Indian community. However, it also fostered a kind of denominational colonialism. Wherever possible, the first mission in power jealously guards its prerogatives against competing religions and even against secular agencies concerned with Indian affairs.

Until the very end of the nineteenth century United States Indian Bureau positions were political appointments, and key personnel changed radically at the national and local level with each new presidential administration. This became an invitation to corruption, as bureau employees were tempted to profit by peculation in what they expected would be short-term jobs. Conscientious and honest people, who actually tried to work in the Indians' interest, often saw any spark of Indian enthusiasm extinguished by Congressional indifference to financial needs and by central office directives that were inappropriate to local situations. However, Indians were not entirely without friends, and their protests led to periodic attempts to reform the Indian Bureau.

The Allotment Act of 1887, along with legislation related to it, was the most ambitious plan to make Indians self-sufficient as quickly as possible and at the same time phase out the need for the Indian Bureau. Both the United States and Canada had experimented on a limited scale with allotment in severalty of Indian lands. However, the American allotment program of the 1880s was to be applied generally. It was based on the explicit reasoning that Indians would inevitably conform to the grand stage of white civilization; that the hallmark of civilization was the concept of private property; that Indians were obstructed in their "natural" course by the reservation system, which preserved tribal practices in the form of communally held land; and that granting each Indian private property subject to American laws of descent and inheritance would encourage him to move rapidly in the direction of civilization.

The whole process was supposed to occur in the space of a generation, figured as twenty to twenty-five years depending on the reservation. During this time the land remained tax free and inalienable. After allotments were made, which worked out to about 180 acres per family, remaining lands were thrown open to sale and the proceeds used to build homes and establish farms for Indians.

The program was doomed to failure because of both its own internal inadequacies and circumstances external to the fact of allotment. Even if Indian people had liked the idea of farming, which most of them did not, patterns of diversified subsistence farming were to prove generally impractical for all Americans in the face of increasing mechanization and improved transportation of produce to expanding urban markets. Small farms rapidly gave way to single-crop or herd enterprises requiring vast acreages. As early as 1891 the Indian Bureau began renting aggregations of allotments to white farmers engaged in the newer operations. This provided a short period of prosperous leisure for Indian "landlords," but after 1900 another development created new problems.

Indian population had decreased steadily during the nineteenth century, but the trend changed after 1900; and as original allottees died, their small estates were divided among expanding numbers of descendants. In time many people held scattered shares in several different allotments. By then rental was the only feasible course. Land could be handled as parcels and the rent money divided among the heirs. As protective provisions expired, many Indians became unable to pay their taxes and stood in danger of losing even their small shares. Tax relief measures were applied; and patents-in-fee, which returned land to taxable status and gave the owner the right of sale, were to be issued only to Indians who were deemed "competent." The concept of competence soon was subject to abuses as unscrupulous whites pressured and bribed superintendents to declare Indians able to sell their land (Fey and McNickle, 1959, 72–79; Lurie, 1966). Allotted reservations became a patchwork of Indian- and white-held property.

It was hard for Indian people to comprehend what was happening or to protest. Land once secured to the tribe had been lost as individual holdings over which the tribe had no control. Although in many treaties Indian "consent" was no more than reluctant resignation, the appropriation of tribal land and wholesale removal of tribes merely demonstrated who held the greater power in the negotiations. The nature of the land-holding group was not questioned. Allotment demonstrated that the government denied the right of Indians to persist as communities.

The sincerely benevolent promoters of the Allotment Act were properly concerned about the abrogation of individuals' rights and even dignity under the oppressive "wardship" administration of the reservations. However, they were naïve about the nature of culture and society. In the late nineteenth century white society was not a homogeneous whole but was segmenting into humanly manageable and usable parts. Individuals formed urban neighborhoods, ethnic communities, and specialized occupational and industrial settlements. Thus, allotment did not permit Indian people to take their place as individuals making free choices among the segments of the larger American society or to create their own segments as others had done; it picked out the rural agricultural segment for them. By and large, they found it unattractive and economically inadequate, as did other Americans in increasing numbers.

For various local reasons relating to the nature of the land or to occasional successful opposition by Indians, some land escaped allotment; and because of mounting problems, the plan was not extended to all reservations. Thus, there are unallotted regions in the Southwest, parts of the Great Basin, and certain mountainous and heavily forested lands.

Both before and after allotment, some tribes became acquainted with new economic opportunities that suited them very well. But even tribes such as the Navaho and the Pueblo groups often had cause to complain about the heavy and capricious hand of the Indian Bureau. Indian preferences, from community organization and religion to clothing and hair styles, were suppressed in both the United States and Canada. In the United States particularly, programs for economic development were subject to frequent change. Indian people greeted each new proposal with less enthusiasm; and the less enthusiasm they showed, the more it was interpreted as inability to manage for themselves. The administration of Indian affairs grew increasingly paternalistic and authoritarian.

Adaptation to Reservations or Equivalent Stabilized Settlements

Bureau personnel encountered sullen apathy, a sense of deep grievance, passive resistance, subtle sabotage, a high incidence of drunkenness, uncooperativeness, and mourning for the past. Among Indians themselves community life became concentrated in areas over which the bureau had little control or knowledge. Ties and mutual responsibilities of extended kinship remained important despite some reduction of function that socioeconomic circumstances imposed on clans and other elaborated systems. Traditions of generosity and patterns of sharing assured group survival at least at a general level of poverty. Subsistence depended on irregular wage work, small gardens, a few dollars in land rent money, perhaps a little hunting, sale of crafts to tourists, mission charity, and occasional emergency rations issued by the government.

Social activities, such as the secular dances known as powwows, became increasingly important as overt expressions of Indian identity and a focus of community interest. Though often deplored by the Indian Bureau, these affairs were not explicitly religious, and as tourists would pay to watch Indians dance, it seemed hardly fair to forbid a source of earned income.

On the other hand, serious factionalism arose within the communities in the search for a satisfactory way of life. Some people turned to new religions, both mission Christianity and Pan-Indian nativistic movements, while others hewed to traditional ideas. Tribesmen who became cynically astute in manipulating the reservation system for personal gain were often favored by bureau personnel because they appeared enterprising in white terms. Many Indian people came to see poverty and uncomprising negativism toward any bureau suggestion as badges of personal integrity. Other people, who for various reasons had become effectively self-supporting and could have been prosperous, curtailed conspicuous evidence of their well-being and shared their wealth with sufficient generosity to maintain community respect and cooperation. To whites these natural leaders sometimes seemed no better than the rest. They appeared to encourage sloth by supporting "lazy" relatives rather than acting as exemplary models of competitive white acquisitiveness with their houses and other possessions. They often left home, weary of the struggle between bureau and community. Thus, a great deal of potentially qualified leadership was regularly spun off the reservations. Leaders who remained behind could usually rally support only in their own factions or for general social activities in which the bureau had little interest.

Meanwhile reservation life fostered an amazing skill in political maneuvering of sources of power, whereby competing missions, the bureau, other agencies of a state and federal nature, and even individual whites were played off against each other in a never-ending game between the factions. This kept everyone very busy, and the Indians at least held the line, if unable to advance on their own terms. Such negotiating had an old history, but the reservation situation corrupted and narrowed it until it became almost an end unto itself (Clifton, 1968; Walker, 1968).

Beyond factionalism there was another obstacle in the way of sincere efforts to involve communities in program development. Most Indian groups prefer to reach decisions by consensus. Although predictably patterned and effective, the methods of consensus are difficult to grasp for people who equate democratic procedure and efficiency with majority rule binding on the opposed minority. When Indian people appeared incapable of following such a simple procedure as presenting an idea and voting on it and insisted on long and apparently irrelevant discussions (which often had to be translated into English), even the best-intentioned, but thoroughly weary, superintendent often concluded that he would have to make the Indians' decisions for them after all. They simply did not understand "democracy." Indian people left such meetings exasperated by the superintendent's obtuseness about fundamental principles for making workable plans; or they accused him of transparent deceit in having said he was going to respect their wishes when he did not really mean it. Often the factions blamed each other for holding up consensus. Naturally, the general situation was far more critical in some tribes than in others.

If reservation people felt over-administered, many nonreservation communities, both within and outside the federal jurisdiction, also felt a sense of grievance. They were often just abandoned. In seeking to make new adjustments they turned for help to state agencies, missionaries, and any friendly whites, but help was usually extended with the same alternative encountered by reservation people: take on white identity or remain poor. The result was that community life took much the same form as on reservations.

World War I marked the beginning of a new phase of Indian policy, which was to end with World War II. Generally, Indians under federal jurisdiction could not be conscripted, nor could they vote. (Provisions for "citizenship" were made in a few treaties and in special legislation for particular groups or individuals.) Nevertheless, Indians volunteered for the armed services in large numbers from all over the country and by 1919 accounted for an astonishing record of heroism. In the United States public opinion was aroused by the realization that such patriotic people were neglected "wards of the government." In 1924 full citizenship was extended to all Indians. More importantly, serious attention was directed to the problems of Indian administration. The result, the so-called Meriam Survey, published in 1928, was an extensive and impartial study carried out under government contract by a private research organization. The facts were depressing; the recommendations bordered on the revolutionary.

While adhering to the idea that Indians would inevitably become assimilated, the Meriam Survey concluded that attempts to force the process simply did not work. Still viable Indian patterns could be used as a basis for program planning and white customs gradually substituted for them. It was timidly suggested that some Indian traits were admirable and did not deserve extinction. The survey reported, but did not understand, a widespread sense of grievance among the tribes regarding long-standing obligations that the government had not fulfilled. It was contended that policy and program improvement would be of no avail until the basic source of discontent was removed by providing prompt and fair judicial review and just settlement of claims. (Meriam, 1928, 805). The fact is that Indian people responded very positively to the administration of John Collier, Sr., Indian Commissioner from 1933 to 1945. Collier understood the essential nature of Indian grievances as anxieties regarding their future as a people. The kind of court procedure recommended by the Meriam Survey—the Indian Claims Commission—to deal with past injustices by strictly monetary compensation was not established until 1946.

The enabling legislation for Collier's programs was the Indian Reorganization Act (I.R.A) of 1934. Designed to encourage self-determination for Indian communities under federal jurisdiction, it granted them the option to organize under constitutions and to negotiate and operate as corporate entities with a real future in regard to credit, education, land acquisition, resource development, law and order, and similar matters. The steady forfeiture of Indian land, a continuing effect of "competency" proceedings, was halted, and a land acquisition program was begun.

Collier has been criticized as an impractical romantic trying to turn back the clock to the point of encouraging spurious Indianness and, conversely, as an uncompromising bureaucrat trying to impose Euro-American formulas of government to further strain remaining and usable Indian patterns. Good specific cases have been made for both arguments. Nevertheless, it is clear that from the start Collier evoked a remarkably enthusiastic reaction from Indian people who had grown apathetic and cynical toward the bureau. Of 263 tribes eligible under the I.R.A., over two-thirds, 192, approved it. Many soon adopted constitutions, charters, and other legal instruments available under its provisions.

Collier made enemies among some tribes, notably the Navaho. For all that, the retrospective view among Indian activists today is that he understood what Indian people wanted and that his administration was cut short before there was an opportunity to make the kind of program adjustments required in the implementation of any radically new policy.

The primary value of I.R.A. was that it reopened negotiations between tribes as communities and the larger society. It was not properly designed to serve all the functions of community self-government expected of it. Most of the highly organized Pueblos that had voted for I.R.A. did not see any need for constitutions. Communities seriously rent by factionalism made their customary internal political capital of the new format for tribal self-government, sometimes to the detriment of general tribal interests vis-à-vis the larger society. I.R.A. worked best where it stimulated old patterns into new life to coordinate community action and relate the community to the national socioeconomic system through the channels provided by I.R.A.

Collier sought Indian guidance, and his efforts were directed to helping communities cherish their distinctive identity while improving their
material welfare. Although his policy built on the findings of the Meriam
Survey, his own thinking had gone far beyond it. For many people in
Congress it went entirely too far. During the war years especially, Congress could remain indifferent to Collier's pleas for adequate support of
I.R.A. for long-range programs, because the immediate economic problems of most reservations were temporarily ameliorated by the prosperity
of full employment. When the war ended, servicemen and factory
workers came home to reservations still in desperate straits, with rapidly
increasing populations to strain limited local resources further. But they
brought back new skills, knowledge of a larger world and its varied
economic opportunities, and enthusiasm to develop programs for community improvement presumably available under I.R.A. By then the
national outlook of the postwar period was one of retrenching conserva-
tivism, felt in Indian affairs as in other branches of government. Ironi-
cally, Collier's policy, which never received proper financial support, was
blamed by Congress for the sad condition of Indian communities after
the war.

Recent Developments in Indian Policy

The transition in Indian policy is reflected in the Indian Claims Commission Act, which was passed in 1946 but under which hearings to
allow preparation of cases did not begin until 1951. The broad grounds,
allowing compensation on proof of fraud, duress, and evidence of governmental dealings that were not fair and honorable, were soon sub-
sumed under a general construction that the act covered only lands.
The Commission's work was scheduled for completion by 1957. Compensation centered on any inequities between the assessed value of the
land and what the Indians actually received through time in cash value.
This essentially simple theory of law is far removed from the expectations
of those who framed the act, and it has entailed incredibly complicated
and time-consuming argumentation for each case. It has also entailed repeated extensions of the tenure of the commission, the most recent
extending it to 1972 (Lurie, 1957; Bureau of Indian Affairs, 1966, News
release).

Although at the outset the Indian Claims Commission Act was hailed
as a long overdue measure of humanity and justice, other legislation of
that same year indicates the direction in which Indian affairs were to
move. Powers reposed by law in the Secretary of the Interior and the
Indian Commissioner were delegated to subordinate officials, and frag-

menting of authority obstructed coordination of programs for Indian community development. The creation of area offices interposed a new administrative hurdle between tribes and final approval of appropriations for their work.

By the early 1950s Congress had enacted legislation to set in rapid motion a process that was to disband and disperse Indian communities and thereby discharge any federal obligations for all time.[9] In 1953 the House Concurrent Resolution 108 was passed, enunciating a policy to terminate federal jurisdiction over reservations. Such a resolution is not binding on succeeding Congresses, but termination acts can be passed if there is enough sentiment for them. Public Law 280, passed the same year, transferred federal responsibility for law and order on Indian reservations to the local states. Federal liquor laws were also revised in 1953 to remove special prohibitions relating to Indians. In 1955 responsibility for Indian health was transferred from the Bureau of Indian Affairs to the Public Health Service (cf. Lurie, 1961, 480–481).

Tremendous complications arose immediately in regard to the specific termination acts of 1954 for the Menominee Reservation in Wisconsin and the Klamath Reservation in Oregon. Although these two tribes had been singled out in the Meriam Survey as soon able to manage their lumbering operations as tribal corporations without federal supervision, the philosophy of the 1950s was aimed at terminating Indian identity. These tribes, designated as prosperous in 1928, are now considerably worse off than they were prior to termination, their carefully husbanded capital used up by schemes promoted by advisers from the business world trying to show them how to join the American mainstream (American Indian Chicago Conference, 1961, 33–35; Stern, 1965, 151 ff.; Lurie, 1969). Public Law 280 specified only five western states in taking over responsibility for reservation law and order, but indicated the trend to sever the Indians' federal tie by all possible means. The philosophy seems to have been that states stuck with the task of policing areas of untaxed land would help to force termination, although Indian people on reservations pay income and other taxes.

The new Indian Division of the Public Health Service endeavored to bring Indian health up to national minimum standards, but Congress was working to disperse Indian communities. It saw no need to allocate money to build or even improve Indian health facilities, as this would imply perpetuation of identifiable Indian communities as a continuing governmental responsibility.

The option to repeal liquor prohibitions on reservations was fundamentally sound, because the law had racist undertones that were clearly discriminatory. Indian communities, however, had become so appalled by the course of federal legislation that some attached symbolic significance to any special *Indian* law and would not vote for repeal. On a few western reservations repeal resulted in the decision to open liquor stores as tribal enterprises.

Although "Collier men" remained in key bureau positions after Collier's retirement, they had no success in trying to change the direction of Congressional sentiment. When Dillon S. Meyer was appointed Indian Commissioner in 1950, the policy of the bureau accorded fully with the philosophy of Congress. Among the major undertakings of the bureau in the 1950s was the "Voluntary Relocation Program." As a matter of fact, Indian people had been relocating themselves for a long time in the effort to find the wherewithal to survive. The Meriam Survey of 1928 devoted an entire chapter to "The Migrated Indians" (667–742). Deploring the squalid camps that had sprung up on the outskirts of smaller cities, particularly in Arizona and New Mexico, it also cited a happy model for the bureau to study. About 1910 the Santa Fe Railroad began establishing Indian colonies along its right of way to handle shop repairs. Decent living conditions, training in skilled work, and standard wage scales created healthy Indian communities in tune with the industrial development of the nation.

The Meriam Survey regretted the dearth of records concerning the adjustment of Indian people who had left for larger, distant cities. The bureau had been content to forget them. We realize today that a great many of these so-called migrated Indians did not make the same kind of adjustments as rural white Americans who abandoned farm and small town forever. The Indian pattern was not to migrate, but to commute, long before burgeoning suburbia made the term fashionable. Although the Meriam Survey suggested that the behavior of city Indians ought to be studied as a guide to program planning, by the 1950s the bureau was aware only that Indian people kept coming home again. No one saw Indian behavior, such as regular weekend trips from Denver or Chicago to Pine Ridge, South Dakota, as a special kind of commuting dictated by the same community imperatives that motivate the modern suburbanite to struggle out each morning to catch the 7:20. Indian people do not seem to view city life as new and different from an old life back on the reservation. Rather, it is an extension of peripheries of an area exploited in order to survive, in the way that hunters, gatherers, even slash and burn gardeners and peoples dependent on trading, venture further and explore new terrain and opportunities when local resources are inadequate.

The Voluntary Relocation Program, however, set out to lose Indian people in the cities. The plan included taking people as far as possible from their home communities to discourage returning. Ultimately, retreat from "problems of adjustment to city life" was to be cut off by terminating the reservations. The bureau provided one-way travel expenses, initial jobs, and housing. Relocated people often qualified only for unskilled jobs of uncertain duration. Urban housing that they could afford was frequently substandard. The relatively small economic recession after 1956 was devastating for many relocated Indians, and the Relocation Offices were not equal in budget or personnel to the crisis posed. To survive, Indians depended on other Indians, both more successful fellow relocatees and old residents who had formed intertribal clubs and centers able to extend assistance.[10]

By the end of the 1950s it was clear that the current policies were not only drawing vigorous and outspoken Indian opposition but were simply not practical. In 1961 John F. Kennedy appointed a Task Force to visit tribes and collect data as a basis for policy recommendations; and in the same year, Philleo Nash, a member of the task force, was appointed Commissioner of Indian Affairs. Although many thoughtful Indians pointed out that the report of the task force still reflected assimilationist sentiment while showing little sympathy for the actual programs of the previous administration, Nash himself took an increasingly pragmatic approach to Indian affairs, committed neither to a general policy of assimilation nor to perpetuation of Indian distinctiveness. He sought to meet the Indians' varied needs on Indians' terms. He encouraged industry to locate in Indian areas, promoted tribal enterprises, rationalized and humanized the relocation program, and expanded the base of financing Indian programs beyond the resources of the Indian Bureau to other federal agencies. He was profoundly aware that most Indian communities had no wish to phase out of existence.

Experiments initiated by some tribes even before Nash took office had demonstrated that Indian objectives were feasible. Since the time of World War II Indians had shown interest and aptitude, derived from their own cultural background, in industrial work requiring careful observation and fine manual dexterity. Moreover, reservation communities are well suited to the national trend to disperse clean manufacture of component parts and small products to local communities. Left to their own devices, Indians proved remarkably innovative, tribalizing management and the nature of the production line to create enterprises ineffably Indian yet comfortably in step with the demands of the modern world. They, however, demonstrated many other talents and vocational interests as well. Efforts were being made to use natural resources along cooperative or corporate lines adapted to tribal values in raising cattle, lumbering, and fishing (Steiner, 1968, 124–135; Deloria, 1969, 225–242). Tourism also appeals to some tribal communities, as it capitalizes on the otherwise often unproductive natural beauty of many reservations and assures keeping the tribal estate intact as a primary asset. Touristry of this kind meets a rapidly growing demand for wilderness areas on the part of an urbanizing society with more leisure time and higher wages to spend on recreation than at any period in our history.

Nash endeavored to build with such articulatory models in mind. But he was obliged to work and show quick results in the face of a prevailing government philosophy that defines Indian populations as mere aggregates of impoverished individuals in need of crash programs to propel them into "the American mainstream," rather than as viable communities seeking satisfactory contractual relationships in regard to the total socioeconomic system of the country. When the Office of Economic Opportunity (OEO) was established, programs were extended to Indian communities. Despite overall commitment to the idea of a "grass roots" approach, OEO has been little more successful in Indian communities in this regard than it has been with other peoples. Any success in Indian work must be attributed largely to the presence of an already developed grass roots program and to effective local leadership, able to prevail against entrenched bureaucratic predilections and canned programs. For many tribes, however, OEO created new problems and smothered nascent self-help efforts, as the Indian Bureau had so often done before. Long experience in survival by means of factional manipulation of the Bureau of Indian Affairs was simply extended to OEO.

Nash's regime was in no way as revolutionary as Collier's, but his term of office lasted less than half as long. Deemed too slow and cautious in extending the benefits of big business to the reservations, Nash had no recourse but to tender his resignation, in 1966 (McNickle, 1966).

The Indians' idea of healthy community development is not to serve as cheap labor pools for mammoth tourist enterprises owned by white syndicates that seek to exploit Indian ethnicity or to punch time clocks in feeder factories of large corporations. Many efforts to create jobs on reservations have ceased operation or require employment of non-Indians to keep going, while Indians become increasingly embittered that they are blamed for the failure of programs over which they had no real control in planning and decision making.[11] Even expert assistance extended to terminated tribes like the Klamath and Menominee has deprived them of a real voice in managing their affairs as communities. And as the problems of poverty and social discontent mount, the Indians' alleged lack of understanding of sound business practices and the years of government paternalism are blamed (cf. Cahn, 1969).

However, the Indians' own established commuter patterns and the broken hopes of developing proper reservation industries have promoted a new sentiment that suggests yet another articulatory adaptation. Reservations should remain exclusively tribal estates, and commuting, including planned alternations of residence between *home* and city, could provide necessary financial support while ongoing Indian community life is maintained. Instead of the usual white pattern of leaving the eight-hour workaday world of home for short, unproductive vacations, Indians suggest a pattern whereby they would live longer periods at home, leaving briefly to engage intensively in economically productive activities. The idea is to systematize on a community basis what is an actuality in varying degrees for many Indians as individuals and families. A model approaching community adaptations of this kind even exists among the Mohawk and some of the other Iroquois people, many of whom are structural steel workers (Wilson, 1959, 3–36; Steiner, 1968, 160–161).

Nash's successor, Robert La Follette Bennett, a Wisconsin Oneida, was far less forceful than Nash in fostering Indian self-determination, but even he was deemed too much a Nash man when the Nixon administration took office. Bennett's appointment had typified the political temporizing with minority grievances of recent years; however, it set a precedent that the job of Indian Commissioner must go, nominally at least, to an Indian. During a six month's search for Bennett's replacement, the administration rejected some half-dozen qualified Indians promoted by intertribal organizations and scholarly advisers to the government. In August 1969, Congress finally approved the appointment of a Republican Indian of Mohawk and Siouan descent, Louis R. Bruce, a virtual unknown in Indian affairs who has dairy interests and has spent most of his adult life in the advertising business in Manhattan. Although much is made of the fact that he considered the termination of Menominee and Klamath a mistake, his own role as a "prominent Indian businessman" causes worry among many Indians that he will find little to dispute in the big business approach to reservation development.

Pan-Indianism and Intertribal Organizations: The Contemporary Movement Toward Unity and Action

The Indian movement toward unity to promote articulatory objectives reflects recent problems, crises, and opportunities. But it remains a logical outgrowth of Pan-Indianism, which unites Indian people ideologically, and of an old tradition of intertribal alliance to provide structures for action. Pan-Indian sentiment has always crossed the Canadian-American boundary: an important recent development in Indian activity, however, is the attempt to organize for action on an international scale and involve not only Canadian and American Indians but even the more traditional tribal peoples south of the United States (*Akwasasne Notes*, 1969).

Although for some scholars Pan-Indianism is virtually synonymous with the relatively recent powwow complex, there seem to be very old common Indian elements that have always transcended local differences of language and culture and that can be properly termed Pan-Indian. The Pan-Indianism discussed here refers to a persisting cluster of core values and related, predictable behavior that give Indian people a commonality of outlook they do not share with people of European cultural tradition. Component characteristics can be enumerated but must be understood as interrelated:

1. As noted earlier, there is preference and relaxed patience for reaching decisions by consensus. While often baffling to the white observer, the process is patterned, and Indian people of widely varying tribal backgrounds are able to conduct business together according to mutually understood "rules." Modern organizations, including those of Indians, must keep records; and parliamentary procedure is easy on recording secretaries. However, consensus was too valuable a technique to abandon, and Indians across the country discovered and began using tape recorders in conjunction with business meetings while such machinery was still very primitive and cumbersome. With this method a complete record can be kept for possible reference use and only final decisions noted in parliamentary terms and duly recorded on paper.

2. A high value is placed on oratory as pure artistry and on reasoned persuasion as a means of achieving agreement. This probably reflects the common preliterate background of all tribes, reinforced by the same circumstances that often produce verbal eloquence in segments of the society that are not excessively dependent on the written word. There is a distinctive quality to Indian oratory, even in English, that is remarkably reminiscent of the many speeches translated and recorded during treaty proceedings of the nineteenth century (see Fenton, Chapter 5 of this book). Even writings in English reflect an Indian style, as evidenced in the dozens of tribal and intertribal periodicals that have sprung up as part of the heightening political activity since the 1950s.[12]

3. There is a special kind of Indian humor. Like other minorities, Indians take delight at the expense of the dominant group, and while many Indian jokes are adaptations of widely used themes, Columbus and Custer figure prominently. Indians have no reluctance to tell a funny story even though they know everyone already knows the punch line. Ridicule, of course, is an important means of social control in all small societies and is used for this purpose by Indian people even in intertribal settings. It is also a sometimes devastating weapon in Indian-white confrontations: "Some scalps aren't even worth taking." Truly Indian humor in ridicule, interpersonal joshing, and formal oration tends to a straight-faced summing up of serious discourse with stunning effect by outrageously funny metaphors, analogies, or puns (sometimes

Indian tipi on Alcatraz Island, overlooking Golden Gate Bridge, February 1970.
The occupation of Alcatraz has proved to be of great symbolic significance to
Indians across the country in their fight for recognition of their rights to land.
(United Press International photo.)

bilingual) between seemingly unrelated universes of discourse (Miller, 1967). An example is the one-word translation of a long, esoteric Winnebago clan name denoting a spirit bear that travels under water and ice: Polaris. Prescribed "joking relationships," usually between brother-in-law and sister-in-law or other potential marriage partners, are observed in many tribes. These require salacious wit in conversation. Beyond this and more widespread is a kind of teasing that may strike the non-Indian as downright cruel, poking fun at physical disabilities or old mistakes, but symbolizing close friendship. Whites may easily mistake for hostility what is a carefully considered overture of friendliness. Whites are also put off when Indians are vastly amused in seeing or telling about antics that result from really painful mishaps to people and animals.

4. Various patterns of institutionalized sharing as an important mechanism for community survival are reinforced by great social esteem accorded the generous. There are consequently strong negative sanctions

on greed, envy, and even excessive material acquisitiveness, as well as on selfishness. Mudslinging is certainly not peculiar to Indian politics, but it is noteworthy that while people may gossip about an individual's laziness, drinking, or sexual behavior, he and his faction are really in trouble when the rumor starts that "Someone took all the money." It does not matter whether there was much money to begin with, or any money at all; if the group does not prosper, or if a plan fails or is delayed in accomplishment, greed must be at work, almost like an evil presence.

5. There is lack of emotional commitment to personal possessions. This is evidenced in the frequent criticism of whites as "too materialistic" or "selfish." Indian people certainly seek decent living conditions and greater economic security. But one hears a frequent disclaimer among Indians whose living standards are those of whites: "These things are nice and I enjoy them, but they are not important to me." Exquisite craftsmanship is admired and prized in such portable, personal objects as Indian jewelry, costumes, and ritual or powwow paraphernalia. But these objects are parted with readily and proudly in generous gestures even to casual acquaintances, particularly if they are admired. Likewise, all gifts are accepted graciously as an honor to the giver, without the conventional white, middle-class protest: "Oh, you shouldn't . . ." —a reaction that strikes Indian people as grossly impolite and selfish. A gift acknowledges a previous gift or kindness from the recipient or implies that some future reciprocation will occur at the other person's convenience or when the giver is in need.

6. Interpersonal relations are characterized by a preference for indirection in attempting to control the behavior of others. To some extent the prevalence of gossip in Indian communities and intertribal organizations is predictable simply as a common social control among members of primary groups. Whatever differences arise, they will continue to need each other to survive and therefore must channel hostility carefully. However, if a person is clearly disruptive to some immediate situation, particularly if he is drunk and beyond rational management, others will withdraw into cold indifference, faces devoid of expression. The troublemaker has no recourse but to subside or depart. Overt aggression or wanton destruction of property as attention-getting devices are coolly ignored, and physical intervention is usually resorted to only if it appears that some innocent person may be seriously injured. This technique is also used widely by Indian parents in controlling children. Direct confrontations, although not unknown, are not indulged in rashly and are reserved for situations in which gossip, teasing, and other indirect controls have failed. Often the one to issue the reprimand is not the injured party, but someone who is especially skilled or re-

spected or who is the appropriate kinsman for the job. The objective is to shame the wrong-doer into an admission of his errors and make him compose his differences with the group. I believe that the unhappiness Indian children experience with white teachers and the anxieties adults experience with white employers and co-workers can be traced in large measure to the fact that scolding and overt criticism are taken far more seriously by Indian people than they are by whites. For the white person a difficulty is usually considered over if he can let off steam, but for the Indian person the situation remains unrepaired.

7. On a similar plane is the concept usually verbalized by Indians as "respect for people." There is comfortable acceptance of long silences to allow another person to mull over new information or simply withdraw into private thought if there is nothing pressing to talk about (Wax and Thomas, 1961). Because Euro-Americans have a low tolerance for silence, they are apt to characterize Indian people as sullen when they do not respond readily to conventional, conversational overtures. The Indian person is politely trying to give careful attention to what the white person produces as a kind of sociable noise he does not expect to have taken seriously.

Respect for people includes wide tolerance of individuals' idiosyncrasies if they abide by otherwise fundamental Indian values. In intertribal activities this also allows for accommodation to great cultural diversity. The forceful Plains politician whose behavior reminds us that his not too distant ancestors recited personal deeds to certify their merit may strike the mild Pueblo person as painfully overbearing and egocentric. The Plains man, in turn, may confide that the Pueblo friend really has excellent ideas and could hasten proceedings if he just were not so diffident. Yet, lest they appear critically disrespectful, both hasten to add the familiar Indian phrase "But that's *his* way." As long as people are sincere and sensible, these differences do not matter.

8. Withdrawal from situations fraught with anxiety, although related to the preceding point, deserves special consideration. It is accepted easily by Indian people but is a source of despair and exasperation to non-Indians trying to work with them. Retreat may consist of no more than sudden uncommunicativeness or an actual departure. When most members of a group are agreed upon a course of action after hearing all dissenting opinions, the dissidents are free to withdraw their participation if they wish. The others may regret their going, but if all arguments are exhausted, well . . . that's their way. Perhaps they can agree on some other issue some other time. The decamping of dissatisfied segments of larger tribal and intertribal entities during the treaty period is illustrative of withdrawal behavior.

9. The average Indian person is simply more observant than the

average white. Children are ridiculed for making the same mistake twice and for making mistakes that could have been avoided if they had been on the alert. Avoidable injury receives little sympathy. Teasing among adults reinforces the foolishness of ill-considered actions. Individuals are expected to be responsible for themselves, which perhaps explains why Indian people are reluctant to offer gratuitous advice even when another's course of action may appear disastrous.

10. Perhaps no more than a complex of much of the foregoing is what sophisticated Indian people refer to as their adaptability, or expediency. We are willing to accept as *Indian* the culture of the Plains based on a European import, the horse, or the herding culture of the Navaho, which was also a late postcontact development. Indians are continuing to make the same kinds of adaptations, working in structural steel; using the automobile to make country and urban resources parts of a general Indian territory; employing tape recorders so they and their children can hear the traditional songs and stories regularly even in a city environment; and preferring employment where intensive spurts of effort pay high dividends, allowing them to have more time of their own.

All these characteristics (and there may well be others) would seem too widespread and predictable to have developed recently or solely as a result of similar experiences in contact with whites. Indian people who live alternatively and with equal success in the white and Indian worlds are aware of shifting gears, knowing on a conscious level what kind of behavior is called for in different situations. Such Indian people are not "marginal"; rather, they thrive on the richness of two traditions in the way the true bilingual does.

All this suggests that alliances and confederacies among Indian groups were expedited by more than the commonly felt threat that whites posed to Indian land and resources. Europeans as a whole, whatever their national differences, afforded a striking contrast, which served to make evident to Indian people the similarities among themselves that they had taken for granted as simply natural human behavior. Alliances occurred early, and with surprising frequency considering the diversity of Indian cultures and languages sometimes involved. Until well into the nineteenth century there was room for differences of opinion among tribes concerning which competing white powers could serve them better and how far they shared specific goals, irrespective of their philosophical commonalities as Indians as a reason for alliance. But with the firm and peaceful establishment of American, Canadian, and Mexican sovereignty, Indians were left to build allied strength only with each other in their own interest. By then, Indians were severely inhibited in exercising old patterns for unifying effort by the exigencies of the reservation system, which froze their political peripheries, both in regard to old alliances and in the making of new ones.[13]

It is surprising that Indians continued to get together at all. Inadequate though Indian resistance was to the policies of the 1950s, the amount of unity and Pan-Indian political sentiment in evidence argues for cultural continuity and a tradition of alliances under exceedingly trying conditions, rather than a lack of strength attributable to the recency of Pan-Indianism and intertribal activity.

Just as control over their own affairs in the local communities was forced to center on matters of little concern to the Indian Bureau or other whites, intertribal activities during the late nineteenth and early twentieth centuries were necessarily confined largely to social activities and pacifistic expressions of religion. It is difficult to say just what factors had the greatest influence in the development of modern Pan-Indianism as a political force, but the historical ingredients can be traced from the time reorganization and stabilization of community life were developing, during the early reservation period.

At least some of the Plains emphasis in modern Pan-Indian costumes began in the last quarter of the nineteenth century, when Wild West shows and Indian Medicine shows became a popular form of traveling entertainment. They usually featured Plains Indians, which contributed to the familiar stereotype of *the* American Indian. A new and prestigious occupation as theatrical performers was a stroke of good luck for the Indians. The Indian epitomized by Plains trappings was a noble and attractive, albeit fearsome, figure. The theatrical image of the Negro in the same period remains a liability, as traveling minstrel shows featured white comedians in blackface makeup who lampooned Negroes.

As the tourist industry expanded in relation to the growth of railroads, Indians quickly recognized new "natural resources" to be turned into cash: handcraft, their own likenesses on film, and costumed dance performances. The white sportsman from the city promoted the occupation and romantic image of the Indian guide. Indians themselves began riding trains to visit other Indians almost as soon as the tracks were laid, and they sometimes held out for free passes as part of the price for rights of way through reservations. Automobiles brought more tourists; they also gave Indians more mobility both to engage in intertribal activities and to explore for work that appealed to them. Information relating to practical matters was diffused in the course of participation in other tribes' social and religious activities.

A type of secular dancing had begun to take form in the nineteenth century, based on ceremonial patterns of the Plains and known as powwows—the word itself probably derived from Algonkian origin.

Powwows last from a day to a week or more and include games, craft displays and sales, giveaway ceremonies, and other features, along with the main attraction, costumed dancing.

It is sometimes alleged that crass commercialism to fulfill tourists' expectations prompts the emphasis on Plains styles and that modern powwows are specious Indianism or at best tawdry nativism. However, the Plains influence is much older, and social Pan-Indianism, even in powwows, involves much more than entertaining tourists.

> The horse not only enabled Plains Indians to become extremely mobile in hunting and "warfare," but also increased inter-tribal contacts. Even a sign language developed in the area to provide communication across linguistic boundaries. In the 1800's not only had intensive "warfare" and very mobile hunting developed but tribes were beginning to ally with one another, camp with one another and inter-marry with one another. Most significant for the later development of Pan-Indianism, the Plains style of life was extremely attractive to tribes on the edges of the Plains area. Plains traits and institutions were spreading to other areas even at the time that Plains Indians were becoming pacified and settled on reservations [Thomas, 1968, 79].

Thus, the modern pattern was set strongly in Plains terms. The result was a dynamic social and esthetic tradition, with local adaptations constantly made on the general pattern and diffused as changing fashions in the Pan-Indian world.

English is used in order to announce programs to white audiences and also because of language differences between participating tribes. Sometimes English is incorporated into the dance songs ("When the big powwow is over . . . I will take you home in my one-eyed Ford") but is obscured to white ears by Indian tonal and syllabic treatment derived from their own, and not Western, musical tradition.

Indian people sometimes resent the term Pan-Indianism when it is meant to suggest that ongoing tribal traditions and identity are melting down into no more than a kind of recreational, dress-up activity for any Boy Scout troop or hippie to copy. For Indians there are two kinds of powwows, both diffusing Pan-Indian traits and reinforcing tribal identity.

One type is planned as an intertribal affair and is usually held on what might be termed neutral ground. Examples include large commercial enterprises involving white entrepreneurs, regular dances at intertribal social centers in large cities, and the dancing that constitutes the social side of otherwise serious intertribal meetings. The greater the number of different tribes represented, the greater the success of the affair.

The other kind of powwow, the tribal powwow, is a local activity. Whether or not it seeks to attract tourists, it is primarily a community effort in which local customs and language are evident despite the overlay of Pan-Plains elements (Rachlin, 1968, 107–111). These powwows build community solidarity. The old man who can sing and train others is no more nor less important than the skilled electrician who handles lights and loudspeakers. Pleasures of dancing are unrelated to religious affiliation, formal schooling, or annual income. The tribal powwow is usually attended by urban workers and helps to sustain the sense of mutual interests among all members of the tribe. It is customary to welcome visitors from other tribes with speeches and formal gift exchanges, thereby reinforcing each group's distinctiveness as guest and host while promoting intertribal fellowship. Since the 1950s powwows have become increasingly prevalent, so that people now can spend entire summers traveling the powwow circuits. Although one Indian observer blames anthropologists for encouraging this phenomenon (Deloria, 1969, 86–87), my own opinion is that it was part of a general response to the growing threat to Indian identity, an effort to make continuing Indianness widely known and to reenforce tribal and intertribal unity.

A few missionaries and their more devoted converts look askance at powwows as heathen dancing and no more than an excuse to knock off work and engage in a drunken brawl. However, obstreperous drunks are considered a threat to the occasion and are often dealt with by customary sanctions of withdrawal, ridicule, and, in some places, action by clans or societies traditionally invested with "police" power.

Intertribal activity includes more than powwows, and there is a good deal of visiting for purposes beyond mere sociability. Concentrations of natural resources, such as fish runs in the Northwest, draw visitors who customarily share them in season with the "owner" tribes. Healers, including skilled herbalists and genuine shamans, sometimes attract an intertribal clientele. Many contemporary Indian communities represent scattered fragments of once larger tribes, and their ties of kinship and friendship are kept alive by visiting. Where tribes share common ceremonies, differing perhaps in local detail, such as the Plains Sun Dance, qualified visitors from other tribes may participate or people may simply reciprocate reverently interested attendance at one another's ceremonies.[14] Among the conservative Pueblos, where Plains Pan-Indianism holds little appeal, traditional religious rituals serve many of the same functions that secular powwows serve elsewhere.

In addition to traditional religious activities, a number of Pan-Indian revitalization movements have sprung up. The Ghost Dance of the Plains—which ended for all practical purposes in the massacre of hundreds of unarmed Indians at Wounded Knee, South Dakota, in 1890—is best known; but others, such as the Dream Dance and Indian Shaker Religion, have persisted. The most widely diffused, the Peyote

Religion, began taking form in the 1880s and by 1915 was chartered as an official denomination in the United States as the Native American Church. Because of the peculiar, although essentially harmless, effects of peyote, the denomination has had to take legal action on many occasions and thus has been a training ground in political aspects of Pan-Indianism (cf. Slotkin, 1956). Most recently, a Prophet Religion has begun spreading across northern Canada as the kinds of culture-contact problems that engender nativistic or revitalization movements are just beginning to have an impact. Likewise, intertribal social dancing and traditional gambling games are increasing as new roads expedite travel by car and bus. Significantly, the new Indian religions tend to be Indian-male dominated, in contrast to mission Christianity, where the clergy is usually white and the strength of the churches rests in the Ladies Aid and similar organizations.

Social and religious gatherings promoted political trends. Because there was ample evidence of outright chicanery, dishonesty, and callous disregard at the local administrative level, few Indian people realized that these immediate hardships were distinct from the difficulties they experienced as the result of consistent promulgation of a benevolently intended assimilationist policy. In organizing resistance, political appeals must be simple, clear cut, and reducible to slogans to attract the largest possible group. Thus, the subtleties of the treaty-defined relationship as Indians understood it became the rallying cry "Broken Treaties," and all grievances were simple proof of calculated "bad faith" on the part of the government. Most tribes have treaties of their own that invest the broad slogans with local, if not always precise, meaning. Tribes that were passed by in the treaty-making period also made common cause under the slogans, presumably because their rightful treaty interests as Indians had been disregarded. Even members of tribes whose reservations have been terminated in recent years persist in the argument that a special treaty relationship exists for all time. The political movement observable today derives from this early and widely diffused appeal to all Indians, fortified in later years by purposeful efforts of more educated Indians to create intertribal organizations to deal with clearly defined problems.

Although the nature of reservation administration discouraged intertribal alliances, the Indian Bureau itself unwittingly contributed to the strength of Pan-Indianism. Well into the twentieth century many children were taken to distant boarding schools, frequently over parental protest. Although some former pupils drifted into the white population or became professional Indians, many of those who maintained Indian ties became community leaders and were among the first active proponents of formal, intertribal political organizations. These people formed a national network of friendships based on the experience of being simply Indians together trying to cope with the larger white world as it had been forcibly imposed on them in the military-style boarding schools. The situation was similar within Canada. Therefore, intertribal unity as promoted initially among the more educated Indians tended to assume that the international boundary was a firm dividing line between groups of Indians and that Indians outside federal jurisdiction and not represented in the boarding schools were not really Indians.

Since the second half of the past century concerned whites working with educated Indians have formed organizations to assist Indians, but the orientation was merely to humanize implementation of the assimilationist policy of the government. Through the years such groups gradually moved toward the Indian orientation, but they tend to be largely run and dominated by whites. The first large-scale and effective organization formed by and for Indian people is the National Congress of American Indians (NCAI) founded in 1944. With headquarters in Washington, D.C., and regional offices around the country, NCAI was initially concerned with helping local groups obtain advice and pool information in utilizing the Indian Reorganization Act and to act as the political lobby of united Indian opinion before Congress and the Indian Bureau. Voting is adapted to tribal blocs, involving a variety of tribal governing bodies, and is also adapted to individual memberships. Of significance, in view of the very outspoken opposition of young Indian activists today toward white meddling, however well intentioned, is that while NCAI has white memberships, even since its inception NCAI required that whites pay twice the dues of Indians and not be allowed to vote.

For present purposes, the political philosophy of NCAI will be designated as moderate, although to many whites it is not "moderate" at all. It is clearly articulatory and sees the government under an old contractual obligation based on treaties and similar agreements to protect the Indian land base and provide assistance in developing channels satisfactory to Indians for interaction with the larger economy. Assimilation should be an open option for individuals, but there should be an honest alternative. All Indians should have appropriate educational and other opportunities and the choice of either entering the larger society at a decent socioeconomic level or remaining identified with Indian communities with decent standards of living. It seeks reform and improvement within the existing structure of government, including the Bureau of Indian Affairs.

In contrast to NCAI are such intertribal organizations as The League of Nations–Pan Am Indians, which is loosely structured. It is difficult to determine whether one organization or several attracting the same personnel are represented by the various leagues, confederacies, unity conferences, and so forth, listed on printed letterheads or mentioned in self-identification of spokesmen. "Traditionalists" will be used to describe their political position as the direct outgrowth of the old surge toward political unity under the rallying cry of treaties.

The traditionalists view the moderates with suspicion as including people who are or were in the employ of the Indian Bureau and, above all, as compromising on the central subject of treaties. The moderates' stress on education and employment, their work with the bureau and other federal agencies, occasional screaming-eagle patriotism, and exhortations to use the ballot, all fall on traditionalist ears as the white man's formula: progress equals assimilation. The traditionalists see no point in the Indian Bureau and consider the granting of citizenship to United States Indians in 1924 and to Canadian Indians in 1951 another abrogation of their treaty rights and a plot to destroy Indian identity by fiat. To the traditionalists the apparent "patriotism" of Indian volunteers in World War I, which got them the vote in the United States, was a treaty obligation of loyal allies. Although more extreme than that of the moderates, the traditionalist outlook derives from the same history of preferences for contractual relationships between Indian and white societies and insistence on respect for all time of the Indian land base, not just as tax-free federal land but as the Indians' sovereign territory.

The traditionalists argue for recognition of Indian tribes as virtual nations or mini-states, in peaceful treaty relationships with both the United States and Canada. Recourse in grievances should not be to Washington or Ottawa, but to the United Nations. Furthermore, the traditionalists seek to restore customary tribal forms of self-government to manage their internal affairs.

Although the attitude is changing, many moderates still consider the traditionalists' position unrealistic, irresponsible, and silly, likely to alienate public sympathy so even moderate articulatory goals will be impossible to achieve. In the 1950s they noted with distaste that traditionalists' demonstrations at Canadian border crossings, for example, lent themselves to colorful journalism playing on quaint clichés of Indians on the warpath and depicting these Indians as harmless eccentrics. However, in fairness to the traditionalists, and despite their occasional fuzzy mysticism and historical romanticizing, their interest in the United Nations reflects a logical political conclusion given their first premise. Like the moderates, they recognize that Indians must make purposeful adjustments and use respected sources of power to survive in the modern world, and they do not expect to survive on wild plants and game. At the same time, they are convinced that they do not have to accept as many white materialistic values and organizational structures as required by the moderate position, which also rejects much white ideology and feels the Indian land base should remain inviolate.

It is hardly surprising that much traditionalist strength derives from the Northeast, where the Tuscarora and Seneca learned in the 1950s that Congress, upheld by the Supreme Court, could abrogate Indian treaties unilaterally in what was deemed the larger national interest and could approve dam building that flooded Indian land. Likewise, in the Northeast are many of the nonfederally recognized tribes, who do not even have the weak reed of Congress on which to lean for protection. But Pan-Indian traditionalism attracts supporters among Indians all the way to the Southwest and Northwest coast. Traditionalism also has strong supporters in Canada. It is proving increasingly attractive to the most militant young people in both countries.

Many formal intertribal organizations developed before NCAI was founded, but none mounted the broad program of NCAI, and they were regional in scope. Such regional bodies began proliferating in the 1950s, and now there is not an Indian area in the country without one or several intertribal organizations. Most seem to be modeled on NCAI and to be politically moderate; but this may only reflect our having better access to information about those that seek state or federal charters to raise funds for programs as nonprofit organizations.

Opposite to both moderates and traditionalists are people who are often members of moderate organizations, attend intertribal gatherings, and are in demand as public speakers before white audiences as experts on Indian affairs. They see integration and assimilation as inevitable and desirable, although they themselves are really "professional Indians" in contrast to the unknown numbers of Indian people who have actually become so assimilated into the larger society that they no longer identify themselves as Indians. Both moderates and traditionalists share a common anguish when professional Indians deny that there is anything left worth saving in Indian social life and culture and attribute the persistence of Indian communities and their attendant problems to the perpetuation of reservations, romantic devotion to the past, and the Indians' own lack of individual initiative, foresight, drive, ambition, and acquisitiveness. Their model tends to be the third generation European peasant who, having become thoroughly Americanized, can indulge himself, if he wishes, in ancestral hobbyism. Although this is a minority opinion among Indians, it is not rare among whites and must be taken into serious account in attempts to assess the future of American Indians. The message is simple and clear. It plays upon cherished American values of progress and the melting pot and suggests analogies to the poor immigrant lad who sold newspapers or the farm boy who had to walk ten miles to school to reach the pinnacle of American "success."

It is probable that until well into the twentieth century few Indians or non-Indians, including Indians who chose the path of assimilation or the role of professional Indian, were fully aware that there was a diametrical opposition between Indian and white objectives. By the 1950s the ideological confrontation became apparent, and the government determined that the white man's philosophy would prevail.

The present movement developed as explicit resistance to what was seen as an ultimatum against any recognition of the Indian position, whether expressed in moderate or traditionalist terms. Existing intertribal organizations were not strong enough in membership or funds to conduct a proper campaign. Communities themselves became divided internally, with some people arguing for active opposition and others trying to follow the usual procedure of just sitting out the latest storm from Washington. The situation was further aggravated because people of heretofore negligible interest in their Indian ancestry began reasserting tribal membership in the hope that pending land claims cases would bring large settlements to be distributed on a per capita basis or that the tribal estate would be similarly divided by termination. The gap thus widened between the tribal community and its city-based members, who often were automatically suspected of threatening the interests of the community.

The only politically militant Indians were the traditionalists. They had always seen the moderate position as a betrayal and made no distinction between the political moderates and the professional Indians. The moderates feared and avoided identification with the traditionalists; their methods were seen as irrational, impractical extremism that would only aggravate the situation further.

In spite of all these dissensions, a common Indian opposition was spontaneously evoked as knowledge diffused regarding the unremitting assimilationist implications of the legislation of the 1950s. It is my opinion that the greatest handicap for Indians was not the moderate and traditionalist differences among themselves hampering formation of a united front, but the climate of liberal white public opinion regarding civil rights. While former Senator Arthur Watkins and a few other active promoters of termination clearly considered Indians an unwarranted burden on the federal government, there is no question that termination and related legislation were strongly endorsed by well-meaning legislators who were influenced by analogies to the Negro movement for civil rights. In the 1950s the concept of civil rights tended to be reduced to a simplistic popular formula as virtually synonymous with desegregation and free exercise of the franchise.

Most Americans, whatever their views on other minority groups, are usually quite well disposed toward Indians; and even politicians who might have had prejudices or prejudiced constituencies where Negroes were concerned could still look good in championing the "first American first" in regard to civil rights. Both bigots and liberals confused Indians' problems with those of Black people and were eager to help them on those terms. Shocking poverty and expressions of dissatisfaction with the status quo are to be found in both groups. Much to the distress of whites active in the civil rights movement, however, most Indians were opposed to demonstrating and, above all, to making common cause with Blacks. They were deemed racist and their own cause ignored because they characterized even the early, peaceful Black demonstrations as "undignified" or "not the Indian way." What whites did not realize was that Indians had problems enough of their own without inviting the additional problem of heightened racial prejudice.

Not being considered "black," Indians who wished could be "white." In fact, to be identified as "not white" entailed the risk of being "black." Integration was a demonstrably open option in the regular spin-off of individuals who could become integrated and assimilated, able to admit and take pride in "Indian ancestry" rather than being forced to "pass." What little we know of the many generations of Indian spin-offs indicates that they entered the general white society with respectable ethnic credentials at all levels. Even Winston Churchill boasted of his Iroquoian ancestry from his mother's side of his family. Indians who were opposed to termination and the philosophy of assimilation behind the general policy of the 1950s rejected the very option that, it seemed to them, Black people were eagerly seeking. What angered Indian people was the abrogation of their rights, supposedly secured by treaties, the Constitution, and early Supreme Court decisions, to persist as self-determining communities in regard to freedom of religion and other cultural practices. To demonstrate like Black people would imply that they sought the same goals and had the same grievances.

The problem was well illustrated in the intertribal "fish-ins" on the Northwest coast, beginning in the state of Washington in 1964. Although the name was inspired by the "sit-ins" in restaurants that discriminated against Black patrons who had the same rights according to law as whites and wanted to exercise them, the fish-ins were intended to demonstrate that Indians had special treaty rights irrespective of state and even federal game laws governing other citizens.

While Indians have felt deprived both on and off the reservations, they had never felt segregated as this word is generally understood. Their own land was always given up reluctantly and under coercion, but they tried to make the best they could of a bad bargaining position, moving to reservations or withdrawing to marginal lands whites did not want. They expected that by dint of long experience in adapting to the presence of whites and by adopting new traits while maintaining their own ethnic integrity they would make their communities the equal of any they had ever known in satisfying group needs, but not necessarily identical to those of the white man. They had none of the sentiment of the lone immigrant or even the lone slave, separated from kin and community by choice or circumstance, endeavoring to survive among strangers in a similar situation.

Many Black people have "passed," but only those who did not look Negroid had this option. Even full-bloods among Indians could be accepted if they took on a white life-style. Black people, locked into a distinctive social status by racial considerations, had little choice but to strive for improvement of their lot by achieving close cultural similarity to the dominant society. Far more than Indians, they were deprived of satisfactory models for group life of their own choosing. The conditions of slavery obliterated sociocultural ties to African communities. With emancipation, slavery was replaced for many Blacks by a condition analogous to that of the oppressed European peasantry. But the peasant could change his identity and become assimilated, because his skin color did not betray his social origins after he altered his behavior as an individual to join the urban elite. Even a peasant origin is acceptable if it is European and several generations removed, as witness the resurgence of white interest in making the costumes and learning the folk dances of grandparents or great-grandparents who struggled to overcome identity as "Hunkies," "Polacks," or "Greenhorns." An ethnic group even validates its Americanization by pride in origin, and we now see the same process at work as the once despised home-grown "soul" and "Afro-American heritage" are embraced by conservative, middle-class Black people. They, too, now have an "old country." Although strict definitions of tribe no longer apply to Indian communities, and historically there were variations on the tribal model, whatever North American Indians were, or are, they have never been peasants aspiring to better their lot in terms of models provided by the urban elite and distinguishing between past and present identities.

Black people have had special problems relating to race and the recency and common knowledge of their previous condition as slaves. They were, and in some respects still are, truly segregated. This entails economic and educational handicaps and personal frustration and humiliation, as a kind of ritual uncleanliness was early imputed to black skin. Although Blacks were subject to many restrictions after emancipation, late in the nineteenth century some Indian groups were actually fenced in on reservations, and their goings and comings required passes from the local agent. But Indians had the proud knowledge that they were so treated as a conquered people still considered potentially dangerous as the dreaded Sioux or Apache. And even in the worst days of the reservations, the individual Indian who denied his heritage could change this identity. Black people were held back as aggregates of individuals united by common problems of social, educational, and economic discrimination. While Black ghettoes have become communities with their own subcultures, they are not old societies supported by centuries of treasured tradition in continuous contractual adaptation to a larger society. Nor can urban Blacks try to move anywhere but out into the general urban and suburban areas. They were propelled to the cities by a desire to escape southern, legally enforced segregation only to encounter northern de facto segregation. They were squeezed out of their ruralism by the same economic pressures that sent much of the white rural population to the cities over the past century, and they cannot go home again.

The Voluntary Relocation Program coupled with plans to terminate reservations with all possible speed nearly succeeded in putting large numbers of Indians in the position of so many urban Blacks, genuinely segregated at the bottom of the social heap. Deprived of their home communities and ill-equipped educationally and in regard to competitive cultural motivations to make their way to higher levels in the urban environment, Indians would have had no escape, socially or psychologically, from the denigrating implications of segregation. The risk of becoming identified with Blacks as a racial, rather than a cultural, minority raised the strong likelihood that Indians, including the spin-offs who were making their way successfully with white spouses, would be subject to the effects of the widespread racial prejudice experienced by Blacks, which Indians in general had thus far been spared.

Increasing numbers of Indians had been coming to the cities; and even during the Depression they had begun making their own quiet adaptations, some as spin-offs, but a good many maintaining their home ties and engaging in their own style of commuting. The problem in the cities was not really economic; those who stayed exploited city resources effectively by their own lights. The big problem was loss of desirable aspects of Indian life in the cities.

Around 1940 Indian centers and clubs began springing up, primarily as social organizations, their constitutions explicitly stressing "preservation of our heritage" and similar sentiments. They engaged in some welfare work, giving newcomers help in finding housing and jobs and, at times, gifts of goods and money with which to get established. The newcomers were usually quite sure of what they wanted and knew urban kinsmen whom they could ask for help without placing excessive strain on the obligations to share by those who could do so. As they prospered, these newer arrivals validated their Indianness, in turn, in this respect. If the city was not satisfactory, the newcomers went home again. In many cities formal organizations were even unnecessary, as corner taverns became Indian gathering places. The taverns served the same purpose as neighborhood family taverns generally, the main difference being that Indians tended to be scattered over the city and would congregate at the favorite tavern from some distance when unable actually to go home. There they knew they would see old friends, catch up on home news, maybe hear some fellows sing around a drum.

With relocation, the existing centers, limited in financial and other resources, were pressed into welfare work they had not been designed to handle, the social problems of unemployable, discouraged, and psychologically distressed people stranded far from home with no city kin. Welfare agencies in many places had residence requirements and could not be of much assistance to Indian newcomers; they were also hampered even in communicating with Indians. The existing centers sought outside help from churches and other private benevolent organizations, and new centers sprang up to meet the crisis of the 1950s. The Indian taverns ceased being sociable havens in many cases and became trouble spots for municipalities as Indians sought traditional solace in culturally defined patterns of behavior (cf. MacAndrew and Edgerton, 1969). The stereotype of the drunken Indian began obscuring the image of the noble red man most urban whites had subscribed to. The spin-offs drew further away; but the crisis revealed a curious lack of class distinction on the part of many prosperous urban Indians, who accelerated efforts by the centers to provide activities as substitutes for drinking as well as to help the impoverished.

One of the most interesting developments in the urban situation is that today it is a rare city with a sizable Indian population that has only one active Indian center. Sometimes new centers can be traced to the budding off of dissident groups, but not always; and even where there was an initial disagreement, people who participate in the activities of one center will usually participate in all from time to time. The different centers' programs are remarkably similar, and one encounters within each the whole spectrum of Indian political philosophy, from moderate to traditional. A few prosperous, fairly regular city residents assume most of the responsibilities of running the centers; but people with problems turn to them for help in large numbers, and many others without problems participate in social activities of various kinds.

My own tentative hypothesis is that the multi-center phenomenon reflects an old reservation adaptation for survival as Indians. Most centers require outside sources of funding to keep going, particularly in regard to welfare responsibilities. It is difficult to obtain such help without obligation. On the reservations, factions assure that no one group, and above all no one non-Indian source of funds that Indians can only manipulate but cannot control, will be in a position to dictate terms that might threaten fundamental Indian community interests. I have the impression that intertribal groups in the city, like intra-tribal factions at home, almost automatically seek means to avoid the risk of having to "play in a crooked game because it is the only game in town." At the same time, no one in on the action wants to miss any part as long as it remains honest.

Figures are unreliable, but at the very least, one-quarter and perhaps as much as one-half of the total Indian population is now resident in cities, although the actual personnel varies daily and seasonally. What estimates we have show that Indians have a high proportional arrest rate compared to other groups in the cities. This may in part be attributed to racial discrimination extending increasingly to Indians as poor, darker-skinned people. But Indian crime is almost always alcohol-related and confined largely to nuisance and petty disorders. For many Indians the fellowship of the taverns rather than the atmosphere of the centers offers a more immediate and total, if short-lived, escape from the personal pressures of urban life and the contemplation of the frustrations of trying to achieve decent community life on the reservations.

Indian leaders were able to discern this tragic course of developments as the fate of many relocatees, and they knew wholesale termination would mean that there would be no place to go home to for any Indians. But they were faced with the task of opposing the policy of the 1950s as it was promoted in Congress and before the public in adaptations of the then popular language of the Black movement for civil rights. The policy was described as offering "freedom for the Indians," and reservations were described as "rural ghettos" and even "concentration camps." There is no question that a good deal of overt anti-Black sentiment was thereby generated among Indians, who were accused of preferring "dependency," "second-class citizenship," and "segregation" when all they wanted was to hang on to their own property and develop it along lines they found compatible.

White Americans who have begun to grasp what Indians want are not universally sympathetic. To some, Indians are somehow "un-American." Others consider the Indian cause touching but unrealistic. Even social scientists find it difficult to imagine economic development of reservations and movement of individuals to the cities (even those maintaining reservation ties) as anything but inimical to persistence of Indians as a distinctive cultural group, let alone a linkage of distinctive sociocultural tribes within the larger whole. Those who argue, as did Collier, that Indian communities may offer useful and interesting experiments in new structural relations for large industrialized societies encounter many colleagues who cannot see this theory—although it has never been tested—as anything but trying to set back the clock of progress (cf. Task Force, et al., 1962, 125–136). (That Indians have had difficulties in trying to convey their message becomes understandable when we observe the dismay of many white liberals in recent years faced with the new Black separatist sentiments.)

In the midst of all the turmoil of the 1950s, however, experiments were going on to build Indian strength and win public support for Indian objectives. These concentrated work through influential segments of the public. Many lawyers had become acquainted with Indians' problems through the more than 800 claims registered with the Indian Claims Commission by 1951, and they became exasperated with the intransigent stand of government as the long history of legal complications in Indian affairs came to light in research on the cases. Indian groups, in turn, began to see lawyers as able to forward various community objectives besides claims cases on a comfortable and familiar contractual basis. Lawyers either work in their clients' interests or the clients can fire them (Dobyns, 1968). Tribes and intertribal organizations have also been able to work out mutually beneficial contracts with scholars and universities on the basis of shared interest. In 1955 a Workshop on American Indian Affairs was established in cooperation with the University of Colorado at Boulder. Since 1959 the six-week summer workshop open to young Indians from both the United States and Canada has been run by American Indian Development Incorporated (AID), a nonprofit organization with an Indian and white staff. The workshop has become the model for similar undertakings on a more localized scale throughout the country, with younger Indians taking more control of such endeavors.

A landmark endeavor was the American Indian Chicago Conference (AICC) of 1961, initiated by the anthropologist Sol Tax and carried out by the largest intertribal representation ever assembled for a common effort. On the eve of the election of 1960, Tax hypothesized that despite the confusion and cross-purposes in Indian reactions to the policy of the 1950s, there seemed to be a common sentiment of opposition among Indians. If Indians were given the opportunity to meet and share views freely without white interference, they might reach agreement among themselves on what they wanted, as a guide to Indian policy for the incoming administration and as a reasoned argument of their position before the public (Lurie, 1961). The *Declaration of Indian Purpose* resulted from the experiment, which began in the fall of 1960.

It involved individual, tribal, and intertribal participation in exchanges of views that were printed and distributed to a growing mailing list; and it culminated in a final, week-long meeting in Chicago in June 1961. In retrospect, the conference not only accomplished its purpose of producing a document reflecting Indian agreement (although Indians are still trying to get their message to the government despite a formal presentation of the *Declaration* to President Kennedy), but it was prophetic of the course of Indian activities to the present time.

The American Indian Chicago Conference may well have helped clarify and hasten subsequent developments, but the elements were already present in the people and events at Chicago. The *Declaration* reflects what has been designated a moderate approach, hardly surprising since in 1961 NCAI was the only major intertribal organization and Tax's initial contact to test Indian interest in the idea. However, traditionalists participated from the start, even on the Indian steering committee. The traditionalists did not withdraw their support until the very end, when it became obvious they could not win others over or find reason to change their own position on treaties. Besides the traditionalists, the conference included mutually suspicious factions of reservation, nonreservation, federally recognized, nonfederally recognized, and urban Indian people, as well as the inevitable professional Indians, who had as many criticisms of the whole idea as the traditionalists. As the preponderance of moderates from all factions gradually explained their positions, the group was able to reach consensus. It was debated whether the few Canadian Indians present should vote, and it was mutually agreed that their role was that of observers to take back ideas, since they were under a different national jurisdiction. Also, the Canadians were not under the same threat as the Americans at the time. This, among other things, tended to discourage the traditionalists, whose political strategy transcends national administrations.

Students on their way to the 1961 AID workshop at Boulder also attended the Chicago conference, where they met other young Indian people. The National Indian Youth Council (NIYC) was formed on the crest of enthusiasm for Indian unity. As it turned out, these young people took a broader view than their elders, who accepted the departure of the vehement traditionalists as a matter of course, withdrew in a state of tight-lipped anxiety from any mention of the Black movement for civil rights, and were politely but only distantly interested in Canadian problems.

At the start a great many people wrote NIYC off as a small group of negativistic young soreheads who would never be important on the Indian scene. Liberal whites found their talk of blood bonds and Indian "right to self-segregation" perilously close to outright racism.

In derision, they dubbed them "Red Muslims," little realizing that the Black movement, knowingly or not, had begun to borrow old pages from the Indian book, which young Indians were only expressing noisily in a new jargon. NIYC frightened moderate Indians too, when they staged the first fish-in in 1964, as they seemed to confuse the Indian-Black distinctions the moderate Indians had worked so hard to make clear. Demonstrations, as the traditionalists had always known and as NIYC recognized, are not peculiarly Black and are sometimes the only technique to make people stop and listen to reasoned persuasion. NCAI had chosen the political technique of lobbying, which was not "the Indian way" either until they chose to apply it to Indian problems. Borrowing from the terminology of the Black movement—"Culturally deprived: a white middle-class suburban child"; "Integration: marrying an Indian in another tribe"— NIYC helped to establish the Indians' distinctive position more clearly than the older Indians' complete withdrawal had done. Perhaps most telling of the ability to see that the whole civil rights movement has relevance for Indians too is the pun "Uncle Tomahawk," the Indian leader who is willing to live with the status quo like the timid Uncle Tom who is the despair of the Black militant (*Indian Voices*, 8). The serious humor and relatively mild militancy promoted by NIYC enjoys a broadening appeal, and Indians all over the country now display lapel pins and bumper stickers proclaiming "We Shall Over Run," "Custer Died for Your Sins," "Custer Had It Coming," and "Indian Power."

The last is worth special note in regard to developments on the Indian scene since about 1967. Although Indians may refer to themselves as red men, the term "Red Power" was not initially popular in the United States. First, there are unfortunate political connotations and, second, Indians see themselves as a cultural, rather than a racial, power block. Nevertheless, during 1970 Indians have begun to use the term Red Power more frequently, perhaps because of Canadian influences discussed below. American Indians usually hasten to say that civil disturbances are "not the Indian way" but will often add comments about Black Power to the effect that "Now they're getting smart; they're proud of who they are." A few Indians even joined the Poor People's March on Washington; but they soon fell out with the predominantly Black participants, because their grievances were still too specialized and only a few of the Chicanos understood anything about treaties. Militant Indian power in the United States has been expressed by holding fish-ins; barring reservations to white sportsmen and vacationists who littered the beaches and defaced rocks; and, in Maine, preventing use of state reservation roads as public thoroughfares.

In Canada, there was never any reluctance to use the term Red

Power in decidedly menacing terms and actions. The development of the Indian movement in Canada has lagged behind that in the United States just as Canadian policy has tended to follow American policy at a distance (see note 9). However, where Canada has never taken advantage of the opportunity to profit by the example of consistently ineffectual Indian policy and programs south of its border, Indians have been keeping closer watch. Forewarned, they have tended to arm accordingly. Canadian Indians have also been able to exploit advantages not available to American Indians. But they, too, have their own special problems (cf. Cardinal, 1969).

The National Indian Brotherhood of Canada was founded some thirty years ago and is roughly analogous to NCAI in political philosophy and in directing work within its own national polity. However, it is organized as Provincial Native Brotherhood Chapters and, because of the relatively greater uniformity of tribal governing bodies from band to band, seems to avoid many of the internal problems of factions and tribal representation that plague NCAI. In addition, there is the Indian-Eskimo Association, begun in the early 1960s but more similar to the early, Indian rights organizations of the United States, which are more or less dominated by whites. Some mutual disdain exists between the two organizations, but at present the Association, as its name indicates, is more active in the far North, where the Brotherhood is just beginning to extend its influence.

The Brotherhood was not very active until about 1966–1967, when a combination of circumstances that had stimulated the American movement caught up to Canada. These included agitation to settle land claims, increasing problems as more Canadian Indians were moving to the cities, serious threats of a termination policy, and a growing cadre of educated Indians arguing for effective community development to ameliorate problems of poverty on the reserves.

Canadian Indians had generally experienced fewer problems with the government during the period when they were being settled on reserves, because during the American Revolution and the War of 1812 most Indians involved in these conflicts, north and south of the border, had been loyal to the crown. When the Americans won the final round, American Indians became a conquered people, whereas Canadian Indians had been faithful allies in an unsuccessful conflict. Thus, Canadian Indian history is not one of wholesale removals and great reductions of tribal land. Canada, with more land and a relatively smaller population, could, for a long time, afford to be generous in treaty concessions. Now the still unassimilated Indians are becoming an ethnic nuisance and occupying large areas that whites could well use. The Canadian Indians are prepared to fight for their land—preferably by peaceful legal means, but they are not afraid of militancy. Most American Indians assumed in the 1950s that the day of *fighting* the white man had passed and that their only recourse was polite, dignified politicking, playing on the nation's moral sensibilities through Congress.

Furthermore, Canadian Indians can avail themselves of the clout of analogies to Black militancy without the risks and fears that caused American Indians to withdraw completely from any association with the Black movement. The relationship of Canadians, Indian and white, to Black people has been very different from the American experience. While Canadians may be no more free of racial prejudice than Americans, the relatively few Blacks in Canada can be comfortably tolerated, and their image in white eyes is generally good. Theirs is the historic tradition of the underground railroad. The first Blacks encountered by Canadians were a selection of people with unusual skills and high motivation to escape slavery and succeed as free Blacks in a white society. It has always been the Indians in Canada who were the poor and socially out of step. Canadian Indians have experienced much more real racial prejudice than American Indians, although assimilation is still easier for individual Canadian Indians than it is for American Blacks. Neither Indian nor white Canadians were particularly informed or concerned about the Black movement in the United States until it reached spectacularly destructive proportions. By then, Black Power, separatism of various kinds, emphasis on new African nations and the tribal heritage, as well as "soul," had replaced the older desegregation watchword promoted so enthusiastically by white supporters of the initial stages of the Black civil rights movement. Black rejection of white leadership and help was also attractive to Canadian Indians.

Canadian Indians can afford to exploit analogies between Red Power and Black Power because, given the nature of the case, these will remain only useful analogies; they do not imply a merging of a Black majority and red minority as a common racial power block in which Indians' special cultural predilections and demands would be lost. Canadian Indians have taken approving notice that Blacks in the United States have wrested concessions and thoroughly frightened the white man by a show of force in areas of concentration of Black population where the ratio of Blacks to the total population greatly exceeds the national figure of 10 to 15 percent.

Talk of Red Power has given law enforcement officers I have spoken to nightmares of Watts and Detroit. In many Canadian reserve towns the white population is relatively small but dominates business and commercial interests. All across Canada there have been hostile, even violent, "incidents"—so far without fatalities—and many more are threatened. These concern local problems of discrimination or grievances about reserve administration, and they usually are not reported in American newspapers or even widely publicized in Canada.

However, where the Canadian movement can safely play on the theme of Red Power, it has special problems of its own to dissipate united strength. These concern the métis people, who can join in the movement and be accepted in terms of problems of racial prejudice and discrimination but whose other social and cultural interests are different from those of Indians. Often they are phenotypically and even genotypically more "Indian" than some officially recognized Indians, and in many places they share a similar life-style and problems of poverty. However, they have no treaties, reserves, or tribal band organizations through which to work in their own behalf, nor do they have other special provisions to make up for the lack of treaties and reserves, such as the protected land and social services enjoyed by "natives," which includes the Eskimo. Complicating matters, there are, in addition to the members of old, established métis communities, people of mixed parentage living in Indian communities who are classified as Indian if the father was Indian and white if the father was white. Yet others have signed off of treaty status but remain in the Indian communities or return to them when unable to avail themselves of the benefits of assimilation, which is the implied governmental objective of the option to sign off.

Urban Indian Centers in Canada are often Indian-Métis Friendship Houses operated under governmental auspices. For many practical purposes of finding employment, housing, and healthy social outlets, Indian and métis can be considered together; but there is mutual suspicion, and Indian groups bud off on their own. The métis, in the present policy crisis, really has nothing to lose and cannot share the Indian's anxiety about threatened termination or join his agitation for support of community development on the reserves on Indian's terms. In the United States many communities that are not federally recognized as Indian identify as Indian; and they are gaining acceptance in the Indian movement as long as they maintain ethnic integrity as Indians and in principle support goals of federally recognized Indians, such as opposing termination. The métis by definition, if not always in fact, represent a hybrid people, racially and culturally, and seek respected recognition and their own distinctive identity. For some, it would be a step down to cast their lot with Indians, and Indians are sensitive to this snobbery, albeit attributing it to sour grapes that the métis have all the disadvantages and none of the advantages of being officially "natives."

At present there are so many things going on—so many new organizations, petitions, special conferences, and Indian newssheets—that it is exceedingly difficult to untangle all the different strands. However, a number of trends can be discerned. While dedicated traditionalists embrace an ultimate goal of a kind of mini-state treaty status in contrast to the moderates' preference for the definition of tribes as dependent, domestic nations, both reject the domestic colonialism of much Indian administration, on the one hand, and the loss of identity by assimilation, on the other. Organizations such as NIYC and conclaves of traditionalists seem to be offering a strategy for uniting Canadian and American Indian strength without obliterating tribal ties or rejecting work within the governmental structures when feasible. They seem to ask that each Indian, no matter what his tribe or where his residence, take on the general welfare of all Indians as his personal responsibility. When any crisis arises in which the local Indian interest is threatened from the outside by government, missionaries, sportsmen, or anyone else, the individual should take whatever immediate action he is capable of. This may mean going off to join a demonstration, buying and wearing a lapel button, flaunting a bumper sticker, writing to congressmen, donating money, signing a petition, or just getting the word around to others who can help more.

Indicative of the present movement toward unity is the increasingly widely read *Akwasasne Notes,* a newspaper appearing ten times a year and reprinting current news stories about Indians from Canadian and American papers and magazines. It is edited at Rooseveltown, New York, and shows a strong traditionalist orientation. Such presently popular singers as Buffy Ste. Marie, a Canadian Cree Indian, and, to a lesser extent, Johnny Cash, who claims Cherokee ancestry, have also had an important influence in informing the general public about Indians' historic and contemporary problems and in rallying Indian people to mutual effort in the Indian interest.

In 1961 the traditionalists could not understand the moderates' concern over termination and abolition of the United States Bureau of Indian Affairs. They now appear willing to support Canadian Indians in their fight against termination and the phasing out of their Indian Office as a means of holding the line against further erosion of any treaty recognition. While moderates in 1961 and before were embarrassed by the traditionalists' treaty ideas of mini-states, many can now support those tribes along the Canadian border who are trying by demonstrations and other means to force both Washington and Ottawa to recognize provisions of the Jay Treaty of 1794, which Indians living on the border claim permits them to travel freely in North America and to cross the border without paying duty, as citizens of the United States and Canada do.

Indians today seem to be molding a movement that is tolerant of, and even eager to encourage, local societies and distinctive cultures as the basis of satisfactory community life. Some go so far as to recommend more variety for the nation as a whole, white and Indian. The range of differences between Indian groups as well as the widely diffused Pan-Indian traits make up the full richness of a dynamic and complex modern Indian culture with which all Indians can identify in Pan-Indian or nationalist terms. It is not necessary for everyone to participate directly in all the different expressions of this culture.

In commenting on the fact that at one time the more acculturated individual had only the choice of conforming to the demands of the Indian community or giving up his Indian identity entirely, a perceptive Indian observer notes:

> It is the process of individual acculturation that is being changed by the Pan-Indian movement. For one thing, the marginal people are not leaving the Indian communities as it seemed they would. The Pan-Indian movement has formed a healing bridge between factions. For instance, it is possible now for a very marginal acculturated Indian to be accepted in his community even by the more conservative Indians if he participates in the institutions and symbols of this Pan-Indian community . . . the general problem of loss of identity and community in America may mitigate against even very urban Indians cutting their ties with other Indians altogether. One could imagine a resurgence of local tribal identity in response to these conditions [Thomas, 1968, 81].

Tribal identity even seems to be encouraged by participation in Pan-Indian urban life (Ablon, 1964; Verdet, 1961).

If American Indians were once appalled at the Canadians' greater militancy, they, too, have come a long way. The 1969 convention of the NCAI was enlivened by pickets and hecklers when the new and controversial Secretary of the Interior, Walter Hickel, appeared as an officially invited guest speaker. It was not just disrespectful, hot-headed youth, who did not appreciate "the Indian way," but a good many angry middle-aged Indians who waved signs and shouted, "Shut up, fickle Hickel!" as shown by network television coverage of the event.

Anti-white sentiments are also being expressed, and Indians seem to be seeking new contractual relationships even with old friends. Anthropologists have come in for severe criticism recently, and many have been shocked and hurt to find that the views expressed by Vine Deloria, Jr., (1969) are far more widely shared than they ever realized. Research among Indians of benefit only to the anthropologists is criticized in the same breath as efforts on the Indian behalf, presumably on Indians' terms, but undertaken without real Indian involvement or advice. There is resentment even when there is total agreement with what whites have to say. Indians want to say it themselves as the best proof that they are ready to undertake what informed whites also say they are capable of.

If some hostility is at present misplaced and even unjustified, it behooves us to realize that this is inevitable when repressions are suddenly thrown off, and to have patience (Lurie, 1970). I do not know whether it was the Canadian willingness to exploit Red Power–Black Power analogies or the message of NIYC[15] and the traditionalists that demonstrations are not necessarily "not the Indian way" that has helped overcome the reluctance to criticize the living, breathing white man as something only Black people do to achieve Black objectives. It is clear that Indian people are becoming convinced that they will not get satisfaction by merely couching their deep and old bitterness in terms of trying to hold the white man responsible and accountable for the sins of his ancestors who "stole the Indians' land" and brought the Indian to his present sorry pass.

The Indian movement forces us to face a basic and exceedingly contemporary question. Do Indians demand special rights and unreasonable privileges or simply a serious reevaluation of the concept of civil rights and liberties that may help to make mega-society more livable for all of us? Black Power and soul, Hippie and non-Hippie communes, and a host of other expressions of dissatisfaction with life in conventional, contemporary society suggest that individual "freedom" to achieve and accumulate is not really enough. What makes the Indian movement worth careful attention is that Indian people have not had to make their delight out of necessity or whole cloth. They have old, tried models of community and culture that have stood the test of adversity and have proved flexible and adaptable to the technological complexities that so many people fear will dehumanize us.

N O T E S

[1] There is always a problem in designating modern Indian societies. Official terminology in Canada applies the term *band* to each sociocultural group with its own census roll. In the United States, the terms *band, group, tribe, community, rancheria, pueblo,* and others are used to designate an administrative unit such as reservation or nonreservation communities under the federal jurisdiction. Following usual Indian practice, I have used the word *tribe* throughout to mean any local administrative unit that sees itself as a defined community of the Canadian and American Indian bureaus, state reservation communities, and communities that identify themselves as Indian, although entirely independent. The intertribal settlements in cities are called *urban communities*. Where the reference is to the pre-nineteenth-century period or to groups not yet brought

under federal jurisdiction during the nineteenth century, the terms *tribe, band,* and *intertribal alliance* are used in a more standard ethnographic sense.

2 This study draws heavily upon *The American Indian Today* (Deland, Fla.: Everett/Edwards, 1968), most of which appeared as a special issue of the *Midcontinent American Studies Journal* VI (2): fall, 1965, edited by Stuart Levine and myself. When asked to help prepare the special issue of the journal, I had been wondering about the accuracy of my own impressions of a current ferment in Indian life. I wrote and distributed a statement, "An American Indian Renascence?", to Indian people, anthropologists, and others (more than eighty people) whom I felt could give me an informed, critical appraisal. I also asked people to volunteer papers for the special issue of the journal. The commentaries on my statement and the volunteered papers were most useful in agreeing that something is definitely stirring, but it is not a "rebirth," and it shows clear continuity with the past. The only really new features are a broader public awareness of Indians and Indians' own efforts to present their views. The information returned to me also gave a deeper view on Pan-Indianism as more than the diffusion of modern "Indianness" and as enriching and reinforcing local identity as well as broadening a sense of Indian unity. Events were moving swiftly on the Indian scene even before the book was published.

3 Recent reading, as well as a brief trip to Norwegian Lapland and the opportunity to discuss the Same (Lapp) situation with Scandinavian specialists during January–February 1966 under a grant from the Wenner-Gren Foundation for Anthropological Research, Incorporated, suggest parallels to the North American Indian picture. Of particular interest is that the Sea Same wish to become integrated as Norwegians, but the Mountain, or reindeer, Same do not. Both have experienced "racial" prejudice, but the Sea Same have experienced severe discrimination in economic competition with Norwegians, with whom they share a more similar cultural outlook as fishing people than reindeer Same do with other Norwegians. Another point worth exploration in the comparison between Canadian and American Indian administration is that Norway in the later nineteenth century was quite intolerant of Same cultural separatism as inimical to the general Norwegian nationalistic movement endeavoring to sever ties with Sweden. Similarly, and more violently, the United States repudiated ties to Britain, which Canada still acknowledges; but as Canada insists more strongly on its own national destiny, Indian policy also becomes less tolerant. Sweden has been consistently more tolerant toward the Same, but has a much smaller Same population than Norway. There is also a Pan-Same movement, at least among Same intellectuals, relating the Same of Norway, Sweden, and Finland.

4 The Social Science Research Council Summer Seminar on Acculturation (Barnett, *et al.*, 1954) has guided my thinking in regard to developing consistent comparative criteria for acculturation study. The seminar suggests that there are three types of end results of continuous culture contact: fusion, assimilation, and stabilized pluralism. However, there are different degrees and forms of pluralism; therefore, I have designated the Indian response as articulatory as a means of refining one type of pluralistic relationship.

5 I have been greatly influenced in the development of this chapter by the

insightful premises that were set forth briefly and tentatively by John Provinse (1965) shortly before his death. Avoiding the terms *tribal* and *peasant,* and drawing upon a world-wide experience as an applied anthropologist, Provinse distinguished between peoples with a tradition of sedentariness and peoples with a tradition of mobility. The latter, given Provinse's criteria, is a better general category than *tribal* to cover the multitude of North American native societies at the time of contact.

Indian people themselves demonstrate an awareness that native peoples all over the world share similar problems and goals, as indicated by an article in *Indian Voices* (1965) concerning the Maori of New Zealand and their relations to the Pakeha or non-Maori society. Newspaper releases from Australia, Japan, and elsewhere, including parts of the USSR, indicate the presence of activities by the native populations comparable to those of North American Indians.

[6] The United States, following British precedents, first dealt with Indians through government authorized trading posts and special commissions to undertake land acquisition by means of treaties. The Bureau of Indian Affairs was created in 1824 under the War Department. In 1849 the Department of the Interior was established, and the Bureau was moved from military to civil control. The bureau "sometimes became the uneasy and unhappy buffer between Indians and the U.S. Army," especially on the Plains. In order to establish the Bureau's authority, in 1862 it was decided to "regard Indians as wards" of the Department of the Interior, rather than as enemies of the War Department. But officially, Indians are not wards, and trusteeship applies to Indian land, not people (Bureau of Indian Affairs, 1965a, 1–3; 1965b, 7.

In Canada and prior to the American Revolution in the American Colonies, colonial governors dealt with Indians until 1755, when the first Indian superintendent in charge of trade and administration was appointed with headquarters in what became New York State. A similar superintendency operated briefly in the southern area. After the American Revolution the northern office was moved to Canada. It was supported by the imperial government until 1860 in Ontario and Quebec, when the province of Canada assumed this responsibility, and Indian Affairs came under the jurisdiction of the Crown Lands Department. Elsewhere Indian Affairs were under various provincial or colonial jurisdictions. Under provisions of the British North America Act of 1867, Indian Affairs came under the government of Canada, Department of the Secretary of State. In 1873 it was transferred to the Department of the Interior. In 1880 a separate Department of Indian Affairs was established, but in 1936 it became a branch of the Department of Mines and Resources. In 1950 Indian Affairs became a branch of the Department of Citizenship and Immigration. Eskimo were administered by the Department of Northern Affairs and National Resources (NANR) (Office of Indian Affairs, 1964, 2–3, 14). In 1966 Indian Affairs was reorganized to cover the Eskimo and was separated from the Office of Citizenship and Immigration.

The present study excludes the Eskimo of both the United States and Canada for lack of data regarding involvement in contemporary political activities. However, where Eskimo and Aleut people were subject to much the same kind of administration as Indians in Alaska, NANR in Canada has apparently tried to work in much closer cooperation with the Eskimo and seems more sensitive to their wants and preferences than has been the case with Indian administration under Indian Affairs (cf. Iglauer, 1966).

7 The 1960 census in the United States, where people were self-identified, listed 523,591 Indians, including those not under federal jurisdiction. In the same year 28,637 Eskimo and Aleut were reported as under federal jurisdiction in the United States. In Alaska there are two reservations and ninety other land areas used by Indians, but owned by the government. Exclusive of Alaska there are 277 separate areas, in effect, "reservations" under federal trusteeship, though all are not so titled, as well as thirty groups of public domain allotments and other federal trusteeship lands used by Indians. In 1964 over 11.6 million acres were held in trust for "tribes" as defined in note 1. In Alaska 4.1 million acres are administered by the Bureau of Indian Affairs. The basic aims of the American bureau are: "(1) maximum Indian economic self-sufficiency, (2) full participations of Indians in American life, and (3) equal citizenship privileges and responsibilities for Indians" (Bureau of Indian Affairs, 1965a, 1, 9–11).

In Canada, as of 1964, there were 211,389 Indians under the jurisdiction of Indian Affairs and approximately 12,000 Eskimos administered by NANR. No figures are available on Canadian Indians outside the jurisdiction of Indian Affairs. There are 551 "bands" occupying 2,267 reserves and 72 settlements not classified as reserves. There are 5,975,646 acres of Indian land (Office of Indian Affairs, 1966, 1–2). "The primary function of the Indian Affairs Branch is to assist the Indians to participate fully in the social and economic life of the country. . . . Indians may vote at federal elections on the same basis as other citizens. With regard to provincial elections, Indians are governed by the electoral laws of the various provinces" (Office of Indian Affairs, 1965, 3, 9).

8 For example, the Lumbee (named for the Lumber River) and Haliwa (for Halifax and Warren Counties) and many others like them on the southeastern seaboard have no remnant of original language and little observable Indian culture. Many of these groups show a range of phenotype among individuals from Negroid through Indian to white. Most could pass as white if they moved to areas where their ancestry was not known. Part of their insistence on Indian identity can be traced to their southern location, where they were not accepted as white and refused to be classified as Negro and to use segregated facilities. They have kept largely to themselves. The Lumbee and a few others have become rural, middle-class people able to maintain their own school systems. Others, such as the Houma of Louisiana (cf. Fischer, 1968), have had virtually no schooling because of this conflict of definition. In making arrangements for regional meetings in connection with the American Indian Chicago Conference of 1961, it was impossible to get meeting and lodging places at any state-supported school in the Southeast because of the tension over integration and the equivocal ancestry of many southeastern Indians. The Lumbee people came forward and offered the use of their college at Pembroke, North Carolina, and the regional meeting was held there. Despite the racial prejudice against Negroes that has become more noticeable among Indians in the 1950s in reaction against confusion of their goals with the Negro movement for civil rights, and despite

the suspicion in which many tribes outside the federal jurisdiction are held by "federal Indians," the Lumbee, Haliwa, and other such delegates to the conference in Chicago were able to gain recognition of their groups as Indians. Furthermore, they showed a surprising similarity of outlook to that of the other Indian people. The Lumbee, *et al.* had a clear option, with the opportunities opening up as a result of the Black movement for desegregation, simply to wait out the immediate excitement in 1961 and to begin availing themselves of the benefits brought by the Negro movement. They chose to identify themselves with the Indian movement. However, involvement in the Pan-Indian movement in terms of powwows and intertribal organizations seems more prevalent among the small Algonkian, nonfederally recognized groups of the New England coast and Maine than among the more southerly groups of mixed tribal ancestry.

9 As the dates in note 6 indicate, Canada underwent shifts of policy somewhat parallel to those in the United States concerning an Indian "dependency complex." The Indian Act of 1876, which was the basic enabling legislation in Canadian policy and certainly outmoded, was replaced by a revised Indian Act in 1951. However, Indians were consulted in subsequent legislation, and the official outlook was that for the time being Indians were to be "encouraged to take control of their own destinies as full responsible citizens while retaining their traditional privileges" (Dunstan, 1963, 8). This situation is changing, and as of this writing, 1970, Canada is considering new legislation with strong overtones of termination and assimilation. Canada presents a distinctive situation in regard to the métis people who comprise communities of a stabilized Indian-white mixture. They are not officially Indians and yet are culturally and socially distinct from whites. In some ways they are comparable to the seaboard groups in the American Southeast. But in the United States people are either Indians or white by their own definition and that of their neighbors, whatever their degree of Indian ancestry. Most métis communities are located in the prairie provinces; and Pan-Indian activity in those areas, especially in urban centers, includes the métis, but they remain a more distinctive society than people of mixed ancestry in the United States. In the far North, Indian communities include nontreaty métis neighborhoods, but biologically and culturally many are indistinguishable from Indians, while unable to benefit from many programs designed for Indians.

10 A particularly telling incident of the 1950s was the Kinzua Dam Case (see Fenton, chap. 5, this volume). It demonstrated that Congress felt no compunction about breaking Indian treaties unilaterally if "just compensation" for land were made and the action could be justified as in the greater public interest. There are serious reasons to doubt that the site at Kinzua near the Allegany Reservation serves as great a public interest as an alternative site, which would not flood a substantial part of the reservation and which the Seneca suggested on the basis of a professional hydrographic study they paid for (Atkinson, 1961). In 1961 John F. Kennedy still had the opportunity to reverse actions begun by a previous administration of the opposite party. He was repeatedly requested to do so by both Indian and white groups. Among such requests was a statement from the American Indian Chicago Conference of 1961,

an unprecedented multi-tribal representation of concern in regard to a matter facing a particular Indian group. However, by then the interests of big business, especially in Pittsburgh, as well as powerful forces in New York State which would benefit by the Kinzua location, were not to be denied.

11 The "Indian Resources Development Act," an "Omnibus Bill" promptly dubbed "The Ominous Bill" by Indian political activists, was presented May 18, 1967, and referred to the Committee on Interior and Insular Affairs. While promising much needed economic development, it embodied many features Indians opposed in regard to implicit threats of land loss if programs did not succeed and in regard to a conventional big business rather than Indian community organization orientation. It was still under discussion when the Nixon administration took office and appears to have been quietly dropped. Nixon promised a new Indian policy; and after controversy, including a good deal of Indian opposition, about the appointment of Walter Hickel as Secretary of the Interior and a long delay in finding an acceptable republican Indian, Louis Bruce, as Commissioner of Indian Affairs, President Nixon finally issued a policy statement on Indian affairs on July 8, 1970. Most encouraging to Indians is the repudiation of forced termination and the admission that terminated tribes are often worse off than they were before termination. Indian people are still assessing its implication; and while they have cause for optimism, experience has taught them wariness. They still need real proof that actual programs will give Indians greater control over their own affairs and the protection of their land promised in the statement. The Menominee and Klamath are particularly concerned as to whether the Nixon policy will allow restitution for the injustices they suffered as a result of termination or whether the statement will only protect other tribes from their fate.

12 In 1965 a list of Indian publications was prepared by the Public Inquiries Staff of the Bureau of Indian Affairs. (The list is available on request from the Indian Bureau.) These include both Canadian and American periodicals. Although a few of the 110 entries are published by religious denominations and other white groups interested in Indians, the majority are produced by and for Indian people. Even this list does not cover all the tribal newsletters and regional newssheets as of 1965, and more have appeared since then.

13 I am particularly indebted to D'Arcy McNickle for criticisms of an earlier draft of this study, which pointed out the confining effects of the reservation system on intertribal political activities; I am also indebted to him for generous sharing of other pertinent data used throughout this paper. Dozier (1961, 161) notes the disruption of certain Pueblo-Plains associations due to expansion of the reservation system in the nineteenth century.

14 McNickle observes:

> I was impressed with the movement between Navajo and Pueblo zones. Of course, this reflects a very old pattern but I suspect that it results in a continuing reinforcement of Indianism in side-by-side societies. . . . When the local (Eastern) Navajos conducted a Yeibechai out of season (in August), the people at San Felipe (Pueblo) knew about it (and no doubt others as well), and were righteously critical although this is a purely Navajo cere-

mony. Is this, then, an older Pan-Indianism which has remained localized? So far as I know, no one has written about it.

He further observes that:

> When Isleta Pueblo recently threw their Catholic priest out of the pueblo, they were reacting to something profoundly disturbing—and probably every Indian in the area felt more Indian [personal communication, Dec. 7, 1965].

[15] My analysis of the National Indian Youth Council and related matters derives from attendance at intertribal meetings in the Middle West, conversations with NIYC members, and the NIYC publications, *A.B.C.—Americans Before Columbus, American Aborigine,* and the mimeographed newsletters. *Indian Voices,* a monthly intertribal newspaper, which is a direct outgrowth of the American Indian Chicago Conference, has also been a most valuable guide to contemporary Indian thinking. My study also draws upon regular reading of a number of tribal and intertribal papers and newsletters from different parts of the country, particularly *Akwasasne Notes,* as well as the regular news releases mailed out by the United States Bureau of Indian Affairs.

BIBLIOGRAPHY

ABLON, JOAN

1964 Relocated American Indians in the San Francisco Bay Area: social interaction and Indian identity. Human Organization 24:296–304.

AKWASASNE NOTES

Published ten times a year at Rooseveltown, New York, beginning in 1968.

AMERICAN INDIAN CHICAGO CONFERENCE

1961 Declaration of Indian purpose. Chicago: University of Chicago, Department of Anthropology.

ATKINSON, BROOKS

1961 Proposed dam that would violate treaty with the Seneca poses moral question. The New York Times, April 21.

BARNETT, HOMER G., *et al.*

1954 Acculturation: an exploratory formulation—the social science research council summer seminar on acculturation, 1953. American Anthropologist 56:973–1002.

Bureau of Indian Affairs, U.S. Department of the Interior

1965a American Indians and the federal government.

1965b Answers to questions about American Indians.

1966 News release. January 19.

CAHN, EDGAR S., ED.

1969 Our brother's keeper: The Indian in white America. Washington, D.C.: New Community Press.

CARDINAL, HAROLD
1969 The unjust society—The tragedy of Canada's Indians. Edmonton, Canada: M. G. Hurtig.

CLIFTON, JAMES A.
1968 Factional conflict and the Indian community: the prairie Potawatomi case. *In* The American Indian today. S. Levine and N. Lurie, eds. Deland, Fla.: Everett/Edwards. pp. 115–132.

DELORIA, VINE, JR.
1969 Custer died for your sins. New York: Macmillan.

DOBYNS, HENRY F.
1968 Therapeutic experience of responsible democracy. *In* The American Indian today. S. Levine and N. Lurie, eds. Deland, Fla.: Everett/Edwards. pp. 171–186.

DOZIER, EDWARD P.
1961 Rio Grande Pueblos. *In* Perspectives in American Indian Culture Change. Edward H. Spicer, ed. Chicago: University of Chicago Press. pp. 94–186.

DRUCKER, PHILIP
1965 Cultures of the North Pacific coast. San Francisco: Chandler.

DUNSTAN, WILLIAM
1963 Canadian Indians today. [Reprinted from Canadian Geographical Journal. December. Available on request from Office of Indian Affairs, Ottawa, Canada.]

FEY, HAROLD E., AND D'ARCY MCNICKLE
1959 Indians and other Americans. New York: Harper & Row.

FISCHER, ANN
1968 History and current status of the Houma Indians. *In* The American Indian today. S. Levine and N. Lurie, eds. Deland, Fla.: Everett/Edwards. pp. 133–148.

FRIEDL, ERNESTINE
1956 Persistence in Chippewa culture and personality. American Anthropologist 58:814–825.

IGLAUER, EDITH
1966 The new people. New York: Doubleday.

INDIAN VOICES
1965 Talequah, Okla. August.

KAPPLER, CHARLES J., COMP. AND ED.
1904 Indian affairs, laws and treaties, Vol. II. Treaties. Washington, D.C.

KUPFERER, HARRIET J.
1968 The isolated eastern Cherokee. *In* The American Indian today. S. Levine and N. Lurie, eds. Deland, Fla.: Everett/Edwards. pp. 87–98.

LESSER, ALEXANDER
1961 Education and the future of tribalism in the United States: the case of the American Indian. The Social Science Review 35:1–9.

LEVINE, STUART

1965 The Indian as American: some observations from the editor's notebook. Midcontinent American Studies Journal 6:3–22.

LEVINE, STUART, AND NANCY O. LURIE, EDS.

1968 The American Indian today. Deland, Fla.: Everett/Edwards.

LURIE, NANCY OESTREICH

1957 The Indian Claims Commission Act. The Annals of the American Academy of Political and Social Science 311:56–70.

1959 Indian cultural adjustment to European civilization. *In* Seventeenth Century America, Essays in Colonial History. James M. Smith, ed. Chapel Hill: University of North Carolina Press. pp. 36–60.

1961 The voice of the American Indian: report on the American Indian Chicago conference. Current Anthropology 2:478–500.

1965 An American Indian renascence? Midcontinent American Studies Journal 6:25–50.

1966 The lady from Boston and the Omaha Indians. The American West 3:31–33, 81–85.

1969 Wisconsin, a natural laboratory for North American Indian studies. Wisconsin Magazine of History. December.

1971 As others see us [forthcoming]. New University Thought.

MACANDREW, CRAIG, AND ROBERT EDGERTON

1969 Drunken comportment, a social explanation. Chicago: Aldine.

MARSHALL, JOHN

1831 The Cherokee nation v. the state of Georgia. U.S. Supreme Court *Reports,* 5 Peters 15–18.

1832 Samuel A. Worcester v. the state of Georgia. U.S. Supreme Court *Reports,* 6 Peters 559–561.

MCNICKLE, D'ARCY

1966 The Indian tests the mainstream. The Nation. Sept. 26. pp. 273–279.

(MERIAM) BROOKINGS INSTITUTION

1928 The problem of Indian administration: report on a survey made at the request of the honorable Hubert Work, secretary of the interior. Survey Staff: Lewis Meriam, technical director. Baltimore, Md.: The Johns Hopkins University Press.

MILLER, FRANK C.

1967 Humor in a Chippewa tribal council. Ethnology 6 (3):272–293.

NATIONAL INDIAN YOUTH COUNCIL

1965 American Aborigine 4:1.

OFFICE OF INDIAN AFFAIRS, OTTAWA, CANADA

1964 The Canadian Indian. (Pamphlet.)

1966 Indian Affairs, Facts and Figures. (Pamphlet.)

PITTOCK, BARRIE

1965 First impressions of Maori-Pakeha (white New Zealanders) relations. Indian Voices. June. pp. 14–16.

PROVINSE, JOHN

1965 Letter to the editor. Human Organization 24:185–187.

PROVINSE, JOHN, *et al.*

1954 The American Indian in transition. American Anthropologist 56:387–394.

RACHLIN, CAROL K.

1968 Tight shoe night: Oklahoma Indians today. *In* The American Indian today. S. Levine and N. Lurie, eds. Deland, Fla.: Everett/Edwards.

ROYCE, CHARLES C., AND CYRUS THOMAS

1896–1897 Indian land cessions in the United States, Bureau of American Ethnology 18 (2), Annual Report.

SAHLINS, MARSHALL D., AND ELMAN R. SERVICE, EDS.

1960 Evolution and culture. Ann Arbor: The University of Michigan Press.

SLOTKIN, J. SYDNEY

1956 The Peyote religion: a study in Indian-white relations. Glencoe: Free Press.

STEINER, STAN

1968 The new Indians. New York: Harper & Row.

STERN, THEODORE

1965 The Klamath tribe—a people and their reservation. Seattle: University of Washington Press.

TASK FORCE ON INDIAN AFFAIRS, *et al.*

1962 Implementing change through government. Human Organization 21:125–136.

THOMAS, ROBERT K.

1968 Pan-Indianism. *In* The American Indian today. S. Levine and N. Lurie, eds. Deland, Fla.: Everett/Edwards. pp. 77–86.

TURNER, KATHERINE C.

1951 Red man calling on the great white father. Norman, Okla.: The University of Oklahoma Press.

UNDERHILL, RUTH M.

1953 Red man's America. Chicago: University of Chicago Press.

VERDET, PAUL

1961 Unpublished summary report on urban Indians, distributed in mimeograph copy at the American Indian Chicago Conference.

WALKER, DEWARD, JR.

1968 Conflict and schisms in Nez Perce acculturation. Pullman: Washington State University Press.

WALLACE, ANTHONY

1956 Revitalization movements. American Anthropologist 58:264–281.

WAX, ROSALIE H., AND ROBERT THOMAS

1961 American Indians and white people. Phylon 22:305–317.

WAX, ROSALIE H., AND MURRAY WAX

1968 Indian education for what? *In* The American Indian today. S. Levine and N. Lurie, eds. Deland, Fla.: Everett/Edwards. pp. 163–170.

WILSON, EDMUND

1959 Apologies to the Iroquois. New York: Random House.

WITT, SHIRLEY HILL

1968 Nationalistic trends among American Indians. *In* The American Indian today. S. Levine and N. Lurie, eds. Deland, Fla.: Everett/Edwards. pp. 53–76.

Index

About the Authors

JULIA AVERKIEVA is Vice-Chairman of the Department of American Ethnography of the Institute of Ethnography in Moscow and Chief Editor of the journal *Sovetskaja Ethnographia*. Her extensive research on the Tlingit Indians of the Northwest Coast has included field work with the late Franz Boas among the Kwakiutl. Available in English translation is her monograph *Slavery Among the North American Indians* (translated by G. R. Elliot, 1966).

T. J. C. BRASSER is Plains Ethnologist with the National Museum of Man in Ottawa. During the years 1962–1969, as Curator of the American and Eurasian Arctic Department at the National Museum of Ethnology of the Netherlands, he conducted a study of the Long Island, New York, Indians and the Stockbridge Indians of Wisconsin. For brief periods he has done research among the Crow, Assiniboin, Plains Cree, and Blackfeet, as well as among the Scandinavian Lapps.

JAMES F. DOWNS is Professor of Anthropology at the University of Hawaii and Chairman of Cross-Cultural Training at the University's Center for Cross-Cultural Training and Research. His widely varied field research has included study among American nudists, the Washo and Navaho Indians, and, in 1966 and 1968, among Tibetan refugees in northern India. His writings include *Animal Husbandry in Navajo Society and Culture* (1964); *Two Worlds of the Washo* (1966); and *Human Variation: An Introduction to Physical Anthropology* (1969), of which he is co-author with Hermann Bleibtreu. In preparation are *Human Nature: An Introduction to Cultural Anthropology* and, with R. B. Ekvall, *Pilgrimage in Tibetan Life*.

EDWARD P. DOZIER, Professor of Anthropology at The University of Arizona in Tucson, is a Pueblo Indian from the village of Santa Clara, New Mexico. His work among the American Indians of the Southwest has included both linguistic and anthropological studies. He has also done field work among indigenous populations of the Philippine Islands. His writings include *Hano: A Tewa Speaking Community in Arizona* (1966); *Mountain Arbiters: A Study of a Philippine Hill People* (1966); *The Kalinga of Northern Luzon, Philippines* (1967); and *The Pueblo Indians of North America* (1970). [Editors' note: On the eve of publication of this book, word was received of the sudden and untimely death of Edward Dozier, May 2, 1971. We mourn the loss of our friend and colleague.]

WILLIAM N. FENTON is Research Professor of Anthropology at the State University of New York at Albany. A life-long student of the Iroquois of his native New York, he is the author of numerous articles and several monographs on their ethnology and history, including *The Roll Call of the Iroquois Chiefs* (1950); *The Iroquois Eagle Dance* (1953); and *Indian and White Relations in Eastern North America* (1957). He is presently at work on a book entitled *The People of the Longhouse*.

JUNE HELM, Professor of Anthropology at the University of Iowa, has since 1951 spent ten field seasons among the Athapaskan-speaking Indians of Canada's Northwest Territories. She has published a number of articles on folklore, kinship, and political and territorial organization in several tribal groups; a general study of a community of Slave Indians, *The Lynx Point People* (1961); and, in co-authorship with Nancy Oestreich Lurie, *The Dogrib Hand Game* (1966). She is the editor of the volume on the Indians of the Subarctic in the forthcoming *Handbook of North American Indians*.

HAROLD HICKERSON is Professor of Anthropology at Simon Fraser University, British Columbia. He has done extensive research on the ethnohistory of peoples of the Northeastern Woodlands, especially the Ojibwa of the upper Great Lakes. Among his many publications on this people are two full-length works, *The Southwestern Chippewa: An Ethnohistorical Study* (1962); and *The Chippewa and Their Neighbors, a Case Study in Ethnohistorical Method* (1970). He is former editor of the journal *Ethnohistory*.

CHARLES C. HUGHES is Professor of Anthropology and Psychiatry at Michigan State University, in East Lansing. He has done research in the areas of sociocultural change, social psychiatry, and behavioral science and medicine, and field work in Nova Scotia, in Alaska among the Eskimos, and in Nigeria. Other writings on subject matter relevant to this book are *An Eskimo Village in the Modern World* (1960); "Under Four Flags: Recent Culture Change Among the Eskimos," in *Current Anthropology* (Vol. 6, No. 1, 1965); and, forthcoming, *The Child Is Father: An Eskimo Life History in Psychosocial Perspective*.

ELEANOR BURKE LEACOCK is Professor of Anthropology at Polytechnic Institute of Brooklyn, Brooklyn, New York. Her extensive field work has included research among the Montagnais-Naskapi Indians of Labrador in Northwest-River, Newfoundland-Labrador, and in Natashquan, Quebec, as well as among the Harrison Indians of the lower Frazer River, British Columbia. In addition to numerous contributions to professional journals, her published works include *The Montagnais "Hunting Territory" and the Fur Trade* (1954); *Toward Integration in Suburban Housing: The Bridgeview Study* (1965), of which she was coauthor; and *Teaching and Learning in City Schools: A Comparative Study* (1969).

NANCY OESTREICH LURIE, Professor of Anthropology at the University of Wisconsin, Milwaukee, has a professional background of field research, ethnohistorical study, and work in action anthropology programs. Her primary field work has included extensive study among the Winnebago Indian people of Wisconsin and Nebraska; three field seasons among the Dogrib Indians of the Canadian Northwest Territories; and research and action endeavors with the urban Indian community in Milwaukee. *The American Indian Today,* edited with Stuart Levine, won the *Saturday Review's* Annisfield-Wolf Award for the best scholarly book on intergroup relations for 1968.

D'ARCY MCNICKLE, Professor of Anthropology at the University of Saskatchewan, the Regina campus, is a member of the Confederated Salish and Kootenai Tribes of Montana. He is a former staff member of the Bureau of Indian Affairs and former Director of American Indian Development, a program in community development. His writings include *They Came Here First* (1949); *The Indian Tribes of the United States, Ethnic and Cultural Survival* (1962); and *Indian Man: A Life of Oliver La Farge* (1971).

MARVIN K. OPLER is Professor and Chairman of the Department of Anthropology and Professor of Social Psychiatry in the School of Medicine at the State University of New York at Buffalo. In addition to research among Japanese, West Africans, and Puerto Ricans, his field work has included study among the Eastern Apache tribes of New Mexico, the Paiute of Utah, and the Ute of Colorado. He has contributed to edited collections of writings on the American Indian and has included material on the Indian in two of his books: *Culture and Mental Health* (1959); and *Culture and Social Psychiatry* (1967). He is editor of *The International Journal of Social Psychiatry.*

WILLIAM C. STURTEVANT, Curator of North American Anthropology at the Smithsonian Institution in Washington, D.C., has specialized for twenty years in the ethnography, history, and material culture of Eastern North American Indians, paying particular attention to the Seminole in Florida and the Iroquois in New York, among whom he has done extensive field work. He has conducted briefer field investigations in many communities of other Eastern Indians, in Mexico and Kashmir, and for a longer period in Burma. He has published many articles and chapters on these and other anthropological topics, served as co-editor of two books, and is General Editor of the forthcoming multi-volume *Handbook of North American Indians.*

GENE WELTFISH is Professor of Anthropology at Fairleigh Dickinson University in Madison, New Jersey. As a long-time member of the Graduate Faculty at Columbia University, she did field work on language, art, technology, and culture among American Indian tribes in Oklahoma, Nebraska, North Dakota, New Mexico, Arizona, and Louisiana. Her published works include articles in professional journals and popular versions of those articles; *The Lost Universe,* based on field, ethnohistorical, and archeological research on the Pawnee Indians, which was listed among the Notable Books of 1965 by the American Library Association; *The Origins of Art* (1953); *Caddoan Texts* (1937); and, with Ruth F. Benedict, *The Races of Mankind* (1943).